Twentieth-Century Music
In Western Europe

Da Capo Press Music Reprint Series

GENERAL EDITOR

FREDERICK FREEDMAN

VASSAR COLLEGE

Twentieth-Century Music in Western Europe

The Compositions and the Recordings

By Arthur Cohn, *1910 –*

DA CAPO PRESS • NEW YORK • 1972

Library of Congress Cataloging in Publication Data

Cohn, Arthur, 1910-
   Twentieth-century music in western Europe.

   (Da Capo Press music reprint series)
   1. Music—Europe—Discography. 2. Music
—Analysis, appreciation. 3. Composers—Europe.
I. Title.
ML156.4.N3E9   1972   780'.94   70-39297
ISBN 0-306-70460-9

This Da Capo Press edition of *Twentieth-Century Music in Western Europe* is an unabridged republication of the first edition published in Philadelphia and New York in 1965. It is reprinted by special arrangement with J. B. Lippincott Company, Philadelphia, New York

Published by Da Capo Press, Inc.
A Subsidiary of Plenum Publishing Corporation
227 West 17th Street
New York, New York 10011

TWENTIETH-CENTURY MUSIC

IN WESTERN EUROPE

Also by Arthur Cohn

THE COLLECTOR'S TWENTIETH-CENTURY MUSIC
IN THE WESTERN HEMISPHERE

Twentieth-Century Music

IN WESTERN EUROPE

THE COMPOSITIONS
AND THE RECORDINGS

BY

ARTHUR COHN

J. B. LIPPINCOTT COMPANY
Philadelphia & New York

FOR MY CHILDREN

ALAN, DEBORAH, AND *LESLIE,*

THIS BOOK, WITH LOVE

FOREWORD

AND ACKNOWLEDGMENTS

No other period of musical history can match the complex diversification of styles, tenets, and exciting innovations of the current century. It is an era of kaleidoscopic change, of fascinating, crowded development. Neoromanticism, primitivist nationalism, atonality, expressionism, neoclassicism, dodecaphonic and serial writing; the techniques of polyrhythm, dissonant counterpoint, polytonality, pandiatonic and panchromatic harmony; the modal speech of Vaughan Williams, the pointillism of Webern, the electronic habits of Stockhausen—all these and more will be found in the music produced by the most representative twentieth-century composers of Western Europe, discussed in the pages that follow.

Some of the men included may disappear with the years, others may emerge from the ranks. In the arts, longevity is speculative and oblivion is not always permanent. The roll of selected composers may be questioned. For example, why Boulez and Stockhausen? In the thirties, the query was why Berg and Bartók? In the sixties such men are among the honored select. In the nineties a number of those who cause shock in the sixties will have become the new elder statesmen. Boulez and Stockhausen are surely in the running for such recognition. They emphasize that music is as healthy as ever and not ready for interment as some critics (professional and amateur) will have it.

Short of encyclopedic encompassment a book has limitations of scope. Here, the term "twentieth-century music" is defined as beginning where Debussy ends. His impressionistic methods had broken the grip of German romanticism and were then absorbed into musical speech as it moved on to newer resources. Debussy's work deserves separate study.

Nothing is discussed in this volume that has not been recorded on a twelve-inch long-playing disk (a pair of ten-inch releases are the sole exceptions). Whether the recording is currently available or not is immaterial. A certain number of stores still carry stocks of deleted disks, reissues are constantly appearing of cut-out items, and a number of individuals are in business to find out-of-print productions. Concurrent use of this book with recordings will enrich the reading and the listening.

Each composer is introduced by an evaluation of his aesthetic criteria. No biographical treatment, not even once over lightly, is given—sufficient data are available elsewhere. The individual essays avoid the cold boredom of measure-by-measure analysis, doubly irritating without the printed score at one's elbow, and even then of interest only to the creative fraternity. Though not geared for the specialist the writing is designed for the knowledgeable listener who does not cringe at a technical term here and there. It also asks for a broadminded listener-reader, not one who, knowing what he likes, likes only what he knows. Since this is a book of information, it cannot avoid being a book of criticism. Accordingly, so far as personal prejudices can be overcome, constructive criticism has been applied.

A word about translations of titles. The inconsistency followed in the text is paradoxically consistent—that is, translations have been given only when they are in fairly common use; otherwise the original language stands. The order of compositions for each chapter follows the plan I used in the preceding volume of this series (*The Collector's Twentieth-Century Music in the Western Hemisphere*, Lippincott, 1961). Thus: *orchestral* (full, chamber, string, brass); *solo instrument with orchestra* (concertos, other works); *instrumental* (with or without accompaniment); *chamber music* (in order of the increased number of instruments employed); *vocal; choral;* and finally *ballets, operas*, and *film music*. Within these categories the titles of the music are arranged alphabetically; with the opus number indicated if such exists.

A. C.

New York City
Christmas Day, 1963

ACKNOWLEDGMENTS

T HIS book would not have been possible without the assistance of a number of executives in the recording industry. Therefore, my thanks to: Peter Bartók (*Bartók*), Ward Botsford (*Vox*), Emory Cook (*Cook*), Ben Deutschman (*Decca*), Walter Diehl (*Vox*), Sidney Finkelstein (*Vanguard*), Jack Freisell (formerly of *Columbia*), Peter Fritsch (*Lyrichord*), Louise Goodman (*Boston*), Sol Handwerger (*MGM*), Herb Helman (*RCA Victor*) and his aide Dale Ford, John Hurd (*London*), Debbie Ishlon (formerly of *Columbia*), Leo H. Kepler (*Deutsche Grammophon*), Lester Koenig (*Contem-*

Acknowledgments

porary), Irving Kratka (*Classic*), John Kurland (*Columbia*), Abner Levin (*Urania*), Paul Myers (then of *Kapp*), Gabriel Oller, Jr. (*Montilla*), Carl Post (then of *Capitol*), Peter Reilly (*Columbia*), Jack Romann (*Deutsche Grammophon*), Bruno G. Ronty (*Bruno*), Michael Stillman (*Monitor*), Peter Sutro (formerly of *Artia*), Clair Van Ausdale (*Mercury*), Earl Walker (*Music Library*), Richard H. Wangerin (*Louisville*), Kurt J. Wycisk (*Concordia*), Saul Zaentz (*Fantasy*).

Personnel of the following firms were most helpful: Audiophile, Austin, Concert-Disc, Dot, Draco, Educo, Mirrosonic, and Word. To Gene Bruck, Horace Grennell, Dr. Herbert Zipper, and Joseph Greenspan (of the Discophile store) my thanks for making hard-to-secure recordings available to me.

A fair number of the essays that follow originally appeared in *The American Record Guide*. They have been completely revised for inclusion in this volume. I am exceedingly grateful to my dear friend, the keenly sagacious James Lyons, publisher and editor of *The American Record Guide,* for permitting me the right to use this material. I am further in his debt for the loan of innumerable recordings from a collection that lacks nothing and for a calmness in the face of my almost consistent failure to meet publication deadlines.

To George Stevens, of my publishers, I convey my gratitude for assistance in planning and for his patience in awaiting the completion of this volume. The final acknowledgment is far from the least. Clarity has been the watchword of my wife, Lois, who typed the final manuscript, clinging to a heavy crayon that made fat question marks. For such a combination of patience, mental alertness, and physical energy, a husband (and author) is indeed fortunate and my thanks are small repayment.

CONTENTS

Contents

PART TWO : THE RECORDINGS

PART ONE
THE COMPOSITIONS

1. MALCOLM ARNOLD
(1921–   )

SINCE in most instances the instrument a composer plays is the piano, it is a rarity to find one who is a trumpeter of the first order. Arnold's orchestral experience—he was a member of both the BBC Symphony and the London Philharmonic—shows in his orchestrational manners. His use of instrumental synonyms avoids monotony and makes his orchestral sound always zestful and exciting. Malcolm Arnold's music is tonal, healthy, attractive, extroverted. Though he refuses to burden his music with heaviness, he avoids the danger zone of sticky sentimentality. It is artistically commercial, and for that reason Arnold has been chosen to write a considerable amount of film music. His background scores prove that the twain (art and utility) can meet if both unbend just a little.

In the English school of composers Arnold represents the imaginative non-experimentalist. He stands in the category of a "best seller."

ORCHESTRAL

¶ A Grand Grand Overture

Arnold's wizardry with the orchestra is proven with this frivolity, especially composed for the high jinks that marked the London concerts arranged by the recently deceased musical cartoonist and expert on the tuba, Gerard Hoffnung. This work reaches into the *musique concrète* field and makes orchestrally respectable such a piece of merchandise as a vacuum cleaner. The score lives up to its title: it calls for orchestra plus organ, together with four rifles, three "Hoovers," and an electric floor polisher! The C major presto postscript of the piece kids the notes off every Suppé, Offenbach, Rossini, and Auber operatic overture.

¶ Beckus the Dandipratt Overture

Though this piece has a programmatic title, the music is the opposite . . . almost. Arnold's "dandipratt" is not a foppy clothes-worshiper, but a human of *dégagé* demeanor, and this unbuttoned mood sweeps through the conception, which is subtitled a "comedy overture."

3

¶ English Dances

These eight dances (divided into two sets) were suggested by Arnold's publisher and focused the spotlight on the composer for the first time. Statistics show that more performances have been given them than any other works by Arnold.

The dances are not stubborn to one concept. Arnold reiterates but tempers his thematic premises; accordingly, the native (but strictly composer-made) attestation is retained, while the arguments and presentations are recolored. The technical means to this objective are cleverly utilized. Modes (the simulative dress for a constructed folk melody) contrast with straightforward major keys, each tempo is different, six varieties of meter are employed, and the orchestral timbres, solo and in combination, are exploited to the fullest. Convivial music written convincingly.

¶ Four Scottish Dances, Op. 59

The "Scottish Dances" attempt to equal the huge success that Arnold's eight "English Dances" enjoy. Continual native correspondence is maintained; the music includes the Scotch-snap rhythmic element, and the terpsichorean catalogue of a strathspey, reel, and fling. These dances contain good imitations of the Scotch flavor, with one tune credited to Robert Burns, but they are denatured.

¶ Symphony No. 2, Op. 40

Arnold is best in the realm of the short piece. Symphonic style escapes him. Though the form and content of the separate movements are apparent, a set of sectional reviews with repetitive designs (changed only in terms of orchestration) is far from being a symphony. This music (an initial joyful movement, a scherzo followed by an elegiac slow section, and a lighthearted finale) is truthful, tuneful, readily accessible, but formally undernourished. The orchestration is overdone, and sometimes slips out of style.

¶ Symphony No. 3, Op. 63

Arnold persists in writing symphonies, but since he is a composer of film music in addition to his concert output, it may well be that he confuses his creative issues. Sequences are of aid to the movie composer (they use up time and decrease the necessity for constant invention). In Arnold's symphonies the sequence becomes the gimmick for attenuation. As a result, the seams show. In layout, the third symphony follows routine intentions. Movement one's sonata design coalesces into a scherzo plan. Then come variations and a rondo derived from three themes.

¶ Tam O'Shanter Overture, Op. 51

Arnold's overture translates Robert Burns's text exactly. In outline, the grisly humorous tale concerns a hard-drinking Scotsman's wild nocturnal ride during a storm. He encounters sorcerers and witches, is pursued by them and escapes, but his mare loses her tail when it is grasped by one of the fiends. The moral for temperance is obvious.

Midnight hags and atmospheric disturbances are just the stuff for pictorial orchestration, and Arnold makes the most of it. For proper native mood he also mixes an excellent musical cocktail of Scotch drone sounds, rhythmic snap, and melodic flavor. No one can do better with a clearly indexed musical story than this young composer.

BAND

¶ River Kwai March

The *idée fixe* in the film score for *The Bridge on the River Kwai,* was a tune called "Colonel Bogey," written in 1914 by an obscure composer named Kenneth Alford. Arnold added a stirring counter theme and the two were combined in a full-scale stimulating march.

ORCHESTRA AND BAND

¶ Excerpts from The United Nations

Cold-war music is represented in this grim satire. A typical Elgarian melody is contrapuntally massaged by a number of bands, each playing its own native-type tune to indicate the international political climate of divided we stand and united we fall.

SOLO INSTRUMENT WITH ORCHESTRA

CONCERTO

¶ Guitar Concerto, Op. 67

Themes for this instrument are generally focused on rhythm, quite often of Spanish cast. Arnold's music is otherwise. He considers the guitar without such creative insularity. The core of the concerto is the

5

elegiac second movement; the music detailed by glides and of blues insistence. While the outer divisions consist of material that does not belie the basic character of guitar language, mere rhythmic patterns and other time-marking methods are absent. Arnold's concerto for the guitar is conservative contemporary music, with a cross-blend that satisfies the ear for tunes and satisfactory harmonies.

CHAMBER MUSIC

¶ *Piano Trio in D minor, Op. 54*

Successful contemporary trios for violin, cello, and piano are in short supply. Arnold's D minor opus does not help alleviate the condition. Motives cannot form a responsible musical structure unless they dovetail and develop. There is a great deal of propulsiveness in the piece but most of it is in unrelated hunks.

¶ *Three Shanties for Wind Quintet*

A triple serving of good, clean spoofing, as animated as champagne bubbles, as titillating as a striptease. Arnold's clever avoidance of fully quoting any phrase of a sailor's tune is akin to brilliant dabs of conversation heard on the fly.

In the first shanty, after skirting around the contours of "What Will We Do with the Drunken Sailor," the use of habanera rhythm is artistic frivolity at its very best. The second piece is hinged on "Blow the Man Down" in a kind of slow motion. A montage of frisky melodic snippets forms the finale. The final cadence is perfect for this chamber-music skit.

BALLET

¶ *Homage to the Queen*

This work was written for the Sadler's Wells Ballet, as a coronation tribute for Queen Elizabeth II. Here Arnold is himself only part of the time. For the rest he takes on the manners of the traditional romanticist. But there should be no pretense if a composer deigns to be quite conventional. The "Homage" consists of representations of the four elements: Earth, Air, Fire, and Water. The best is the third, which has ravishing orchestration, vitality, and plenty of brassy brilliance of effect.

FILM MUSIC

¶ *The Bridge on the River Kwai*

If one can suffer through the whirl of sounds that are meant to convey the sense of jungle mystery, enervating heat, and assorted exotica, plus the entire paraphernalia of orchestrational trickery utilized to underline screened images, then this score still has only a march to recommend it.

¶ *The Inn of the Sixth Happiness*

Arnold's lush score is appropriate as background commentary. The music alone is somewhat forced and artificial.

2. BÉLA BARTÓK
(1881–1945)

In the first part of the twentieth century it was quite fashionable for composers to experiment. Possessed of a thorough technical capacity, Béla Bartók would have none of this specious originality, produced by so-called talents. Intuitiveness and erudition, applied to a going beyond ordinary art restrictions and conventions constitute his great creative endowment. The music he wrote was nonschematic and not based on the narrow pronouncements of theorists; it was beautifully unfashionable and therefore had all the attributes for long life. In its dynamic impulses, sureness, mastery, and continuity of growth, it matched the individuality of Beethoven's music.

Bartók's style was not Beethoven's but both had formal security of special order. Both had the means and the mentality to express the thought that realism is the seeking of logic. Since the peak of classicism is identified with Beethoven's work, Bartók should be a neoclassicist. But Bartók represented the direct antithesis of the neoclassical composer. He brought into service some of the chordal materials of the style, but he pressed them into far different shapes. He did not consider the retrospective spiritual kinship that was the dogma of twentieth-century classicism. He championed the complete striving for intelligibility of the classic tradition—which meant form and formal advance simultaneously.

Folk song was the driving impetus behind much of Bartók's music. His entire evolution was concerned with it. Though not the complete estimate of his work, it was its heartbeat. Actually no composer in history had been so completely the national artist because of his use of native material, and thus, in being the unmistakable Hungarian, Bartók became a universalist. It was the folk-song resource which bound his expressive melodies and was, in turn, embraced and exposed by exceedingly explicit and direct harmonies. With Bartók dissonance was as prime as any other part of musical grammar; consonance a lesser tension; color a method of portraying and identifying these. Rhythm harnessed all the material and became interallied with all other parts of the compositional scheme.

Bartók's work, as Beethoven's, was divided into three periods with string quartet compositions marking the divisions. The first—the period of the barest use of native datum—ended just after the first string quartet. The second span, concluding with the fourth quartet, was one of broadening and absorption. The third period consisted of more concentrated resources and complete synthesis. To this part of the Bartók story belong the fifth and sixth string quartets.

In none of Bartók's works are there superfluities. In all of them there is manifested a tremendous creative imagery. This man was one of the greatest constructivistic composers of the last hundred years.

ORCHESTRAL

¶ Concerto for Orchestra

Bartók never repeated himself. While this indicated a recast personality it did not mean a lessening of technical depth. Because of the popularity of the concerto some have accused Bartók of "writing down." The fact is that his style had simply resolved into refinement.

The "Concerto for Orchestra" is a suite-like affair in five movements. The title derives from the use of orchestral components in a soloistic fashion, especially in the second section entitled "Giuoco delle coppie" ("Game of Pairs"), wherein differently paired instruments play tunes in turn and for diverse intervals. The opening is "stern" (the composer's description); the third part is an "Elegy." Bartók's fourth movement title "Interrupted Intermezzo" defines matters to a *T*. The utilized rondo form is split by the "interruption," a mad take-off of a cheap tune (beautifully disguised, but patently clear) from Shostakovich's *Seventh* (*"Leningrad"*) *Symphony*. In the finale, fugal technique is supreme, encased in a volatile perpetual motion of sound. According to the composer, it symbolizes "life assertion." The entire piece revamps the conventions of concerto form.

¶ Dance Suite

Indigenous content and spirit identified Bartók's creative doctrine, whether internalized within the design or comprising the cardinal compositional element. The combined Hungarian, Slovak, and Rumanian folk resource became coalesced into his musical language. He thereby represented the artistic voice of his countrymen.

This union is the creative refrain of the "Dance Suite." The thematic material is totally Bartók's, yet the focus is native song and dance. A Bartók scholar has called this work an example of

9

"imaginary folk music." No better example of such artistic alliance exists.

¶ Deux Images, Op. 10

The stamp of Hungarian and French (impressionistic) qualities is on the first piece. Though unique for this composer, it is explained by the early date of the composition—1910. More typical Bartókian dialect is heard in the kinetic, shifting-tempoed "Village Dance."

It is rare to hear these orchestral representations on concert programs, probably because of the hip-pocket repertoire of most conductors.

¶ Hungarian Peasant Songs

Originally a set of fifteen piano numbers (*see page 19*) composed between 1914 and 1917; Bartók orchestrated nine of the pieces sixteen years later. The expressive power and emotional force of Hungarian nationalistic art are made more graphic in the larger settings, without disturbing the fundamental truth. They anticipate the commanding discourse of the quartets and the other large-scale compositions.

¶ Hungarian Sketches

Bartók transcribes Bartók in this instance. So much of this composer's keyboard music lends itself to orchestral arrangement that it is surprising he did not indulge more often. Three of the five parts of the suite are program music miniatures; namely, "Evening in the Village," the very pointed "Slightly Tipsy," and the savage "Bear Dance," surrounded by a full-bodied ostinato.

¶ Mikrokosmos Suite (arranged by Tibor Serly)

Those who know the eight items chosen for orchestration (the first of the set is *not* from "Mikrokosmos," but the third of a group of piano pieces Bartók contributed to a memorial album in homage to Paderewski) will appreciate the way Serly brings new elements to light in this second look.

All the colorings are a delight. Included are such images as an up-dated Bourrée, a flip and explicit scherzo called "Jack-in-the-Box," and one of the most brilliantly successful examples of musical onomatopoeia in the orchestral literature, "From the Diary of a Fly." Close your eyes when listening and you're likely to reach for the swatter.

¶ *The Miraculous Mandarin, Suite from the Ballet, Op. 19*

One of Bartók's most breathtaking pieces—the suite covering about one half of the total ballet. The stage tale concerns a prostitute and her three male confederates who rob and beat a pair of victims. Their next intended prey is a mandarin. He is robbed, but all attempts to dispose of him by smothering, stabbing, and hanging are unsuccessful. His longing for the woman unsatisfied, he refuses to die from the brutal treatment. It is only when she shows pity and embraces him that his desire is appeased, his wounds bleed and he dies.

No choreographic association is necessary to appreciate the score's rhythmic proliferation, concluding with a real "chase" sequence in frenetic fugal fashion. Even in its relaxed moments the music is an orchestral "Allegro Barbaro," with pulsatile muscle and blood supply. The violence, reiterative patterns, and glaring glissandi display Bartók's primitivistic style.

¶ *Suite No. 2 for Orchestra, Op. 4*

Berlioz once described music as containing both sentiment and science. It is this principle that makes possible the enjoyment of a complex art by both the lay and the technically informed audience. The former will appreciate the fundamental Hungarian thesis of the music. The latter will realize how fantasy propounds the elements of this work, wherein basic classical form is molded into Bartók's individual patterns. Far from determined suite construction, the four movements are a complex of multisubject debate.

Quite early in his career (the "Suite" was written between 1905 and 1907, revised as late as 1943 without change of its stylistic tone) Bartók rejected native expression in the direct manner and substituted a natural nationalism of his own make.

¶ *Two Portraits, Op. 5*

Despite Bartók's "for orchestra" indication in his title, there is no arguing the principal role of the violin in the opening portion. Further, this part duplicates the opening movement of an earlier violin concerto, which was thought lost until rediscovered in 1958. The second movement also exemplifies self-borrowing, being an orchestration of the last of the "Fourteen Bagatelles," for piano.

No uncertainty concerns Bartók's musical drawings. The imagery is sharp and severely contrasted in length and type. The first of

11

the pair is lyrically contrapuntal (identified as "The Idealistic"), the other ("The Distorted") is a surly presto waltz.

¶ *Two Rumanian Dances, Op. 8a* (arranged by Leo Weiner)

A splendid realization of Bartók's contemporary coinage of indigenal shapes. The dances are entirely original though sounding as if drawn out of a folk-tune storehouse.

¶ *The Wooden Prince, Suite from the Ballet, Op. 13* (see page 35)

CHAMBER ORCHESTRA

¶ *Music for Strings, Percussion and Celesta*

One of the masterworks of the twentieth century, employing a unique instrumental combination. No composer has ever chosen the orchestrational plan involved, or defined the placement of the instruments in so sonorously constructive a manner. By dividing the ten-part string body into two orchestras, placed left and right, with the other instruments allocated in between, Bartók anticipated the stereophonic era. This results in multiple string writing, opposed and unified sound masses, with colorful polyphonic and textural differences. The exceptional inclusion of percussions as well as the specialized timbres of the celesta and harp are sufficient to designate the opus one of unconventional make-up. With the use of the piano and a full-scale employment of timpanic glissandi, polychromic resource is further illustrated. (Bartók's thinking is patent in his title. He does not single out the piano or harp; these are, therefore, string and/or percussion instruments. The separate definition of the celesta can be argued. A bell-keyboard instrument is as much a percussion quality as a string-keyboard piano.)

Bartók was not partial to singular instrumentation. (The "Contrasts" for violin, clarinet and piano and the "Sonata for Two Pianos and Percussion" are the only other examples of specialness.) It was a particular blueprint for the exercise of his vigorous creative curiosity, a spur to artistic discovery. The fugue that opens this composition is a view of a brave, new contrapuntal world. Movements two and four (both in fast tempi) contain wondrous invention, structural clarity, and stand in contrast. The first of these is motival, classically grained, with magnetic rhythmic discourse; the

12

other is decisively marked with national characteristics. Movement three is a slow-paced music that was Bartók's invention; color is as paramount to the structure as its themes. It is impressionistic, to be sure, but its darkness and mystery are as distant from French style as can be imagined. "Music for Strings, Percussion and Celesta" is a work of genius.

¶ Rumanian Folk Dances

Catchy tunes occupying one of the top rungs of Bartókian popularity. No heavy make-up was applied to these dances and their sensitive beauty projects a warming immediacy. Following the composer's lead (the dances were originally for piano), the suite has been transcribed for strings, violin and piano, and other instruments—even the somewhat ridiculous combination of mouth organ and accordion! Regardless, the pieces wear well.

There is considerable variety in the seven-part collection. Tempi range from the gentility of the "Horn Dance" to the animation of the last pair, each a "Fast Dance." Metrical definitions are squarely duple for the most part; the "Rumanian Polka" is oddly birhythmic. The types are as colorful as the names identifying the areas of origin. In addition to the four mentioned, there is a "Stick Dance," a "Sash Dance," and a cute "On the Spot" (or "Stamping Dance"). Bartók's native capers range wide, representing melodies drawn from the districts of Mezöszabad, Egres, Bisztra, Belényes, and Nyágra.

STRING ORCHESTRA

¶ Divertimento for Strings

This work is the equivalent of a thesaurus of string orchestra techniques. Bartók's instrumentation is not merely machinery to move the "Divertimento." It punctuates, highlights, places the material into proper perspective, and is an organic part of its totality.

The title of the composition is deceiving. Bartók's "Divertimento" is no airy amusement. It has plentiful cheer, but balances this with throbbing emotionalism plus introspective intensity. It has concerto grosso particulars and a goodly portion of contrapuntal engagement (canons and a fugue in the finale). These are decorated with the fanciful embroideries of a fiddle cadenza of quasi-Gypsy turn and a short, tongue-out polka in pizzicato color.

¶ *Rumanian Folk Dances* (arranged by Arthur Willner)

Completely effective, and, in fact, more often performed in this setting than the small orchestra version (*see page 13*). Stringed instruments give fluidity to the dances.

SOLO INSTRUMENT WITH ORCHESTRA

CONCERTOS

¶ *Concerto for Viola and Orchestra*

Death from leukemia prevented Bartók from finishing the viola concerto. Unlike the third piano concerto (on which he worked simultaneously), which only required some seventeen measures of orchestration for completion, this one was left a rough draft of fifteen un-numbered pages without any logical sequence. It was up to composer-violist Tibor Serly (a pupil and very close friend of Bartók's) to unravel the tangled hieroglyphics of the composer's musical shorthand. Serly spent some two years in his task of reconstruction. Naturally, it will be forever unknown how much of the concerto is as Bartók would have had it.

It may be hindsight, but the viola concerto persistently indicates autobiographical overtones. Bartók knew he was dying as he sketched the piece and this fact entwines itself within the lines, not in black-striped emotion, but in a certain despondency within the *adagio religioso* movement and a somewhat ironic concept that jars the Hungarian cast of the finale. The confusing mood of the opening (spliced with Magyarian elements) is weak; the music is patchy. This does not carry over to the deeply expressive slow movement. There, the pathos is a foil for the defiance found in the following division. Was this Bartók's final show of strength in his swan song?

¶ *Concerto for Violin and Orchestra (No. 1), Op. Posth.*

Composed for Stefi Geyer, a Hungarian violinist, this concerto was believed lost until facts uncovered after her death proved otherwise. Geyer had kept the score hidden for fifty years and willed it to Paul Sacher, with the request that the work be given its first hearing by him. This took place on May 30, 1958, at a Bartók Festival held in Basel, with Hans Heinz Schneeberger as the soloist and Sacher conducting.

The first movement of the pair comprising the composition is a duplicate of the initial piece in the "Two Portraits" (*see above*). This could mean that Bartók was dissatisfied with the concerto and simply retained what he wished of the opus under a different title. However, despite the finer craftsmanship of the opening (slow) movement, built on a single, generating theme, the second part has interest beyond mere historical reference. It is rhapsodic but not Hungarian, of concerto size yet formally loose. In totality, the formation proposes a fantasy constructed around a number of themes, with abrupt shifts of mood.

¶ *Concerto for Violin and Orchestra (No. 2)*

[*The published music for this concerto—composed in 1937–38 —does not bear a number. For a long time it was thought to be the only concerto Bartók had written for the violin and thus had no need of chronological identification. However, a two-movement concerto had been completed thirty years earlier* (see above). *To avoid confusion, the habit of speaking of "the Bartók violin concerto" must be abandoned.*]

This violin concerto is among the few that have been taken into the repertoire since the mighty examples by Bach, Mozart, Beethoven, Brahms, Mendelssohn, Tchaikovsky, and Sibelius. Bartók's concerto balances variations in the middle part with sonata designs in the terminal movements. Serge Moreux terms the opus one of the composer's "most spectacular" compositions. Though partly true, the description might well be misconstrued. The concerto is music first: a fusion of subtle (read mellowed) nationalism with drama that lacks bombast. Its technical bravado feeds artistic demands, accounting for its unusual early success.

¶ *Concerto No. 1 for Piano and Orchestra*

Bartók's initial piano concerto is a miracle of coloristic creation, especially the middle movement, which is for the most part a remarkable duologue for piano and percussion. The entire work shows an industrious affection for rhythm. Bartók indicated that his concerto reflected a study he had made of pre-Bach music. Scarlattian clarity is abundantly present, but though the opus may have been born of classical parents, it seeks unclassical, pulsatile paths. Concerto design is validated by the rhythmic properties, plus the type of unsentimental nationalism that Bartók preached. It displays a mastery that damns the lack of concert attention to the composition.

15

¶ *Concerto No. 2 for Piano and Orchestra*

Formal classical apparel is fabricated with native cloth in Bartók's second piano concerto. The designs are neat, enhanced and embroidered with engaging color. The allocation of thematic material to both protagonists is rooted in the systems of the eighteenth century; the structural development, rhythmic thrust, instrumentational vitality, and percussive pressures are strictly twentieth century. The orchestration is a study in vivid contrasts of dark and bright combinations. However, one senses the neoclassic temper of the whole, especially in the polyphonic formations employed. It totals a brilliant blend.

¶ *Concerto No. 3 for Piano and Orchestra*

Relaxed, almost quiet music, but far from laconic. It is a conception that places poetry above drama, with a recital that covers more repose than strife.

This romantic example in Bartók's catalogue was composed during his last days and was shy seventeen measures of orchestration when he died. (Tibor Serly carried out the necessary work.) Some see the music's lighter conduct as signifying Bartók's plan to leave to his wife (also a pianist) music which would be acceptable to the largest segment of the public and thereby provide her with an assured source of income. No proof exists for this theory.

SOLO PIANO WITH ORCHESTRA

¶ *Rhapsody for Piano and Orchestra, Op. 1*

Comparing this production, composed in 1904, with Bartók's later work, reminds one of Haydn's remark after he had completed his first three dozen string quartets. Now, he explained, his music would be in an "entirely new special style" ("*Ganz neue besondere Art*"). Unlike the belly-whopping vigor and gusty individuality of his subsequent output, Bartók's first opus ("first" only in numerical designation, there were earlier pieces) breathes the simplicity and poetically assorted airs of romanticism; the climate is that of mild nationalism.

The earlier realization of the composition, for piano only, lacks the cheerful orchestrational fires that warm the ear and lend needed contrast. Bartók was wise in amplifying his "Rhapsody" not only texturally, but also in terms of length.

SOLO VIOLIN WITH ORCHESTRA

¶ *Rhapsody No. 1 for Violin and Orchestra*

Bartók spins an honest musical tale of Hungarian rural society in place of the pseudo café society yarns of the Gypsies in this two-movement piece. The capriciousness of the style equals total artistic nationalism. Bartók's touch is light and entertaining in this case, his mood mostly gay, though probing. In the initial section there is the free flow of rubati, its measures marking a fluctuating improvisational type of "Lassú" lassitude. The second part—a fresh "Friss"—is directly opposite in content.

¶ *Rhapsody No. 2 for Violin and Orchestra*

Like the first rhapsody, the pair of sections forming this work consist of restyled Hungarian folk melodies. Though a solo work that contrasts rhapsodic terms with those of block-busting propositions, the music is dedicated to a full artistic objective and not designed for the adulation of a performer.

¶ *Two Portraits, Op. 5* (see Orchestral above)

INSTRUMENTAL

CELLO

¶ *Rhapsody No. 1 for Cello and Piano*

This exposition of the piece is just as definitive, if of less coloration, as the original for violin (*see above*), since it is the composer's own alternative setting. Bartók had wanted the accompaniment orchestrated and had approved its being done by a former pupil, Géza Frid, but due to wartime difficulties the project was never accomplished.

CELLO QUARTET

¶ *Fifteen Hungarian Peasant Songs* (*Nos. 7–15*) (arranged by Laszlo Varga)

Granting the extreme rarity of music conceived for four cellos, nothing is more futile than a senseless transcription for the medium.

17

One is reminded of the most infamous arrangement of all time: Handel's "Hallelujah Chorus" boiled down into a version for two unaccompanied flutes! Bartók's faultless, sensitive idealizations are ruined in this transfer.

HARMONICA

¶ *Rumanian Folk Dances*

The pocket-sized wind instrument is an apt intermediary for Bartók's pithy folk attractions. The authenticity of these tunes is recertified when heard in a timbre that simulates unrefined, native quality. Definitely, this instrument worthily serves the original conception.

HARP

¶ *Evening in the Country from "Hungarian Sketches"*
¶ *For Children* (arranged by Aristid Von Wurtzler)

However acceptable Von Wurtzler's ideas may be, they are rather colorless. The reason for a transfer of Bartók for the piano to Bartók for the harp seems to be native kinship (the harpist-arranger is Hungarian).

"Evening in the Country" is the same as "Evening in Transylvania" for piano. The "For Children" designation is confusing and irresponsible. Only part of its random assortment is drawn from the pair of volumes with this title, the balance is from other elementary material.

HORN

¶ *For Children* (*Nos. 17 and 33*) (arranged by Joseph Eger)

Though the horn is extensively used in chamber music combinations of varying make-up, its solo literature is limited in terms of the fullest artistic meaning. Eger's translation of these miniatures is neat, truthful, and valuable.

ORGAN

¶ *En Bateau*

A little-known piece (some studies on the composer's works do not even list it), with a title that minimizes the scope of Bartók's pithy musical logbook, which includes a description of seasickness.

PIANO

¶ *Allegro Barbaro*

Intense, with pugnacious pulsatile drive, and as tight as a drum, this concentrated savage piece is a key to Bartók's percussive, steely rhythmic style. Once termed the work of a composer traveling down a blind alley, it constitutes one of the most important contributions to contemporary piano literature. Bartók's music thunder-strikes the ear; it haunts the memory.

¶ *Fifteen Hungarian Peasant Songs*

The over-all pattern of these "15 Magyar Parasztdal" derives from the folklore research that Bartók carried on, while the *modus operandi* divides the composition into four sections: the outer portions' tunes and dance melodies balancing the inner parts, designed as a scherzo and variations on a ballade theme. Despite the insular material employed, and regardless of the fact that melodic purity is not disturbed by sophisticated frills and furbelows, the settings display a catchy inventiveness. The idealized folk music of Bartók's suite represents a synthesis of the highest order.

¶ *For Children—Volume 1* (Based on Hungarian Folk Tunes)
¶ *For Children—Volume 2* (Based on Slovakian Folk Tunes)

Bartók and Kodály collected genuine Hungarian peasant melodies. They scoured the entire country and covered other areas where Slovakian and Rumanian dialects only were to be heard. This research constituted the most decisive influence on Bartók's work.

The music in these collections represents samplings from the findings, tastefully and simply clothed for display. For the time being, Bartók wished to familiarize students and listeners alike with his discoveries. Though designed for pedagogic purposes at the lower grade levels, the pieces are not bound by the confines of the teaching studio and have fully established artistic power.

"For Children" was written in 1908 and 1909. At first it consisted of eighty-five pieces, separated into four parts. When Bartók revised the collection in the year he died, the total was reduced to seventy-nine and divided into two volumes. Of these, forty-eight are spotlighted by a succinct descriptive title.

¶ *Four Dirges* ("Nénies"), *Op. 9a*

Recitative qualities predominate in these funeral chants. Some see a kinship with Debussy in the style. There are color splashes and

19

chordal blocks, yet the intensity is far removed from the Frenchman's world. Bartók's phrases are longer than Debussy's—the music *sings* more. And the inquietude of the harmony is additional evidence that the rhetoric is Bartók's own.

¶ *Fourteen Bagatelles, Op. 6*

Bartók in miniature, outlining (in 1908) what his future creative course would be. The "Bagatelles" parallel, in a way, the initial signs that Schoenberg gave of his later conduct in his "Six Piano Pieces."

Twelve of this set are right out of Bartók's inventory, like the polymelodic routine of the first piece and the motoric ostinato surrounding the harmonic rub of the second. A pair are defined as folk songs (numbers four and five, Hungarian and Slovakian, respectively), tinted and festooned by the composer. Only the final two bear titles: "She is Dead," and "Valse—My Darling is Dancing." The last of these forms the second of the "Two Portraits" for orchestra. Its melodic and harmonic acridity are just as fascinating in the restricted palette of the keyboard instrument.

¶ *Improvisations, Op. 20*

A suite of eight pieces (the seventh in memory of Debussy) sometimes indicated as "Improvisations on Hungarian Peasant Songs." Folk melodies are the starting point for independent originality. Plenty of gritty sand rubs against the strands of these simple tunes. Unburdened of any romantic thought, the "Improvisations" are concerned only with a supersophisticated formula that has special fascinations. The effect of Bartók's sharp vertical and horizontal shapes is like knives dug into sound.

¶ *Mikrokosmos*

Bartók's compositional catechism is traced through the one hundred and fifty-three pieces that comprise the six volumes of "Mikrokosmos." These range from the most elementary to the virtuoso level, the reasoning process embracing an amazing number of musical facets. Strict concentration on a pertinent problem is the objective of numbers devoted to legato, staccato, dynamics, and the like; others concern modes, some cover dance constructions. Programmatic forms, folkloric identification, and many more ideas are included; the scope for each movement disposed from a tidbit to a work of fair length. It would be difficult indeed to find any fundamental resource lacking—even such subjects as wrestling and the buzzing of a fly are to be found in the descriptive pieces.

Planned as a pianistic course of initiation into the essences of contemporary techniques the doctrinaire impulse is totally absent. It is pure music that Bartók is preaching, not the gospel that merely produces an instrumentalist. These are art pieces from first to last. Simultaneously, "Mikrokosmos" offers the means of tracing the composer's own development. It presents in review the technical and aesthetic diary of a master.

¶ Nine Little Pieces

Concentrated polyphony, contemporaneous formality, satire, and nationalism are contained here. Bartók had been studying pre-Bach music at the time he composed this suite in 1926 (published in three parts). The influence is apparent in the first four "Dialogues," where classical two-voiced counterpoint becomes translated into Bartók's language.

The remainder is less important, though neither the "Menuetto," "Air," nor the "Tambour de Basque" is exactly derivative. The second of these has a childlike inquiry, the last is more pulsatile than usual. Completing the survey are a "March of the Beasts" and a two-part "Preludio—All'Ungherese." These are rather obvious and somewhat pedantic contributions.

¶ Out of Doors

A descriptive précis need not accompany certain music to identify it as programmatic. In three of the five parts of this suite the forcible directness of Bartók's speech is a sufficient guide—the militaristic and ceremonial tone of "With Drums and Pipes," the assorted sonic susurrations of "The Night's Music," and the triggered action of "The Chase." Each projects a vivid, wordless scenario.

¶ Petite Suite

Adaptations of numbers 28, 32, 38, 43, 16, and 36 from the set of forty-four violin duets. The "Quasi Pizzicato" and the "Bagpipe" are not as colorful on a keyboard instrument as they are when presented by a pair of fiddles. At any rate, there is no denying the charm and simplicity of the six pieces.

21

¶ *Rhapsody, Op. 1* (see page 16)

¶ *Rumanian Christmas Carols* ("Colindes")
Further evidence of Bartók's intensive folklore investigations. These interesting tunes are drawn from a compendium of no less than 484 melodies and slightly elaborated for the piano. The collection (published in Vienna in 1935) bears the title "Die Melodien der Rumanischen Colinde." Heard in succession the twenty pieces tend to monotony even with the utilization of asymmetrical arrangement.

¶ *Rumanian Folk Dances* (see page 13)

¶ *Second Fantasy*
Make a wager with your erudite musical friends that they can't identify the composer of this piece. It sounds very much like a pot-boiler written by a bearded mid-Victorian. Historically interesting (one of the "Four Piano Pieces," produced at the age of 22), but musically the very opposite.

¶ *Seven Sketches* ("Esquisses"), *Op. 9*
If these are meant to be brief accounts, the use of sprawling form negates the objective. Further, there is a blend of expressionism with some indigenal melodic material. The stylistic merger is far from successful.

¶ *Sonata*
Primitivism stalks through Bartók's largest work for the solo piano. It is tumultuous in the opening, thrice so in the finale, and tense in the central movement. There is no compromise with dissonance; the harmonic language employed bypasses the triadic in favor of the secundal smash, the barbaric vociferousness of sevenths and ninths, the simulation of bass and snare drums depicted by tone clusters. The effect is magnificently orchestral, a concord of sweet percussiveness. The artistic rawness of the piece makes it one of the most powerful of all contemporary piano sonatas.

¶ *Sonatina*
Strictly speaking, a sonatina is a diminutive sonata, minus development. Bartók's "Sonatina" is certainly diminutive (its running

time is a fraction under four minutes), but its contents make it a minuscule three-part suite. The first two sections are descriptive ("Bagpipers" and "Bear Dance"), the last is a bit coolly identified as "Finale." Actually it is a string of dance tunes from the region of Transylvania. Nothing special in this instance; the outcome simply substantiates the assembled native facts.

¶ *Suite, Op. 14*

Bartók described the "Suite" in his own words on a recording that he made. He indicated that it has "no folk tunes, it is based entirely on original themes of my own invention." His objective was quite special—a "refining of piano technique into a more transparent style . . . of bone and muscle."

The opening has all the turns, accents, and playfulness of peasant musical language; the imitative style is as rich as any authentic, earthy dance tune. No adornments are hung on the scherzo, and the wild homophonically packed third movement is similarly lean. Bartók's "bone and muscle" purposes are fully verified. The final slow and sustained portion parallels the close of the second string quartet, composed during the same period.

¶ *Ten Easy Pieces*

"Easy" is not precisely the case. In a few instances the technical scope is several cuts above the elementary. Though the pieces are wedded to simplicity they have an engaging depth of meaning—even the one devoted to fingering problems.

Two of the pieces are orchestrally represented in "Hungarian Sketches"—the "Evening in Transylvania" (renamed "Evening in the Village" in the instrumentally amplified version) and the exciting "Bear Dance."

¶ *Three Burlesques, Op. 8c*

Piano compositions which prove Bartók's wizardry of musical description. No stories are detailed to the last comma in this threefold depiction, yet each sketch is patently clear. The first is a quarrel, the second a slightly drunk person, the last a capricious individual. In his musical processes Bartók does not demand a story-following listener. If one wishes, the imagination can float along with these pungently harmonized lampoons.

¶ *Three Etudes, Op. 18*

Etudes exclusively for pedantic use are horribly dull; concert studies, such as these, designed for the public's ears as well as the practice room, are quite the opposite. The general characteristic of the form—to display one type of special technique, exposing it musically and, at the same time, consistently—is partially followed in this opus. What is uniform is the dissonant sonority plan.

The first of the group is a headlong toccata, full of *brio,* the second is an impressionistically conceived idea with sharp edges. Bartók's stance here, insofar as musical *sound* is concerned, is more in Vienna's postromantic territory than on his native soil. The finale is an essay in rhythmic and agogic unrest.

¶ *Three Hungarian Folk Songs*

One vivacious and two quiet settings of melodies originating in the Csik district of eastern Transylvania. No capriciousness, instead, the utmost simplicity rules.

¶ *Three Hungarian Folk Tunes*

More national music documentation. The harmonies are exceedingly reticent, as though they did not want to intrude on the *parlando-rubato* quality of the tunes, all in moderate speeds.

¶ *Three Rondos on Folk Tunes*

The first of the rondos (composed in 1916) is charming and light-weight music, trimmed with modality. This is in direct contrast to the remainder, written eleven years later, which have greater depth and leaner textures. The difference in performing difficulty is just as marked. It is interesting to note the use of folk material (the tunes are all Hungarian) here: quite obvious in the first of the three pieces, fully fused into the composer's language in the last two.

¶ *Two Elegies, Op. 8b*

"A return to the old romantic afflatus" is the way Bartók described his "Two Elegies." Such discursive, quasi-Lisztian writing is perhaps a delight for some pianists, though it offers minimal returns to the listener. The inflated substances are neither elegiac nor stamped with the Bartókian insignia of creative authenticity.

¶ *Two Rumanian Dances, Op. 8a*

Not to be confused with the "Rumanian Folk Dances." This is completely Bartók's product. Bravura is the axiom that guides the dances. No gentle and swaying *graziosos* relax the rhythmic dynamo that powers every measure. The vehemence and restless violence is like a Rumanian cousin to the "Sacre du Printemps."

TWO PIANOS

¶ *Sonata for Two Pianos and Percussion*

Bartók's "Sonata" is a tour of a fascinating new timbre world. Always emphasizing the percussive qualities of the piano, Bartók employs it as part of a complex that calls for pitched and non-pitched wooden, membranous, and metal pulsatile instruments. These include small drums with and without snares, plus bass drum, thereby affording graduated relative pitch. The same ratio exists among the suspended and clash cymbals, the sopranino triangle, and the bass-gamuted tam-tam. Further melodic interaction is realized between the wooden ictus of the xylophone and the string accentuation of the piano.

The integration of instrumentation continues into a considerable application of massed formations of sound, either by chordal counterpoint or by two-dimensional harmony. This magnificent array of tonal power is not employed for mock experimentation. Though the designs of the three movements (sonata allegro, ternary, and rondo) are standard, they are given a complete new look by the color properties employed.

VIOLIN

¶ *For Children* (Excerpts) (arranged by Ede Zathureczky)

Eight of the total seventy-nine piano pieces in a discreet arrangement approved by the composer.

¶ *Rhapsody No. 2 for Violin and Piano*

Familiarity with the violin and orchestra version makes for dissatisfaction with the more neutral setting.

¶ *Rumanian Folk Dances* (arranged by Zoltán Székely)

For reasons of timbre scope and singing lines these attractive pieces are beautifully apt for the fiddle. Székely's edition is tasteful

25

and nicely colored; the harmonics utilized in the third dance are especially delightful. (Székely was honored with the dedication of Bartók's violin concerto and was the soloist in the world première, given in 1939, with Mengelberg conducting.)

¶ *Sonata for Solo Violin*

Unaccompanied music for a stringed instrument poses an intellectual challenge (and strain) to composer and listener alike. There have been few successes in this field of music. Most of the harmony must be implied in the melodic continuity, and counterpoint is limited to tightly linked bands, often imaged by spatial relationships of completely separated lines. Though coloristic techniques (pizzicato, harmonics, muting, glissandi) expand the resources, these possibilities must remain minor in the total conception.

Bartók's "Sonata" for violin alone is music for a virtuoso; it is virtuosic music as well. Its demands extend to the auditor. However, despite the limits of the medium the sonata's formal organization is beautifully exposed. The "Tempo di Ciaccona" has sonata implications, it also has some Magyarian contours. Part two is a three-part fugue, followed by a "Melodia" with thematic proposals that richly bear out the title. The finale is a kinetic, presto-tempoed affair that alternates between darting insectlike sounds and choreographic frenzy. Considering its huge emotional and technical range, this work is the equivalent of a symphony for a single violin.

CHAMBER MUSIC

¶ *Forty-Four Duos for Two Violins*

Far from ordinary duets, these are among the most original compositions in the entire literature for two violins. Though pithy, concentrated, almost raw, the duos serve a double purpose—as important chamber music in their own right and as a succinct index of the composer's artistic aesthetic and technical style, paralleling the huge "Mikrokosmos" for piano. In these tender and strong images (replete with color but absent of trick effects) one again perceives Bartók's imposing individuality.

Certain formal possibilities are not scanned because of the restrictions imposed by the medium of two string voices. Nevertheless, this does not prevent an example of Bartók's unique musical graphicism from being included. In "Mikrokosmos" one of the most vivid portions bears the tantalizing title "From the Diary of a Fly." The same insect appears in the twenty-second duet, "Dance of the Fly," with dulled sound, cross rhythms, and open fifths outlining the flight and drone of the pestiferous hero. Another instance of sonic onomatopoeia is the "Limping Dance." The play of contrapuntal accent in addition to emphasis on the strongest pulse portrays the idea vividly.

One of the most haunting pieces in the opus is the "New Year's Song No. 1." A part of its theme will remind many listeners of Stephen Foster's "Jeanie with the Light Brown Hair." The initial use of muted and unmuted tone, with the recapitulation section in totally muted timbre, enhances the music's undertone. And only a genius could have dictated the final cadence of this miniature.

¶ Sonata No. 1 for Violin and Piano

The *klangfarbe* of the violin and piano in Bartók's hands is unique to the concerted sonata repertory. The keyboard instrument provides a radiant combination of colors, from flutelike swaying cascades to sharply enunciated brassy-brash percussions, while the violin sings or scintillates with abandon. This wondrous power of sound makes performance exceedingly difficult. Bartók's complicated method, however, is ingrained within his fantastic speech; the instrumental problems represent his normal language. Bartók does not play to the gallery. He is not an exhibitionist.

The sonata was composed in 1921, at a time when Bartók was moving toward a synthesis of the native material he had gathered during his investigations and was casting off, at the same time, the type of euphony that can be termed semiromantic nationalism. It was a period of sinewy and dogmatic aggressiveness. No warm breezes are permitted to enter the music's territory. The sonata storms, is violent but fortified with new conventions. The creative decree reads: free harmony, chord combinations joined by sharp spikes, vehement rhythm, almost a ravishing of the sonority body. Not for shy ears.

¶ Sonata No. 2 for Violin and Piano

There is no basic design to the Magyarian arabesques of the first movement. The objective is one of motival extemporization. Though the changes are manifold, a centripetal force of balance is present. This is obtained from the violin's initial phrase which peeps through the dynamic flow and holds it in control. The other part of the sonata is an abstraction of Hungarian folklore.

27

The sonata employs harmony with free circumstance. Inosculated sounds (academically catalogued as foreign tones) are not supplementary color sheaths or overlaid on chords; neither are they concerned with twelve-tone technique by any means. Bartók may suggest the dodecaphonic application, but his motive is far from that sphere. Regardless of the dissolution of a key center a tonal basis applies to his work.

¶ Contrasts for Violin, Clarinet and Piano

"Contrasts" was composed specifically for the combined talents of Joseph Szigeti, the erudite violinist, and Benny Goodman, who has bridged the gap between dance hall and concert auditorium by appearing as a soloist in both. Both string and wind instruments are given plenty of technical acrobatics to do and are accorded equal time for cadenza display in the outer movements (both dances). The piano is, in great part, antiphonally featured in the middle part (titled "Pihenö"—"Relaxation"). In comparison to Bartók's other chamber music, "Contrasts" says the least, though it has the genuineness and intelligence expected of him.

¶ String Quartets

[*Bartók's six string quartets furnish an index to his creative career. The first was composed in 1908, during his early period of work. Romantic elements are present but checked by special use of rhythm. Tonality is only somewhat confirmed; Bartók merely hints at the folk tales brought back from his travels. The second quartet appeared nine years later. It shows the hand of a more subtle artist, without a definite changing of style. The folk issue is not separate but ingrained in contemporary harmonic forms.*

[*A period of ten years elapses between the second and third quartets. All previous techniques are now reshaped; the formal procedures are new, the writing for the instruments is of amazing individuality. The pizzicato and glissando ideas and the style of the texture itself give evidence of integral creation, not merely superficial invention. Romanticism has been cast off; the period of elaboration has arrived. Only one year passes before the fourth string quartet appears, indicating that assimilation has begun. This work is on the periphery of the third quartet's boundaries and not quite into the territory of the final works in the medium. With the composition of the last two string quartets (in 1934 and 1939) Bartók arrives at his final period of work. All elements—technical and aesthetic—have been solidified. The product represents mature reflection.*]

¶ *String Quartet No. 1, Op. 7*

The thesis-antithesis of the first two movements is polyphony answered by homophony. In like manner the recitative conduct of part three is contrasted by the sharp-pointed, determinative rhythm of the final section. Thus opposites attract and are brought into balance. There is further total cohesiveness in relation to these four qualities by the fact that the tempo plan is one of increasing rapidity. The speeds move from *lento* to *allegretto,* to *allegro,* and finally *allegro vivace.* The pace continues in the coda, ending in *presto.*

Folk music is little used in this work, but the stress of weighted sounds off the beat is an indication of Hungarian musical dialect; the chordal and ostinati beating are primitive.

¶ *String Quartet No. 2, Op. 17*

Of Bartók's six quartets this is the only one in three movements. Both of the outer divisions are in slow tempo but contrasted in terms of meter and emotional quality. The opening sways with transitory melodicism while the other contains stolid resignation, even remorse, and grayed desolation. This provides the co-ordinated marks and plasticity similar to a painting which has more than one vanishing point for the eye.

Movement two is Bartók without gloves and with heavy peasant-styled boots on his feet. The stamping, violent authority of this music is a magnificent exploitation of rhythm and drive, plus the inculcation of Hungarian fantasy, capriciousness, and rubati.

¶ *String Quartet No. 3*

A hard-fisted essay abounding in polyphonic syntax. As a result the tonality is complex, but is completely outside the pale of bitonality or polytonality. Those techniques demand the striction of the separate keys on their own planes in order to register comprehensively as keys. Without individual identity the double or triple tonal combination is unproved, unheard, vague. Bartók's third quartet is free, but the tonality provides strong anchorage.

There are further matters of newness in this quartet. It is the only one-movement composition in Bartók's chamber music. The individual plan consists of two parts, called *Prima Parte* and *Seconda*

29

Parte, with a *Recapitulazione della Prima Parte,* plus a coda. The latter is actually a recapitulation of the second division, just as the first part is summarized in the section preceding the coda. But the binary story has a new twist. Both of the resurveys are completely devoted to fresh developments and are freely constituted quotations, not exact ones.

Bartók's unique application of concentrated counterpoint and form is paralleled by his innovations in instrumental color. He introduces special bowing techniques concerned with placements of attack, *glissandi, col legni, ponticello,* and other exciting spontaneities. Modified in the later quartets, here these original timbres are a syllabus of eloquent sensations possible to the stringed instrument family.

¶ *String Quartet No. 4*

Timbre and the tincture of music reach an intensity and quality unknown in string quartet history in Bartók's new patterns of sonority and scoring for the instruments in the fourth quartet. The use of mutes to dull the scramble of an exceedingly fast movement and thereby excite by tone color behavior is a marvel of chamber-music conduct. The discovery of new plucked sounds, once and for all expanding string techniques too long static is to string quartet color, and color as a whole, as was the evolution of the sonata form to design.

The five movements consist of a violent *allegro,* a *prestissimo* of sheen and dexterous, slippery subtlety, a declamatory portion equal to a Hungarian landscape touched by morning, noon, twilight, and deep night all rolled into one; a completely plucked sound scherzo and a very rhythmic, frenzied finale—as indigenous a piece of music as Bartók ever wrote.

There is difficulty in finding music comparable to the second movement. Completely muffled in impact this part is a nervous transmittal of a scherzo topic that sounds like a wild whisper. The elastic third movement slowly squeezes the shaped elements of Hungarian folk music in contrasts which mark the deadness and aliveness of nonvibrated and vibrational tone. It is completely recitative; haunted, at times, by the junglelike night sounds familiar to several of Bartók's works. The fourth part of the quartet is, in a way, the most striking single movement in Bartók's catalogue. Devoted to pizzicato it is a veritable dictionary of resources. Regular plucking is related to legato-connected pizzicato, and arpeggio formations of softness are compared to twangy guitar simulations. Normal pizzicato style is contrasted to percussively snapped delivery, average timbre is opposed to desiccated tone. A breathtaking invention, it is a landmark in the evolution of instrumentation.

¶ *String Quartet No. 5*

Movement one is contrapuntally set in sonata form. The texture of movements two and four (both in slow tempi) are of tissue-paper weight. Color is the principal strength in these examples of gossamer antidynamicism. Bulgarian rhythmic flux makes its bow in the scherzo. The four voices hang on a fantastic web of asymmetrical rhythm with a triple pulse taken apart to form a unit of 4:2:3. Contrasting this are three differing arrangements of decuple meter. The result is a musical cliff-hanger of wonderful breathlessness.

The other new feature in the quartet is the very odd (probably autobiographical) inclusion of a hurdy-gurdy tune in the midst of the finale. It is marked "con indifferenza" and is to be played "mec-canico." This signal of a dream world is not explained and can only be termed development by disorder, for the very prime order of this section in A major is like a chipped ear in an otherwise perfect set of cups. It is a "double take" in a precipitate rondo that includes a fugue based on a thematic portion drawn from the initial movement. The use of silence, that most delicate of all "noises," is part of the finale's design and is a significantly dramatic springboard that gives aural thrill.

¶ *String Quartet No. 6*

The cyclic spade digs deep in this work. A germinal theme prefaces each of the first three movements and as these develop so does the unifier. The logic of this idea is enhanced by the time span for the successive introductions, each of which is recurrently longer. Finally, this thematic summary moves away from its partnership with the other movements and individually matures as the *complete* concluding movement, one practically equal in length to the previous three preludes. Thus it is the ultimate synthesis of the generator into the maturator.

For the first time in any of Bartók's quartets, character pieces typify movements. The scherzo gives way to a "Burletta" and a "Marcia" is utilized for the second movement. Color is also pushed further. Bartók's stinging rhythmics had previously turned their way into his harmonies and counterpoints, wherein secundal and septuple forms predominated. He intensifies such frictions by using intervals which span the micro-distance of a quarter tone.

31

The final *mesto* which emancipates the motto theme further unifies the composition by quotation of the initial movement's pair of principal themes. Its final *pianissimo* hush concludes this last work Bartók conceived on his native soil. The remaining six years of his life were spent in voluntary exile from the political oppression that suffocated Hungarian life.

VOCAL

¶ *Eight Hungarian Folk Songs*

Bartók fashioned settings of a considerable number of folk songs for solo voice with piano. "Four Songs" comprised the initial group, produced in 1904, followed by a volume of "Twenty Hungarian Folk Songs" in association with Zoltán Kodály, issued in 1906. The eight under discussion were arranged between 1907 and 1917, and a collection of twenty more was completed in 1929.

The vitality of the eight songs (like Bartók's others) is fascinating; each song containing unequal phrases, quartal and pentatonic contours, and intriguing rhythmic rubati. In their own special way these minuscule conceptions have as much depth as many large symphonic documents.

¶ *Five Songs, Op. 15*

This opus had never been performed anywhere until it appeared in recorded form (*see page 376*). The blanket of silence that covered Bartók's music after its composition was drawn by the composer, who refused to divulge the author of the texts he used and therefore could not obtain publication. It has been suggested that one of the reasons for this secrecy was that the poems border on erotica. This is farfetched, since not even the prissy minded could consider the anonymous love strains voluptuous. Neither is there any *al fresco* nationalism in these almost grim, tightly sparse songs. They are like arias without colorful cadences or extrovert effect.

¶ *Five Songs, Op. 16*

Ballad-type compositions, minus folkloric reflection—a special brand of Bartókian creation. The introspective dark-tinged atmosphere of these songs, set to texts by Endre Ady, defines them as belonging to the expressionistic school.

¶ *Twenty Hungarian Folk Songs*

Bartók called the native tunes his countrymen heard in public surroundings the work of "domestic folk-song factories." Comparing these with the truly indigenous melodies he culled on his travels accentuates the artistic difference that exists between manufactured popularisms and the simon-pure product. The squared regularity of the former is obvious and controlled, the latter is alive with pronounced differences of line, rhythm, and formation.

¶ *Twenty Hungarian Folk Songs* (in collaboration with Zoltán Kodály) (see also: Kodály, page 171)

Between Franz Liszt and the great school founded by Béla Bartók and Zoltán Kodály there is a tremendous hiatus in Hungarian musical history. Likewise, between Liszt (who absorbed cosmopolitan tenets by spending more time in Paris, Vienna, and Rome than in Budapest) and Bartók, there is a huge aesthetic gap.

Liszt's so-termed Hungarian music does not have the natural national speech which was the fruitful result of the research carried out by Bartók and Kodály as a team. An absolute, authentic summary of folk music is presented in this collection (followed by others which each composer published separately). In addition to endemic truth, there is more warmth, depth, and flavorsome enjoyment to be found within these melodies than in all of the Liszt rhapsodies.

¶ *Village Scenes* ("Dorfszenen")

The depiction of a Slovak marriage. No outward reference is made to native disposition in the five songs, which have a stunningly conceived piano support, yet the essential melodies are firmly rooted in native (here Slovakian) culture.

CHORAL

¶ *Five Slovak Folk Songs*

Straightforward realizations that back up the original tunes with harmonies that are neither boldly contemporary nor rigidly tuned to scholastic conventions.

¶ *Four Slovak Songs*

Here is rugged vitality containing a full measure of the composer's personality. Bartók shows how to present folk song without harmonic clichés in a group consisting of a wedding song, a "Song of the Hay-harvesters," and a pair of dancing melodies from two different localities (Medzibrod and Poniky). The setting for mixed voices can be performed with or without accompaniment. Either way the spontaneity of these native tunes is refreshing.

¶ *Twenty-Seven Choruses*

Authentic, native material is at the core of this striking assortment for two- and three-part voices. (The score is for either women's or children's voices with ad libitum accompaniment.) Bartók's music is of gentle dynamic order with subtle chordal intensities, the result of a blend of the traditional and the sophisticated. In this composite it is impossible to know where indigenous tunes leave off and Béla Bartók steps in.

CHORAL WITH ORCHESTRA

¶ *Three Village Scenes* (on Slovakian Folk Songs)

A score bright with virtuosity of plan. The "Scenes" concern a wedding, a lullaby, and a dance, with instrumentational delights peppering the voice lines. The double dimension of this suite is an extraordinary accomplishment that combines tartness with sugar—a fusion of harmonic percussiveness and instrumental sharpness with female vocal suavity, a purposeful contrariness of antiromantic sonorities linked with folksy tunes.

There is no paradox in this combination of the vocal portion's emotionalism and the cold objectivity of the orchestra's procedures. This conflict is obsessive and forms its own style.

¶ *Twenty-Seven Choruses* (see Choral above)

CANTATA

¶ *Cantata Profana*

The "Cantata Profana" is based on an old Rumanian folk ballad. A man's nine sons are changed into stags while on a hunt. Welcoming the complete freedom they now enjoy the sons tell their father they will never return home. He reminds them of the love their mother has for them, the warmth of their home life, the plenitude of food. They still refuse and tell him their antlers do not belong indoors, their

34

dainty legs are not made for confinement within a house, that they no longer want father, mother, or human existence.

In the main the tale is told by the chorus; the vocal soloists (tenor and baritone) represent the oldest son and the father. Despite the naïve subject matter (the moral is unclear, though some contend it was Bartók's protest against restrictions on individual liberty in Hungary) the music is powerful. It is like a symphonic poem enriched with voices, containing a commentarial use of the orchestra and an instrumentalized treatment of the chorus.

BALLET

¶ *The Wooden Prince, Op. 13*

The complete score of a ballet may be authentic, but quite often it lacks the tight construction that is necessary for music separated from stage action. Bartók looks longingly at his old-fashioned fairy-tale plot and over-celebrates the matter. There are only a few interesting sections in this opus marked by eruptive rhythms and abrasive harmonies, and these are contained in the orchestral suite. The pickings are slim here and so is the inspiration.

OPERA

¶ *Bluebeard's Castle, Op. 11*

Why Bartók's only opera (in one act) has not become part of the international repertory is difficult to understand. Encased with rich melody and color, dealing with the fascinating subject of the psychological barriers existing between man and woman, and provocative in its suggested sadism, it has all the elements for success. (With only two singers required, the matter of economy should be appealing.)

Though this Bluebeard tale differs from the usual legend, it is just as grim and bloodcurdling. Bartók's opera concerns Bluebeard's wife, Judith, who discovers the secrets of his castle: each door as it opens reveals a different setting—including a torture chamber, a garden, a lake of tears—with everything drenched in blood. Ultimately she ascertains what has happened to Bluebeard's previous three wives and realizes she will share their fate. The wives, who represented the morning, noon, and evening of life, are now to be

35

joined by the wife who will be "all the nights forever." The symbolization is clear: man's inability to find fulfillment in woman.

This is music not for the "Traviata" multitude, but for the "Pelléas" and "Wozzeck" class. There are no set pieces, arias, or duets, but almost constant musical dialogue. This is an opera that has acute instrumental discourse. Underlining, paneling, and channeling the action, the orchestra is the third member of the cast.

3. ALBAN BERG
(1885–1935)

Though Arnold Schoenberg was an illustrious teacher, only a few of his many pupils achieved the rank of first-rate creators. Only two— Alban Berg and Anton Webern—stand on a level with their mentor. No greater homage can be paid a teacher than that the mysteries he has unfolded will not remain dormant but will be continued and detailed even further. Berg's compositions carry on the Schoenberg tradition but are authenticated by his own independent contribution. (Significantly, Schoenberg's doctrines continue as the root force of the challenging musical aesthetics of the present day.)

In considering Berg's style it may be said that he opened his studio window and permitted the air of romanticism to waft into his music. Schoenberg abhorred and argued against romanticism. Berg permitted only the cleanest and purest elements to come through his creative filtrations. Compared to Schoenberg's distant, lean and cool music, Berg's is warm and well-fed . . . approachable. He proved what could be accomplished with a new technical approach combined with stylistic elements of the most recent past. Since Berg's work provides a bridge between tonality and serialism (torn apart by Schoenberg's dodecaphonic engineering) he can be labeled a creative reconstructionist.

The great variety, the lyrical exteriorization of Berg's music is important. It utilizes the power that sweeps through Schoenberg's system of composition. But an isolated technique cannot exist without feeding on itself; it needs subsistence, which Berg provides. He showed that productive variation of Schoenberg's individual creation was possible and with variation, growth, proof that the original organism was healthy. Thus, Berg (and in a far different way, Webern), not Schoenberg himself, substantiated for all time that the precepts of twelve-tone technique result in meaningful musical language.

ORCHESTRAL

¶ *Interlude before the Final Scene from "Wozzeck," Op. 7*

This portion follows Wozzeck's drowning and covers a change of scene before the final section of the opera. It offers a commentary on the horror of watery death in masterly, concentrated orchestral sound. In a little less than four minutes Berg's music encompasses a powerful miniature symphonic poem.

¶ *Lulu Suite*

During Berg's work on the opera "Lulu" (never completed due to his death) he designed a set of five "Symphonische Stücke" from the composition-in-progress for concert performance. Published as the "Lulu Suite" (also known as the "Lulu Symphony") Berg hoped thereby to stimulate interest in the entire opus.

The five pieces vividly delineate the emotional temper, the nightmarish and fatalistic quality, and technical mode of the opera. They begin with a "Rondo," drawn from material in the second act, then an "Ostinato" (this accompanies a film scene in the stage work) which divides in half, the first part swinging in retrograde direction in the second half. The third piece is a fifty-measure coloratura soprano solo with orchestra ("Song of Lulu"). This movement serves as a dedication within a dedication. It is inscribed to Webern for his fiftieth birthday; the entire suite is dedicated to Schoenberg's sixtieth. The fourth movement is a set of four variations on an old lute tune that has a haunting contour (serving as an interlude in the opera). Finally there is an "Adagio" climaxed with Lulu's death cry, a monster twelve-tone chord embracing fifty-four instrumental voices and covering a bit more than a four-octave range in *triple fortissimo*. The coda consists of another exceedingly short (only ten measures) apotheosis to Lulu, to be performed by the same person who sings the "Song of Lulu" (!) (in the opera it is sung by a Lesbian countess, who has befriended Lulu).

Most operatic music defies separation from the stage, especially when one has had the experience of knowing the opera, but the dramatic force of the "Lulu" excerpts is incontestable.

¶ *Three Orchestral Pieces, Op. 6*

In the opinion of Willi Reich, a friend and Berg's most important biographer, Opus 6 is one of his greatest works. Conceived for a huge orchestra, the music has delicate textures as well as emotional heat, and bristles with technical difficulties. Heavy chromaticism rams its way into the composition but does not take full possession.

Berg's titles, "Prelude," "Round Dance," and "March," are mere springboards for use in considering the music. Some of the sound combinations will seem sheer musical sensationalism, but this is simply a full exhibition of the orchestration. The pieces have magnificent shock appeal.

STRING ORCHESTRA

¶ *Three Movements from the "Lyric Suite"*

Movements two, three, and four of the string quartet composition, instrumentally enlarged by the composer. It has proven to be successful at concerts, but there is greater truth in the same three parts of the quartet version. Berg notwithstanding, the "Lyric Suite" is not music for an instrumental crowd.

BAND

¶ *March from "Wozzeck," Op. 7*

A very short and pungent excerpt. Played offstage in the opera as dynamic counterpoint to a very tense scene, it can stand alone as concert fare.

SOLO INSTRUMENT WITH ORCHESTRA

CONCERTOS

¶ *Chamber Concerto for Piano and Violin with Thirteen Wind Instruments*

Vivid contrasting colors of the winds pitted against the individually timbred solo instruments characterize the concerto, and musical acrostics are woven into it. (The German musical letters contained in the names of Schoenberg, Webern, and Berg are presented in a five-measure motto that precedes the opening movement and form the basic working material.) In the three movements the total chromaticized spectrum is aglow with fresh sonorities presented in a special manner: the violin is silent in the initial section, the piano is not used in the slow movement; both join with the winds in the final part after a dramatically arabesqued double cadenza.

39

The concerto is full of relationships and permutations, such as mirror forms, inversion, retrograde inversion, and so on. The final part draws on a combination of the previous pair of movements, as though proving their validity by way of a powerful summation. Yet, schematic as the work may be, Berg understands that theoretical sport alone is as artistically cogent as the game of blindman's buff. The venture must be expressive, relate a range of sensitivity and vision. His "Chamber Concerto" is a remarkable demonstration of this ability to be emotionally perceptive as well as technically astute. It has heart as well as brain.

¶ *Violin Concerto*

If nothing else the modern violin concerto has put to rest the schmaltzy, sentimental solo pieces that once drew applause. The "ten-twent-thirt" of "Zigeunerweisen," and the like have been abandoned in favor of works with the stature of the Elgar and Bloch, the Sibelius, Bartók, and Berg concertos. The formal plan still requires technical display (else why a concerto?), but a display for artistic ratiocination only.

Berg's rich concerto is for the brave fiddler. Very few care to pit their skill against this opus which draws its resource from a freed, individually-free dodecaphonic method. It is not only difficult per se, but its passage work and fingering problems are dissimilar from the violin music of the preceding era; the demolition of the major and minor key systems necessarily demanding new patterns with new speech. Nonetheless, the spanking fresh concerto of today still retains its heritage: contrasted color apportionment, interplay, interpolation and opposition between solo voice and orchestra remain.

Berg's concerto bristles with enough thorny formations to satisfy any virtuoso, but places them in a richly poetic frame of reference. The orchestra has just as much to say and is as virtuosic. Within the structure of two movements, each subdivided, Berg has woven a remarkable amount of material in his dodecaphonic web, including Viennese waltz shapes and a Carinthian folk song. More pertinent is the symbolic delineation of the young girl (Alma Mahler Werfel's daughter) that inspired the composition. Her death affected Berg deeply, and it triggered much of the concerto's spiritual ecstasy. The girl's passing is pictured by a section marked "catastrophe" and is followed by her transfiguration, in which a Bach chorale is amazingly woven into the music's fabric without altering its technical style. A violin and orchestra requiem that can be considered a masterpiece.

40

INSTRUMENTAL

PIANO

¶ *Piano Sonata, Op. 1*

Berg's preoccupation with polyphony is well illustrated here. Written in the extremely chromatic style of the dying Tristanesque period, it simmers with the flavors of the composer's mature work. Vacillating harmonic and contrapuntal ingredients hold full sway in a pithy one-movement discourse that is restless from the unquiet of the tonal zigzag. Of a period somewhat unfashionable in the jet age the sonata pianistically represents the pantheistic symphonism of the Mahlerian world.

CHAMBER MUSIC

¶ *Lyric Suite for String Quartet*

Berg's "Lyric Suite" is a work of triple-weight importance. First, it is significant chamber music for all time. Second, it stands as one of the most important musical examples of the twentieth century, not only codifying both the ultimate goal of romanticism and twelve-tone technique but also combining them. Third, it is undoubtedly one of the great works of the total produced by the twelve-tone school's "Big Three"—Schoenberg, Webern, and Berg. It forms, with the "Violin Concerto" and opera "Wozzeck," three of the most individual pieces in modern music.

The "Lyric Suite" has delicate textures as well as emotional heat, but, like most of Berg's music, it gives softer explanations than Schoenberg's. Though chromatic restlessness is present, Berg's craftsmanship guides the accidentalized sounds and they are not permitted to free a range. In combining twelve-tone technique (about half of the quartet is in that style) with extended romanticism, a balance of technical power is maintained; accordingly, no belligerently free chromaticism runs riot. The composer's aesthetic is ingrained to such an extent that the fusion does not result in shifts between style.

The six movements of the suite alternate in progressively fast and slow tempi. In this manner the end movements stand in absolute contrast to each other. Tempo becomes a secondary development within a formal development.

Each movement contains one or more succinct mood descriptions.

41

None of these picturesque explanations (cheerful, amorous, mysterious, ecstatic, passionate, frenzied, gloomy, disconsolate) is the sign of a fanciful composer, but of proper insight—all are kin to the expressive streams of consciousness which Berg sets moving with various rates of speed.

These are the psychological factors inherent to Berg's music but without any program. His quartet story is of plunging silence that makes its way without need of definition. The whispers here and the loud tones there are dynamic in total, regardless of level. The cyclic tracing of a theme from one movement to the next is further evidence that Berg's thoughts are not isolated but developed and crystallized as the music progresses. It totals a dramatic tragedy set in a chamber-music medium—one of the most thrilling combinations of sound to be found in any work. Its proper place is with the great last set of string quartets by Beethoven.

¶ *String Quartet, Op. 3*

The Opus 3 quartet, marking the last work Berg composed under the supervision of Schoenberg, is intense to the point of incredibility . . . "wondrous strange." The emotion of the piece is of driven force from start to finish. There are no bald spots in the composition. The peaks are constant; when there is descent it is slight. The music never drops into relaxation or weakness. This is an early work, so it is not surprising that some Wagnerian harmonies come forth, but none are of the sweet-tooth variety. Berg's tonal curves and ecstatic pronouncements are of a world which Wagner never knew.

Berg's quartet is polyphonic and does not include any squared-up themes. The music is organized in one large, continued, endless development. In a sense, Berg's work is a synthesis of elaborative devices with formal looseness being the very means for compactness. In place of thematic thesis-antithesis the components individually pivot, instead of being related and compared. A powerful composition unhampered by formulas.

VOCAL

¶ *An Leukon*

Though filled with an abundance of chromatic sounds, the key sense of Berg's early (1908) song (initially published as a musical appendix to Willi Reich's book on Berg) is quite apparent. However, the composer is too preoccupied with formal content and there are a few specks of dryness.

¶ Four Songs, Op. 2

Romanticism enjoys its last gasps here, where the tones of the chromatic scale jostle one another freely and constantly. The opus includes no bonbon melodies, but rather constitutes a kind of musical chewing tobacco. Berg's songs may be non-Wagnerian, but they resemble Wagner's composing habits, dressed up with additional sharps and flats.

¶ Seven Early Songs

Chordally free, harmonically slightly left of center, the style is related to Mahler's interlocutions. Some of the texts are by such major poets as Hauptmann, Lenau, and Rilke, but the words are of little importance. In these urgent, somewhat poignant, angular songs, Berg sounds like a tonally concerned Schoenberg.

VOICE WITH ORCHESTRA

¶ Der Wein, Concert Aria for Soprano and Orchestra

Berg's reasonings in "The Wine" have a strong relationship to tonal ideology, though the work is based on twelve-tone precepts. Refusing to be a parochial composer he combines the formal stability of classicism and linguistically-free harmony with serial technique. The tri-composite arrives from the use of sonata design to frame the three songs which comprise the aria (the texts from Baudelaire's *Les Fleurs du Mal,* but in a German translation by Stefan George) with a tone row that is a D-minor scale in its first half portion. Thus, the horizontal elements tend to look to the past and the vertical components to the present. No incongruity—actually a compelling affirmation that tonalism and serialism are distant kinfolk. If Schoenberg had cut off old ties, Berg was attempting to make friends again.

¶ Five Orchestral Songs to Picture Postcard Texts by Peter Altenberg, Op. 4

Berg wrote his Altenberg lieder in 1912. They created a riot when first performed and the police intervened before they could be completed. Have a riot and one is sure a masterwork has been un-

43

veiled. There is plentiful proof, including the first hearing of Stravinsky's "Sacre."

Almost half a century later we find excitement and highly colored post-romanticism in the music that scared the Viennese; music born of Wagner and Mahler, yet subtle chamber music (though scored for a very large instrumental apparatus). In these songs Alban Berg is a German impressionist (no pictorial landscaping). The music is free-willed but fantastically appointed. Attention to the most minute scale of instrumental dynamism is equivalent to the careful chiseling, polishing, and sandpapering a sculptor makes on the stone which he works. It is music of impressionism without exterior effects.

¶ Seven Early Songs for High Voice and Orchestra

Originally composed between the years of 1905 and 1908, Berg made his orchestration of the supporting piano part twenty years later. This instrumental afterthought underlines the varied moods. Berg did not tamper with his youthful music, but his mastery of orchestral resource added compelling interest to the songs without impinging on their initial style.

¶ Three Excerpts from "Wozzeck," Op. 7

A sampling from his opera which Berg made at the suggestion of conductor Hermann Scherchen. The performance of these extracts was important in stimulating the initial presentation of the complete work.

The first part consists of a short preamble, the military march music in the opening act, and Marie's song to her child. Section two deals with the bible scene, a mixture of *Sprechstimme* and full song set in variation form, completed with a fugue. The final excerpt begins with the exceedingly frightening music that describes Wozzeck's search for the knife with which he has killed Marie (measures of the most unearthly sound) and leads into the final scene of the opera.

OPERA

¶ Lulu

A study in depth of female carnality played against a Krafft-Ebing décor. Berg's potent music drama has enough grisly perversions to warrant a study by the Kinsey staff. The shock element is apparent from the story line: Lulu, with a long history of sordid affairs and tragic marriages, murders her husband and flees with his son. Involved in a life of degradation, she becomes a whore, and is eventually murdered by a character recalling Jack the Ripper.

Each character is assigned a definite musical form which persists throughout the opera; for example, a scene between Lulu and one of her husbands is cast as a sonata movement, including full development and recapitulation. Despite such rigid use of classically orientated controls Berg does not merely prove his point of technique but cannily employs it for dramatic purpose. The cohesiveness is confirmed by the use of a single tone row from which all themes and motives are drawn. In Berg's hands the twelve-tone ordering produces music that propels a plot of such lurid literalism, that, in comparison, the sexual pathology in Strauss' famous "Salomé" and "Elektra" becomes a fit subject for presentation to Sunday-school audiences.

¶ Wozzeck, Op. 7

A great work is often greeted with sneers and closed ears, save by the cognoscenti, and public recognition comes too late. Thus did Berg's gigantic opus join the operatic list.

Seven years in the making, the opera is a creation of sweeping revolution, one in which musical design and dramatic content merge with uncanny unity. The music is cast in the form of old dances, a passacaglia, a complete five-movement symphony, sets of inventions and variations, plus a fugue. To plan this to meet the concurrent needs of a fifteen-scene drama might be considered a frenzied desire for novelty. But Berg's brilliant intellectual vision materialized, and "Wozzeck" turns out to be one of the profound achievements of the century.

The opera traces the tragedy of the soldier Wozzeck, ridiculed by his fellows. His inamorata, Marie, has borne him a child, but she is unfaithful and Wozzeck kills her. In turn he drowns when he attempts to find the murder weapon. Within the composition, every minuscule point of sound has a relationship to the others and to the whole conception, and yet a tremendous variety of means is utilized: speaking, half-sung and half-spoken passages, full voice delivery, offstage instruments, parodies, even an out-of-tune barrelhouse piano.

Iain Hamilton has pointed out that Berg's opera emphasizes "ferment, decay and death." It is truly a work that transcends the fate of its characters as it bares the psychotic phobias and diseased morality of contemporary times.

45

4. ARTHUR BLISS
(1891–   )

Bliss's early works slanted toward the picturesque, even the grotesque. He experimented in the use of special timbre combinations. For example, his vocal compositions were a music of syllables rather than words. This gave way later to the so-called "absolute" method of composition. Although the maturer works are more structurally regulated, Bliss did not forget his less restrained younger days. They infiltrate all his music, and account for his continued fondness for ballet and motion-picture composition.

As one of the elder statesmen of English composers, Bliss was appointed Master of the Queen's Musick in 1953. His compositional habits follow the guarantees of the present-day romanticist, making him a proper choice for the post. Bliss's music is enriched by certain lush Brahmsian resources which predominate in love of thick contours. Tonal ambiguities are absent. His music is warm.

ORCHESTRAL

¶ *A Colour Symphony*

Bliss has said that mental color images come into his mind when he is composing. Thus, it is not surprising that the divisions of his symphony are defined by color names (purple, red, blue, and green) in place of the usual Italian tempo traffic signs. But Bliss's tinted aspects do not deter one from imagining his own set of color frames. The movements are in the usual distinct relationship of a large-scale symphonic work: a broadly paced initial section, a scherzo, music in slow tempo, and a polyphonic finale. Contemporary romantic faith is maintained harmonically and orchestrationally throughout.

¶ *Dance of Summer from "Adam Zero"*

Bliss respectably blends this excerpt from the suave flavors of Adam, Delibes, and other utilitarian ballet composers. An example of the most rugged nonindividualism.

¶ *Discourse for Orchestra*

Bliss has been honored by many commissions (Coolidge Foundation, the BBC, among others). This work represents the product of the latest commission he has received—from the Louisville Orchestra —which meant not only a number of public performances of the piece but a guaranteed recording.

"Discourse for Orchestra" is a set of continual and partially recapitulated variations described as moods: gay, contemplative, and so on. The technical qualities are par for the course, but the music stays rooted to a central gamut and amounts to dull talk.

¶ *Introduction and Allegro*

Though Bliss is a romantic, he is not the usual postromantic type. His music is more athletic than that of composers basking in the post-Wagnerian light. Only in his penchant for weighty textures is there a modicum of relationship. The move-and-go of this piece keeps the music in balance; it is terse and contemporary in its energetic excitement and rhythmic inquisitiveness.

¶ *Suite from the Ballet "Miracle in the Gorbals"*

Bliss's fondness for graphic music is illustrated with lush resource in these nine sections drawn from the total of fifteen which comprise the complete stage work. One will be reminded of the ballet music of Tchaikovsky and Glazunov, with Anglicized flavor. All the moods of the story of life in the slums of Glasgow are outlined with Hollywood flair: the loneliness of the girl who commits suicide, the finding of her body, the appearance of the mystical stranger who performs a miracle, and his death. Not exactly British music, not precisely artistic music, but definitely serviceable music, and very easy to listen to.

¶ *Suite from the Film "Things to Come"*

Extraction from the complete score of a motion picture creates a mixed bag. But if one doesn't mind, this assortment of à la light Delibes ("Ballet"), pseudo-modern ("Pestilence"), and so on, will satisfy. Old-fashioned moving-picture music despite Bliss's know-how with the orchestra.

¶ *Welcome to the Queen*

The pomp and circumstance of ritually majestic England according to Arthur Bliss. When a composer writes to order he must conceive his music traditionally à la mode, but those who wish real ceremonial music with Englishness written all over it should try Elgar's "Pomp and Circumstance."

STRING ORCHESTRA

¶ *Music for Strings*

The British tradition of contemporary string orchestra music has been quite strong, reaching from Purcell's "Fantasias" to present-day works by Tippett, Berkeley, Bush, Searle, and many others. Bliss's string composition is one of his finest. It is lusty, British in its airiness, and romantic—but not a potboiler of sliding harmonies. Its spirit is daring, its materials consciously related, yet not belabored. It is astringent, but polyphonically flavorsome and full of verve. The composer exemplifies the theorem that one of the most satisfactory of all instrumental media is the string body, in this case of tender sound and volatile brilliance.

SOLO INSTRUMENT WITH ORCHESTRA

CONCERTOS

¶ *Concerto for Piano and Orchestra*

It is difficult to reconcile the date of this work (1939) with its contents of grandiose musical manners of the last century. Though Bliss's full-size concerto (almost forty minutes in length) is not music of total recall, it is not applicable to the present times. The god-fathers of the opus are Tchaikovsky and Rachmaninov, minus Slavic *Weltschmerz*.

For those who like it that way, the composition contains plentiful, full-blooded virtuosity, some fair tunes, spirited rhythms, and Lisztian-Griegian bravado. And the orchestra puts up a good show. Still, with the exception of portions of the tender slow movement, the music is overpopulated by the ghosts of war-horse piano concertos.

¶ *Concerto for Violin and Orchestra*

Just as Bliss turned out his best chamber music works when severely contrasting colors were used, so did he here. In addition to color, he concentrated on timbre weight and its effect on the texture.

Only the length of the work is to be decried, although Bliss is concise in the scherzo and discusses his witty topics to the point.

SOLO VIOLIN WITH ORCHESTRA

¶ *Theme and Cadenza for Violin and Orchestra*

Bliss's reputation, already considered by some to be moving in reverse, is not helped in this instance. The "Theme and Cadenza" is lush, terribly commonplace; a rich man's "Warsaw Concerto." It might be termed a contemporary musical aphrodisiac, but more potent ones are available. I couldn't find the "cadenza."

CHAMBER MUSIC

¶ *Conversations*

Although merely titled and without a story attached to any of the five pieces, the forcible directness of Bliss's musical speech removes his "Conversations" (for flute alternating with bass flute [an error, Bliss means an *alto* flute], oboe alternating with English horn, violin, viola, and cello) from the category of absolute music and places them directly in the field of program music. Bliss's suite was composed during his significant early period of work. At that time, he was more the revolutionary creator than the evolutionary composer.

Movement two ("In the Wood") is a short nineteen-measure pastoral, the third piece is a "Soliloquy," for unaccompanied English horn, and the fourth part ("In the Ball Room") is a semi-scherzando waltz, in cut-and-dried tripartite form.

The most illustrative movements are the outer ones—"The Committee Meeting" (a gem of musical humour) and "In the Tube at Oxford Circus." The instruments of the first of these are to play "with the utmost force and vigour throughout," while the violin plays "a monotonous *mf*." Thus the violin represents a chairman who doggedly tries to keep to his point of agenda, while the committee members (the flute, oboe, viola, and cello) altercate and break all the rules of an orderly meeting. The chairman monotonously insists six times on his very dry point. Apparently he wins, as the final D major chord snaps Bliss's musical meeting to a close.

At the beginning of the urban sketch the conversation in the London subway is very animated and the cello imitates the rumbling

49

BLISS

of the underground. No trains are heard, however, in the middle of the movement. These musical pleasantries are stimulating examples of properly proportioned chamber music combined with clear wit and sparkle.

VOCAL

¶ The Buckle

Folksy charm that perfectly fits the four 4-line verses of the text. By enveloping the sweet vocal line with gracefully sprayed instrumental dissonance, Bliss makes every second of his 78-second song live.

BALLET

¶ Checkmate

The dramatics of chess equated in a ballet wherein love and death are the principal characters. Though the tale has a tragic ending, most of the music is bright and tuneful. It proves Bliss can write for the dance and can spin melodies with nicely framed rhythmics. No intellectual jugglery in this score. Bliss is not concerned with musical corroborative evidence of the moves of his chess pieces. His musical prose is polished and no boundaries are broken in the process.

5. PIERRE BOULEZ
(1925–   )

THERE has never been a creative hiatus in the history of French music similar, for example, to the break that occurred in England, where it took a long time to remove Germanic infiltration and end the timidity of the nation's composers. The line has stretched tightly from Couperin, Rameau and Lully to Berlioz, Chabrier and Fauré; onto the important stage of impressionism, a violent counteraction against Wagnerian thicknesses. With the chaotic aftereffects brought by the end of the First World War, a reaction set in again, this time against the refined textures of impressionism. Two new styles were emphasized—formal conciseness and textural hardness, but with the clearly sharpened lines of Roussel, and the "music with the ax" of Honegger, Milhaud and Poulenc. With the ending of the Second World War the trend was strengthened with two powerful artistic philosophies. One was founded on a type of religio-theologic dogma, with the premise that humanism could find its salvation only in musical form (Messiaen was the most important member of this group); the other preached the twelve-tone gospel. It is noteworthy that some serial elements are to be found in the music of the former group and that certain rhythmic functions predominant in the work of the Messiaen school have been embodied in the output of the dodecaphonists, French or otherwise. (Boulez, the most important of the latter coterie, studied with Messiaen, as did other serialists, such as Barraqué, the Belgian, Goeyvaerts, and the German archdeacon of avant-garde—Stockhausen.)

Twelve-tonism was almost an immediate method for Pierre Boulez. He has remained a serialist, but with one difference. "Continuity" (meaning total consistency) has been an all-encompassing tenet. In his view the doctrines of Arnold Schoenberg were incorrect, since Schoenberg had embraced his new technical formulation with traditional methods of procedure and the resultant synthesis was a stylistic misfit. According to Boulez the twelve-tone act justifies the total organization of all elements according to serial means. (Totality, therefore, rather than stylistic interfusion.) Thus, from his early works in dodecaphonic form (such as the "Sonatine" for flute and piano) Boulez moved into the saturated sphere wherein rhythm, meter, dynamic, density, register, and all components in the design were rigidly dealt with according to serial law. This ascetic symbiosis reached its ultimate point in the "Structures" for two pianos, the piece that made Boulez one of the leading voices in musical composition of the last ten years.

A large body of composers has followed in his footsteps; some to such an extent that degrees in mathematics, physics, and engineering seem necessary adjuncts to the composition of music. Regardless of the supreme objectivity of all this output, and disregarding some of the sheerest technical nonsense by a few of the younger men, there is a developing and not a perverting of the artistic ideal in such strikingly new and different compositions. The tonal constitution of music was rewritten by Schoenberg. In turn, his law has been amended and enlarged by Boulez, Stockhausen, and their followers, into a complex serial code. Since art is above restrictions when it is genuine, all styles will continue to exist. (The scientifically punch-drunk composers have their purpose also. They will supply at least a few lively footnotes for future historical treatises.)

The superpolyorganized state of Boulez's music may bewilder a listener, since much of its declared systematization will not be apparent to the ear. But controls (whether they be diatonic chords or the severest application of involved formula) are a composer's problem. Further, any worthy composer will refine his work, and refinement precedes communication. This is apparent in "Le Marteau sans Maître," which is as sensual as the "Structures" are a set of icy cold intellectualities.

INSTRUMENTAL

TWO PIANOS

¶ *Structures*

Although the description "abstract" may come to mind in listening to "Structures," it is decidedly inexact. "Concrete," "positive," or "constructive" better defines Boulez's huge musical edifice. The music is analogous to abstract painting only in the broad terms of an entity which is not referable to nature (equated in music by tonality, chordally based on the overtone series); undeviating formal arrangement gives this music its entire meaning.

"Structures" may sound like a fleeting improvisation, but it is planets removed from the unpredictable in its absolute, harnessed plan. Each split second is predetermined from a musical blueprint. These include the note series: twelve tones arranged to move forward, backward, inverted, and inverted backwards; a set of durations, one dealing with dynamic strengths (ranging from quadruple *piano* to quadruple *forte*), and one based on types of attack and accent. Similarly to the pitches, all these are permutated and transposed. The role of each of the substances—separately and in combination—is strictly planned from charts, tables and mathematical precepts. If the cry be that this is cold science and completely uninspired, let it be recalled that each creative device reacts upon a previous one and there is more than a tenuous link between Bach's planning of a fugue and Boulez's method of organizing his "Structures."

Boulez's technical plan is further intensified by double series working simultaneously. For that reason the use of *two* pianos; the choice of similar instruments being made to retain the most clarified objectivity: i.e., no changing tone color other than that defined by the dynamics and accents. Melody is absent from this woven network of pitches, isolated durations, planes of strength, and means of articulation. When sounds come together they are not meant to be (nor will they sound like) chords—they are combinational happenstances from the progress of pitches and rhythmic values.

"Structures" consists of three parts. The first part covers eleven short sections, separated by terse caesuras. There are ten divisions in part two; the tempi change at each point and are so related that, working backwards, the last four portions equal the first four, the middle two acting as pivotal differences. Part three consists of varying rapid speeds.

There are complications that arise in the pragmatic plan of this music. The critical matter of durations becomes so rarefied that it is difficult to characterize varying fractional snippets of sound. Further, some dynamic differences tend to be unrecognizable, since it is virtually impossible to express the change between a *pppp* followed immediately by a *ppp* (dynamic indications are relative terms to begin with, and no one can distinguish one minutely set marking from another without a defined contrast as a point of reference). Regardless, Pierre Boulez's "Structures" represents a turmoil of craft, a brilliant effort, and a musical discovery.

CHAMBER MUSIC

¶ *Sonatine for Flute and Piano*

A compound of serial and rhythmic elements outlining a fully drawn sonata within a single unit. This is twelve-tone music to be sure, but minus any smug conformity to rules out of dodecaphonic textbooks. Technical and dramatic ingredients are mixed. Though there are restrictive functions because of the compositional system employed, these do not interfere with the commentary of Boulez's musical tale.

His twelve-tone world communicates with a language of extreme line skipping and violent register changing; the flute is unharnessed so that it growls, shrieks, and rolls its sounds as much as it sings them. This drains out the usual intimacy of chamber music and replaces it with fevered instrumental dialogue.

VOCAL

Voice with Instrumental Ensemble

¶ *Le Marteau sans Maître*

Despite its scoring for only seven performers (a solo voice and six instrumentalists) Boulez's work has imposing symphonic qualities. "Le Marteau sans Maître" pushes beyond the chamber periphery into the area of the miniature orchestra. It can be performed without a conductor (one realizes it would be best not to have the waving arms or baton of a director as this magical and sensitive music unfolds), but at severe risk. The difficulties are enough to test the ablest of musicians, no matter how expert and sympathetic, and with the absence of coalesced sounds in this post-Webernian cycle the need of a directing rod of authority is mandatory.

Boulez's opus comprises nine movements; four are settings of three surrealistically-styled poems by René Char. The other portions are instrumental commentaries on the texts. These commentaries (Boulez is fond of literary terms and forms—his "Third Piano Sonata" has sections titled "Texte," "Parenthèse," as well as "Commentaire") are matters before and after the vocally-stated facts, used and then, once employed, disassembled. Each movement is scored differently, ranging from the third for voice and flute duo, to the final one, which calls for the complete ensemble. The dream world interchange of the poems sets the key for the composition. The French language is quite syllabic, but in Boulez's hands the words turn into sound images as their meaning is deliberately disintegrated, making a seventh instrument, as it were.

"Marteau" can be considered neo-impressionistic serialism. It is a far cry from the music of Schoenberg and Webern; remotely related to the former by fantasy, and somewhat to the latter by the use of sonic pulverization. The peripatetic, dissected rhythms are also reminders of the nervousness found in the Stravinsky domain. However, there are no intrusive recognizable duplicates of any of these composers; the fluid result is pure Boulez—a music of perpetual variation in color and pitch. "Le Marteau sans Maître" is a plastic transformation of strict serial composition. Its music stings while it expresses a Freudian world in sound.

6. BENJAMIN BRITTEN
(1913–   )

I N the early 1940's Britten was considered the heir apparent to the throne of English music, continuing the line of Purcell, Elgar, and the then reigning Vaughan Williams. He was the "big success" story of England's music. His rise had been so meteoric one could hardly keep abreast with his performances. Britten has not maintained his pace, though he retains his place as England's leading entry in the ranks of the world's most important composers. It may well be that Britten cannot reach the top rung because of his facility. (Some say he has written himself out, though this writer contends he has outwritten himself.) It is rare to find creative dexterity and greatness combined in one person. How many can astonish like a Mozart?

Though Britten states subjectivistic writing is a thing of the past he does not adhere to this dogma. While his music is formally certain, it has romantic attributes. The greatest deterrent to Britten's greatness is the eclecticism which stains many of his works. His music therefore lacks a distinctive profile, in the sense that one can immediately recognize a Bach, a Debussy, or a Bartók. But he can write magnificent melodies and he can sense the appropriate conditions demanded for the specific project at hand. It is this uncanny apprehension and interesting solution of the creative situation that makes him a composer with whom one must reckon. Britten may someday burst out as one of the individual voices of the century; thus far his classification is that of a top-professional contemporary composer of consequence.

ORCHESTRAL

¶ *Four Sea Interludes, Op. 33a and Passacaglia, Op. 33b from "Peter Grimes"*

These excerpts have become a conductor's favorite. Britten's "Grimes" music is a present-day evergreen, similar to the "Bolero," the "Firebird," and "Mathis." The pieces are of varying characterizations, but achieve the status of a five-movement suite conveying the general mood, tone, and effect of the opera.

¶ *Matinées Musicales, Op. 24*

A companion set of five pieces to the five contained in Opus 9 (*see below*). In this case two of the movements were drawn from Rossini's *William Tell* ballet music, and the remainder from the bonbons the Italian composer turned out in his late years. The "Matinées" are well-bred examples of musical cross-breeding.

¶ *Sinfonia da Requiem, Op. 20*

The argument here is leisurely disclosed: a solemn consideration of symphonic form, set in a quasi-programmatic frame of reference. The three connected parts (two slow movements embrace the middle portion) refer to the moods of the Requiem Mass: Lacrymosa, Dies Irae, and Requiem Aeternam. Though Britten has a long chain of colors at his command, the scrupulousness of the orchestration is the most interesting facet; the musical material is restricted in scope and rather scrappy.

Britten's composition was ordered by the Japanese Government to celebrate the 2600th anniversary of the Mikado's dynasty, but was refused after completion on religious grounds. Some might agree with the Japanese, for other than religious reasons. The music is dull.

¶ *Soirées Musicales, Op. 9*

Britten says his suite of five movements is "after Rossini" but, except for orchestration, the Rossini originals are fundamentally untouched.

Both the Swiss movement ("Tirolese") and the Spanish evocation ("Bolero") take on humorous twists and are light musical coinage. In addition to a "Canzonetta" and the concluding "Tarantella," the "Soirées" begin with a "March," originally the "Pas de Soldats," contained in the third act of *William Tell*.

¶ *The Young Person's Guide to the Orchestra, Op. 34*

The compound of vaudeville, musical midway, and didactic consideration known as the "children's concert" has brought to the repertoire a few genuine pieces: from the Soviet Union, the best-seller "Peter and the Wolf" by Prokofiev; from America, "Tubby the Tuba" by George Kleinsinger, and Don Gillis' "The Man Who Invented Music"; and from England, Britten's Opus 34, which is evolved as a set of variations plus fugue on a Purcell theme. Save for the last, none of these compositions prevail as absolutes. Conceived with commentary, they cease to exist without it.

Britten's published score allows for the elimination of the narrator's part, but once having heard "The Young Person's Guide" with narration (*see* Narrator and Orchestra *below*) it is frustrating and annoying to have the narration lacking.

CHAMBER ORCHESTRA

¶ *Sinfonietta, Op. 1*

Four woodwinds, a French horn, and five strings equal a dectet. Save for the usual fondness for variational form, this early Britten piece (he was 18 when it was composed) does not have the broader emotional content of most of the later music. It is unpretentious and serious despite the mixture of musical metaphors; French purity and Straussian complexity.

STRING ORCHESTRA

¶ *Simple Symphony, Op. 4*

Early music, written between Britten's ninth and twelfth years, edited and polished by the hands of the composer-come-of-age. For pops concerts or music to read liner notes by.

¶ *Variations on a Theme of Frank Bridge, Op. 10*

Britten's basic means of variation rely on a freedom of departure from the thematic base, with the principal idea represented more in spirit than in its individual characteristics. The ten variants are mainly patterned on specific nonclassical propositions—some of them with a wonderful sense of parody (the fourth, "Aria Italiana," is snide Rossini; the sixth, "Wiener Waltz," pulls the tail of that musical form), others with an engaging color and textural plan. The embellishments do not twine on or flow out of the theme, but disport by themselves in the form of new settings. Myriad activity and change point up the essential diversional aspects of Britten's engaging piece.

NARRATOR AND ORCHESTRA

¶ *The Young Person's Guide to the Orchestra, Op. 34*

A variational wraparound (six thematic statements and thirteen variations) on a Purcell theme (from "Abdelazar," or "The Moor's Revenge") with the purpose of identifying the orchestra's components.

This is followed by a fugue which displays the entire apparatus in sections and full tutti. All this is given with the assistance of a verbal M.C. who points out the instrumental landmarks.

Initially conceived as the sonic data for a documentary film "Instruments of the Orchestra," its rich effectiveness without pictorial support, but with the original commentary, is undeniable. The narrator serves a dual purpose. He calls the timbre tune and is the liaison between orchestra and audience (program notes in the flesh).

Though all the instruments are given a place in the spotlight this is not a mere tone-color catalogue. Allowing that Britten's guide was educationally conceived, this is music that never forgets its artistic conscience.

SOLO INSTRUMENT WITH ORCHESTRA

CONCERTO

¶ *Concerto for Violin and Orchestra, Op. 15*

Britten probes a different concerto plan than usual, in this darkly colored work for solo violin and orchestra. The first movement discourses around suspenseful rhythmic motives. A virtuosic scherzo follows. The influence of Shostakovich is pertinent, but the music refuses to take on a gay air. In the final, solemn part of the concluding movement (a passacaglia) the concerto reaches its finest moment.

SOLO PIANO WITH ORCHESTRA

¶ *Diversions on a Theme for Piano (left hand) and Orchestra, Op. 21*

Piano compositions designed for the left hand alone sometimes have the objective of specialized virtuosic display. This reminds one of Paganini's deliberately playing on one string of his violin; it is acrobatic fun, little more. But in the case of piano music written for a one-armed virtuoso the limitation is a virtuous requirement.

This concerto-sized piece was composed for Paul Wittgenstein, a concert pianist who had lost his right arm during the First World War. In order to continue his career Wittgenstein rebuilt his technique from scratch, and acquired the ability to play music with his one hand that would tax the unhandicapped average performer. Assured of his artistic capabilities once more, he ordered works from a number of outstanding composers: Prokofiev, Strauss, and Ravel among others. Britten's commission was fulfilled in 1940, and bears out its title by consisting of a set of eleven diverting variations. Nothing profound is presented but a thorough-going display of expert variational technique.

INSTRUMENTAL

ORGAN

¶ Prelude and Fugue on a Theme by Vittoria

A minor item in Britten's catalogue. This is his only work for solo organ and is based on a theme from Vittoria's motet "Ecce sacerdos magnus."

PIANO

¶ Holiday Diary, Op. 5

A suite (originally titled "Holiday Tales") of four pieces, easy to digest, quite unimportant in terms of Britten's music in general.

RECORDER ENSEMBLE

¶ Scherzo

A short work for a quartet of recorders. Britten has taken an active interest in the revival of the *Blockflöte,* and, with Imogene Holst (the daughter of the late composer), has published a number of original pieces and transcriptions for the recorder. The "Scherzo" is correctly spirited. With the bittersweet sound of the instruments, it is also quite enjoyable.

CHAMBER MUSIC

¶ Sonata in C for Cello and Piano, Op. 65

No extravagant devotions are present in this subtly strong work. It combines suite formation with sonata principles, though most of the time the movements originate from a monothematic basis. Tonally, there are controlled explorations outside the defined home point. It is again apparent that Britten is a nonconformist in terms of design (his works often have pertinent subject reference points, but he does not permit himself to be driven into formal inclosures). The sonata has five titled movements—"Dialogo," "Scherzo-Pizzicato," "Elegia," "Marcia," and "Moto Perpetuo"—each of which probe these subjects succinctly and successfully.

What is striking is the use of·Bartókian references—varying plucked timbre in the second movement, plus the intervallic tightness of the opening division and severe spatial contrasts between the instruments. But it is not pugnacious eclecticism. The sonata displays a powerful direction of purpose, without any of the elusory elements that mark the composer who rests in a musical bed still warm from a recent occupant.

¶ *Phantasy Quartet for Oboe, Violin, Viola and Cello, Op. 2*

Britten's talents were in early evidence. His second opus was composed in two months in 1932, before he had reached voting age.

Though a fantasy, the form of this oboe quartet is circular, passing through varying tempi and semisectional aspects, determined, in part, by the use of free variation. When these are completed the main theme returns, followed by the original introduction. Toward the end, the instruments drop out one by one, just as they entered.

¶ *String Quartet No. 1, Op. 25*

A mantle of germinal construction covers both the opening movement and the vehement second part of this quartet. Movement three is variational. Britten is attracted to this technique. His juggling of theme is neither ordinary nor representative of the hard-boiled veteran who has performed the same act many times; the treatment and color are fresh. The final movement shows the composer forming his sounds from a motival denominator. The motive is not elaborated, but rather imitated and maintained as an accompaniment.

VOCAL

¶ *Folk Songs*

Britten's versions are sensible and do not obscure or overdress the basic tunes. This is creative reasoning at its most artistically honorable. Only the reactionary purists will complain. In their tight little world, traditional tunes can only be supported by traditional harmony. They consider it a violation of good taste to have a folk song converted into a miniature work of art.

Britten has made thirty-seven folk song arrangements, published in five volumes. The first, third, and last of these are devoted to material from the British Isles, volume two concerns France, and the fourth volume is titled "Moore's Irish Melodies." Since these airs were revamped and had new texts set to them by Thomas Moore, a famous Irish poet and modern troubadour, they are not folk songs at all. However, in their more than one hundred years of life melodies like "The Minstrel Boy" and "The Last Rose of Summer" have acquired folklore status. Their inclusion in Britten's compendium is justified.

¶ *The Holy Sonnets of John Donne, Op. 35*

Britten employs the poetic form of the sonnet in the nine parts of this cycle devoted to the general theme of death. The prose elements serve as intensifications and the composer reacts by being creatively free.

¶ *Let the Florid Music Praise! from "On This Island," Op. 11*

It is difficult to argue about Britten's command of word setting. In this early opus (a set of five songs with words by Auden) there are no mannerisms, or stark clichés; each song is unified and defines the poem's meaning, form, and purpose. The first is one of Britten's best songs; its fanfare D major opening and bravura vocalization are pertinent to the words and yet balanced in reference to musical style.

¶ *Seven Sonnets of Michelangelo, Op. 22*

Britten, according to most critics, is a determined English composer. In Opus 22 he uses an Italian text but maintains his Anglicism. This may seem impossible, but the sensitive loveliness of the cycle is an artistic point of proof. Some of the word-handling is odd, but the music gives sufficient compensation by its inspiring warmth of conception. A full piano background is utilized; it is scaled properly, but the use of patterns is overdone.

¶ *Six Hölderlin Fragments*

With this cycle (composed in 1958), all the basic languages become represented in Britten's song portfolio. The international coverage embraces the many examples in the composer's native tongue, the Italian texts of the "Seven Sonnets of Michelangelo," the French words of "Les Illuminations," and the German of this very expressive opus. In every instance musical and prose character run parallel, a subtle blending difficult to accomplish.

Of the "fragments," "Die Jugend" is the lightest—a combination of waltz and scherzo. "Der Heimat" illustrates canonic expertise. The most powerful song is the last of the set, "Die Linien des Lebens," a stark inspiration with a black-white control of harmony as the acute dissonant chords merge into final consonant resolution.

¶ *Three Canticles*
  Canticle I—My Beloved is Mine, Op. 40
  Canticle II— Abraham and Isaac, Op. 51
  Canticle III—Still Falls the Rain, Op. 55

As the opus numbers indicate, Britten composed his triptych in piecemeal fashion (the years of composition are respectively 1947, 1952, and 1954). Each part calls for a different setting: the first is for tenor and piano; the second for tenor (Abraham), alto (Isaac), and piano; and the last for tenor, horn obbligato, and piano. (Odd note: by combining the voices in the second "Canticle" to represent the character of God, Britten invents a third type of "voice.") Despite the disparity in time of composition and the variety of combination, the pieces have a unity bolstered by sensitive contrast.

An archaic beauty hovers over the "Abraham and Isaac" tale. It is more tender than profound. "Canticle I" embraces the equivalent of a four-movement design; it is as identifiable as a Haydn minuet, its language merely more sophisticated. The poem consists of six verses, each of seven lines. Britten balances verses one and two with the final pair in slow tempi, and contrasts these with recitative and quasi-scherzo sections. Variational treatment is utilized for the last of the set, its text a wartime poem by Edith Sitwell. This black-bordered music, marked by an intervallic descent, can be described as a secular "Kol Nidre."

The cycle has an enchanting clarity (Britten's magical ability to write for the voice is his compositional trump card). These canticles support the axiom that the finest creative messages are often the simplest.

¶ *Winter Words, Op. 52*
Although some portions of this eight-song cycle, set to poems by Thomas Hardy, denote a musical interpretation of the poetical points

(ostinato for the train in "Midnight on the Great Western or The
Journeying Boy," and the piano making like a fiddle in "At the Rail-
way Station, Upway or The Convict and the Boy with the Violin"), by
and large Britten's method is one of artistically flexible musical prose.
While the lyricism is shaped to underline meaning (waltz style to
match lines reading "the pines like waltzers waiting," proper mood
to fit "Before Life and After"), it is also permitted its own existence
and in this manner produces a fine example of modern art song composition.

VOICE WITH ORCHESTRA

¶ *Les Illuminations for Tenor or Soprano Solo and String Orchestra, Op. 18*

One of Britten's most sensitive works—an opportunity to hear
large-scale vocal music shaped by intimate reasoning. Instead of a
big-sounding spectacle Britten concerns himself with a tight, concentrated, and thrilling drama in his ten settings of poems by Arthur
Rimbaud. Regardless of mood the details are pictured by chamber
music adaptations. Romantic passion and symphonic amplitude are
always kept in balance. The orchestra of strings becomes an instrumental chorus of many divided voices. In its splendor this work is
akin to a heady wine.

¶ *Nocturne, Op. 60*

When a composer binds himself to writing a song cycle with a
precise, interlocked subject, it is a difficult task to reconcile such
concentrated plan with the demands of structural balance. If the
design includes searching color individuality to substantiate the narrative, the problem increases unless some technical factor overcomes
these clashing conditions.

"Nocturne" embraces eight songs of different mood, by as many
poets (including Shelley, Wordsworth, Keats, and Shakespeare), and
each is scored for strings with a different obbligato instrument. Since
every poem is concerned with the subject of sleep and dreams, Britten
attains his objective and the necessary formal stability by the original
slant of his scoring without any eccentric instrumentational behavior.
The opening part uses muted strings, they are joined by the bassoon
in the second song, by the harp in the next portion, and so on, until
the full tutti reigns in the eighth and final section. The poetic subject

matter becomes dramatically positive through the musical and orchestrational context.

¶ *Serenade for Tenor Solo, Horn and String Orchestra, Op. 31*

In the "Serenade" Britten's power to fit musical line to the poetry of Tennyson, Blake, Jonson, Keats, and Cotton is magical; the scoring no less evocative.

The haunting six major sections of the "Serenade" (in addition to a prologue and epilogue) are like a synthesis of archaic, yet fresh sound. Sweetened with the bouquet of horn tone, the composition has a gentle nocturnal breath throughout its measures. It defines the essence of music itself. In fact one realizes how Benjamin Britten might have been a younger Ralph Vaughan Williams.

CHORAL

¶ *A Ceremony of Carols, Op. 28*

To write purposefully under wraps, for treble voices and a mere harp as instrumental support, is difficult. Britten's gentle and genuine result is unique vocal chamber music. Devotional in content (most of the words stem from medieval poetry), and with hardly a punctuation of contemporary inflection, the effect of Britten's music is to turn the clock back. But complacent style is not entirely absent from contemporary music.

Britten's employment of plainchant is sensitive and atmospheric. The effect is paradoxical—secular music with religious feeling.

¶ *A Hymn to the Virgin*

Spearheaded by modality rarely employed by the composer, this little composition which predates Britten's official Opus 1 (the "Sinfonietta" for chamber orchestra) was written in 1930 and revised four years later.

Churchly but not conventional, an anthem but not academic, the music contains keen differences of texture with neat antiphonal effects. Some four minutes of real beauty.

¶ *Choral Dances from "Gloriana," Op. 52*

Music for a chorus to accompany an Elizabethan masque that appears in the second act of the opera Britten composed for the coronation festivities in 1953 for Elizabeth II.

In this instance, however, purpose does not change method. These *a cappella* choruses are of general facture, styled in differing tempi and contrasting harmonic and polyphonic style. As usual the choral medium shows Britten to advantage, though originality is lacking.

¶ *Hymn to St. Cecilia, Op. 27*

Quite often choral music merely sets the text per se. In the "Hymn to St. Cecilia," Britten *translates* the music inherent in the beautiful words Auden wrote. It is as though the music and poems were inseparable; created simultaneously. The codification exhibits both sensibility of structure and sensitivity of prose meaning and mood. This is a work for unaccompanied five-part (divided sopranos) chorus with incidental solos. Especially appealing are the varied colors of the voices, to a degree imitative of instrumental timbres, plus a scherzo section that is as close to light string instrument style as a chorus can achieve.

CHORAL WITH ORCHESTRA

¶ *Spring Symphony, Op. 44*

To Britten, symphonic form does not mean relying on past conformations. His "Sinfonietta" is small-scaled, formally and instrumentally (scored for a chamber orchestra); the "Simple Symphony" turns out to be a suite, its blandness matched by a plain string setting. Next comes the "Sinfonia da Requiem," with programmatic overtones, and last, Opus 44, which is a choral symphony.

It is true that words can disturb symphonic purity, but in the "Spring Symphony" the text is integrated with the formal concept. The poems (written as far apart as the thirteenth and twentieth centuries) deal with a concentrated theme (the spring season) and give birth to a large, four-movement design, with contrasts and relationships as beautifully invested as in an instrumental symphony.

Britten orchestrates with vividness; various groups are chosen for their specific quality, and special colors are emphasized: the alto flute, bass clarinet, and a wholly extraordinary cow-horn. As a result, the restricted use of orchestral tutti becomes that much more effective. This is paralleled by an instrumentalized approach to the vocal forces of three soloists, a mixed chorus, and a boys' chorus, who whistle and hum.

Purists may argue that this work is no symphony, since Britten avoids substantiated practices. Never mind! This vivid creation has substantial symphonicism even though it skirts the usual areas.

¶ *War Requiem, Op. 66*

The precept of this imposing work is found in the quotation on the title page of the score: "My subject is War, and the pity of War./ The Poetry is in the pity./ All a poet can do is warn." These lines were written by Wilfred Owen, a poet who served as an officer in the British Army during the First World War and was killed in action at the age of twenty-five. Britten's "War Requiem" is no vocalized fanfare for measuring manhood by battle, no orchestral song about the circumstances of "glorious" combat. It is an antiwar manifesto of overwhelming power, within which words and music are equally potent and important.

To define his document (almost eighty-five minutes in performance time) Britten requires an imposing array: a very large orchestra with plentiful percussion, piano and organ, a chamber orchestra of a dozen players performing on eighteen different instruments, a harmonium (or portable organ), mixed chorus, boys' choir, and three vocal soloists. These sing a combination of the Latin words employed for the Mass for the Dead and the modern English lines of nine of Owen's poems; the texts being contrasted, intermingled, and joined. The juxtaposition of the traditional liturgy for mourning and Owen's words of protest is conveyed by a triple dimensional disposition of instruments and voices. Styles and sonorous contexts contrast yet fuse subtly in these three categories. The first group—consisting of the solo soprano, mixed chorus, and orchestra—represents the liturgical element and is dramatic and brilliant; the second, with the tenor, baritone, and chamber orchestra, identifies worldly quality and is dry and almost gritty in sound; the third section (boys' voices and harmonium) is always veiled and ethereal in content and defines the heavenly innocent.

Tremendous publicity has followed in the wake of performances of Britten's requiem and a number of critics have hailed the opus as the greatest of the century. Some may not term this a masterful work, but they cannot deny that Britten's handling of the work is masterful. Even though it is derivative in spots (the "Dies Irae" recalls the stylistic manner of Carl Orff), it is his greatest achievement to date, worthy of company with the famed requiems by Mozart, Berlioz, and Verdi. In the "War Requiem" Britten has proven that tonal music is not a dead language.

CANTATA

¶ *Cantata Academica* (Carmen Basiliense), *Op. 62*

Fittingly titled and constructed to fit, Britten's thirteen-sectioned cantata was written in 1960 as a result of a commission from the University of Basel, to help celebrate its quincentenary.

Academic, yes, though not strictly conventional. Britten puts on formal cap and gown but wears them with a dodecaphonically fashioned slant. Each of the movements is based on a different pitch for its key span, and thus the work encompasses twelve tones (the thirteenth section returns to the polarity of the opening). Serial organization is thereby considered, accepted peripherally, but otherwise cast its lot tonally. The tone row is only used as a row in the eighth part, and even there it is disguised as E flat major harmony. The forms are a dictionary of devices, such as chorale, canon, recitative, arioso, scherzo, and fugue, combined with techniques galore: ostinato, inversion, retrograde, stretto, pedal points, imitation, and so on.

While all this is professional, it is also professorial, perhaps because Britten considered his scholastic commission too scholastically. Measured by the formal slide rule, Britten's cantata is quite resourceful; estimated by dramatic criteria it is found wanting.

¶ *Rejoice in the Lamb, Op. 30*

A cantata in ten sections, the text drawn from the poem by Christopher Smart (1722–1771), which is, in the apt description of H. F. Redlich, a composite of "cloudy and mystical religiosity." Britten's music is most moving in its simple "Allelujah" portions (parts three and ten), most curious in a division devoted to the poet's cat, Jeoffry. This latter division includes a motive in the organ which politely delineates feline characteristics.

¶ *Saint Nicolas, Op. 42*

It is noteworthy that Britten, more than any other contemporary composer, has utilized the touching quality of children's voices for cogent artistic effect. In "Saint Nicolas" the young voices enhance, in a contrapuntal-color manner, the manifold forces of a solo tenor, a mixed chorus, and a four-ply instrumental aggregate of string orchestra, percussion, organ, and piano duet.

Dealing with nine episodes in the legendary tale of the patron saint of children, seamen, and travelers, Britten planned his work to include audience participation in the singing of hymns at the conclusion of the fifth and final sections. The score lives up to the composer's statement that the instrumental parts are "not very sophisticated." Lyrical, colorful, unassuming, this attractive work is easy to listen to.

BALLET

¶ *The Prince of the Pagodas, Op. 57*

Britten's ballet tale is confused and overloaded with characters and situations. Despite some good portions the music is a mixture of utilitarian assignment with overtones from early and late Russian ballets (Tchaikovsky and Prokofiev).

OPERA

¶ *The Little Sweep, Op. 45*

A contemporary counterpart of the joyousness that permeates *Hänsel und Gretel*, "The Little Sweep" is actually the last act of an "entertainment for young people." It is preceded by a story about children and their elders who plan some holiday fun and decide "Let's Make an Opera" (the title of Britten's "entertainment"). The opera concerns a poor boy who as a chimney sweep is dominated by a pair of bullying masters, and his adventures in a school nursery where the action takes place. The lad is rescued by being placed in a trunk and returned to his family.

Britten's music is light and tuneful, a real delight to the ear. Far from a set of pieces in simple style, the composition includes invigorating formal usages, such as cross rhythms, a passacaglia, and so on; the refreshing themes are always those of whimsy and humor. Instrumental color is limited to strings, four-hand piano, and percussion, and these timbres are a delicate aid to the musical Dickensian flavor of the whole. Though there is an air of folk song within the opera, Britten avoids such currents; "The Little Sweep" is truly English—a specifically national music without defined extraction from folk source. In the serious art form of "children's music" Benjamin Britten has no equal.

69

¶ *Noye's Fludde, Op. 59*

Compositions for children (but artistically acceptable to any age) form a special part of music's history. Britten's contribution, "Noye's Fludde," is the most ambitious and significant of his total output in this category. In his setting of a Chester Miracle Play of the Middle Ages Britten has succeeded in making a union of disparities. He calls for a cast that combines adults with children—meaning, professionals with amateurs—and the result is enchanting magic art.

God, Noah, and his wife are the only adult voices; the first a narrator's part. Noah's sons and their wives, all other parts, and the chorus call for young people. The orchestral division is also largely assigned to children, playing string and percussion instruments (including the clean sound of handbells), recorders and bugles, contrasted to a professional chamber combination of string quintet, piano duet, recorder, percussion, and organ.

The tale is presented with expressive simplicity, intensified by the colorful Middle English text and includes three hymns sung at key points by cast and congregation (the opera is meant for church performance). Sheer inspiration marks the processional march of the animals into the ark, heralded by bugle calls and interspersed with the singing of a "Kyrie eleison." No less inspired is the subtle sense of the storm scene, set in passacaglia form, followed by the scene of the dove's flight and return with an olive branch. The bird is represented clearly by a dulcet recorder, flutter-tonguing included.

Music of tremendous charm and effect. Britten surely took pleasure in writing this composition.

¶ *Peter Grimes, Op. 33*

The success of this opera makes its absence from the repertory an enigma. Britten was commissioned to compose "Peter Grimes" by the Koussevitzky Foundation. It received its première at the Sadler's Wells Theatre in June of 1945, then was performed at the Berkshire Music Center, and the Metropolitan. Despite a huge number of European productions, "Grimes" has been silent in America since the Met season of 1948–49. What price operatic expression when a major contemporary work must be sacrificed to the depressing merry-go-round of the old stand-bys?

Britten's opera is grim and powerful. It concerns a violent and sadistic fisherman whose two apprentices meet with accidental deaths. The villagers do not believe the facts; only one person, a widowed schoolteacher, whom Grimes wishes to marry, understands. When she discovers Grimes's harshness, she realizes there is no hope for him. Grimes takes to the sea and scuttles his boat.

The *dramatis personae* is distinguished by superbly contrasted characterizations; a retired sea captain, a constable, a nerve-frazzled widow, a druggist, among others. The chorus plays an important role. It represents the "crowd," the unified protagonist pitted against one personality who will not merge with the others.

Britten's music is free of artificialities that might disturb the story line. "Peter Grimes" is a continuous drama, although it contains all the usual ingredients: arias and duets, storm, crowd, pub, and church scenes, plus the serious techniques of canon, passacaglia, and fugue. The orchestra itself represents a member of the cast. And in this stage work the text is set without any marking of time; there are no scene-setting recitatives.

The musical profits of "Peter Grimes" are gigantic, and once the listener is caught up in the plot he will experience a virtuoso operatic experience. The conventions of large-scale opera are not smashed, but neither are they painfully followed. They have been given a fresh scope of tremendous excitement.

¶ *The Turn of the Screw, Op. 54*

Rarest of all operatic types is that of a ghost story, packed with quiet, psychological terror. Britten's composition, based on the bone-chilling Henry James tale, holds the attention as it relates the supernatural grip of a man and woman on two children in the care of a governess. The manifestation of this evil power is not precisely disclosed and the tale becomes more frightening in the play on the listener's imagination. The effect is heightened further when ghosts are seen and heard—an important difference from the original story.

With uncanny ability, Britten conveys the horror of this ghastly domination. Despite the inclusion of some children's tunes, the score retains a sombre, threatening polyphonic quality from prologue to completion. The technique of thematic variations is still another binding device, but is governed freely so that it does not stem the flow. These variants are formal weights that aid the musical equilibrium. The theatrical impact of this opera gains by the use of compressed instrumentation. Britten uses five strings, four woodwind players (performing on eight instruments), horn, harp, piano, celesta, and percussion to produce the tragic, macabre totality of this work.

7. LUIGI DALLAPICCOLA
(1904–   )

Luigi Dallapiccola is not only the unquestioned leader of Italy's twelve-tone composers, but one of the outstanding exponents of this technique in any country. He adopted the dodecaphonic style without studying with Arnold Schoenberg, any of his pupils, or, for that matter, any devotee of the system. He is a twelve-tone classicist compared, for example, to the younger Italians Nono, Berio, and Maderna, who are left-winging dodecaphonic extremists. These avant-couriers of the avant-garde compose in a rigid totally serialized style that splinters the already tiny elements that constitute musical pointillism. The romantic serial imagery of Dallapiccola is quite a different story.

Dallapiccola is a rare member of the twelve-tone fraternity, for he does not abandon traditional premises; these are defined and apparent in his music no matter how much the material is freed. They are found in the use of melodic and harmonic intervals together with spiky sevenths and nippy ninths, and include the clear octave. Further, the link is indicated by the triadic suggestion found within his music, the often-heard Italianate sweep of the melodic lines, and the hinting of tonal center equivalences. Thus, Dallapiccola paradoxically endows tonality with nontonality—the strictures of the latter permeate the laxness of the former.

His work is different from the Viennese dodecaphonists. While it shares their dramatic impetus and color sensitivity, it is of clearer texture, hardly heavy or nervous, and never scratched with *Weltschmerz*. Accordingly, his music gives full proof that twelve-tone music is not a dead-end; is, in fact, anything but the musical mathematics the snide critics say it is. The development of dodecaphony warrants the existence of the technical idea, and Dallapiccola is one of the few composers to bring in aesthetic synthesis. In his case theory did not overpower creative artistry.

ORCHESTRAL

¶ *Variazioni per Orchestra*
Dallapiccola's "Variations" are continuous, but demarcated by acute differentiations of texture and mood. There is no diffuseness; the objectives are clearly presented by the fully realized power of variational technique, and the syntax is embellished by stunning orchestration.

SOLO INSTRUMENT WITH ORCHESTRA

SOLO VIOLIN WITH ORCHESTRA

¶ *Tartiniana for Violin and Orchestra*
Tartini's thematic material, selected from his sonatas, is combined with harmonic and contrapuntal developments drawn and orchestrally colored to scale and perfect fit by Dallapiccola. Serial methods are utilized for tonal materials, enhancing the 18th-century melodicism.

VOCAL

¶ *Quattro Liriche di Antonio Machado*
Dallapiccola exempts himself from any solemn use of serial technique in these four songs. The freedom lends a fresh touch to the style, making the vocal shapes quite different from the angular patterns found in the Schoenbergian school. Loosening the bonds of formal discipline gives the music a benignity that beautifully fits the outer pieces which deal with springtime. The more brooding lyricism of the other sections provides perfect contrast.

VOICE WITH ORCHESTRA

¶ *Cinque Frammenti di Saffo* ("Five Fragments of Sappho")
Part one of a trilogy of "Greek Lyrics" (the second part titled "Sex carmina Alcaei," for the third, *see* "Due Liriche di Anacreonte" *below*). This cycle ushered in Dallapiccola's total employment of twelve-tone technique. The pieces are minatures, each a probing con-

73

centrate. But there is no Teutonic grey coldness. The disposition is of southern climate, each song has the decisive stamp of quiet _bel_ (read "twelve") _canto_. Constructivistic though the music may be, in Dallapiccola's hands the technical system is secondary to the emotional expression.

¶ _Concerto per La Notte di Natale dell'anno 1956_ ("Christmas Concerto for the Year 1956")

Dallapiccola's form of musical worship is not marked by commonplace hymn singing in this concerto for soprano voice and seventeen instruments. The voice is employed in the second and fourth movements, and the translated tempi (animated, jubilant and impetuous, violent) underline the apodictic tone of vehemence that shows the worship of God is as powerful (if less sweet) as ever. The poetry consists of three excerpts (a total of twenty-two lines) from the thirteenth-century mystic writer Jacopone da Todi. An instrumental prologue initiates the composition and the second vocal section is preceded by an intermezzo and concluded with an epilogue. It is possible to describe these divisions as _cantus lateralis,_ literally "song side by side," since the continual growth of the material not only reaches new points of information but provides constant fresh ideas of instrumental color.

VOICE WITH INSTRUMENTAL ENSEMBLE

¶ _Cinque Canti per Baritone e Alcuni Strumenti_ ("Five Songs for Baritone and Several Instruments")

This opus (the vague indication employed in the title, "alcuni strumenti," covers eight instruments) changed the line of Dallapiccola's previous work. Composed in 1956, the style is much more nervous. Dallapiccola's previous creative suavity is uprooted. These "Cinque Canti" sound as though they should bear the German title "Fünf Lieder."

¶ _Due Liriche di Anacreonte_ ("Two Anacreontics")

This is the last part of a trilogy of "Greek Lyrics," translated into Italian by the 1959 Nobel prize winner Salvatore Quasimodo (the initial part of the cycle—"Cinque Frammenti di Saffo"—is discussed above, _see_ Voice with Orchestra).

Diatonic-Italian music colors every sound, though the piece is dodecaphonic. A diminutive form cannot express too many sides to the musical angle. It must concentrate on essentials. Accordingly, Dallapiccola sets his two songs (both concern Eros) in canonic and variational format. He codes his music with germane timbre, employing a pair of clarinets (one being the high-pitched, thinner-toned E flat), viola, and piano. Expressive music with expressive results.

¶ *Goethe Lieder*

The language of these seven concise pieces illustrates how potent twelve-tone speech can be in place of the overgushing conversations of the post-romantic tonal elite. Regardless of the total polyphony (the harmony results from the juxtaposition of moving lines; it is not measured to fit specific vertical rule) there is no harshness. Dallapiccola's active support of dodecaphonic language is warmed by his Mediterranean accent; it speaks with passion, but passionate neatness.

The "Goethe Songs" constitute lyrical chamber music for the unusual combination of a voice and three different clarinets: the small (E flat), normal, and bass. Although the aid of the score is required to decipher the assorted tone-row permutations, this is unnecessary; musical content and merit need not be determined or proved by technical premises. This music glows; it is also very moving.

CHORAL

Choral with Orchestra

¶ *Canti di Prigionia*

These "Songs of Prison," with modality, chromaticism, and pantonality, represent the composer's protest against Fascist aggression and totalitarian rule. Dallapiccola's persistent belief in democracy and his love of man's freedom are expressed in these three pieces which comprise a prayer, an invocation, and a farewell (the later "Canti di Liberazione" testifies to the composer's optimism for the future). The music, powerfully acute, eliminates all strings and winds in its percussively pointed orchestration (two pianos, two harps, xylophone, vibraphone, eight tubular bells, three tam-tams of different size and therefore pitch, suspended and clashed cymbals, triangle, timpani, snare and bass drums), and is harsh only in its aura of desperation.

75

8. MANUEL DE FALLA
(1876–1946)

CONSIDERED one of the superior creative voices of the twentieth century, Manuel de Falla is undoubtedly the greatest of all Spanish composers. This does not imply his art was constricted, bound by indigenous rule, even though the label "Made in Spain" vividly identified his output.

Falla's music reached beyond a national setting because he was not baldly intent on turning out an endemic product. The unyielding nationalist—unyielding in the sense that he believes creative patriotism is exhibited by the literal and exclusive employment of folk data —cannot produce first-rate work. Such a credo puts independence and truth into a deep freeze.

The special tone in Falla's work is its subtlety. He was not insensitive to flamenco heat and Mediterranean passion but kept such moods under control. Falla's Spanish emotions were reflective rather than dogmatic. The evocation of Hispanic atmosphere and the intonational curves of native musical speech strengthened his work. He reflected on and developed the racial characteristics of his country's musical temper and avoided any blatant mimicking of its popularisms. Not a single cheap, artificial "tune" can be found in Falla's music.

Like Bartók, Falla studied the melodies of his countrymen. But he purified them, extracted their flavor, refined and re-created the basic material. Despite certain impressionistic colorations Falla's music, as a result, is objective, i.e., classical in its printing.

Excessively critical (often the concomitant of a retiring personality), Falla wrote very slowly and his catalogue is exceedingly small —two ballets, a one-act chamber opera, a lyric music drama, single works for orchestra and for piano with orchestra, a unique type of harpsichord concerto, some songs, piano pieces, and a few short miscellaneous items. Worth, of course, is not measured by output. The impact of Falla's work proves its masterful values.

76

ORCHESTRAL

¶ *El Amor Brujo* ("Love, the Magician")

A simple plot surrounds the music of "El Amor Brujo." A young Gypsy girl finds love, but her romance is haunted by the ghost of her former paramour. Attempts to exorcise the phantom (the music for this portion is the famed "Ritual Fire Dance") are unsuccessful. Another girl accompanies the lovers to their next meeting; the ghost is distracted, succumbs to the new face, and the couple find peace and happiness.

Despite the conception of "El Amor Brujo" as a one-act ballet, it is rarely seen in that form; the huge number of performances as an extracted suite of a baker's dozen numbers has led to the adoption of Falla's inspired work as a symphonic piece with or without voice, or with instrumental substitutes for the latter (*see* Voice and Orchestra *below*). The music displays moods ranging from the starkly primitive to the mournfully evocative. Brilliant and alive with color the score is fundamentally Andalusian (considered the most characteristic region of Spain). The orchestration is a marvel of effect though the instrumental forces are restrained—only pairs of horns and trumpets are utilized in the brass section.

¶ *Ritual Fire Dance from "El Amor Brujo"* ("Love, the Magician")

This is the piece that caused Manuel de Falla to become a household name. The orchestral setting is straight from the original ballet. No brave, new arrangement can match its color and fire.

¶ *El Sombrero de Tres Picos* ("The Three-Cornered Hat") (Suites Nos. 1 and 2)

Here is the fullest promulgation of Hispanic sensations and the criteria for authenticity in nationalistic art. The liberating folk force not only shapes the profile of Falla's composition, but gives it stamina, while also serving as a point of departure.

If wit is paramount in the ballet's story (*see* Ballet *below*), the orchestral suites form a crescendo of color and rhythmic bewitchment which ravishes the senses. Inspired by traditional native dance forms, the music is stylized by discriminating sophistication. No one-two-three-four pulsed monotony blemishes Falla's measures. In "The

77

Neighbors" Mozartian motility contrasts to seguidilla snap. The farruca-styled "Miller's Dance" is mild and also violent, a flamenco both tamed and untethered—its heel-stamping conclusion raises the temperature. And no better illustration of rhythmic ambivalence can be given than the final dance of the ballet composition, where ideas whirl along sometimes in duple beat, sometimes in triple. Presumably this is a jota, but no national dance remained static in Manuel de Falla's hands.

¶ *Homenajes* ("Homage")—*Suite Sinfonica for Orchestra*
The last work Falla completed is a weak effort and certainly not in the class of his ballets and other major compositions. It consists of a fanfare, two transcriptions of earlier guitar and piano pieces, plus a final movement so passive that attention lags.

¶ *La Vida Breve* ("Life is Short") (Interlude and Dance)
Poignant atmosphere and ethnic veracity are contrasted in this double portion from Falla's opera, his first creation for the stage. The "Interlude" covers a scene in which the heroine, forsaken by her lover, approaches the villa of his new sweetheart, where a wedding party is being held. This leads into the companion piece which forms a part of the festivities. Evocative sensualism permeates the dance. The effect is eloquent.

ORCHESTRAL ARRANGEMENTS

¶ *Dance of the Miller's Wife from "El Sombrero de Tres Picos"* ("The Three-Cornered Hat")
Though a fair number of arrangements have been made for the solo guitar, this is the only one that seems to exist for the unusual combination of an orchestra of plucked stringed instruments.

¶ *Ritual Fire Dance from "El Amor Brujo"* ("Love, the Magician")
Popular fare for the pop, jazz, and fad arrangers. None do Falla justice.
The boys have been busy with this piece ever since Paul Whiteman began to "jazz the classics." But the verdict is strictly thumbs down. Even the latest trick of plenty of peppery percussion hasn't helped.

SOLO INSTRUMENT WITH ORCHESTRA

SOLO PIANO WITH ORCHESTRA

¶ *Noches en los Jardines de España* ("Nights in the Gardens of Spain"), *Symphonic Impressions for Piano and Orchestra*

Paradoxes pile up in this triple set of nocturnal impressions. It is a concerto, minus exhibitionism, conceived in terms of concentrated chamber music. It is orchestrated in French pastels that trace Spanish contours. It combines coolness with sensual warmth. It indicates picturesque titles but tells no story.

Falla's "Nights" was written with no pretension of being descriptive. The composer said the music was "merely expressive," meant to evoke "sensations and sentiments." Nevertheless, many annotators have foolishly attempted to wrap the piece in a purple cloth of programmaticism. "Nights in the Gardens of Spain" grows increasingly rhythmic and excited as it progresses; but, whatever the mood or tempo, it contains all the elements and persistencies that make for impressionism—meaning that it is suggestive and not positive. Falla's themes are too languorous, too dipped in color, and are not squared sufficiently to be rooted out and developed methodically. In this colorful instance Hispanic impressionism clearly produces its own brand of clarity and powerful effect.

INSTRUMENTAL

CELLO

¶ *Ritual Fire Dance from "El Amor Brujo"* ("Love, the Magician")

A much more satisfactory arrangement than the overworked one for piano. The roughage a cello supplies is good for this kind of musical diet.

¶ *Seguidilla Murciana from "Siete Canciones Populares Españolas"* ("Seven Popular Spanish Songs")

Folk song is given the full-dress treatment in this transcription of the first of Falla's set of seven songs.

¶ *Spanish Dance No. 1 from "La Vida Breve"* ("Life is Short")

A beautifully realized translation which respects the original while understanding the stringed instrument's potential.

¶ *Suite Populaire Espagnole*

This is the secondary title for the "Seven Popular Spanish Songs," used when the transcription of six of the group was made first for violin and then for cello by Paul Kochanski and Maurice Maréchal, respectively.

GUITAR

¶ *Canción del Fuego Fátuo* ("Song of the Will-o'-the-Wisp") *from "El Amor Brujo"* ("Love, the Magician")

Despite the imitation of guitar technique in Falla's orchestration, this resetting makes little sense and has no depth, even though it was accomplished by master guitarist Miguel Llobet.

¶ *El Círculo Mágico—Romance del Pescador* ("The Magic Circle—"The Fisherman's Song") *from "El Amor Brujo"* ("Love, the Magician")

This transcription represents a poor attempt to add to the repertoire for guitar.

¶ *Homenaje: Pour le Tombeau de Debussy* ("To the Memory of Debussy")

The original setting of the piece, later incorporated in the orchestral suite "Homenajes" (*see* Orchestral *above*). An elegiac mood is maintained within a basic habanera metrical design. By employing an instrument most representative of his native land, Falla pays further homage to Debussy's evocative Spanish-styled and colored music.

TWO GUITARS

¶ *The Miller's Dance from "El Sombrero de Tres Picos"* ("The Three-Cornered Hat")

Even a half-dozen guitars couldn't make this arrangement convincing. Falla's dance needs the guts of an orchestra, of bows hammering in *martelé* style on the strings, not fingers plucking them.

HARMONICA

¶ *Ritual Fire Dance from "El Amor Brujo"* ("Love, the Magician")

If transcriptions must be, this will do. The trills and color contrasts possible to this distinctive instrument show off Falla's hackneyed piece with telling effect.

HARP

¶ *Dance of the Corregidor from "El Sombrero de Tres Picos"* ("The Three-Cornered Hat")

A portion of the ballet rarely utilized for transcription. Its zestful content makes for satisfactory results.

¶ *Jota from "Siete Canciones Populares Españolas"* ("Seven Popular Spanish Songs")

There are a number of instrumental substitutes for Falla's original vocal and piano piece. In this case the harp is a sound medium.

¶ *Spanish Dance from "La Vida Breve"* ("Life is Short")

The element of *legato* is as important in this beautiful bit as its rhythm. Since true *legato* is not a primary attribute of the harp, it is obviously an unfitting choice for the translation of Falla's effective gem.

ORGAN

¶ *Ritual Fire Dance from "El Amor Brujo"* ("Love, the Magician")

Georges Montalba's arrangement (for organ with percussion!) is vulgar, consisting of muddy trills, ponderous, stuffy rhythms, and a tinkly xylophone.

PIANO

¶ *Canción and El Paño Moruno from "Siete Canciones Populares Españolas"* ("Seven Popular Spanish Songs")

Most often, versions of these songs are heard in cello and piano or violin and piano combinations. The solo piano draft was made by

81

another Spanish composer, Ernesto Halffter, who had been one of Falla's pupils. The pieces are rarely performed in this form and can be considered novelties.

¶ *El Amor Brujo* ("Love, the Magician")

The keyboard version, arranged by the composer himself, blights Falla's catalogue. The "Ritual Fire Dance" illustrates how negative his music is when converted from its orchestral setting.

¶ *El Sombrero de Tres Picos* ("The Three-Cornered Hat")

The ebullient rhythms of Falla's ballet have sufficient strength to withstand keyboard arrangement. Nonetheless, real art is found wanting in such piano reductions.

¶ *Fantasía Bética*

Falla's last and longest composition for solo piano (approximately twelve minutes in length) is a musical mural that portrays a cross section of Hispanic sensations. Merging agitated rhythms, guitar sound synonyms, broad lines, and keyboard song—it is a compendium of Manuel de Falla's creative credo. The "Fantasía Bética" (or "Baetica," the ancient Roman name for Andalusia, where Falla was born) has the identifiable slant of folklore but is unlocalized. It is not a sonorous postcard for a tourist in search of a picturesque snapshot.

Unfortunately, few pianists choose to play Falla's strong work. Despite its technical demands, there is no valid reason for such avoidance. It was composed (in 1919) for and dedicated to Artur Rubinstein, who gave the initial performance in New York City some forty years ago. After a few other presentations he apparently has never played it since.

¶ *Homenaje: Pour le Tombeau de Debussy* ("To the Memory of Debussy")

Falla's version of his guitar piece which he again used for purposes of orchestral treatment (*see* Guitar *and also* Orchestral ["Homenajes"]).

¶ *La Vida Breve* ("Life is Short")

Falla made sterling piano transcriptions of two dances from his opera. The simple partnership of melody and rhythm is neatly detailed.

82

¶ *Nocturno*

Stylistically in the Chopin manner, with not even a modicum of Falla's usual accent. Tuneful and colored by its minor tonality.

¶ *Pour le Tombeau de Paul Dukas* ("To the Memory of Paul Dukas")

The French periodical *La Revue musicale* published a number of musical supplements, including certain grouped pieces dedicated to famous composers. In the issue of May-June 1936, nine piano compositions appeared with the title "Le Tombeau de Paul Dukas," written by Falla, Schmitt, Pierné, Ropartz, Rodrigo, Krein, Messiaen, Aubin, and Barraine.

Falla's forty-two measure contribution in memory of his friend is not comparable in size to its emotional cogency. The music has no Spanish slant, no contrapuntal communication, merely dark, paeanic harmonies set in F minor, which conclude in a poignant, unresolved addition to the tonic chord. ("Pour le Tombeau de Paul Dukas" forms part of the "Homenajes"—*see* Orchestral *above*.)

¶ *Quatre Pièces Espagnoles* ("Four Spanish Pieces")

In this suite, the harmony is woven and the color applied in representative Falla style, while the indigenous authenticity of the forms remain unaltered. Save for the third piece ("Montañesa"), where the sounds are wrapped in a perfumed, impressionistic cloth, the music has the fullest Spanish identity. The guitar imitations of the "Andaluza," the jota patterns of the "Argonesa," and the irresistible beat of "Cubana" represent the enthusiastic combining of formality with native illumination. Falla's early work (published in 1909) illustrates how to utilize the simplest domestic elements and still propound forceful artistic logic.

¶ *Serenata Andaluza*

Not to be confused with the "Andaluza" that constitutes the last of the "Four Spanish Pieces." Pahissa, the composer's biographer, makes no mention of this lollipop. No shame for Falla, no credits either.

¶ *Valse Capriccio*

An early pianistic snapshot, in style a salon daguerreotype.

83

TWO PIANOS

¶ *Jota and Nana from "Siete Canciones Populares Españolas"* ("Seven Popular Spanish Songs")
The duo-piano version made by the Whittemore and Lowe team is commendable.

¶ *Ritual Fire Dance from "El Amor Brujo"* ("Love, the Magician")
In the solo piano setting the results are less than fair. Twice the number of instruments offers no pains and no gains.

VIOLIN

¶ *Asturiana and Jota from "Suite Populaire Espagnole"*
Parts three and four of the original vocal work "Seven Popular Spanish Songs" transcribed by the Polish violinist-composer Paul Kochanski. The quality of these miniatures makes them perfect vehicles for string vocalism.

¶ *Canción Populare from "Suite Populaire Espagnole"*
A popular tune from the area of Granada, with the characteristic Falla touch which makes it an original creation. The "populare" portion of the title is not used in the original set of songs from which this suite was drawn, but is a true description.

¶ *Jota from "Suite Populaire Espagnole"*
See above: "Asturiana and Jota" from "Suite Populaire Espagnole."

¶ *Nana* (Berceuse) *from "Suite Populaire Espagnole"*
An Andalusian cradle song differing from the general aspect of lullabies by its rhythmic kick (dynamically quiet) at the beginning of certain measures. The mixture of subdued impressionism with the assimilation of folklore elements forms a pellucid miniature as effective as extended music of intense complexion.

¶ *Pantomime from "El Amor Brujo"* ("Love, the Magician")
The common point of view is that the musical bonus (*i.e.,* the encore) should be pithy, a positive contribution—exuberant and

84

pyrotechnic, or staid and chastely classical. Actually, the real value is music chosen because it is difficult to place in the regular program. This piece fulfills the definition of a worthy concert gratuity.

¶ *Spanish Dance from "La Vida Breve"* ("Life is Short")

Fritz Kreisler's "La Vida Breve" transcription is probably the most famous of any made from Falla's catalogue. The sensuousness of the music lends itself to multicolored violin sound. Kreisler was a master of musical resetting, avoiding cheap effects and unstylistic bargains.

CHAMBER MUSIC

¶ *Concerto for Harpsichord* (or Piano), *Flute, Oboe, Clarinet, Violin and Cello*

The title of Falla's work has led to severe differences of opinion as to whether it is a solo vehicle accompanied by five players, or a work for six players *in toto*. In form, content, and instrumental style, the conception harks back to the days of the *sonata da camera* or *concerto da camera; i.e.,* a chamber work in sonata or concerto form. The "Concerto" is certainly ensemble music, not only because it is limited to six players but because the composer has indicated that all are "soloists" (read: equal to each other). Furthermore, while more grandiloquent speech is given to the keyboard instrument, the balances of the piece are those of chamber style.

Falla's three-movement work is less Spanish than broadly neo-classic. The composer sits in the twentieth century and muses in retrospect. Notwithstanding the formula of free tonality and shifting harmonic roots, with some chordal brushing that uses the paints of combined keys, these deliberations do not interfere with the refined quality that cannot be termed other than classic. The "Concerto" becomes as much a hybrid of means (in harmony, form, and color) as is its title.

The basic compositional style can be realized at the very start. The harpsichord plays in clear D major, but its rhythm is complicated by two rates of combined periodicities. To this, sharp string chords are pinned, one instrument being in the distinctly opposed key of E♭ minor. Thus, tradition mingles with modernity. In the final *vivace,* a pertinent Spanish rhythm is employed, combining duple with triple patterns. Casting such rhythmic binomials in an eighteenth-century tonal setting shows the neoclassic hand at its best. Falla connects his own art with those of his forebears in a composition singular in his entire output.

VOCAL

¶ *Seguidilla*
The final song in a set of "Trois Mélodies," set to poems by Théophile Gautier. Avoiding any stock gambits, Falla joins poetic romanticism with light national *características* to form a striking example of vocal chamber music.

¶ *Siete Canciones Populares Españolas* ("Seven Popular Spanish Songs")
Falla disliked his music to be called "delicate." Regardless, the integration within these songs illustrates a delicate fusion between free will and folk winnowing. Neither is emphasized. Mirroring the native ethos and remaining himself at the same time, Falla creates a fresh music, honestly Spanish, totally removed from the pseudo-provincial shallowness that marks self-conscious "Spanish style."

The songs contain the procedures Falla utilized from the start of his career: an enlargement of triadic harmony, a romantically blended *cantabile* undertone, intensely proportioned rhythm, framed in designs that display the contents without rigidity. Clear and powerful the songs speak of Spain with the individual diction of Manuel de Falla. In this manner indigenous art has universal effect.

VOICE WITH ORCHESTRA

¶ *El Amor Brujo* ("Love, the Magician")
The voice adds drama and excitement to the instrumental spectrum (*see* Orchestral *above*). In the full setting, rhythm and accent, and the sweet and pungent timbres are exhibited at their most propitious intensity.

¶ *Two Arias from "La Vida Breve"* ("Life is Short")
A pair of moving monologues not only of full operatic sweep and grandeur, with curious reflections of Puccini, but touched with native turns of phrase. Both arias are anguished declarations. "Vivan los

que ríen!" ("Long Live People Who Laugh!") is from the first act, "Allí Esta! Riyendo!" ("There He Is! Laughing!") is from the final act. The first concerns the heroine's fear of coming disaster, the second confirms it.

CHORAL

¶ *Five Songs*

Not original Falla, but very original "choralstrations" of five of the "Seven Popular Spanish Songs" (numbers one and three are eliminated).

BALLET

¶ *El Sombrero de Tres Picos* ("The Three-Cornered Hat")

A ballet tale about a flirtatious miller's wife, the attempts of the old *corregidor* of the province to seduce her, the seeming compromise of the wife, and confusion by mistaken identity. With the eventual clearing of the village air all ends happily and the old roué gets his just deserts. It is almost like a Viennese operetta transplanted to Spain.

Though the excerpted set of three dances so often heard (*see* Orchestral *above*) is exhilarating, the complete ballet (first produced in the summer of 1919) is thrice so. Here we have the total that enhances the sections commonly known. Most ballets gain by excerpting, Falla's great score does not.

OPERA

¶ *El Retablo de Maese Pedro* ("Master Peter's Puppet Show")

Operatic conventions take a holiday in this one-act marionette musical play with grand opera trimmings. Falla's "El Retablo" is an adaptation of classical Spanish idiom into neonationalism, mixed with *authentica* (such as street cries), and a tinge of secularized liturgicalism. Everything is concentrated and intimate, even the orchestra, which includes a harpsichord.

The tale is based on a section from Cervantes' *Don Quixote*. Don Quixote and Sancho Panza are watching a puppet group act out a

Castilian adventure dealing with a captive fair lady, freed by her man in armor from the villainous Moors. Thinking the puppets to be real, Don Quixote attacks them, destroying the little theatre of Master Peter. Two sizes of puppets are required: miniature ones for the show and larger ones for the onlookers—the singers are in the orchestra pit. Falla was meticulous in his instructions, indicating that the singers must avoid all theatrical mannerisms, and minutely specifying the exact way each of the puppet characters was to be vocally portrayed.

The unusual format of "El Retablo" has limited its presentation. However, the crystal-clear, picturesque music offers plenty of interest even if no staging takes place. In its avoidance of clichés Falla's score represents an ideal of musical purity, without forsaking operatic dramatics.

¶La Vida Breve ("Life is Short")

Active and assertive, "La Vida Breve" is a tragedy that fits in the operatic cubbyhole neatly and comfortably. Salud, a blacksmith's daughter, is in love with Paco. He deserts her for a girl of the upper class. Salud breaks into the wedding celebration, reproaches her seducer, and then falls dead.

There's plenty of Spanish lace in Falla's creation, also plenty of Italian fringework. Nevertheless, the stylistic merger is neatly made and acceptable. Falla was a young composer when he wrote his opera, but no cheap compositional histrionics interfere with the music's progress.

The orchestral color (save for the famous "Dance" and a choral-dance section) has a subdued cast. Even in the most native-tempered sections Falla avoids a "big guitar" sound. The dark timbres employed fit this score which unfolds like a gigantic set of lieder.

9. PAUL HINDEMITH
(1895–1963)

PAUL HINDEMITH was a born composer, a composer's composer, one who met the demands of every type of music from home to concert hall, from teaching pieces to motion-picture scores, for performance at a school or in an opera house, for old and for young, for amateur or professional, cast for every conceivable instrumental possibility from an unaccompanied solo to a brass band. His role in twentieth-century music remains very powerful in his influence on other composers and on the public as well. Hindemith's entire output was marked by care and concern. He maintained (no matter what the medium or purpose) the highest technical proficiency, never deviating from his own creative personality or character. The result is an unusual contemporary musical link between composer and performer.

Hindemith is not to be classified with the atonal tag so often incorrectly attached to him. Tonality was as important to him as is the gravitational pull that keeps peoples' feet on the ground. He was a direct descendant of the classic and romantic schools (the latter is manifested quite often in the beauties which sensitize his slow movements, the former is illustrated in his formal precision). He did not mimic these schools of thought, but continued their arguments logically and inevitably. His early works showed consideration of Brahmsian-Regerian doctrines. Later, lush sonority turned to clear, but bristly texture.

Hindemith's second period of work was based on freed tonality. It expressed purer thought and avoided luxuriance by keenness (but not thinness). To liberate himself from romanticism and its packed harmony, Hindemith adopted the procedure of linear assembly. In so doing, he maintained musical strength, since horizontalism moves on long phrases and is not clipped or punctuated with commas. Romantic despotism was ousted by polyphonic liberty in abstracting the tersest possibilities of freedom. While dissonance came first, all of Hindemith's compositions at that time were devoted to tonal release, not tonal discontinuance.

In his latest creative period Hindemith synthesized all the elements found in his previous music, merging the initial romanticism with the later employment of tonal license. Thus, diatonic and chromatic selections combine, triadic and other types of chords are confirmed— all based on an obedience to rooted areas of tonality, with all varieties of harmony moving within that position.

Though part of the early freshness (because it was of special newness) disappeared and because he had a tendency to overproduce (there was an evident tempering of this *furor scribendi*) his later music displayed, at times, a too scrubbed complexion. The beauty of Hindemith's iconoclastic slap-on-the-cheek harmony and the value of his "wrong" notes in the right places made a beautiful slingshot to cast against the smug potbelly of postromantic music. Some of this ammunition is missed because listeners still want their music to be more pungent than intellectual. But Hindemith's later output is in no way a deterioration. It is not aged, but still has the clearest dynamic vision.

Paul Hindemith proved that the expressively acute composer can only be one who has the boldness of confirmed purpose. His music has character, strength and permanence. He is one of the most important composers of this age.

ORCHESTRAL

¶ *Concert Music for String Orchestra and Brass Instruments, Op. 50*

Every musical composition has its problems of balance—some solved with more subtle effect than others. Despite the fact that a piece may have pointed ideas, a lack of equipoise in their arrangement is defeating. But Hindemith gave fullest regard to matters of adjustment. Opus 50 is organized with discrimination, a reshuffling of classic order, with sensible elimination of all superficialities. Five divisions are spliced into the two parts; a vigorous opening merging into a broadly paced section and a finale (fugally designed) intersected by a second slow portion, defining a tripartite design. The inner contrasts of the pair of movements produce an equilibrium of finesse, with a "rondo" alternation of speeds.

Harmonic blend is far from Hindemith's thoughts. It is the mingling and clash of the lines that give the music its strength. This work appears lean and healthy compared to the corpulent music of the Strauss era.

¶ *Concerto for Orchestra, Op. 38*

Concerto Grosso design viewed through a twentieth-century mirror. The title seems contradictory, but is proven correct in the way the instrumental combinations are assorted within the full orchestra range. These include a concertante offshoot (of oboe, violin, and bassoon) in the initial portion and the sole use of the woodwinds for the third part, a "March." Hindemith also exhibits his penchant for massed, layered orchestration (especially in framing the kinetic scherzo-styled second movement), as well as peripatetic contrapuntalism. These blend with the formal plan which culminates in a parade of variational devices deployed over a septule-pulsed bass ostinato. Hindemith's orchestra concerto is thrilling.

¶ *Cupid and Psyche, Ballet Overture* (1943)

[*For a long time Hindemith used opus numbers for his compositions, but stopped doing so after reaching the half-hundred mark. Thereafter he adopted the "new" manner of identification (following the practice of many others) and only listed the year of composition.*

[*Some of the composers treated in this book use the "year" method for locating their music, but this has not been indicated because they have not followed the plan consistently. (When an opus number exists it has been noted, however, providing it is part of the "official" title.) In Hindemith's case the code of an opus number or year of composition has been steadfastly maintained and accordingly has been followed in the listings within this chapter.*]

A slight departure from Hindemith's general characteristics is found in this six-minute piece inspired by the frescoes in the Villa Farnesina in Rome which describe the old Apuleius tale. The texture is thinner than usual, a delicacy of statement is manifested in the motivally engendered score. Contrast spells out the formal word. The fast pace of the beginning is balanced by an even speedier coda (dynamically set at the lowest point) and is severely opposed by the central portion, its tempo five times slower than the opening.

¶ *Nobilissima Visione* ("St. Francis"), *Suite for Orchestra* (1938)

Originally part of a ballet with its subject derived from the life of St. Francis of Assisi. The somewhat mystical music of the suite (in three movements, comprising five parts) typifies a relaxed composer. While contrapuntal spinning continues (without it there is no Hinde-

91

mith), the yarns are less bright than usual and thus the patterns fuse more subtly. Within a lyricism that is similar to the "Mathis der Maler" music one will find stressed the engaging techniques of fugue and passacaglia; the latter in the final movement, consisting of nineteen variations based on a six-measure theme. Few contemporaries can match such highly geared polyphonic invention.

¶ *Sinfonietta in E* (1950)

Hindemith's artistic calligraphy shows in this work. Movements two and four combine a slow section with a fugato and a recitative with a spicy rondo. The opening is fast, the third movement based on ostinato. The initial part is Hindemith *en rapport* with Bach, a factor that distinguishes most of the motoric allegros; ostinato and fugue are two of the major forces of Hindemith's technical arsenal—very few of his pieces omit either. The recitative brings "Mathis der Maler" immediately to mind, but who can quibble at such self-remembrance? Another of his favored practices is apparent in this very fluent symphony (its little-over-twenty-minute length makes the "sinfonietta" too modest a title)—a fondness for special instrumentation. A full orchestra is required, but the brass is condensed: three in place of the usual four horns, only one trumpet, and two trombones rather than the customary three.

¶ *Symphonia Serena* (1946)

The "Symphonia Serena" bursts with ideas handled with creative sagacity. Movement one is akin to a set of textural and instrumental variants on a propulsive idea. These are not merely deployed in juxtaposition, but combined in an engaging new sonata design interlocked with concerto grosso methods.

Hindemith, like other composers, borrowed melodies and bent them to his own will. The present symphony includes a delightful, sportive section in the second movement, molded from a Beethoven military march. And, like begetting like, instrumentational influence carries over to this part, scored only for winds and percussion, plus celesta. A startling freshness also sweeps through the third movement, a "Colloquy" for double string orchestra alone. Themes are stated separately, then combined, and further interstices occur with solo instruments playing on and off stage. In this instance the whole is as fascinating as its parts.

All parts of Hindemith's composition bring invention and discovery. Place them together and they correspond as much to a twentieth-century depiction of suite form as they do to a symphony. Hindemith's "Serena" adds a vivid page to symphonic lore.

¶ *Symphonic Dances* (1937)

Music with a fanciful title that does not match the facts. The terpsichorean force is of exceedingly minor impact in Hindemith's "Symphonic Dances," though there is a sufficient quantity of rhythmic interest. This is a straightforward symphony, with four movements in slow, lively, very slow, and energetic tempi. It does not reveal more than Hindemith's habitual polyphonic purposes, nor does it have the intriguing invention of the other symphonic works.

¶ *Symphonic Metamorphosis of Themes by Carl Maria von Weber* (1943)

Weber, by way of Hindemith, and what a wonderful way it is! This suite is without doubt Hindemith's most delightful and approachable orchestral work. Weber's original themes form only a small parenthesis in the text, but the romantic glow is unmistakable, notwithstanding the contemporary festoons of harmony and counterpoint, and a plethora of nice percussion sounds, persuasive flute roulades, and a wholesome, jazzy fugato.

The major part of the source material (used in the first, third, and fourth movements) stems from a rather obscure work Weber wrote for piano, four hands, called "All' Ongarese." This is implanted in a swinging allegro, crammed with kinetic sixteenth notes and set in Hindemith's favored sectional scoring, a haunting slow movement and a lusty march. Movement two is derived from Weber's incidental music to Schiller's play "Turandot." It displays a jaunty scherzo in which variations of color and associated material twirl around and embrace the solitary subject. Hindemith's speciality—fugal sport—supplies the requisite contrast.

¶ *Symphony "Die Harmonie der Welt"* (1951)

Akin to the "Mathis der Maler" symphony, this suite is drawn from an opera *The Harmony of the Universe.* The subject matter is the life of Johann Kepler, a seventeenth-century philosopher and astronomer, and emphasizes his speculations concerning the music of the spheres. This is just the sort of material that would stimulate

Hindemith, especially in the dazzling counterpoint that inhabits the composition.

There are some who contend that polyphony is an intense factor in compositional technique, but that it is not the most dramatic means of expression. This three-part symphony (especially the compelling final passacaglia) argues against such a theory. There is much *vital élan* in this heady work, a virtuoso document for the orchestra. It shows the potency of Hindemith's creativity. And it makes one anxious to see and hear the complete opera.

¶ *Symphony in E♭* (1940)

For "E♭" read tonal polarity. In his later period Hindemith is not concerned with constrained keys but employs tonality centers. All sounds are related by the measurement of one center to other points, which affords (depending on distance) tension or repose, stability or motility; furthermore, modulations from one area move to another and, in turn, give a particular tensility compared to release, and so on. Thus, Hindemith "keys" his music in terms of new controls. It is the contemporary manner of tonal etiquette.

Formally, the symphony follows the traditional four-movement procedure. The vigorous opening portion is followed by a dirgelike slow movement, then a scherzo that avoids the light hop-skip-and-jump of Mendelssohnian style, and a summational finale. In content, the paramount technical element is polyphony. Hindemith refuses to disguise his love for horizontal construction.

¶ *Symphony "Mathis der Maler"* (1934)

Actually not a pure symphony or a suite, but an orchestral triptych drawn from Hindemith's opera dealing with the life of Matthias Gruenewald, with each movement titled after a painting by this artist. The music has soft bite, is an aesthetic culture drawn and refined from Hindemith's earlier conceptions, and contains a sonority of sculptured tonal proportions. It is not "tonal" in the rigid sense, but solidly concerned with orientation of key center in its contemporary manifestation. "Mathis" has elocutionary power that dovetails Mozartian clarity into Hindemith's rhythmic drive.

Few contemporary works have achieved the success of Hindemith's opus—the most widely performed of his orchestral pieces. A standard item in the concert repertoire it deserves all the plaudits given it, for "Mathis der Maler" is a forceful work of art, a high point in the composer's output.

94

CHAMBER ORCHESTRA

¶ *Kammermusik No. 1, Op. 24, No. 1*

Music of the twenties that is just as smart and effective in the sixties. Music of wit, of irony, of power, of violent vitality, scored for twelve players using twenty instruments. The end movements have toccata propulsiveness, and in the final section a 1921 dance tune of another composer and the wail of a siren are expertly stitched into the fabric. The piece is all muscle and tone. A wonderful affair, with Hindemith in a smirking mood and on a hot kick.

STRING ORCHESTRA

¶ *Eight Canons in First Position for Violin Choir, Op. 44, No. 2*

[*Since this work, as well as all others in the string orchestra category, "Morning Music" (see Brass Instruments below) and "Trio for Recorders" (see Chamber Music below), fall under the heading of* Gebrauchsmusik, *it is important to understand the meaning of this generic form of music in connection with Hindemith's work as a whole.*

[*Hindemith first came into contact with* Gebrauchsmusik *at a music festival held at Baden-Baden in 1921. The attempt to bridge the gap between contemporary music, with its terrifying newness, and the usual stuffiness fed children in schools was the prime impetus of the examples he heard. Teachers who persisted in following a syllabus of 1899 vintage naturally could not mold young people's minds for readiness to listen to twentieth-century music. A new way had to be found.* Gebrauchsmusik *was the manner of approach, though as it developed it proved important in its new premise. It was a two-fisted potential contestant. Not only was the composer aided by writing simple music which gave him wider benefits materially and otherwise; not only were future customers for his other products thereby given a preliminary taste of things to come, but a new category of fine concert-hall music was developed simultaneously. For* Gebrauchsmusik, *which was written for children, was found to contain another value. The hard-boiled adult audiences found in its simplicity and freshness a music they could enjoy as much as those for whom it was specifically written.*

[*There has been some criticism that to translate the term* Gebrauchsmusik *as "utility music" is incorrect. It is and it is not. In the sense of a composer's writing to order so as to meet workaday demands, the term is proper. In the sense of the word "utility" defined literally, the term is not so good a choice, since* Gebrauchsmusik *consists of every type of specified music outside the general territory to which concert music is devoted. It is music for children, for political groups, for schools, home and fireside; music for playing and singing, or both together, or for the ad libitum fun obtained by the improvisational exchange and substitution of instruments in connection with any or all of the individual parts of a piece of music.*

[*The technique of* Gebrauchsmusik *was one of simplification. Above all the composer's idiom was to remain unchanged. (The basic purpose of this educational propaganda was to quietly agitate for the acceptance of contemporary music manners.) Further, the precept of all utilitarian compositions was to teach by stimulation so that the making of music would ultimately be arrived at; it was better to play the false note oneself than to pay to watch someone else avoid it. And active participation would speed understanding of modern style.*

[Gebrauchsmusik *was not new. Composers had long before written to order, and had scaled down their musical semantics so that a pocket-sized vocabulary was used in place of an unabridged one. But in Germany the movement took root with great rapidity in the 1920's. A large number of composers went to work in the field of* Gebrauchsmusik. *The leader of the group was Paul Hindemith; Kurt Weill and Carl Orff were among the others. Though Hindemith stopped composing "utilitarian" music per se, he continued to meet the demand for many types of music. And many composers in other countries practised the idea, without terming their product* Gebrauchsmusik. *When Aaron Copland wrote "The Young Pioneers" for piano or Igor Stravinsky composed "Les Cinq Doigts" (very easy pieces limited to five sounds) they too added to the store of* Gebrauchsmusik. *And so did Vaughan Williams with his "Household Music" for almost any conceivable combination of instruments.*]

There are not many extended canons which have the virtue of eloquent expression in place of bald artifice. Because of its restraint this technique of polyphonic imitation quite often results in the dullest type of musical fare.

In this work Hindemith illustrated the gift he possessed as a spontaneous contrapuntalist, and also proved how pleasurable music can be written within the most restricted means and without change of personal style, providing the composer is in full control of his craft.

¶ *Eight Pieces in First Position for String Choir, Op. 44, No. 3*

The pieces are a synthesis, a concentrate of Hindemith's early but not initial style. To listen to them is to hear a capsule version of Hindemith's art. All his methods are detailed as a representation, a sampling of the larger compositions. True, the set is written to limits of the first position in order to obtain the attention of younger players and secure performance from them. But this only compresses the tonal compass, and does not affect the quality of the conception.

¶ *Five Pieces in First Position for String Orchestra, Op. 44, No. 4*

It little matters here that the range for the instruments is purposely circumscribed. No burden rests on Hindemith's fecund talent, since he makes these pieces sound as if they were written without any technical restraint whatsoever. The first position anchor is no more a deterrent to the scope of the music than is the fact that a work for the piano may be limited to performance by the left hand alone. Especially compelling is the final movement, a kinetic knockout, with a solo fiddle riding on top of the full string body.

Actually, concert performers avail themselves of higher positions in order to obtain more pertinent color and dynamics, thereby giving deeper meaning to the music as a whole. Hindemith's ability to create a meaningful composition with limited resources is not minimized thereby. Whatever way these pieces are exhibited, their beautifully precise settings make perfect art jewels.

¶ *Nine Pieces in First Position for Violin Choir, Op. 44, No. 1*

Save for the last pair of pieces this music promises sure boredom for all but the tyros for whom it was expressly composed. The "Nine Pieces" are in bare two-voice textures, with an occasional thickening via an added open string. Some *Gebrauchsmusik* is creatively anemic; Hindemith's is rarely so, but this is an exception.

BRASS INSTRUMENTS

¶ *Morning Music from "Plöner Musiktag* ("A Day of Music at Plön") (1932)

[*The nine miscellaneous works which comprise Hindemith's "Plöner Musiktag" came about from a visit he made to the Plön school, during which he noted the wonderful spirit displayed by the students and promised to arrange a music festival for the school to*

take place in June 1932, and to write music especially for it. Hinde-
mith found all types of musical groups at Plön, even very young
children who were only capable of performing on miniature-sized
recorders. Thus Hindemith overlooked no possibility in his commis-
sion, since his music accompanied every part of the institution's
activity—morning, noon, and night.

[*Hindemith never forgot the day he spent when he returned to*
Plön. Music was the exclusive consideration. It was an event that left
all exhausted but filled with joy. This was the most absolute definition
of Gebrauchsmusik.

[*The music Hindemith composed comprises four divisions, each*
for use at different occasions during a day's span. The first is "Morning
Music," for brass instruments, to be played from the top of a tower.
Section two, "Table Music," is a set of four pieces to be played at
table during a meal. The third section is a cantata on Martin Agri-
cola's words which admonish young people to study music. Part four
is an "Evening Concert" and consists of a half-dozen compositions,
the proper assortment for a full-scale concert. Included are two pieces
for massed instruments (playing in triple-divided parts), a pair of
pieces for solo instruments with string-instrument accompaniment, two
duets for violin and clarinet, and a trio for recorders (see Chamber
Music below).]

Hindemith's composition is a modern equivalent of baroque tower
music. It calls for trumpets in two divided parts (flügelhorns, etc.,
may be added at will to each of these), and horns and trombones also
combined in two parts, with an ad-libitum tuba. Though conceived
originally for a massed combination of performers, the three movements are written strictly in four voices throughout. Triple aspects of
mood are realized: a proclamatory initial part leads to a "Song"
(played through twice), while the contrapuntal and antiphonal scoring of the last section produces music of triumphant character.

BAND

¶ *Symphony in B♭ for Concert Band* (1951)

Hindemith's entire dogma is based on the universality of the
musician, who must be able to write and perform, teach and conduct,
and compose for all kinds of audiences. This twenty-minute opus was
written for the U. S. Army Band and once more proves there are no
limits to Hindemith's creative vision.

The décor of the symphony has all the usual Hindemith touches.
Exploring the band medium artistically and resourcefully, he singles

98

out certain colors that are pertinent (example: the counterplay between alto saxophone and cornet in the middle movement). Paul Hindemith does not approach contrapuntalism with timid diffidence. The fugue in the final movement confirms this polyphonic empathy. It is bravura music, at one point combining the fugal subject with a new theme and one from the initial movement. Such audacious inquiry brings rewards.

SOLO INSTRUMENT WITH ORCHESTRA

CONCERTOS

¶ Concerto for Cello and Orchestra (1940)

This piece is actually Hindemith's second cello concerto; his first bears the opus number three and remains unpublished. Nor should it be confused with "Kammermusik No. 3," which is for cello and ten solo instruments. The concerto represents Hindemith's first sizable piece composed in America. (Forced to leave his native land by the Nazis, Hindemith first resided in Switzerland, then came to the United States and was appointed to the faculty at Yale University in 1940; during that summer and the following one he was on the faculty at the Berkshire Music Center at Tanglewood. The cello concerto was completed there in September of 1940.)

In this work, similar to the violin concerto produced the previous year, Hindemith is no longer rash and fervently contrapuntal in his creative demeanor. The counterpoints still sting, but with melodic antidotes. The right of the cello to be heard in solo is a paramount premise, and no cellist can complain he hasn't an opportunity to display a singing tone or a flashy finger-and-bow technique; all are available to the soloist in this rich conception. It is cast in the average three movements: the slow movement encloses a scherzo particular, and the finale is in a marchlike, somewhat peppery vein. Traditional form is employed but the concerto is not traditionally academic.

¶ Concerto for Clarinet and Orchestra (1947)

A significant avoidance of monotonous solo timbre is to be noted in Hindemith's clarinet concerto. The concerto is a vehicle for the orchestra as much as it is for the woodwind instrument. Despite the need for soloistic definition, any lack of equipoise in a concerto is a double defeat—for the work itself and for the principal protagonist. The latter's arguments have the greatest force when they are made

99

during equal debate. In this instance the functions of all participants balance to the greatest degree.

¶ *Concerto for Horn and Orchestra* (1949)

Creative fatigue is always a danger in an artist's output. When the total is great the peril increases. It is to Hindemith's credit that, although his music varies in quality, he rarely is other than an expressively alive composer. The horn concerto displays the fact that Hindemith's inventiveness was as keen as in his younger days. Only the early satire and snide instrumental sneer have been removed, otherwise the music is smart and totally up to date.

The horn writing fits the instrument as perfectly as the famed Mendelssohn concerto does the violin. If any music could be termed "hornistic" (minus fanfare passages, hunting calls, and other assorted bread-and-butter ideas), this is it, with brass vocalism pervading the entire atmosphere.

The last part is twice as long as the first two portions. Imbalance thereby creates balance. Actually, the design is a shrewd and subtle one; the first two movements whet the appetite, and the final one satisfies it.

¶ *Concerto for Trumpet, Bassoon and String Orchestra* (1949)

Hindemith's gingered drive did not lessen throughout the years. The vagrant waltz idea included in this work is evidence. The bright and dark colors of the soli are contrasted beautifully in the modern translation of concerto grosso design. A rare contribution to the limited literature of double concerti.

¶ *Concerto for Violin and Orchestra* (1939)

No angry, bleak, icy, cutting music here. Hindemith's concerto is not illustrative of the heedlessness that so often makes modern pieces for the violin a stifling of the instrument's personality. Instead, it proclaims a romantic contemporaneity that sings with liquescence (and therefore conviction), making the fiddle sound like a violin.

For the most part the music sounds un-Hindemithian, but this does not damn him; rather, these delights have beautiful persuasion. The concerto is lyrical, a scrutiny of *cantilena* that is as exciting as all the flying trapeze technique required by music of the note-loose, virtuosic school. This ardent vocalism is even present in the third movement, the most rhythmic and spirited portion of the piece.

With the cry that there is a dearth of worthy contemporary violin concertos, one might ask why this work rarely appears on concert programs? Few performances have followed the initial one in 1940 by the Boston Symphony Orchestra, with Koussevitzky conducting, and its then concertmeister-assistant conductor, Richard Burgin, as soloist. A work so wealthy with suave melodies should receive the attention (and gratitude) of the fiddling set.

¶ *Concerto for Woodwinds, Harp and Orchestra* (1949)
A divertissement, though labeled a concerto. While the sounds often clash, they are of subdued quality, mollified by the colorful timbres of the four solo winds and the percussive suavity of the harp. Cadenzas? Yes, applied with taste and tact. The fun of the last movement, which plays volley ball with the Mendelssohn "Wedding March," is high jinks on a high plane.

SOLO ORGAN WITH ORCHESTRA

¶ *Kammermusik No. 7* (Organ Concerto) *for Organ and Chamber Orchestra, Op. 46, No. 2*
The severity of Hindemith's musical speech is well suited to the organ, and so are the gritty harmonic synonyms that season his language. Motoric style is the plain-speaking objective of movement one. The finale is just as unequivocal: a fugue that concludes matters properly with rousing toccata energy. On the other hand, the central movement is immersed in canonic imitation. Compared to the outer portions it is rather disappointing. The timbre freshness offered by the concerto is the opposite.

SOLO PIANO WITH ORCHESTRA

¶ *Concert Music for Piano, Brass Instruments and Two Harps, Op. 49*
Hindemith plots the combination of keyboard timbre, plucked sonority, and brass choir (four horns, three trumpets, two trombones, and tuba), so that the musical canvas of the "Concert Music" is of drypoint style. Rampant soloism is checked, and more attention paid to total integration, without negating specified individual highlighting.
The quietude of the initial movement is realized only after hearing the linked second movement, where the piano is predominant. The variations of part three are also a study in color proportions. The piano and harps alone are utilized for the theme and the first three

101

variants; full-scale scoring thus not only indicates the next section but brings dramatic emphasis, in turn balanced by the simplicity of the terminal portion of the work. In this manner a tripartite instrumentational design blends the final paired movements.

¶ *The Four Temperaments* (Theme with Four Variations) *for Piano and String Orchestra* (1940)

Notwithstanding the pinpointed names of the movements ("Melancholic," "Sanguine," "Phlegmatic," and "Choleric") this is not a programmatic suite, but music originally conceived for ballet—an idea abandoned by the composer. However, the score eventually became the basis for a ballet, choreographed by the famous Balanchine.

Give Paul Hindemith string instruments (he played three himself, in addition to several others of different classification) and he coined some of his best ideas. Writing "for the hand," as it were, the material flows from one beautiful point to the next.

SOLO TROMBONE WITH ORCHESTRA

¶ *Trauermusik* ("Music of Mourning") *for Trombone and Strings* (*see below* Solo Viola with Orchestra)

Davis Shuman, a trombonist of exceptional skill, transcribed the "Trauermusik" with the composer's permission. The complexion of the music is much healthier with a solo profile that is not so well scrubbed as a trombone.

SOLO VIOLA WITH ORCHESTRA

¶ *"Der Schwanendreher"* (Concerto for Viola and Small Orchestra) (1935)

Two special points concern "Der Schwanendreher." First, the three movements are based on four folk tunes with which Hindemith makes polyphonic sport, though there are sufficient homophonic sections to give relief and contrast. Second, there are neither violins nor violas in the orchestra, thereby placing the solo instrument in bold outline.

The title of the concerto is derived from the seventeenth-century song exploited in the finale, "Seid ihr nicht der Schwanendreher?" ("Are you not the ————?") The blank in the translation points up the arguments as to the meaning of the key word. Some call the "Schwanendreher" a hurdy-gurdy player; others, one who roasts swans on a spit. The latter is certainly more appetizing—one wishes the music were likewise. Unfortunately, "Der Schwanendreher" is all busy technique, its emotions are quite tepid.

¶ *Trauermusik* ("Music of Mourning") *for Viola and Strings* (1936)

Even a minor Hindemith work has conviction. This short four-movement piece (funereal music, but stated in full Hindemith terms) was begun the day after the death of King George V of England, and performed the following evening.

SOLO VIOLIN WITH ORCHESTRA

¶ *Kammermusik No. 4* (Violin Concerto) *for Violin and Large Chamber Orchestra, Op. 36, No. 3*

Hindemith's seven-part "Kammermusik" series covers six solo concertos for piano, violin, viola, viola d'amore, cello, and organ, respectively, plus one work for chamber orchestra. Within all of these the opposition to romanticism and packed harmony is manifested by linear assembly. Such style maintains strength, since horizontalism moves on long, unpunctuated phrases.

Though Hindemith's work resembles "chamber music," it is basically a concerto. Furthermore, the orchestra does not include violins, so the principal voice is sharply focused. Only in the opening "Signal" is the solo violin silent. Elsewhere it is the commanding voice: vigorous in the second part, lyrical in the "Nachstück," sportive in the following movement, which peppers the fugal pattern with easy-going jazz (very light German barrelhouse), and performing ghostly glides in the perpetual action of the finale. The music is of happy effect.

INSTRUMENTAL

HARP

¶ *Sonata* (1939)

Composing for the harp demands a milder dynamic speech, but with no lessening of intensity. Regardless of the instrument Hindemith chooses, there is creative rapport; accordingly, his use of ratioed simplicity to companion the harp's restricted chromaticism. Since there is a touch of medievalistic modalism within its three movements, the sonata is of softer impact than is most of Hindemith's other music.

ORGAN

¶*Sonata No. 1* (1937)

Excluding the output of Messiaen, and with the exception of an occasional short piece, music for the organ is not characteristically found in the catalogues of the important contemporary composers. However, Hindemith puts his acute instrumental knowledge to work. His three organ sonatas (a welcome addition to the literature), are imaginative, modern without unsuitable aggressiveness. Above all the organ is made to order as a vehicle for his linear language, though the "Phantasie" portion is somewhat loosened from Bachian postulates.

¶*Sonata No. 2* (1937)

The least diagnostic of the three sonatas. A concord of traditional form is displayed, ranging from a robust, typically Hindemithian opening movement, to a quiet and gentle pastorale section, and concluding with a fugue based on a zigzag subject. If Hindemith is not very exciting in this case at least he is not boring.

¶*Sonata No. 3* (1940)

Each of the three movements is based on an old German folk song. The tunes are used as the basis over and under (and around) which polyphony is woven with neo-archaic coloration and intertwined with mild lyricism. In Hindemith's organ sonatas his sly humor is held in check until the last movement of this, the last of the set.

PIANO

¶*Kleine Klaviermusik* (Easy Five-Tone Pieces), *Op. 45, No. 4*

The commercial music world (especially the publisher) has always sought compositions that represent the composer's style and yet are capable of being played by students in the early grades of development. For every work of worth by a recognized composer, a few hundred are issued that are exactly the opposite, only because it is virtually impossible to fulfill this objective. To scale down technically is a simple matter, to retain simultaneously one's personal style is horrendously difficult.

Hindemith was a realist and a composer of extraordinary skill. He neither changed nor renounced his doctrines—merely edited them to fit. These "Little Piano Pieces" offer the proof. They total a dozen tidbits limited to a five-tone gamut, but are as Hindemithian as his symphonies.

¶ *Ludus Tonalis* (1942)

Subtitled "Studies in Counterpoint, Tonal Organization and Piano Playing," this extensive opus could well be called "The Processes of Tonal Order According to the Rules of Paul Hindemith," since the music defines his theoretical principles (spelled out in a number of textbooks). "Ludus Tonalis" consists of a dozen fugues, including such polyphonic attractions as inversion, stretto, and palindrome. Twelve "interludes" intersperse the fugal cycle. These cover a variety of moods, including a waltz, a pastorale, a perpetual motion affair, and a solemn march. The suite is completed by a "Prelude" and "Postlude"; the latter a mirror inversion of the former.

"Ludus Tonalis" is a contemporary "Well-Tempered Clavier," with some modern glances at Bach's "Kunst der Fuge." It tempers didacticism with down-to-earth good music. That not too much attention has been given the composition since its première (in Chicago, on February 15, 1944) proposes a partial historical parallel that may ultimately run its full course. At one time Bach's "Forty-eight" was also considered a dry educational tract. Today, we recognize the pervading affectability of the "Well-Tempered Clavier." Tomorrow may do the same for Hindemith's imposing undertaking.

¶ *Shimmy and Ragtime from "Suite '1922'," Op. 26*

Hot jazz, written in a tight and hard, intensely syncopated style. Some serious composers turn out feeble specimens when they try their hands at this special art; as usual, Hindemith is quite expert. The "Shimmy" and "Ragtime" are the second and fifth parts of the suite. (The remainder consists of a "March," a lyrical "Nachstück," and a slow waltz titled "Boston.")

Hindemith's admonition to the pianist to strip away all his inhibitions (in the final movement) is worth repeating: "Forget everything you've learned in your lessons . . . play this piece . . . like a machine. Use the piano as a percussion instrument. . . ." In the "Shimmy" the slow cooch is sexy and properly uncivilized. It will remind one of Strauss' "Salome's Dance"—perhaps Hindemith had this in mind as a satire. Composed in 1922 this music is still "hep."

¶ Sonata No. 1 (1936)

A large five-movement affair, inspired by a Hölderlin poem, "Der Main." Like most of Hindemith's keyboard compositions the materials are slung on a bed of counterpoint—linear design is the significant purpose. However, the exchange and horizontal interchange of sounds are not mere creative mumbo jumbo. Hindemith's sonata co-ordinates discipline and finesse with style and excitement.

¶ Sonata No. 3 (1936)

There is no denying the fulsomeness that marks much piano music and nullifies artistic validity. Hindemith defines pure white and black values in his third piano sonata; many times spacing the voices widely, a very literal way of avoiding any romantic descant. Further anti-romantic viewpoints are to be heard in the second movement, wired for nervousness by asymmetrical insertions at strategic places.

Polyphony, the reigning doctrine of Hindemith's aesthetic demeanor, is a power in the sonata. It constantly accents, agitates, and flares within the homophonic sections. Finally, it explodes in a tremendous double fugue as the culminating part of this outstanding composition.

PIANO DUET

¶ Sonata for Piano, Four Hands (1938)

The repertoire for certain media is meager. There have been very few contemporary works for two players at one piano that can be considered a close match for the beauties left by Mozart and Schubert. Hindemith's sonata can be nominated for that honor, together with Ravel's "Mother Goose" gem, Stravinsky's droll sets of pieces, and Debussy's "Six Epigraphes antiques."

Formal clarity and thematic warmth are the artistic working tools of this three-movement piece. Within are contrasted elements, such as the dramatic drive and keen kick of the middle part (representing the scherzo) and the gentle polyphony of the final movement which is a synthesis of slow and fast divisions. Here is clear music, music immediately recognizable as Paul Hindemith's; music that will doubtless endure.

106

VIOLA

¶ *Sonata for Viola Alone, Op. 25, No. 1*

An unaccompanied stringed-instrument work might seem to propose a dismal listening experience, or at best a monotonous aural condition. In most cases it does. It takes the genius of a Bach or the wisdom of a Hindemith to formulate music of deep meaning for a lone violin, viola, or cello, while little able to do more than skeletonize harmony or counterpoint.

Contemporary composers have given the homophonic solo goodly attention, covering all types, including the believe-it-or-not use of the bass clarinet and the tuba without accompaniment. (There have also been pieces for timpani alone!) Hindemith has produced six pieces for various string instruments, of which this is one of the very best. Made for a virtuoso, it turns out to be not one whit less intense in its bare form than music written for thrice the number of players. The sonata's propelling excitement is today's equivalent of Bachian prosody, save the wild fourth movement which brings to mind a set of drums percussed by steel beaters.

VIOLIN

¶ *Sonata for Violin Alone, Op. 31, No. 1*

The sonata's main characteristic is its melodic flow. This is a rare instance of Hindemith suppressing his learned contrapuntal vocabulary. The single violin voice is propped occasionally with supporting chords or figuration that places a pedal point into perspective. Otherwise, the five movements alternate in tempo, each part clear in shape, with sonorous similarity overcome by a developing fluidity, and by use of muted sound in the final *prestissimo*.

This music falls gently on ears attuned to Cage and Stockhausen. Hindemith's solo sonata was once termed "ugly." Its neatness and clarity show that critics quite often stumble when they judge quickly.

¶ *Sonata for Violin Alone, Op. 31, No. 2*

The precept is simple: four strings on one instrument do not make a string quartet. The boundaries stare one in the face. To enlarge these only modestly, without monotony, demands the most subtle methods of changing the demarcations and refurbishing the ground.

Hindemith is not found wanting. The four movements of the

107

sonata follow the motto affixed to the score: "Es ist so schoenes Wetter draussen." It is certainly "so nice" music; lyrical and songlike in all of its four parts, including the variations on a Mozart tune employed for the finale, and the all-pizzicato third movement.

CHAMBER MUSIC

¶ *Kleine Sonata for Viola d'Amore and Piano, Op. 25, No. 2*

This represents the first of two examples within Hindemith's massive catalogue that call on the rarely used tenor viol. (The other instance is its employment as the solo voice in a concerto.) Regardless of a fairly extensive literature by seventeenth- and eighteenth-century composers, and samplings by such men as Meyerbeer, Charpentier, Puccini, Strauss, and Loeffler, contemporary composers have given the highly individual viola d'amore scant attention. (Doubtless the principal cause is that there are few practitioners.)

Though tunings for the seven-plus-seven stringed instrument vary, the richest is an *accordatura* of D major. Hindemith takes advantage of a sure thing and makes this the key focus of the sonata, especially in the vigorous final movement, where the closely positioned D major triad appears as a repetitive fanfare device some twenty-eight times.

Sharp contrasts heighten the music's pithiness. The "Invention" (basically three-voiced) has baroque bounce; the very slow movement to which it is connected is almost bleak in comparison. In the final part sharp rhythms and pulsatile chordal blocks enjoy a workout. Few can carry off this type of learned levity as well as Paul Hindemith.

¶ *Sonata for Bassoon and Piano* (1938)

Although a composer cannot be a meek personality if he wishes to turn out a competent work of size for bassoon and piano, he cannot display overostentatious disregard for the problem he faces. If the bassoon is given the demand to pit itself against merciless thick piano tone it can only mean artistic defeat. The bassoon is not a timid instrument, but it is fragile in terms of sonorous density. Care must be given it, and Hindemith's work is exemplary in that regard.

In the first movement and at the conclusion of the second, rustic feeling is predominant. In both instances this is indicated by a barcarolle-mannered pleasantness, swung along in duple meter. The final "March" is one of Hindemith's formal identification marks. Here too

108

there is no cross-grained instrumental purpose—the bassoon is used properly for the truly lyric voice it represents.

¶ *Sonata for Cello and Piano, Op. 11, No. 3*

Music with backlash and recoil, of violent reaction compared to the earlier works that share the opus number (*see below:* Sonatas in E♭ major and D for Violin and Piano, Op. 11, Nos. 1 and 2). The energy and motor drive of the first movement show an athletic composer pitchforking his sounds as if an engine were propelling them off the ground. A slow march occupies the first half of the second movement and progresses into the finale. Rhythmic action with free-conducted lines persist in this instance. In direct conflict, the general dynamic level moves from a *forte* to a concluding *triple piano*. The cadential plan offers a shrewd climax.

¶ *Sonata for Cello and Piano* (1948)

It is of historical importance that in the years surrounding the Second World War four of the greatest foreign composers of the century resided in the United States; namely, Bartók, Schoenberg, Stravinsky, and Hindemith. Living in a complete change of environment one might expect definite change on the part of an artist. But in all four instances the haven found in America offered freedom for thought and work without resulting in any new constructive absorptions, though in each case the man's artistic maturity increased.

Hindemith, with a long established code of practice, turned out music with even greater clarification than previously. This cello sonata is one of his American products (completed at New Haven, Connecticut, on March 8, 1948). Dynamic best describes the opening "Pastorale," central movement, and concluding "Passacaglia." The word may seem odd when used in connection with a "Pastorale." But the noiseless tenor of quiet music has its own predominant strength. The bold simplicity of this portion is one of the most attractive parts of the sonata.

¶ *Sonata for Clarinet and Piano* (1939)

Notwithstanding four distinct and concrete patterns in this composition, there is an interlink that gives a duodimensional reality to the utilized balanced conventions of a four-movement sonata plan. The first, second, and fourth portions conclude in a *pianissimo* dynamic, the third in *piano*. The natural intensity levels of the fast, scherzo, slow, and pertly demeanored divisions are of minute but

109

communicable effect to the general reticence of the final cadences. It is just such magic that marks the expressive composition from the ordinary.

¶ *Sonata for English Horn and Piano* (1941)

This represents the first example of an English horn sonata by a composer of distinction. Though Hindemith does not belabor the most common method concerned with the instrument (to depict suburban facets of music; the shepherd's voice, and so on), neither does he miss such opportunity. He balances all possibilities so that a melancholic atmosphere is compared with a more cheerful view. In addition, the spice of variety stems from the shifting commentary basic to variational form.

¶ *Sonata for Flute and Piano* (1936)

Virtuosity is not lacking in Hindemith's music, but he never indulges in it for sheer pretension. The use of the agile flute in connection with the exposition of a sonata might lead some to make such an error—Hindemith does not. The content explains the instrument's character and type of personality. It is not simply conventional, but exercises proper discrimination for the charming wind instrument. Thus geniality and light niceties dot the surface of the music's conversation.

Especially appealing are the final pair of movements. In comparison to the preceding pair these are much gayer and released in decorum. Hindemith's fondness for the form in question is shown by the concluding "March." The pulse of this homespun design is of more than minor importance to him. Its crispness is refreshing; the effect irresistible.

¶ *Sonata for Oboe and Piano* (1938)

Hindemithian orthodoxy is illustrated: motival co-ordination, fluctuating tonal polarity, and cleverly disposed rhythm. The favored telescoping of movements is followed in part two. A total double binary pattern is realized by combining slow-tempoed music with scherzolike liveliness. Running through the operation twice, with but one exception—in the recapitulation—the scherzo becomes a fugue.

¶ *Sonata for Trombone and Piano* (1941)

Hindemith's trombone and piano sonata does not indulge in fantasies foreign to the majestic breadth and stability of the most sonorous of all brass instruments. There is a firmness and a sententious quality in this one-movement conception that is parceled into definite quadruple sections (the last of these using themes from the first). Wide-spaced intervals are utilized, giving the enthusiastic and healthy "well-to-do" disposition most proper for brass-timbred thematics. In Hindemith's hands the trombone is a prancing instrument (but retains its footing); it dominates and is resolute, it calls to order without any theatrical manner. Notwithstanding a scherzo-mannered portion and folk-style deviations (section three is based on an English tune, "Swashbuckler's Song"), Hindemith's trombone sonata is one of declarative power.

¶ *Sonata for Trumpet and Piano* (1939)

Trumpet music equals music of authoritative character. Most often, determined clarion intervals are used in its subject matter, together with short jets of simulative bugle calls (as in part one here), plus proclamatory evidence (movement three). This sonata is conceived instrumentally *à la mode;* harmonically and rhythmically it is completely under Hindemith's control.

An odd point arises with a theme employed in the second movement. The imprinted play projects an ironic view of "Ach du Lieber Augustin." If Hindemith's tune is totally original and its shape is merely coincidental it remains just as unique. If the tune is included purposely, then it illustrates the gentle type of musical snicker.

¶ *Sonata* (No. 4) *in C for Violin and Piano* (1939)

Each one of the three movements of the "Sonata in C" has the patent nobility that shows real achievement. Movement one offers cohesive stability and contrast simultaneously by forming both of the principal themes from the same starting sounds. Movement two embraces a scherzo span within its deliberate pace.

The sonata's most demonstrative part is the "Fugue." Fugues are often pretentious, and more often of the academic variety. But Paul Hindemith can muster a fugue that is always dynamic. The ceremony of contrapuntal composition is one he most willingly (and cheerfully) attends. In this case the "Fugue" is a triple fugue. Three subjects are separately announced and then artfully combined. The movement's climax is obtained by a fully fed augmentation of the initial subject as the music pulls into the terminal C major.

¶ *Sonata* (No. 2) *in D for Violin and Piano, Op. 11, No. 2*

Hindemith surveys the back country of romanticism here. The diagonal bend of semidissonance is prominent; linear aspects are

111

definitely shadowed. Notwithstanding the point that the work pays testimony to its ancestral forebears—Brahms and Reger—there is a goodly amount of the young composer in it. No snug glance observes and copies in this case. While tradition is recognized, Hindemith is not blinded. He aspires to kindle a new flame and, in trying, realizes a remarkably terse sonata that stands apart from the usual clogging product of Germanic postromanticism.

¶ *Sonata* (No. 1) *in E♭ major for Violin and Piano, Op. 11, No. 1*

Hindemith's first violin and piano sonata shows that he will have none of the schematics proposed by dry and stuffy textbooks. Notwithstanding that Hindemith at this early period cannot be false to his love of Brahms, he begins to shake loose from him. The sonata is short, containing only two movements. This conciseness is later recanted by the composer, though he never deserts the sonata's dynamic pithiness of expression.

Little harmonic spikes are thrust into the romantic tissue of the music. As this is done, it is accompanied by dance pulse gestures. Stiff Teutonicism starts to vibrate from its hinges, and the resultant rhythmic reckoning becomes a specialty of Hindemith composition. Simultaneously, romantic rubato ceases to exist.

¶ *Sonata* (No. 3) *in E for Violin and Piano* (1935)

In this sonata Hindemith concerns himself with the past, but not too strongly. Such evolutionary distinction is but one of the marks which point to his proper place in the line of great German composers. Any reluctance to continue and enlarge a specific tradition forfeits consideration of a composer from a historical viewpoint. While Paul Hindemith holds no laws in awe, he obeys and reasons. He enhances and thereby strengthens the Germanic tradition of music.

The sonata has a relaxed manner, containing vernal qualities rather than the *Sturm und Drang* of the earlier compositions. Even in the faster, concluding section the matter of flow is basic to the conception. Throughout, there is a definite connective principle that formally binds the work. This is brought about by tonal centers in the first movement, with some cyclic assistance that relates the opening part to the last. In turn, the latter is connected with the slow-tempoed preceding part.

¶ *Trio for Recorders from "Plöner Musiktag"* ("A Day of Music at Plön") (1932)

The revival of the flute's immediate predecessor, the recorder (a vertically played instrument), has been so enthusiastic that today it is an important part of the music manufacturing industry. The recorder's tone quality may be described by saying it is to the flute what the parlor harmonium is to the full organ. Marked tonal sweetness is its biggest asset, while the dangers of false intonation have left many a red mark in the ledger of performances.

Marchlike pertness is the determining point of much of the trio. And, of course, with Hindemith, polyphony. Accordingly, the concluding movement is a "Fugato."

¶ *Trio for Violin, Viola and Cello, Op. 34*

A work of transcendent power; the working material is handled freely, the horizontal impulse being the paramount objective. There is muscularity in the trio, depicting a small-sized Hindemith composing music thrice his strength. Strength of color predominates in the third movement. Save for the last few measures (where the cello changes to bowed sounds) the three instruments are completely muted and fully concerned with pizzicato throughout.

Hindemith's incessant concentration of polyphonic purpose in his work for three instruments posts a high mark in the record books of string-trio literature. The indomitable vigor is so tremendous it is almost terrifying.

¶ *Trio No. 2 for Violin, Viola and Cello* (1933)

Music based on exceedingly unconstrained tonality; but one is reminded that atonality is not Hindemith's way of work. There are composers who write with complete negation of key, who do not at least "reinsert," as it were, a tonal zone to focus the ever-circling music. For such, the term "atonality" is correct; for Hindemith, in spite of some opinions, the word would not be applicable.

The trio is a clear realization of tonal matter, but with plastic freedom. Hindemith's music recoils and leaps, tenses and relaxes, and forms its own kind of tonics and dominants. It is not glued to a key, but is mobile; the tonality as motile as the rhythms.

¶ *String Quartet No. 3, Op. 22*

Of all the Hindemith string quartets the third work has a place which matches those compositions of classical distinction in the

113

confirmed repertoire. This proves that music lying outside the territory of the major and minor tonal systems can also obtain proper response. Hindemith's mature manner of more than thirty years later is perhaps more solid, but does not depart very much from the style and sensitive quality of his Opus 22. Nor was he able to go much beyond the individuality of the third string quartet.

This is the only string quartet which Hindemith wrote that consists of five movements. Each part displays clarity of form and theme, and the melodic lines ripple with beauty. There is no sonata design within the quartet.

A free fugato opens the work; movement two is a stream of power channeled through the most violent and barbaric kind of sonorous action. The third movement is the most captivating of all, accomplishing such convincing loveliness that Hindemith was hard put to duplicate it in his other works, chamber music or otherwise. In muted power this movement sounds dissonantly, but intimately, stimulated by ostinated quintal intervals. The fourth section is a wild toccatalike affair, improvisational in its course through free fantasy. Hindemith serves up a final fugal movement of almost chaste quality to make a fitting conclusion to one of the special quartets of the century.

¶ *Kleine Kammermusik for Five Wind Instruments, Op. 24, No. 2*

One of the most widely played of all contemporary works for wind instruments. It is scored for the traditional forces of the woodwind quintet—flute, oboe, clarinet, bassoon, and horn—with a piccolo being substituted for the flute in the second movement. This is without doubt one of the composer's most charming pieces.

The quintet embodies humor, parody, and irony; some of the passages must have been written with acid. Its dance-slant attitude, in typical post-World War I style, equals a musical hedonistic view of life presented in cameo style. The dissonant chordal bite of the very first beat outlines and sketches the type of aesthetic axiom that the composer will propound; the quintet's tonality is to be free and friction harmony will persist.

In proper place, soft sounds have as much influence as the bombastic explanation. For example, it is a quiet dynamic use which implies the most concentrated and pungent detail in musical parody. This fact is demonstrated in the second movement ("Walzer"), not related to any "Blue Danube." And the same relish is obtained throughout this music with spiculated texture.

¶ *Octet* (1958)

The instrumentation for the "Octet" represents attention to timbre variance in the larger media of chamber music. Semidiaphanous qualities predominate, with the darker, mellower winds (clarinet and bassoon) and horn associated with a string quintet of violin, two violas, cello, and double bass definitely pitched toward smoky colors. The consanguinity of form and content integrates the richness of the composer's varied, masterful modern polyphony. Counterpoint is almost the whole means of regulating the expression, yet the linear bargain is not overdriven into boredom. The contrapuntalism in each of the five movements has a different point to explain: a sonata-styled initial part, variations, a slow-paced division, a gingered, dry scherzo description, and a novel twist to a fugue which intertwines "drei altmodische Tänzer" (waltz, polka, and galop).

VOCAL

¶ *Das Marienleben* (1948)

Quite a history surrounds this huge cycle of fifteen songs. Rilke's poems on the life of the Virgin Mary were written in 1912 and were chosen by Hindemith as his text in 1922. After the completion of the composition (listed as Opus 27) in the year following, very few singers dared to present "Das Marienleben." Its difficulties of range and style were not the only problems—physical stamina was an important one. In a way strain was part of the basic style of the cycle, bearing in mind that this element adds its own type of urgency to a composition's dramatic progress. (In the hands of the first-rate, pyrotechnical passages may seem to require much more effort than they actually do. "Strain" is a foreign term in this reference. Hindemith's pure music was taxing because of its formal and vocally unorthodox syntax.)

In 1948, after seven years of work, Hindemith completed a sweeping revision of "The Life of Mary." The new "Marienleben" was not meant to eradicate difficulties, but to reset the work in Hindemith's later style, one removed from the heated musical atmosphere and rugged counterpoint of the nineteen twenties. Only one song remained as it was originally; the others were, for the most part, rewritten entirely. Fundamentally, the revampings replaced restlessness with smoothness. But sharp musical sculpture has been changed into a polished engraving. "Das Marienleben" is still powerful, difficult

115

to perform, effective and monumental; but young, instinctive veracity has been superseded by older, cautious learning. We have lost the dynamistic image of music conceived without theoretical extenuating circumstances.

The cycle divides into four parts. According to Hindemith the first section treats of Mary's personal experience; the second "an array of people, landscapes and circumstances." In the third part we observe "Mary as the sufferer," and the last portion is "an epilogue in which ordinary mortals and the affairs of man no longer play a part." Various devices are used: passacaglia, basso ostinato, fugato, theme and variations, and so on. The cycle is one of the great examples of lieder; in size it is the equivalent of an oratorio for solo voice.

¶ *Geistliche Motetten* (Three Motets) *for Soprano and Piano* (1941–1944)

Sacred definition is not served in this instance. Secular sunshine streams over these motets. Gospel texts are utilized (from Matthew, Luke, and John), but these furnish the only ecclesiastical touch. Otherwise, each of the motets sounds like a canzonetta, or a villanella, or an ordinary art song.

CHORAL

¶ *Liederbuch für Mehrere Singstimmen* (Five Songs on Old Texts), *Op. 33*

The title in parentheses is naturally not a translation of the German, but represents a second setting. Hindemith's "Liederbuch" (also called "Lieder nach alten Texten") was composed with German texts in 1923. In 1936 Hindemith took numbers 1, 2, 3, and 6 (the last) of the original group and made a new version in English and German; *i.e.,* "Five Songs on Old Texts." The reconstituted group, used as numbers 3, 2, 5, and 4 respectively, is filled out with the addition of "True Love," to words by H. von Veldecke.

In either form the choral technique is without floridity; clear chromaticism dovetails into diatonic purity. The perceptive regard for neatly tailored harmonies makes the euphonious music a compact delight, especially "Of Household Rule" ("Vom Hausregiment") to a Luther text; "Lady's Lament" ("Frauenklage") emphasizing women's voices, and "Mercenary's Drinking Song" which is an alphabetical gem in German: "Landsknechtstrinklied."

¶ *Six Chansons* (1939)

No surprises in these settings of poems by Rainer Maria Rilke and little illumination of Hindemith's profile. For the most part chordal conduct directs procedures, and, though agreeable music, it is rather conventional and terribly unimportant. A second-class product by a first-rate composer.

CHORAL WITH ORCHESTRA

¶ *Requiem "For Those We Love"* (1946)

Music of haunting spirituality. A requiem (but not a "Missa pro defunctis") that finds proper place alongside works in the same genre, fully as telling as those by Brahms, Verdi, and Berlioz. Composed after the conclusion of the Second World War, "For Those We Love" can be considered as testimony for those lost in conflict and a memorial to the composer's native land destroyed by Nazi ideology.

The elegiac text is from Walt Whitman's "When Lilacs Last in the Dooryard Bloom'd," part of a Lincoln memorial tribute. The formal scope is diversified, chosen to best present the mood of the material. It includes a gripping prelude projected over a pedal point, a dynamic fugue, a duetted hymn, and keen color in the use of parade drum and bugle in a march sequence. Formal guidance never interferes with the quiet fervor of the music. And in this manner Hindemith's creative virtuosity spreads a magical liturgic sheen over his inspired threnodic speech; a truly profound "symphonie funèbre."

BALLET

¶ *The Demon, Ballet Pantomime, Op. 28*

Hindemith composed this dance mime in 1924. Some of the titles of the fourteen sections cause anticipation, but the musical cards are stacked against any excitement. For example, the "Dance of the Poison" is little different from the "Dance of the Whipped Animal," and so on. The story deals with a prehistoric character, an exemplification of evil, who seduces two young girls and then practices sadism on them. It turns out to be quite ridiculous, not helped by music that is uncommonly dull and monotonous.

117

¶ *Hérodiade* (1944)

Despite its brooding color and interesting technical content, Hindemith's score needs the choreographic partnership that stimulated its birth. I am also convinced that the narration of the poem by Mallarmé, from which the idea of the ballet was derived, is essential. One cannot overlook the fact that Hindemith subtitles his work "Récitation orchestrale." He does not mean a reciter *with* orchestra, but a blend of dance and/or poetry with the music is almost crucial. As pure orchestral fare "Hérodiade" subsists on half rations.

OPERA

¶ *Mathis der Maler* (1934)

Hindemith's opera (best known by the orchestral "symphony" he drew from the score) considers the rightful place of the artist in society during times of stress. Based on a mostly fictional account of events in the life of the sixteenth-century painter Matthias Grünewald, it tells of his belief that he should join with the underprivileged in their revolt during the violent German Peasants' War of 1524. Grünewald abandons his art only to find that injustice knows no class distinctions. Assailed by constant doubts and not capable of coping with the intrigue and violence that surround him, Mathis returns to his painting, having learned that the artist serves his fellow men best by his work.

Much of the score is concerned with a declamatory style that will remind one of late Mahler, but at that point the similarity ends. "Mathis" is a solemn, somewhat mystical conception, but it is Hindemithian to the core, with the single exception that a great deal of the orchestral background for the voices is quite conventional compared to the strictly instrumental portions. But the warmth of the vocal lines negates any criticism. Derived from medieval turns, elements of Gregorianisms, and colored by neo-Baroque grandeur, "Mathis" is a marvel of contemporary lyricism. It is one of Paul Hindemith's supreme inspirations.

10. GUSTAV HOLST
(1874–1934)

THERE are composers who stand apart because of intense individuality and there are composers about whom the critics constantly disagree. Holst is in the class where the doubts and the convictions clash. Some contend he was too self-conscious a nationalist and too coldly intellectual at the same time (the word "manufactured" has been used to describe his music). Others have leveled the charge that he could not handle large forms. His defenders claim originality, that he was a composer of ingenuity, a master of orchestral craft.

Despite his English purpose, despite his use of native subject matter and folk song, Holst is for the most part as un-English a composer as one can find. His music poses a paradox, for it not only contains modernity far beyond any to be found in British music of his time, but it is (in some cases) severely neoclassic, haunted by the shadows of Hindemith and Stravinsky. In still other instances it is in the pure English tradition. Holst once told a friend that when he composed he considered himself a mathematician attacking a specific problem. Here, again, is a contradiction, for Holst's music, even in its most vehement address (it is never severe), is emotional, though it may be on the cool side.

It is important to elucidate a man's ideas and carefully judge them. It is a dodge for the critics to say, without proof, that Holst is not important and that he once was fashionable, but is no longer so. In all fairness his music is the creation of a craftsman-musician, and it is absorbing art. Of course, one can challenge this conception of Holst's work. The challenge is readily accepted, for Gustav Holst remains, more than a quarter of a century after his death, an important artist, a notable contemporary voice in the wilderness of creative dogmas.

ORCHESTRAL

¶ *Egdon Heath, Op. 47*

A pastoral study, but entirely without bucolic gentility, "Egdon Heath" represents desolation at its gloomiest. Loneliness, despair, and

119

the effect of limitless space are brought to mind by its measures, inspired by a quotation from Hardy's novel *The Return of the Native*.

The introspectiveness of Holst's composition is obtained by an intensely checked orchestral condition. Despite a full instrumentation (but no percussion, not even timpani) the entire orchestra is only used in one measure. Elsewhere, there is fractional scoring; the strings are divided for the greater part, and further thinned by being split into muted and non-muted groups.

Although none of the books dealing with Holst points it out, a subtitle exists for Opus 47: "Homage to Thomas Hardy." Holst wrote his piece for the New York Symphony Orchestra, which gave the première in February of 1928, under the direction of Walter Damrosch.

¶ *The Perfect Fool—Ballet Suite, Op. 39*

Though Holst's oddly parodistic opera on opera lies in peaceful rest, the ballet remains one of his better-known pieces and is truly exciting fare. It is certainly unusual to open an opera (let alone one in a single act) with a ballet. The three dances—representing the spirits of earth, water, and fire—open Holst's stage piece. Thus it has come to pass that with the opera's demise its beginning has become its entire representation.

Despite the similar melodic shapes of the principal tunes of the pieces, their contours are varied expertly. A clever septuple metrical plan is employed in the first part, cool orchestration surrounds the middle section, and the final section has powerful thrust. There is no stock response to any of the ideas, and the orchestration is handsomely brilliant.

¶ *The Planets, Suite for Large Orchestra, Op. 32*

Holst's magnificent essay for a huge orchestra (including alto flute, bass oboe, six horns, tenor and bass tubas, large percussion array, two harps, organ, and so on, plus a six-part female offstage chorus in the seventh movement) represents instrumental painting that can also be defined as absolute music. The suite can be judged as an astrological whole or its structures can be considered separately. Each movement has a set design (sometimes framed by ostinati), pertinent subject temper, and undeceptive allegiance to both pattern-scoring and composition.

The subtitle of each movement specifies a mood that Holst carries out vividly. "Mars, the Bringer of War," is a battering ram of quintal rhythm framing parallel chordal violence; tender and quiet ideas symbolize "Venus, the Bringer of Peace." Other divisions indicate the contrasts of speed and jollity, then desolation ("Saturn, the Bringer of Old Age"), followed by magic (plus grotesqueness and comedy), and finally quietude ("Neptune, the Mystic"). These seven images represent an anthology of Holst's ideas of orchestration, texture, and speech (a good parcel of Englishry is contained in the music). Nonetheless, he exhibits a liberal technical viewpoint.

It is strange that the success of this work distressed Holst. But it is not strange that this music of opulence and grandeur has retained its popularity. Originality makes its way—Holst's music of the outer spaces is not stamped with the hallmark of any "schola."

STRING ORCHESTRA

¶ St. Paul's Suite, Op. 29, No. 2

In listening to this work, one notices its allegiance to the spirit of the dance. (The title has no religious connection; the suite was composed in 1913 for the orchestra of the St. Paul's Girls' School, where Holst was in charge of music from 1905 until 1934.)

Rhythm and folk melody mark the music. The modal jig of the first part, the ostinato whip of movement two, and the sixteenth-century country dance tune of the finale (the "Dargason") cleverly counterpointed by "Greensleeves," furnish the proof. Contrast is provided with the more majestic contours of the "Intermezzo." Though Holst's suite uses catchy themes, there is nothing trivial about its overabundance.

BAND

¶ First Suite in E flat, Op. 28a

In three movements: a chaconne, intermezzo, and march. Though the formal horizon changes, the basic material is drawn from the opening section of the chaconne. More effective band writing is difficult to imagine, for Holst's formal, harmonic, and rhythmic leadings give coloristic life to the entertaining properties of the suite. Holst's scoring produces an organic totality to his "bandstration"; the organlike sonorities illustrate expertise in a medium that few composers have mastered artistically. And he discovered a fresh way of dealing with the chaconne design. Variants there are, but the music is so recognizably British that the basic neutrality of the form is erased. The same goes for the intermezzo; the march is a humdinger.

121

¶ *Hammersmith: A Prelude and Scherzo, Op. 52*

Music dealing with implied programmaticism. Aside from the proper noun of the title, which describes a London borough where quiet and noise, respectability and hedonism, homes and machine shops are in jagged counterpoint, there is the contrasted impact of the two moods of the subtitle. The prelude can be termed a humid nocturne; it can also reflect (as suggested by Holst's daughter, Imogen) the Thames that flows through Hammersmith. It is the scherzo that makes a thousand picture possibilities spring to life. Pace and temper constantly prod each other, chameleonlike, in this earthy movement. This is rather unusual in that the final portion of a large-scaled work is usually definite. It can be argued that Holst had absolutism in mind while composing this band masterpiece, but the soft-hardness of texture is further evidence of the music's multifarious (qua programmatic) character.

The facts surrounding the work are just as picturesque. Commissioned by the BBC in 1930, it was not performed. Holst later transcribed it for orchestra. The band score was thought lost until uncovered by an American, Robert Cantrick, who conducted the world première in Pittsburgh in 1954. The musical world remains in Cantrick's debt for bringing to light a major Holst composition.

¶ *Mars from "The Planets," Op. 32*

The music finds potent expression in the band's colors. Notwithstanding this fitting transcription there is just as much relentless fury and even more tension contained in the orchestral original.

¶ *Second Suite in F, Op. 28b*

Though rooted in folk song, Holst's band suite has a fresh viewpoint. The last movement, "Fantasia on the Dargason," which Holst later transferred to his "St. Paul's Suite" for string orchestra, is magnificently timbred contrapuntalism, combining "Greensleeves" with the principal theme.

VOCAL

¶ *Persephone, Op. 48, No. 9*

Holst's solo songs are rarely heard, but reward the listener when they are. Most of them have an economy of expression that frames the words with impeccable style and aptness.

"Persephone" is one of a group of "Twelve Songs" composed in 1929. In this instance, modal style is maintained as the minimal resource.

CHORAL

¶ *Abroad As I Was Walking*

A mastery of choral technique makes any Holst work for voices a treat. This arrangement of a Cornish folk song has an introspective sweetness which illustrates his method of artistically polishing a simple tune.

¶ *A Dirge for Two Veterans*

Similar to a number of other composers, Holst was influenced for a time by the poetry of Walt Whitman. At the age of 25 he wrote (but did not publish) a "Walt Whitman Overture," Op. 7. Later he composed a piece for soprano and orchestra—"The Mystic Trumpeter," Op. 18 (also unpublished). Published compositions based on Whitman texts are the "Ode to Death," Op. 38, for chorus and orchestra and "A Dirge for Two Veterans," set for male voices, brass instruments, and drums.

Holst matches the text with a type of choral processional, squared securely but sensitively with a constant rhythmic outline and framed with demanding brass flourishes. The emotional words are paralleled naturally. Choral music of sensitive content that is expressive without going outside the tonal hierarchy.

¶ *A Dream of Christmas*

Designed with precise symmetry of five verses and a refrain. The slight poignancy of the latter is especially charming. This short piece of Christmas music is deserving of popularity.

¶ *Eternal Father*

A short anthem in which Holst displays a partiality to textural contrasts. Bells and organ are employed as a frame for varied choral writing, including an incidental soprano solo, and, in the coda, arpeggiated female voices intoning a decoratively composed Alleluia. The piece is an example of a drive to climax by the opposite device of decrescendo.

¶ *Lullay My Liking*

We have an abundance of drama, tragedy, and tense emotional moods in the *Zeitgeist* of today. A carol like "Lullay My Liking" is a refreshing reminder of the simple beauties and expressiveness to be found in the tonal past. It is a perfect gem.

¶ *Matthew, Mark, Luke and John, Op. 36, No. 3*

An unaccompanied "choral folk song" from a set of six. It can be described as part modern organum, enclosed in pedal points, setting forth a carol tune of a bygone era. But if composition is merely a process of discovery, Holst has found how to invest two minutes of choral music with entrancing beauty.

¶ *Personent Hodie*

A Christmas carol with majestic sweep. The emotive power of the sixteenth-century tune is displayed in Holst's unadorned setting.

CHORAL WITH ORCHESTRA

¶ *The Hymn of Jesus, Op. 37*

Religious music, but as different from the musty, mummified Stainer tradition as is Stravinsky's "Symphony of Psalms." Holst sings to the Saviour with ecstatic spiritualism. The "Hymn to Jesus" (the text drawn by the composer from the apocryphal *Acts of St. John*) is violent as well as devotional, with acrid combinations of sound jostling plainsong effects.

Holst's daughter has described this work as one of "fierce exaltation." Unorthodox in its setting, requiring two choruses, a semichorus of sopranos and altos, orchestra, and organ, the sharply coded shapes of Holst's huge hymn are as fiercely concerned with tone color, textural flux, and dynamic accent, as they are sacred.

There are faults in the composition, especially some time-marking via sequences, but they do not vitiate the artistic triumph of this strangely beautiful conception. "The Hymn of Jesus" is one of the memorable items in Holst's catalogue.

¶ *148th Psalm*

Actually, Holst titled this piece "Lord, who hast made us for Thine own." It forms the second of "Two Psalms," for chorus, string

124

orchestra and organ, which he composed in 1912 (as in a great number of his works, no opus number was assigned).

When the principal tune (based on a sixteenth-century hymn melody) is set in augmented time values and counterpointed above, the effect is telling. This builds to a neat climax that is gently thrilling.

11. ARTHUR HONEGGER
(1892–1955)

Honegger's music is lyrical and athletically vigorous. The lyricism, combining acridity and sweetness, is based on freely chromatic harmony—almost atonical in its range—yet bypasses any rigorous setting and placement of the twelve tones. Because of a liking for sturdy contrapuntalism there is a Bachian innuendo in all of this Frenchman's music, but romantic textural rotundity and sentimental thickness are missing. Honegger's music is rather clipped and tight, partial to the tautness of twentieth-century energy. Quite often Honegger's melodicism seems austere because he is not tempted to excess.

Honegger's musical prose is richly chromatic. Polytonality does occur, but it is not the ordered setting of lines in separate keys against each other. It is parenthetical—employed to embellish (and thereby verify) the basic tonal fluxion. Like Bach, Honegger derives his main musical grammar from contrapuntal juxtaposition. But unlike Bach, Honegger's polyphony embraces specific vertical combinations of the diatonic system, and adds up to a total of *chordal* counterpoint. These combines make the musical structure rock-ribbed with superpositioned sounds which place foreign elements on otherwise recognizable triads, seventh and ninth chords. Activity is constant, the parts interlocked and interwoven in the fabric. His compositions illustrate the polyphony of today; they codify the school of modern counterpoint. Unless one accepts these facts, Honegger's music cannot be effective or understood.

ORCHESTRAL

¶ *Chant de Joie* ("Song of Joy")

Honegger's music is energetic; it displays a vigorous appetite for sound. His sonorities are heavy-laden, but without any surplus deadweight. The piece under discussion is evidence of Arthur Honegger's mastery of contemporary polyphony. It fulfills its title admirably with sufficient contrast in its tri-part form.

126

¶ *Mouvement Symphonique No. 3*

Music in the absolute manner, identified so patently by the title. Honegger's symphonicism is implicitly chromatic, not only in the ebb and flow of its harmonic conduits, but in its melodic shapes as well.

This quality delivers a frictional invigoration that avoids the balm of chords in thirds and sixths. It is the semiacid harmony applied to the lines that creates the highly sonorous exuberance—an exciting example of orchestral music. Honegger skirts wholesale bitonality and polytonality. He is not the rigid servant of such music, as is Darius Milhaud. Rather his is contemporary music with the clear properties of classicism.

¶ *Pacific 231* (Mouvement Symphonique No. 1)

Mention of Honegger generally brings this work to mind. "Pacific 231," a fascinating description of an American locomotive, is now rarely performed, but during the 1920's and the modern *verismo* period of musical composition it was a program best seller. The piece does not concern itself with the locomotive in static grandeur, but with the dramatic drive of the machine in motion. It starts with scratching slowness, moves gradually into full speed, and then reverses the process as it slows down and finally stops. In total, the music is like a rhythmic bibliography.

A composer may be classified incorrectly through hackneyed short works or a *pièce d'occasion*. While Honegger's "Pacific 231" is one of the cleverest examples of musical programmatics, it is a trick, the work of a creative magician. Arthur Honegger, the true composer, is heard in his "King David," in his chamber music and late symphonies.

¶ *Prelude, Fugue and Postlude*

One might think that the severity of a set contrapuntal design, a fugue, would be somewhat mechanical in the hands of a composer who thinks polyphonically most of the time. With the talents of a Honegger the results are dramatic. Thus the demand for intellectual listening (which is part of the joy of hearing music) is matched by the emotional response of the expressive content.

Balanced on either side of the fugue is music of intensity and quiet. The triptych so formed makes a moving composition.

¶ *Prelude to "La Tempête"* ("The Tempest")

Truly a tempest, but not too appetizing a prelude. This music is dictated by free, heavy harmony and a polyphonic mixture derived from liberated lines. The result is of almost unburdened dissonance. Underneath the harmonic overcoat are triadic chordal combinations but these are obliterated by the sound.

Honegger's composition is very busy and extremely loud. It is a cold running of music, without sentiment or mood; its inordinate chromatic usage and thick texture are self-defeating.

¶ *Rugby* (Mouvement Symphonique No. 2)

Honegger created his own brand of audience psychology in this piece. The title was the result of a newspaper story which stated that the famous French composer was present at a rugby match in order to orientate himself with the proper atmosphere for his next orchestra work. Though contrary to the facts, Honegger thought the idea was excellent and composed "Rugby."

"Rugby" is a vigorous, sonoric abstraction replete with blocked counterpoint and motile part activity. The interlocking and interweaving of the voices produce a polytonal web, which could be descriptive of something or nothing at all. It is the music *plus* the significant name of the piece that provide mental levers for the auditor. Without title—no rugby match. With title suggestion translates the music into images of the teams dashing up and down the field, the contact of player, against player, etc. (Note that the first performance of "Rugby" took place at an athletic field during the intermission of an International Rugby match between England and France, held in the Stade Colombe in Paris, on the last day of the year 1928.)

¶ *Suite Archaïque*

Honegger proves that linear style is only successful if it has clear form and clean, direct counterpoint. The color surfaces in this suite are indices to the forms. The outer movements complement each other: the stark, brass-dressed hymn tune in the "Overture" becomes the march resource of the "Processional." In the "Pantomime" flutter-tongued flute sound is primary, and in the "Ritournelle et Sérénade," solo string variants.

This piece was commissioned by the Louisville Orchestra. It is not great music but an example of excellent creative skill.

¶ *Symphony No. 3* ("Liturgique")

Charles Munch, the Boston Symphony's conductor from 1949 to 1962, was honored by the dedication of this symphony. He considers Honegger's "Liturgical" symphony to have certain symbolic foundations ("the problem of humanity vis-à-vis God"). This opinion is as valid as any other, since Honegger's symphony is colored by the Latin subtitles given its three movements: "Dies Irae," "De Profundis Clamavi," and "Dona Nobis Pacem." These definitions are expressed dramatically in the opening movement by a quality of nihilism and fear combined, by the sense of anxiety and pleading in the second part, and through the mood of militancy which climaxes in a hymn of aspiration in the final portion. However, if there are almost sacred objectives in this composition, they are more mystical than spiritual.

It is useless to seek programmatic purposes in Honegger's work. The "Liturgique" is a true symphony, illuminated by its movement headings, but not confined by them. The orchestral coloring is a clue to the emotional depth of the symphony; it is mostly drawn from the darker timbres and combinations. But no matter what meaning is applied to this work, one will recognize the deep poetry of the music, with its most individual melodicism—not "tunes" but architectonic lines that have more probity than so-called "melody." Just because Honegger's themes are not easily whistled, they are no less perfect.

¶ *Symphony No. 5* ("Di Tre Re")

The sonorous and linear thicknesses found in many of Honegger's compositions are eliminated in this one. The dissonances are poised on thin but strongly incisive lines, which are just as probing as massed layers of sound.

Honegger's composition is an indictment against the superficial chicanery of many a so-termed "symphony." It also serves as a document to confirm the sincere and ever-fresh significance of his contemporary thought. We have heard so much "modern" music our ears are coated with stale sounds, and much of the "new" music is boldly unoriginal. A composer of honest-to-goodness creativity is rare these days; Honegger's "tre re" proves his stature as a real symphonist. It is also proof that Honegger sang while he dotted his music with rhythmic vitality.

(The "Re" in the subtitle means the tone D. Each of the three movements ends with this sound.)

CHAMBER ORCHESTRA

¶ *Concerto da Camera for Flute, English Horn and String Orchestra*

Virtuosity surrounds any solo concerted work, but the crudity (we can term it blatant showboating) of the super-duper concerto finds no place in the artistic product of a contemporary composer. Honegger's substantial opus contradicts neither the terms of the chosen form nor his personal style. His chamber concerto is conceived in the classical sense; the virtuosity is interfused and thereby pertinent to the working material; the polyphony is refined, lucid, and delightfully communicative. Contrasts and color combine in the three movements, making one of the purest of Honegger's compositions. This work exemplifies twentieth-century music of substance; its natural rhythms and flow related to the pulse choices of the eighteenth-century composers.

¶ *Pastoral d'Eté* ("Summer Pastoral")

For Honegger, this is a rare example of relaxed music. Nevertheless, his quiet rustic rumination does not meander; there is a well-balanced demeanor between purpose and method. Thematic consideration is emphatic, the working material based on a pair of subjects. Honegger's summer music (for four woodwinds, horn, and strings) is neither breezy nor stormy—simply gentle.

STRING ORCHESTRA

¶ *Symphony No. 2*

A magnificent work that cannot be indexed exactly, because a trumpet joins the strings at the end. (Since the brass instrument is ad libitum the opus is conveniently considered for string orchestra.)

Honegger has stated that there is no program to his second symphony. Nonetheless, the feeling persists that the dark mood, the hurtling figures, the dynamo that is let loose in the violent opening movement, and the optimistic peroration (a singing chorale in which the trumpet adds its fervent voice) present graphic reactions. No "enigma" in this case; the second symphony was conceived in 1941, in the dreadful days when the Nazis occupied France. (Honegger worked in the heat of inspiration, for though his room was without warmth he never ceased composing.) The music moves from strength to strength in a parade of somber, emotional intensity as ostinati power the opening movement and a passacaglia shapes the central part. Only in the final *vivace* is some of the tenseness removed. But even here the sense of struggle is maintained, as harmonies and rhythms are set in opposition. It is not exaggeration to say that this is Honegger's most important symphony, and one of the most dramatically probing in the literature for strings.

BAND

¶ *La Marche sur la Bastille* ("The March on the Bastille")

Truly a decided contribution to band (and march) music. Honegger's piece is music macabre, its colors heavy, its attitude certain and frightening; the ending in the very bowels of the gamut is grim music.

"La Marche sur la Bastille" was written as part of a commission given by the French Government to Honegger, Milhaud, Ibert, Auric, Koechlin, Roussel, and Lazarus for short pieces to accompany a pageant by Romain Rolland called "Le Quatorze Juillet" ("The Fourteenth of July"). The first presentation was given at the Paris Exposition of 1937.

SOLO INSTRUMENT WITH ORCHESTRA

SOLO PIANO WITH ORCHESTRA

¶ *Concertino for Piano and Orchestra*

In this approximately ten-minute piece one can enjoy a lighter representation of the Honegger catalogue. In comparison to most of his other compositions, the "Concertino" is a wonderful conceit, a delicious delicacy. The style is Parisian low-down, sounding like a jazzy Mendelssohnian prospectus. It has the proper décor: snide tunes, stop-and-go rhythms, blue notes, wail and rag scale. Really fun.

INSTRUMENTAL

FLUTE

¶ *Danse de la Chèvre* ("Dance of the Goat")

Honegger's short piece is one of the small total of worthwhile unaccompanied flute music, the most important being Debussy's "Syrinx." In three-part form, its outer portions are akin to a soliloquy rather than a dance, while the main middle portion is a delicate scherzo, smoother in flow than one would expect from the music's title.

131

ORGAN

¶ *Choral*

Music in a deep freeze, sterilized against warmth. In its lack of aural speculation, Honegger's hermetic harmony illustrates musical sparseness (Spartanism?). Very logical, but damnably uneventful and unemotional.

CHAMBER MUSIC

¶ *Second Sonata for Violin and Piano*

Sonata reasoning has become freer through the years, but maintains its place as the first among all musical forms. Many composers have shifted their sonata scenes with abandon; some learned (as did Honegger) that it was possible to obtain a new significance to the old design without creating an emphatically different one.

Movement one of this sonata is a case in point. Its broad subject is a swinging and sensuous "echt-Brahms" item (in meter only!) fitted by triple- and quadruple-pulse patterns. A fugato neatly substitutes for the development section. The slow movement is monothematic; changes of the theme are merely designs woven around the main subject. In the finale note the oddity of introducing two principal themes in the extreme bass zone of the piano.

¶ *Sonatine for Cello and Piano*

This composition (a clarinet may be substituted for the cello) represents relaxed Honegger. The compressed and concentrated three movements define a residue of true sonata form. There is such condensed depiction that if one is not aurally quick the subtle Honeggerian order will pass by all too swiftly. In the first part the composer uses a lazy type of theme, a short fugato (wherein the subject is heard in augmented rhythm), and a recapitulation. A synthesis of ternary form is employed in the *Lent et soutenu*. The finale consists of thirty-seven measures and includes some nimble jazz glides. Actually, this work is a "sonatinette."

¶ *Sonatine for Two Violins*

Proof that proper climax can be obtained even with the minimal means of two-voiced polyphony is ably expressed in the opening movement of this work. (The "Sonatine" was dedicated to Honegger's colleague, Darius Milhaud, with whom Honegger first performed the work in 1921. This was certainly an historic affair, since two famous contemporary composers were the instrumentalists.) Thematic relationship is made clear by alternating homophonically coupled statements, and by four-part writing. Contrasts are also detailed by color (muted timbre in the middle movement). Fugal design defines the final movement.

Unfailing craftsmanship is demanded so that a work for a pair of unaccompanied violins registers effectively. This "Sonatine" adds more credit to Honegger's record.

¶ Sonatine for Violin and Cello

A composer who is fond of polyphony would be drawn to the possibilities available in combining homophonic instruments. In this duet artful contrapuntalism is linked with smart rhythmic ideas. As usual with Arthur Honegger, there is tonal independence. Though the first movement begins in unisoned G major, assorted tonal vein work quickly appears from within. Principally, there are two main motives, both in duple meter; one swings, the other plunges.

The large three-part slow movement is in aria style, followed by a fugal section (an ornamental development of the first part) and then a return to the initial manner. The last movement is somewhat whimsical. The halt-and-go of certain rhythm is of somewhat Stravinskian manner, but the gay E major theme is decidedly French.

¶ Petite Suite for Two Instruments and Piano

A charming bit of semi-whimsy; an odd item in Honegger's catalogue, also singular in several other ways. In its simplicity, the suite is an example of French *Gebrauchsmusik*. The "two instruments" are not named by Honegger, thus permitting a great latitude in choice.

Three categories of combinations are used in the same total of movements. The opening division calls for one instrument and piano, the last for all three players, while the middle section employs the two instruments without piano. The music is tonal, served by a handful of chords and only in a few measures of the final movement are bitonality and birhythm found. Honegger composed this music for his niece and nephew, but—as is so often the case—adults will also enjoy it.

133

¶ *Rapsodie for Flute, Oboe, Clarinet and Piano*

This quartet (originally for a pair of flutes, clarinet and piano, or two violins, viola and piano; the change of instrumentation had the composer's approval) was an early work with an impressionistic cast. Rhapsodic deference is present more in the curvatures traced by the sounds than in the form, which is tripartite. The two outer portions are retouchings, in a way, of Debussy's and Ravel's art; while the central section is a more precise and direct rhythmic march. Compared to other Honegger works the "Rapsodie" indicates a relaxation from formal stringency and harmonic astringency.

CHORAL

CHORAL WITH ORCHESTRA

¶ *Cantique de Pâques*

The technical viewpoint of this *Alleluia* is polyharmonic, couched in a linear style that avoids romantic descant, yet it is totally a work of clear, sacred force. Clarity is demanded for black and white values, and Honegger depicts the Resurrection without fuss. Its utter concentration indicates that he knew how to portray a religious scene as expertly as he designed a symphony or described a streamlined locomotive. The solo voices are textural contrasts in the sonorous movement and with the fine-line orchestral background the music is beautifully appointed.

CANTATA

¶ *Cantate de Noël* ("Christmas Cantata")

Why this moving contemporary music has not found a secure place in the Christmas music category is unfathomable. Furthermore, the "Christmas Cantata" is not merely a seasonal work. It contains both Yuletide and concert music. Honegger's cantata displays a magnificent clarity of polyphonic thought (honest-to-goodness polyphony, not simply harmony turned on its stomach and stretched horizontally). This is set in a true Bachian manner, with the abrasiveness usual to Honegger's strong contrapuntal language honed down to the minimum. Woven into the cantata are French, German, and English carols, together with a pair of Latin hymns. All this is accomplished with taste and stylistic tact.

ORATORIO

¶ *Jeanne d'Arc au Bûcher* ("Joan of Arc at the Stake")

A monumental work with a tremendous complexity of forces employed—combinations of narration, singing, and orchestral playing. The declamation is delivered by two persons, at times with underscoring; the choruses are intertwined with the narration or are separate, and the orchestral forces are used both as a supporting group and as an individual body. The whole is of utmost concentration despite the tremendous area and scope of Honegger's conception, which treats the life of the heroine symbolically.

Although Honegger had composed his "Joan" as a stage production with full-scale scenery, costumes, lighting, and so on, it is just as vivid as a concert piece. It illustrates a revitalization of the oratorio medium, fusing its style with operatic trappings.

¶ *Le Roi David* ("King David")

An oratorio in concept, termed a "dramatic psalm" by the composer, this powerful piece combines chorus, solo voices, and narrator with orchestra in terms of operatic sweep, and purity of thought. "Le Roi David" was initially music for a play by René Morax, instrumentally conceived without string instruments. Two years later it was orchestrally enlarged for full resources and reset as a concert work. A composition of mixed genre, this oratorio-opera is divided into three major sections, and consists of twenty-eight different numbers.

"King David" is stark music, both radiant and brutal because of its subject. It is like a huge mural as it traces David from shepherd to king, by way of psalms, fanfares, incantations, lamentations, marches, and dances. Because of its varied scope the contrasts are extremely vivid, obtained by chord and discord, Bachian classicism compared to audacious "Le Sacre" types, pure harmonic constructions set off from polytonal counterpoint. Though each scene has its individual evocative power, the extremes of style content do not make a hodgepodge. The sections are related one to the next no matter how different. Nothing artificial, nothing mannered, "Le Roi David" shows how an abundance of variety can serve dramatic purposes and create its own colorful balance. The rewards are eloquent.

135

¶ *Les Cris du Monde*

Depicting modern man's destiny in his machine-ridden environment, the entire picture of "The Cries of the World" is gloomy, weighted with piercing sadness, and verging on the ultratragic. It is rare that a work can be formed successfully from one absolute, undeviating mood. Usually there must be some relief. However, no anodyne is used to lighten the pessimistic character of Honegger's oratorio.

DRAMATIC WORK

¶ *Nicolas de Flue*

In his sprawling three-act *Festspiel* (termed a "dramatic legend"), Honegger has permitted too much stress on the narration. It traces the life of Nicolas de Flue, a heroic figure in Swiss history, who reestablished peace in his country after it was threatened by civil war. There is far too much talk and insufficient musical action in the use of Denis de Rougemont's poem. Quite often a choral section has hardly begun when it is either counterpointed by the speaker or totally cut off. What music there is, is disparate—children's songs, chants, fanfares, dance ideas, neo-Handelian climaxes; plain and fancy, original and eclectic. But this assortment is like a minor added attraction to the narration. In terms of concert fare, Honegger's opus is rather poverty-stricken.

12. JACQUES IBERT
(1890–1962)

Most composers should be classified by their best efforts rather than their entire output, which may show conflicting attitudes. The separation into time and style periods, applied to Beethoven, for example, does not pose a classification quandary. In his case, growth was not accompanied by sharp change, but by acute adaptation. Beethoven's technical action was variable, but his aesthetic deportment did not yield to it. With Stravinsky, strenuous artistic change defies a pigeonholing of all his music.

Ibert was consistent, even though he was not of Beethovian intellect. In his output there is no fleeting attention to the creative reasoning of others. The type and style of all his compositions are individually sensitive if not progressively reshaped with more vital and deeper thoughts. Though Ibert's chromatically incised diatonic music avoids empiricism as well as sensationalism it just as emphatically seeks the expression of pleasure and comes gift-wrapped in marvelous colors. To know one of his compositions may well be to know them all, but the vigorous regard he had for the strict maintenance of idiom is not monotonous as one passes from one work to the next. His choice of synonyms not only avoids dullness but shuns patterned speech and furnishes a pleasant surprise, notwithstanding the fact that the listener knows what to expect. Jacques Ibert was a master of sheer musical pleasure.

ORCHESTRAL

¶ *A Louisville Concerto*
Rather disappointing music from this witty composer. The piece is mainly devoted to activity of line but the resultant zest is not very interesting, merely very busy.

¶ *Escales* ("Ports of Call")
Ibert's reputation is pinned to this work, inspired by a trip through the Mediterranean, and his "Divertissement," a "pops" program per-

ennial. The color bravado of the music, its single-minded idea of a terzetto of Italian, African, and Spanish settings, signifies the composer's acute knowledge of style, for "Escales" represents more than mere imitative creative sport. There is so much ingenuity in the composition that it is difficult to believe that Ibert was not from the environments he described.

¶ *L'Amours de Jupiter*

Ibert's ballet suite is a representative item but does not emphasize his tongue-in-cheek humor, or his extremely colorful demeanor, as expressed in "Escales."

¶ *The Little White Donkey from "Histoires"*

The whimsical is realized to perfection in this piece written originally for piano, especially defined in its orchestral setting. Ibert's sharp musical camera catches the donkey's lively, untiring trot and his brays.

CHAMBER ORCHESTRA

¶ *Capriccio*

Fluid music, racy and rhythmic music, describes the "Capriccio." The composition moves on the axles of active, zestful counterpoint and pleasantly astringent harmonies.

¶ *Clowns' Dance from "Invitation to the Dance"*

A cute bit with colorful circusy orchestration. The main attraction is the imitation of a wheezy three-piece band of toy instruments. Ibert's score includes a lot of percussion, plus a quaint instrumental debut: a pair of scissors.

¶ *Divertissement*

Doubtless the most typical work in Ibert's output. An orchestration of caustic wit, its zip governed by tonal and harmonic bite, and full of the musical wisecrack. Watch for the spoofing of Mendelssohn's "Wedding March" amidst some jazz and a mock procession; catch the thumb-to-the-nose Viennese waltz, listen to the pianist simply bang the instrument, and laugh with the graphic vulgarisms (including a police whistle) that mark this parody.

Ibert's suite is an assortment of succulent Parisian bonbons. Origi-

nally written as music for a farce ("Le Chapeau de paille d'Italie")
it fulfills this titillative objective in the concert hall.

¶ Suite Symphonique "Impressions of Paris"

A delightful and frolicking set of pieces describing the Paris subway, a restaurant scene, a parade, and three other snapshots. The
music is free, sensibly immodest, and the timbres exhilarating. As is
usual with Ibert, much mischievous fun is displayed along with an
alert ear for program-painting via the orchestra. Smart Parisian music
and still fashionable (for those who refuse to be artistic snobs).

SOLO INSTRUMENT WITH ORCHESTRA

SOLO SAXOPHONE WITH ORCHESTRA

¶ Concertino da Camera

In France, the saxophone suffers no relegation to the rear of the
musical ranks and is given proper pedagogic and artistic attention.
It is not considered the instrumental chimera it represents in many
other regions. A few virtuosi do make solo appearances, mainly performing works especially written for them. Because of the French attitude, composers have written seriously for the saxophone and it
now has mature status (the credit for its invention belongs, however,
to a Belgian).

Ibert's is considered the most important solo work for the alto
saxophone. The "Concertino" summarizes fascinating triple aesthetic
qualities of high spirits, fun in proper style, and polyphonic excogni-
tion. It also exhibits the essentials of concerto format, splitting two
movements into three parts, and giving additional solo privileges by
reducing the accompaniment to six instruments plus strings. The
syncopations and melodic curves are typical of Ibert.

INSTRUMENTAL

ORGAN

¶ The Little White Donkey from "Histoires"

Ibert's light gem, so beautifully delineated in his suite for the
piano, becomes a listening torture in a heavy organ texture. What
desperation caused Mario Salvador to make such a transcription!

¶ *Trois Pièces*

Can organ music (*real* organ music, not pushbutton science) ever be whimsical, light, sonically diaphanous? Apparently not. But, as illustrated in this case, it can fall short of heavy ponderosity. Ibert casts aside his Parisian fillips and writes seriously, but not overseriously; the polyphonic subtleties of the music (ideal for the organ) reflect this notably.

PIANO

¶ *Histoires* (Ten Short Piano Pieces)

Ibert's musical conduct always resulted in good taste. He was a composer of excellent aesthetic breeding—it showed in his polished manners and suave wit. Though miniature forms tempted him, none of these turned out to be mere trifles, because of the subtle and pleasing refinements of which he was a master.

The ten pieces exemplify a light but sure touch and demonstrate how Ibert could form delicious sounds, here portrayed by lively and dainty music. (Like Debussy with his "Préludes," Ibert is modest in setting forth his titles—they appear under the final measure of each piece, enclosed in parentheses, as a suggestive description.) One of the set, "The Little White Donkey," is a favorite encore, but each part of the suite is made for hearty enjoyment.

CHAMBER MUSIC

¶ *Entr'acte*

The special coloring of certain instruments would draw a composer of picturesque intent to them. Ibert's "Entr'acte" for flute and guitar (composed in 1935) creates a definite mood of romantic poesy. It courses its way by busy figurations, its tunes creating the effect of an idealized dance. The guitar equals Spain, and the music bears a native monogram.

¶ *Jeux—Sonatine for Flute and Piano*

Another example of Ibert's suave and cheerful demeanor, exemplifying the playful title. The two sections of the duo compare animated and tender ideas. *Animé* is feathery and gay, written in tripartite style, jumping on the feet of quintuple pulse. *Tendre* constitutes vocal music for the flute; sung first with simple accompaniment, resung in canonic form.

¶ *"Le Jardinier de Samos"—Prelude to Act Two*

Odd in format (for violin and cello alone) and odd for Ibert (somewhat plain), but novel in its conception as part of the incidental music to a dramatic work. Although "The Gardener of Samos" was never presented, the concert suite of five numbers calling for five contrasted instruments (flute, clarinet, bassoon, violin, and cello) is heard occasionally.

¶ *Trio for Violin, Cello and Harp*

It is not required that a composer plainly imitate set patterns in order to relate his musical story simply. It can be expressed convincingly and managed expertly in a style that is basic to the premise of the work.

In this trio Ibert does not use long-strung classical forms since his themes will not permit undue development. Excellent and impressive music results because it is placed in simple frames that match its character.

Measures containing extra beats inserted at strategic points in the thematic line give additional kick to the first movement. Compared to the outer movements the middle one is rather serious. A breezy type of scherzo (totally opposed to Beethoven's dramatic handling of the form) is called on for the finale. Ibert's magnificent sense of color is exhibited in this section—his symphonic works display orchestrational perception just as acutely.

¶ *String Quartet in C*

An unfamiliar work, even to chamber-music devotees. Ibert's chamber piece has received less than a half-dozen hearings in this country since it was completed in 1942. Akin to his supple orchestration, the quartet is deft, yet retains a relaxed profundity. Its key feeling is C major, but in terms of the twentieth century. That is, the tonal anchorage is C; the deviations are many.

The French are known for refinement, grace, and wit in their music; Ibert proves it in the simulated march that embraces the finale. There are similar attractions in the preceding, all-pizzicato division. (The penchant of contemporary composers for movements of plucked sound in their string works has become a definite vogue.) Ibert does

141

not employ more than the ordinary type of pizzicato in the third part of his quartet, and yet the ear does not tire during the entire two hundred and fifty-one measures. The slow movement is quite different. Ibert said it depicts his reaction to the Second World War. In this chamber work Ibert shows how all-embracing French musical art really is.

¶ *Trois Pièces Brèves*

With the exception of Hindemith's "Kleine Kammermusik," this is the most favored contemporary work in the wind quintet category. Ibert employs simple designs for the very cogent reason that the medium can quickly pall (woodwinds, no matter how expert the players, never jell as does a string quartet; the kaleidoscopic change can tax the ear if it is retained over a long period of time). His tuneful themes do not require enlargement by argument. These pieces, for a delightful and frolicking pocket-sized orchestra, are examples of true hedonistic music; they combine paprika with soda pop—a pleasure to the ear, a delight to play.

VOCAL

VOICE WITH ORCHESTRA

¶ *Suite Elizabethaine*

Music of interlaced quality: some of the themes of the nine movements are based on ideas by Elizabethan composers, and others are pure Ibert . . . but Ibert with a classical mask on his face. The result is enchanting: the solo voice and chorus giving a warm contour to the dance forms employed.

13. LEOŠ JANÁČEK
(1854–1928)

NATURAL musical speech is generally evolved from certain (almost formal) material, then expanded in the particular style of the composer. It has long been a common thought that composers were inspired by nature; not exactly in the sense that one musically translates the trees, the sky, the sun, but rather in that specifics of nature become the internal factor of a work, the dictum, creed, inspiration. So it was with Janáček.

He made copious notes as he listened to people, noting the inflection of their conversations. He drew on the sounds of birds and animals in the woods, tirelessly noting, checking, and studying. As a result, his compositions sound as if people were speaking in cryptic, terse, and violent tones, slow or fast. The water wheels of ostinati, pedal points and rhythms turn this into a music more individual than most other compositions infused with native materials.

Neither the instruments nor the orchestrations are restricted to traditional roles. Janáček's pleasure in color (not for sheer luxury but for defining his aesthetic intonations) is evident in the searching use of odd combinations in a complete work or within sections of a large composition. He had command of instruments. Cellos are tenor-bass instruments, but in his scores they also perform woodwind arabesques; trombones take on a soprano stance, and so forth. Above all, padding and fillers are nonexistent.

Freed of specific rules, this man's work is anything but problematical. It is a music that is novel, daring, and completely nationalistic, yet moistened with the atmosphere of international language. In this poised creative ambivalence between folkloric primitivism and contemporary sophistication, with the ruggedness of the former strengthening the latter, Janáček has no equal.

ORCHESTRAL

¶ *The Ballad of Blaník*

A programmatic piece about armed knights who hide on a mountain, and a Czech Rip Van Winkle character. When he awakens after a century's sleep the knights are no longer fighters but workers with hoes and ploughs. Presumably, this tale was chosen by Janáček for orchestral portrayal in order to substantiate his theory of "the patriotism of effective work."

Nothing wrong with this point of view. But the music doesn't stimulate with its pale material and formal looseness.

¶ *The Fiddler's Child, Ballad for Orchestra*

Janáček's is like Liszt's idea of a symphonic poem. A line-by-line orchestral translation of events is bypassed, although specific clues are given by using isolated instrumental colors to signify characters and events. Despite the fact that Janáček's score is more concerned with structural balance than with musical picture-painting, there is sufficient literalness to realize the death and transfiguration theme that shapes this symphonic ballad.

¶ *Lachian Dances*

A half-dozen folkloric exemplifications; bright, gay, and with none of the compositional monkeyshines that create havoc with simple utterances. The dances are in the Dvořák "Slavonic" tradition, with just enough variety to sustain the naturalness of the music.

The publication of the score for the dances (their titles are as melodious as the music itself: Starodávný, Požehnaný, Dymák, Čeladenský, and Pilky) contained an introduction by Janáček which included the dedication: "In praise of my native district, my Lachia . . . ," and the hope that the music might ". . . spread happiness and bring forth a smile on all faces." It should.

¶ *Sinfonietta*

Urban refinement and sophistication combine with rural earthiness in this singular work, containing a range of orchestration that is bewitching. Janáček's spacing methods give weirdly wonderful personal sounds that haunt the mind. The other processes of the composition are as select. With this composer development procedures were as special as his consideration of harmony (all chords had emotional clues . . . of calmness, of agitation, and so on).

The many extra brass instruments (twelve trumpets, two bass trumpets, no fewer than four trombones, and a pair of tenor tubas) caused Janáček sometimes to refer to his piece as a "Military

144

Sinfonietta," but the martial quota is extremely small. Nevertheless, the coolness of classical order is foreign to the essence of the Sinfonietta." Lushness (in correct proportion), richness, and coloristic fantasy are the related objectives. They make the composition a rhapsody of themes, though some relationship and recapitulation exist. This five-sectioned composition is powerful evidence of Janáček's significant creative voice.

¶ *Taras Bulba, Rhapsody*

The profile of nationalism (a Moravian comprehends a Russian story [by Gogol] about a seventeenth-century war with Poland, in which a Cossack leader and his two sons meet death) is very strong in Janáček's programmatic, three-movement suite. The music is spontaneous and not formally stiff so that it loses its urgency. Story detail is clear, but not to the point of a minute inventory. Janáček's orchestration is especially inventive, including a fine use of the organ as a special timbre.

STRING ORCHESTRA

¶ *Suite for String Orchestra*

Early Janáček (his post-student period), pro-Dvořák in concept and content. Despite the use of set classical designs such as an allemande, sarabande, and scherzo, the native idiom is not completely subsurface. A romantic outlook permeates the suite.

SOLO INSTRUMENT WITH ORCHESTRA

SOLO PIANO WITH ORCHESTRA

¶ *Capriccio*

Unusual facts surround the work. It would be expected that music for but eight players would fit easily into the category of chamber music, but Janáček's "Capriccio" is for piano (left hand alone) *with* seven wind and brass players. This alone places it in the rare area of a concentrated solo vehicle, not with chamber orchestra accompaniment, but with a distinctive septet group. There are exceedingly few such compositions in the literature. The full scale of the four movements approaches concerto style but falls just short of it. Janáček's

145

extremely odd coloration (a flute alternating with a piccolo are the only woodwind representatives, the remainder consists of a pair of high trumpets, three trombones, and a tenor tuba) and his avoidance of virtuosity turn the "Capriccio" into an octo-timbred sonata for concerted instruments. Thereby, it fully straddles the field of chamber and solo-accompaniment music.

The piece was originally called "Defiance." It is music of solemn disapproval, contrasted with passages more intimate and quiet in mood. The succinct melodic curves simulating speech and the cryptic motives so habitual with this composer are in bold relief. They make for a tense emotional condition, heightened by the uniqueness of the instrumental combination.

¶ Concertino for Piano and Chamber Orchestra

A hybrid plan of concerto (prominence of the piano), chamber music (seven instrumentalists), and symphonic elements (despite the opening pair of movements calling only for two instruments each), make this work unique. The sound is expressly and expressively nationalistic with a tough accent—not by way of tunes and dances, but by naturalism in the lines, which are never cut to fit squared phrase lengths or smoothed to ordinary balances. A maximum sonority is obtained by minimal means. The frictions are mild but powerful. Janáček's "Concertino" is an example of Moravian musical philology set within an extraordinary concerto design.

INSTRUMENTAL

PIANO

¶ In the Threshing House

Four pieces shaped like Moravian-Chopinesque rhapsodies. There are no redundancies, no reiterative thematic manipulation; the ideas unfold from one section into another. The fantasia-like behavior is somewhat of a sequel to the fifteen pieces that comprise "On the Overgrown Path." Janáček is also concerned with nostalgia; thus the reason for the alternative title: "In the Mists."

¶ October 1, 1905

Actually, the subtitle (written on the manuscript in European fashion as 1. X. 1905) of a "Street Scene Sonata." Janáček's piano

146

work joins the list of requiems, memorial pieces, and compositions of protest that dot music's history. Its genesis was the Austro-Hungarian government's proclamation (on October first of 1905) refusing to permit the establishment of a Czech university in Brno. Street demonstrations and clashes between the people and the army resulted. On the next day many Czechs, singing patriotic songs, paraded through the streets in dissent from the decree. One, a young unarmed workman, was bayoneted and died soon after.

Janáček, a fervent advocate of Czech independence and national identity, was quick to react and add his voice to those fighting for social and economic freedom. He composed a three-part sonata (one writer insists it was a cycle of fifteen pieces) with the dedication "in memory of a worker stabbed to death during a manifestation for the University of Brno." Later he destroyed the last movement (a Death March), but retained the first and second sections titled "Premonition" and "Death." These have intense power and potent illustrative meaning, made even more exciting by the knowledge of why they were composed.

¶ On the Overgrown Path—Set I

While many of the germinal impulses of musical composition are rooted in indigenous materials, the difference is wide between a work in folk mood as contrasted with one employing definite folk song. Janáček composed his suite in the former sense.

Each of the ten items is titled. However, a few of the translations are at odds with one another. Thus, one listing denotes the sixth piece as "My Words Stop," another calls it "We Could not Agree," and a catalogue of the composer's works titles this part as "Uncompromising." This indefiniteness does not interfere with the music's logic. These pieces are retrospective miniatures of the composer's younger days and are simply presented, as if musical stories being told by a nonprofessional.

¶ On the Overgrown Path—Set II

The popular habitat of the first part of this cycle is now invaded by an almost explicit use of formality; the change of view confirmed by Janáček's shift from titles to mere tempi designations. The gentleness and poetics of the initial ten pieces are replaced by more reflective moods and much less cohesiveness in the second set of five. Here, the music tends to overlength. If part one had homely lucidity, the second portion has the fault that the professional hand does show.

147

VIOLIN

¶ *Dumka for Violin and Piano*

The long-arched melodic line of this piece of balladic character is an example of imitative musical manners. It represents a style rarely to be observed in Janáček's important output.

The *dumka* (a Russian term) has varied tempi, sometimes fast, sometimes slow, and literally means "lament" or "elegy." Dvořák used it in many works, definitely or by implication. In his hands it became an idealization of the form, used as a mold for a slow movement, even at times for a scherzo-type section. In Janáček's hands it turns into a prosaic piece of secondhand fare.

CHAMBER MUSIC

¶ *Sonata for Violin and Piano*

Janáček's primitive (but knowledgeable) style (one critic has compared him to Charles Ives in this respect, but the comparison is incongruous) will be noted in the sonata, composed in 1913, revised during the First World War, and completed in 1921. The opening movement, with abrupt changes from a single fast theme to a completely opposed tempo, conveys the subtleties of Moravian language. The "Ballada" that follows alternates two subjects, in unadorned style, with the final statement in ad libitum manner. There is no sense of *two* instruments; the combination is *one*. The final portion of the work has a special fascination in terms of rhythm. It is charged with elongation, contraction, and attendant irregularity. This is characteristic Janáček.

¶ *String Quartet No. 1*

Janáček tells us the motivation for his quartet. After a rehearsal prior to its première he wrote of the work: "I had in mind an unfortunate woman, suffering, beaten, ill-treated, just as Tolstoy describes her in his 'Kreutzer Sonata.' " (A piano trio based on the same creative source had been composed late in 1908, but the manuscript was either destroyed or lost.)

In no sense is there a scene-by-scene portrayal of Tolstoy's novel. What Janáček depicts are the furtiveness, cruelty, and passion of the tale. One need not know the story. The listener shares in a chamber-music drama that requires no precise thematic analysis, since it is conveyed by the power of perfectly integrated music.

¶ *String Quartet No. 2* ("Intimate Letters")

An unhappy marriage caused Janáček, in the latter part of his life, to turn to another woman, Kamila Stössel. Thirty-eight years Janáček's junior, she was of the greatest influence on his work and was the inspiration for this quartet, originally titled "Love Letters." (The composition was initially scored for a viola d'amore in place of the viola. This choice of the fourteen-string instrument, with its lovely, passionate tone underlines the composer's feelings.) It was just five months and three weeks before his death that Janáček completed his intensely intimate musical document, expressing his sentiments in a letter to Kamila: ". . . you have been mine without knowing it . . . you have been everywhere in my compositions, wherever there are deep feelings, sincerity, truth, passion and love."

The entire quartet is pervaded with transient thoughts and fleeting ideas, bound by determined pronouncements, articulations, and punctuations. Technically speaking, these are obtained by changing meters, dislodged accents, and other refractional permutations. (Janáček's music is as seen through mirrors giving various shapes.) The dominating repetitive patterns are sometimes overemphasized, but such is the Janáček method. Throughout, there is intertwined a Tristanesque emotionalism without Wagnerian overtones.

¶ *Mládí* ("Youth")

Janáček's creed that one develops national music by listening to the voices of the birds and by drawing from nature is fully developed in "Mládí," a suite for wind sextet. The country of Moravia is expressed in this musical travelogue of the forest, the creatures that inhabit it, the land, and the people speaking. The only bow to musical form (in the classic sense) is the increasing speed of the four movements, but only in general terms, since the tempi constantly change within each section. Janáček's ideas of wind scoring are as far from the traditional as possible, including the rare chamber-music use of the flabby-toned bass clarinet.

The four-four beat of the second movement, interrupted eight times and stretched an extra sixteenth, is a delightful rhythmic anachronism. And the catchy march (movement three) is a pert parody.

VOCAL

¶ *The Diary of One Who Vanished*

An unusual conception which can be classified either as a mono-drama or a miniature concert opera (Janáček wanted dim lighting throughout a performance, unobtrusive entrances and exits, and no breaks within the twenty-two "stanzas," or divisions, of the work). It is designated as a vocal composition because this comes closest to the means employed.

The score calls for a tenor, who has the major role in the cycle, an alto, a piano (of solo proportions), plus three female voices. The story (a true one which came to light when poems were found in the room of a young man who had mysteriously disappeared) is extremely concise and simple, of high moral tone. It kindled an intensive reaction on Janáček's part, after he had read it in a newspaper, and triggered one of his most powerful works. It concerns a farmer's son who falls in love with a Gypsy girl, who has a child from the affair. The boy cannot forget her. After much inward struggle he runs away from home to join the girl, despite his intense love for his parents, and though this means leading a nomadic life.

Janáček's music has the same fundamental artistic truth as the tale it describes. Language is no barrier to understanding the poignancy of the tale. The contrast between the emotional conflict of the youth and the sensuality of the woman is telling, underlined by the commentarial color of the miniature chorus and piano. Exciting and unusual music set for a unique combination.

CHORAL

¶ *Elegy on the Death of Daughter Olga*

Janáček's daughter died of typhus just as he was on the verge of completing his great opera "Jenůfa," and the title page of the "Elegy" score bears the inscription "In memory of my daughter Olga."

Without knowing this music's title one will recognize the fervent grief that impregnates its measures. It has a lengthy prelude for solo piano that emphasizes a leitmotiv of funereal persistence. Even the attempt to be optimistic in the middle section does not mask the fact that within the work stalks the tragedy of a young person's death.

¶ *Folk Nocturnes*

Music that documents Janáček's deep research in musical ethnography. The results of his study are found in the hundreds of published Moravian, Slovakian, and Czech songs, many in collaboration with František Bartoš, a specialist in Moravian folk art. They also illuminate the distinctly titled folk settings for solo voice, chorus, and piano, and shape the dialect of the orchestral, chamber music, and operatic productions.

The "Folk Nocturnes" (subtitled "Slovak Evening Songs from Rovný") comprise the second section of a four-part cycle of folk ballades. Each of the seven pieces is limited to duet writing, most often introduced by a solo voice, followed by two-part response, with additional piano support. The music is super simple. Interest lags because of Janáček's preoccupation with sweet harmonies that do not budge from wholesome consonance. By repeating their tales the folk wear out their welcome.

¶ *Male Voice Choruses*

O Love
Oh! The War!

Dedicated to Dvořák "as a token of the deepest respect," Janáček's music shows its bias by more than a passing Dvořákian influence. One misses contrapuntalism in these choral pieces. The music does not linger in the memory.

¶ *Male Voice Folk Choruses*

Our Birch Tree
The Wreath

Composed as independent items between 1873 and 1914 these compositions, plus two others, were published as a collection in 1948. They utilize folk poetry ("The Wreath") and verses by Eliška Krásnohorská ("Our Birch Tree"). Either way, the effect is of simplicity, without fuss or special personality.

151

¶ *Moravian Male Voice Choruses*

If You Only Knew
Evening Witch
Parting

Choral treatment that is not overly fancy but possesses rich contrast in its handling of the medium. The moods vary from folksy vitality to dark-toned aspects (the key of the last piece is A flat minor). A prime illustration of Janáček's keen vocal sense.

¶ *Songs of Hradcany*

Three elegiac *a cappella* female choruses in as many different settings: the first for chorus alone, the other two having interleafed solo passages for coloration, with a flute in one and a harp in the other. Hradčany is a section of Prague and Janáček pinpoints it by utilizing native folklore in the music.

¶ *Three Mixed Choruses*

Autumn Song
Wild Duck
Our Song

Composed as individual pieces at five-year intervals (1880, 1885, and 1890), this set of *a cappella* choruses did not reach publication until 1950, when they were issued as a unit. This expediency does not bring balance; the neutral (like a secular motet) style of the "Autumn Song" becomes drab in its drawn-out facture. In contrast, the other two items are concise and folksy with neat harmonic accommodations. "Wild Duck" was originally conceived for school groups, but is in no way limited in appeal and concludes with a most telling cadential whimsy. "Our Song" is dance music for voices. Janáček's catchy choral polka has a Bartókian sound—with its nails trimmed.

¶ *Truthful Love*

Chorale-styled choral music, minus counterpoint. This could be anyone's conventional music for men's voices. Though at the age of twenty-nine Janáček was still immersed in the classic-romantic tradition, there are better examples from this period of his work.

¶ *The Wolf's Footprints*

A minuscule drama for multiple female voices plus piano. The tale tells of a captain discovering the tracks of a wolf that turn out to be the footprints of his wife's lover, whom he shoots. (The thought comes to mind that Janáček had anticipated the connotation of the word "wolf.") The ballad doesn't come off, mainly because it is set for women's voices; the characterizations are quite hazy. It is neither music of great depth, nor mature Janáček.

CHORAL WITH ORCHESTRA
CANTATA

¶ Amarus, Lyric Cantata for Soli, Mixed Chorus and Orchestra

Music wedded, for the most part, to despair and tragedy. Janáček's five-part tale (written in 1897 and twice revised, in 1901 and 1906) is a lesson in how to achieve intensity without plangent hammers. The scenes are infused with emotional accents of melodic line, the harmonies anguished with chromatics, the instrumentation rarely moving into any of the brighter orbits.

The story is simple. A monk, born out of wedlock, prays for death because he cannot forget his mother's sin. An angel tells him that his wish will only be granted if he neglect the performance of one of his duties. The monk observes two lovers praying and fails to refill the altar lamp with oil. He is found dead on the grave of his mother the next day.

The final section, though of processional shape (mostly for orchestra and colored with bells), conveys, in an artistically underplayed manner, the sense of acute, inexorable pain. It seals the grimness of the cantata perfectly. And by using ideas from the initial part, the composer forms a cyclic design. Janáček's "Amarus" is a profound musical drama that haunts the listener.

MASS

¶ Slavonic (Glagolitic) *Mass*

Not music for religious purposes, but rather a composition celebrating God in a secular, self-determined, quasi-pagan manner (one of the reasons why this work is also known as a "Festival Mass"). Though Janáček's mass follows the usual format, it interlards several features uncommon to the plan, in addition to being set in the old ecclesiastical Slavic language rather than the usual Latin. The Credo divides into several sections of pure instrumental character, and after the final Agnus Dei there is a brilliant organ solo plus an Intrada. There is no simple psalmodic tone or even pulse; the rhythms are

153

restless, irregular, bold; the mood tense and charged with vocal electricity.

Probably no single piece better explains and illustrates Janáček's technique and aesthetic courageousness than this mass, one of the last compositions he wrote. It is the product of an individualist, a composer stating truths, even though these are of nonliturgical order paradoxically set in a sacred musical form. (Janáček's score is headed with the remark "God is gone up with a shout.")

OPERA

¶ *The Cunning Little Vixen*

A stage work which parallels animal and human life poses a difficulty for a composer. Janáček's opera is not only unique, it is sheer delight, a spacious nature poem recited in sound.

"The Cunning Little Vixen" developed from drawings with captions called "The Adventures of Fox Sharpears" that Janáček saw in a newspaper. The gay story, with a slightly sad ending, contrasts the freedom and love of animals with the conflicts of humans. Though the vixen is killed by one of the humans, who then presents his bride with a fox muff as a present, the vixen's cubs remain and as Janáček stated the moral, ". . . so evil and good make their round through life anew."

The prelude to the opera, the various interludes, and the orchestral background furnish a veritable anthology of Janáček's deep-felt sensitivity to the communications of intrinsic sounds (he described this as "the eternally young rhythm of nature"). The vocal lines retain an uncanny exposition of the same data; their flow and placement make them intensely real, conversational, and untypically operatic. This fable, illustrating the full lure of Janáček's native musical diction, is an off-beat contribution to a field in which few composers succeed.

¶ *From the House of the Dead*

Janáček's manuscript for the last of his ten operas (completed just a few months before his death) bears the motto "In every creature there is a spark of God." It explains the composer's sympathy for the underdog and the oppressed which had attracted him to Dostoevski's autobiographical tale of the days he spent in Siberia as a political prisoner.

"From the House of the Dead" concerns a group of convicts and the varied incidents that brought them together. The cross section of personalities defines the drama; the treatment realizes the objective of compassion and understanding. In a sense every character is a star, which almost makes Janáček's score secondary to the raw story. Nonetheless, it is a commanding mark of stark realism and sensitive music, ranging from folk integration to bristling contemporary-colored harmonies.

¶ *Jenůfa*

"Jenůfa" is Leoš Janáček's *opéra d'resistance*. Its dramatic tempo persistently moves forward like the Moussorgsky tradition, plus all the intensity of Debussy's "Pelléas et Melisande." The story treats of lust and infanticide, enmeshed in jealousy, resolved by expiation and hope. In "Jenůfa" expressivity is paramount. There is no massive retardation of action by formal cut-to-pattern constructions. Janáček projects his opera by way of declamation woven into song—a potent method of maintaining urgency and yet meeting lyrical demands. Plot and musical shape become correlative; the expression of the former defines the latter. The design therefore permits, without irritating static stage representation, the inclusion of a mad scene, an Ave Maria, a splendid climactic duet. However, unlike Debussy's operatic orchestra, Janáček's does not become part of the *dramatis personae,* though it is far from mere accompaniment.

Delayed recognition is no startling event in the world of art, and "Jenůfa" is an example. Initially performed in a small theatre, it took twelve years before a major company (in Prague) produced the work. This was no temporary success: the opera took full command of the stages of the leading houses in Europe and even achieved production at the conservative Met in 1924. Although the Prague National Theatre has shown "Jenůfa" more than two hundred times, it is rarely scheduled elsewhere. The star system that breeds box-office contentment should not be allowed to smother "Jenůfa." It is magnificent musical theatre.

¶ *Kata Kabanová*

This is an opera that illustrates Janáček's characteristic ability to blend the rise and fall of his score to the moods of his text. There is passionate lyricism (an exciting example is the music that ends the second act, an amalgam of pure and profane quality that expresses the surging love of an unfaithful married woman), storm music (not of chromatic tissue nor hot diminished seventh sequences), and tragedy (explained by understatement and thereby gaining double the impact). All of this is cast in the Moravian's fusion of primordial elements with Debussyian language that gives significance to the music. Much of the orchestration is traditionally based, yet with Janáček's spatial techniques the results are fresh, vivid, and instrumentally inventive.

All of this is placed at the service of a drama which concerns illicit love in an atmosphere of personal despotism. The main character (Kata) rebels against a loveless marriage and her dictatorial mother-in-law, but lacks the strength to free herself. She resolves her problems by suicide.

¶ The Makropulos Affair

The theme of Janáček's next-to-last opera is longevity. A girl in search of eternal youth finds the proper potion, but three hundred years of life bring boredom and aimlessness in place of joy.

This exemplifies Janáček stripped of his folk clothes, a composer attracted to the richness of timbre, rhythm, and melodic kernels, using the operatic orchestra as a dramatic element against the voices. The color play of the cryptic designs that make up the composition disproves the nonsense that in opera the music must be neatly tailored to words and stage action. "The Makropulos Affair" is an abstract of Janáček's style framed with expressionism. It fits the story line.

14. ANDRÉ JOLIVET
(1905-   )

Jolivet completely rejects facile methods in his work. His music, technically atonal (atonical), has a remote kinship with expressionism. For the most part Jolivet is devoted to an esoteric musical philosophy; a probing, as it were, of subconscious trauma, as though the music were being analyzed on the psychiatrist's couch. This may recall Scriabin, and in a way there is a relationship to that composer's otherworldliness. Textures and special colors point to Messiaen, but Jolivet does not follow that composer's quasi-theologic viewpoint. Rather, his music has the brass, aluminum, and steel trappings of today, controlled by specific sound orbits in which the patterns fluctuate.

Sound is principal and principle in André Jolivet's output. This stems from study with Edgar Varèse, but he does not imitate Varèse's method of forming musical compositions by sheer sound forces and frictions. Jolivet gives full credit to Varèse for making him realize music "as a magical and ritual expression." His music is as spiritual as that of Mozart and Beethoven, but it is so violent as to cause one to forget (or overlook) the spirituality and concentrate on the sonic bravado. Priapean creativity describes André Jolivet.

ORCHESTRAL

¶ *Suite Française*

Movie music, but so conceived that film matter followed the aural fact. Jolivet's suite had sufficient changes of pace in each of its four movements for Edouard Logereau, who thought of reversing the usual process of combining music with film.

Six sections of France are described, and, in the final section, the hustle and bustle of auto and plane travel, and the spirit of the atomic age. The chief resource is orchestral color, ripe with percussion. Jolivet's harmony reminds one of a drama first played on one level, then simultaneously combined with others on different stages. This is a piece of secret program music, a work for an orchestra of forty-five with the powers and timbres of thrice the number.

¶ *Suite Transocéane*

In the words of the composer the title has no significance save that it "symbolizes a liaison between the two continents of Europe and America." The composition is not clarified by this vague description.

Despite its line and detail, the activity and fussiness of this work are fatiguing. Jolivet's music is unmistakably highly expert, but in this case shows a fanatical *idée fixe* of undue contrapuntal confusion.

CHAMBER ORCHESTRA

¶ *Rapsodie à Sept*

A septet commonly constitutes chamber music, but not in the hands of André Jolivet. This music demands a conductor, and thus is included in the chamber orchestra category.

The instrumentation of the "Rapsodie à Sept" is the same as that chosen by Stravinsky for his "Histoire du Soldat," but the language of the piece is far different. There is some rub-off from jazz, but the facts are those of a roving commission of sound and fancy. There is no mechanical response to form, but rather composed improvisation (last movement). In the first two-thirds of the work there is an insistence on gliding sounds, a link from one place to the next. Thus the material is unified despite Jolivet's various sound complexes.

¶ *Suite Delphique*

In any art, style must be in an absolute manner if the conception is to be clear and correct. Although Jolivet simply enlarges on Greek modes in each of the eight movements, he can be forgiven because he is serious and does not stray from the subject.

The music concentrates on color, most pertinent in the use of the electrical instrument, the Ondes Martenot. Its timbre ranges from a simulated saxophone to that of sonic aeration; included in its resonances are violent glissandi, the super-microtonal type, and brutal grunts that are quite frightening. It is sound, rather than theme, which is the crux of this work, just as defined tonality (with attendant modulations) is the pivot of a Mozart work, or a row of tones the axle of a Schoenberg composition.

STRING ORCHESTRA

¶ *Andante for Strings*

Originally the second movement ("Allant") of Jolivet's first string quartet. Its heavy, sensuous sequences have sonorescences that seem to be derived from the twelve-tone system but are not. This short work supposedly illustrates Jolivet's viewpoint that "music should be a manifestation of sound in direct relation with the universal cosmic system." Though this thesis is not explained, it produces valid music, best described as sound for sound's sake.

SOLO INSTRUMENT WITH ORCHESTRA

CONCERTOS

¶ *Concerto for Bassoon, String Orchestra, Harp and Piano*

The athletic tone of the music is its cardinal point. Jolivet is insistent that the demeanor of a concerto must be (soloistically) extrovert. Accordingly, the bass wind instrument is treated with dogmatic virtuosity—its testimony remains constantly fresh and exciting.

Like the majority of Jolivet's scores this one is linear, with moderately heavy textures modified by motoric rhapsody. Formally balanced by alternative slow- and fast-tempoed music it embraces recitative, a concentrated sonata section, a plaintive nocturnal poem (one of the most moving of all Jolivet's creations), and a snappy, multitonal fugue. The bassoonist fraternity will welcome this lusty addition to their very slim repertoire—so should the public, since Jolivet writes a contemporaneously cultured, solidly constructed music that bypasses the latest fads and fashions.

¶ *Concerto for Harp and Chamber Orchestra*

In the musical galaxy of techniques, rhythm is more than important. It is the soul of the working idea, and is the primary source in Jolivet's piece. Rhythmic shifts of duple and ternary pulses characterize the scherzo of the opening part, and rhythm is again

159

the driving point of the quietly jazz-imbued closing movement. The central, slow section exemplifies Jolivet's introspective side.

As a solo instrument the harp has come a long way, and for this the French composers, more than any others, are responsible. But in the musical complexities of Jolivet's world, the harp, primarily a diatonic voice, imposes fetters since it is pedal chained. Because of the instrument's inability to command ultrachromatic communication, this harp concerto is parochial instead of universal.

¶ Concerto for Ondes Martenot and Orchestra

A far cry from generic concerto depiction. Any careful listener will find that the initial incomprehensibility is almost beautiful by itself. The use of an electrical timbre as a solo voice portrays Jolivet's general mode of thought more clearly than any other instrument. And if one can be patient during the first movement, a fantastic scherzo-minded, diabolical musical montage unfolds which is worth the listening.

¶ Concerto for Piano and Orchestra

Whatever the philosophy of this composer, his music falls in the avant-garde department. He is concerned with sounds in his own kind of "frequency modulation," embedded in a thick texture, containing tints of thousands of differences. Though the orchestral forces in the piano concerto, with the addition of a saxophone, are normal, Jolivet "goes for broke" in the percussion department. No fewer than twenty-eight pulsatile instruments are required—and these are no mere noise-makers. The percussion is more important than the other instrumental families in this concerto which ostensibly evokes Africa, the Far East, and Polynesia.

It is important to realize that the concertante situation is avoided in Jolivet's solo-with-orchestra works. These are all virtuosic, but of a virtuosity based on the fullest speech interchange of the solo voice with the mass totality.

SOLO TRUMPET WITH ORCHESTRA

¶ Concertino for Trumpet, Piano and String Orchestra

Despite free tonality Jolivet's structure is as carefully organized as that of those who use pandiatonic orientation. It is as controlled as works employing fluid tonality which sprays from a central source. The form of an introduction, a theme and a set of variations exemplify neat and concentrated design. Within are the potentials today's composer expects from a brass instrument.

No nineteenth-century concerto décor here. Jolivet abhors that tradition. He describes the soloist's role in such music as "a virtuoso chatterbox." His viewpoint is proven by the expert contemporary logic of the "Concertino." It does not include one measure of small talk.

INSTRUMENTAL

PIANO

¶ *Chanson Naïves*

Jolivet under wraps. This music resembles Ravel's earlier efforts. The question arises: should a composer, when writing "occasional" music, change his personality? The answer (in reference to music for children) seems to be No, as witness Prokofiev, Casella, Hindemith, to name only a few. Jolivet disagrees, and his children's codifications exhibit little that is substantial.

¶ *Mana*

Piano style quite unlike any other. Percussion power, ejaculative bunches of notes, and extreme use of the keyboard range are the features of Jolivet's suite of six pieces. Despite the Couperinesque titles (for example: "L'Oiseau," "La Princesse de Bali," "La Chevre") this is a set of incantations, with sound, color, and rhythm serving as the principal agencies.

A fascinating work, and a true discovery in the field of piano literature.

CHORAL

¶ *Epithalame*

Tradition demands that vocal and choral compositions must remain just that. Thus, one reads of the hell-fires of "nonvocal" melody. But composers can only help themselves when they free themselves. Tradition has long benumbed the powerful properties contained in writing for voices; it has remained for the contem-

161

porary school to prove there is more to choral music than the sweet movement of conjunct or chordal sounds.

Jolivet's "Epithalame" is a unique example of twentieth-century choral composition. In this case the chorus is turned into a vocal orchestra, divided into twelve instrumentalized parts containing not only melody, harmony, and counterpoint, but involved rhythms, percussive qualities, manifold color, accent, and effect as well. The composer's own text is full of letters and syllables which give cries, snaps, rolls, sibilations, glides, and other properties. (Examples: pTap, Glap; Pi-Té-Pi-Ta-Pit; Dla Nang.)

There are three major sections; the scherzo (for voices!), within the first of these, the most vivid. Jolivet has the voices move with the speed of a Mendelssohn allegro, combining the breathless excitement of the tempo with polyphonic excogitation.

15. ZOLTÁN KODÁLY
(1882–   )

Bartók and Kodály are to Hungarian music what the three B's are to German music. And in their different ways the two are as great and important as the three.

Kodály formed, with Bartók, the core of true-principled Hungarian musical creation. Together they collected native musical material, analyzed and described the findings. Kodály has shown how amazingly trenchant and new are the old secrets of folk sources. As is the case with Bartók, the music of Kodály is made subtle by assimilating the treasure house of folk song.

But two composers believing in basically similar creative gospel still express themselves individually. Rhythm was more than a clothesline on which Bartók hung his musical garments. Bartók's violent asymmetric rhythmic plans were drawn for instruments susceptible to the supple art of mensural interpretation. Kodály's rhythmic demeanor is more vocal, more choral, like the naturalness of speech inflection. Kodály's nature is more melancholic than Bartók's, and his power is of quiet strength.

No more fastidious composer exists in the field of contemporary music. Kodály's musical glossary furnishes one of the best illustrations of authentic, national musical language. He has no intellectual artificialities: the music pours out in free style, yet is as balanced as the most precise phrase that Mozart fashioned. It is tamed music but roams freely on the tether of subtle Hungarian accent.

ORCHESTRAL

¶ Concerto for Orchestra

All the frictions and dynamism of Kodály are found in this work, commissioned for the 50th anniversary of the Chicago Symphony Orchestra (first performed by them in February of 1941). While the idiom is unmistakable (as are the neoclassic

163

squared rhythms) and the results pleasant enough, the total is rather unimportant. Kodály's one-movement piece is only a fair example of eighteenth-century concerto trimmings on modern models. The premise is sufficiently outlined, but the arguments, aside from the restrained virtuosity, are somewhat tedious; the music is almost pretentious. The cool sweat of Kodály's chamber music (especially the solo cello sonata and string duo) is absent. Kodály is not a composer who is at his best with bounded formalism.

¶ Dances of Galanta

Kodály's attractive themes were chosen from a book of Gypsy dance tunes issued in the early nineteenth century. He thus preserves tradition and pictures true Hungarian music in terms of quantitative apportionment.

The Galanta Dances were composed to commemorate the eightieth anniversary of the Budapest Philharmonic Society. Kodály's *Tzigane* document was a fitting gift. It also shows that one does not need to be a creative exhibitionist to write exciting music.

¶ Háry János Suite

Kodály's most-performed work is a colorful display of sound that has assorted ramifications: from poetry to satire, from intimacy to healthy orchestral richness. The music of "Háry János" is nationalistically tuned, and fervent melodic turns of phrase rule the suite which Kodály drew from his opera "in four adventures, with a prologue and an epilogue."

The fun begins with an orchestral simulation of a sneeze. Kodály's orchestral pen then draws masterly pictures of a Viennese musical clock and a mock battle, among others. He includes, in two of the movements, a cimbalom, a Hungarian instrument rarely encountered in concert (though Stravinsky used it in "Renard" and in his "Ragtime for Eleven Instruments").

Opulence is not the major point in "Háry János," though there is a sufficiency of the big *tutti*. Rather, it is tasteful refinement of thought and a pinch or two of humor that lend Kodály's musical tale its force and bring its highpoints to the fore.

¶ Marosszék Dances

Authentic Hungarian folk materials from the Transylvanian district of Marosszék form this set. They were collected by Kodály and later (1929) made the basis for a piano work (*see* Piano *below*). The following year, at the request of Toscanini, they were transcribed for orchestra.

No matter how nationalistic Kodály's feelings, he never permits his folk indoctrination to outweigh his interest in proportional balance. The dances illustrate this. By using the introductory subject as a link between the various sections Kodály composes a set of delightful dances with rondo overtones. There is no pyrotechnical posturing, but there is quiet excitement in his amalgam of native elements and formal logic.

¶ *Peacock Variations* (Variations on a Hungarian Folksong)

There is a difference between variations on a theme and thematic modifications. In the former case, the principal idea or one of its components becomes reorganized and totally developed; in the latter, the main characteristics of the theme are retained within defined statements.

Kodály's set of variations on the folk song "Fly, Peacock, Fly" illustrates the values of controlled modification. The theme is treated to varying types of development: scherzo, funeral march, dance type, and so on, producing an orchestral showcase of colorful gems.

¶ *Symphony*

Kodály waited until he was seventy-nine before writing his first and only symphony. At such an age one can expect to share some new horizons, but none are reached in this case. The three movements are classically ordered as to design, with quartal intervallic spans the most characteristic point of all the principal themes. The music is a synthesis of Kodály's earlier output, rolled into a package of nice, folksy tunes, conservatively orchestrated with proper attention to mass scoring methods. Real depth is lacking. The variational slow movement, based on a quintal-metered idea, has an engaging beginning, but meanders. Kodály's status is not strengthened by this potpourri of self-eclecticism.

¶ *Theatre Overture*

A proxy operatic overture, composed for the Budapest performance of "Háry János." It is faithful to native reflections, containing a heady *csárdás* among its several themes. Though felicitously scored, it lacks the technical virtuosity of the "Peacock Variations" and does not have the exhilaration of "Háry János." The best that can be said

165

for this relatively minor item in Kodály's catalogue is that it is styled
well. However, he is guilty of routine practices.

CHAMBER ORCHESTRA

¶ *Summer Evening*
Intimacy pervades Kodály's warm weather nocturne. There are
no perplexing musical arguments in this suave score. Because Kodály
was young, (it was composed in 1906 and revised twenty-three years
later) his characteristic personality does not appear. He was still too
close to his academic study and his newly found folk *bona fides* to
stride fully on the mature stage. In this music of poetic rhapsody,
native musical curves companion impressionistic patterns. The combination is of faraway dreams with some echoes of folk dances.

INSTRUMENTAL

CELLO

¶ *Sonata for Cello Solo, Op. 8*
Music for an unaccompanied string instrument is always compared to the six great solo compositions that Bach wrote for the
violin. There have been examples in fair number since Bach, and
perhaps Reger's contributions can be granted second place. But,
among all of the contemporary literature for a solo string instrument,
no work (not even Bartók's great violin sonata) can come close to
matching Kodály's fabulous contribution for the cello. Not only does
he exploit the instrument's technique (only a master performer can
cope with the sonata), but he never departs for a single measure from
his distinctive Magyarian personality. Kodály's composition runs its
course with unshaken belief in its technical and aesthetic purposes:
brutal demands which convey the feeling that two, three, and even
four players are simultaneously at work, not one; and the presentation of an intrinsic Hungarian musical document.
    The sonata consists of three movements, beginning with a majestic
emphasis on declamatory lines. In the slow part melodic urgency
(sustained thoughts preceded most often by fast-jetted sounds) is
contrasted to savage cadenzas. Pedal insistence, simultaneous pizzicato with bowed ideas, gives further color, sometimes banking the
melodic stream above and below (extremely difficult to perform). The
barbaric finale is an ingrained transmutation of Kodály's study of his

country's melodies. The weavings of this movement are not only aural excitement; they are its language.

PIANO

¶ Children's Dances

Self-limitation is practiced in this set—music on the black keys only, thus technically employing the pentatonic scale. The boundary of five sounds is cute and educationally valuable though somewhat tiring if the dozen pieces are heard in immediate succession. Kodály is very clever in the way he handles his small folk-tune ideas, but the lack of tonal change is wearing on the ear.

¶ Háry János (Viennese Clock, Song, Intermezzo)

Andor Foldes made a keyboard version of movements two, three, and five of the orchestral suite which presumably received the composer's approval. Its deadly accuracy is honest transcription, but of impotent result.

¶ Marosszék Dances

Kodály's "Marosszék Dances" for piano are rarely heard these days since he transcribed them for orchestra (*see* Orchestral *above*). They are pleasant enough, even in the restricted black and white range of the keyboard instrument.

¶ Seven Piano Pieces, Op. 11

Ordinary music from this extraordinary creator. The compositional manner is akin to light and shadow; folk moods companion impressionistic inclinations à la Debussy.

VIOLIN

¶ Adagio for Violin and Piano

Kodály had not yet reached voting age when he wrote this rich, soaring melody. It has very little Hungarian quantity, but contains real quality.

¶ Dances from the Village of Kálló

Folk material in measured balance; immediately identifiable. The dances consist of sectional depictions, a slow one being followed by a fast set, which grows increasingly livelier in tempo.

167

¶ *Three Hungarian Folk Dances for Violin and Piano*

These terpsichorean pieces (arranged by one Feigin) present formal (but not academic) definition with the stimulus of native roots. Naked folk tunes must be dressed up, to be sure, but in appropriate style. In this connection, Bartók's metaphor "town clothes are too tight and do not fit," is very apt. Kodály heeds his colleague.

CHAMBER MUSIC

¶ *Duo for Violin and Cello, Op. 7*

The minimal means with which Kodály is concerned causes him to employ a striking new technique, one in which he stretches the instruments to equal, at times, sonorities of twice their number. This is not collateral enlargement, but enlargement that remains subservient to the truthfulness of the creative idea.

Most of the first movement is of broad continuity, perfectly balanced between the two instruments which often break into exultant song. The extent of Kodály's rhapsodic vocalizations doesn't matter. The movement's form and its allied tonalities are as clear as his allegiance to Hungarian style. The result is one of the two greatest works (the other is Ravel's composition) instrumentally limited to a violin and a cello.

The Magyar feeling in the adagio is somewhat subdued. The final Presto (with a *parlando* preamble, presented antiphonally) is in huge binary form, twice surveyed, with the addition of a coda that seals the work with a wild conclusion. Kodály's duo displays the deep-rooted emotions of a composer who works with his own people's music and thereby understands and loves his countrymen. With such deep comprehension he makes others understand the Hungarian people as well.

¶ *Sonata for Cello and Piano, Op. 4*

In its closest sense sonata design is typified by triple sections: those of exposition, development, and recapitulation. The dynamic tension of the central development section is to prove the contentions brought forward by the themes announced in the exposition, while the recapitulation modifies and reconfirms the basic premise. Music has still to find better formal logic than the sonata form. With the broadest "modern" outlook, Kodály shows how this design may be expressed cogently by a musical journey afield yet not too far from the boundaries of classical sonata territory.

Movement one of Kodály's cello and piano duo is a "Fantasia." It proposes the mood of the work by dialogue and loosened rhythmic exhortations; it also sketches the composition's warmth and Hungarian manner. Three shadings, therefore, indicate the complexion of this general exposition. Movement two integrates and tightens rhythm, sweeping along with dance motility, which confirms ("develops") the spirit of the initial part of the sonata. At the end of the second movement the first section reappears in concentrate; thus formal recapitulation. Sonata terms have been fulfilled, yet this is less a sonata of two movements with semicyclic inference than it is a work of one panel drawn in colors which complement each other.

¶ *Serenade for Two Violins and Viola, Op. 12*

Few critics will demur at the statement that Kodály's "Serenade" and Dvořák's "Terzetto" are the two superlative works in the severely restricted category of string trios calling for a pair of violins and viola. It is sad to realize that with the completion of this work Kodály has never returned to chamber-music composition, the heart of his total output and that which marks him as one of the important composers of the present century.

The three movements of the "Serenade" could well have titles affixed—"Activity," "Dialogue," and "Dance." Movement one is in intimate but not introspective style, portrayed by a bouncing theme which is activated by the nimble tempo. The most individual part of the trio is the middle movement. Kodály's unerring manipulation of instrumental detail is beautifully expressed as the first violin and viola converse with each other in an example rare to chamber music, one akin to operatic recitative of the boldest order. Such declamatory writing is program music in spirit, without detail. Whipped rhythm and repose are neatly blended in the finale. The color of pizzicato pulsation is paramount, while some of the gentleness of this choreographic music is Mendelssohnian.

¶ *String Quartet No. 1, Op. 2*

Although Kodály's initial quartet shows great interest in the terms and turns of old Hungarian music, his characteristic method of portraying it beyond the arbitrary, classic-romantic manner, is not as yet displayed. Nevertheless, Kodály's later personality is present; future possibilities and solutions are simmering.

169

Of all Kodály's chamber-music works this is the only one in four movements—a sign of his preliminary attitude in contrast to later decisions. The first two movements are derived from the cello's opening theme, which is defined principally with a measured dip of an intervallic fourth. Movement three (*presto*) represents the scherzo part; its subject is of decided national cast. A set of variations is called on for the finale.

¶ *String Quartet No. 2, Op. 10*

The speech of the four stringed instruments is produced here from indigenous Hungarian musical dialect which accents "open-air" intervals; its rhythms move through the Magyar slow *lassu,* the frenetic *friss,* and the *alla zoppa* of limping syncopation, its vocabulary extended by the *rubati* of rural Gypsy melisma. There is no better identification of Kodály's art, which conveys the subtleties of idealized musical folklore. It has all of the fertile and mysterious variables that make a sensitive composer independent of scholastic calculations.

This quartet bears a relation to Kodály's first work in the same medium as does the freedom of the late Beethoven quartets to the more imitative first half dozen. In the first quartet, Kodály examines his newly found jewels of folk song; in the second quartet he wears them.

VOCAL

¶ *Hungarian Folk Music*

Refinements of the crude, basal musical stuff that Kodály found in his researches. The styling is superbly artistic, a gentle editing of the native materials with pastel-colored crayons. All the songs depict superb craftsmanship.

¶ *Recruiting Song*
¶ *Soldier's Song*

Folk items not stylistically dressed to kill the primordial quality of the tunes.

¶ *Six Songs, Op. 9*

Kodály's early period of work was marked by a large number of vocal compositions. Within the first nine *opera,* numbers 1, 5, 6, and 9 consist of sixteen, two, seven, and six songs respectively. In the Opus 9 set the moods are mainly on the dark side. Thus, "Sappho's

Love Song" is pessimistic, and both "At Night" and "The Forest" are mainly adumbrated by the *Weltschmerz* of inner turmoil. No national musical turns regulate these songs; they are introspective sketches by a composer who had yet to find his identity.

¶ *Twenty Hungarian Folk Songs* (in collaboration with Béla Bartók) (see also: Bartók, page 33)

The fascinating results of Kodály's partnership with Bartók in the field of Hungarian folklore, a tremendous untapped resource before their research took place. The results of the project were first made known in this collection, issued in 1906; independent publication of folk materials followed. Though given professional polish the beauty of the native melodies is not hindered by worldly technique. Both Bartók and Kodály reserved that for their own music which stems from the indigenous background they probed.

CHORAL

¶ *A Christmas Carol*

Kodály's carol is bedecked with colorful counterpoint, moving in imitation, excited by use of minute syncopation. Though one loves the well-known carols, a new one is like pure, fresh air.

¶ *Akik Mindig Elkésnek* ("Those Who Are Always Late")

One of the characteristics of Hungarian music is the wide inter-vallic descent (quite often of a fourth). This tonal birthmark is quite plain and markedly important in Kodály's very haunting, short choral piece, written to a poem of the revolutionary Hungarian poet, Endre Ady.

¶ *Christmas Dance of the Shepherds*

A charming and catchy Hungarian carol for two-part women's voices. The march tempo neatly and deftly defines the follow-the-leader use of canon. The carol is unaccompanied in the initial part, delightfully colored with piccolo in the latter portion. A real "sleeper."

¶ *Evening*

Composed early in Kodály's career (1904), "Evening" is music written in a neutral, unassuming manner. It portrays a quiet nocturnal mood. It is relatively unimportant.

171

¶ *Jesus and the Traders*

A moving, fascinating work that interweaves baroque austerity with some plainchant brought up to date, colorful polyphony (more than one usually finds in Kodály's music), and Hungarian tints. "Jesus and the Traders" is a motet of split personality and split divisions, yet paradoxically creating a clear conception because of its sensitive contrasts.

The scoring for unaccompanied chorus is anything but foursquare. There are telling spacings, especially the splitting away of top voices from the lower ones. Kodály's textures are in constant change. They are truly exciting.

¶ *Scenes from the Mátra District* (Mátra Pictures)

Catchy snapshots of coloristic nationalism. Kodály's folksy pictures warm the ear and heart. No questions are posed, no demands made; this is as artistically vital as music of symphonic dimensions.

¶ *Stabat Mater*

A fully chordal chorale, hymn-styled; the same music states each of the four stanzas. Simple, yes; recognizable as the work of Zoltán Kodály, no. Clearly a historical item, written when the composer was a youth, but compelling nonetheless.

¶ *Veni, Veni Emmanuel*

A simple setting of a melody Kodály found in a French missal. It is modal, and minus any national fingerprints. Kodály matches the mood and flow of his music to the solemn Latin words. A minor work in his catalogue but of major effect.

CHORAL WITH ORCHESTRA

¶ *Kálló Double Dance*

More Hungarian than any other work Kodály has written. The three dances are folk-pop in style. No dismembering of melodies, no fancy counterpoints, nothing but the native truth is heard in the suite, which becomes increasingly faster in tempo as it moves along. Documentary rural music scored for a village ensemble of three clarinets, two cimbaloms, and strings, plus mixed voices.

"Kálló" is the shortened name for a town "Nagykálló"; the "Double Dance" originally was performed by one couple, today it is danced by groups of young men and women. The first records of the tunes Kodály employs date from 1674; his setting was made in 1951.

172

¶ *Psalmus Hungaricus, Op. 13*

The 1923 commemoration of the fiftieth anniversary of the unification of Buda and Pest proved to be a red-letter event in music. Commissions by the Hungarian Government produced Bartók's colorful "Dance Suite" and Kodály's powerful "Psalmus Hungaricus," the text of the latter an adaptation of the Fifty-fifth Psalm by the sixteenth-century Hungarian poet, Michael Vég. The nonliturgical interpolations and extensions that Vég made amount to a paraphrase of the Biblical prose.

Kodály's nationalistic temper is tenacious. Formality is secondary to the aesthetic truth of his piece—a one-movement symphony for tenor solo, chorus, and orchestra that portrays music of Hungarian substance. However, the scope and emotion of the "Psalmus Hungaricus" could not be evoked by a provincial composer. It is steeped in native melos, but also contains the direct expressiveness and dramatic strength that are understood universally.

¶ *Te Deum* (Budavari Te Deum)

In spite of its devoutness and a richness of traditionally telescoped polyphony, the true characteristics of Hungarian peasant music are present in the "Te Deum" (sometimes called "Budavari Te Deum"). Vivid and forceful alternations of mood occur, combining religious praise with national spiritualism. This does not constitute superficial compromise but a modern duologue. Kodály proves in his work (written to commemorate the 250th anniversary of the freeing of Budapest from the Turks) that kinship of folk disposition need not be of mere outward reference in the medium of sacred music.

MASS

¶ *Missa Brevis* (in Tempore Belli) ("In Time of War")

Despite the fearful days of the Second World War, Kodály remained in Budapest continuing his creative work. It was during this period (1945) that he wrote the "Missa Brevis (in Tempore Belli)." It has as much conviction as his "Psalmus Hungaricus," but is far simpler in formulation. In this contemporary mass Kodály's methods are never extravagant; the dominating effect of the music is its subtle, native characteristic, with a bit of intermingled quasi-Gregorian qualities.

Kodály's piece has ecclesiastical meaning without loss of individual style. The "Missa Brevis" is a self-sufficient art work, no less

173

fitting, however, for liturgical use. Kodály worships God in his own special way. It is as sincere, respectful, and correct as the cheerfulness by which Haydn paid homage to the Deity in his masses.

OPERA

¶ Háry János

The orchestral suite from "Háry János" is so well-known that concertgoers have always been curious about the complete work. This curiosity has been difficult to appease, since only one American production has been given (by the Juilliard School of Music, thirty-four years after the Budapest première of October 1926). The bald fact is that "Háry János" is far less than an opera; it is a play, with background music—talk is the major element.

Kodály's opus concerns the legendary adventures of one Háry János, who among other exploits, singlehandedly captures Napoleon. The broad farce of Háry's engagements makes him the Hungarian counterpart of a Baron Münchhausen. Listening to the opera one will find that the picturesque sections used in the orchestral suite are mere aural hinges in the stage work and offer no surprise. All of it fits very well; it fits even better when it exists orchestrally apart and does not support stage action. The small amount of music that was not used in the orchestral suite is neat, folksy, and quite lovely, but incidental.

¶ The Spinning Room

For cataloguing purposes only, this can be indexed as an opera. The twenty-one numbers in the seven scenes of Kodály's "Spinning Room" total a theatre piece that is paradoxically a concert work. Whereas "Háry János" is a big play with supporting music, the "Spinning Room" is all music hung on the merest skeleton of a play.

Kodály's intensive research in folk song gave him a vast amount of source material. He has taken a number of songs, ballades, and dances and strung them together expertly. However, his "plot" is cellophane tape; it concerns a woman, her suitor, some young people, and a character disguised as a long-nosed flea. The police are searching for a man who has committed some wrong; the culprit seems to be the suitor, it turns out to be the flea. This tepid material is in striking contrast to the genuine aspects of the music.

16. ERNST KRENEK
(1900–   )

Eʀɴsᴛ Kʀᴇɴᴇᴋ's career reminds one of Walt Whitman's "Whoever you are, to you endless announcements!" No one of the present century can match Krenek's compositional travels. He was prolific and changed his style often.

Krenek's works were first overloaded with the weight of late romanticism. Then came a period during which he courted linear counterpoint, flirting at the same time with the then fashionable cult of atonality. A jazz phase came next—dropped in favor of complete atonality. Whether the atonal market was glutted, or whether he felt he had exhausted its possibilities, Krenek completely changed his manner in the late twenties and became a conservative romanticist, his music spiced with contemporary Schubertian syntax. The aesthetic itch could not be mollified; a further change (the most positive of all) took place around 1930. From that date most of his compositions were written in twelve-tone technique, which has led to an increased concentration on predetermining all elements of a work; *i.e.,* total serialization. The creative journey continues: Krenek has already turned out electronic compositions.

All this might signify a composer with an overopinionated mind, one who constantly seeks new loves because of mild hatreds in the past. More to the point, it indicates that Krenek wishes to retain his creative youth and throw off any identification with older phases of modernity.

Though it is quite clear that he delights in solving new problems, Krenek is no mere musical faddist. His compositions are thorough, supremely logical, intellectually satisfying, with all their plotted complexity.

ORCHESTRAL

¶ *Eleven Transparencies*

Like Debussy, in his "Préludes" for piano, Krenek gave suggestive subtitles to the "Transparencies" after completion. Because of such guidance a listener is not prone to push the composer's reactions aside and is therefore captive to predetermined images. Once told a movement is "Sparks Cascading," or "Knocks and Dashes," it is almost impossible to draw one's own pictures.

However, with Krenek's twelve-tone dogma such aids are welcome, for they make the fantasy much simpler to understand. The music is sullen, its colors are sallow. In its relentless way Krenek's "Transparencies" is frighteningly effective.

STRING ORCHESTRA

¶ *Music for String Orchestra*

There are no light charms in Krenek's piece. Neither are there any sensual soporifics or sonorous intoxications. All is dark: harmonically, contrapuntally, and texturally. All is tightly meshed from a concentrated motivic weave; making for a sensitive abrasiveness that is quite telling.

The gloomy tread of this composition makes one think of a "Non-Verklärte Nacht." By all means a "Very Serious Music for String Orchestra."

BAND

¶ *Drei Lustige Märsche* ("Three Merry Marches"), *Op. 44*

A vintage from the days when "modrin" music was in flower, but still wonderful fun and highly enjoyable. Krenek's band sound is peppy, properly brassy; the pieces are flavored with a zestful, dissonant icing.

SOLO INSTRUMENT WITH ORCHESTRA

CONCERTO

¶ *Double Concerto for Violin, Piano and Small Orchestra*

There is no tonality précis here, but the twirls and twists of atonality (thus atonicality) are supported by serial particulars. Krenek makes no compromise: the concerto is harsh and refractory, its language governed by tensions and slight releases.

Within the seven movements the solo instruments make severely serious discourse against a type of neutral, bland scoring using four woodwinds, a pair of horns, trumpet, and strings. On the whole

Krenek's concerto is dried of emotional content. Music of grim countenance.

INSTRUMENTAL

ORGAN

¶ *Sonata, Op. 92*

The organ does not thrive on heavily packed writing, or a puzzling cipher of unidentifiable sounds results. Krenek's one-movement, twelve-tone work is shaped well as a successful conception for this difficult and restricted medium; its slow section is especially appealing. Recommended to those who believe that organ literature began with Bach and ended with Franck.

PIANO

¶ *Sonata No. 3, Op. 92, No. 4*

If the specific order of tones is related to the dynamic inherencies of a motive in tonal composition, the matter of *understanding* twelve-tone music becomes less difficult. With dodecaphonicism the expression becomes the complete structure; form is not cut away from emotional meaning, the form *is* the intrinsic expression. It is thus with Krenek's sonata.

Accepting the amazing order and logic of Schoenberg's method, Krenek has developed its principal distinctions without blindly following the leader. He divides the twelve-tone row and obtains contrasting qualities; furthermore, by a process of rotating the order of the pitches in each row he fashions a new type of modulation. Though dodecaphonicism is the rib work of Krenek's serious piano piece, he is most certainly an independent serialist.

¶ *Sonata No. 4*

Again (as in the third piano sonata) Krenek pursues the serial muse differently from Schoenberg. The basic twelve-tone row turns into a dozen different series as the original row is splintered into three-note groups, permutated by the rotation of the sounds within each. The entire sonata is drawn from combinations of these sets.

There are four movements: the first rather free in form, the second in ternary design, the third a rondo, and the last a set of variations.

177

Krenek's brute and unshaken belief in his brand of twelve-tone music is somewhat stiff; it does not make for constant interest.

¶ *Sonata No. 5*

The disassociative, almost stuttering type of twelve-tone music, with its damning static adherence to a blueprint, has been a plague for which even those who have mastered the dodecaphonic craft have been blamed. The fault lies solely with the peripheral small-fry creators who turn out long-winded trifles with unmasterly eclecticism.

Krenek's fifth sonata fills the dodecaphonic shell with real substance. It is of Schoenbergian vintage, but with a virtuosic flavor rare to twelve-tone piano music, especially emphasized in the last movement. Unconventional and ripe serial music that deserves plaudits, even though there are no sweet tunes to whistle.

PIANO DUET

¶ *Four Bagatelles* (Sonata) *for Piano, Four Hands, Op. 70*

Music without a trace of floridity, yet with lines that are very articulate and rhythmically zestful. Rarely has Krenek been so lyrically engaging. The composition is fully chromatic but pays attention to tone-center gravity, which neither represses nor tends to vagueness, yet is fluid without overzealous, astringent dissonance.

Hardly a "sonata" as the term is defined. Nevertheless, these "Bagatelles" must not be considered in the French meaning of the word ("trifles"), but in the pure musical sense of short pieces; they are compact but not of small importance. Together they provide beautiful balance.

CHAMBER MUSIC

¶ *Sonata for Viola and Piano*

Easily identified music of tone row ideology, but not easily digested, because of the almost arid preoccupation with intellectual note-spinning. Krenek has done much better than this. The music is certainly knowledgeable, but emotionally cold.

The average condition of a three-movement compounded work is reversed; the end parts are in slower tempo, the fastest in between. In a way this matches the more restrained, broader tone of the string instrument employed. Within the last movement the dual elements of sustainment and release by scherzando propulsion cross each other.

VOCAL

¶ Fiedellieder, Op. 64

Though spoken with the tongue of Krenek, the accent in this cycle is slightly Mahlerian. The set of seven "Minstrels' Songs" are totally romantic in construction and freely romantic in spirit.

VOICE WITH INSTRUMENTAL ENSEMBLE

¶ Sestina for Voice and Instrumental Ensemble

Compared to his other music, Krenek's "Sestina" is as driving rain to sunlight. In this work there is a brute and unshaken belief in the rigid organization and regulated distribution of all elements. Tones, textures, spacings, time values, tempi, dynamics, and even the text are determined by the row system. All the art is in the serial science. Any free thinking is disallowed. The condition is dogmatic—that of ordered order; a totalitarian form of the art process.

Thus, an example of the unharnessing of twelve-tone technique, and in its way as different from Schoenberg's work as his was from the tonalists. There is formal discipline in the "Sestina" even though the control is completely different from its traditional meaning. The forms of the triadic world of harmony are predicated on key relationships and the premise of consonance and dissonance. Using one of the "standard" forms would be like trying to construct a limerick in free verse.

However, the technique in the "Sestina" is not original. Krenek has never been very late in trying his hand at the newest fashion and in this instance he imitates the Boulez-Stockhausen methods. Undeniably, there are aural portions of this piece that are remarkably fascinating. The structural implications are twice as intriguing.

CHORAL

¶ Die Jahreszeiten ("The Seasons"), *Op. 35*

This surveyal of the four periods of year was inspired by Friedrich Hölderlin's poems. The tonal flexibility, which bends most gracefully, shows Krenek's perceptive regard for subtle harmonic progress. It also illustrates an aloof, restrained kind of romanticism.

The change of the seasons is not very decided: "Winter" has as much warmth as "Spring." However, the energy of "Summer" is more invigorating than one expects, obtained from contrapuntalistic push. "Autumn" is mainly constructed in chordal blocks.

179

¶ *Five Prayers Over the Pater Noster as Cantus Firmus*

Polyphonic music for four-part unaccompanied women's choir, a bit freed from the tonal vine. The five portions are enclosed—fore and aft—with the unison singing of The Lord's Prayer; the music knitted by the varied contrasts of each of the sections devoted to the "Litanie" of John Donne. It is a composite structure—*durchkomponiert,* as the German phrase aptly describes it.

¶ *Lamentatio Jeremiae Prophetae* ("Lamentations of Jeremiah"), *Op. 93*

Undoubtedly the longest and most serious sacred work written in dodecaphonic technique. Krenek's opus draws its text from the liturgy of the Roman Catholic Church, used during the Tenebrae services held during Holy Week. There are nine parts—three *lessons* each for Maundy Thursday, Good Friday, and Holy Saturday.

Despite the strictness of Krenek's compositional system, based on a twelve-tone row split into a pair of hexachords, each further divided by rotating the progress of the sounds, and manipulated by transposition and more rotation, his unaccompanied choral composition ranges far beyond cold investigation. Krenek has mixed his materials with imitative Gregorian chants and old polyphonic features, but this does not cause a stylistic potpourri, rather a reassessment and refurbishing of Schoenbergian language in terms of *ars antiqua.* The spirit of the work evokes music written in mensural notation transcribed into serial equivalents.

Significant feeling must go beyond calculated plan, of course. The "Lamentations of Jeremiah" have all the wizardry of polyphonicized predisposition: canon, augmentation, diminution, *cancrizans,* and the like. However, the quiet vitality of the work proves that its encyclopedic technique serves emotion fully. Krenek's sentiment is without ecstatic shock, and is inexorable; it is deeply expressive nevertheless.

CHORAL WITH ELECTRONIC SOUNDS

¶ *Spiritus Intelligentiae Sanctus, Pfingstoratorium für Singstimmen und Elektronische Klänge—1. Abteilung* ("Whitsun Oratorio for Voices and Electronic Sounds—1st Section")

Electronic music eliminates performers; it is sound of assorted types placed on tape and heard over loudspeakers. To attempt to compare an exclusive electronic piece with any musical work (regardless of whether it is conceived with such extremes as tonality or aleatory principles) is to indulge in rodomontade. Of course, there are rhythms and pitch levels, textures and the like, but everything is set forth with a totally different treatment to anything that has preceded in music's history. This newness is so startling that only by a frank erasure of musical desiderata can one properly cope with it. The human element must be canceled, since the electronic concept is of human plan but not of human manufacture. Man arranges, but the machine proposes and realizes. There is no emulation of "music." Electronic analysis speaks of sinus tones, phones, blank noise, modulation (a musical word, note well!), equated by amplitudes which are considered periodically or statistically, and so on.

The combination of human voices with electronic sound is employed by Krenek in the "Whitsun Oratorio" in a way that makes the voices synthetic substitutes not only for themselves but for the electronic elements. How valid a practice this is can be argued, for if electronic techniques are so Gargantuan in concept and possibility, why must nonelectronic means be employed at all? One can foresee the combination of musical sound with that of electronic manufacture (Varèse has already done this), but most electronic creators are opposed to such an alliance.

Krenek's involvement with taped datum is rather restrained in comparison to other composers. He is, however, a man who has tried each new phase of technique as it has appeared. It is not surprising that he would put his foot (even though very gently) into the hot hellwaters of electronic composition.

OPERA

¶ The Bell-Tower

Krenek fashioned his own libretto for the opera (which covers four scenes in its single act) after a Melville story. The tale of a bell caster who murders both the girl he loves and her father and then is killed by the mechanical contrivance he has built is silly. Its repolished consideration of the Frankenstein myth is crossed by mystical mishmash.

The opera is entirely serial, but the adherence to technique at all costs does not bring any profits. Krenek's regard for rigorous technical manners overburdens the piece. In the dogma of serial music, calling a composer to task for being technically strict is tantamount to heresy. So be it.

17. GIAN FRANCESCO MALIPIERO
(1882–   )

Malipiero is one of the most original creators in Italy's musical history. He has no direct tie to traditional manners, save that he has been inspired by the straightforward, epigrammatic decisiveness of the old Italian masters. For Malipiero there is no such thing as thematic development, per se. All of his music is of plastic continuity, architectonically formed and directly plotted by sectional statement; each part a unit unto itself, each particularly spontaneous, yet each a link in the total chain.

No other composer has had the audacity to compose in chunks, yet Malipiero, with full *unrestraint,* captures the integration that other composers attempt to formulate by *restraint* itself, so that their music is spanned and co-ordinated by one, two, or three central ideas developed to form the whole. Formal schematicism is abnegated by Malipiero; musical condensation takes its place. He looks to the end result without parenthetical references, footnotes of instrumental explanation, or strings of musical adjectives. Such style has no counterpart. It makes the work of this composer incapable of classification with any other.

Once considered very advanced, Malipiero's compositions offer no complexities to the ears of today. Thus the young radicals attack him as severely passé. However, the years have not diminished the freshness of his creations. A composer who bypasses time-honored routine methods, avoids mundane mechanics of harmony and form, eliminates any false hurly-burly, and sounds tonally spontaneous, is bound to remain a fresh voice.

ORCHESTRAL

¶ *Fantasie di Ogni Giorno* ("Fantasies of Every Day")

Solitary formal titles are the exception in Malipiero's catalogue. Most often these are accompanied by a parenthetical, semipictorial explanation. Such combinations bypass detailed musical reportage

182

and paradoxically hint at a story. Thus this work, a Louisville Orchestra commission, has no programmatic intent but is merely a set of thoughts rolled into one. One idea moves into the next—a series of inferences shuffled into a musical huddle, but yet not a pastiche. This is Malipiero's method of order.

¶ *La Cimarosiana* (Cimarosa-Malipiero)

Tasteful versions, for a medium-sized orchestral group, of five pieces by the eighteenth-century Italian. For the most part Malipiero does not show his contemporary hand; the few spots that he does merely heighten the color scheme.

SOLO INSTRUMENT WITH ORCHESTRA

CONCERTOS

¶ *Concerto No. 3 for Piano and Orchestra*

This work, which is in one piece, is defined by differentiated degrees of tempo for its three linked sections. The solo piano is considered as a basic, chordal personality, and when it is given melodic lines these are in a form it can sustain successfully. Malipiero does not attempt to duplicate a fully singing string or wind instrument.

Throughout there is a neobaroque positiveness, with the sunny side up. Malipiero looks to the end concerto result without showy capers, cadenza spotlighting, or virtuosic gimmicks. The concerto is a celebration of composition without rigid system, producing music in a singing style.

¶ *Violin Concerto*

Neither the accepted classical form nor its derivatives employed by the later period composers, including the most up-to-date contemporaries, interest Gian Francesco Malipiero. This opus defines a modern spelling of concerto design, in lightly tart linear style, pandiatonic as to harmonic vocabulary, with a spontaneity of sonorous instrumental flow. The violin alternates in its role: it is a homophonic character and a contrapuntal resource.

There is a cadenza, but no mere emotional *portamenti* or flying triple stops. It forms a separate sonatina for unaccompanied violin— almost a short composition set within a large one. This surprise is a Malipiero twist. Formality bends in this composer's hands. One recalls

183

his "Sonata a Tre" for piano, violin, and cello, which uses cello and piano in movement one, violin and piano in the middle part, and only becomes a full-fledged trio in the finale. And one also remembers the set of variations Malipiero wrote for piano and orchestra but "senza tema" (without theme)!

INSTRUMENTAL

PIANO

¶ *Poemi Asolani*

These three pieces ("La Notte dei Morti," "Dittico," and "I Partenti") represent Malipiero's typical manner of piano composition —fragmented ideas held together with slight programmatic clips. (The main title concerns Asolo, a small Italian town, near Venice, where Malipiero has lived since 1923.)

CHAMBER MUSIC

¶ *String Quartet No. 4*

A work in a single movement integrated by the use of ritornel. It contains the usual Malipiero brand of diatonically stabilized polyphonicism, which means it is like the clear, open air, and far different from the stuffy atmosphere found so often in the late German romantic school. Tonality is present, but it does not wither away in the underbrush of academicism. Through the insistence of the counterpoint the instruments are freed. In this way the strings reverberate, the sonority opens wide, the quartet is full-chested.

¶ *String Quartet No. 7*

Although the seventh string quartet shows Malipiero's fixed attention to disjunctive structural technique, he pays considerable heed to the opening motive. This appears often, as a thread that stitches the many colorful bits of the work with one distinctive hem.

One will hear Malipiero's individual form of speech, diaphanous with pandiatonic shades of meaning. There is also a symbolizing of the instrumental qualities of the Renaissance period expressed by twentieth-century string scoring. It is this freshness of sound that marks Malipiero's individuality as a composer of quartets.

¶ *Sonata a Cinque for Flute, Violin, Viola, Cello and Harp*

Malipiero considers his sonata "for five" in the truest and most elemental meaning of the word "sonata"—that is, "to sound." The sonata's loose compilation, held within a single movement, illustrates the full essence of the composer's style. In its close resemblance to the seventeenth-century canzona one realizes that Malipiero's work has a soft coherence with older musical eras. The same properties are exhibited: a number of sections in contrasting mood and tempi, an alternation of homophonic statement with contrapuntal argument.

Retentive memory serves Malipiero nicely. His sonata is music of neoclassic intensity, a true token of past heritage invoked in modern paraphrase.

VOCAL

¶ *Tre Poesie di Angelo Poliziano*

Delightful variety is offered in these three short items. The vocal menu consists of an appetizer (close to ornamented recitative), a clever echo song (restatement in a contrasting register of the terminal part of each of the eight short lines), and the heaviest course last (a dramatic "Ballata"). Typical light contemporary Italianate song, with no showy operatic intrusions.

18. BOHUSLAV MARTINU
(1890–1959)

THE general withdrawal from romanticism that took place prior to the First World War in most European countries affected Czechoslovakia very little at first. The roots of love of country went deep with the Czechs, and the work of Dvořák and Smetana was not forgotten in the music of the contemporary school. As usual, however, musical styles developed from the performance of many foreign compositions. Cosmopolitanism cut deeply into the romantic ranks. Many Czech composers joined the composers in other countries intent on using the forms of classicism and romanticism, but accenting these with a present-day tongue.

Martinu proved to be the most international minded of the entire Czech group. Though a stay in Paris brought him slightly under the influence of Stravinsky and Hindemith, the stream of Czech nationalism was never filtered out of his work. After a short stay in Portugal Martinu came to the United States and entered his most prolific period. He followed a classical choice of forms: concerto grosso, serenade, ricercare, etc. His music was neatly plotted, with tonally clear themes dipped in dissonant harmonies and marked by sharp and precise (though not always symmetrical) rhythms. Martinu's contemporary translation of classical ideology defined him as a Czech neoclassicist.

ORCHESTRAL

¶ *Estampes*

These "prints" have an allegiance to impressionistic scoring and composition. They are not of a particular school but are somewhat an anthology of typical French styled texture, speech, and correctness. No superintending subtitles, but the quality suggests the outdoors.

¶ *Fantaisies Symphoniques* (Symphony No. 6)

Mainly because of a tendency to rely on literal restatement, Martinu's ability to construct a true symphony has been debated. It is true

186

that his work is episodic, yet it shows observance of the symphonic objective—big expression and development of material. The composer anticipates certain critics by clear titling, *i.e.* "symphonic fantasies." The color imagery of the sixth symphony alone gives it a unique place in Martinu's output. The critics of New York City were pleased—bestowing on it their annual award as "the best new orchestral work" in 1956.

The orchestration is most compelling. Martinu knows how to balance matters between the artistic and technical, and accomplishes his fascinating sonority and pigmented schemes without any outré effects or special instruments.

¶ Intermezzo

An accumulation of Martinu's past compositional memories almost hashed together, saved only by the composer's craftsmanship. Aside from an injection of Czechian flavor in the middle portion, this is routine, impersonal orchestral fare.

¶ Les Fresques de Piero della Francesca (Three Frescoes)

Notwithstanding the picturesque title, all divisions of this work fall in the orbit of objective music. Inspired by the fifteenth-century painter, Piero della Francesca, whose frescoes he had often admired in his visits to the church of San Francesco at Arezzo, Martinu described his intent thus: "I have tried to express in music the kind of solemn frozen silence and the opaque, colored atmosphere. . . ."

No late romantic laxity will be heard, nor any huge "letting loose," but merely some Czechized Respighi (without brass orgy, gramophone nightingales, and overcelebrated orchestration). Martinu's musical frescoes have a firm solidity of detail. Orchestral color is used freely but rigidly, mass against mass. The product is one of darkened lyricism aided by motival technique and martially brilliant instrumental potencies. The work is inventive; the effect just a bit too attenuated.

¶ Memorial to Lidice

In this threnodic piece Martinu is conscious of contemporary harmonic overtones, but not apathetic to national expression. These combine in a fervent musical testament that reminds a listener of the agonizing horror of Hitler's blood bath.

The music sings in a vocal sense and is organized on the theory

187

that melodic lines keep trim the musical body. Martinu's quality of expressivity will remind some listeners of the ecstatic portions of Roy Harris's third symphony, but to use this as a critical weapon is to disallow the so-called internationalism of art. The sonorous material is expertly assigned, especially hairpinned ramifications of dynamically-terraced colors (sometimes beautifully abrupt). This is paralleled in harmonic shifts between major and minor modes.

Martinu's Lidice piece is sincere, moving, and sensitive. It is music of direct, sustained utterance.

¶ The Parables

Despite the allegories that presumably define this suite (the subtitles are indicated as "Parable of a Sculpture," "Parable of the Garden," and "Parable of a Labyrinth") there is no connection with program music. In fact, Martinu added the "explanatory" texts to the second and third pieces after he had completed the composition. He uses a maximum dynamic scale as the sounds splash and overluxuriate in a Respighian Roman bath of orchestration. The rhythm pumps unceasingly; the music is gripped by febrile excitement, regardless of different tempi. It is all too slick and sounds like the background score for a super film production from Hollywood.

¶ Serenade

National *característica* are submerged in most of Martinu's music, though they create a subtle flavor here and there. He cared much more for the formal address and objective. Nonetheless, the four movements of this piece prove that Martinu could never retreat into fully strict formalism (any more than Schoenberg could desert Viennese atmosphere, no matter how abstruse his musical linguistics).

The sonorities of the "Serenade" are of modern cast, while the harmonies are only somewhat removed from classical-romantic style. These, by their chromatic direction, free the lines from vertical rigidity and stimulate the inner texture.

CHAMBER ORCHESTRA

¶ Concerto for Two String Orchestras, Piano and Timpani

One of the best pieces in Martinu's large output. Its movements form a triptych, with the surrounding of a slow movement by two fast ones. And what sheer motor drive! But the concerto is far from the "machine" music reminiscent of 1920 fashions. The very first beat of the initial measure richochets as if from a slingshot. Ostinati, cross accents, asymmetrical phrase divisions—all form a breathless drive that does not halt for one second. This is felt in the slow-paced division as well. Nor is this exceedingly peripatetic subscription lessened by the fact that Martinu's hand shows some guidance from Stravinsky's "Sacre." The panting excitement and urbane glorification indicate Martinu gave more than a passing glance to his contemporaries. In this marvelous chunk of sonorous sculpture the essential facts of Martinu's abilities are present. The composition is significant.

¶ *Sinfonietta La Jolla for Chamber Orchestra and Piano*

A three-movement essay typical of the composer with a tinge of Czech flavor in the final movement. The clearest of structures is used, with a writing style that replaces stringent diatonicism with astringent formations. The energetic thesis of the opening has a deep-felt middle movement response; the finale is a dance.

Martinu treats the piano in a subsidiary manner. It is in no way a solo instrument, but simply an obbligato voice. The term "La Jolla" has no programmatic meaning—it appears because the composition was commissioned by the Musical Art Society of La Jolla, California, which offers an annual music festival.

¶ *Toccata a Due Canzoni*

Three separate moods leave their imprint on this work, but there is a relationship between the mysterious impetus of the opening portion and the middle section of the second canzona. A further affinity exists between parts of the last canzona and the first. As a whole, this richly colored music is a suite, especially illustrative of canzona style; a derivative of lyric poetry, wherein formal balance and textural variety define the poetic stanzas.

An example of Martinu's neoclassic aliveness and non-stereotyped creative approach.

STRING ORCHESTRA

¶ *Partita* (Suite I)

Persistent and insistent rhythm gives this work its spice. The emphasis is on motival-like formations; continuity, contrast, and balance are arrived at by the manipulation of brief ideas. Whatever melodicism there is derives from the musical architecture. Spun, catchy lines or juicy themes are not the way of the composer in this instance. This is exhilarating music.

189

BAND

¶ *Little Suite from "Comedy on a Bridge"*

Martinu composed his one-act opera in 1937 and revised it some thirteen years later. This sketchy compilation includes a garish march, an instrumentalized aria, and a second march (a happy one) as a finale. No one is charged with the band arrangement.

SOLO INSTRUMENT WITH ORCHESTRA

CONCERTO

¶ *Concerto for String Quartet and Orchestra*

There have been attempts to successfully combine the most efficacious chamber-music group (the string quartet) with the modern symphony orchestra, but the ratio does not work. Though one violin can pit itself against an orchestra, two violins, a viola, and a cello cannot seem to make the grade. This may be because the assimilated soli apparatus tends to disassociate itself from the orchestra and lacks soloistic individuality because of its numerical strength. Whatever the reason one can not compare this contemporary idea with its older relative, the concerto grosso. In the latter case solo strings are pitted against multiplied strings and the contrast is much more refined and sensible than the modern orchestra sweeping its sonorities against four stringed instruments.

Three-movement form generally binds a slow movement with two outer fast sections. Further balance is pertinent here with duple meter bracing both the opening *Allegro vivo* and the terminal *Tempo moderato*. Otherwise the musical horizon is changed; the initial part is quasi-variational, the finale a polka-flavored rondo. Though Martinu's concerto is not fully a formal success it is a brilliant attempt.

INSTRUMENTAL

PIANO

¶ *Les Ritournelles*

Adequate run-of-the-mill music, consisting of six short pieces relatively slight in weight and effect.

190

¶ *Three Etudes*

These are taken from three volumes of piano études and polkas, composed in 1945. Martinu had a fondness for the étude design, writing sets of rhythmical études for violin alone, cello alone, and violin and piano. The emphasis on one facet of construction that marks an étude can often be boring, but Martinu accomplishes his objective with artistic meaning.

¶ *Two Polkas*

Martinu practices neo-Smetana art in these extracts from a set of sixteen pieces, wherein an étude is followed by a polka throughout. This Czech identity almost lapsed into extinction in his late compositions.

CHAMBER MUSIC

¶ *Duo for Violin and Cello*

The duet for homophonic instruments poses severe difficulties, unless the writing is to be mundane, elementary, or, in the case of string instruments, stretched into chordal virtuosity, wherein the instruments attempt to produce music for twice their number. Of all the duet combinations, those using soprano and bass are patently the best, since the total gamut gives the widest range. Use of high-low ranged instruments also affords (even if both are from the same family) a color differential that aids in setting forth the most concentrated type of writing, despite necessary liberal counterpoint dosages to help the minimum of voices move with maximum force.

Everything in this musical twosome is paired: two instruments, two movements, two formal aspects. Part one's method is chromatic and linear, the second is more clarified and straightforward. The first ("Preludium") evolves around a cross relationship of two centers of harmonic flux; the second, a "Rondo," is clearly defined by its harmonic-contrapuntal delivery. This portion contains two tremendous cadenzas, one each for the two instruments.

¶ *Five Madrigal Stanzas for Violin and Piano*

In the sense of regularly planned arrangement (not specifically of sectional length, but in the connection of similar groups), the "stanzas" can be immediately understood. In the matter, however, of "madrigals," the polyphonic liberty of the form that flourished from

191

the fifteenth to the eighteenth century is reversed; the madrigal was freer in its lines than Martinu's transliteration, which is disposed toward rhythmic transportations.

Philosophy, physics, and science were among Martinu's absorbing hobbies. He dedicated this work to Albert Einstein.

¶ Sonata for Flute and Piano

Style falls into neat, contrasting casings in this display. Martinu does not spread his wings, but writes very competent and pleasant music. This does not mean a cancellation of neat polyphonic detail, nor are contemporary touches absent from the sonata. This is lucid, convincing music.

¶ Sonatina for Clarinet and Piano

Martinu's harmony is transparent, spaced for the air to come-through. Chords in a pandiatonic cloth dress the ternary form of the opening movement and the fast flowing and Czechish rhythmic patterns of the last part. The essentials of sonata form are cut to the bone; likewise in the slow portion, which is more a preliminary to the terminal movement than a section by itself. Martinu may be imitating a generally moderate contemporary style, but his formulations are sound, agreeable ones.

¶ Three Madrigals for Violin and Viola

While there are many types of madrigals, their free contrapuntalism was the attraction for Martinu. He places the form in a predominantly dissonant, slightly polytonal instrumental setting, with defined melodic outlines.

Sonorities are all important in this opus. Densities occur at climactic points, registering with effectiveness (though enlarging the concept of the duet beyond its two-voiced scheme).

There has been criticism of Martinu's penchant for motoric rhythm—the blocked pattern of rhythmic repetition. There is a great deal of this churning in the last movement. But the so-termed fault is a value in disguise. By establishing his automotive drive, Martinu is able to enhance the middle section by complete duo-lined, contrapuntal argument.

¶ Trio No. 2 in D minor

Contrast, together with fine-grained balance, is the hallmark of this fine trio; the outer fast movements are almost exactly the same length, the *adagio* half again as long. The initial part has Czech savor, with a liquidity of theme and development; it breathes gently, is folklike and easily comprehended. In the slow movement the nationalistic spirit is much absorbed by the music's detail.

Martinu sports his choreographic impulses in the final part. Everything—themes, development, and subsidiary material—stems from the opening idea. It is cut apart and splintered for use in a formal movement, but retains its identity. The surge of this kinetic music is one of the most informative and exciting movements in all trio literature.

¶ *Piano Quartet No. 1*

Those who contend Martinu is an incorrigible rhythmist make a valid point, but only when he commits the sin of overemphasis. When the pulse patterns are as spontaneous as in this work, technique becomes secondary to artistic effect. Strong and virile rhythm is characteristic of this composition and the man who conceived it.

CHORAL

CHORAL WITH ORCHESTRA

CANTATA

¶ *Liederstrauss—auf Worte der Volkspoesie* ("Bouquet of Songs —on Words of Folk Poetry")

A very rare item from Martinu's extensive catalogue. (The writer cannot recall any American performance, since its première in Prague, in 1938).

The composition divides into an overture and seven parts. These consist of five ballades (the last in two sections), with an "Intrada" for the orchestra (a large group including two pianos) preceding the fourth vocal portion. Turn to any page of the score and there is evidence of nationalism. Martinu's musical folk tales represent only partial allegiance to contemporary factors. Native concord is in the forefront.

MASS

¶ *Field Mass, for Male Chorus, Baritone and Orchestra*

Martinu's "Field Mass" is a compound of secular and sacred moods (the text is a composite of psalms and poems by Jiří Mucha), neo-ecclesiastical and folksy style, modal choralism, and fancy brass fanfares. Composed in Paris at the start of the Second World War,

193

and conceived as a testimonial to the composer's countrymen who volunteered for service in the French army, it partly lives up to its title by being militaristic in tone. (There are no strings in the small orchestra: nine wind and brass instruments, piano and organ, plus plentiful percussion.) On the other hand, the design of the piece is much more a cantata than it is a mass.

The material matches the formal hybrid, with robust sounds flattened against somber ones. It is strung out, more melodic than generative. It has variety and continuums of nice, rich sonorities, but these are not sufficiently architectonic to register effectively. Too many fish swim in Martinu's musical pond.

19. OLIVIER MESSIAEN
(1908–   )

MESSIAEN's aesthetic viewpoint is unique. An independent voice, his music is not only enmeshed in heavy rhetoric but includes the sounds of bells, the calls of birds, and mensurally scans Hindu patterns. His devotion to ornithological song and the witchery of complex and exotically complexioned rhythms amounts to a passion. A very devout Catholic, his love for his religion is of tremendous intensity, involving his compositions in a ritual that reminds one of Scriabin, so unilateral are the creative practices. Messiaen's heavy colors, fat chords, and pseudo orientalisms equal a model of verbosity which has always been a mark of the musical mystics as they sermonized their way in sound.

To preach the word of God is Messiaen's entire and sincere purpose. As he has stated, "I am above all a Catholic musician. My . . . music . . . expresses the end of time, the ubiquity of glorious bodies, the divine and supernatural mysteries. . . ." But he does not weary his concert parishioners with dull monody or dressed up plainchant. Part of the rite is made into a delight by titillating the auditory senses with voluptuous sounds. The other side of the coin is less exciting—an overexpansiveness of similar content (a staticness) that fogs the senses.

It will be observed that Messiaen does not sing of the honesty of the Christian faith by simple means that the flock will understand, as they do Bach today. Nonetheless the imagery is spectacular. Messiaen's theoretical evangelism may use complex words and be overtaxing by its seeming redundancy, but it is always fascinating. The intriguing textures, new melodies, harmonies, and timbres, the perpetual rhythmic change may be technically fussy and fustian, but the music is rewarding because it rings true (even the disbeliever will vouch for the technical truths that are expounded). Above all, Messiaen is an advocate of sonorous outpour. Sustaining instruments are dominant in his music, the opposite situation is found in the majority of the post-Webernian school (Boulez, Stockhausen, and others). In this respect Olivier Messiaen is actually the last of the pure romanticists.

ORCHESTRAL

¶ *L'Ascension* (Four Symphonic Meditations)

With the exception of the third meditation, this cycle was originally composed for organ, in 1933, and transcribed for orchestra the following year. The scoring shows the hand of Messiaen the organist. (Oddly enough the last movement is scored for strings alone.) And the program furnished shows the hard-core philosophy of Messiaen the devout, the text being drawn from the Catholic liturgy. "The Ascension" partly parallels Messiaen's general creative conduct—it is low-keyed ecstatic music .

¶ *Turangalîla Symphony*

A symphony, yes; but forget all average ideas of the form. "Turangalîla" (meaning freely a "song of love") is an impassioned musical document for the brave and patient only. It embraces ten movements that cover almost an hour and a half of playing time. This mammoth projection is full of fervent sound surges, violent colors, and rhythmic counterpoint. Messiaen's piece is the equivalent of "Tristan and Isolde" converted into orchestral fantasies by way of Hindu-promulgated metrical plans. (The symphony is an outgrowth of three "Talas" for piano, Ondes Martenot and large orchestra.)

Some of the movements are titled, but there is no storytelling attempted. Type characterizations are used based on four cyclic themes: a fierce "statue" subject, a supple "flower" motive, a very important love theme, and a chordal idea. The cycles are interwoven and developed, as well as restated. They are supercharged by a huge orchestra plus a smaller group within it of glockenspiel, celesta, vibraphone, piano, and metallic percussion that lends a sonority like a Balinese Gamelan ensemble. The staggering piano part is almost a solo role.

"Turangalîla" poses a set of paradoxes. It is heated, pagan music, yet devout. It is complex in construction, yet totally understandable. It is exciting and volatile, but its relentless paroxysms are also irritating. It has tuned balance and orgiastic climaxes, but seems to be in a constant tumescence.

196

SOLO INSTRUMENT WITH ORCHESTRA

SOLO PIANO WITH ORCHESTRA

¶ *Oiseaux Exotiques*

In his book "The Technique of My Musical Language" Messiaen states that one of his teachers, Paul Dukas, said "Listen to the birds. They are great masters." And he has followed Dukas's dictum in this work for solo piano, wind instruments, xylophone, glockenspiel, and other percussion. The "Exotic Birds" which Messiaen depicts are not merely a compilation of birdcalls, but include a many-faceted multitude of roving rhythms. These encage and engage the avian representatives with Hindu and Greek patterns (no fewer than eleven of the former and eight of the latter). The partnership is indeed singular.

Birds have been described throughout musical history (Mozart, Beethoven, Delius, and Wagner will come immediately to mind), but never like this. According to the composer, forty birds are represented. To try to identify each one is useless. What is profitable is the timbred orgy that results in a mélange of dazzling luminescence.

Though this is music without any standard of comparison it is as convincing as it is assured, and worthy of everyone's attention. Some listeners will think they detect sounds similar to the talk of the post-serial elect. Hardly—in comparison with that group Messiaen speaks with the tongue of a classicist.

INSTRUMENTAL

FLUTE

¶ *La Merle Noir for Flute and Piano*

Although it bears a descriptive title ("The Blackbird"), Messiaen's piece is not a musical chronicle. The skittering passages (for unaccompanied flute) may remind one of the feathery tribe, but mainly the music bathes in soaring, disjunctly curved canons. There is a grace to these measures, but they are not graced by cut-and-dried metrical patterns—no time signatures compress this contemporary music. One cannot quarrel with Messiaen's devotion to bird-song interpretation. It is a kind of "my bird music, right or wrong, but my bird music."

197

ORGAN

¶ *Apparition de l'Église Éternelle*

In its slow pace and incessant progression of block chords, this is music of stolidity, without needed contrast. The coalescence is shaped by an arched dynamic plan. Messiaen's mystical organ picture is restricted in appeal by its constraint.

¶ *La Nativité du Seigneur* (Nine Meditations for Organ)

Messiaen has been quoted as saying that "God being present in all things, music dealing with theological subjects can and must be extremely varied." And "varied" means in this case a formal relaxation for each of the nine parts (divided into four books, three "meditations" in the first and third, two in the second, and one in the last). The style resembles improvisation, but is actually motival repetition. While the accent, rise and fall of rhythm are very flexible, none of the music is rhapsodic. Each meditation has a specific mood; some examples: pastoralism is the flush that colors "Les Bergers," a hazy nocturne defines "Desseins Eternels," fanfaric optimism marks the final "Dieu Parmi Nous."

The cycle gains strength on repeated hearings. Messiaen's representation of Christ's birth must be considered in total montage. To expect to recognize every small documentary detail is to lose sight of the essential grandeur and positive depth of the music.

¶ *Le Banquet Céleste*

It was this short work that brought Messiaen to the attention of the European music world. Composed in 1928, before he had attained voting age, "Le Banquet Céleste" exhibits the usual symbolism that prevails in all of Messiaen's compositions. (The music represents the Last Supper; the "celestial banquet of Holy Communion.") The hermetic harmony gives a desolate and sad tinge to the slow motion of the piece, bound further by motivic constancy. Notwithstanding, it is as purely ecstatic a declamation as Messiaen's pyrotechnic orchestral pronouncements.

¶ *Messe de la Pentecôte*

Despite its title the "Messe" is a gigantic fantasy stuffed with the composer's favorite plainchant shapes, embroidered with counterpoints, and amorphic rhythmic patterns. Included are countless bird songs, transformed and reinterpreted.

The interposition and mass combination of Messiaen's sound complexes, though exceedingly long in performance time, are not tautological. It is sonority that captivates regardless of the method. Messiaen's statement is worth recalling: "It is a glistening music we seek, giving to the aural sense voluptuously refined pleasures." But this is raw music despite the pious garb worn by the composer.

¶ *Prière du Christ montant vers son Père* (Movement 4 from "L'Ascension" [Four Meditations])

Regardless of the apparent craving for programmatic delineation, most of Messiaen's music does not follow any story. Instead it codes a specific emotional expression. The background of unceasing chordal movement presents a decisive image of beseeching, fully bearing out the mood: "Prayer of Christ Ascending towards His Father."

A music of muted florescence and shadowed inquiry that illustrates the sounds of service in the church of Olivier Messiaen. It is strangely moving.

¶ *Transports de joie d'une âme devant la Gloire du Christ que est la sienne* (Movement 3 from "L'Ascension" [Four Meditations])

This third movement is entirely different from that of the orchestral version (*see page 196*). It utilizes the full dynamism of the organ and is a tour de force of instrumental injunction in its sonic expulsions.

PIANO

¶ *Cantéyodjayâ*

Although Messiaen bases his preemptory music on rhythmic pronouncements drawn from Çârngadeva (a Hindu theorist of the thirteenth century, who formulated a set of one hundred and twenty *deci-talas* [Hindu rhythms]), his composition goes beyond mere systematic propositions. "Cantéyodjayâ" is a symphonic essay for solo piano, ranging from concentrated intensity to furious sonorescence. The piano simulates bell timbres, xylophones played with a variety of beaters, and timpanic and drum sounds.

This orchestra of one produces free music, yet obeys a form consisting of variated episodes linked by a ritornel. There is not a commonplace sound in Messiaen's score.

MESSIAEN

¶ *Vingt Regards sur l'Enfant Jésus*

Messiaen enmeshes his doctrines with occult definitions which practically require a concordance to understand. In this huge work he is describing (but never in severely ordered, programmatic fashion) the "'Contemplation of the Child-God of the Crib and the Glances which fall on Him." He utilizes certain harmonies to simulate the design of stained glass, the heavenly rainbow, and so on; or, as in section fourteen "Glance of the Angels," his remarks begin: "Flickering, throbbing; powerful blast from the trombones. . . ." These directions are translated into overly charged chordal combinations thrown about in semitortured melodic lines. The atmosphere is heavy; the effect is stifling.

Constantly astir and severely untempered in contrast, the "Vingt Regards," like Messiaen's other lengthy compositions, are taxing for a listener. The point is that too much Messiaen defeats him. For best results, his exhortations in sound should be heard in small portions.

TWO PIANOS

¶ *Visions de l'Amen*

Seven solemn ratifications of wide range, including the creation, desire, and the agony of Jesus. Messiaen claims that his musical speech is "essentially material, sacred, universal." But in speaking and singing instrumentally to his God, Messiaen does not speak for humanity. There is a caste system in his work that makes it less universal than he presumes. The music is decidedly motival, and engendered by permutative development. It tends to meander and is attenuated. "Visions de l'Amen" holds the attention mostly by its science, far less by its emotional impact.

20. DARIUS MILHAUD
(1892–   )

DARIUS MILHAUD can be considered a dual musical citizen. Since the end of the Second World War he has alternated between France and the United States, combining guest-conducting and teaching with his creative career. His advice has been sought by large numbers of eager students. Milhaud's regard for young composers makes him uniquely humanitarian.

His life has been most varied, including study with the famous d'Indy and service as an attaché at the French Legation in Rio de Janeiro (a stay which later inspired Milhaud's well-known "Saudades do Brasil"). In 1919 Milhaud returned to France, where he joined with five other French composers (Auric, Tailleferre, Poulenc, Honegger, and Durey) in the formation of "The Six." The main credo of this group was simplicity. However, the strength of personalities eventually caused the partnership to dissolve. "The Six" is now important only in a historical sense.

Milhaud is extremely prolific (he has composed almost four hundred works!), yet this spontaneity does not result in mere shallowness or banality. Most of his compositions have individuality and profile, fluency and freshness. There runs through his music the true French spirit of outright clarity and engaging simplicity. The common sense of his work perpetuates the French tradition that began with Rameau, and led to Berlioz and Debussy. It evolves in his hands, braced by the most contemporary spirit.

Any discussion of Milhaud must take cognizance of his use of combined key schemes; the greater part of his music is concerned with the technique of bitonality and polytonality. This determines Milhaud's pure lines, with their cogent and extremely expressive melodicism. (The writing of simple, yet not elementary melodies is a difficulty frustrating many composers, but not Darius Milhaud.) By careful use of chromatically cleansed thematic strands the various keys are uncompromisingly indicated. Milhaud stands in first place as the modern lyrical poet of polyphonicism.

Combining various keys does not form a geometric tonality cube. There is never any sense of atonalism or total key negation. Milhaud goes the opposite way from Schoenberg. Both are expressionists. Milhaud outwardly, deliberately stating defined tonality; Schoenberg inwardly, purposely excluding any sense of key. Milhaud has order and reason, the strictest premise of tonality extension short of collapse by use of simultaneous key centers.

ORCHESTRAL

¶ *Kentuckiana* (Divertissement on Twenty Kentucky Airs)

Milhaud is so prone to thematic combination that it is almost an injustice to expect him to do otherwise. Such avidness for polyphony is given a heady workout in this collocation, wherein twenty Kentucky tunes are employed without inhibition. Yet Milhaud knows that excessivity can lead to sonorous indigestion and that the antidote is the tuneful diatonic shape of an instrumental voice so that it does not become too difficult to extract from the total mass. The listener must assist . . . by using both ears. It is rather fun to hear "Sweet Betsy from Pike" and other lusty American airs in the colorful intonations of a Frenchman.

¶ *La Muse Ménagère* ("The Household Muse")

Musical representation is the method in this case, manifested by the use of very specific descriptive titles. However, Milhaud's orchestral picture-painting is more idealized than actual. It is exciting to await a composer's tonal realization of "Cooking" or "The Cat," for example, but these particular movements sound almost the same as others named "Household Cares," and "The Laundry." Darius Milhaud is no Richard Strauss in portraying his "domestic symphony."

¶ *Ouverture Méditerranéenne*

Milhaud's overture, written for the Louisville Orchestra, shows middle-age sag. One can be charitable and say that it is light, moves along at a nice pace, and has a neat tune here and there. However, it doesn't say a thing that the composer hasn't said before, and said better. The Mediterranean elements (*sic?*) are to be found in the dance melodies of the central part of the piece. For music written by a masterly composer, the pickings are lean.

¶ *Protée—Symphonic Suite No. 2*

The high spirits of this five-sectioned suite are most apparent. "Protée" is devoid of any pose; it is fresh and sometimes arrogant

202

. . . sophisticated, with a devil-may-care attitude about it, yet never cheap. The music is chatty, but not gibberish . . . nervous, but not strained.

Our norms of behavior differ widely, and no law dictates how we should behave at concerts. Nowadays, it is rare to have spontaneous disapproval registered at an artistic affair. In 1920, when this work was first produced in Paris, it incited behavior comparable to a gang fight. Milhaud describes the brawl in his book *Notes Without Music,* and it covered everything from musicians slapping each other to police intervention. Disapproval by reactionaries tends to make a work significant rather than producing artistic sanctions against it. We listen to Milhaud's opus today wondering what sort of climate there was in Europe that could cause such a "succès de scandale."

¶ Saudades do Brasil

Originally composed for piano, Milhaud transcribed this suite of dances at the request of the conductor, Vladimir Golschmann. (For details, *see* Piano *below.*) The fertile polytonality that covers the score is clarified by the instrumental color streams, and the rhythmic *chic* is likewise enhanced by the varied timbres. These salty and swingy "recollections" are full of surprises—one example: the final cadence of "Laranjeiras," which offers a musical O. Henry twist.

¶ Serenade

Baroque rhythmic bustle and gay melodies describe the end *Vif* movements. This joyously diversified ebullience (stimulated by smart harmonic-contrapuntal key conflict) is retained in a more placid state in the song contours of the *Tranquille* section. Milhaud's characteristic, but not overemphasized polytonality is no anachronism in the format of a modern serenade for orchestra.

¶ Suite from "Maximilien"

Taken from one of the three operas Milhaud has composed about the Americas ("Christophe Colomb," and "Bolivar" are the others). The operatic conception of the ill-fated Emperor of Mexico has not been produced often; the severity of the polytonal range has been an aesthetic barricade against acceptance. Key combinations are the compass that directs the music. While this simultaneity of opposed tonalities is strikingly bold and clear, its overpossessiveness reacts in reverse and enfeebles the work. Though the suite consists only of orchestral interludes and the overture from the opera (which forms

203

the finale here), it offers sufficient proof of why Milhaud's other stage works are quite superior.

¶ *Suite Provençale*

Old period themes are a fruitful resource for many a composer. In the eight movements of this suite Milhaud utilizes eighteenth-century dance tunes of his native Provence and some themes by André Campra, a French composer who lived from the middle of the seventeenth century to the middle of the eighteenth. Though the tonality scheme is somewhat removed from the 1700's there is a more than passing regard for classical simplicity and purity.

The "Suite Provençale" is a charming work of superb lyricism and sunny disposition. Musicality springs forth from every measure, contrary to the stereotyped pedanticism so often found in compositions based on material from earlier eras. Milhaud's folksy music is both documentary and personal; it is irresistible.

¶ *Symphony No. 1*

In his initial full-scale symphony, Milhaud is a bit preoccupied with pat formulas. The opening "Pastoral" is no rural reflection, but jogs on moderately animated feet in a "busy" fashion, while the second movement is a consideration of stereophonized lines. The third section turns out to be a wonderful waltz harmonized with iced spice and some heated vinegar. The final part is, again, a mechanical development of the basic theme—a dissonant chorale. All of this is unmistakable Milhaud, but symphonically hardly rewarding.

¶ *Symphony No. 2*

One of the noteworthy (the pun is intended) examples in the Milhaud catalogue. Composed for the Koussevitzky Music Foundation, the second symphony is in five movements, each defined by mood indications rather than tempi. The first is "Peaceful," the second "Mysterious," succeeded by a superb section titled "Painful." The music's grave character hints at elegy. Such temper is a Frenchman's melancholy moment—his *triste*—and not uncommon to many of that country's composers. Movement four is marked "With Serenity," and the symphony is completed by an "Alleluia." This last portion is jammed with counterpoint, but Milhaud's triumphant fugue is not overcrowded and fussy.

Orchestration is a unique art in Milhaud's hands. Many pages of his scores would seem to be poorly balanced, overdetailed, heavy, with too many people residing in the orchestral house at one time. But

204

performance under a skillful conductor proves these fears unfounded. The second symphony is imaginative and telling; the orchestration is a dominant part of its coherence and variety.

¶ *Symphony No. 4* ("1848")

In 1947 Milhaud received a request from the Minister of Education of France for a work to celebrate the centenary of the 1848 Revolution. As usual, it took little time for Milhaud to compose the piece. He set his symphony in the common four-movement arrangement, subtitling the divisions to represent "Insurrection," "To the Dead of the Republic," "The Peaceful Joys of Regained Liberty," and "Commemoration 1948."

Polyphony is presented here to its usual large degree. It denotes an abstract, cold compositional logic, though within the woven lines and conjugated melodies the ideas of each movement (with an assist from the descriptive titles) are fairly clear. Nevertheless, the feeling remains that the symphony is almost a vain effort to show off an ability for linear musical arrangement. As a result, not one of the themes remains in the memory.

CHAMBER ORCHESTRA

¶ *The Globetrotter Suite*

Milhaud's talents as an imagist have long been proven by his excellent film and ballet scores. His ingenuity is displayed in works dealing with large, dramatic subjects; his spirituality is evidenced in cantatas, psalm settings, and a service for the synagogue. No matter the goal, Milhaud has been able to portray successfully whatever he wishes. And most of his work has been by rule of art, and not by the academic thumb.

It is a novel and challenging idea to illustrate the representative personalities of various countries in a work for a small group of instruments. Each sketch is animated by clever, musical cartooning, in deft, yet not overdone style. The chicness of France, the nonchalance of Portugal, and the general temperaments of Mexico, Brazil, Italy, and the United States are each delineated. No nation is flattered or given a vague silhouette in these orchestral profiles.

¶ *The Joys of Life* (Homage to Watteau)

The psychological factors which often block a composer's production when he is requested to write in a specified medium are not the

205

case with Darius Milhaud. Commissioned by Irving Mills of Mills Music, the publishers, for a composition that would help shape the taste and proficiency of the younger generation, Milhaud wrote the score for this six-movement suite between February 8 and 19 of 1957. Employing his talents in pleasurable focus, Milhaud utilizes an instrumental combination of classical chasteness (flute, oboe, clarinet, bassoon, trumpet, and four strings) to display musical solutions of the present.

The Watteau reference concerns scenes from the painter's "Les Charmes de la Vie." Liquid sonorities, sense and sensitivity mirror the past in the minuet, gigue, serenade, and musette. These portions are akin to writing on a slate with very soft chalk, compared to "The Indifferent" and "Masquerade," which are the equivalents of painting with bright oils on a canvas.

¶ *Three Rag Caprices*

Originally for piano (*see page 213*) and orchestrated for a small ensemble five years later. Milhaud captures the philosophy of the jazzmen's work, merely changing their language with bitonal and polytonal synonyms. Cute and colorful, expressive and entertaining.

STRING ORCHESTRA

¶ *Symphony No. 4 for Strings*

Milhaud has duplicated the numbering of the first six of his eight symphonies. Though this is confusing, there is a difference in the two groups. First composed was a set of six "petite" symphonies (meaning not only small in size and scope but chamber-styled in instrumentation), each scored for a different combination; then followed the symphonies numbers one to eight for large orchestra (the third with chorus).

The first three of the "petite" group are titled: "Le Printemps," "Pastorale," and "Serenade"; the fifth is a dectet for winds; the sixth, with no title, calls for the unusual combination of oboe, cello, and vocal quartet! The fourth is actually a dectet for four violins, and two each of viola, cello, and double bass, though the parts may be multiplied. Like all the other "petite" symphonies it has three movements.

"Symphony No. 4" is music of utopian timbre intensity, with Bachian strength and contrapuntal mobility in the "Ouverture," an umbrageous "Chorale," with uncompromising harmonic acidity, and a breathtaking polyphonic acrostic in the final "Etude." This section is doubly contrapuntal by sheer force of individual line and direct fugal sensibility. It may be criticized as a mechanically conceived music, but it is magnificently apportioned.

BAND

¶ Suite Française

Originally composed for band, but very often heard in transcription for orchestra (an unusual reversal of matters). Milhaud's purpose was to write for the average school group, but technical boundaries do not suffocate art. The product (including some contemporaneously dressed folk tunes) is a work of brilliance and virtuosity without requiring virtuosi.

SOLO INSTRUMENT WITH ORCHESTRA

CONCERTOS

¶ Concerto for Percussion and Small Orchestra

All Milhaud needs to do is rub his creative lamp and music jumps to his command. In this unique concerto one percussionist plays a number of instruments: timpani, five types of drums (one with cymbal attachment), metal and wood blocks, cymbals (clashed and suspended), triangle, tam-tam, castanets, slapstick, and rattle, accompanied by four woodwinds, two brass, and a small group of strings. The usual concerto compound is compressed into one movement and ends quietly. The percussion unit furnishes rhythmic commentary and obbligato points, as well as colorful soloism. This is a standard Milhaud production, though no mundane results are implied by such description. (*Note:* there have been a few percussion concerti composed for solo timpani and orchestra or percussion group with orchestra; Milhaud's was the first.)

¶ Concerto No. 1 for Cello and Orchestra

This is one of Milhaud's best concertos. Its architecture is very stable, set in patterns which follow the traditional validity of three-movement plan, with contrastingly balanced tempi (moderate-slow-fastest). In the middle part (marked *Grave*) Milhaud reaches an emotional plane he rarely seeks. Like matched opponents, orchestra and cello create a trenchant concerto drama by their opposition, in this case conveyed by the timbres themselves as much as the themes. After this strong musical dish, the following portion, "a sort of Italian saltarella," is like a serving of dessert.

¶ Concerto No. 1 for Piano and Orchestra

The music's bittersweet polyphony (with an ending that seems to be a tonal *non sequitur*) is typical Milhaud. The composition will doubtless represent atypical concerto fare to those who think the medium means rousing romantic roulades. Symmetrically tempoed in its end movements, the opus has a Milhaudian reformation of a barcarolle in the center, which is extremely rare in the concerto world. One fault—a major one: the insistence of the solo voice is almost crucially inflexible and tends to be too Herculean.

¶ Concerto No. 2 for Violin and Orchestra

Milhaud substantiates Milhaud here. The method employed combines classical clarity with polytonal address. It is observed in the opening theme which is embraced with chordal counterpoint that touches various keys. It continues with the clear and somber (yet limpid) melodic line of the inner movement against a shifting grey-colored background, with all individual points carefully stating their tonal affiliation. It is certified by the impetuosity of the last movement. The bracing technique of the composer offers rewards when it is so clearly utilized.

¶ Concerto No. 4 for Piano and Orchestra

Milhaud's target is most apparent in this three-movement work, commissioned by the pianist Zadel Skolovsky, and written in 1949, during one of the composer's sojourns in the United States. Neatly dovetailed, the music alternates between the sport of dance rhythms and pace and the atmospheric nostalgia of Paris, circa 1920, that has never departed from the composer's thoughts. The peppy last movement is most individual, with expedient "wrong note" harmony, and the appetizing busyness that motivates most of Milhaud's fast music.

SOLO PIANO WITH ORCHESTRA

¶ Cinq Etudes ("Five Studies") for Piano and Orchestra

Darius Milhaud's polytonal worship exists in the "Cinq Etudes." His contrapuntal legerdemain is given the fullest exposure; the effect

208

is fantastic and fascinating. The third section, for example, is a composite of four simultaneous fugues: one each in the winds, strings, brass, and piano!

Milhaud has indicated that each study deals with "a different problem of harmony and construction," and by use of multitonality he obtains "a more subtle sweetness and a greater intensity of violence." With little exception, the instrumental conversation of these fairly short conceptions is like a boisterous musical cocktail party where all the guests talk at the same time about different things.

At the first performance, in 1921, the result was audience bewilderment and, according to Milhaud, "the hall became rowdy." This perplexity can continue unless the performance is in the hands of a conductor who realizes exactly what goes on in Milhaud's cyclonic multiplicity. For that matter, the listener must give the music his undivided attention, even when the conductor is fully comprehending. Unfortunately, for the time being, no one seems to want to give Milhaud's galvanic invention the opportunity of being heard.

¶ *Le Carnaval d'Aix*

The subtitle of this work denotes the original source of its material: "Fantaisie pour Piano et Orchestre d'après 'Salade'." Milhaud took twelve sections from his *ballet chanté* and turned them into a witty and scintillating work for piano and orchestra. It has no pyrotechnical premises, no momentous musical moralizing; it is highbrow honky-tonk. The carnival of characters (including a peppy Polichinelle) and dance turns (such as a polka, tango, maxixe, and waltz) form a real frolic; rarely sober, quite often ribald. Milhaud's music travels between light limericks and the brash musical revues to be seen in Parisian cafés. Almost forty years old, it is still fresh.

¶ *The Four Seasons* (*see below* under individual instruments for: "Concertino d'Automne," "Concertino d'Hiver," "Concertino d'Eté," and "Concertino de Printemps")

[*Since Milhaud, in his recording of this cycle, approved the above title, we must accept it. However, it should be realized that this was a decision made long after the creative facts. The composition of the works, covering a seventeen-year period, did not follow the solstitial order. Milhaud's conceptions of the seasons interlocked. They began with spring, then jumped to autumn, followed by summer and winter (the years of composition are 1934 for the first, 1951 for the next*

209

two, and 1953 for the last). The parallel to Vivaldi's famous "Seasons" occurred to Milhaud later, accounting for the lack of such heading in any of the published scores.

[*The four concertinos are distinct, and are usually performed separately. Each calls for a different solo voice and varied group of instruments in support. "Autumn" is for two pianos with two winds, three horns, and three strings; "Winter" is scored for trombone and strings; "Summer" calls for viola accompanied by four winds, two brass, two cellos, and double bass; while "Spring" is set for violin and chamber orchestra. However, a recording is available of the cycle as a unit.*]

Two Solo Pianos with Orchestra

¶ *Concertino d'Automne for Two Pianos and Eight Instruments*
The main theme is simple and gentle. Then the music develops into contrasting, cross-patched counterpoints; the fresh tunes swimming in a bath of dissonant colors and lathered lines. Milhaud's autumnal tints are on the darker side, employing three horns, two violas, and a cello, lightened only by a flute and a oboe.

Solo Trombone with Orchestra

¶ *Concertino d'Hiver for Trombone and String Orchestra*
Of the works in Milhaud's "Seasons" "d'Hiver" and "de Printemps" most closely identify with the descriptive titles. "Winter" is adumbrated by the trombone's low gamut . . . it growls. General timbre disassociation from the supporting string body indicates a partial pictorial realization that Milhaud undoubtedly sought. Thus the coolness and aloofness; the thematic material could apply to any time of the year.

Solo Viola with Orchestra

¶ *Concertino d'Eté for Viola and Nine Instruments*
Patterned thinking and a ternary design are manifest here. The first is a codification of style heavily drawn from clichés in Milhaud's own inventory. Attenuated in construction, Milhaud's summer music is unimportant and dull. The "Concertino d'Eté" is the weakest part of the "Four Seasons" cycle.

SOLO VIOLIN WITH ORCHESTRA

¶ *Concertino de Printemps for Violin and Chamber Orchestra*

A charming example of concentrated music, its solidity contains no extraneous packing. What is particularly enchanting is the manner in which Milhaud symbolizes the vernal atmosphere while retaining his style of carefully combined tonalities. A number of thoughts are discussed in the piece: each is stated, reconfirmed, quickly concluded, and then the music skims off to the next idea. The coda, which disassembles one of the themes while the solo violin skitters like a bird, is a marvelous way of clinching a proposition without long-winded musical oratory.

RECITER WITH ENSEMBLE

¶ *Cantate de l'Enfant et de la Mère*

Milhaud's "Cantate" is on the periphery of chamber music, since the vocal part is conceived as rhythmic recitation and thus fuses with the string quartet and piano. The text (divided into twelve sections) is by Maurice Carême, a young Belgian poet. Though the composer's beloved harmonic frictions are included, in the main the music is gentle, floating along with the beautifully formed prose. The piece conveys general mood impressions rather than narrative detail.

Milhaud's choice of string quartet and piano with reciter was dictated by a desire to combine the talents of some of his friends. The composition was written for the twenty-fifth anniversary concerts of the Pro Arte Quartet (of Belgium), a group that had been closely associated with Milhaud's music. Paul Collaer, long a close comrade and biographer of the composer, played the piano, and Milhaud's wife was the reciter. The composer conducted the initial performance (May 18, 1938).

INSTRUMENTAL

HARMONICA

¶ *Chanson du Marin*

In 1942 Milhaud composed, as his 234th work, a "Suite" for harmonica and orchestra, most often heard in an alternate version for violin. The composition had been commissioned by Larry Adler. (He

211

and John Sebastian, represent the most distinguished virtuosi of this once-humble instrument.)

The "Chanson du Marin" is the middle movement of the three comprising the suite. It matters little whether the solo voice is supported by orchestra or piano in Milhaud's sensitive and quiet expression of Gallic nostalgia. It matters much that some important composers have recognized and taken advantage of the special capabilities of this miniature instrument: including Vaughan Williams, Villa-Lobos, Gordon Jacob, Malcolm Arnold, Tcherepnin, and others. Approve or condemn the harmonica, it cannot be ignored any longer.

ORGAN

¶ *Pastorale*

If there is no special individuality to this short item, at least it does possess charm in its vernal, *bel canto* style. Above all it avoids the curse of much organ music: pedantic and dusty voice couplings.

PIANO

¶ *L'Album de Madame Bovary*

Seventeen extracts from the score Milhaud composed for the film "Madame Bovary," produced by Jean Renoir. A compendium of Schumannesque melody, sensitively colored by Milhaud's special harmonic synonyms. The suite gives full evidence of the composer's lyrical gift, reminding one of the fundamental warmth, the flow, spirit, and clarity of the French clavecinists.

¶ *La Muse Ménagère* ("The Household Muse")

Program music is difficult with a keyboard instrument. A better guide is available in the orchestral setting (*see page 202*), even though Milhaud's explanations are rather vague.

¶ *Saudades do Brasil*

One of the most enjoyable of Milhaud's multitudinous compositions. Composed in Paris, in 1921, after he had returned from a stay in Brazil, the pieces reflect his memories of Brazil's musical climate. Each of the dozen items is distinctly Latin-American in rhythm, but folk tunes are not used at all. No fiery, passionate mannerisms are exhibited, but rather uninhibited Parisianism (festooned with Milhaud's picturesque harmonic combinations) framing the native elements. The various titles (colorful by themselves, such as "Sorocabo," "Boto-fogo," and "Copacabana") mean nothing. They simply identify municipal districts in Rio de Janeiro.

¶ *Three Rag Caprices*

Milhaud traces ragtime's rhythmic reflexes and charts these with his own type of harmonic crayon. The textures are economical, the music elastic, with primal style and hedonistic tone. (The version for orchestra is discussed on page 206.)

¶ *Touches Blanches and Touches Noires* ("White Keys" and "Black Keys")

These pieces are so short they almost sound like elusive improvisations. The first is a waltz and the second resembles a lullaby. Both show Milhaud's ability to spin a tune.

Two Pianos

¶ *Scaramouche*

The title may recall Sabatini's novel of the same name. It is purely coincidental. Milhaud's choice is predicated on the word's meaning—*buffoon* or *scamp*—borne out by the music's diverting representation, for the most part, of mischief-making temper. One of the "classics" of contemporary two-piano literature, "Scaramouche" was actually derived from music written for two plays. Such self-helping is found in a number of places in Milhaud's catalogue. All to the good, since only a fractional total of incidental music has lasting properties, whereas "Scaramouche" is one of Milhaud's triumphs.

"Scaramouche" is cross-sectioned by brashness. This is especially noticeable in the music-hall potpourri of the opening, which carries strains of many light tunes, including the old radio chorus "We want Cantor." Movement two has a bittersweet pertness. Dash and flash return in the final portion, a Brazilian souvenir that rocks and rolls (officially a samba).

Four Pianos

¶ *Brasileira from "Scaramouche"*

A little doctoring of the two-piano score for purposes of a group known as "The Original Piano Quartet." (No credit is given for the arrangement, but it is doubtless by one of the team members.)

213

VIOLIN

¶ *Danses de Jacarémirim*

Three Brazilian evocations (a samba, tango, and chôro), each of diminutive size. The melodies contain a modicum of spice and are covered with winy, harmonic sauce. No complexity to this slightly intellectual salon music. It is thoroughly enjoyable. (The title "Dances of the Little Alligator," though picturesque, has nothing to do with the music.)

¶ *Saudades do Brasil*

Six of the dozen pieces within the original piano suite (first transcribed by the composer for orchestra) were arranged for violin and piano by Claude Lévy (another version of portions of the suite exists for cello and piano).

CHAMBER MUSIC

¶ *Sonata No. 2 for Violin and Piano*

In this early work (written at the age of 25) Milhaud concludes his adolescent romanticism, and goes on to examine tonality.

The first movement of the sonata (dedicated to André Gide) is a "Pastorale"—a mood present often in Milhaud's works. It includes the parallel movement of unrelated keys such as the triple combination of B♭, D, and A♭ major. Partnered tonality is very marked in sections of the slow movement, with C major triads cascading against pentatonic sharped tones. The last part is free in form and implies a bitonal conclusion.

¶ *Sonatine for Flute and Piano*

In coupling a wind instrument with the piano balance is all important. Milhaud's balance of sound makes this piece a gem. All the flute's registers are used; it functions as a cosmopolitan instrument in a work that can well serve as an example to other composers. In words expressed several centuries ago by William Byrd, the English composer, Milhaud's "Sonatine" is "well sorted and ordered."

There is no slow movement. The first (marked "Tendre") is smooth in texture, highlighted by a constant piano motive of seconds, used either singly or combined. The "Souple" second movement is barcarolle-like, joining flowing rhythm with jazz punctuations. Part three ("Clair") is tightly strung; its brilliance is a decided dramatic stroke, while subtle humor is not ignored by the exceedingly soft, final cadence. All this adds up to neat music, not thought-provoking, but the production of an expert.

¶ *Pastorale for Oboe, Clarinet and Bassoon*

A clear, light effusion, so light that it could serve as background music for a fashion show.

¶ *Sonata for Two Violins and Piano*

Milhaud's trio for the less ordinary string combination of two violins (instead of a violin and a cello) with piano is an example of chamber-music transparency. The music is beautifully measured by pastoral tints with an elasticity that is the result of relaxed and free artistic vigor.

An early Milhaud item, the "Sonata" is as good as the later-period works. Composed in the country, it illustrates the composer's ideas of impressionism, written with a two- and three-pronged polytonal pen. The second movement is especially bucolic; the atmosphere is clear and the arabesques give the suggestion of feathery flight.

¶ *Suite* (d'après Corrette)

This woodwind trio for oboe, clarinet, and bassoon is very light and Parisian, very much a Milhaud production, and saturated with semi-archaic fundamentals. Milhaud's opus (originally played as incidental music for a "Romeo and Juliet" production) is based on themes by Michel Corrette, a French composer of the first part of the eighteenth century. Its eight designs include a "Tambourin," "Musette," "Rondeau," three rigidly measured minuets, and the like. The essential point of the music is pithy and tart, a set of fancies so disciplined by the composer that the classic shapes of the work are cozy, yet alive with imaginative temper.

¶ *Suite for Violin, Clarinet and Piano*

Contemporary chamber music not only differs from that of the earlier periods in form, harmonic style, and rhythm. Very often it delights in using a combination that consists exclusively of mixed timbres.

Milhaud's trio is a study of some of the color and sonority possible

215

in the combination of a string, wind, and keyboard instrument. Matching these textural shifts is the French manner of Milhaud's musical illuminations. Rarely has this composer been as charming and gracious.

¶ *Sonata for Flute, Oboe, Clarinet and Piano*

Since the tone quality of the woodwinds is so distinctive, their use in counterpoint is very productive. In the association of keys instead of lines the same value is derived. Polytonality becomes more striking, more lucid, as in this quartet.

The ternary-designed first movement has the pastoral blend so typical of the composer. His technical turn of expression is immediately recognizable in the second part. However, by instrumentational definition Milhaud avoids the tonal mud that might occur from his prodigious polytonal mixture. Movement three ("Emporté") also joggles the keys freely, producing percussion by way of the tonality clash. In the last section ("Douloureux") the feeling is akin to a funeral march. Tight rhythms, pulsed trumpetlike fanfares, and bell-like sounds give a dimly screened picture of gray-black catastrophe. The unrest and key obscuration are only released into pure C major in the very last measure. Milhaud's amalgamations are no blatant stunt; they produce music of meaning and importance.

¶ *String Quartet No. 6 in G*

Al fresco music for four stringed instruments. Each section is precise, balanced, and fluidly controlled without superfluity. In this work, Milhaud reaches the mellow period of urbanity in his string-quartet compositions. This opus shows him at peace with his poly-tones and polyharmonies.

The first portion is supple in feeling, animated in spirit. This is followed by music slow in tempo, irregular in pulsation, toasted to a contrapuntal turn. The last part of the quartet is a rhythmic alert. Practically every measure calls on a different gauge, such as 3/8, 4/8, 2/8, 5/8, and 6/8—no interference with the movement's catchiness, however. This finale displays Milhaud's winning scherzo manner, obtained by tossing the rhythmic ball about in 103 metrical changes!

¶ *String Quartet No. 12*

Milhaud's work, composed in memory of Gabriel Fauré (on the hundredth anniversary of his birth) expresses a very definite classical clarity. Movement one is of individual plan; it is paced by an introduction that appears as the epilogue as well, embracing a large, fully developed ternary design. The noble four-measure subject of the middle section of the quartet appears nine times during the course of the movement. Part three is excited by determined imitation and the pile-up of *stretti*.

Though Fauré did not believe in the combining of keys, he was no creative bigot. As one who turned his back on the academicism of the late nineteenth century he would have had to admire Milhaud's brilliant quartet, regardless of its polytonality.

¶ Divertissement en Trois Parties for Wind Quintet

The thrust of moving voices is paramount in this triple serving of chamber music. Line cross-checks line and keys do likewise here; the most pointed portion being the middle "Dramatique." Rhythmic pertness and melodic tunefulness prevent boredom. All of it has been said before by Milhaud and illustrates his retentive memory for his own music.

¶ La Cheminée du Roi René—Suite for Woodwind Quintet

According to the score the king in this chamber-music tale was born in 1409 and died in 1480, lived in Aix-en-Provence (Milhaud's birthplace), and was beloved by his subjects. The king often walked on what is now a main boulevard called "La Cheminée du Roi René."

Non-narrative in form, Milhaud's seven-movement work has the feeling of the times it celebrates. The poetic moods and engaging pulsatile swing of these miniatures describe, in a general way, such things as a "Cortege," "Jousts on the Arc," and "Hunting at Valabre." Nothing intellectual, but enjoyable woodwind musical exhibits.

¶ Two Sketches for Woodwind Quintet

Deeply felt short pieces (a "Madrigal" and "Pastoral"), with the composer exceptionally restrained. Part one casts off formal anchors. The rhythmic flow of part two is animated by combining duple- and triple-pulse points within the steady flow of two beats per measure.

This music was composed in 1941 and consists of sections one and two of a work entitled "Four Sketches," for orchestra, or clarinet with piano, or solo piano. The original first movement (the second "sketch" in the woodwind quintet edition) is titled "Eglogue," not "Pastoral."

VOCAL

¶ *Chansons de Ronsard*

Music written for a coloratura specialist (Lily Pons), with no holds barred. There are positive differences in the four songs. The first is a Frenchy, nineteen-twenties portion, the second an ornately fashioned romantic bit, followed by a vocal exhibitionistic concoction which reminds one of a whiz-bang operatic "stop-the-action" aria. It concludes with a grand-scale quasi-folksy piece.

¶ *Poèmes Juifs*

Milhaud begins his autobiography, *Notes Without Music,* with the statement: "I am a Frenchman from Provence, and by religion a Jew." He has composed a number of works on Jewish subjects, but very few of these display any Hebraic musical traits. Though the eight songs comprising the "Jewish Poems" are fluent and fluid pieces, they offer no vital connection with the unified title; the music could fit any poetry, despite the original Hebrew from which the texts were translated.

VOICE WITH ORCHESTRA

¶ *Air de Manuela and Berceuse from "Bolivar"*

Though it held the boards for two successive seasons, "Bolivar" passed into apparent oblivion after its last presentation in Paris during the 1951–52 season. The first excerpt displays an admirable way of handling an involved chromatic line with finesse. For the most part the lullaby bears out its title, though it arches into an involved, contrasting section that is anything but restful.

¶ *Chansons de Ronsard*

The setting with piano (*see* Vocal *above*) will charm many; with orchestra (the original version) it has more merit.

¶ *Fontaines et Sources*

The six parts of "Fontaines et Sources" include the counterpointed textures so dear to the composer but have the supple purity requisite

218

for a satisfying and dramatically effective vocal work. Combining a voice with a busy orchestral background always poses a problem of balance; it is accomplished successfully in this case.

¶ *Les Quatre Eléments*

Beautifully conceived formulations of four poems by Robert Desnos, originally composed for soprano and tenor with orchestra, but changed later to a setting for solo soprano. The four substances: water, earth, fire, and air are not considered in any descriptive sense. In fact there is a somewhat aristocratic order to these songs. Most of the color is assigned to the orchestra.

CHORAL

¶ *Psalm 121*

Chordal force is a traditional device in choral music, but in Milhaud's hands the harmonies run contrary to the textbook facts. In this sixty-seven measure piece (identified incorrectly in Milhaud's catalogue of works as "Psalm 126"), composed for the Harvard Glee Club, some pure diatonicism can be heard, but before everything else it is music of partnered tonality. A particularly expressive point is the murmured conclusion set in six parts which juxtaposes F and G major. Save for a little spray of canon the work is practically void of counterpoint.

CHORAL WITH ORCHESTRA

¶ *Sabbath Morning Service*

Ranging far and wide, Milhaud's catalogue includes a number of compositions pertaining to Hebrew topics. Among the more important of these are the "Poèmes Juifs," a Purim opera "Esther de Carpentras," the "Candelabre à Sept Branches," several pieces dealing with Palestinian songs and dances, the opera "David," and the "Sabbath Morning Service." By far the strongest and most fervent is the last, a major opus in four parts, divided into twenty sections.

In this production for the synagogue, Milhaud demonstrates his doctrines in more orthodox ways than usual. While choral thrust is matched by chordal incisiveness, diatonic disposition forms the major realization of the text. Structural balance with warm, devotional feeling replaces uncompromising polytonal viscidity. Milhaud adapts his style to the eloquent content of his chosen subject.

219

CANTATA

¶ *Cantate Nuptiale*

Four excerpts from the "Song of Songs," written in 1937 as a miniature cantata to celebrate the golden wedding anniversary of the composer's parents. The words are not clarified by the music, but there is no mistaking the composition's sentiments. An essentially French composer is pouring out clear, vernal melody.

¶ *Le Retour de l'Enfant Prodigue* ("The Return of the Prodigal Child")

Opposites detract from each other in Milhaud's cantata for five voices and twenty-one instruments, written to a text by André Gide. A relatively early opus (Milhaud's forty-second), composed in 1917, the polytonal fat in the instrumental fire splatters the constant declamatory vocal line. And that is all there is to this very long work wherein over-logic destroys the basic logic. Milhaud's method is crucially inflexible, especially because the cantata is all talk, no action, lacks a climax, and is minus dynamic and textural contrast.

¶ *Les Deux Cités* ("The Two Cities")

A type of baroque grandeur is established in this musical edifice. The plastic lines are engaged constantly in new projections (Milhaud does not repeat himself exactly) as subtle contrasts distinguish the three sections ("Babylon," "Elegy," and "Jerusalem").

The first of these is more vertically disposed than is the final portion, which is triumphant both in text and contrapuntal exhibition. In the "Elegy" there is recitative inquiry. Divisionally planned, yet compact and stylistically related, Milhaud's miniature *a cappella* cantata shows how to deal with an old form in terms of modern estimation. "The Two Cities" is a little known small masterpiece.

BALLET

¶ *La Création du Monde* ("The Creation of the World")

The easygoing assurance with which Milhaud usually fashions his music (wholesale polyphony crisscrossed with multitonalism) is anything but romantically lyrical. It becomes almost noisy, in the artistic sense. When the very same formula is disposed with subtlety the effect is thrice powerful. Whereas scholasticism can be argued in many of the symphonies and quartets, because Milhaud cherishes his own tradition, the same technique, mingled with 1920-style American jazz make "The Creation of the World" one of the composer's most exciting and delicious pieces.

Milhaud's admiration for jazz (most of his research was made in New York's Harlem district) has been asserted by utilizing the idiom, either explicitly or as a metaphorical means, in many portions of his compositions. In "La Création du Monde" the inventory includes a blues, a jazzy fugue, ragtime beat, trombone smears, and other sonic accouterments of the popular dialect. A dance combo type of instrumentation makes a perfect frame for the structure; the score calling for 16 soloists plus percussion, with an alto saxophone replacing the viola in the string quintet. The orchestrational lingo produces jazz as it should be spoken—properly improper. All this is decidedly apt for a ballet and just as fitting for concert listening.

Milhaud's "Creation" was one of the first sizable works in the jazz genre, antedating George Gershwin's "Rhapsody in Blue" by a year. Oddly, the former has many Gershwin-like turns, but by following correct chronology one would have to state that Gershwin's famous piece reflects a great deal of Milhaud ideas. Either way, Milhaud's synthesis of neoclassicism and juicy jazz remains a masterpiece.

¶ Le Boeuf sur le Toit

Originally, "Le Boeuf sur le Toit" (its English title is "The Nothing Doing Bar") was conceived as a "cinema symphony" to be used as the accompaniment for a silent movie comedy. Its high-class, honky-tonk, five-and-dime prattle would have served this objective admirably. Instead, it was "imagined and arranged" as a ballet by Jean Cocteau, who invented a mad stage concoction that anticipated the era of Surrealism.

Made from Brazilian tangos, sambas, maxixes, and so on, with one tune binding the mélange (appearing fifteen times!), the score is sophisticated, yet properly low-down. The cocktail tunes, spiked with polytonality, produce a wonderful sweet and sour jam session. Milhaud's marvelous farce music requires no dramatic action.

¶ Les Rêves de Jacob ("Jacob's Dreams")

Milhaud's "suite chorégraphique" was planned to meet two objectives—a ballet with chamber-music instrumentation and a quintet for

221

concert purposes. Therefore, the published score is without descriptive subtitles, though it retains the picturesque principal heading.

The several episodes in Jacob's life are not markedly identified. In the second dream portion a vigorous fugue, in *fortissimo,* is rather opposed to "lutte avec l'ange et bénediction." Further, the first dream sequence, indicated as "l'échelle des anges," follows a severe musical blueprint. The last forty-nine measures are an exact retrograde version of the initial forty-nine measures. No more perfect symmetry is possible, of course, than the running of music backward, sound for sound, rhythm for rhythm. Such technical magic is always fascinating, but it has nothing to do in this case with a Biblical scenario.

¶ L'Homme et Son Désir

This music is run on polytonal wheels within polyrhythmic wheels. Complete independence of material rules: melody, tonality, and rhythm each goes its own way. The musical media are just as individual: a wordless vocal quartet, five wind instruments, a string quartet, double bass, trumpet, harp, and fifteen percussion.

The story of Milhaud's early ballet (his forty-eighth work) concerns the primitive strength of the Brazilian forest at night and the mystical forces that hold sway therein. Milhaud's sonorous texture is as complex as the jungle setting. His quadrupled layered counterpoint of motival snippets, noises, fractured and fractioned pulsations, framed by exotic instrumentation is exciting. Traditional methods of cohesion are lacking, but in this super-expressionistic vehicle they are not required.

OPERA

¶ Le Pauvre Matelot

Subtitled a "lament in three acts," Milhaud's four-character stage work, based on a Jean Cocteau text, has a simplified style in comparison to his other operas. Its succinct story tells of a sailor who returns home after a fifteen-year absence without being recognized, and learns that his wife has remained faithful. Posing as a rich friend of her husband he tests the wife's loyalty further by stating that her husband will soon return but that he is still poor. The woman murders the stranger so that she will have riches for her husband when he does return.

In a novel manner, Milhaud reverses usual procedures. He underplays the tale, depicting everything in a quiet, semistatic manner, supported by a somewhat snide orchestral commentary. Nothing precipitate occurs. Such lack of agitation turns into a binding force and places a magical spell on the proceedings.

¶ Les Choéphores

A musical blockbuster of sound and fury, containing one of the strongest doses of polytonality in this composer's inventory. The savage power of Milhaud's opus is not only illustrative of the vehemence of combined tonalities but is a compendium of vocal techniques, many invented by the composer. The versification has a remarkable puissance which is maintained from start to conclusion, especially in places where the narrator is surrounded by sonoric contrapuntal vocalized timbres, and a battery of percussion in chordal components of varying tensility.

"Les Choéphores" ("The Libation Bearers") is the second part of Aeschylus' trilogy "Oresteia," with text arranged by Paul Claudel. The Electra-Orestes tragedy is divided into seven sections, each with a varied scoring (one for soprano and six-part mixed chorus alone, two others for narrator, chorus, and fifteen percussion instruments). Structural heaviness surrounding the complex chordal textures predominates. The impact and emotional fierceness is stunning. Milhaud's score is as exciting and new today as it was when conceived in 1919.

¶ Les Malheurs d'Orphée

This opera is creative adventure, first, in the sense that the characters, while defined, form their own chorus. Secondly, the orchestral requirements are modest and unusual, calling for a quartet of woodwinds, trumpet, harp, glockenspiel, percussion, and five stringed instruments—thirteen in all.

The classic Orpheus legend is no new entry in the operatic world. In Milhaud's hands the myth is modernized to the hilt and transferred to a rustic Provençale milieu—it doesn't suffer thereby. Orphée, a peasant, marries Eurydice, a Gypsy. He loves animals and tends to their illnesses. Eurydice falls ill, but Orpheus cannot be of any help and she dies. In turn, he is killed by the Gypsy's sisters. The lovers are thereby united in death.

Lyricism is dominant; the entire score is pure song. Extremely pithy, the three acts cover a mere forty-five minutes. One questions the extreme compression, which makes the music a sketch rather than a whole opera.

223

21. CARL ORFF
(1895–   )

Here is an independent voice in contemporary music. On the strength of his "Carmina Burana" (completed in 1936 and first brought to American attention by recorded performance rather than live presentation) Orff has become one of the "big names." All of his succeeding compositions are large stage works, including a new setting of "A Midsummer Night's Dream." His catalog contains but a single piece for orchestra and that was written in 1928. This work ("Entrata") is Orff's only composition remaining before "Carmina Burana"—all the others have been disowned.

What sort of composer is this man? His aesthetic is based on the premise that melodic simplicity and primary rhythm are the pertinent, all-embracing elements of music. He turns away from current styles or recently fashionable ones, believing that all such are finished, as representing the end of a dead-end street, and this includes neoclassicism, neo-neoclassicism, new romanticism, dodecaphony, and everything else. In their place he turns back to writing in a superfine primitivistic style—superfine, but bluntly calculated. There is solidity in the compositions, but no solid grace. Orff does mix his metaphors slightly, since the rhythmic constancy of his music stems somewhat from Stravinsky's "Les Noces" combined with a baroque squareness. This is not a stylistic mishmash, but selective, and new in its oldness. It can be classified as neomedievalistic.

Orff generally overwhelms the listener, knocking him in the aisles at the first hearing. After the first time Orff is much less exciting. To some, a little Orff now and then is sufficient . . . others praise him, no matter. What creative potion does he stir to cause this? First, innocent music—innocent of any complexity, dedicated to primogenial sounds. These are ostinati, pounded over and over again, then an interjection followed by a new ostinato. There is not a trace of counterpoint. Orff writes in vertical blocks of primary harmony, *sans* frictions, *sans* chromaticism, outlined with basal pulsation. In a way his music invokes the primitive religion of the Gregorian age. Melody is a concatenation of one simple idea swung around and around almost into insensibility. While these tunes have their own colors the orchestration is an orgy of rhythmic determination. Copious percussion is utilized (with many unusual instruments), and pianos are employed in multiple strength and only in a percussive manner. The voices are also directed toward a paganistic objective: they shout, whisper and hum, talk and half-speak, imitate drums and string plucking, as much as they sing. The words they utter are not mere pegs on which the music is hung. Orff's texts are as musically organized as the music with which they are combined.

Sometimes the effect of all this is God-given, other times it is exceedingly vulgar, verging on the obscene. Orff's music seems to stand still . . . and yet move forward. It is all very special, all very carefully collated, all ordered with Germanic precision. Most certainly this composer's independence makes him a distinct personality in the music of this age.

ORCHESTRAL

¶ Entrata after William Byrd

Beautiful obstinacy is the virtue of Orff's lone instrumental composition, a setting (composed in 1928 and fully revised in 1943), for quintuple orchestra, based on a keyboard piece ("The Bells") by William Byrd. Actually, the "quintuple orchestra" is a set of five choirs—far from the staggering total the description would seem to indicate—comprising 11 woodwinds, 16 brass, pairs of harps and pianos, strings, organ, and (for Orff) very moderate percussion.

The tonality is static, the bass generator a mere pair of chords. "Entrata" sticks to its unremitting point as bell sounds crisscross, engage and re-engage themselves. Its ostinato delights create the impression of a processional ceremony.

CHORAL

CHORAL WITH INSTRUMENTAL ENSEMBLE

¶ Music for Children ("Das Schulwerk") ("The School Work")

Orff does not step out of character with his "Musik für Kinder." His work to train the young is composed in the same spirit of independence as the stage compositions. It contains the same audacity.

225

The five volumes of "Das Schulwerk" constitute powerful artistry, absent of any eccentric pedagogy.

All the do-re-mi folderol, all the make-money theories about teaching music to the young seem quite pathetic when compared to Orff's remarkable ideas. How many of us were initiated to music by the severe handicap of systematic ear training and the much nicer, easier (but just as hidebound) course in "music appreciation"? Orff teaches by natural participation. He uses songs, dances, speech songs, instruments, acting, etc., in progressive fashion, beginning with a pair of sounds. He does not employ any instrument that requires special and precise muscular co-ordination—hand clapping, toy drums, tuned water glasses are just as effective. Rhythms found in enunciating words are still another aid. Nothing is pat and rigorously ordered. It is possible to add to an already sketched idea of Orff's or create one in similar manner. Anyone who has had to cope with the difficult problem of teaching will be excited by this constructivistic system.

STAGE WORKS

[*The term "opera" is not an exact definition for Orff's theatre works. None are so described by him. Therefore, I have classified them as "stage works."*]

¶ *Antigone*

A fusion of Greek classical drama with Orffian style occurs in this conception of the Sophocles tragedy, rendered freely in German by Friedrich Hölderlin. The atmosphere of "Antigone" is of stark austerity, projected by the vocal orchestration typical of Carl Orff.

There is no setting of music to a text. Speeches replace arias, expressive syllabication is avoided, everything is directed toward clarifying the prose, without any fancy framing or digression. Because of Orff's percussion and rhythm, declamation (quite often on a single pitch) and chanting, whispering and screaming replace mellifluous or sensuous vocalized gestures. Only some cadences and an occasional dramatic point deviate from the pattern. In Orff's hands Schoenbergian *Sprechstimme* turns into an oratorical telegraphy that sweeps the *word* into first place.

There is no arguing against the potent specialness of Orff's music for this tragic tale. The instrumentation is mainly percussive, but the emphasis on the text makes this instrumental battering ram subservient. "Antigone" lasts well over two hours. It can wear a man down.

¶ *Carmina Burana* ("Trionfi"—Part 1)

Orff's reputation stems from this scenic oratorio (or cantata). It defines his stylistic tenets.

For his text, Orff chose twenty-five poems from the thirteenth century, in all instances representing a revolt against the conventional prose of the times. The hour-long work is divided in three parts, covering Springtime, In the Tavern, Courting and Love (read: the restless season, drink, and sex), preceded and followed by a section titled "Fortune, the Empress of the World." These generalities go into many matters of living, including the delights of feasting, wining, and wenching—especially the matter of love in its fullest physical sense. Nothing is taboo, even rousing singing about the joy of deflowering virgins. In toto, this is a musical Rabelaisian tale, quaintly described as "Cantiones profanae, cantoribus et choris cantandae comitantibus instrumentis atque imaginibus magicis" ("Profane chants, performed by singers and chorus accompanied by instruments and magical representations").

There is no cerebral speculation required; Orff drives home his arguments in the simplest and most direct fashion. Any criticism of redundancy is canceled out by a plan which is totally based on supersaturation. Repetition and still more repetition is used for melodies, rhythms, words, and orchestration. The arch-primitivistic language of the composer is thoroughly in keeping with the musical plot; it may be called banal by those who wish a much more sophisticated method, but it is no more artificial than any other "system." "Carmina Burana" is a vivid example of musical pleonasm exploited to its fullest.

¶ *Catulli Carmina* ("Trionfi"—Part 2)

"Catulli Carmina" is the middle piece in the trilogy that opens with "Carmina Burana" and is completed by "Trionfo di Afrodite." Erotic poems by Catullus are the basis of the text for Orff's "Ludi Scaenici" (scenic play), which can be properly described as "for adults only." Because of its earthiness most translations that are furnished for concert and recording purposes are edited.

The setting begins with the pledging of love and devotion by groups of young men and women. Another group of older men dispute these vows as "unbounded foolishness." The story of the poet

227

Catullus and Clodia (known as Lesbia) is re-enacted as evidence (the method of a play within a play). Her faithlessness is offered as proof that promises of everlasting love are nonsense. The young people are not convinced and the play ends as it began, with their pledges of "In eternity I am yours."

Orff's music is vivid, violent, and frenzied. Its repetitive patterns remind one of super-propelled Gilbert and Sullivan. The instrumentation is a bath of spectroscopic timbres, with four pianos, four timpani, and approximately a dozen players for other percussion instruments (including two types of xylophones, stone sounds, maracas, cymbals, etc.). "Catulli Carmina" is a fascinating experience.

¶ *Der Mond* ("The Moon")

Orff based "Der Mond" on a Grimm fairy tale. In the main this is a piece of mnemonics: from the field of Wagner, from music-hall ditties, out of low-down jazz, out of Puccini, Strauss and Mahler, by way of beer-cellar ditties and pop tunes; even to the inclusion of a nursery tune. The subtitle—"Ein kleines Welttheater"—may explain the assortment. This "small theatre of the world" or "theatrical microcosm" (as one writer has termed it) means that one must accept Orff in terms of a vaudeville show, music drama, oratorio-*cum*-symbolism, narrative opera; light, comic, and heavy.

There is something for everyone in this wacky story of four chaps who steal the moon from a neighboring village and install it in their own hamlet. As each dies he takes a share of the moon with him. When the moon is reassembled St. Peter claims it and places it where it belongs, in the heavens. A tale of sheer nonsense, but with a sufficient frame for Orff's musical effigies. These are quite evocative, despite their differences. One either delights in the musical antics or becomes annoyed. No middle course is possible.

¶ *Die Bernauerin* ("The Bernauer Woman")

Music of such primitiveness that it makes one cry for full chromatic nourishment. Orff is so extravagant with his boom-booms and drum rolls that he blots out any sense of contrast, tension, and release. He seems bent on a pilgrimage into a land where musical denial flourishes. This tale ("Ein bairisches Stück" is Orff's subtitle) of "more than five hundred years ago" is a poor product.

The story line is uninvolved. It is derived from a ballad about a beautiful girl who marries a prince. The rub is that she is a commoner;

228

the daughter of a barber. The prince's father is vehement in his opposition, denounces the girl as a witch and has her drowned.

Most of "Die Bernauerin" is carried along by pure monologues or dialogue, and in a language that few will understand (Old Bavarian dialect). Aside from some choruses and short solos, the musical part of Orff's stage piece is poverty stricken.

¶ *Die Kluge* ("The Story of the King and the Wise Woman")

Despite the usual caravan of Orffian materials: duplicated ideas, rhythmic squareness, folklike melodies, and additional plain cargo, "Die Kluge" is very tuneful. The music has fun and a jauntiness that carry over beyond the dialogue of the plot (also a Grimm fairy tale). It tells of a peasant girl who becomes a queen by answering riddles, and then outsmarts the king by solving an even greater poser.

In this stage parable Orff reconfirms his antiromantic stand. There are no lush, juicy arias; there is a great deal of pitter-patter song speech and plenty of supercharged rhythmic attenuations. Since "Die Kluge" is a long work with lots of recitative, some may not be willing (even with a knowledge of the stylized German) to wait for the real musical moments to come along. Be patient, those moments are worth waiting for.

¶ *Trionfo di Afrodite* ("Trionfi"—Part 3)

Like the other parts of the trilogy, the "Triumph of Aphrodite" is heated music. The lines don't pull any punches as Hymen, the God of marriage is invoked, a young couple are brought together and wed, and Aphrodite, the Goddess of sensual and spiritual union appears. Everything is nice and neat, sacred and profane, zealous and zippy.

If Orff has accomplished nothing else, he has succeeded in bringing sex into the concert hall. Lusty words equal lusty music in the Aphrodite score and are conveyed by orgiastic ostinati and the give-and-take of antiphony. These are delivered by a huge instrumental apparatus, including three guitars, three pianos, two harps, percussion, the usual woodwind, brass, and strings. In addition there is a large group backstage, consisting of two pianos, harp, and various string and percussion instruments.

22. FRANCIS POULENC
(1899–1963)

POULENC was once considered a type of *enfant terrible,* chiefly because he believed that music should be immediately accessible and gladden the ear. His hedonism did not presuppose coarse or perverted art. He assumed, quite correctly, that a fresh assortment of sounds would inject new blood into the music of prolix romanticism and artificial impressionism; that contemporary music could give pleasure to those who lolled on street corners or sat in parks as well as to concert-goers.

Time has confounded Poulenc's critics. It has shown that he was a little ahead of his detractors and that his sardonic demeanor disguised clear Mozartian-Frenchified features. A musical extrovert was at one time considered to be damned, but the "damned" are now on the side of the angels. Poulenc's early-period music was never trivial. It had charm and lacked self-consciousness. Though his youthful art mellowed with the years, it was not enfeebled by age. Music of such exuberance, vitality, and élan survives time.

Poulenc's later output had a wider emotional content with more finesse and seriousness. However, the basic objective did not change; the pedantic was always detoured. Many of these works can be described as simple music written with a learned, relaxed hand. The most serious are the significant compositions based on sacred themes. Although an uninhibited Parisian, Poulenc was a fervent Christian and carried this disposition over into a number of pieces on religious subjects, including an opera ("Les Dialogues des Carmélites"), sets of motets, a "Stabat Mater," and a "Mass." Expressive, but never of Beethovian profundity, these works are sweet and poetic rather than intellectually probing. In the nihilistic art world of today Poulenc's music represents innocence. It is indeed refreshing.

ORCHESTRAL

¶ *Les Biches—Suite for Orchestra*
    Poulenc's "Les Biches" (meaning "The Does"—in French slang, females that represent themselves to be innocent) is light-swinging,

salonesque ballet music. It is totally relaxing, smart but not arrogant, whimsical but not flippant, lightly sexual—a French music-hall transplant of a Broadway musical.

CHAMBER ORCHESTRA

¶ Suite Française

A British writer has accused Poulenc of "illiterate trifling" with the music of Claude Gervaise, a sixteenth-century composer, which furnishes the original genesis of the seven pieces comprising the "French Suite." Though the content is simple, it is not "trifling," and in his approach Poulenc certainly respects the stylistic source. The air of the old period is allowed full circulation in these dance pieces, ever so slightly channeled by neoclassic controls. (Poulenc also made a piano version: *see page 236.*)

SOLO INSTRUMENT WITH ORCHESTRA

CONCERTOS

¶ Aubade, a Choreographic Concerto for Piano and Eighteen Instruments

Originally cast as a ballet, Poulenc's composition loses nothing in separation. He termed it "amphibious," because it was a blend of media. "Aubade" is less than a full-blown concerto and more of a concerto grosso.

The "Aubade" is in eight movements and can be listened to as absolute music or in a semi-programmatic conception, following (in a general way) the original scenario which concerns the goddess Diana, who suffers remorse because she has vowed to be bound by the laws of chastity. The score is lightly theatrical, mostly lyrical, with the solo voice and orchestra posing questions and responses, as well as rebukes, to each other. This is discreet Poulenc with a complete French sense of order and charm.

¶ Concert Champêtre for Harpsichord (or Piano) and Orchestra

The "Concert Champêtre" has direct eighteenth-century consanguinity. Classical diatonicism blends with harmonic pepper, resulting in a typical Parisian (Poulenc) concoction. It is of seriousness laced with lightness—sugar with bitters.

This composer is more than capable of handling the difficult

231

balance of a harpsichord and a modern orchestra. Themes and episodes are set off against each other, and when combined the action has the pace of a speedy basketball game. No jollier example of fast-charged music can be heard in these days of serialized polyphonic shuttling. The end movements are as clear as Haydn. The orchestral quality is effervescent, a virtue in itself. And the relaxed, contrasting slow movement is an ingratiating *siciliano*. The entire score offers genuine entertainment—many of the themes can be recalled long after performance.

¶ *Concerto for Piano and Orchestra*

Poulenc's concerto attitude leads him astray in this instance. Rather than flowing, hedonistic French discourse, of which he is a master, he resorts to writing a collection of musical limericks. The lines of the piece are ruled off, making a smug island of tunes. There are some pert ideas, but Poulenc jigs and joggles these over and over again. It's all meant to be a diversion, but the cuteness falls flat. In the last movement the resemblance of one idea to "Swanee River" is quite striking. If this was meant to be a tongue-in-the-cheek reference, it, too, misses the mark.

¶ *Concerto in D minor for Two Pianos and Orchestra*

The simplicity of this work at times comes perilously close to banality. Poulenc's music is supertonal, but festooned with dissonant cellophane. Facile and silky for the most part, the concerto has the air of super-styled salon music, running the gamut from frankhearted Mozartian imitation to spoofery.

Poulenc's double concerto is so disarming that by the time it has run its course one is willing to grant him all the benefit of artistic naïveté. In the long-hair musical world, successes of this kind of unabashed parody are very rare.

¶ *Concerto in G minor for Organ, Strings and Timpani*

Although there is a plentiful supply of contemporary solo organ music, little of it is outstanding. The same applies to the limited number of concerti that have been written for the instrument. Poulenc's is one of the standouts. His colorful opinions are a cultivation of things heard before and remembered. His eclectic "originality" has neither poverty nor riches, but is to be listed in the middle class of musical wealth. (For the record, Poulenc considered this composition to be one of his very best.)

The concerto is attractive in its medieval nonpolyphonic Bachian seriousness, together with refurbished Saint-Saëns and Delibes. This is quite a mixture, but Poulenc was always master of his kitchen, and the combination is appealing. The design of the music consists of varying sections tied into a single movement. Near the conclusion, continuity and balance are strengthened with the reprise of material heard earlier.

NARRATOR AND PIANO

¶ *The Story of Babar the Little Elephant*

An exception to the rule: narrator with solo piano, rather than with orchestra. And no exception to the rule—music and talk for children, more thoroughly enjoyed by adults.

After his mother has been killed, Babar comes to the city and is befriended by a rich old lady, who gives him fine clothes and an automobile. Eventually, he becomes dissatisfied with civilization, returns to his native soil and is chosen King (his predecessor died from a poisonous mushroom). The tale concludes with Babar's marriage to his cousin, Celeste. Descriptive and pertinent to the story the score is not a mishmash of mickey-mouse variety. In writing this excellent musical vaudeville, Poulenc doubtless had as much enjoyment as his listeners will.

INSTRUMENTAL

HORN

¶ *Elégie*

Most often, works composed for the horn tend to be severely academic, or merely designed for the inflated exhibition of technical abilities. Only a handful of excellent sonatas exist (by Beethoven, Hindemith, and the American Anthony Donato, for example). Despite its striking timbre and responsivity, the literature for the horn (except in combination with other instruments) has suffered neglect.

To the limited repertory of worth one must add Poulenc's "Elégie," composed "in memory of Denis Brain," one of the great horn virtuosi, who died in 1957 as the result of an automobile accident. Poulenc's piece illustrates the conviction that a lament need not

233

be doleful sentimentality. Its ecstatic moments are of raw, chromatic urgency, and its logical coherence and commanding sweep mark it as one of the best pieces for the brass instrument.

PIANO

¶ *Humoresque*

Possibly encore material, definitely salon music. A musical bonbon with nothing to chew on.

¶ *Improvisations, Books I and II*

A sophisticated collection of twelve numbers, not virtuosic music but requiring more than a mere playing of the notes. There is no smart-alecky attitude in the "Improvisations" but there is some salt. If impropriety is not the way of politeness, Poulenc proves it is the soul of wit. He remains the life of the contemporary music party.

Poulenc's skill in shifting from Ravelian moments to Russian moods, and yet remaining himself all the time is paradoxical, but artistically successful. He illustrates how a composer can reshape conventional musical factors and make them his own. It is nothing more than musical plastic surgery.

¶ *Les Animaux Modelés*

In 1941 Poulenc completed his ballet "Les Animaux Modelés," based on six fables by La Fontaine, in which animals possess human qualities. As is usual he made a piano reduction of the orchestral score. From this, the concert pianist, Grant Johannesen, drew material for a solo piano suite. The deadly monotony (the piano sounds like the background of an old silent movie) is not Johannesen's doing.

¶ *Mélancolie*

Old wine in an old bottle. This six-minute dissemination of sentimentality is a concord of semisweet, old-fashioned sounds. Without composer identification one would place the date of "Mélancolie" in the 1850's. If Poulenc was kidding, his jest falls flat.

¶ *Mouvements Perpétuels*

These three compact pieces, composed in 1918 are the most frequently played of Poulenc's piano compositions. They display a waggish demeanor on Poulenc's part. Like an acrobatic clown prancing on a tightrope, his music makes all the gestures of falling on its face, but everything is controlled during the excitement.

The attenuated, unchanged rhythmic doodling of "perpetual motion" pieces is completely absent from Poulenc's designs. The material is concentrated, the action alive, the effect one of slyness with an engaging smile.

¶ Nocturnes

Trust Poulenc not to be dogmatic. In his hands the plan of a nocturne is extremely fluid, sometimes a very animated sketch, sometimes semi-programmatic. In the set of eight he composed, only one is extremely slow and traditionally nocturnal. The others vary in faster tempi, including one delivered in presto speed, entitled "Phalènes" ("Moths")! Further variety is maintained by a moderate waltz (number 4, subtitled "Bal Fantôme"), a light ballet diversion named "Ball of the Young Girls" (number 2), a bell piece (the third of the set), and the quasi-sentimental flavor of the sixth of the group.

According to Debussy, music was meant to "humbly seek to please." Poulenc's miniatures consistently do so. Only the main title is misleading, since most of these "Nocturnes" are more expressive of morning and midday than they are of night.

¶ Novelette in C major

Nothing novel is offered in this minor item. Poulenc contrasted his poetic tidbit with a second "Novelette," in the key of B minor.

¶ Pastourelle from the Ballet "L' Eventail de Jeanne"

In musical composition collaboration has been attempted in a few isolated instances; in the anthological sense there are a number of examples. Among the most important are the orchestral "Variations" on the tune "Cadet Rouselle," a compilation by British composers; a set of "Fanfares," commissioned by Eugene Goossens for opening the Cincinnati Symphony Orchestra concerts during the Second World War; the septuple setting of the passages from the Bible, "Genesis," by Schoenberg, Stravinsky, Toch, Milhaud, Tansman, Shilkret, and Castelnuovo-Tedesco. Also of interest are a number of string quartet pieces produced by late-nineteenth-century Russian composers to honor Mitrofan Belaiev, who spent a fortune in publishing his countrymen's music.

Poulenc's "Pastourelle" is the ninth part of an eleven-movement

235

children's one-act ballet in which ten composers co-operated by furnishing one piece each (Ravel's "Fanfare" is used twice, as the opening and as part six). The partnership developed as the result of a commission by René Dubost, in whose home the first performance was given on June 16, 1927 (the initial public presentation was scheduled much later—on March 4, 1929).

Originally for orchestra, the "Pastourelle" is kin to the "Mouvements Perpétuels." Its charming principal B flat major theme, undisturbed by a single chromatic, shows Poulenc at his tenderest. No counterpoint is used; it is unnecessary for the diatonic breeze that floats through Poulenc's mellifluous measures.

¶ Presto in B flat

The title tells the tale of this virtuosic savory. In ninety seconds the music drives ahead unceasingly and signs off with a smiling thumb-to-the-nose cadence. *Voilà tout.*

¶ Seven Pieces for the Piano

[*Poulenc never composed a set of "Seven Pieces." A recording has been issued with the title, the music drawn from four of his separate compositions (considered individually elsewhere in this section).*

[*The confusion that arises from any invented title is considerable when the compilation consists of extracts from sets of pieces specifically designated by the composer as "Improvisations," and the like. It is worse when a complete opus (the three "Mouvements Perpétuels") is disguised and forms part of the spuriously titled package.*]

¶ Suite Française

The piano text of this suite (*see* Chamber Orchestra *above*) displays the neat contours of its neo-archaic contents, but the orchestral setting adds timbred sharpness. The black and white of instrumental antiphony can only be hinted at by a keyboard instrument.

¶ Three Pieces

[*Still another counterfeit title bestowed on a recording of pieces drawn from Poulenc's piano catalogue. Since Poulenc actually wrote a set of "Trois Pièces," the muddle is compounded. The compositions involved ("Humoresque," "Improvisation [No. 5]," and "Valse in C") are discussed in their proper alphabetical place in this section.*]

¶ *Trois Pièces*

In this collation of diverse pieces, stylistic mimicry is apparent but after it has passed through Poulenc's Gallic sifter it is refreshed and new.

The "Pastorale" is impressionistic, containing a nostalgic nuance that is closer to an urban nocturne. In the "Toccata" (a frenetic piece of virtuosity) the quartal harmonies color the traditional form with contemporary chalk. The third piece is a "Hymne," more profane than sacred. A grand conception of broad utterance, it includes a contrasting section that sounds suspiciously like a Chopin review.

¶ *Valse in C from "Album des Six"*

Short-hair music written by a young long-hair. This light caricature represents café music for the concert hall. Catchy, concentrated, and no oom-pah-pah monotony.

¶ *Villageoises*

Tunes for whistling, with slightly salty harmonies, placed in pithily defined forms: waltz, march, a melody, polka, and a round dance. Though this music is simple it is packed with Poulencian wit.

PIANO DUET

¶ *Sonata*

Quite often, the music of a young composer brings returns. Poulenc's concise and witty three-movement piece, written at the age of nineteen, delights the ear with its nicely colored ideas and filamented textures. The surfaces are crystal clear; the dissonances slight scratches thereon. There are no complex curvatures or heavy gravities in the sonata; it simply floats.

Ernest Ansermet, the conductor, spoke of this piece with admiration; mentioning its subtlety, joviality, and occasional spirit of abandon. One notes other points that decorate the concentrated designs: pentatonic touches, childlike tunes, and cadences that smirk. Poulenc's four-handed piano sonata displays typical French *savoir-faire*.

TWO PIANOS

¶ *Sonata*

If not heavy, Poulenc's music is never slight, and though it is amusing, it is never corny. There are some well-worn (by Poulenc) clichés in the "Sonata," but they are minor blemishes to the major congruities found in the work. The balancing of sonority is especially successful in a medium that can well sound like too much of a muchness. In this opus, Poulenc is like a French Mozart with patent leather shoes and pomaded hair. There are some serious moments, but for the most part the music is urbane. It is potent enough to keep any listener interested.

CHAMBER MUSIC

¶ *Sonata for Flute and Piano*

Music which stems formally from classical orientation need not be primitive or imitative. Though the three-movement flute and piano sonata does not contain hedonistic oversimplicities, there is no indulgence in Promethean stormy oratory. It has a neat cyclic reference for its terminal portion, is set in nicely dissonantized harmony, and its textures are as delicate as china. Despite the descriptive "malinconico" of the initial allegro, this part is as Parisian-made as the final *presto giocoso*.

¶ *Sonata* (To the Memory of García Lorca) *for Violin and Piano*

Here, Poulenc's style is romantic—quite different from the many flippant examples in his output. Mind sails far over matter; the opening movement especially seems to be concocted from Brahms plus Russian Five leftovers and Franckian sequences. There is a superfluity of material and too much goes on.

Further, the expected threnodic temper is absent. Lorca's memory is only called to mind by the quotation of one of his lines as the motto for the second ("Intermezzo") movement: "La guitare fait pleurer les songes." A major-sized work with minor impact.

¶ *Sonata for Horn, Trumpet and Trombone*

Brass chamber music is common today, but when Poulenc composed this trio in 1922, it was considered a daring exploitation of timbre. The piece was criticized as bizarre, *outré;* the result of a brash young man sowing musical wild oats. Musical audiences have now become more sophisticated; neither brass music nor varied currents of tonal electricity shock them. Poulenc's "Sonata" can only be criticized in certain portions which overemphasize the rakish Bohemian smugness practiced in much music of the early 1920's. But those who claim this is not a composition to be considered seriously are unjust.

The outer movements are the freshest. Gayest of these is the "Rondeau," with some touches of French popular song, though the themes are all original. The final cadence is a joy to hear, with clamped seconds up to the last moment, whereupon the pure D major chord solves everything. The "Allegro moderato" is warmer in its flow, but contains a somewhat similar bouncing spirit; one portion is like a soft-shoe dance.

¶ *Trio for Oboe, Bassoon and Piano*

Poulenc's keen sense of scoring know-how is worth the undivided attention of his listeners. In this oboe, bassoon and piano trio the scoring is so coupled with the instruments that the very essence of the music would vanish if any substitution were made.

The gay first movement frames a headlong Mozartian finale. In the slow movement Poulenc's attractive spirit recalls the melos of a Bellini and a Gounod. The last part (in gigue style) is as merry as can be.

¶ *Sextet for Piano, Flute, Oboe, Clarinet, Bassoon and Horn*

Parisian wit has always been considered first rate. It is quite convincing in this tinseled and glittering sextet. The lyrical element is somewhat low-down, the choreographic simulation is heated by jazz, while the expressive slower sections (within the middle movement, a "Divertissement") remind one of late-afternoon tea music. Over all hangs the charming temper of escapism.

Poulenc always had a sure hand for the light stuff with proportional nonsense. Musical effervescence of artistic value is not easy to create. The sextet is one of the best illustrations of this composer's ability to write breezy and scintillating instrumental music.

VOCAL

¶ *Air Vif*

The concluding song from the set "Airs Chantés." (The other parts are "Air Romantique," "Air Champêtre," and "Air Grave.") Poulenc's slightly droll melody is like a comic opera excerpt.

239

¶ *Attributs*

A bittersweet vignette. "Attributs" is the initial piece in the "Cinq Poèmes de Ronsard." I would argue with Henri Hell, who, in his book on the composer, states that Poulenc became "severely critical" of this group of songs.

¶ *Banalités*

Kurt Weill said he was writing for the present and didn't "give a damn about posterity" when he composed his "Three Penny Opera." This thought came to mind when listening to the five songs set to texts of Guillaume Apollinaire that make up "Banalités." Once heard, it is difficult to recall any exact musical phrase within these songs; however, the style will be remembered, especially the fact that the moods are so definitely opposed to the words. This results in vocal music truly independent of poetic calculation.

Of all the pieces in the cycle, the most beautiful and sensitively intimate is "Hôtel." Though held under dynamic wraps, this song is suffused with feeling, despite such lines as "I don't want to work/I want to smoke." It is only in terms of the texts that the title "Banalités" has proper meaning. This is further exemplified in the colorful "Voyage à Paris." The setting of this portion makes the keyboard instrument sound like an ancient player piano, its mechanical waltz rhythm tracking the gentle, semi-repulsing vocal line.

¶ *"C" from "Deux Poèmes"*

One of the most important and popular songs of the composer. The title has no musical significance, being derived from the text (a poem by Louis Aragon) wherein each line ends in "Cé." It concerns the happy days before France was occupied by the Germans. No rampant patriotism is indicated, but a restrained, nostalgic sweetsadness conveyed as aptly in the music as in the words of the song.

"C" was first performed during the German Occupation in Belgium, and resulted in a tremendous ovation for Pierre Bernac, the baritone, and Poulenc, who was at the piano. Fortunately, the Germans did not understand what was behind this tremendous response. There was no question that Poulenc had triumphantly proven his theorem that "poetry and music should evoke the other."

¶ *Calligrammes*

From the angularity and disjunctiveness of the lines of the songs in speedy tempo, it is apparent that Poulenc was more influenced by the decorative arrangements (the calligrams) of Apollinaire's poems, than the actual text. The rest is just short of being conventional. Vocally, a somewhat uneven cycle; the instrumental support is far superior.

¶ *Ce Doux Petit Visage*

One of Poulenc's favorite poets, Paul Eluard (five song cycles, three individual songs, and several choral pieces were written to his texts), provided the subject matter for this bit. It has quiet expressivity, illustrative of the composer's mastery of vocal melody, French style.

¶ *Chansons Gaillardes*

The peppy texts employed (anonymous, from the seventeenth century) do not preach prudity with wine or women. Poulenc does not go constantly for the "hard sell" in his settings. In the "Chanson à Boire," a song devoted to the joys of drink, the music is slyly sedate. On the other hand, "La Belle Jeunesse," which advises young men to love 'em and leave 'em, is as musically racy as the subject. With one exception the other songs follow suit. The spontaneity of the eight pieces is exhilarating and typically Gallic.

¶ *Chansons Villageoises*

The drolleries of Maurice Fombeure's poetry set the tone in this set of six songs. Poulenc's gay temperament sprinkles these pieces with admirable affinity.

¶ *Fiançailles pour Rire*

Though the moods of "Engagement for Laughter" vary, they convey the meaning and spirit of each of the six parts without stylistic shifts. Song presentation demands flexibility, and Poulenc follows suit, but always retains control of his individuality. Thus the artistic naïveté of "La Dame d'André," the agile flow of "Il Vole," the waltz that marks "Violon," the lyrical, yet not conventional status of "Fleurs," and so on. All are in Poulenc's clear, economical style, with awareness of the poetic compass.

¶ *Le Travail du Peintre*

Texts devoted to the "work of painters," including Picasso, Chagall, Braque, Gris, Klee, Miró, and Villon. No musical pilotage in

241

pictorial waters is made, as Poulenc is deadly serious in setting Eluard's poems to long-breathed lines. Since few know the personalities of the painters involved, but many know their work, it is difficult to remove the conflict between the styles of canvases seen and that of the music heard. Despite this, Poulenc's emotional lyricism is quite telling.

¶ *Les Chemins d'Amour*

Light as a feather and of light content. Poulenc's updating of his Gounod-styled song brings little consequence to the music.

¶ *Main Dominée par le Coeur*

Once again Poulenc's affiliation with Gounod is to be noted, but the special transparency of texture makes this contemporary transplant successful. The freely designed music that surrounds the Paul Eluard text makes for agreeable coexistence.

¶ *Miroirs Brûlants*

As befits a song dealing with hate, Poulenc is propulsive in the music for "Je Nommerai Ton Front." He is just as opposite in the companion piece, which concerns an unloved woman. The former is of romantic fervor, the other a long-spun piece somewhat of classical cognizance. Both songs have lines which represent fertile, frank melodic subjects. In this instance, Poulenc is a twentieth-century composer using the well-sharpened tools of the nineteenth.

¶ *Reine des Mouettes*

The first song in the three-part cycle "Métamorphosees." Set in a tempo that is fast "and breathless" the music is suave and flowing, with a tinge of sensuousness. Poulenc's "Queen of the Seagulls" does not belong to the innocent, pastoral world.

¶ *Tel Jour Telle Nuit*

Not a trace of Parisian scamper is to be heard within these nine songs. Even the few faster-tempoed representations are well within the elegance that represents the mainstream of French song literature. The shadowed melancholy of the two longest pieces in the cycle (the opening "Bonne Journée" and the final "Nous avons fait la Nuit") are among the finer examples in Poulenc's large vocal catalogue.

CHORAL

¶ *Litanies à la Vierge Noire*

This represents Poulenc in his most saintly demeanor. The neo-ecclesiastical writing for three-part women's or children's voices parallels the old technique of psalmody, colored by violent intersections of the organ in response. A regard for native heritage makes itself felt here in music contemporaneously related to the *Ars nova* of the fourteenth century. An extremely subdued exultation is rare in Francis Poulenc's output; the "Litanies" is one of the exceptions.

¶ *Quatre Motets pour le Temps de Noël* ("Four Christmas Motets")

Quite (and properly) lucid, in the sense of straight choral writing. This eminently respectable Christmas music avoids any linear ligation and is resolved in terms of homophony. No vigorous contemporary flourishes are executed, save a light tinge of dissonance that serves to animate the general serenity of the pieces, especially in the initial "O Magnum Mysterium."

¶ *Quatre Motets pour un Temps de Pénitence* ("Four Penitential Motets")

Unaccompanied choral music rigidly pegged at the vertical level. There is not the slightest hint of counterpoint in these thrillingly dramatic, yet chaste Lententide pieces. Belief that sacred music is only proper in traditional dress is false. Poulenc shows how modern tonal worship can express Bachian piety and yet include the incisiveness of frictional harmony.

CHORAL WITH ORCHESTRA

¶ *Gloria in G major*

From the very beginning, Poulenc's "Gloria," written to fulfill a commission by the Koussevitzky Foundation, met with acclaim. It was given its world première in Boston, on January 20, 1961. Less than a month later it was heard in Paris, and recorded the next day by the same forces that performed it. In the meantime it was cited by the Music Critics Circle of New York, following its initial New York presentation.

Poulenc comprehends the traditional objective of his liturgical subject, recognizes its requirements, yet avoids staid orthodoxy. Completely fresh, fully contemporary in manner, the music's religious quiet is powerfully expressed. This is a reverse form of moderation. For example, the snappy syncopations in the "Laudamus Te," and the pert use of a Bach-Poulencized ritornel in the "Domine Fili Unigenite."

Analysis discloses that the warmth of the "Gloria" is arrived at by cooly determined procedures—at times a bit eclectic (Stravinsky and Ravel will be heard). Nonetheless, by Poulenc's breadth of consideration the meanings of his "Gloria" are not confined any more than true religion is bounded by the four walls of a church. It is a superb contribution.

CANTATA

¶ *Le Bal Masqué*

Lusty music set to locomotive texts, couched in surrealistic *sub rosa* style (one example: "she had thick blood was bachelor of arts and had charge of classes."). This gives Poulenc the right-of-way for a veritable field day of tuneful tomfoolery in his secular cantata consisting of six movements, half with voice, half for an ensemble of eight players, the equivalent of the pit combinations of old vaudeville days: oboe, clarinet, bassoon, cornet, violin, cello, percussion, and piano.

Satire is Poulenc's signal for music that is fast-kinetic, jazz-banked, scherzo-spiced. "Le Bal Masqué is a perfect gem of cartooned flamboyance. The later opera "Les Mamelles de Tirésias" is a distinct outgrowth of this racy dissertation.

¶ *Sécheresses*

A cantata with a more sober outlook than usual (fundamental to the texts by Edward James, which describe "Locusts," "The Abandoned Village," "The False Future," and "The Skeleton of the Sea"). Staidness, with Francis Poulenc, becomes sharp-edged music. The preciseness of the settings for "Drought" makes for heady, strong brewed stuff.

One author has described "Sécheresses" as a quasi-surrealistic opus. This writer disagrees (despite the surrealist form of the text). The composition represents the whole relish of modern choral style, intensified by neo-modal accentuations. One realizes again that few contemporary composers can equal Poulenc's handling of the voice alone or in combination.

ORATORIO

¶ *Stabat Mater*

The text of the "Stabat Mater" has been the source of important music by Palestrina, Pergolesi, Haydn, Schubert, Rossini, Verdi, and Dvořák; but only a few twentieth-century composers have been attracted to it. Poulenc's concept of the form is faithful to the liturgical objective and yet does not abandon his Gallic pellucidness. The "Stabat Mater" has the strength of simplicity; its traditional dignity remains unimpaired even when contemporary dissonance is added to the harmonic vocabulary.

MASS

¶ *Mass in G major*

Poulenc dedicates this sacred work for mixed *a cappella* voices to the memory of his father (a devout Catholic). It is in five sections (the *Credo* was not included) and, for the most part, in a style far removed from the twentieth century. The simplicity of writing is proper to the subject matter, but the music lacks impact. Too much solemnity is not becoming to this extrovert composer.

OPERA

¶ *La Voix Humaine*

Poulenc enlarges the definition of opera by contraction of resource in a production that calls for a cast of one. There have been a number of monodramas, but these consist of recitations with music. The opera-for-one is a distinct rarity.

The theme of "La Voix Humaine" may call to mind Schoenberg's "Erwartung," which also deals with a woman's soul-searching experience (seeking her lover in a forest and eventually finding him dead). But Schoenberg's expressionistic text does not constitute actual straightforward operatic drama. In "La Voix Humaine" a woman carries on a telephone conversation with her lover, as a final leave-taking after five years. One learns she has attempted suicide as she passes through a complete cycle of fear and bravery. She lies, she scorns and attempts to be lighthearted. Eventually she promises to be strong but cannot, and breaks down tragically at the end. The special point of Poulenc's work is that one is caught up in the monologue (expertly planned with slight interruptions due to the telephone's party line) as though more than a single person is on stage.

To convey this impassioned tale with its erotic overtones (based on a Jean Cocteau play) Poulenc employs a lyrical recitative structure. There are no heaven-storming arias, no motivic play, no development per se; simply the constant illumination of the story as the woman pours out her soul. The orchestra serves as a companion, projecting a simultaneous instrumental translation of the tale. The combination is as powerful as it is novel.

¶ *Les Dialogues des Carmélites*

The "Dialogues" is a drama with strong psychological overtones, set at the outbreak of the French Revolution. Blanche, a young girl, seeks to escape from her problems by becoming a Carmélite nun. However, her previous inability to cope with life and her undefined fears are hardly lessened by the new experience. The convent is besieged by the Revolutionaries and Blanche seeks refuge in her father's home. It is only when the nuns are condemned to die on the guillotine that the girl finds security, undergoes a spiritual awakening, and willingly accepts a martyr's death.

Poulenc's music is wide of true sacred association. He knows how to set words, and the score has excellent color, but the "Carmélites" will strike more than one listener as a pastiche (Moussorgsky, Debussy, and filtered Puccini), wherein the plot moves forward but the music draws the other way. The latter has a certain theatrical force, but it never projects the girl's turmoil and her eventual redemption.

¶ *Les Mamelles de Tirésias*

Bald, ribald, witty, and with a good dose of double entendre. No one should listen to this musical burlesque without realizing its essential point: Poulenc's opera is a grand (and very successful) attempt to avoid pointing out a moral.

A woman decides to leave her husband. She becomes a man and grows a beard after her breasts (differently colored!) float away. The man dresses as a woman and with the aid of a special incubator makes children by the thousands. Things continue to happen in this same skimble-skamble vein. Eventually the woman is reunited with her husband and the public is advised to go ahead and make babies.

"Les Mamelles de Tirésias" is top-grade foolishness and as such it is a refreshing departure from operatic mores. Froth and bawdiness are not new (Wolfgang Amadeus Mozart and Richard Strauss are sufficient examples), but the sexuality is subtly costumed. Poulenc is not quite so refined in his scatologically peppered, existentialistic opera.

23. ALBERT ROUSSEL
(1869–1937)

Roussel began composing comparatively late in life—he was twenty-nine when he enrolled at the famed Schola Cantorum, where César Franck's disciple, Vincent d'Indy, held sway. Impressionism had entered the French artistic arena as still another violent reaction against Teutonic-Wagnerian thickness (a patriotic rebirth had begun after the Franco-Prussian War, concerts of purely French music became the vogue, the national spirit had reawakened). Although impressionism beckoned, Roussel yielded only temporarily to its delineative qualities. He was drawn to the more clear-cut premises of formal design and construction. But this did not mean that Roussel could fully subscribe to the superattenuated brand of hyperacademicism practised and taught by d'Indy, an archdeacon of the rulebook. Roussel recognized the magnificent value of classical doctrines, but expressionism (slightly colored, somewhat pictorial, but earthy and opposite to impressionism) was a magnetic attraction. Accordingly, Roussel's creative demeanor changed to combine both Gallicism and neoclassicism.

The shift came late in his career, but still permitted Roussel to produce a quantity of outstanding music. His work was not defined by precise boundaries. The older Roussel became increasingly freer in his outlook, assimilated much of the harmonic vocabulary of the nineteen twenties, but never at the expense of purity of language or loss of individual direction. His music is an intermarriage between intellect, of the type to delight any learned musician or attentive listener (which leads some to call him a cold fish or a mechanical technician), and sentiment of the polite French kind (which means not sensational, avoiding mawkishness, but touchable).

Roussel's style combines polyphony with, or on top of, chordal threading. In his mature period the musical material is formed from harmonic types, classic and diatonic in birth, but altered in their vertical and horizontal existence. His polyphony does not simply embellish a straight and simple thematic thought, but crosses and imposes itself on long, muscular melodic lines. The astringency of the harmony makes his music exceedingly contemporary. The contrapuntalism causes a special type of bitonality, but it is basic to traditional order. Order, above all else, makes Roussel's work clear and enjoyable. This is music where action exalts further action, a music that has the necessary stamina to live.

ORCHESTRAL

¶ Bacchus et Ariane, Suites Nos. 1 and 2, Op. 43

There is no precise sonic pictorialism in the "Bacchus and Ariane" ballet. The music is charged with full imaginative grasp, but the style is as newly classical as the tale on which the work is based. The legend deals with the celebration of Theseus and Ariane, after the slaying of the Cretan Minotaur. Bacchus appears, drives Theseus away, and seizes Ariane. She forgets Theseus after Bacchus bestows on her the kiss of immortality. The end of the ballet is of vehement virtuosity—a rousing bacchanale.

Roussel's habits are for formal shapes not pruned to fit each and every situation. One can listen to this score almost as a piece conceived in absolute manner, without any stage picture in mind. Roussel's conception is ages removed from the successful, but principally choreographic, values of ballet scores by Tchaikovsky, Glazunov, Adam, and Delibes. Thus, each of the suites, representing music drawn from each of the two acts of the ballet, is a completely synthesized dance symphony . . . in one elongated movement, as it were. This is orchestral music with no programmatic ideology.

¶ Concerto for Small Orchestra, Op. 34

Neoclassicism in its optimum state: large-spanned melodic lines, extended tonality floating within a key scheme, flexible meters, demarcated colors rather than blended ones—all these are contained in this three-movement affair for an orchestra of double woodwinds, two horns, trumpet, timpani, and strings. Roussel's opus is a concerto grosso with a new look, pitting groups within the orchestra against each other, but never settling for one highlighted color as in the older use of the form. A cogent example of traditional formality with contemporaneously enriched content.

¶ Petite Suite for Orchestra, Op. 39

This represents the mid-eighteenth-century instrumental serenade idea characterized by mixture of forms and scored for a compact

249

ensemble (double woodwinds, pairs of horns and trumpets, percussion, and strings) reminted in terms of the twentieth century. The designs are changed to modern equivalents: an "Aubade," real open-air exhilaration gliding in tenfold meter; a "Pastorale," plus a "Mascarade," which is a brilliant showpiece with Rousselian decorum. The entire suite has piquant modernism and appeal.

¶ *Suite in F, Op. 33*

Pure music, formally straight, but freed of trite formula. Old forms are newly illuminated in this three-movement opus. Serge Koussevitzky must be credited with introducing the work (properly, it was dedicated to him). The sections are a sinewy "Prelude," a sampling of concerto grosso style refurbished with tart harmonies; a chromatically curved "Sarabande," with a long line that is of more grandeur than this dance usually signifies, and a free-driving, but not nervous "Gigue."

Roussel's neoclassicism is direct; in comparison, Stravinsky's is argumentative. The pure sound of this suite and its pithiness explain a great deal. Roussel proves that in the hands of a master craftsman no musical design becomes yellowed with age. Truly exciting music.

¶ *Symphony No. 3 in G minor, Op. 42*

This symphony was commissioned for the fiftieth anniversary of the Boston Symphony, which gave the initial performance on October 24, 1930. (Among some of the other works written for the same celebration were Stravinsky's "Symphony of Psalms," and Honegger's first symphony.)

Though rugged rhythm marks the first movement, the adagio is a superb example of dynamic lyricism. The light-weight (for Roussel) third movement might be described as a spastic valse, while the final section is of almost aristocratic profile. As a whole it is an astute type of modern superclassicism, but far from mere precision of construction. Roussel's symphonic message is delivered by direct application of form and legible style, but with a perceptive diversity that avoids a paraphrase of stock patterns.

¶ *Symphony No. 4 in A major, Op. 53*

Roussel's full-fledged symphonicism does not negate compactness. His many-throated instruments do not depend on their mass for effect. Textural elasticity is to be found within the design of this symphony. To realize the meaning of the music one must listen polyphonically, or else the individuality of the lines, which probe and project the essential *whole,* is lost. Only the third movement, based on a giguelike subject, is more vertical a concept. In this symphony the points of argument are as clearly ordered and defined as any found in a Beethoven symphony. In short, it is a neoclassic composition, straightforward in form, and yet new in its manner of filling each part of the symphonic mold.

CHAMBER ORCHESTRA

¶ *Le Marchand de Sable qui Passe* ("The Sandman"), *Op. 13*

Enjoyable music, mainly important as an early period work. Roussel composed the music in 1908 for an ensemble of flute, clarinet, horn, harp, and strings, as incidental music to a play by Jean Aubry. "The Sandman" is exceedingly simple, tuneful, written with taste, but somewhat attenuated and in a similar mood throughout its four movements. Quite different from Roussel's large-scaled mature pieces, it is similar to hearing an early Haydn piano trio as compared to a late Beethoven string quartet, without denying that there are significances in both.

STRING ORCHESTRA

¶ *Sinfonietta, Op. 52*

One of the most appealing compositions of the composer. Music concentrated in scope, as precise as the jeweled works in a woman's wrist watch. It sounds as it appears on the score page—clear, of pellucid definition as though all sounds, rhythms, and phrases were made with a ruler. Roussel's string piece is contemporary simplicity in its most exigent and therefore exciting form.

The initial movement is asymmetric, slightly nervous; like the other portions of the work it is diatonic as the alphabet, yet dissonant. In the slow division the effect is bitonal; but this is a paradox, for Roussel is not a bitonalist but a pantonalist, permitting diatonic tones to have constricted congress with each other—a type of celibate harmonic marriage. The finale is smart, joyous, based on a "chasing the tail" idea, with episodes both dramatic and of semi-jazz snap. The threaded points of ostinati bind the texture. No mumbo jumbo for Roussel, his twentieth-century music is substantial art; it wears exceedingly well.

251

SOLO INSTRUMENT WITH ORCHESTRA

CONCERTO

¶ *Concerto for Piano and Orchestra, Op. 36*

None of the pyrotechnical bombs of the Grieg, Tchaikovsky, or Rachmaninov concerti, but all the technical chemistry that makes Roussel's music fresh is present here. There is virtuosity, but it is subsidiary to the corporate work. This is why few pianists know it, and fewer play it. The loss is theirs and unfortunately ours.

Roussel employs his favorite three-movement design, with outer sections in moderately fast pace balancing a somber, restrained middle division. As is often the case he utilizes the force of ostinati in the opening movement, but in the last part the power is driven by a variational system. Happily there is no cadenza.

INSTRUMENTAL

GUITAR

¶ *Segovia, Op. 29*

A true portrait—line, design, and correct instrumental timbre to match. A rhythmic Spanish (but not stereotyped) piece for the guitar which perfectly delineates the famous virtuoso. In its less than three-minute scope this sketch is a little gem. (Roussel also made a version for solo piano.)

HARP

¶ *Impromptu, Op. 21*

In 1909, Roussel journeyed to China and India. This trip to the East inspired the composition of a set of three symphonic poems ("Evocations") and an opera-ballet "Padmâvatî." Roussel's interest in Hindu aesthetics was not permanently retained in his creative outlook, but its clear expositions left their mark on all his later music.

This indirect response is present in the sole work Roussel wrote in 1919 for the plectral harp. Although the identification of the "Impromptu" is mainly French, due to its clarity of line and form, the Eastern element is recognizable in the music's accent and sense of languor.

PIANO

¶ *Sonatine, Op. 16*

This composer's neoclassic activity, with tonality livened by fan-wise spread, is evidenced by the pithiness of his Opus 16. Without going beyond the fluidic limits of twentieth-century classicism Roussel brings stylistic unity and balance to the two parts of the "Sonatine" (each further divided, so that the first movement bridges into a scherzo and the slow movement is partner to an animated finale).

Roussel's aim is to be intelligible, and he is. The perspicuity reminds one of Mozart speaking in today's language. Pianists would do well to consider this music of tenderness, wit, and rhythmic bravura.

¶ *Suite pour Piano, Op. 14*

There is no adherence to formula in Roussel's suite, though the pat titles of movements two and three ("Sicilienne" and "Bourrée") lead one to expect it. The minor-keyed "Bourrée" contains a tense vitality and drama reminiscent of Beethoven. It is as remote from the spirit of the French seventeenth-century court dance as is Igor Stravinsky from Edward Elgar. Roussel's "Sicilienne" is long-lined, moves with chromatic inquietude. The outer movements come closer to their titled identifications of "Prélude" and "Ronde," though they are not obvious. The point is that Roussel's music remains always dignified and serious, even when its tempo is accelerated.

¶ *Trois Pièces, Op. 49*

Music of different inclination from the deep emotional content found in most of this composer's output. Roussel seasons his neo-classicism with plenty of paprika. In taking over the lighter Parisian franchise, Roussel refuses to relinquish a single delight. But such resolution and stubbornness do not defeat him. It is all quite satisfying.

CHAMBER MUSIC

¶ *Trio for Flute, Viola and Cello, Op. 40*

Aside from his habitual polyphony, Roussel exploits this medium's possibilities, but not at the expense of intrinsic musical quality. This is especially noticeable in the pert last movement, where tricolors form the opening subject in the shape of pizzicati for the cello, and viola arpeggios combine with a typical flute-shaped idea. The use of timbre to identify and regulate the themes and subsidiaries holds true throughout the entire movement. In this fashion the polyphonic points are conveyed advantageously. Color also advertises the ternary form of the slow movement. In the opening part of the trio—a graceful allegro—free polyphony, based on the system of the pandiatonic (semichromatic, however) hierarchy is the functional method.

Some have called Roussel's chamber works, "music for musicians" —a snide inference of overintellectuality. But the fluid and fluent course of this opus, together with the terseness and balance of its polyharmonic and polyphonic arguments, nullifies this point of view. There is a fervent contemporaneousness in the flute, viola and cello trio, which is far from the hermetic label some critics apply to this composer's chamber music.

¶ Trio for Violin, Viola and Cello, Op. 58

Never does Roussel lose himself in the somewhat sullen, tense, and introspective style of so many of the German neoclassicists. A pert French spirit helps Roussel's polyphony get off the ground. Austerity (not to be confused with seriousness) was foreign to him. A perfect illustration is offered by the polished clarity and poignancy of this trio, Roussel's last work. (After it, he began a trio for oboe, clarinet and bassoon, but death came before the work could be completed.)

Most of the music's dividends are drawn from counterpoint. Significantly, the polyphony does not obviate melodic profile, as in the case of the opening theme, set in chromatically festooned A minor, or the principal theme for the viola in the second movement. Only the third part of the trio is more vertical, based on a giguelike subject. It would be difficult to better this musical testimony of Roussel in his most characteristic vein.

¶ String Quartet in D major, Op. 45

Roussel's string quartet displays all of his mature compositional habits. Joining his French colleagues, Fauré, Debussy, and Ravel, in producing a single example in quartet form, he has stated in it his entire creative creed.

The music would seem to be heavy and thick, almost glutinous, when inspected from the score itself. But the sharp harmonic outline and clear rhythmic plan employed prove otherwise. The quartet is titled in "D major," but this defines a tonal polarity magnet, not an example of major-minor buttressing. This music of dynamic tensility is not for relaxation in the drawing room. It is adventurous, highly effective, and profound. The final movement is a fugue, wherein Roussel freely and successfully casts his tonal lines, though restricted by the most severe of forms. Strangely enough, there are two explicit and almost separate codas—both as far from the fugue's flavor as sour is from sweet.

¶ *Serenade for Flute, Violin, Viola, Cello and Harp, Op. 30*

There is constraint in this quintet of mixed timbre. Roussel's frequent polyphony gives way to more vertical states and definite attention is accorded the colorful resources of one wind, one plucked, and three stringed instruments. The deftness of harp glides, arpeggios, and light ictuses help pigmentate this cheerful work, composed for the famous (no longer in existence) Quintette Instrumental de Paris.

The freer the lines, the more the urge to let each pursue separate paths. Limitations of one key can be overcome with the insertion of particular tones which move the tonalities side by side, instead of spreading one tonality between various voices. The slight application of such means is exhibited in the second movement, where the flute is mainly a solo voice against the three strings; the harp awaits the call for coloring the second portion, again mostly a solo, this time for the cello. The third section is a reprise in differentiated treatment. Both the outer movements exemplify the elements with which Roussel worked—the sobriety of classicism contemporaneously revitalized.

BALLET

¶ *Le Festin de l'Araignée* ("The Spider's Feast"), *Op. 17*

A charming score different in sound from the usual hard-core neoclassicism of the composer. In this case Roussel's music is as delicate as brush work, its textures of lazy, dusted substances. Although not impressionistic in style, one realizes how intensely beautiful Debussy can be in the translated terms of Albert Roussel.

The scene of the ballet-pantomime is a garden; the cast is headed by a spider, and includes ants, butterflies, beetles, fruit worms, and others (no human beings act as human beings). Woven around various episodes, some humorous (one, especially, depicts worms crawling into an enormous apple), the tale mainly concerns the villainous spider, who, after feasting on various insects, is finally killed by a praying mantis. Wonderful exotica—matched by music of such finesse and sensitivity that it seems to spin on the point of a needle.

24. ARNOLD SCHOENBERG
(1874–1951)

F EW men in music have caused such controversy as Arnold Schoenberg. It is indeed a rare day when the matter of a composer's musical technique reaches the editorial pages of daily newspapers, but Schoenberg achieved that honor in his lifetime. To understand the reasons, one must study Schoenberg's aesthetic progress, with its revolutionary (evolutionary) results.

His periods of work are marked as clearly as the boundary lines on a map. First there is the romantic spirit in vogue when he began to compose. Schoenberg used this in its most elaborate state: a Wagner-Mahler-Bruckner cosmos of tone enriched to such an extent that the aural appetite became surfeited. Realizing the dead end, Schoenberg began to pull away from the perpetual shifts and tonal fluxion of romantic musical language and to set his house of tones in order. Disciplining his conceptions by temperate editing, Schoenberg eliminated sonorous lushness, even though his music was still heavy, and entered the period of semitonality. (Schoenberg's. so-called "atonality" is only partially correct. His was actually tonality without rooted control, yet not without subconscious remembrance of tonal days past.)

In the third and last period, Schoenberg reached creative liberation. The unhampered sounds were gathered, reset, and revitalized into the startling invention of twelve-tone technique. This method was not discovered overnight but was developed by constant testing and rejection until the artistic light came through the technical mist. In later years, Schoenberg brought more and more polish and clarity of thought to his brain child. The more he produced the more logical and yet freer the system became. Nonetheless, this technical maturation had grown out of an already existing synthesis.

Twelve-tone technique is determined by the structural formation of the twelve pitches used in Occidental music. However, unlike the arrangement that guides major or minor tonalities, there is no relationship whatsoever to a focal or ground tone, a pivotal basis, or any type of polarity. Actually, the polarity is the entire set of dozen tones. This makes the music *fully* chromatic, completely abolishing

256

diatonicism, wherein seven of the dozen pitches are the total basic working material, with the remainder employed for modulation and coloration.

The twelve sounds are arranged (the "tone row") to determine the music's scope; therefore, they are a generator, defining its mode and mood as well. This constitutes the composition's entire existence—vertically, horizontally; melodically, harmonically, contrapuntally. The row is not shackled, however, so that it appears only in its original chronological order. It is permutated: in retrograde, inverted, and inverted in reverse; telescoping occurs, even at times at the point of the row's initial announcement. Shifts in sequence are made, equaling inner qualification—a variation on the tone row itself. Partial rows and split rows are also employed, each of which has its own interlocked changes. All these alterations are bound to the original statement. By transferring the tone row to any of the other eleven pitch levels and repeating the pattern, a modulatory parallel is established.

Nevertheless, Schoenberg's music stands not on this consummate logic, but on its authoritative content. It must be considered simply as a newer kind of musical rhetoric, without endeavoring to trace every chord and tone to its row root. True, Schoenberg's work gives perspicuous proof of a staunch structure. His emancipation of music from the tonal doctrine, initially met with impudent scorn, is now an orthodox discipline of the majority of today's composers.

ORCHESTRAL

¶ *Begleitungsmusik zu einer Lichtspielszene* ("Accompaniment to a Cinema Scene"), *Op. 34*

Schoenberg's Opus 34 has a subtle power rarely encountered in illustrative music, perhaps because he was not constricted by any scenario, since the "Accompaniment to a Cinema Scene" has nothing to do with any actual motion picture. The "film" is imaginary, coded by situations defined as "Threatening Danger," "Fear," and "Catastrophe." A double synchronization occurs; the music intensely defines the three-ply emotions and technically operates within strict dodecaphonic boundaries. Coloristic reflections and shifting contrasts (the orchestra is only of fair-sized total—far from Mahlerian "*Monumentalinstrumentation*") are a vivid double counterpoint as the composition unfolds its view of terror and tragedy.

257

The first American performance of Schoenberg's piece, on July 23, 1933, was presented, appropriately, at the Hollywood Bowl. It was conducted by the adventurous Nicolas Slonimsky. Was this Slonimsky's subtle way of giving the movie capital of the world an example of how film music could be written without resorting to the usual eclectic mishmash?

¶Choral Prelude—"Komm, Gott, Schöpfer, Heiliger Geist" ("Come, God, Creator, Holy Ghost") (Bach-Schoenberg)
¶Choral Prelude—"Schmücke Dich, O liebe Seele" ("Deck Thyself, Bright Soul") (Bach-Schoenberg)

Baroque style is liquidated in the coloristically detailed romantic address of Schoenberg's translation of Bach's texts. The moment one scores an organ piece for full orchestra, stylistic supersedure takes place. This does not signify any irreverence for the original. It does signify, in Schoenberg's case, a luminificent orchestration of Bach's black-and-white conceptions. Indeed, it may seem inappropriate to hear triangle and glockenspiel, plus harps (in the first of these preludes), and celesta (in the other), but all these timbres are fitting for the horizontal dignities of the music.

¶Five Pieces for Orchestra, Op. 16

Music that overreaches the boundaries of late romanticism (though clearly indicating the tonal sod that nurtured it), but is not yet dodecaphonic. The set of pieces is marked by microscopic orchestral camera work. Schoenberg's sensitive colors may bring to mind impressionistic relationships, but they are too subjectively abstract to be so categorized. They could be paradoxically described as "expressionistic impressionism." Each portion is formally free, remotely describing such conditions as "Premonitions," "Summer Morning by a Lake," and so on.

In essence this music is a five-part study in orchestral pigmentation. Melodic statements and harmonic ingredients contribute only minimally; the coloristic metamorphosis makes this so. Nothing like this had ever been attempted when Schoenberg completed his suite in 1909. Sonorities are dematerialized with a total absence of pedal-padding to weight the sound, thereby transferring the intimacy of chamber music to the large stage of the orchestra. There is no bombast in these essays even when the scoring is in a state of turbulence.

258

¶ *Pelleas und Melisande, Op. 5*

Schoenberg first considered "Pelleas and Melisande" as the subject for an opera, without knowing that Debussy had anticipated him. However, the length of the symphonic poem he produced (approximately forty-five minutes in length) makes it the equivalent of a one-act opera for solo orchestra. Schoenberg's overcharged and passionate consideration of the tale is in direct antithesis to the mystical, twilighted repression that marks Debussy's score.

More than a modicum of eclectic significance (meaning Richard Strauss, who suggested the use of Maeterlinck's tragedy to Schoenberg) is blended by leitmotif into the opus. Regardless, the particulars of craft are truly magnificent and are put to work to clearly outline the story line. Schoenberg's royal-purple orchestration is somewhat perfumed, somewhat overluxuriant (a massive apparatus is required), but meaningful. His intensely heated chromatic polyphony is controlled; the counterpoint *sounds*. It is not a mere receptacle for academic waste. Regardless of compositional perspicuity, a musical message must sonorize emotional factors. Schoenberg is not wanting in this respect.

¶ *Prelude and Fugue in E flat major* ("St. Anne") *for Organ* (Bach-Schoenberg)

Like his transcriptions of a pair of Bach's choral preludes (*see above*), Schoenberg boldly utilizes the instrumentational palette for his scoring of two parts from the same composer's "Clavierübung." Especially, the fugal magnitude is allied to superb orchestrational authorship.

¶ *Variations for Orchestra, Op. 31*

Considered the first actual twelve-tone orchestral work, the organization of the "Variations" offers a vivid testament of Schoenberg's craftsmanship. There is more than mere note-spinning in this creation. The generating tone row is exploited thoroughly, providing a remarkable emotional range that is spiritual, delicious, and exciting. These qualities are contained in the introduction, thematic statement, nine variations, and finale that comprise the composition. Further, the opus is a study of intense orchestrational design with a gamut that contrasts massivity and chamber style.

A work of this creative conviction proves the validity of Schoenberg's dodecaphonicism. It also shows the poverty of small-fry

259

disciples who employ a new "system" for each of their works, not one conceived from inner conviction. In their cases the "system" is an end as well as a beginning.

CHAMBER ORCHESTRA

¶*Kammersymphonie for 15 Solo Instruments* ("Chamber Symphony"), *Op. 9*

(This work is *not* in E flat major, despite the sale of scores indicating that key; it is, as Schoenberg insisted, in E major.)

The symphony is for eight winds (flute, oboe, English horn, three types of clarinets, bassoon, and double bassoon), a pair of horns, and one each of strings. Composed in 1906, it marked the completion of Schoenberg's initial period of work. It also indicates a dichotomous aesthetic stance. One part is in Straussian territory, the other in the superlogic land in which the composer was ultimately to settle. Although for a small orchestra, it signifies Schoenberg's initial employment of individualized timbre. The "Kammersymphonie" is a gigantic one-movement compilation with interlocking material. The parts of the structure are clear; including exposition, scherzo, development, slow movement, finale, and recapitulation.

¶*Second Chamber Symphony, Op. 38*

An odd set of facts surround this composition. As far back as 1906, when Schoenberg was an exponent of verbose German romanticism, he completed the first movement. Twenty-nine years later he reorchestrated it, and five years afterward wrote a second (and final) movement. It takes courage to compose at the age of sixty-six in the style one used at the age of thirty-two, yet Schoenberg was fully capable. Aside from matters of honesty (completely rewriting part one to match a maturer voice in part two would have been creative opportunism), Schoenberg understood he was courting stylistic failure if his advanced technique were not bent back to the previous method employed.

All this might be chasing one's shadow. Regardless, the accomplishment is quite successful. Schoenberg's symphony, with its youthful head uncovered, is heartily concerned with the days of "Verklärte Nacht." However, one can perceive a sharper technique, a subtler orchestration, a more powerful voice in the concluding section than in the initial one, even though this may be considered as critical hindsight.

260

¶ *Three Little Orchestra Pieces*

These midget-sized items (the last of the set is incomplete) were found among Schoenberg's papers after his death. (As of this date they are unpublished.) Elliptical expression and instrumental concentration are combined in the work. The lengths of the pieces are twelve, seven, and eight measures, respectively, and they employ, in turn, an octet, a dectet, and a dozen instrumentalists. Within the few phrases minuscule motives change like a bird in flight. The colors are shuffled like a pack of cards.

STRING ORCHESTRA

¶ *Verklärte Nacht* ("Transfigured Night"), *Op. 4*
(See further discussion of this work under "Chamber Music.")

Quite a number of critics and listeners use the orthodoxy of Schoenberg's "Verklärte Nacht" to confute his later output. Nevertheless, Opus 4 is not illustrative of the real Schoenberg, since it is only preliminary to his ultimate achievement—the liberal tonal lull before the systematized serial storm. Because of its somewhat lush emotionalism, "Transfigured Night" remains Schoenberg's most-played composition. (It is popular as the ballet, "Pillar of Fire.")

Although Schoenberg preferred the original sextet setting (composed in 1899) he never banned the string orchestra version that he made in 1917. In fact he produced a second, definitive edition in 1943 for the large string body. However, the buoyant urgency and clarity are not bettered, and in fact are lessened by multiplying the number of players.

BAND

¶ *Theme and Variations, Op. 43a*

A telling work that displays the band's special timbre of frank and candid brightness, even in the softer dynamics. It is a rare contribution to the literature (composed for school bands, but rarely so heard because it is not easy to play; performed just as rarely in a second version for orchestra). The design consists of seven variations and a finale on the theme, in Schoenberg's ultrachromatic (but tonal, not twelve-tone) writing.

261

SOLO INSTRUMENT WITH ORCHESTRA

CONCERTOS

¶ *Concerto for Piano and Orchestra, Op. 42*

Composed when he was close to seventy, the piano concerto represents Schoenberg at the very peak of his career. The technical logic is fascinating, properly a means of producing music of sculptural strength. Lyricism pours through the measures with colors that reflect old on new. These are set in a concerted plan whereby the keyboard instrument almost moves over into the orchestral territory. There is solo virtuosity, but politely stated. The music requires a top-echelon pianist.

While fantasy is proposed by a single movement, divisional definition is clear (the equivalent of variations, scherzo, slow movement, and rondo). Tonality remembrances shadow the music. These are not in the fat, early Schoenbergian (post-Wagnerian) sense, but, in his later manner, lean and bony. The "bogy" that tone-row music cannot be immediately meaningful is put to rest here. Those who insist that Schoenberg's music is mechanistic, formed on the drawing board with T-square and slide rule, are refuted by his expressive piano concerto.

¶ *Concerto for Violin and Orchestra, Op. 36*

Both the violent linear contours and the rhythmic restlessness of Schoenberg's intense concerto have led to the critical cry of "hysterical." Almost three decades later young composers label the piece "old fashioned." Two wrongs don't make a right.

The disdain for patterns that would fit the fingers, a coloristic, romantically inclined bravado, and volatile virtuosity do not exemplify an aesthetic gone amuck. These within balanced shapes (in three movements; moderately fast, slow, and marchlike, including a cyclic reference in the finale to the opening) define a classicist.

There is no doubt that Schoenberg's concerto fuses the subjective with the objective. He accomplishes this within a strict application of "composition with twelve notes related only to one another." He includes the conventional cadenza displays (none are conventional in style!) without interrupting artistic meaning or technical purity. Schoenberg's partnership of strict structural elements with sheer virtuosic demonstration is an exciting emotional and intellectual blend.

262

INSTRUMENTAL

ORGAN

¶ *Variations on a Recitative, Op. 40*

Fully chromaticized tonality (centered on D but permitted the fullest opportunity to roam) is illustrated in this huge production, one with Bachian grandeur and Regerian textural heaviness. This is Schoenberg's single contribution to organ literature. At first he planned and began the composition of a sonata, then discarded the idea in favor of the variations. Meant to be a short piece, all the stops are pulled out in consideration of the "king of instruments," and a long and complicated structure resulted.

Improper registration can make a shambles of the contrapuntalism. It is a common "right" of organists to countersign a composer's work by their own ideas of registration (excusable only by the exigencies of the instrument they may use). This kind of home rule often pads the lines, contrary to the composer's stylistic purposes which demand constant minute adjustments of color quality for true balance.

No cut-and-dried traditional theories of variation are employed in the set of ten, followed by a cadenza and a fugue of marvelous polyphonic utterance. However, the deployment of the theme (meaning the recitative) pays respect to bygone days. It is present in each of the variants, sometimes shortened, at other times slightly changed and/or ornamented, woven into all parts of the texture. The music's romantic complexion contains a goodly number of dodecaphonic behavior patterns. The twain meet.

PIANO

¶ *Five Piano Pieces, Op. 23*

There is a somewhat curious air about this suite; its expressionism is meaningful yet almost cold. Schoenberg is on the verge of integrating his musical fantasies with the concrete method of dodecaphonicism. While the conflicts show, the contents are sharply codified; including a quasi-fugue and a waltz.

¶ *Piano Piece, Op. 33a*
¶ *Piano Piece, Op. 33b*

These are the last pieces Schoenberg wrote for the piano, an instrument he did not play but for which he composed with great

263

skill. Both are a mature synthesis of the dodecaphonal method and are extremely approachable. The first is dramatic and the second of poetic contrast, exemplifying Schoenberg's stipulation of atonical romanticism. Lush munificence is avoided and, in place, is a cool (almost flinty) expression.

¶ Six Little Piano Pieces, Op. 19

Wondrous, spidery-fine, short, aphoristically considered music. Each of the portions is a perfect gem. Each of the objectives is a fascination for the ear. In the second piece a reiterative intervallic third holds the balance of power; in the third, *pianissimo* is required throughout in the lower part with variously deployed dynamics in the upper. Part four is bald melody propped by harmony. The final piece is an amazing bit constructed entirely from a single chord, presented in strengths no louder than *piano* and ranging to a dematerialized *quadruple piano*. A Webernian Schoenberg opus.

¶ Suite for Piano, Op. 25

Technical symmetry joins formal symmetry here. One tone row is utilized as the basic working material for all five movements. Because of the designs (a "Prelude," "Gavotte with Musette," "Intermezzo," "Minuet with Trio," and "Gigue") classical plan matches twelve-tone method. In turn, the minutely balanced objectives of the former are colored by the rhetoric of the latter. Though Schoenberg's "Minuet" does not swing in trinal oompah beat, the drone of the "Musette" (granting contrast to the almost piquant "Gavotte") and the rhythmic brilliance of the "Gigue" will be immediately apparent.

¶ Three Piano Pieces, Op. 11

Neither tonal nor twelve-tone, these pieces are in the no-man's land between—generally called "atonal." Minus a positive system of pitch arrangement the music's logic is obtained by motivic construction, repetition, and imitation. Inasmuch as there is no key, consonance and dissonance, in their tonal meanings, vanish. In their place, tensions and releases, together with shadings of lines (primarily contrapuntal, all chords being the result of this) furnish the balances.

Tradition is shunned, yet the past is present. This is especially the case in the first pair of the set, where late romantic urgencies develop. The third piece is violent, a motival tour-de-force.

264

VIOLIN

¶ *Phantasy for Violin with Piano Accompaniment, Op. 47*

The word "Accompaniment" explains why Opus 47 cannot be strictly defined as chamber music. Schoenberg's final instrumental work (the compositions that followed were for either voice or chorus), conceived in 1949, is honestly described. Though the piano is far from a mere handservant it is a secondary support to the principal voice. (According to Josef Rufer, a pupil of Schoenberg's and later his assistant at the Akademie der Künste in Berlin, Schoenberg first composed the violin part and then added the piano accompaniment, in order "to maintain the desired soloistic and virtuoso character of the piece.")

Though the free flight of imagery is the focal point of any phantasy, its improvisatory tendencies must be controlled. This compact piece wraps in one package the constituents of several movements. It begins with a declamatory theme contrasted to a lyrical second subject, the latter then developing with a dance lilt. A tripartite scherzo follows, leading to a changed and compressed recapitulation. The "Phantasy" illustrates Schoenberg's sensitive formal wisdom.

CHAMBER MUSIC

¶ *Canon for String Quartet*

A glimpse into a composer's workshop. This snippet (performance time approximately forty seconds) was written for Thomas Mann, as one of three supplementary pieces to the "Three Satires" for chorus.

¶ *String Quartet No. 1 in D minor, Op. 7*

One of the largest quartets in the literature, not only in performance time but also in scope. A one-movement compendium, it holds fast to classical tradition and at the same time kicks it to the side. The formal audacity, which is linked to Beethoven, moves much further afield.

Schoenberg's Opus 7 is boiling and seething, an emotional unification of the classical era and the romantic school. At the same time, it gathers up all that Wagner and Strauss had done. The synthesis

265

occurs in a technical *coup de grâce* that finds Schoenberg resistant thereafter to such manner of composing chamber music.

Tonality is very much in evidence, but inherent, not vertically displayed. The linear truths which Schoenberg later preached are being tested in this work. There is utter independence from confined tonality as the harmony soaks in a full contrapuntal bath. The single movement is devoted to fast-paced and scherzo concepts, a section in slow tempo, and a finale. These are tied together into a symphony for four stringed instruments.

¶ *String Quartet No. 2 in F sharp minor* (with Soprano Voice in Movements 3 and 4), *Op. 10*

Classical definition of form (sonata design in the end movements, scherzo and variations in between) mingles with a distinctive new-ness of sound material creating an original method of chamber-music presentation. The second string quartet has formal stability, but there is no compromise with free expression of tonality, which sweeps through the piece to such an extent that the final move-ment marks the starting point of a new chapter in musical history. This is Arnold Schoenberg's final work to bear a key signature— lying ahead is the emancipated land of twelve tones.

Here, too, for the first time instrumental and vocal chamber music become partners. In the first two movements the medium is strictly four stringed instruments; in the last two, a soprano singing words by Stefan George joins in, transforming the in-strumentation. George's text is dovetailed into the design and the quartet turns into a quintet by natural growth.

In view of what was to follow in Schoenberg's career, it is prophetic (if only coincidental) that the words of the last section begin "I feel the air of other planets." Impressionistic color is used with expressionistic detail, both at the service of a chamber-music drama. Schoenberg is now exempt from the traditional tenets of romanticism. He is not calm, however. The dodeca-phonic storm is to break soon.

¶ *String Quartet No. 3, Op. 30*

Schoenberg's third quartet is in his mature, strict style of twelve-tone composition. Within it concentrated thematics are used to establish precise architectural stability. The sounds remain romantic, though far from sweet, making a neutral blend of balanced sonority. The work also illustrates a type of classicism, but is as far from

Stravinsky's neoclassic brand as Wagner's *Ring* is from Debussy's *Pelléas.*

Schoenberg's handling stretches the classical line to a new point. Thus the permutations of the tone row accompany and parallel permutations within the sonata, variation, "Intermezzo," and "Rondo" forms. There is no static impulse; development proceeds to development, and symmetrical recapitulation is replaced by further evolution.

Interestingly enough, the word "moderato" figures in the tempo designations of all the movements, except the slow one. Decidedly, the most resolute consequences are achieved from "moderato" consideration.

¶ *String Quartet No. 4, Op. 37*

In this work, Schoenberg accomplishes a unique synthesis in which he contradicts neither classical form, nor his own technical premises. To combine the special system of a tone row and its zigzagged equivalence with nineteenth-century arrangement is a feat; it also has telling effect. Each movement of the fourth quartet is classical in design and each is ordered by the generative tone row. Both serial and traditionally styled music are honored simultaneously by Schoenberg's exceedingly well wrought, fascinating chamber-music contribution.

¶ *Quintet for Flute, Oboe, Clarinet, Horn, and Bassoon, Op. 26*

Schoenberg is the archromanticist of twentieth-century composers (Stravinsky *was* its archclassicist). The term applies to the inner creativeness involved, not the technical style. Schoenberg is the vital deputy of chromaticism, and that is precisely why he represents romanticism. This does not mean structural and textural thickness. Schoenberg's single work for the accepted combination known as the "wind quintet" (slightly modified in that a piccolo substitutes for the flute in the second movement and again for a short section in the fourth) is illustrative. It is heavily laden, but its weight is brought by the *action* of the sounds, not their static mass weight or the density resulting from heaped sonorities.

Architecturally, Schoenberg represents the most traditional composer of the contemporary musical revolutionaries. While this does not mean Haydnesque simplicity, it has the advantage of an identity better known than any other. Thus the sonata form of the initial movement, the "Scherzo," the ternary construction of the slow move-

267

ment, and the final "Rondo" offer secondary frames of reference to the dodecaphonic fluency that moves within.

¶ *Verklärte Nacht* ("Transfigured Night"), *Sextet for Two Violins, Two Violas and Two Cellos, Op. 4* (see also: String Orchestra)

Schoenberg's "Verklärte Nacht" is detailed program music, best understood with the Richard Dehmel poem as a guide to the tale. (It represents the first example of the symphonic poem form in the field of chamber music.) Schoenberg's rich scoring technique figures in the composition, as well as his tonally sensuous, *echt*-Wagnerian manner. It was from this super-romantic mania that Schoenberg fled because he did not want to be drawn into and then crushed by the cul-de-sac of Wagnerian doctrines.

The story deals with a conversation between a man and a woman which ends in the man's complete self-renunciation when the woman confesses that she is to bear another man's child. The man urges her not to feel guilty, that she shall bear the child for him—all this while walking through a dark forest, its coldness lessened in part by the moon above.

The fervent emotional premise is fully proven in this romantic drama. The conversation is amazingly conveyed by the give-and-take of Schoenberg's lines. The moonlight music is superb tone painting. Its fabric (subdued by mutes and low-keyed dynamics) is made from arpeggios, lightly plucked sounds, and a warm high-gamuted melody. This "white" music is ravishing.

¶ *Suite, Op. 29*

Though this unusual combination of three different types of clarinet, string trio, and piano, is proportioned by family groups, the color factor is applied to nurture the individual properties in each instrument. The composer also masses the timbres and relates his scoring to the serial system.

Divertimento representation is the formal beam of light for the music's path. The opening "Ouverture" is a sonata, followed by a "Tanzschritte" ("Dance Steps"), which resembles portions of the preceding movement. Schoenberg's instrumental choreography is entirely in duple meter; embroidered, transformed, skippy and slippery with full rhythmic exploitation. The governing rod of thematic variations aids in following the design of the third movement, and the suite concludes with a "Gigue" set in free sonata style.

This is music of trenchant complexity; a contrapuntal puzzle for the uninitiated. After sufficient study, familiarity will reveal the secrets of the score.

¶ *Serenade, Op. 24*

This music is gaily Viennese. The instrumentation is of serenade character with the plectral mandolin and guitar, lute-like equivalents with timbres unique to the field of chamber music. In addition to clarinet, bass clarinet, and a string trio, a low voice is used in the fourth of the seven movements (the text a sonnet by Petrarch).

There are innumerable humors and delights in the "Serenade." Schoenberg has rarely exhibited a lighter touch than in the squared rhythmic pungencies of the "March." This reappears in the finale, together with quotations from other movements. The "Minuet" is tart, yet as gracefully molded as any by Haydn. And in the "Dance Scene," as is so often the case in music by Austrian gentlemen, the triple waltz pulse of the cafés stands out. The more serious portions ("Variations," "Song Without Words," and the section with voice) do not detract from the serenade style. In his Opus 24, Schoenberg shows how cheerful and charming his music can be. To those who think of his work as forbidding and grim, it should be quite revealing.

VOCAL

¶ *Fifteen Songs from "Das Buch der Hängenden Gärten"* ("The Book of the Hanging Gardens"), *Op. 15*

To know Schoenberg's works one must be able to differentiate between the dodecaphonic works and those that immediately preceded them. At Opus 15 the long line had been crushed to short and severely demarcated ideas. This is musical suppleness and in vocal writing it amounts to mobility—quasi-recitative. Tonality is now free; cohesiveness is obtained by the musical shapes; polarity of mood substitutes for tonality; the crutch of key gives way to the central subject or idea which holds everything in place by magnificent logic. This is expressionism freed of objectivism.

Schoenberg selected a set of fifteen poems from a volume by Stefan George, which are colored by symbolism, exotic and rarefied to a great degree. The music he composed has no heavy perfume hanging about; it is subtle, extremely free and flexible, yet is one piece. The voice is not solo; it is an instrumental part of a duet. The composition is true chamber music for two performers.

269

¶ *Songs*

> *Eight Songs for Voice and Piano, Op. 6*
> *Four Songs with Piano, Op. 2*
> *Six Songs with Piano, Op. 3*
> *Two Songs for Voice and Piano, Op. 14*

Vocal composition was Schoenberg's strongest interest in his early works; two, four, and six songs, respectively, are included in the first three *opera*. These were followed by a set of eight (Opus 6), though chronologically a half dozen with orchestral accompaniment preceded, designated as Opus 8. Few voice and piano works came from Schoenberg's desk thereafter. In 1906 he composed "Two Ballads" (Op. 12), and, in the year following, two songs listed as Opus 14. The music to poems by Stefan George ("The Book of the Hanging Gardens") is a different conception, representing a closed cycle, and dissimilar to the miscellaneous vocal pieces. In the remaining period (from 1908 until 1951) Schoenberg produced only two song sets—a group of four with orchestra, completed in 1915 (Opus 22), and the three pieces for low voice and piano, written in 1933 (Opus 48).

The songs contained in opus numbers 2, 3, 6, and 14 are far from orthodox. The breaking of aesthetic lances can be heard in many instances. Affinity to traditional style is avoided by the freedom of both voice and piano; the latter is never accompanimental, and hints of Schoenberg's later disavowal of post-Wagnerian romanticism appear.

¶ *Alles, Op. 6, No. 2*

Restlessness is intensified by the use of wide, disjunct intervals. However, Schoenberg employs delicate textures to contrast the abundant chromaticism.

¶ *Am Wegrand, Op. 6, No. 6*

Music of passionate lyricism and controlled intensity.

¶ *Der Wanderer, Op. 6, No. 8*

The longest and largest-scope song in Schoenberg's Opus 6. The motivic manipulation is fascinating.

¶ *Erhebung, Op. 2, No. 3*

Though the leaps in the melodic line may portray "Exaltation," most of the text is set to a complex, yet richly sonorous texture. (The words are by Dehmel, the poet who wrote the lines on which "Verklärte Nacht" is based.)

¶ *Erwartung, Op. 2, No. 1*

Not to be confused with Schoenberg's monodrama of the same title. The mood of "Expectation" is realized by tonal properties, yet the desire to expand the aesthetic view is indicated by the use of quartal harmonies.

¶ *Freihold, Op. 3, No. 6*

No innovation, no groundbreaking, merely a song that revolves around G minor. Dika Newlin, in her study of the composer, points out the prophetic line included in the poem: "I stand alone, yes, all alone." It is not borne out by the music of "Freihold."

¶ *Ghasel, Op. 6, No. 5*

Music replete with the polyphonic devices that emerge in full flower in Schoenberg's twelve-tone compositions. Augmentation and diminution are utilized in this somewhat intimate, yet Oriental song, set to words by Goffried Keller, a Swiss poet.

¶ *Hochzeiteslied, Op. 3, No. 4*

A different creative attitude is displayed in this instance. "Hochzeiteslied" is split into two parts with the piano in between, again functioning soloistically at the close. The diatonic simplicity in the vocal line contrasts sharply to the all-pervading chromaticism of the songs in the preceding opus.

¶ *Ich Darf Nicht Dankend, Op. 14, No. 1*

A wintry cool piece. Tonality gasps for breath within thirty measures of slow, duple pulses. The two Opus 14 songs are historically and musically significant.

¶ *In Diesen Wintertagen, Op. 14, No. 2*

If the companion song in the opus is of cold temperature, this one has the feeling of warmth and sun. In the seventy-one measures, thirty-one are for the piano alone. The chordal vocabulary is used with the freest functionalism, while the vocal line obtains its coherency by motivic assembly.

271

¶ Jesus Bettelt, Op. 2, No. 2

This is also known by the first words of the poem: "Schenk mir deinen Goldenen Kamm." Chromaticism of Tristanesque extravagance is on display. Schoenberg's restless harmonies are in a state of perpetual modulation.

¶ Lockrung, Op. 6, No. 7

"Enticement" is in the key of E flat major, but is not a plain fabric. Its diatonic weave is laced and buttoned with chromaticism.

¶ Mädchenlied, Op. 6, No. 3

One-sided music with little effect. The piano portion is quite involved and commands whatever interest one can muster.

¶ Traumleben, Op. 6, No. 1

Schoenberg's method of yanking intervals out of their sockets in his later works is given a trial run in this song. Long leaps (especially of ninths) are in full evidence. It still is Wagnerian, though slightly corrupted.

¶ Verlassen, Op. 6, No. 4

As in the previous song of the group ("Mädchenlied"), the piano is almost a feature by itself, the voice a motival instrument counterpointing it.

¶ Waldsonne, Op. 2, No. 4

Some subtle ideas here, though on the whole a song with commonplace expression. "The Forest Sun" is the weak sister of this opus.

¶ Three Songs for Low Voice, Op. 48

As is so often the case in vocal composition, antipodal conditions rule this opus. The music (set to poems by Jakob Haringer) is romantic in shape, though not in its intervallic spans and motions. Similar response is maintained in the piano.

VOICE WITH INSTRUMENTAL ENSEMBLE

¶ Herzgewächse, Op. 20

This short item for soprano voice of wide range, plus harp, celesta, and harmonium, immediately precedes "Pierrot Lunaire" and can be considered a preliminary study for it. A clearly defined piece, its extensive curves would tax the best of singers. Musical importance before vocal comfort is the credo here.

¶ *Pierrot Lunaire, Op. 21*

These settings of twenty-one poems (oddly enough, Schoenberg's opus number is the same) by Albert Giraud, in German translation by Otto Erich Hartleben, for speaking voice and instruments, are focused on the vocal protagonist. They represent, therefore, a fascinating hybrid of theatre presented in chamber-music style.

"Pierrot Lunaire" once chilled the marrow of most critics. The famed James Huneker described Schoenberg's opus with sadistic implications: "he mingles with his music sharp daggers at white heat . . . he twists the knife in the fresh wound." As recently as 1952, a venerable American critic was still unable to understand the subjective climate of Schoenberg's moonstruck Pierrot or unwilling to realize the music's expressionistic validity as a proven contemporary classic. He wrote: ". . . the listener leaves . . . this work doubting his own sanity."

"Pierrot Lunaire" has shocked principally because the vocalist does not sing, but emotes midway between song and speech, thereby emphasizing both the prose contours and the musical content. A set of five players play eight instruments supporting the voice. However, the instruments do not *accompany* the *Sprechstimme* or act as a programmatic tool.

Schoenberg's music is complex because of its novel dualism: the atonical, fragmented lines are entwined in a colorful and concentrated instrumental weave, and are associated with the dramatic speaking voice. The product is a music of constant and unremitting tensility. Its colossal individuality makes it an enduring monument in the art world of the twentieth century.

CHORAL

¶ *Canon: The Parting of the Ways from "Three Satires," Op. 28, No. 1*

A concentrated gem of fun. The opening words "tonal or atonal" give the clue, and the polyphonic play follows suit. The effect is Elizabethan in modern full-dress clothes. Schoenberg's choral inspiration gives rise to a paradox: the more it is heard the more the beauty comes through and the less the satire.

¶ *Friede auf Erden, Op. 13*

An eight and one-half minute *a cappella* composition (completed the same day Schoenberg began his second string quartet) that spans his early luxuriant bravado and the later application of serial logistics. Tonality is present, its rays obscured by chromatic clash. Modulation has harmony by the throat, and classical chord construction is soon to be strangulated.

In this broad expanse of shifting colors, depicted by diatonic and chromatic elements, the effect is hypnotic. However, the texture is heavy-laden; the perpetual variation conduct of twelve-tone writing is previewed in the incessant chordal motion. The ear will tire if it is overloaded by such sonic weight. Fortunately, the length of "Friede auf Erden" is just short of a too-muchness.

CHORAL WITH INSTRUMENTAL ENSEMBLE

¶ *Four Pieces for Mixed Chorus, Op. 27*

Short, unaccompanied settings (except the last which employs a mixed quartet of violin, cello, clarinet, and mandolin) of texts by the composer in the first two pieces, and Chinese poetry in the last pair. Music from the twelve-tone realm, therefore polyphonic. Polyphonic, therefore of linear fluidity. The lone negative point is that the contrapuntal engagement interferes with depiction of the word meanings.

CHORAL WITH ORCHESTRA

¶ *Friede auf Erden, Op. 13*

The presentation of this piece with orchestra is a negation of the composer's objective. "Friede auf Erden" is for voices alone (*see above*) and no record exists that Schoenberg made or contemplated making a second setting with instrumental accompaniment. The orchestral doubling of the choral lines denies the purity of conception, despite Schoenberg's later viewpoint that his music was *probably* unsingable unless instrumentally supported.

¶ *Gurre-Lieder*

The "Gurre-Lieder" is a stupendous document of operatic totality wherein the fervency of Wagner and the orchestrational purple prose of Strauss are combined. Except for one section which affords lighter relief, everything is deadly serious.

274

A massive scope matches the two-hour length. The forces employed include five solo singers, a speaker, no less than three male choruses of ninety-six singers, a mixed chorus also of ninety-six, and a colossal orchestra, providing more for the exploitation of homogeneous timbre than for the mere enlargement of sound. Though gigantic orchestras mark much of the music of the late Romantic era, few composers indulged themselves as did Schoenberg with, for example, seven clarinets (three types) and seven trombones (four types). Aside from percussion, one hundred and thirty-eight players are demanded! Little wonder that the work has rarely been heard as producers stand in their own economic defense.

The "Gurre-Lieder" is intense love music mingled with grimness, drawn to a medieval Danish Tristanesque text. The apogee of liquid tonality is reached as Schoenberg begins his opus with creative eclecticism and concludes with an individual process—the employment of "Sprechgesang" (spoken melody), anticipating its expanded (and conclusive) use in "Pierrot Lunaire." Schoenberg wrings every passion from his inspiration. It has not cooled off in its half century of life. A far cry from the sober world inhabited by the serial works, it shows that a composer bares his beauties in many ways.

¶ Kol Nidre, Op. 39

One can read into the writing of this work Schoenberg's own desire to repent (*see below:* "A Survivor from Warsaw"). The text describes how all may pray together, asking for the annulment of selfish acts, and leads to a call for penitence. In his orchestration Schoenberg suppresses purely descriptive tactics; the subject data and technical style are sufficiently meaningful. A method of continued variation is applied to tonal material, interweaving the six-hundred-year-old "Kol Nidre" melody which is sung at the beginning of the twenty-four hours marking the holiest event in the Jewish liturgical year: the Day of Atonement (Yom Kippur).

¶ Prelude to "The Genesis Suite," Op. 44

This represents Schoenberg's contribution to a seven-part work in which six other composers were independently involved. The project of portraying the initial part of the Old Testament was the brain child of Nathaniel Shilkret, who commissioned the pieces and wrote one movement himself. Castelnuovo-Tedesco, Milhaud, Stravinsky, Tansman, and Toch were the other men concerned in the joint effort. (Coincidentally, all were residents on the West Coast.)

Schoenberg's "Prelude" is decidedly atmospheric in its beginning, a true translation in orchestral sound of ". . . the Earth was without form." It then moves into definite shape (dodecaphonically fugal), though of decided complexity, and proceeds to some wordless choral partnership. The conclusion resolves matters into clear tonality and a dynamic fade-out. It is as clear a piece of program music as Richard Strauss's "Don Quixote," though no guide was supplied by the composer.

CANTATA

¶ *A Survivor from Warsaw, Op. 46*

It should be recalled that Schoenberg rejected Judaism and became a Protestant, later renouncing that faith as well. Finally, in protest against Hitlerism, he returned to the Jewish faith in 1933. The Hebraic works are special, but *de facto*. In addition to settings of some psalms, these include the magnificent "Kol Nidre," the imposing opera "Moses und Aron," and this pithy six-minute cantata for speaker, male chorus, and orchestra, written in 1947.

The "Survivor" score is chillingly clear, describing the brutality and horrors of a Nazi concentration camp, the preparation for death in the gas chambers. Schoenberg's choice of different languages makes for biting naturalism. The narrator employs English and changes to German when representing the Nazi monsters, while the Jews' traditional, ritualistic *Shema Yisrael* ("Hear, O Israel") is delivered by the chorus, naturally, in Hebrew. This last is one of Schoenberg's greatest inspirations. Intertwined with anguished twisting lines it creates a second dimension of gripping emotion against the background of turmoil. In addition, colors are utilized for concise, strong impressionistic purposes. The orchestra is no frame for the voices; it is a prime member of the *dramatis personae*.

¶ *The New Classicism from "Three Satires," Op. 28, No. 3*

Supposedly, a snide view of neoclassicism. However, the joke is told in serial-shaped slang and will be rather ambiguous to all but a select few. In fact some of the points are so smoothly communicated that a listener may well miss the humor and not realize Schoenberg is snickering at the pandiatonic camp.

That one can ridicule neoclassicism in the midst of manipulating tone rows is not proven here. Like so many great men Arnold Schoenberg was egocentric. In "The New Classicism" he is a bit hysterical. For the most part Schoenberg's scoffing turns into self-mockery.

OPERA

¶ *Die Glückliche Hand, Op. 18*

Symbolism becomes Schoenberg in this allegory devoted to man's suffering, disillusionment, and shattered hopes. It can well be considered a self-portrait in tones. Unfortunately, Schoenberg's home-made libretto is embarrassingly corny. Fortunately, it concerns only a fraction of the composition's eighteen-minute length. The action is principally pantomime, guided by meticulously detailed and complex stage and lighting directions. Within the orchestra the darker elements are featured, interposed with stabs and jabs that make each register with the impact of a hammer stroke.

"Die Glückliche Hand" has the violence, the colorative excess, and the formal stream of consciousness that describe the world of expressionism. It is morbid, hard-edged, and remorseless. It whiplashes the emotions. It isn't pretty.

¶ *Erwartung, Op. 17*

Schoenberg's monodrama permits a listener to draw his own conclusions. "Erwartung" concerns a woman who goes to a forest to meet her lover and finds his murdered corpse instead. Its four scenes can be considered in two sections: first, the woman's fear of the woods, her wait and search for the man, and eventual discovery of his body; second, a soliloquy addressed to the dead person. The principal facets are hysteria and eroticism laced with hate. Nothing is explained in a scrutiny that moves through a Freudian world of dreams. "Erwartung" could be descriptive of a real experience, signify the actions of a deranged person, or simply constitute a staged nightmare. The question mark that surrounds it is a neat dramatic subterfuge.

The single character has a feverish vocal line, as orchestral in its gamut of exposure as the orchestra itself. Together voice and instruments counterpoint the moods and colors of a moonlit forest, the thoughts of anxiety, jealousy, and love, the terror of the climax. Never erupting but always on the verge are the seismic intensities of the imagery. It is this suspenseful, never-resolved condition that builds up the heat of "Erwartung." No contraction takes place within its tumescent state of neurotic ecstasy.

277

¶ *Moses und Aron*

Schoenberg's magnum opus (it occupied him some twenty-five years), in terms of conception, forces employed and deployed, and technical magic (the entire opera is constructed from a single tone row). This emotionally powered, beautiful music with uncanny dramatic magnetism holds one captive.

Schoenberg himself wrote the text, succinctly defining his two principal protagonists. Moses personifies thought (the world of God), Aaron illustrates action (the reality of life). To underline this contrast of the sacred and the profane, the former is given a speaking role and the other assigned to a tenor voice. The Biblical tale is not exactly translated but rather depicted in symbolic experiences. The scope is vivid: God's message conveyed through Moses, the performance of miracles, the refusal of God by the people, Moses' absence for forty days, the descent into sin and worship of the Golden Calf, the return of Moses with the Tables of the Law, his destruction of them, and his final despair. This brings the musical work to an end; another act exists with only the text. Despite conflicting viewpoints the opera can be accepted as complete—as complete as Schubert's "Unfinished."

The demands of "Moses and Aaron" are prodigious, including thirteen "leads," with other groups totaling as few as "six to eight," and as many as seventy! Six solo voices are situated in the orchestra, itself a large aggregation calling for a big percussion section, piano, and a pair of mandolins; a stage orchestra is also required. The erotic orgy and sacrificial scene, if staged as Schoenberg wanted them, would be a censor's field day. The virgins in this opera are to be stark naked, and the frenzy, drunkenness, and sexual play during the bacchanal to end all bacchanals ("The Dance Round the Golden Calf," the third scene in the second act) are a powerful enticement for bluenoses and assorted Mrs. Grundys.

Schoenberg's operatic sense makes nonsense of the criticism that twelve-tone technique is incompatible with the broad, diverse needs of a large-scale stage work. Serialism serves every required purpose meaningfully and retains its own stylistic purity at the same time. The fascinating rhythmic contours are another denial of the prejudices that have arisen about dodecaphonicism. And the instrumental dimensions are new in the field of orchestration. "Moses and Aaron" is truly a phenomenon in Schoenberg's legacy.

25. KARLHEINZ STOCKHAUSEN
(1928–   )

THE figure of Stockhausen stands in bold relief among the most important of present-day (especially postwar) composers. To some he is the latest *enfant terrible,* to others he is a special pleading experimenter, a few classify him as a tormentive sensationalist. He is terribly concerned with theories, he *is* an experimenter, but the provocative torment he raises is merely the seeking of uninhibited cutaway-from-the-past music. Stockhausen never repeats himself exactly. Each new work is unique and only tenuously related to a previous one. Each opus is newer new music. His followers are many, and his importance is not to be underestimated.

Godfather to his writing (as to so many of the young avant-garde, like Nono, Berio, Maderna, etc.) is Webern in his late-period. In turn, the chain of command has made Stockhausen father of the twice-left-of-center school, represented by Kagel, Nilsson, Bussotti, Pousseur, etc. Stockhausen was attracted by Webern's radically new sensibility, his "formal purity." Formality has warmed Stockhausen, even come close to consuming him, for it has led to a coldly calculated virtuosity, whereby the multicomplex construction of every element in a composition is predetermined.

There is a danger in this kind of planned morphology of the musical structure. The intense, dogmatic practice of equality which diffuses contrasts and eradicates the give-and-take between melodic, harmonic, rhythmic, metrical, and other aspects may be strikingly disciplined but decidedly futile. Stockhausen bypasses his hair-shirted, rigid technical precepts by enlarging them into further creative discoveries. His aesthetic is austere, but this does not mean it is ineffective.

His concepts have caused an enlargement of music's vocabulary. A few examples: *parameters*—mathematically decided, serial considerations applied to the height and depth of sounds, color, mode of attack, tempi, etc.; *time fields*—visual depiction of sounds rather than ordinary notes with stems, beams, etc. (this partakes of guided improvisation, since the performer makes his own translation of the shapes in regard to thickness and length); *sound objects*—electronic treatment of sounds not possible with the usual instrumental classifications.

Beginning with music styled in the desiccated post-Webern manner, Stockhausen proceeded to compositions (utilizing electronic instruments and music composed on tape) that eliminated the interpretative performer. Eventually he turned to the opposite concept, requiring a large number of performers plus conductors, as in his "Gruppen" for three orchestras, thereby coincidentally touching on another facet of his work: stereophony and spatial designs in music. In between came the exciting matter of combining rhythmic complexity with controlled improvisation ("Zeitmasse"), productions with infinite choice permitted the player (thus chance merges with prearranged defined form). These compositional inventions are sometimes interlinked. In "Kreuzspiel" not only rigorous calculation of material exists, but directions are given for the placement of the four players involved (oboe, bass clarinet, piano, and percussion) as well as the height of the platforms on which the instrumentalists are to sit and perform.

Stockhausen is an intrepid musical explorer. His expositionary output is vast. The manifestations of his sounds go far beyond the tonal conveniences of the distant past, the ordered freedom of the twelve-tone system of the recent past. Stockhausen makes no reidentification, calls on no creative mnemonics. The prospectus of his music is radically new; his devices absolute innovations.

ORCHESTRAL

CHAMBER ORCHESTRA

¶*Kontra-punkte* ("Counterpoint")

One enters, in this piece, the post-Webern, pointillistic world of sound. Stockhausen's aesthetic conduct is one of pure formal arrangement of instrumental colors contrapuntally blended and compared in minute proportions. His method is nonlyrical, non-melodic, discontinuous; the ideas develop only within a timbre play of ten instruments deployed in six basic components: flute and bassoon; clarinet and bass clarinet; trumpet and trombone; violin and cello; piano; harp. Intermutation, tension and release, pitches, agogic receptivity, and all other fundaments are abrogated in favor of the instrumental spectrum.

In this unthematic music each texture is stretched (by its fragmentation) until the total sonorous gamut is of gigantic scope, much larger, in fact, than a tonal orchestral work for seven times the number of instruments. Stockhausen's piece is quite indifferent to formalism. It is a substantial example of a vibrating color image.

¶*Zeitmasse* ("Tempi")

In the orders and disciplines of most of today's advanced music, rhythms have been unshackled to a point where they almost cease to have specified shapes and lack a relationship to mensural binary and ternary divisions. In "Zeitmasse" Stockhausen goes still another step forward and splinters tempo.

Traditionally (and this includes the disparate styles of such twentieth-century composers as Bartók, Schoenberg, Stravinsky, and Varèse) tempo has been a basic premise; whether the unit speed increases or decreases, a relationship is apparent and defined to a central pulse rate, regardless of multitudinous shifts. The commanding speed equaled the monarchy of the key within tonal music, the pivotal tone in freer realized music, the tone row of dodecaphonic music. "Zeitmasse" (which means "tempi" or freely "time measures") is like no other musical composition in its disordered tempo and abrogation of metric continuity. It contrasts and combines metronomically set speeds with those that are slowed down or made faster according to the performer's will. It juxtapositions tempi of different ratios (not precisely polyrhythmic since nothing is rigidly fixed); it makes tempo unrest the prime sensation.

The patterns within the music follow this disintegrative range, and for the most part consist of values disassociated from any fundamental time phase. These designs parallel the lack of tempi cohesion and consist of fragmentary and/or super-cadenza whirlwind notes. Dynamics follow suit in their agile shifts. In some twelve minutes Stockhausen creates a species of musical atomization. He proves his statement that time is most experienced when all sense of time is lost.

PERCUSSION ORCHESTRA

¶*Refrain*

Keyboard instruments are combined with percussion for each of the three performers in this composition. The distribution is as follows: first player, piano and three wood blocks; the second, celesta and a set of three antique cymbals; the third, vibraphone, three cowbells, and glockenspiel. Further, the players utter sounds as additional percussive equivalents; human and instrumental detonations are thereby coalesced.

Stockhausen's score is printed on curved staves. A transparent attachment with various signs on it can be swung on the face of the score thereby changing the reading in relation to that portion with which the supplementary device comes in contact. This proposes the element of chance. The notation of Stockhausen's composition therefore includes both rigidly fixed indications and symbols that are mere pictorial representations for interpretation.

Despite the kaleidoscopic range of choice the outcome can be described. "Refrain" is a skeleton of soft contentious sounds; the rhythms drugged so that a fundamental pulse is eliminated. Melodic ellipsis takes place as tones are fragmented, isolated and disconnected. The central argument consists of dynamic contrasts and timbre extremes, with the nuance of expression piloted by the dart of sound from polarized registers.

The rituals of Stockhausen's "Refrain" indicate a further and further departure from the realms of ordinary instrumental conduct and sound like the equivalent of electronic sonorities translated backwards, as it were, into instrumental terms. With the use of percussion Stockhausen conceives a music which is nothing more than a constant vibrating concussion of accentuations.

INSTRUMENTAL

PERCUSSION

¶ *Zyklus* ("Cycle")

Stockhausen devotes his creativity to the matter of chance in this piece for one performer using marimbaphone, vibraphone, guiro, assorted drums, bells, cymbals, triangles, and gongs. The percussionist has a score of some sixteen pages and may start on any page but must then play "a cycle in the given succession." The notation offered is an amalgam of few notes plus many shapes; the latter are a stimulant for the performer—a pictorial bridge—since they are translated at the will of the soloist. The explication (an award should be given to anyone who can make sense of the composer's explanatory notes) is far more ambiguous than the music itself.

Because of its major reliance on unpitched instruments with related *types* of sound (metallic, membraneous, and sibilative), "Zyklus" follows the tenets of athematicism. There is no development; only a free, very independent, and ever-fresh unrolling of pulsatile demonstrations in one basic and general mood. There is artistic

282

balance within Stockhausen's monologue regardless of the freedom of choice offered the interpreter.

PIANO

¶ *Klavierstück 6* ("Piano Piece 6")

To understand Stockhausen one must realize his ancestral bond with Webern, and to recognize this one must comprehend Schoenberg. Schoenberg's desire for order without tonality, the cancellation of the precept that one sound could be more important than another, led to his startling new system distinctly removed from the diatonic orbit. His pupil, Webern, went still further in his late compositions, reorganizing tone colors and intensities, with a special emphasis on silence itself. Webern was moving toward a totality of serial principles; any clinging forms of the past (recognizable in Schoenberg's music) were eradicated. This was to be irrefutable anticlassicism, antiromanticism. Karlheinz Stockhausen arrives at Webern's goal and goes far beyond it.

This piano music is not an example of discontinuity. What Stockhausen is practising is exhaustive regulation. Pitch, registration, duration of sound (as well as silence), intensity, articulation (type of touch), are all as carefully and precisely knitted as the twelve tone-row system.

Compared to Schoenberg's weighty textures, Webern's are extremely thin. In turn, Stockhausen's "Klavierstück" is much more transparent, though more brittle than Webern's music. Stockhausen's *contrecoup* may disturb or shock but it has historical sequence in its favor. On this basis it must be seriously considered by the auditor.

ELECTRONIC COMPOSITIONS

[*At one time, the advocates of so-called "mechanical music" hoped for electrical means to extend music's boundaries. The inability of a bassoon to go beyond a tenth above middle C, the limit of true violin timbre bounded by its pivotal G string, and so on—all such restrictions would be eliminated once the forces of science were put to work. Present-day instrumentation would remain intact, as would the most complex rhythmic combinations. But here, too, the laboratory would produce a machine to solve the problems in terms of perfect string, wind, brass, or percussion qualities. Electronic music is altogether*

*another essence. The Hammond organ is its only counterpart in
modern instruments. (Even though this sickly, deep-set sonority is but
a small portion of the electronic catalogue, it poses a drawback because of the association the sound immediately brings to mind.)*

*[It seems apparent that electronic music is incorrectly named. The
term "music" implies that relationships exist between electronic discoveries and traditional procedures of composition and playing. But
electronic "music" needs no performer as the intermediary. The tape
recorder is the instrument that "performs" through loudspeakers what
the composer has put together in a special electronic studio, using
sinus tones and frequencies, mixtures, noises, complexes and impulses,
et al. That composers have transferred (subconsciously and consciously) their experiences to the problems of electronic sound (a
preferable term) goes without saying. But it is clear that while empty-
ing the chromatic bath they have thrown out the musical body with it.]*

¶ *Gesang der Jünglinge I* ("Song of the Youths I")

Much variety exists in the "Song of the Youths." There is tremendous tension in this work which combines a young boy's voice
with the electronic vocabulary. The human voice also undergoes tape
arrangement-disarrangement, and the fragmentation gives startling
effects. The expressive assortment includes intelligible words, a sweetness jelling with the very opposite.

Stockhausen's piece is an experience. To the listener faced with
this new art no short cuts or listings of maxims of behavior will
suffice. He must be prepared to remove the "warder of the ear."

¶ *Kontakte*

Normal musical procedures do not prevail here. "Kontakte" includes no themes, countersubjects, harmonies, or heterophony (though
hocket technique will be noted by sly listeners). Rather, one hears
recoil from sonic impulse, approach and recession, patterns of attraction and repulsion, an ingress and egress of sound objects.

Some of Stockhausen's fancy inventions will remind one of the
instrumentational atmosphere, though this is actually not the proper
way of considering "Kontakte." The parallels must be indicated,
nevertheless. They include an organ, a quintuple *fortissimo sul ponticello* abrasion in the low cello register, a cymbal rolled with tin
beaters, a double bassoon playing an octave below its lowest "possible" point in flutter-tonguing style, a contrabass banjo-mandolin,
etc. Less heard as a mosaic of sound and rather considered as aurally

"viewed," the composition is a fascinating exploration of sonic objects turning into forms—the movement of these shapes rear and front, in symmetry and distortion (symmetry in sequences found in the composition), sharp and blunt, rough and smooth, open and perforated. At the same time the action of these formations depicts a second level of association, wherein motion and quiescence contrast.

In this manner "Kontakte" lives up to its title and has a stirring, fiery irritation. Listening to it the meaning of weightlessness of sound is realized. There are other discoveries—the violent braking of speed (in the final section of part one) accompanied by a descent into the electronic bowels of the apparatus being used is "climax" as never before experienced. The initial division is broad and dramatic. The twice-as-long second portion is a scherzo equivalent, fundamentally proposing snapped dabs of sound, giving a sense of suspense that is ultimately unresolved as the composition terminates in the most finite type of decrescendo.

Only the length raises a problem. "Kontakte" will crumple and corrugate many an ear, but the shirring and smocking would be eliminated (almost) if the piece were cut in half instead of running on through its two movements for well over a half hour. Regardless, the evidence is boldly clear. With his "Kontakte" Stockhausen has jumped the field with his colossal knowledge of electronic techniques.

¶ *Studie I*
¶ *Studie II*

Though Stockhausen calls his pieces "Studies" they are not coldly pedantic. They include defined areas of tempi and register; dark timbres are contrasted with heated high combinations, and these contrast in terms of speed. The range of experience (related only to constructive arrangement, not to recognizable musical procedures) deals with quantities, qualities, and proportions. One point is clear: the permutations of Stockhausen's chosen elements are very noticeable. The very opposite of instrumental music, the pair of electronic études have definite effect on the unbiased listener.

26. ERNST TOCH

(1887–1964)

THERE are some composers whose names are unfamiliar to the great majority of concertgoers, though they are included in the select roster of internationally important creative musicians. Ernst Toch is such a one. Once his work is examined, it will be recognized immediately as being of the very highest rank. Toch turned out a large number of compositions during the time that Hindemith, Stravinsky, Schoenberg, and Bartók were making their presence felt. Why, then, has he remained in the background?

Toch manifested all the original thinking one would expect from a young composer writing in the twenties and thirties. Included in his output were chamber operas, works for band, mechanical organ, and an amazing fugal conception for four-part speaking chorus. This was no attempt to revolt, but actually an enthusiasm for the sensitivities of sound in all its prismatic possibilities. Toch evinced an independent freedom of any technical dogma—retained his personality by disavowing pretentiousness. His linear counterpoint was not the motorized vehicle that drove Hindemith from one continent to the next; his was not a music that would draw Stravinskian hisses on *Sacre* beats; no twelve tones were arranged and advertised; he made no folkloristic excursions. Although Bartók, Schoenberg, and the others made no attempt to sell their wares; these were wrapped in bright new paper— one was drawn to look inside.

These days a composer must be a press agent, directly or indirectly. Ernst Toch's refusal to patrol the musical market place, more than any other reason, has isolated him. Humility is a virtue often preached, rarely practised. Toch was content to compose music and practise humility.

Though the cool-warm qualities of Brahms are only noticeable in Toch's very early music, the classic-romantic hybrid rationale was never completely eliminated. This mode of speech with contemporary inflections governed Toch's aesthetic. His compositions contain free yet decidedly formal strength and intense feeling for color. The excitement of spontaneity is paramount, for Toch was a nonconformist in terms of general design and instrumentation. His works evolve; they are not driven into formal enclosures. Even in its most exciting documentation Toch's music is always ordered with beauty. He was an earnest composer, a distinct personality in the music of this age.

ORCHESTRAL

¶ Circus, an Overture

Toch's carnival music is infiltrated with lively description. However, "Circus" should be considered as a *jeu d'esprit* rather than of fully positive programmatic content.

Aside from the stimulus of the title, there are sections dealing with the roar of wild beasts, the cracking of the ringmaster's whip, and clowns' antics. Finally, a beautifully percussive chord. Toch has had fun! So will the listener.

¶ Notturno, Op. 77

Unique tonal pigments are prime in the cool and veiled effects of this one-movement composition. The gloved instrumentation does not include string basses, and though it calls for three trombones these are used for only a few chords toward the end; the sole percussion is a xylophone that does not crackle. Toch disposes the orchestra into groups, deploys these forces as though composing a hundred-and-one different chamber-music duets, trios, quartets, quintets, sextets, and so on—there is not a single measure of full orchestra tutti!

This unorthodox sonorous poetry is more devastating in its effect than the music of a tone-protesting composer. The arguments of this three-part nocturnal essay are not from Chopin but out of a "midsummer night's dream." However, the light and shade of timbre and sonority are but part of the instrumental inquisitiveness of this bold composer; the "Notturno" also offers impressive musical imagery.

¶ Peter Pan, A Fairy Tale for Orchestra in Three Parts, Op. 76

Regardless of the history of the scherzo—the dramatic ones by Beethoven and Bruckner, the gossamer examples by Mendelssohn, and Chopin's fantastic types—its form displays music of motility, vigorous rhythm, whimsy and surprise. Though Toch's Opus 76 is not designated as a scherzo, it is of the fanciful scherzo genre, broadly fulfilling all its elements and framed by color that sets off the ideas.

"Peter Pan" has balanced design yet is improvisational as the orchestral components are tossed around. Formal adventure, not formal pedantry is found in Toch's work. In this delightful projection of

287

motival thoughts one will find a fresh experience of formed sounds rather than sounded form. In the big noise of contemporary music little has been produced that is more exquisite than the second movement. It consists of sixty-five measures in moderate tempo, where everything moves on carpeted sonorities.

¶ *Third Symphony, Op. 75*

Good thematic material is often nullified by being set in stereotyped design. This composition is a fascinating exploitation of distinctive ideas which do not negate the requirements of full-scale symphonicism, and yet the structures are molded to suit Toch's own purposes. The music avoids the foregone conclusions of fashionable styles, substituting directness for scholastic neoclassicism, using gusto in place of bulky neoromanticism. It is a potent rebuttal to academicism . . . new or old.

Four-movement design coalesces into three-movement order in the symphony. Two-thirds of the piece is basically lyrical (the second portion telescoping a slow movement with scherzo factors); the last part exemplifies bold dramaticism. Carbon-copy recapitulation is avoided; the structural pliancy of the score is paralleled by its tonal flexibility. Fresh in conception, the symphony bears out its motto (from Goethe's "The Sorrows of Young Werther"—"Indeed am I a wanderer, a pilgrim on the earth—but what else are you?"), which Toch indicated was a spiritual prop for his creation.

The "Third Symphony" was awarded the 1956 Pulitzer Prize. The orchestration is drawn from a palette of spectacular assortment, including Hammond organ, vibraphone (sometimes requiring two players), and a hisser (a tank of compressed gas—its flow, controlled by a valve, producing the sound). Unfortunately, at the time of the symphony's première much publicity attended the use of these instruments (and some others, since removed from the score), so that undue emphasis was placed on matters which were never considered for shock purposes.

INSTRUMENTAL

PIANO

¶ *The Juggler, Op. 31, No. 3*

The "hit" piece of Toch's piano output. Its popularity is fully deserved. "Der Jongleur," the last of a set of "Burlesken," is a brilliant scherzo sketch.

¶ *Ten Studies for Beginners, Op. 59*

The last part of the *5 x 10* cycle of piano music that covers Toch's *opera* 55 through 59; five sets of ten pieces, each in a decreasing range of difficulty. Though the material is simple, the miniatures hold one's interest through their effortless craftsmanship. One will be reminded of Schumann with light salt.

CHAMBER MUSIC

¶ *Serenade in G major, Op. 25*

While three-part construction is sufficiently difficult for a composer, the string trio formed from two violins and a viola is fraught with severe restrictions. Since a true bass is lacking, this medium deals with soprano and tenor gamuts. But it is actually the *lack* of bass tone that gives Toch's trio its rare charm.

The "Serenade" (it has a parenthetical title, "Spitzweg," explained by the source of inspiration—a painting by this nineteenth-century German) flows throughout in its restrained color. It is relaxing, undramatic music, with all the power inherent in well-formed, romantic harmonies. Only four measures depart from the openhearted swing of duple meter. For the most part the music whispers a Viennese *Gemütlichkeit* long lost.

¶ *Sonatinetta for Flute, Clarinet and Bassoon, Op. 84*

Tidy productive habits are illustrated in Toch's pithy opus so that wheels within wheels do not turn in the music. In the opening part there is a charming élan which reminds one of a contemporary Mozart. In the concluding movement Toch moves his allegro with whimsical lightfootedness. The tender discourse of the inner division begins as a solo, turns into a duet, and finally achieves full trio status. The colors dart hither and thither. They are exciting elements in this example of sonorous freshness.

¶ *String Trio, Op. 63*

Music not submissive to dogma, yet as clearly balanced as any opus of the classical school. Its tempi are in symmetry (two allegros flank an adagio); the moods of the fast movements are dramatic and propulsive, that of the slow portion a dark intermezzo. Toch intertwines harmonic and polyphonic textures with keen craftsmanship and obtains further subtle contrasts.

289

Rich in romantic quality, the trio is raked with chromatic teeth which dig the tonality out of its bounded fields and cover it with delicate abrasions. Erudition and logic are here, but not at the expense of meaning. Only the last movement seems diffused; not labored, but slightly belabored.

¶ *String Quartet in D flat major, Op. 18*

Toch's first published string quartet followed a half-dozen works in the medium, written when he was in high school. Opus 18 was conceived at the age of 22, and the music displays a harmonically chromatic, richly diverse, romantic text. It also contains the Germanic-Austrian predilection for length, spanning five movements: an introductory division ("Quasi Prologus"), a pair of scherzi surrounding a slow movement, and a rondo-styled finale. Coming events cast their compositional shadows—the scope and travel of the initial theme of the last movement are indicative of Toch; aggressive subjects were used in all periods of his work.

Hearing this quartet without knowing the composer, one would immediately recognize it as Viennese, a combination of Brahms and post-Brahms. The music is warm with the tender sentimentalities and passionate rhythmic habits of these periods; the eclecticism is traceable to its source. Regardless, there is integrity of style and feeling.

¶ *String Quartet No. 10* (on the Name "Bass"), *Op. 28*

Varying stimuli have caused musical action. A favorite child may inspire a lullaby; Honegger's love for locomotives was exalted in his "Pacific 231"; love of homeland actuates a symphonic poem. Another example is the translation of a person's name into music (as much of it as possible, or assigning specific tones to match the letters that have no musical representation). Bach's name has been excellent game. Not only is it revered, but all the letters in his name have pitch equivalents ("B" in German equals "Bb," "A" and "C" stand as is, and "H" in German is synonymous for B natural).

To pay tribute to his cousin, Toch used this form of musical anagram, basing his quartet on his relative's cognomen, "Bass." All the sounds are based on German terminology. As noted above, the "B" equals "Bb," the final "S" turns into an "Eb," and by combining the two middle letters, the sound of "Ab" is obtained.

All themes of the four movements employ this technique. It turns out that Bass's name is susceptible to all shades of feeling. The designs are clear-cut: rondo, variational aspects of song form, scherzo, and a free disposition of sonata shape. There are many delights in the quartet, especially the vivid streaming lines and chromatic figures of the "catlike" third movement. Rhythmically speaking, the last movement is just as agile.

¶ *String Quartet No. 12, Op. 70*

There are other assets in this quartet besides its healthy contemporary lyricism. These are the memoranda of subtly deployed string qualities. In addition to the elegance of the part writing (superb color realization by itself) fascinating items include a pair of quarter-tone chords, and a glissando-arpeggiated pizzicato cadence that is a fillip to the haunting melody of the "Pensive Serenade."

Differences exist between mere polyphonic pugnacity and genuine contrapuntal mating. The initial movement is of semicontrapuntal order, outlined with an ostinato-formed rhythmic plan. Here the music is active yet relaxed—it might be described as tender counterpoint. Polyphony continues in the chromatic second movement. Only at the end is the music homophonic. And in the final division the contrapuntalism is intensified by use of *stretto*. In Toch's hands none of this is starched polyphonic music but expressive realization. This is a quartet of sound feeling as well as sound technique.

¶ *String Quartet No. 13, Op. 74*

Behind any good art there must be the *primum mobile*. Though Toch utilizes twelve-tone technique here (he had never employed it previously) he has twisted the tail of this technical animal so that he is its master. And having mastered, he departed from the scene. The thirteenth quartet signified a fresh-sounding, productive contribution to Toch's output, but he did not intend to use the dodecaphonic system in the future. (Toch's credo was explicit: ". . . twelve-tone writing can be an enrichment—by liberal incorporation into the store of the past—as well as it can be an impoverishment—by dogmatic rejection of everything outside of it." And further: ". . . I do not belong to the . . . twelve-tone composers and . . . I do not intend to join. . . .")

This music does not exemplify rampant serialism. It is simply of different character from Toch's other works, yet it has Toch's imprints; the chinky-chunky, propulsive rhythmic style, the formal solidity, scoring that contrasts violence and repose, and the poetic quality of dramatic counterpoint. The marriage of convenience (Toch did not deliberately set out to compose a twelve-tone work; his initial theme led him to it) has produced a healthy child, if not a lusty one.

¶ *Quintet for Piano, 2 Violins, Viola and Violoncello, Op. 64*

The instrumentation of Toch's piano quintet is most interesting. This medium can easily convey an overdue amount of thickness. Toch's solution pits the strings against the piano in one, two, three or four voices. Combining them in quintet formation is an exceedingly minor part of the total. The slow movement is the best example wherein the quintet functions as a totality in only a dozen of the 129 measures.

Antiphonal color is utilized in the ternary-scaled second movement; the dynamic intensity enhanced by full string muting. The third movement is actually a compendium of timbre—part one with strings alone; part two with solo piano; part three a return to the string quartet and a preliminary to the coda which levels all the forces together. While there is more five-instrument writing in the final movement, the contrapuntal rhythmic plan cuts off instrumentational coalescence. Thus, the four movements, each with a distinct mood (the divisions are called "The Lyrical Part," "The Whimsical Part," "The Contemplative Part," and "The Dramatic Part"), are framed differently. The quintet is freely tonal (not twelve tone), laced with a chromaticism that enjoys a vivid life without forgetting its tonal center.

All these details add up to a composer of the twentieth century who did not find it necessary to thump on experimental tubs in order to make his point. The structural heritage of this music can be traced to the great classical tradition, but the notes are not inked in with a blunted neoclassic pen. Toch wrote his piano quintet in individually bold modern script.

¶ *Five Pieces for Wind Instruments and Percussion, Op. 83*

A modern conception of the *divertimento* plan with an added twist. Toch creates a form within a form; a color variance that engenders added interest. Four woodwinds are employed in the initial part, a snare drum adds rhythmic kick in movement two, and in the next piece the winds become a sextet with the addition of a pair of horns. In the final pair of movements the entire instrumental complex is employed and what began as a quartet ends as an octet.

The vertical and horizontal elements are of contemporary format, but work their way around a tonal center. The rhythm is fluid, but not nervous; everything spins and spreads in romantic phraseology.

VOCAL

VOICE WITH ORCHESTRA

¶ *The Chinese Flute, for Soprano and Chamber Orchestra, Op. 29*

Not only the texts by Li Tai Pe, Sao Han, and Confucius trace the Oriental profile of Toch's opus. "The Chinese Flute" explores matters of sensitive ostinato-derived music, the material treated with an orchestration of soft brushwork. The soprano (used in three of the cycle's seven sections) is less than a solo, merging into the textures as an instrument vocalizing words.

To a certain extent this is impressionism given special national citizenship. From the technical viewpoint each section illustrates expansion from a single idea—quantities drawn from the smallest initial measure. In its fitness of mood this composition confutes the fake Moslem, pseudo East Asian music that has been poured into the drugged ears of millions by movie, radio, and television background scores. Toch's mintage is not counterfeit.

27. JOAQUÍN TURINA
(1882–1949)

IF Ravel's music is typically French, if Grieg's works are representative of Norway, if the country of origin of such compositions can be identified from the sounds alone, then the musical inflections of Turina are recognizably Spanish from first note to last. The constancy of the Iberian style does not make his music stiff-backed—its rhythmic and coloristic life takes care of that.

Turina makes a deliberate point of being Spanish, but his music does contain some foreign elements. He studied with Vincent d'Indy, therefore Franckian arguments are present, including a chromatic vocabulary and cyclic form. Working in France and encouraged by Debussy (as well as Ravel), Turina compounded the substance of impressionism into his compositions. The result can be termed pictorial nationalism. Large designs containing organic development were bypassed by Turina. He favored thematic opposition, its repetition varied by timbre. This proposes a lighter music, less devoted to the higher forms, with an acceptance of some clichés. The value of the music is not diminished.

A prolific composer, Turina wrote for all media; although the largest segment of his catalogue was devoted to the piano. It is immaterial that much of this output is based on the small thought restrung and restated, rather than on the musical inquiry spun out symphonically or propounded in the form of a sonata narrative. A man speaks with his own accent and gestures. Turina was essentially a poet, not an orator.

ORCHESTRAL

¶ *Danzas Fantásticas, Op. 22*

One of the most popular of Turina's efforts, illustrating music with an unmistakable geographic heartbeat. Though Turina was no innovator, neither was he a hard-crusted academician. Without providing a new style, these pieces offer as pure a national music as any innovation.

The dances are not "fantastic," but rather are fanciful depictions of three different moods: "Exaltación" is a moderate-tempo affair, "Ensueño" is dreamy, but for the greater part in 5/8 meter (defining the Zortziko, a Basque dance rhythm which uses uneven division of each measure in a 1/8 plus 2/4 process), and "Orgía," which is red-blooded but politely so. Quotations from the writings of José Más precede these sections but need not be read to understand the warm musical context.

¶ *La Procesión del Rocío, Op. 9*

Turina has provided a description of the scene he had in mind, which places his "Procession of Our Lady of the Dew" squarely in the realm of program music. The annual honoring of the Virgin reverses the usual order—celebration precedes the religious procession in this case. March and dance moods are contrasted to the spiritual, furnishing an allegro and andante tempo relationship.

¶ *Ritmos* (Choreographic Fantasy)

Music commissioned by a dancer (the famous "La Argentina") is bound to have rhythm as an ordained part of its projection. But, in this composition, Turina is overly preoccupied with the rhythmic aspects. Despite the varied dances employed in this five-in-one compendium (including a "Slow Dance," a waltz, and a "Garrotín") the metrical facets are squared and academic; there are no inner textural responsivities. The rhythmic patterns are affiliated with a redundant *molto*-sweet type of music. Turina belabors his love of pat ideas, and the product suffers accordingly. Perhaps this is why La Argentina never performed the work she had requested.

¶ *Sinfonía Sevillana, Op. 23*

The formal element gives way to individual enthusiasm for native melody and rhythm in this three-part work, a sonorous panorama of the city of Seville, the river that flows by, and a fiesta. More a suite than a symphony, Turina's sinfonía poses no intellectual quandary, needs no detailed analysis. Earlier aural experiences of Spanish music make this opus accessible, pleasant, and convincing. A nationalist substitutes dance forms (the garrotín and zapateado) for objectively detailed first and second subjects (in the final movement, for example). Requisite clarity is not beclouded, though such method is most often found in the smaller forms or in a rhapsody. Thus the way of Turina's style. It is effective, if not deeply erudite.

295

STRING ORCHESTRA

¶ *La Oración del Torero, Op. 34*

Turina's most popular chamber-music work, and thrice as popular in its enlarged string-orchestra form. "The Bullfighter's Prayer" was originally written for, and dedicated to, the very famous members of the Aguilar family, known as the Aguilar Lute Quartet, now disbanded.

In this one-movement piece (divided into precise tempo differences), Turina draws both delicate and vivid impressions from the string instrument family, aided by the special color of mutes, pizzicato and *sul ponticello*. "La Oración del Torero" is Spanish in its swaying rhythms, but is fervent impressionism in its pictorial, symbolic curtseying. Block-columned tertial chords, producing the astringencies of ninths and elevenths, provide stylistic flavor. More than a hint of sadness permeates the work, but if there is a story depicted by the music it was never told by the composer. Turina's toreador speaks of the Spanish night more than of his afternoon's work.

SOLO INSTRUMENT WITH ORCHESTRA

SOLO PIANO WITH ORCHESTRA

¶ *Rapsodia Sinfónica for Piano and String Orchestra, Op. 66*

A rhapsody, yes; symphonic, hardly. This one-movement divertissement strings together a series of tunes; very Spanish at the outset, less so later on. Lukewarm romanticism is expressed in contrasting sections. Despite the solo instrument there is no virtuosity, merely a strong obbligato keyboard voice.

This avoidance of formal independence adds up to a stylistic ambivalence. One hurries from native atmosphere to the perfumed drawing room. A more decisive creative attitude would have softened the severity of change.

INSTRUMENTAL

GUITAR

¶ *Fandanguillo*

Although the title signifies a diminutive type of fandango, Turina's dance is a full-fledged affair, with vivid contrasts, mainly in slower tempo. It is much more nostalgic (and more sinister) than a fandango.

¶ *Homenaje a Tárrega: Garrotín and Soleares*

Guitar music in honor of Francisco Tárrega (1852–1909). Tárrega represents the nineteenth-century peak of guitar playing, and all contemporary guitar pedagogy is indebted to his teaching.

The first of the set of pieces is a dance with some neat percussive effects; the second is an Andalusian folk-song example, its poetry heightened by pedal formations.

¶ *Ráfaga*

An example of the melancholy that permeates the "cante hondo" of Spanish music. Turina's two-and-one-half-minute piece is fluid with tempo change, strongly colored by modal, plangent harmonies. Here is Gypsy music in its full glory.

¶ *Sacro-monte from "Danzas Gitanas," Op. 55*

A number of transcriptions have been made of this, the fifth of ten dances for piano, published in two sets of five each. Extremely colorful and striking in its varying orchestral arrangements, it is just as effective for the solo guitar.

Translated, the title means "sacred mountain," but the frictioned bite and wild surge of the rhythms point to an irreverent dance scene.

¶ *Sevillana*

In this dance (related to the seguidilla), Turina successfully blends his ways of musical speaking, and displays metaphorical mannerisms of both dance and rhapsodic-improvisational style.

¶ *Sonata, Op. 61*

Turina's Opus 61 has the working materials for a sonata, but is organized instead into a large suite. The technique reflects French and Spanish style. The writing is vivid. Turina's piece bears the insignia of authoritative Spanish guitar music, magnificently designed for the instrument.

HARP

¶ *Sacro-monte from "Danzas Gitanas," Op. 55*

Because of its rhythms a goodly portion of Spanish music is excellently suited to harp transcription. Turina's impetuous short Gypsy piece makes a fitting display item in plucked sonority.

PIANO

¶ *Ciclo Pianístico*
> *Partita in C major, Op. 57*
> *Preludios 1–5, Op. 80*

The "Ciclo Pianístico" covers a range of compositions in addition to those indicated above, including a "Toccata and Fugue," the "Rincones de Sanlucar" (Op. 78), and a few shorter pieces. In the "Partita" one finds some of Turina's best piano writing. The four movements combine Baroque forms with Spanish meaning and the hybrid is fascinating. There is also classical effusion in the sobriety and tempered style of the five preludes. None of the picture postcard musical texts that adorn so much of Turina's piano catalogue are found here. National propaganda is not entirely absent, but what there is constitutes dignified prose.

¶ *Cuentos de España, Series 1, Op. 20*
¶ *Cuentos de España, Series 2, Op. 47*

These fourteen "Impressions of Spain" exemplify Turina the miniaturist. Most of his vast output for the keyboard instrument seems to have been produced for the market place, if one judges the music by its preponderance of entertaining materials.

Various regions are "visited" in the first set, such as Málaga, Barcelona, and so on, while the town of Córdova is central to the second group. All the sketches are characteristically native, none make thunderbolts in the musical atmosphere.

¶ *Danzas Fantásticas, Op. 22*

Like Falla, Turina transferred an orchestral composition to the completely opposite medium of the piano, though transcriptions generally work the other way around. Thus this second setting of Turina's three dances (*see* Orchestral *above*), and which bears the same opus number.

¶ *Danzas Gitanas, Series 1, Op. 55*

Five dances of which the last ("Sacro-monte") is the best-known. (A second set also consists of five dances.) Turina is not a composer of defiance, but of deduction. His Gypsies are more sensual than torrid; the erotic is clothed in these melodic lines and swaying rhythms. But even in their smoldering quietness, Turina's dances reveal Hispanic facts with no hiding in technical cubbyholes.

¶ *Le Jeudi Saint à Minuit, from "Sevilla, Suite Pittoresque"*

Music covered with a shawl of devout feeling. The programmatic viewpoint is implicit in the title ("Holy Thursday at Midnight") and in the subtitle which concerns a religious procession passing through a little street. Turina conveys this by a muted march with occasional imitations of a distant fanfare. His inspirational response to a sacred theme resulted in sensitive poetic music for voice and orchestra ("Semana Santa" in the "Canto a Sevilla") and for orchestra alone ("La Procesión del Rocío"). This third example is just as telling.

¶ *Mujeres Españolas, Op. 17*

Three profiles of Spanish women: classical, sentimental, and coquettish. Regardless of their varying temperaments all are dressed in crinoline and lace harmonies. No recognizable Turina and practically no Spanish features in these sadly old-fashioned portraits.

¶ *Niñerias, Op. 21*

In place of minuets, variations, and the like, contemporary composers group isolated pieces together, title the assortment suggestively, and produce a suite minus any defined formal plan. Thus, "Niñerias," which Turina dedicated to his three children, delights in old divertimento style. The eight movements span a variety of ideas, including soldiers, dolls, a lullaby, games, and one piece titled "? . . ." so one can have fun in guessing what's what. The best is the first, a prelude and fugue, which thumbs its nose at all the finger exercises written for unlucky pianists; its fugal subject is a simple scale line!

("Niñerias" was composed in 1919. In 1931 Turina added a second series, also consisting of eight pieces under the same general title.)

¶ *Poema Fantástico, Op. 98*

Turina's opus is a set of four pieces with picturesque titles, none explained by the composer or the music. Its poetry is close to the salon. A bit of Spanish icing tops this concoction. Expertly written, somewhat dull piano music.

¶ *Recuerdos de la Antigua España, Op. 48*

Turina's penchant for programmatic insinuation is apparent in this four-movement opus. But the titles make little impact in the first number "La eterna Carmen," or in the last part—what difference is

299

there between a moderately paced music or one called "Estudian-tina"? And movement two ("Habañera") is a pat dance. Part three ("Don Juan") leads one to expect a great deal. However, it delivers none of the titillating amorous adventures of this chap; only the imita-tive tolling of bells, by which we know he has come to his end.

CHAMBER MUSIC

¶ *Second Sonata* (Sonata Española) *for Violin and Piano, Op. 82*

A duo-sonata by title, but a suite for violin with piano accompani-ment by demonstration. Turina's opus is a simple mirroring of the violin's grand ability to sing soloistically (also in a two-voiced man-ner) and the piano to furnish harmonic and rhythmic elaboration. Turmoil and dramaticism are at a minimum; Hispanic atmosphere conveyed by a succession of charming themes is paramount. Color spikes this musical drink—plucked sounds, a muted conclusion to the variations in the opening movement (also some of Turina's fa-vored quintal rhythm), and a little snarling (*ponticello*) timbre in the middle *vivo*.

¶ *Trio No. 2 in B minor, Op. 76*

The frame of this work was partially built in the days when Turina studied in Paris at the Schola Cantorum under Vincent d'Indy. Cyclic tools are used—César Franck's trademark is quite clearly seen. But the difference in workmanship is apparent: the method was germane and natural to Franck and had an affinity to the thematic shapes he employed; with Turina the system is merely a means of extension, sometimes almost irritating by its redundancy. On the other hand, Turina employs a type of thematic staticness in his trio—ideas are contrasted but not developed. Sonata design is sketched, not com-pleted. The cautiously controlled large form is not in the picture at all.

Paralleling the cyclic interplay of small forms within a presumably large design is romantic largesse opposed to rhythmically suave Span-ish expression. In his principal themes, Turina is a cosmopolitan, in his secondary (sweeter) subjects he becomes a homebody.

¶ *String Quartet—"De la Guitarra"*

Turina's chief mannerism in the quartet (the subtitle derives from some resemblance to the open string pitches of the guitar—no plectral sonorities are imitated) is a change of tempi to regulate his extension of thought, rather than thorough development of previously stated ideas. The rhapsodic attributes are summed up in the finale, with a tabulation made of earlier references. Turina must have his cyclic coat to keep his music warm. It is to be expected from one who studied with Franck's pupil, d'Indy.

This does not deny the employment of more than a modicum of nationalism. One example: the Zortziko movement, with its quintal metrical sway. This highly indigenous rhythm is spotlighted by the contrasting central section. Hispanic accents within equal measures are also articulated. Sensualism is minimal, but Turina's quartet is not stiff-backed, its rhythm takes care of that.

¶ *Escena Andaluza for Viola, Piano and String Quartet, Op. 7*

Spotlighting one member of the string quartet body in a somewhat solo capacity (without losing sight of chamber-music logic) is very rare. Notwithstanding differences in technique, form, and expression, this work can be considered an analogous companion to the Chausson "Concerto," which calls for a violin and piano with string quartet. While Chausson uses an instrument already doubled in the quartet, Turina employs the darker viola to help formulate the more poetical, warm content of his music. However, there is this dissimilarity: Chausson's rhetoric is Gallic, Turina's is markedly Spanish in a work that is only partly evocative, despite its pictorial title and subtitles.

In the opening "Twilight" the long preamble of the piano, followed by the song of the viola, can be considered akin to the usual use of the guitar as the preludial instrument to most Andalusian songs. Song and dance elements cover the "Serenata" and "Habañera," but Turina's cyclic habit appears in the final portion "By the Window," (music of pure Hispanic expression with a touch of the impressionistic) when the third movement is recalled midway.

VOCAL

¶ *Farruca from "Triptico"*

An illustration of Turina in his *modest* folkloric demeanor. But this does not signify timidity. The profile of Spanish song is quite clear in this case; the composer permits it to be so.

¶ *La Giralda from "Canto a Sevilla," Op. 37*

Movement six of the suite—"La Giralda" is the name of the bell tower which adjoins the Cathedral of Seville.

¶ *Las Locas por Amor*

All the expected intensity of a proclamation of love is depicted in this short song. It contains only the slightest hint of Spanish nuance.

¶ *Poema en Forma de Canciones, Op. 19*

Folk essence is subsidiary to the romantic, partially Debussian cast of this five-movement cycle, the first of which is for solo piano. The indigenous surge and urgency of the "Cantares," the best-known portion of the set, offer a vivid contrast and thus emphasize the healthy romanticism.

¶ *Saeta en Forme de Salve a la Virgen de la Esperanza*

The darker side shows infrequently in Turina's music. One of the most thrilling examples is the plaintive thrust of this sacred plea for voice and piano. It carries out the responsibilities demanded by the text, artistically and emotionally.

¶ *Tu Pupila es Azul*

Simply and directly, Turina's song traces its romantic subject ("Your eyes are blue") by way of *bel canto* style activated by Spanish rhythms and marked cadences. The lines are neat and clear—Turina's songs are never difficult to grasp; the expected always happens. This offers its own kind of satisfaction.

VOICE WITH ORCHESTRA

¶ *Canto a Sevilla, Op. 37*

Music codifying insular spirit and individual identity is beautifully demonstrated in this composition devoted to a sonic view of the composer's native city. In conception it equals the tribute Respighi made in his Rome pieces; in mood it is emotional from first note to final double bar line.

Turina emphasizes the roles of voice and instruments by combining them in only four of the seven movements, using the orchestra alone in the other three parts. The poems are by José Muñoz Román (six other poems may be narrated alone between the movements— a further contrast). The score includes disparate evocations of Holy Week, fountains, a festival, ghosts, and a tribute to a famed bell tower. Robust and sad, secular and sacred, the music is a delight of authenticity; an aural visa that makes clear the melancholy and voluptuousness of Spain.

28. RALPH VAUGHAN WILLIAMS
(1872–1958)

Rᴀʟᴘʜ Vᴀᴜɢʜᴀɴ Wɪʟʟɪᴀᴍs's musical heritage shows clearly through his compositions, many considered masterpieces. Though his work is British to the core, it is not insular. For the most part, Vaughan Williams based his output on folk song, not in the inculcated style of a Percy Grainger, but steeped in all of its natural flavors. Rather than an external preaching of the native cause he drew upon it for its synthesizing effect. Nationalism blended into internationalism as Vaughan Williams's Englishry conveyed universal meanings.

Vaughan Williams enjoyed a reputation which few creators have equaled. He was a down-to-earth man, easily accessible, and one who welcomed human contacts. Can we wonder at his going to Maurice Ravel to polish his orchestrational technique, although he was the man's senior? Shortly thereafter (1914) he produced the famed "London Symphony." Vaughan Williams wrote nine symphonies, the sixth, in the opinion of many critics, one of the great symphonic documents of this century. His other music is no less significant.

The heart of his technique was a natural love for modality—those types of archaic-sounding combinations which reflect calmness even when dissonantal frictions are applied. It is this *bas relief* of modal contour that is the principal pigmentation of his important works. It is present no less in the tumultuous pieces than in the pastoral ones. This fundamentally pure and stylistic affinity was not mere repetition (a creative cliché), but basic to constant exploration and expansion.

While some composers never solidify their separate skills, Vaughan Williams had a sharpened over-all technique which he combined with masterful workmanship. Never did he juggle technical formulas for sheer effect. He had irreproachable taste, and was primarily a melodist and harmonist of subtle beauty. His total work (embracing all media from the short piece to the full-evening opera) embodies a diversity of moods from the rhapsodic to the poetic, from dry wit to sonic philosophy. All that is traditional in English nationalism is encompassed in the productions of this composer, who spoke with noble belief in musical refinement. Famous during his lifetime,

303

Ralph Vaughan Williams remains an honored and important composer in the musical world.

ORCHESTRAL

¶ *A London Symphony* (No. 2)

Vaughan Williams did not write a systematic program symphony in this case, but the work is picturesque. Thus the misty beginning, the fog of the introduction, the Big Ben chimes at start and finish of the composition, the use of "Sweet Lavender" and the hansom cab jingles in the second movement, the mouth organ imitation in the "Nocturne," and the plodding march of the final section. Folk phrases that twine their way through the measures are added identification.

The composer has asked that we listen to his conception as pure music, as a "Symphony by a Londoner." However, a title gives an auditor's viewpoint more than a philosophical pinch. Let us call V. W.'s musical spades for what they are—a picture of a great city framed in symphonic form.

¶ *A Sea Symphony* (No. 1) (see Choral with Orchestra)

¶ *English Folk Song Suite*

One of the best known of Vaughan Williams's works. Originally, this three-movement suite was written for band (*see* Band *below*); then, with the composer's permission, it was transcribed for orchestra by Gordon Jacob (a former pupil), considered one of England's top orchestrators. The eight conjoined melodies are sea songs, for the greater part, plus homespun tunes from the region of Somerset.

¶ *Norfolk Rhapsody No. 1 in E minor*

The employment of folk tunes within this score is only one part of the composition's enchantment. The modal beauties of its harmonies and its orchestrational pigments give rise to images of dawn: grayness melting into color, half light to full radiance, dawn to day. It is an abstraction of nature, conveyed by song. In a conception swept by tender emotions Vaughan Williams has written a miniature "pastoral symphony."

The rhapsody illustrates English impressionism, but the choice of design is classic—a condition the impressionists considered, but never truly liked or followed. In the "Norfolk Rhapsody" the initial section reappears as the coda. Thus the full formal circle.

¶ *Pastoral Symphony* (No. 3)

There are no scenic impressions, no babbling brooks, no maypole dances, not even some distant thunder to break the spell of this introspective poetic work which suggests an impressionistic essay. Impressionism, however, is broadly defined as being of pictorial origin, musically suggested by way of individualization of instrumental colors. In the "Pastoral Symphony" Vaughan Williams is only parenthetically an impressionist. The countryside is his inspiration, it does not give rise to coloristic imagism. Intensely fluidic, no thrusting dynamic blobs interrupt the contemplative flow. Even the fastest movement (the third, marked *moderato pesante*) is simply activized meditation. Emphasis takes place by direct de-emphasis.

The "Pastoral" is an abstraction of nature conveyed by orchestral instruments plus two small bits for a wordless, disembodied soprano voice. Diatonicism is the ruling technical principle, strengthened by the use of modal counterpoint, a polyphony not of line but of chordal blocks. No music has better illustrated the enchantment and spiritual depth of rural England. Tovey described the symphony as of "massive quietness." It is also of radiant stillness.

¶ *Sinfonia Antartica* (No. 7) (see Choral with Orchestra)

¶ *Symphony No. 4 in F minor*

After three subtitled symphonies without numerical designation, Vaughan Williams elected to number and define the tonality of his fourth symphony. Formality of title is matched by a different compositional character. The fourth symphony is built from a few motives, linked thematically and bound cyclically. It is dark and brooding music; in its undisclosed stimuli there are tragic-torn elements.

Triadic language marked Vaughan Williams's first three symphonies. The fourth does not eliminate the common chord, but it makes the secundal stringency just as common in the musical syntax. From the beginning, the impact and bite of sound are relentless, especially in the scherzo, a *danse macabre* moving with explosive bluntness. And the fever does not subside in the contrapuntal cast of the final section. In this Berliozian panorama Vaughan Williams conceived a new kind of symphony, without casting off formal compatibility.

¶ *Symphony No. 5 in D major*

Notwithstanding the pertinent designations of a "Preludio," "Scherzo," "Romanza," and "Passacaglia," Vaughan Williams's opus

305

has the feeling of a "sinfonia sacra." It also has some affinity to his third ("Pastoral") symphony. The difference is that the D major composition is less vernal and much more meditative. (Perhaps his fifth symphony, written during the Second World War, was Vaughan Williams's way of bringing a message of hope for the future to his countrymen.)

The dynamic plan of the music is never convulsive; the loud planes of sonority avoid instrumental turbulence. Most of the symphony is quiet; the speediest movement (the "Scherzo") floats mainly in a *piano* atmosphere. The rhythms are placid and portend neither anxiety nor anger as they move with fundamental order. Even in the mixture of duple and triple pulsations within the "Scherzo" (the only really fast movement) the effect is refreshing without special excitation. The temperament of Vaughan Williams's music is that of a choral symphony without chorus.

¶ *Symphony No. 6 in E minor*

Eloquent grimness describes the sixth symphony, a blood relative to the fourth. There is little peaceful suavity; the music has an almost hard core. Although a total unit (one movement moves into the next without pause), the four main sections are clearly apportioned. First, the toccata energy of the opening part, then a sinister second movement, conditioned by a rhythmic figure which rides herd on the music; the pattern is never resolved and forms an overwhelming and terrifying ostinato. The scherzo that follows is no musical joke, but unremitting, jagged music, monitored by fugal controls.

All of these white-heated arguments are in severe contrast to the suspended tautness of the finale. The claustrophobic quality of this part is truly frightening. For some twelve and a half minutes (106 measures all in 4/4 meter save for a single exception) the orchestra plays under wraps—*sempre pianissimo e senza crescendo*. This pitiless, unyielding dynamic desolation is unique in symphonic literature and is more crushing in effect than virtuosic orchestration. Despite the hazards of musical crystal-gazing, one can prophesy everlasting life for Vaughan Williams's sixth symphony.

¶ *Symphony No. 8 in D minor*

Perpetual invention marks Vaughan Williams's symphonies. No two are exactly alike, in mood or character, form or color. In this essay symphonic design is revamped into a huge suite scored for divisible orchestral components.

A "Fantasia" subtitled "Variazioni senza Tema" opens matters.
These variants "without a theme" (incidentally, a title used in 1922
by Malipiero for a piano and orchestra piece) are not permissive improvisation. Evolved from motival material the variations are like
seven inventions for full orchestra. Movements two and three comprise a "Scherzo alla Marcia" and a "Cavatina." Though plentiful
scherzi are to be found in symphonies, few resemble the shape of this
grotesque piece for winds and brass. The title of the slow movement
and its use of strings alone are similarly rare. And the finale, "Toccata," also strikes out in modern address, with the full orchestra plus
a huge array of tumultuous percussion (including glockenspiel, celesta, xylophone, vibraphone, tubular bells, and gongs).

¶ *Symphony No. 9 in E minor*

Many a composer modifies the basic, proven musical forms, since
none of the sequences which mark classical-style patterns are im-
mutable. In this sober symphony Vaughan Williams is as clear as any
classicist, but freed from rigidity.

The opening and final movements balance each other: elements
from the initial part finding development in the last. Antithetical material dictates the slow movement (pastoral and somewhat barbaric
ideas) and the scherzo as well (pictorial and mystical moods). Age
changed, yet did not change Vaughan Williams. His favored healthy
modal sets of triads are to be heard, but as harmonic sandpaper
against unrelated chords.

The color imagery so exceedingly vivid in Vaughan Williams's
seventh and eighth symphonies is heightened even further in his ninth
and final work in the form. Three saxophones are utilized, and for the
first time in the serious world of the symphony a flügelhorn makes its
appearance as an important solo voice. Such exception to routine
does not violate a composer's style. Vaughan Williams had his own
distinct creative voice, but he never overcelebrated himself.

¶ *The Wasps, Suite*

The simmerings of the musical pot Vaughan Williams was to bring
to his particular boiling point show unmistakably in these five extracts from the music he composed (in 1909) for Aristophanes' play.
Warm, intimate folk-shaded melodies and modal harmony are the
chief features. No complexities, no Greek musical forgery is represented, merely British *Innigkeit,* demonstrated in a vigorous overture, a pair of entr'actes, a march, and a snappy finale.

Only the "Overture" has established itself in the repertory. It sketches the personalities of the principal protagonists of the play, and includes the picturesque buzzing of the wasps (representing the Athenian jurymen satirized in Aristophanes' comedy). However, no dissonant sting is felt in Vaughan Williams's homespun music. The march deserves more attention. Its quaint title "March Past of the Kitchen Utensils," comes from its use as background music for a mock trial; a house dog is the defendant and calls on a plate, a knife, and other kitchen tools as his witnesses. The quasi-militaristic G major tune and the contrasting minor-keyed broader melody match the oddball solemnity.

Chamber Orchestra

¶ *Fantasia on "Greensleeves"*

The enchanting melody of "Greensleeves" stems from the latter part of the sixteenth century (it was then known as "A New Northern Dittye"). Transcribed in multitudinous ways it remains one of the enchanting tunes of all time.

Vaughan Williams used the song in his Falstaffian opera "Sir John in Love," contrasting it with another folk tune, "Lovely Joan." For concert purposes the version used is an adaptation for string orchestra, harp, plus two flutes.

String Orchestra

¶ *Fantasia on a Theme by Thomas Tallis*

The mysticism of this archaic stringed instrument drama is not conveyed by its title. Fantasia design is exposed by the full contrapuntal development of the basic theme. But there are other riches in this, one of the greatest of Vaughan Williams's compositions. The majestic polyphony and modalistic flow are enmeshed in a golden sonorous beauty that is the instrumental equivalent of superfine massed human voices. This is obtained by monolithic scoring patterns drawn from a three-ply organization of two string orchestras (one an echo group) plus a solo string quartet unit. In this manner, antiphony of musical material is emphasized by antiphony of instrumentation. Vaughan Williams's music is akin to a gigantic secular hymn. Composed in 1910, it is *not* of its age at all.

¶ *Partita for Double String Orchestra*

Vaughan Williams's modern realization of partita format proposes a diverse collation of designs. With a bow to eighteenth-century concerto grosso principles, it is scored with purposely uneven distribution of weights. The first orchestra, minus double basses, contains occasional solo passages, while the much larger second group has the full string body. The violins of both components are a corporate body without division into firsts and seconds.

Though modality—pure, contrapuntal, and dissonantly tinged—is a prime point, rhythm rules the four pieces. This is especially true in the polyphonic chasing of the second movement, a "Scherzo Ostinato," which lives up to its title by the persistent investigation of its main figure (augmented to form contrast) and by its dogged combination of duple and triple pulses within the bar lines. The "Intermezzo" which follows is subtitled "Homage to Henry Hall," a dance-band conductor. Accordingly a syncopated, ostinato pizzicato figure occupies the second orchestra. It begins as though a "vamp till ready," but turns out to be a "vamp al fine." No vulgarization—merely a precisely muted tap-dance support for the healthy melody which moves above it.

BAND

¶ *English Folk Song Suite*

Band music is most accessible when its sonorous plan and textures are its own and not related in any way to orchestral music. Unfortunately, for this reason, there is a paucity of responsible literature.

Vaughan Williams's suite has a marvelous and telling sense of band style and sound, with a rare perception for the idiom. It has become a classic in the repertoire and has also realized wide popularity in its orchestral transfer, a rare reversal of the transcription procedure (*see* Orchestral *above*).

¶ *Toccata Marziale*

Music that lives up to its designation. There is real drive (constant rhythmic impetus) and thus a toccata. There is martial spirit and festive tone and thus "marziale." There is also suburban atmosphere and Vaughan Williams's favored modal vocabulary describing it. While the composition is not based on folk materials, Vaughan Williams expertly weaves native colors and melodic patterns into his toccata design. It is an English product.

SOLO INSTRUMENT WITH ORCHESTRA

CONCERTOS

¶ *Concerto for Oboe and Strings*

Pastoral tinges predominate here (from the use of a woodwind instrument long associated with such moods in orchestral pieces). Since the creation is actually of three facets: a "Rondo Pastorale," a "Minuet" combined with a "Musette," and a "Finale-Scherzo," it is much more a suite than a concerto, despite the elaborate cadenza included in the first movement.

¶ *Concerto in D minor* (Concerto Accademico) *for Violin and String Orchestra*

The secondary title is an unfortunate choice for those who do not know Vaughan Williams's piece. The meaning, feeling, and sensitivity of the concerto is far from academic. It is doctrinal only in its parallel to old classic format; *i.e.,* three movements: an allegro, adagio, and presto, and in the string instrumentation of the accompanying orchestra. Yet it is positively classic in its clarity, with a total elimination of any fuss or furbelows.

The sheer black-white contrasts of the concerto recall the eighteenth century, but this factor is set modally to rights. The concerto contains a Bach spaciousness (many commentators have overemphasized the Bachian concept of the work) but under a Vaughan Williams guardianship. The magic triads of the slow movement and the jig scamper of the finale are proof.

INSTRUMENTAL

CLARINET

¶ *Six Studies in English Folk Song for Clarinet and Piano*

Early, practical (alternative versions for violin, viola, or cello), all-native Vaughan Williams in quality and style. The composer's nationality need not be known for one to immediately identify the rural English enchantment contained in these very short essays. No fast tempo intrudes until the final piece, which forms a sort of postscript to the cloistered beauty of this sensitive traditional folk music.

ORGAN

¶ *The Old Hundredth*

Vaughan Williams arranged this venerable psalm tune, traceable to the early part of the sixteenth century, for use at the Coronation of Queen Elizabeth II in June of 1953. Tradition and dignity were properly served by his choice. His setting made several production possibilities feasible, including the largest for mixed choir, congregation, orchestra, and organ (*see* "All People That on Earth Do Dwell," in the choral section). Bach used this hymn and Vaughan Williams matches him in the thrill and drama of his version.

¶ *Prelude on the Welsh Hymn "Hyfrydol"* (No. 3 of "Three Preludes Founded on Welsh Hymn Tunes")

An eloquent presentation of a swinging sacred melody, minus any insensate counterpoint, but colored by an enhancement of the melody. The modal touch will be recognized in this short piece.

¶ *Prelude on the Welsh Hymn "Rhosymedre"* (No. 2 of "Three Preludes Founded on Welsh Hymn Tunes")

Meticulous regard is accorded the principal idea, with the harmonic frame always shaped to bring the melody into prominence. Though these preludes are minor segments in V. W.'s catalogue they represent the composer seeking material in traditional areas. (The first of the set is based on the tune "Bryn Calfaria"; preludes 2 and 3 have been arranged for small orchestra by Arnold Foster.)

TWO PIANOS

¶ *Fantasia on "Greensleeves"*

An arrangement of the Vaughan Williams representation made by Hubert J. Foss (late head of the music department of the Oxford University Press).

VIOLA

¶ *Suite for Viola and Piano*

An incorrect title, since the work consists of three suites in one— "groups" is Vaughan Williams's designation, with three pieces each in the outer sets and a pair in the middle. The grouped organization

311

is not the only oddity of the work. The movements deal with ideas not often associated with the concert suite. These include a "Polka Mélancolique," a "Christmas Dance," and a civil-mannered, delightful "Galop." The latter is much more a canter along the English countryside on a spring afternoon than fast horse music. It displays ruddy humor. The "Carol" and "Musette" are typical of the composer's heart-touching melodicism.

CHAMBER MUSIC

¶ Sonata in A minor for Violin and Piano

A "Fantasia," "Scherzo," and "Tema con Variazioni" constitute Vaughan Williams's sole concerted sonata. Composed in his eighty-third year it indicates the constant freshness of viewpoint even in his very late period of work. (This mental alertness brought new concepts of orchestration into his symphonies and conceived solo compositions for such instrumental second-class citizens as a bass tuba and a harmonica.)

There is no neutral straightforwardness in this sonata. The opening bithematic movement weaves its counterpoint for dramatic effect; the scherzo contrasts and freely mixes its basic metrical pattern. In the set of variations the theme is let loose and permitted to wander in fresh surroundings.

VOCAL

¶ Folk Songs

[*Vaughan Williams's catalogue of compositions does not include this specific title, though he made innumerable folk-song settings; many published separately, others issued as collections. The titles noted below constitute a representative selection; others are discussed in the "Choral" section.*]

> *The Cuckoo and the Nightingale*
> *Down by the Riverside*
> *The Jolly Plough Boy*
> *My Boy Billy*
> *The Painful Plough*

312

Folk song served as an early nourishment for Vaughan Williams. His research left a permanent imprint on his creative thinking. At times it served as the prime proposal (in such works as the "Norfolk Rhapsody," "English Folk Song Suite," and "Five Variants of 'Dives and Lazarus' "). In other instances it swirls in the blood stream of his music, an unmistakable ingredient in the sound substance. It was folk song that made Vaughan Williams's music emotionally and spiritually English.

Folk-song pieces comprise many versions: voice and piano, vocal duets, unison and part songs for every type of combination, with and without accompaniment. Ideally realized, there are no artifices, no interference with the raw material, save fitting harmonic and polyphonic clothing and proper artistic polish. The direct simplicity of "The Cuckoo and the Nightingale," as well as the other songs, is immediately apparent. In each instance the repetition of the tune matches the exactly proportioned stanzas of the text. The primitive sweetness of it all is perfect.

¶ *Linden Lea*

"Linden Lea" is proof of how Vaughan Williams assimilated his study of native song. This sounds exactly like a folk tune, but it is all Vaughan Williams. None of his songs can be termed hackneyed, but this one (like "Silent Noon") comes close.

¶ *Seven Songs from "The Pilgrim's Progress"*

Especially in America and Great Britain few home-grown composers have been able to crack the barrier of snobbery that halts the acceptance of native operas. Vaughan Williams wrote his share (a half dozen) but none have succeeded. Opinion has it that his operas are much present in the spirit and much absent in content. This set of samplings from his stage work (described as "A Morality in a Prologue, Four Acts and an Epilogue, founded on John Bunyan's Allegory") does not confirm the view. Some of the songs are religious in tone but minus the murkiness of most sacred pieces. One of these even has a slight swashbuckling quality, while "The Bird's Song" is a version of the Twenty-third Psalm that is highly rewarding. Severely opposite in tone is the rousing ribaldry of "The Song of Vanity Fair."

¶ *Silent Noon* (No. 2 from "The House of Life")

The best-known of the six songs that comprise the cycle composed to sonnets by Dante Gabriel Rossetti. Vaughan Williams's love music

313

is restrained in dynamic power, simple in its utterance. There is nobility here, but there is tenderness too.

¶ Songs of Travel

Here is the mature young voice of Ralph Vaughan Williams. Composed just after the turn of the century, the songs forewarned the burial of academicism. The only exception proved to be the romantically individual music of Elgar. No one was lulled by Vaughan Williams's melodies. As Frank Howes has succinctly stated: "This was new music for a new century." And it remains fresh today.

There are eight parts to the "Songs of Travel." Originally, all but the last were produced in two volumes. Recently, the complete cycle has been reissued by the publishers in one volume, including the eighth song (composed later, in 1912) and a short epilogue added posthumously (the composition date is unknown).

Though folk influences are present (especially in the eighth: "Whither Must I Wander?") the cycle is not cakes and ale music. Vaughan Williams set Robert Louis Stevenson's texts with careful attention to their meaning.

¶ The Watermill

A "Lied Domestica" without any semblance of Straussian furbelows. The piece is almost singsong; cute in style and folksy in its text about a miller and his wife, their daughter, her suitors, and the family cat.

VOICE WITH INSTRUMENTAL ENSEMBLE

¶ On Wenlock Edge

The six songs on texts from A. E. Housman's "A Shropshire Lad" have been labeled impressionistic. Actually, they can be so termed only if the word means clarification and intensification of the compositional process. Though "On Wenlock Edge" does contain some pictorial symbolism and twilight colors, its objectives are more expansive, merging a suffusion of folk song with exalted lyricism. Modality, the harmonic specialty of Vaughan Williams, predominates, with chromatic cohesiveness and diatonic detail utilized as foils of contrast. The piano and string quartet outline, but do not overstress, the prose meanings in this supremely English-flavored work.

CHORAL

¶ *All People That on Earth Do Dwell* (The Old Hundredth Psalm Tune)

(For another version *see* Organ *above.*) The plan contrasts organ fanfares before the first and fourth stanzas and after the fifth verse, with an ever-changing consideration of the voices.

¶ *A Song of Thanksgiving*

Originally designated "Thanksgiving for Victory," to fulfill a BBC commission for use when Germany surrendered in the Second World War. The new title has a wider purpose.

To make his meanings direct and clear, Vaughan Williams calls on a speaker, solo soprano, mixed chorus (including a children's semi-chorus), and large orchestra. The choice of text drawn from the Apocrypha, the Books of Chronicles and Isaiah, Shakespeare, and Rudyard Kipling parallels the imposing musical forces. However, the composition endeavors to cover too much ground in too many different ways. It is best in its final section (a setting of Kipling's "Land of Our Birth We Pledge to Thee"), with a metrical interplay of quadruple and quintuple pulses that gives impetus to the hymnlike conception.

¶ *At the Name of Jesus*

A fine old melody based on the tune "King's Weston." Vaughan Williams's anthem is a refreshing contribution to a literature overloaded with sentimental rubbish.

¶ *Down in Yon Forest* (from "Eight Traditional English Carols")

A lilting thesis balanced to a *T* by the antithesis and repeated exactly for the six verses. More than a bit of monotony here.

¶ *Five English Folk Songs*

This anthology of "freely arranged" material appeared after research on folk songs from the "Eastern Counties" and Sussex. It includes the familiar "Wassail Song," a healthy example of a folk tune which Vaughan Williams has translated in a solid polyphonic manner. The others are "The Dark Eyed Sailor," "Just as the Tide was Flowing," "The Lover's Ghost," and "The Spring Time of the Year."

New beauties are unfolded in these settings; the music belongs as

315

much to Vaughan Williams as to the anonymous people who sired it. Obbligati, imaginative harmonies and counterpoints are blended in styles that range from madrigal to pure fantasy.

¶*Folk Songs* (see note concerning this title under Vocal above)
> *A Farmer's Son So Sweet*
> *An Acre of Land*
> *Bushes and Briars*
> *Ca' the Yowes*
> *Greensleeves*
> *John Dory*
> *Loch Lomond*
> *Ward the Pirate*

A tasty sampling from the folk songs that Vaughan Williams stored in his creative work files. Note the span of years he devoted to this music; the earliest is "Bushes and Briars" written in 1908, the latest is the 1945 conception of "Greensleeves." Vaughan Williams described the material as "containing in embryo all those principles which are at the basis of the fully developed art of music."

Although the Scotch song "Loch Lomond" is an old favorite, "Greensleeves" has become an international hit. The V. W. version puts matters to right and clears the distorted atmosphere. "Ca' the Yowes" accompanies words by Burns, which identifies its Scotch source; "A Farmer's Son So Sweet" is from Somerset. No two settings are alike, variety adding to the infectiousness of the songs. In "John Dory" rhythmic and contrapuntal byplay are featured, in "An Acre of Land" (included also in the cantata "Folk Songs of the Four Seasons") a solo soprano and antiphonal response are the highlights.

The throbbing beauty of the Essex song "Bushes and Briars" contains spatial effects that haunt the memory. Vaughan Williams first heard it sung by an old shepherd. The melody, he related, "set all my doubts about folk song at rest."

¶*Linden Lea*
Early Vaughan Williams, originally for solo voice (*see* Vocal *above*), later arranged for mixed voices.

¶*Lord Thou Hast Been Our Refuge*
Somewhat mixed in its elements, containing unison singing, choral recitative, spurts of polyphony, and fugato, this motet tussles with its basic inspiration. It is scored for full chorus and semichorus.

316

¶ *Oh How Amiable*

Is orthodoxy a requisite for religious compositions? Not necessarily. Yet, many present-day composers often adopt a pale neutrality when writing sacred music. This anthem (from Psalms 84 and 90) is neither dull nor old-fashioned, neither is it contemporary in approach nor representative of Vaughan Williams. Its neo-Stanford style makes it deserving of only very faint praise.

¶ *Prayer to the Father of Heaven*

Classically orientated, though the spiritual climate of this unaccompanied motet is in no conventional zone. Much choral music has been produced in composers' studios. Little of it is sensitive. Most of it is banal. Though the "Prayer" is not great Vaughan Williams and is simple in format, it has the mark of his personality.

¶ *The Souls of the Righteous*

The important points in this motet are derived from modal stimulations, balancing the intimacy yet eloquence of the piece. (Vaughan Williams's music was composed for the Dedication Service of the Battle of Britain Chapel in Westminster Abbey in 1947.)

¶ *The Turtle Dove*

A nostalgic and tender love song. The crystalline beauty of this folk tune rivals the famous "Greensleeves," and once given proper attention could achieve as great a popularity. Vaughan Williams made three different settings of this piece: for male voices, unison chorus or solo voice, and mixed voices. In whatever form the music is entrancing.

CHORAL WITH INSTRUMENTAL ENSEMBLE

¶ *O Clap Your Hands*

A panegyrical motet with voices contrasting and partnering brass and percussion instruments as well as organ, in fanfaric excitations. This is a *fortissimo* piece of choral theism, employing words from the Forty-seventh Psalm. Vaughan Williams's praise of the Lord is simply designed and, despite its triadic language, avoids imitation of past configurations.

317

Choral with Orchestra

¶ *A Sea Symphony* (No. 1)

Architectural detail is always the special concern of composers who combine voices and orchestra in a large-scale work. The problems increase if the shape is to parallel the orchestral symphony. With proper finesse Vaughan Williams has merged his voices and instruments to fit the symphonic pattern by following the time-tested design of an allegro, slow movement, scherzo, and a finale in rondo style.

Utilizing Walt Whitman words this sea music bypasses any "Fingal's Cave" drive (save some oceanic currents in movement three, "The Waves") or specific "La Mer" mood-painting. The symphony is devoted to a philosophical consideration of watery expanse. The voices are free and the role of the orchestra somewhat compressed. Melodic sweep is the primary virtue of Vaughan Williams's choral symphony, including sufficient salt spray in the orchestration to warrant the title.

¶ *Fantasia on Christmas Carols*

Though sectionally constructed the fantasia is no cheap catchall of yuletide tunes. The four carols that comprise the work undergo succinct development, intertwined with counterpointed references to other carols. One of the delights of this score is its subtle color devices (including "instrumentalized" singing with fully closed and half-closed lips). Another is the variety of the principal themes. From the beginning with its mystical Aeolian mode tune to the extremely soft conclusion, Vaughan Williams charms the ear with his special Christmas celebration.

¶ *Five Tudor Portraits, A Choral Suite*

"Tudor Portraits" represent the slightly satiric brand of musical humor. Its lusty and rollicking fun are paramount, with some delicate sentiments making a neat balance.

The racy cast of the first part begins with a female who brews strong drink; the orchestration is no Londonderry Air. There follows a love song and music to a macaronic text. The fourth movement, a lament for a sparrow, is a fanciful choral-orchestral soufflé with some marvelous mock pontification in which a spoof of the *Dies Irae* appears. Although the finale bogs down somewhat it is of small moment in relation to the persuasive earthiness of the rest.

318

¶ *Serenade to Music*

The serenade is in the polydiatonic style brought to maturity in
the music of Vaughan Williams. A ravishingly sweet principal theme
splices the leaves of the work (it has the composer's usual kinship for
the pastoral mnemonic). It twines its way among the modal pillars of
the piece, the plangent, consecutive parallel triadic chords mixing the
major form with the minor, with an occasional dissonance rippling
across the vertical stream. This is music of the English landscape
school, with only a small bit of hard ground pictured here and there.
(The text is from "The Merchant of Venice," beginning with "How
sweet the moonlight sleeps upon this bank.")

Composed in homage to Sir Henry J. Wood on his silver jubilee,
the "Serenade to Music" originally called for sixteen vocal soloists
(Wood had requested this so that those singers who had been associated with his career might also be honored); the vocalists forming
their own chorus *inter alia*. Vaughan Williams indicated that performance was possible with only four solo voices and chorus or all
the solo parts might be sung by sections of the chorus. No matter
what vocal choice is made, the effect is entrancing, quietly radiant.
A later version for orchestra alone is proof that the inspirational force
of the work is found in its music, not in its text.

¶ *Sinfonia Antartica* (No. 7)

Huge in proportion (five movements and close to three quarters of
an hour in performance time); immersed in color (large orchestra,
much percussion, including a wind machine, harp, celesta, piano, and
organ), amplified by vocal instrumentation (a solo soprano and a
chorus of female voices, none using words), the "Sinfonia Antartica"
is somewhat absolute and mostly programmatic music. Not only the
quotations which preface each movement place the "Antartica" in
the descriptive category, but graphic orchestral painting of frigid tem-
peratures, loneliness, icy landscapes, and bleakness.

¶ *Toward the Unknown Region*

Described as a "song for mixed chorus and orchestra," Vaughan
Williams's "Toward the Unknown Region" has the proportions of a
cantata. Whitman's text, concerning liberation of the soul, is dealt with
with proper mysticism. The score is also majestic, yet a stolid *nobil-
mente* style is its principal point. This early product is more ecclesiastical than secular in tone—a brand of church music for concert hall use.

319

Vaughan Williams had not yet broken through the boundaries of the traditional English choral world.

ORATORIO

¶ *Sancta Civitas* ("Holy City")

In "Sancta Civitas" sixteenth-century modalism is reshaped by a twentieth-century hand. The temper is mystical in the harmonic style as well as subject matter. Here the triad is god and it rules in many ways: singly, in combination, and grouped in bands of chordal counterpoint.

Of far less importance is the text, aspiring through its fluidic constancy to conditions of spiritual order.

MASS

¶ *Mass in G minor*

The Mass and the Requiem (the "Mass for the Dead") have been fertile forms for masterworks. In most instances the music is fully conceived in the image of the composer's style, but Vaughan Williams's blends his individual method with a reconstruction of Tudorian practices.

The G minor mass is neo-modal all the way. The music is forwarded by harmonic blocks, colored by bare, parallel intervals, dramatically emphasized by linear cross relations. It is all grand, mystical, and dramatically reserved. Vaughan Williams's merger of Elizabethan sublimity with contemporary enrichment contains the full tide of religious and artistic eloquence.

BALLET

¶ *Job, A Masque for Dancing*

Composed with both ballet and concert hall in mind (the problems of obtaining stage production raised doubts about the former), "Job" has turned out to be capable of a double life. The source of inspiration derives from William Blake's famous "Illustrations for the Book of Job." Vaughan Williams achieved a strong synthesis; the score is a powerful adjunct to the miming and dancing of the "masque," and at the same time an independent composition of symphonic amplitude.

In the nine parts of "Job" a number of formal dance designs are utilized: saraband, minuet, pavane, and galliard. None of these are academic. Ultraformalism is bypassed. Sacred dignity and fervor, simplicity and drama, blend and are laced with modal harmonies. Despite its multitudinous scenario directions the music unfolds like a mural and not a mixture of separate balletic bits. "Job" outlines stage action if need be but it can stand firmly on its own orchestral feet.

¶ *Old King Cole*

A ballet hitched onto folklore. Plot means little in this instance (though the King's pipe, bowl, and three fiddlers make their appearances). Notwithstanding a fair dose of *brio* in "Old King Cole" the score suffers from a lack of strong thematic identity. Here, the usual nationalistic benefits pay scant dividends.

29. WILLIAM WALTON
(1902–   )

WILLIAM WALTON stands aloof from today's hectic artistic pace. He works slowly practising his credo of severe self-criticism. A self-trained composer, one of the most serious of the contemporary British school, he prefers larger forms to bread and butter compositions.

Walton has been tagged as a romanticist. The description is only partly true. He is too much of the twentieth century to indulge in the bloated discomfort of overluxuriant style. Walton's sensitive intellect and artistic dignity stave off the abstruse, subjective wanderings of the full-scale romantic creator. Neither has he given any attention to the matter of folk song. His music is rich and lyrically robust but is devoted to traditional climates; especially in its harmonic punctuations, formal equilibrium, and well-chosen, not ostentatious colors.

Walton's importance as a composer lies in his devotion to perfection of detail. Unending creative discovery is quite unlike the commercialized artistic humbug which makes initial impact but has only superficial (extemporized) glitter. Walton refuses to accept data resulting from frivolous woolgathering in the name of progress. He composes with meticulous care. His is music of class. It is music of honesty.

ORCHESTRAL

¶ Crown Imperial: Coronation March, 1937

Walton has been twice commissioned to compose coronation marches. "Crown Imperial" was the result of the first request, made by the BBC for the Coronation of King George VI in 1937 (*see below:* "Orb and Sceptre" for the second one). Bearing a quotation from William Dunbar (1465–1520) "In beawtie berying the crone imperiall," Walton's march is a stunner, with a tingling beat and fanfaric trumpets in triadic formations. The trio portion is less memorable. Walton takes second place in inevitable comparison to

Elgar's famed tune in the first of his "Pomp and Circumstance" marches. Otherwise the coronation offering is tops.

¶ Façade—Suites Nos. 1 and 2

The effervescent music that Walton wrote as an auxiliary of the Sitwell text in "Façade" leads a healthy double life. It is superb with the declamation, it is just as successful without it. "Façade" was truly a profitable undertaking.

In its setting within the "entertainment" (*see below*) "Façade" calls for a flute alternating with piccolo, a clarinetist doubling on bass clarinet, saxophone, trumpet, percussion, and one or two cellos. From the twenty-two sections of the original (a purely instrumental "Fanfare" and the remainder for reciter with instrumental ensemble) Walton formed a suite of five movements and amplified the score to full orchestra dimensions. A second suite of six other sections was then selected. However, a third performance possibility was offered by combining the pair of suites in a prescribed order so as to achieve proper contrast and climax. The reckoning makes another "entertainment" that is decidedly attractive and orchestrally tasty. Smart and sophisticated music, quite unlike Walton's later output, the "Façade" pieces remain fresh and undated four decades after their creation.

¶ Johannesburg Festival Overture

An overture that blows off a healthy head of steam from first note to final double-bar line. Commissioned for the seventieth anniversary celebration of the city of Johannesburg, Walton's opus is jubilant and proves he has the rare knack for composing a successful program opener (or closer).

"Johannesburg" does not have the rowdiness of the earlier overture "Portsmouth Point," but it does have the triple attributes of kineticism, jazz-banked coloration, and zip. An example of brilliant professional know-how of style and scoring.

¶ Orb and Sceptre: Coronation March, 1953

Commissioned by the Arts Council of Great Britain, Walton's second enthronement march was composed for the Coronation of Queen Elizabeth II in 1953. It is much inferior to the earlier "Crown Imperial." One of the proofs of a march's success is whether one can

323

whistle or hum (or merely remember) its principal tune after hearing it. I doubt whether anyone can do this after listening to "Orb and Sceptre." It has no push or drive, little profile and its stirrings are somewhat feeble.

¶ Partita for Orchestra

Walton's music has much rhythmic charm and exploration. In two of its three parts it resembles dance style and displays a modern link to the much older *partita* format. But in the expressed élan of most of the score, with its teeming orchestral virtuosity and color, the suite is nippy, contemporary hedonism.

Walton's neodivertimento outlook is not a set of displays which go up quickly in pyrotechnical smoke. The forms (toccata, siciliana, gigue) are truly profiled, as defined as the tonalities in which they are set. The lines are fired by quick-trigger action; dissonance gives sharpness to the harmony. In this orchestral entertainment Walton employs old prototypes in modern manner.

¶ Portsmouth Point—An Overture

Rhythmic ribaldry, spirited sport, nicely noisy—these phrases describe "Portsmouth Point," a musical translation of a print by Thomas Rowlandson (1756–1827), picturing a waterfront scene before the fleet's departure. Though not a measure-by-measure depiction of the pictorial image, all the elements—dancing, intoxication, sacred and profane lovemaking, and the crowded vista—are portrayed by high-spirited, asymmetrical music. The sounds drive ahead without cessation. They include some folksy curves, but always with bustling, booming, snappy orchestration. This rhythmic holiday is impious music, but correctly so.

¶ Scapino—Comedy Overture

The merry music of this overture (its full title is "Scapino, A Comedy Overture for Full Orchestra, after an Etching from Jacques Callot's 'Ballet di Sfessania,' 1622") was the result of a commission given Walton by the Chicago Symphony Orchestra as part of its fiftieth anniversary celebration. Good contemporary overtures are at a premium—Walton's eight-minute "Scapino" is a decided contribution.

Gay, colorful, and clever, the composition constitutes a miniature "Till Eulenspiegel," minus any programmatic trappings and grisly finis. "Scapino" is correctly insolent and as such lives up to its name. It should enjoy long life.

¶ *Symphony* (No. 1)

True symphonic constructivism, in the documentary scope of Bruckner and Mahler. However, a large part of the melodic curves, sharp edges and ripeness of color can be traced to Sibelius.

This is not to damn Walton's moderate eclecticism. His work has sufficient personal authority to be ranked as music of importance. The traditional symphonic machinery is oiled very expertly, especially in the malicious scherzo, containing jagged rhythms, deliberately false accents, and dramatic spurts of silence. Just as forceful is the fugal finale, giving the opus true climax by way of tempered athleticism.

¶ *Symphony No. 2*

Twenty-five years separate Walton's pair of symphonies. His harmonic language is much more unleashed in the second. The chromaticism is now severely on top of the music, not surrounding it in webs. A sense of rhapsody takes hold but does not loosen the designs, permitting the ideas to slip away. At the same time, Walton uses the colors of the orchestral assemblage with insistence on primary qualities; the sonorous dyestuffs do not casually blend into neutral shades.

Polytonality, collisive counterpoint, and tonal serialism warm the music. But William Walton is no rebel. His symphony is in the exultant romantic vein, despite its sophistication. Tonality retains its validity in the 1960's even though indeterminacy is the status symbol in the chic musical circles.

¶ *The Wise Virgins—Ballet Suite* (Bach-Walton)

Johann Sebastian Bach made harpsichord settings of some sixteen concertos (most were for the violin) by such composers as Marcello and Vivaldi. In turn his own music has been transcribed more than that of any other great composer. Walton chose his score from five cantatas and a chorale prelude of Bach. The fourth movement, "Sheep may Safely Graze," is the most familiar. It includes the introductory recitative, never utilized in other versions, which adds tremendously to the effect.

Musical taste is sensitively illustrated in Walton's orchestration. It stands as a model of Bachian reworking.

325

CHAMBER ORCHESTRA

¶ *Siesta*

In terms of title this short piece (for flute alternating with piccolo, oboe, bassoon, a pair each of clarinets and horns, plus strings) is somewhat Spanish, but the midday rest is considered with some sly musical touches. Walton's piece is light and lyrical, yet simultaneously sensuous and serious. It is as if an unstated story lies behind the music, though the composer furnishes no such key.

STRING ORCHESTRA

¶ *Two Pieces for Strings from the Film "Henry V"*

Walton's film music (especially those scores made in association with Sir Laurence Olivier, for "Henry V," "Richard III," and "Hamlet") illustrates a composer who refuses to sacrifice artistic integrity for the sake of money. Walton writing for motion pictures is the same as Walton composing for the concert hall. Proof lies in these two excerpts. The first is a poignant passacaglia (the "Death of Falstaff"); the second, a moving "Touch Her Soft Lips and Part," that resembles madrigal technique applied to string instruments.

BAND

¶ *Crown Imperial: Coronation March, 1937*

Although written for orchestra (*see page 322*) "Crown Imperial" is infinitely better in "bandstration."

¶ *Orb and Sceptre: Coronation March, 1953*

Walton's coronation piece (*see* Orchestral *above*) is not improved in its band arrangement. Despite the more martial sound, "Orb and Sceptre" remains music written in good faith and with good taste, but is not a *good* march.

SOLO INSTRUMENT WITH ORCHESTRA

CONCERTOS

¶ *Concerto for Cello and Orchestra*

There is more improvisational effect in Walton's concerto tale than adherence to classic customs. In this respect, he displays a contemporary and very personal accent. Agreeing with the essential nobility of the solo instrument's address the initial movement is lyrically gentle, orchestrally transparent, and it is this mood which hangs over the third part. The material is so woven that first movement patterns are spliced into the epilogue. Cadenzas, *per se,* are cast aside; in their place, unaccompanied solo sections twice form "improvisations" on a theme. Two other "improvisations" are stated by the orchestra without the cello.

Save for a catchy cadence the middle movement is disappointing. It is presumably a bow to the cello's ability to set off its own brand of instrumental fireworks, though it sounds best when permitted to sing lustily. Unfortunately, the motility of this section sounds like nothing more than "Fiddle Faddle" in dress suit and spats.

¶ Concerto for Viola and Orchestra

Not only plot but pace is demanded of great music. Walton's sense of timing in this glorious lyrical work is faultless. He does not include the traditional slow movement in the central part of the concerto, but conveys a reticent tempo at the beginning, moves into a jazzed-nervous scherzo, continues the smart speed, then reduces it and eventually returns to the mood and theme of the opening. This reminder of Goethe's remark, "Begin, and then the work will be completed," is illustrative of cyclian technique. The metrical argument of the middle movement is irregular; the fashioning of fun and contest serves as a foil to the song facts with which the concerto is concerned. Above all it exhibits Walton's acute dramatic sense, a perceptivity that applies throughout so that form and content are one.

The texture is richly tonal, fully chromaticized for expressiveness. Walton's solo voice does not deal with supertechnical extremism (which may make immediate contact but has no lasting appeal) but with virtuosic intimacy. Every idea in the score is related to the timbre nature of the viola. This is not a concerto composed and then *applied* to the viola. This is a *viola* concerto, without doubt one of the most important in all string literature. (Going out on a limb, I say it forms, with Ernest Bloch's "Suite," the greatest solo works written for the tenor string instrument.)

¶ Concerto for Violin and Orchestra

To achieve proper definition of a concerto's protagonist and yet fuse the orchestral portion so that it is more than mere accompaniment is a test for the composer. Walton passes it with flying compositional colors. His concerto has all the ingredients: tasty tunes, interesting color, hearty rhythms, a definitive orchestral frame, and plenty of display without bogging down into flying figurations or superimposed ornamentations.

The opening melody is one of typical Walton facture. In the second movement dance figures line up with pep, vitality, swing and sway. The finale meanders a bit but resolves matters by thematic relationship to the initial movement. Walton's work fulfills the soloistic concept, yet is more symphonic in its approach than many other contemporary concertos.

NARRATOR AND CHAMBER ENSEMBLE

¶ *Façade* (an Entertainment with Poems by Edith Sitwell)

High-brow poetry with low-brow music; poetry freely shaped and entwined with music of a decided beat; new verses read, old forms played—thus the mating of words with music in "Façade." The Walton-Sitwell depiction of a serious idea with a humorous objective was a type of premature surrealism (first presented in 1922). In its individual way, "Façade" is a small masterpiece.

Sitwell's poems are totally abstract; the designs not only are formed from word colorations, assonances, dissonances, and the play of syllables, but from the effect of rhythm and tempo in delivery. Walton's music is genuinely witty, grotesque, and rowdy. Its parody is subtle and cunning. Illustrations: a take-off on a tap-dance routine in the "Popular Song," the Rossini "William Tell" off-key quotations in the "Yodelling Song," the naughty mixture of waltz and duple pulse in the "Tarantella." Sitwell's and Walton's verbal-music partnership is a frothy, superbly entertaining monodrama.

CHAMBER MUSIC

¶ *Sonata for Violin and Piano*

Walton's only two-instrument sonata was written for Yehudi Menuhin, who gave the first performance, with Louis Kentner, in 1950, at the Drury Lane in London. The composition is compressed into a pair of movements, mainly of lyrical material but with sufficient dynamicism to clarify the designs. Classical allegiance to tonality is followed, though its moves are fairly free because of Walton's pungent use of frictions.

In the first movement the role of the string instrument is that of a *cantabile* personality, blending its thoughts in the duo conversation. In the seven variations of the second part the thematic digressions are nicely balanced, defeating the sectionalism that often haunts such a formal plan.

¶ Quartet for Piano and Strings

The quartet was composed during Walton's studies at Oxford, when he was only sixteen. It has youthful ardor, little of the strong dynamic force of the later works, yet is precocious music for a mere lad.

Two facets appear which are not utilized in the maturer works; the insistent modal flavor of the first movement and the Ravelian-colored contours of the third part. More important, the young Walton had already conquered the scherzo problem, by no means the least difficult form of composition. (Walton's scherzi have always been among his best accomplishments; their muscularity and rhythmic physiognomy are marked with individuality.) There is more than matter-of-fact scherzo control in the second movement; fugati occur which are nearly a carbon copy of the initial movement's theme, only rhythmically diminished and metrically changed. Matter long after the fact, of course; but the professionalism of Walton's teen-age piano quartet cannot be denied.

¶ String Quartet in A minor

The viola, a favorite instrument of Walton's, defines the intro-spective mood of the opening, one in full keeping with the composer's seriousness. Walton's earlier tendencies toward Sibelian harmonies and Stravinskian rhythms are little in evidence. Both themes of the slow movement are also assigned to the viola. The writing here is almost that of the semi-cramped thickness of Max Reger, but only in its weighted solidity.

The scherzo has a pithy kernel of two sounds. Kaleidoscopic juggling of every conceivable turn of the phrase and its permutations follows. The pulse is driven, the tempo unrelenting. A similar sense of vitality is found in the finale, taut with nervousness, only short silences separating and cutting the kinetic rhythms. Walton's A minor opus is a brilliant example in contemporary quartet literature.

VOCAL

¶ *Three Songs*

Texts by Edith Sitwell furnish the basis for these essays "*nello stile inglese*," "*nello stile spagnuolo*," and "*nello stile americano*." The first is discreetly romantic; the remaining pair are disappointing re-settings of movements ("Through Gilded Trellises" and "Old Sir Faulk") from "Façade."

CHORAL

¶ *Make We Joy Now in This Fest*

Lilting music that has the joyful character of a carol.

¶ *Set Me As A Seal Upon Thy Heart*

An anthem which sticks to form, yet is not limited by convenient theories of choral composition. Gently fervent music, with chromatic harmony that gives the recitation a distinctive touch.

ORATORIO

¶ *Belshazzar's Feast*

Few contemporary works in the vocal-orchestral category have the particular barbaric splendor and volatile sweep of this piece.

The text is a dramatic version of the Fall of Babylon, the material from the Scriptures rewritten by Sir Osbert Sitwell and including passages from a pair of psalms. Walton's oratorio begins with Isaiah's prophecy of Babylonian captivity, continues with a lament (the psalm "By the Waters of Babylon") and then moves on to descriptions of Babylon's riches and its orgies. Then follow the scenes of the handwriting on the wall ("Mene, mene, tekel upharsin"), the death of Belshazzar, an exultant hymn of praise, and the final paean of *Alleluias*. Walton has set this for solo baritone (in the role of a commentator), mixed chorus (often divided), and a huge orchestra, with organ, piano, and two additional brass choirs.

There are no stale sensations in the work, which is colorborne on explosive intoxications of sound. Some critics have termed Walton's piece "theatrical," a few have described it as "garish." Others have hailed the opus as one of the outstanding and most exciting choral products of modern times. The verdict from this corner is that

"Belshazzar's Feast" is a triumph because Walton mastered the one important theorem of musical composition—the engendering of informative substance that contains personality and creative character —a positively new contribution, not an imitation.

OPERA

¶ *Troilus and Cressida*

If expressive melody is the backbone of the drama-plus-music structure, "Troilus and Cressida" stands erect. The work contains the ingredients of good theatre. It does avoid any individual solution to operatic procedures, being designed in a fairly traditional manner, including dramatic recitative and various set ensembles.

The libretto is based on Chaucer's poem "Troylus and Criseide." Walton's score has a romantic profile. However, there are no pat harmonic clichés, nor is the orchestral characterization a simple one. The combination of symphonic richness and vocal sweep (the emphasis is on the voice) is effective.

The highlights are Troilus' aria in the opening part, the love music in the second act, and the aria sung by Cressida before she kills herself.

FILM MUSIC

¶ *Henry V*

Walton's contributions to film music have been considerable. His motion picture scores are written without superficial formula, or Hollywoodian vulgarity. He is never on the defensive—Walton's music is as much a part of the production as the settings and the action of the camera.

The music for "Henry V" contains Purcellian simulations when required and is colorfully and convincingly French-styled in other places. The quiet movements (for two illustrations, *see* String Orchestra *above*) are as vivid and as moving as the climactic battle scene. The latter can stand alone without screen images. It avoids a single measure of padding.

Walton's score for "Henry V" neither distracts the viewer of the film nor fulfills a merely functional role. Only a handful of composers are capable of such an accomplishment.

30. ANTON WEBERN
(1883–1945)

WEBERN'S complete departure from traditional styles (except in the individualistic way he uses the twelve-tone system) demands a changed musical attitude. His touch was so unique that bewilderment and frustration will follow unless music habits are adapted willingly. Few of Webern's works (particularly those of the first half of his career) can be understood by comparative processes; the music by men that preceded and followed his entry on the scene may sound like Sibelius's or Strauss's, Hindemith's or Honegger's, but it hasn't the slightest resemblance to Webern's. He was an artistic hermit.

Webern's music divides into two work periods, with extremely short compositions marking the first of these. However, the somewhat longer pieces of the later output contain the same concentration of working material. Development does not increase quantity as a matter of course; the total measures may be more, the number of sounds not necessarily so.

In the earlier compositions a crystallization takes place in melody, harmony, counterpoint, rhythm, color, and form to such extent that all are combined in one—epitomized within seconds and split seconds. Webern's music has the scope of a sonata in a piece of ten or twenty measures.

In bringing the initial period of his work to a close, Webern realized that he had stretched the technique to the point of exhaustion. Further extension could only add up to a few sounds, or silence, absolute zero music. In order to enlarge his musical structures Webern turned to the dodecaphonic system of composition for the necessary working tools. His early works consisted of the free association of sound, without key, tone row or any other device. They were marked by tone specks of vertical and horizontal outline, oblique and "dot-dash" rhythms, glazed and flat-wash colors. Twelve-tone technique gave him the means to shape and develop his ideas without repetition and free from the looseness that marks athematic style. In this respect Webern was as constructive as he had been in his concentrated compositions. He applied Schoenberg's revolutionary method wholesale to the components (thematic, structural, textural, coloristic) of musical organization.

332

It is almost impossible to codify technically (in the common analytical manner) the essentials of Webern's early productions. There can be no analysis by dissection. And though we can chart and tabulate the later works as to rows and intervals, we cannot describe the unique sonorous pointillism of this stripped music. The listener is given an immaterial, astral plane of sound arrangements in Webern's music, up to the end of Opus 11. The parallel means of essential concentration, of sifting so that only the purest *materia* remains, exist in the dodecaphonically designed *oeuvre*. Compared to the longhand in which Schoenberg described his twelve-tone inventions, Webern's are noted in an abbreviated type of shorthand. Through the choice sounds (as well as the amazing and eloquent use of silence) in Webern's music there exists a completely new and very beautiful art world.

ORCHESTRAL

¶*Fuga* (Ricercata) *a 6 Voci* ("Six-Voice Fugue")—*No. 2 from "Das Musikalisches Opfer"* ("The Musical Offering") (Bach-Webern)

One of a set of contrapuntal pieces based on a theme first extemporized by Bach and now dipped into a bath of *Klangfarben* orchestration by Webern. It emerges with ruddy complexion and in full health. The classical text is broken up into units as Webern italicizes the motival coherence of the fascinating polyphony.

Some may shriek that Bach has been led astray and mocked, but Webern's ultrasensitive recasting of this magnificent fugue by a disciplined radiation of single timbres makes perfect artistic sense. The transcription is the equivalent of an acute aural analysis of the score.

¶*German Dances* (October 1824) (Schubert-Webern)

Webern's role as an orchestrator is properly reticent. Though one realizes immediately that the scoring is just a bit un-Schubertian it is completely un-Webernian. The result is an orchestral gem.

¶*Passacaglia, Op. 1*

Here is Webern straddling the fence between traditional territory and the new frontier. The largesse of Brahms and Mahler are the essentials of this first opus (well-developed formal aspects), though Schoenberg (breadth and chromatic framing) enters in.

333

Twentieth-Century Music

The "Passacaglia" is tonal (D minor) but the atmosphere is charged with Webern-to-be. The orchestral texture is transparent and it governs the aesthetic disposition of the variations (the formal viewpoint that was so emphatic a part of Webern's later style). Despite the twilight of romanticism that streaks the music, the future casts its shadows in certain technical events: wide-spanned voicing, muted brass instruments, the utilization of silence, the devotion to textural conditions.

¶ Six Pieces for Large Orchestra, Op. 6 (Original Scoring)

Webern's miscellany calls for a jumbo orchestra, including sixteen winds, six horns, six trumpets, six trombones, and a tuba, in addition to percussion, strings, harp, and celesta. The set constitutes a group of musical "shorts," the longest less than three and one-half minutes, most of the others just a little over sixty seconds.

In Opus 6 harmonic and contrapuntal suppression is Webern's method of timbre affirmation. Each piece registers in its individual parts. This music illustrates *collage* in orchestral translation. The varied weights of brass or strings, the oscillation of a *tremolandi col legno,* the swish of a rute roll, etc., are the equivalents of paint, newspaper clips, hunks of light cloth, wood, and other material. Color *is* the melody, and the pitches are mere pegs on which to hang the variegated swatches and sonic merchandise. This represents a stinging and provocative new type of musical art.

¶ Six Pieces for Large Orchestra, Op. 6 (Revised Scoring)

Webern composed his Opus 6 in 1909 and revamped the orchestration in 1928. The winds and brass were reduced to more normal numbers. Though the instrumental palette is smaller and some very special colors (for example: alto flute and E flat clarinet solos in the fourth movement) give way to more ordinary qualities, the seductive positiveness of Webern's originality is not lessened.

¶ Variations for Orchestra, Op. 30

Webern's last purely instrumental work has his sparse dodecaphonic syntax and rapid-fire color changes. Though the details of construction are highly involved, with such matters as retrograde movement, rhythmic augmentation and diminution, the expressivity and pungency of the orchestration are enchanting. Despite the extreme economy of the material and its instrumental treatment there is constant discovery as pitch and timbre arrangement become continually transformed.

334

Again Webern illustrates the theorem of perpetual change in order to obtain a maximum of variation.

Some may insist that Webern attempts to shock. However, the wish to activate sound potential by severe organization is purely a desire to find the ultimate in structural clarity. This rigid formal situation from which all the incidents of the piece emerge is thus explained by Webern: "everything . . . is derived from the two ideas stated in the first two measures by the double bass and oboe." And if the "Variations" sound involved it is because complicated music demands a complicated method of expression.

CHAMBER ORCHESTRA

¶ Concerto, Op. 24

Webern's Opus 24 is a nine-ply instrumental affair, its virtuosity solely concerned with music-creation impervious to display, and minus any decorative cadenza. The only remote resemblance to a concerto is that it covers three movements.

The "Concerto" is magnificently and uniquely organized. One each of four different tone types is used, in totals that descend sequentially (three woodwind, three brass, two string, one piano). Webern also divides his twelve-tone row into four groups (three tones in each). This split emphasizes the relationship of mass to individual. It makes possible permutates of the whole and of each portion simultaneously and oppositionally.

In movement one, almost every instrument states three sounds and drops out for the moment. This three in-and-out address changes in the middle movement, where, for the most part, only two consecutive sounds in any single timbre are used. The triple sets in a similar color return in the final movement, forming a symmetrical plan. This shifting instrumentational pattern propels the manifold canonic devices that shape the music. It also adds colorific light and shadow, textural thickness and leanness. Apart from analysis the "Concerto" is compact and communicative, an artistic achievement as well as an illustration of superb scholarship.

¶ Five Pieces for Orchestra, Op. 10

The fluctuating, pigmented intonation of these pieces once again illustrates the "Klangfarbenmelodie" theorem, whereby the principal line is fragmented between assorted instrumental colors, rather than presented in a centralized hue. The gilded and spotlighted assortment

335

of tone quality includes guitar, mandolin, and harmonium, and these are part of an instrumentational plot of tremendous compactness. Super-legato in movement and fluidic in its orchestration, Webern's aphoristic music has the strength and the sway of a spider's web.

In the expressive symbols that mark Webern's transparent orchestral sounds there is beautiful, quietly violent power. Nothing in the entire orchestral literature is like these "Five Pieces." Such divinely original music reflects the genius of Anton Webern.

¶ Symphony, Op. 21

Webern's symphony bypasses traditional definition, consisting of two concentrated movements; the first in moderate tempo containing 130 measures, the other a theme with seven variations totaling 99 measures. The opus can be described as synoptic music, its expressivity expounded by minute and constantly changing textures, accents, dynamics, and colors.

All these points are rigorously controlled but as logically ordered as a Bach fugue; the discourse as nakedly defined. In the initial movement assorted canonic procedures determine a sonata-styled music. In the second part variation particulars are the feature. Again canonic method plays an important role (thus technical procedure interlocks the movements without interfering with formal contrast).

This exceedingly discretionary music has more than twelve-tone superacademic formality. The small orchestra of clarinet, bass clarinet, two horns, harp, and strings without double basses traces the flow with the freedom and plasticity of a super-diffused (but magnificently refined) color scheme. When listening to this chromoscopic orchestra the ear must not define the timbres as isolated; each sound is acutely related to the next. In this world of contractive sound, symphonic flamboyance is smothered to death.

STRING ORCHESTRA

¶ Five Movements for String Orchestra, Op. 5

This is Webern's own setting of the string quartet pieces with the same title and opus number (*see below*). The sonority scale is expanded, naturally; but some will prefer the original four-instrument version. When heard in its enlarged state a great deal of the quartet's subtle imperatives of color, line, and disjunct transformation (each with its own sensation) are underlined, rather than interlined. Greater illumination, in this manner, rejects fantasy.

336

INSTRUMENTAL

PIANO

¶ *Variations, Op. 27*

This represents Webern's sole excursion into the solo piano medium. In a set of three very concentrated movements, variation expands into perpetual change. Gone are polyphonic alterations of Handelian days, the melodic figurations that embroider the music of the classical composers, and the semi-descriptive piece that caught the fancy of the romanticists while making their variational discourse. And gone, of course, thematic functions, replaced by the totality of serial functionalism.

Webern is relentless in the mutation of his substances. Not only pitch and duration shift, but dynamic and mode of attack as well. The controls of the vehicle are the twelve tones, meshed in great part by intricate canons. There are no lush sonorities in the "Variations"; instead, the utmost complexity of organization is detailed by minute segments of sound. The beauty of Webern's "Variations" lies in their structural purity.

CHAMBER MUSIC

¶ *Four Pieces for Violin and Piano, Op. 7*

The four movements of this suite contain nine, twenty-four, fourteen, and fifteen measures, respectively. Dynamic polarity is most important to these epigrams. The first and third are undertones in which the sonority is never louder than a *pianissimo* and is represented mostly in *triple piano*. Webern further underlines the veiled messages by muted tone. Movements two and four are sharply defined by the contrasted highs and lows of dynamic intensity.

These codifications point up the theorem that art requires no historical obligation to confirm its truth. Wonderfully strange music, Webern's brief pieces last long in the memory.

¶ *Three Small Pieces for Cello and Piano, Op. 11*

With only thirty-two measures of music it is significant that Webern calls this set "small," as against the "Four Pieces" for violin and piano, which totaled sixty-two measures (*see above*).

In this opus Webern's skeletal statements are further de-em-

337

phasized by delivery through instrumentalized veils. By checking and stifling Webern reaches the borderline between musical sound and its cessation. He can go no further and can only turn away from an aesthetic that exhibits such exclusion.

¶ String Trio, Op. 20

The motival principle is the root of twelve-tone composition style since the basic tone row is the equivalent of a motive. Like a tonal thematic cell it undergoes combination and separation as well as juxtaposition and variation. But here the similarity stops, since there are no privileged tones in the row. The unity of the trio stems from the mutual equality of its sounds, and it is this point which is basic to its formal plans.

In the slow-tempoed first movement tenderness is the cardinal quality. Its mobility permits Webern to trace a type of free rondo in variation fashion. The sound in the second movement is more tightly knit; the sections are in greater contrast to each other. First a vigorous rhythm is framed in very slow tempo and then is related to a faster division, played through twice with absolute literalness. Thereafter, development takes place in the freest manner.

Thus Webern illustrates his incessant-developing type of sonata design. Poles apart from classical large form, its balances exist just as acutely.

¶ Five Movements for String Quartet, Op. 5

In size the last four pieces of this quartet suite stand apart in relation to the first. Likewise, formal content is dynamically produced by integrated variation and the convolution of two fundamental textures in the first movement; while in the remaining four parts each design is reduced to the most direct and cogent miniature (miniature only in comparison to a large-scaled work). It must never be forgotten that Webern is *not* a miniaturist; his works are spun musical strands which care for all the exigencies met in huge compositions.

The first movement turns on two determined tempo points, with the faster of the pair accompanying more vertically arranged sound patterns than the second. Movement two is an unbroken line passing from one instrument to the next. A single thought expresses the music's completeness. The third part has certain pedal formations— it is a brutal, burning scherzo. It also enjoys uniqueness in Webern's catalogue because the final two measures are strictly in four-part octaves. By the clear sense of its design, the fourth piece divides itself almost exactly in half. In its twenty-six measures the fifth movement displays a fantasy-like desire.

¶ Quartet for Violin, Clarinet, Tenor Saxophone and Piano, Op. 22

The carefully mixed instrumental colors of the quartet are an advantageous means of formal conviction. In the first movement Webern exemplifies the developments which arise from motival variation by four different instrumental types. The themes develop, branch out, intertwine, and move forward and backward. Thus an entire movement is designed from the fundamental expression of canonic narrative, in turn dissected into small, precise substances on which the dabbed instrumental color equals pointillistic application. The instrumental timbres emphasize the difference of ideas, as well as define the canon's progress. They do not exist as colors for individual display but for background illumination.

While the general style of the second movement (a fairly long one for this composer) is looser, the lines of motive supply are still as short as in the opening movement, but there is a sense of widerspread sound, a more settled quality in relation to the first part. In terms of balance the last part is the "allegro" to the previous "andante."

¶ Six Bagatelles for String Quartet, Op. 9

Webern dedicated these pieces (totaling fifty-seven measures) to Alban Berg with the Latin adage "Non multa, sed multum" ("Not many things, but much"), to which Webern added, "How I hope that is true of what I offer you here."

The truth found in these six dissections is well-nigh the ultimate in string-quartet color. Webern's procedure is to explain a theme through its tints, such as will be found in the first measures of the opening piece: a cello harmonic, a *ponticello* sound for the viola, then a wispy, natural tone for the first violin. Thus the music staples itself on wings which are iridescent—mixed and changed from dark to bright. Webern's musical sobriety is only in total count of sounds; the vibrational result is turbulent, paroxysmic.

¶ String Quartet, Op. 28

Canonic device prevails in great part throughout, but the ear won't realize this as well as the eye might in perusing the printed score.

Although the structures of the three movements bear classical affinity (ternary type, scherzo with trio, and a more elaborate scherzo minus a trio), the textures are almost those of static sound placements, despite the elaborate devices employed. These furnish not only the thematic and developmental sections but serve for the complete expansion of the composition. The play of the tone row (distributed in acute, contrasted registrations and constantly permutated) is accompanied by the percussive subtlety of accentuation plus instrumental entrance and departure that make for lively structural resiliency, difficult to follow without repeated aural exposure. The narrative manner is novel, as new to the ear as were Schoenberg's early works in twelve-tone style.

Webern's Opus 28 does not have the same instrumental tinge as his early sets of pieces for four strings. Assorted coloration is not the paramount concern, but its use (in the concentrate) is firmly present. The timbre palette is more disposed toward gray, black, and white.

¶ Quintet for String Quartet and Piano

Predating his first official opus (the orchestral "Passacaglia") by two years, Webern's quintet is lushly romantic. It is heavy with Brahmsian sighs and sentiments, plus the *ferne Klang* of sensuousness that maintained Strauss and even Schoenberg for a time.

In one movement, the quintet is built on a pair of themes which constitute the feeding ground of the entire work. Webern's later style simmers in this composition, by way of beseeching diminished octaves, long, lean leaps, the oscillation of *tremolandi,* and the use of imitatory ideas. It shows Webern's youthful creative potency and how he made the most of it. There is no reason for apologies.

VOCAL

¶ Five Songs, Op. 3
¶ Five Songs, Op. 4

In these two sets of songs to poems by Stefan George tonality is present, but in a somewhat dissolved state. Anchored tonality is avoided. The keynote is mood realized by free melody—melody already shaped by Webern as a continuity of timbre differences. There are no recurring *leitmotifs* in these expressionistic songs; symmetry gives way to the sound itself, its subtle disguises in register, dynamic, and contrast. Nor are there any joyful, tuneful strikings (never in

Webern!), but the seriousness does not becloud clarity. In this respect
these early Webern songs avoid the blatant romantic habit of obscuring formal definition.

¶ *Four Songs, Op. 12*

Larger-scaled songs than those included in Opus 3 and Opus 4,
but with the same lucid, concentrated style of the composer. Although the texts are not used as a program for the music, the lyric
poetry serves as a phonetic part of the total structure.

The Opus 12 group is opposite in effect to the heavy, quasi-
morbidity found so often, for example, in the songs of Schoenberg.
There is a parallel introspection but the range of intensity is different.
One might say that Webern depicts the glow of afternoon, Schoenberg
deals with twilight time.

¶ *Three Songs, Op. 23*
¶ *Three Songs, Op. 25*

Both groups are set to poems by the Austrian painter-poet Hildegard Jone, who, from the year (1934) Opus 23 was composed, was
the only one to whom Webern turned for the texts of his vocal works.
In addition to these six songs Jone's poems were utilized in "Der
Augenlicht," Op. 26 and the two cantatas, Op. 30 and 31. (At the
time of his death Webern was working on a third cantata, also to a text
by Jone.)

In comparison with the terseness in his previous compositions,
Webern is lyrical and expansive in these songs: the first set dealing
with love, the second with nature. The ability to invent new combinations of sound and project the spirit of a text without disturbing formal
logic demands creative mastery. Indeed, it is a feat to retain individuality without deviating from a specified technique which holds
style in place. That Webern carries out all of these obligations is
eloquent proof of his unique achievement.

VOICE WITH INSTRUMENTAL ENSEMBLE

¶ *Five Canons on Latin Texts, Op. 16*

A fusion of words taken from the Breviary, set in strict polyphonic
style, for an extremely odd trio combination of soprano, clarinet, and
bass clarinet. The unity of canonic procedure is unstinting; three of
the set are three-voiced, the remainder are two-voiced, and both

341

types include examples of contrary motion. Insistence on technical method does not mean merely a fascinating blueprint. These canons offer sincere music with a Webernian brand of beauty.

¶ *Five Sacred Songs, Op. 15*

Compared with romantic style, free-toned music (atonal is a poor description) is harsh and refractory. Within its own orbit, the relationships of the first four of Webern's "Geistliche" songs are planned with the same fundamentals of tensions and releases.

But unhampered tonal language can seek other controls, and Webern begins this superintendence in the last song, "Ascend, Fair Soul," with a double canon run in contrary motion. It is canonic regulation which helps the serial organization of Webern's later works, for canon deals with diagonal relationships which are paramount to twelve-tone structural arrangement. The appearance of canon in the end part of Opus 15 is not only a conclusion but a prelude of coming events.

¶ *Four Songs, Op. 13*

Not a single Webern song cycle calls for a male voice. Of the dozen works he wrote for soprano as the sole vocal color (of these one is for medium range and two for "high soprano"), five are with piano and the others with various instrumental groups. The latter vary considerably, the smallest being for two players. Opus 13 requires the largest combination, with fourteen instruments (winds, brass, strings, keyboard, and percussion) covering a full range of tone colors. Further, each movement (based on poems by Kraus, Trakl, and a pair from "The Chinese Flute" by Bethge) is scored differently.

The minute diffusion of timbre is fundamental to these songs. Despite the longer presentation this Webern mannerism is never eliminated. Webern's thoughts are always conveyed in essence, never lengthened by multisyllabic words or parenthetical asides.

¶ *Six Songs, Op. 14*

Sounding like dodecaphonically designed music, Webern's Opus 14 is elastically polyphonic, much less fragmented than his previous output. Integrated with the counterpoint are instrumental colors, consisting of E♭, B♭, and bass clarinets, with soprano and bass string instruments (violin and cello). Webern's refusal to permit static rhythm adds further appositeness to the rich polyphony of these songs to Trakl texts.

¶ *Three Songs, Op. 18*

Fully organized, fully sensitized twelve-tone vocal music, with words about a sweetheart and redemption, concluding with an "Ave, Regina." The texts, however, serve as a convenience for settling the composition's form, rather than outlining and defining a specific mood or circumstance. The technical precepts do not interfere with music of sensitive meaning, which avoids artificial dodecaphonic conventionality. But coloristically Webern is unconventional. No other song cycle comes to mind that uses a raucous E flat clarinet and a guitar as instrumental partners.

¶ *Three Traditional Rhymes, Op. 17*

It is an odd twist that Webern's first pure serial work includes the word "traditional" in the translation of its German title. (Actually, the rendering of the original "Drei geistliche Volkslieder" could also be "Three Folk Texts," or "Three Spiritual Folksongs," but the word "folk" is no less odd.) The texts are prayers to the Holy Trinity, the Virgin, and Jesus. However, the music's persistent intervallic jaggedness—the vivid birthmark on the body of twelve-tone music, especially in its early age—has nothing to do with religion except perhaps a reverence for dodecaphonic principles.

¶ *Two Songs, Op. 8*

Economy is the analogue to the fastidiousness and purity of Webern's compositions. This pair of songs (to Rilke texts) illustrate Webern's creative aloofness. It totals the shortest work he wrote (performance time: one and three-quarters minutes). The eight performers required (playing nine instruments) furnish a few timbred punctuation signs to the words expressed by the singer. Value does not depend on size. This brief music has intense power.

CHORAL

¶ *Entflieht auf leichten Kähnen, Op. 2*

Clarity and comprehensibility are the key words in regard to canon, and canonic technique is a key element in Webern's compositions. In this early opus for *a cappella* mixed chorus, to a text by Stefan George, the complete procedure is the coherence and consistency of canon, framing free tonality.

CHORAL WITH INSTRUMENTAL ENSEMBLE

¶ *Two Songs, Op. 19*

Despite the complexities of twelve-tone style its idiom has flexibility. Webern's opus for mixed chorus or vocal quartet is fully governed by the doctrines of tone-row manipulation, but it also has a freshness, a lightness, a play of rhythmic agility that is quite uncommon to his output. Part of this limpidity occurs because of very close imitations and contrasting vocal coloration, plus an active instrumental spray. None of this concerns the poems, which are from Goethe's "Chinesisch-Deutsche Jahres- und Tageszeiten." The music (as is so often the case in serial composition) is foreign to the texts. But if any Webern music can be called "delicious," this is it.

CHORAL WITH ORCHESTRA

¶ *Das Augenlicht, Op. 26*

Webernian ellipses of sound are absent in this instance; the flow of the voices, regardless of wide-spanned intervals, is far from the streamlined late instrumental pieces. Webern has weighted his textures, but has not modified his technique or aesthetic. Most twelve-tone music lacks the traditional "vocal" essence, but the intensity of "Das Augenlicht" (for mixed chorus with an orchestra of fourteen different instruments plus strings) is arrived at by the sweep of the voices, opposed to the somewhat jagged quality of the instrumental sound.

CANTATA

¶ *Cantata No. 1, Op. 29*
¶ *Cantata No. 2, Op. 31*

Change is apparent in these late-period compositions. More substantial textures and less angularity of intervallic movement mark the cantatas. Both pieces, to texts by Hildegard Jone, emphasize the solo voice. In the first cantata the second part is for solo soprano. In the other, Webern's final completed work (and aside from the early quintet, his longest composition—over ten minutes), solo voices comprise three of the six sections, while in two other movements a solo soprano is contrasted to a three-part women's chorus and a four-part mixed chorus, respectively. Only one portion of the composition is for chorus and orchestra. In this manner Webern changes his working forces as productively as his tone-rows.

Notwithstanding the decisive serialism and the firm objectivity of the music, there is an eloquence far beyond the feeling that one is simply being led by the technical hand. (Webern compared the second cantata to the sacredness of a *Missa Brevis.*) In these pieces Anton Webern has transcended method, especially in Opus 31. The articulated expression of the cantatas bears testimony to his creative magic.

PART TWO

THE RECORDINGS

PREFACE

THE RECORDINGS considered in this study embrace all releases up to January 1964 and include a carefully selected number of foreign issues. The frequent problem of current unavailability for purchase can often be solved by hearing records that friends own, borrowing them from a record club or library, or listening to the programs of radio stations that specialize in serious music.

With only a few exceptions, a discussion precedes the listing of recordings when there are two or more represented for a composition (excerpts, recorded in addition to the complete opus, are considered separately). The releases then follow in order of the author's preference. (If contained in an issue with a special title this fact is given.) In most instances, no mention is made of the poorer performances, though all recordings appear in the listings. The collector is given sufficient information to select from the best; consideration of why the poorer ones are poor is, most often, superfluous.

When only a single recording of a composition has been issued, it is discussed only when some special information had to be supplied or when some point regarding the performance required emphasis. Without a discussion these single recordings are prefaced by stars which define the performance thus:

★★★★	exceptional
★★★	very good
★★	good
★	fair
(no symbol given)	poor

For compactness in the listings, most organizations are coded (*see page* 352). Last names only of performers are indicated. The instrumental or vocal classification follows these, contained in parentheses and abbreviated (*see list on page* 351). Names of conductors always appear last in a listing, preceding the catalogue number of the recording. A code (*see page* 356) also is used for the names of recording companies. Since the letters that sometimes preface a record's catalogue number are of inconsequential value to a purchaser these have been eliminated. Catalogue numbers are given only for monophonic releases; if a stereophonic version is also available (S) follows the monophonic number. (It is a simple matter to locate a stereo disk if one has the monophonic catalogue number.)

In those few cases where only a stereophonic disk has been issued, the number itself appears in parentheses in place of the (S). For the sake of concentrating on the specific work under discussion, companion compositions contained on a recording are rarely mentioned and have not been included in the listings.

LIST OF ABBREVIATIONS

(*a*)	alto		(*n*)	narrator
(*b*)	bass		(*o*)	oboe
(*bar*)	baritone		(*om*)	Ondes Martenot
(*bn*)	bassoon		*Orch.*	Orchestra
			(*org*)	organ
(*c*)	cello			
(*ce*)	celesta		(*p*)	piano
(*ci*)	cimbalom		(*per*)	percussion
(*cl*)	clarinet		*Phila.*	Philadelphia
(*cn*)	contralto		(*pic*)	piccolo
Co.	Company		*Prep.*	Preparatory
Conn.	Connecticut			
(*ct*)	counter-tenor		*Q*	Quartet
Dept.	Department		(*s*)	soprano
			(*sax*)	saxophone
(*Eh*)	English horn		*Sq*	String Quartet
			Sy.	Symphony
(*fl*)	flute			
			(*t*)	tenor
(*g*)	guitar		(*tb*)	trombone
			(*ti*)	timpani
(*ha*)	harmonica		(*tp*)	trumpet
(*har*)	harmonium			
(*hn*)	horn		(*v*)	violin
(*hp*)	harp		(*va*)	viola
(*hps*)	harpsichord		(*vib*)	vibraphone
			Vol.	Volume
L.A.	Los Angeles			
			(*x*)	xylorimba
(*m*)	mandolin			
(*ms*)	mezzo-soprano			

PERFORMING ORGANIZATIONS

ACC   Orchestre de l'Association des Concerts Colonne

ANSC   Orchestra and Chorus of Accademia Nazionale di Santa Cecilia, Rome

BAV   Bavarian State Orchestra

BAVR   Bavarian Radio Symphony Orchestra

BBC   British Broadcasting Co. Symphony Orchestra

BCE   Boston Chamber Ensemble

BE   Barylli Ensemble

BM   Bamberg Symphony

BNSO   Boyd Neel String Orchestra

BP   Boston Pops Orchestra

BPO   Berlin Philharmonic Orchestra

BR   Berlin Radio Symphony Orchestra

BRC   Bavarian Radio Chorus

BRS   Brno Radio Symphony Orchestra

BRSO   Brno Symphony Orchestra

BSO   Boston Symphony Orchestra

BSP   Brno State Philharmonic Orchestra

BU   Budapest Radio Orchestra

BUC   Budapest Radio Chorus

BUP   Budapest Philharmonic Orchestra

CAO   Concert Arts Orchestra

CBC   Canadian Broadcasting Corporation Symphony Orchestra

CG   Concertgebouw Orchestra of Amsterdam

CHI   Chicago Symphony Orchestra

CLE   Cleveland Orchestra

CLEP   Cleveland Pops Orchestra

COL   Columbia Symphony Orchestra

COLC   Columbia Chamber Orchestra

CR   Cologne Radio Symphony Orchestra

CSO   Capitol Symphony Orchestra

CSW   Chicago Symphony Woodwind Quintet

CZ   Czech Philharmonic Orchestra

DET   Detroit Symphony Orchestra

DRE   Dresden Philharmonic Orchestra

ER   Eastman-Rochester Pops Orchestra

EW   Eastman Symphonic Wind Ensemble

FA	Fine Arts Wind Players	LPO	London Philharmonic Orchestra
FAI	Fairfield Wind Ensemble	LRP	London Royal Philharmonic
FRT	French National Radio-Television Orchestra	LSF	Little Symphony of San Francisco
FWQ	French Wind Quintet	LSO	London Symphony Orchestra
G	Morton Gould and His Orchestra	LZ	Leipzig Philharmonic Orchestra
H	Houston Symphony Orchestra	M	Minneapolis Symphony Orchestra
HAR	Hartford Symphony Orchestra	MCO	Monte Carlo Opera Orchestra
HB	Hollywood Bowl Symphony Orchestra	MLS	Maurice Levine String Sinfonietta
HCO	Hungarian Concert Orchestra	MO	Moscow Chamber Orchestra
HP	Hamburg Philharmonic Orchestra	MSP	Moscow State Philharmonic
HRS	Hungarian Radio Symphony Orchestra	N	National Symphony Orchestra
HS	Hungarian State Symphony Orchestra	NAQ	New Art Wind Quintet
I	I Musici	NCO	Netherlands Chamber Orchestra
IP	Israel Philharmonic Orchestra	NE	Netherlands Philharmonic Orchestra
IZ	I Solisti di Zagreb	NSC	New Symphony Chorus
KO	André Kostelanetz and His Orchestra	NSO	New Symphony Orchestra of London
LA	Los Angeles Philharmonic Orchestra	NTS	North Texas State University Concert Band
LAM	Orchestre des Concerts Lamoureux		
LF	Lucerne Festival Strings	NY	New York Philharmonic
LOF	L'Orchestre National de la Radiodiffusion Française	NYW	New York Woodwind Quintet
LOU	Louisville Orchestra	OCM	Orquesta de Conciertos de Madrid
LPC	London Philharmonic Choir		

353

OCPT	Orchestra and Chorus of the Prague National Theatre	PW	Philadelphia Woodwind Quintet
ONE	Orquesta Nacional de España	RIAS	RIAS Symphony Orchestra
ORCOH	Orchestra and Chorus of the Royal Opera House, Covent Garden	RP	Royal Philharmonic Orchestra
		RU	Rundfunk-Sinfonie Orchester, Leipzig
OROH	Orchestra of the Royal Opera House, Covent Garden	S	Leopold Stokowski and His Symphony Orchestra
ORS	L'Orchestre Radio-Symphonique de Paris	SDCC	Orchestre de la Société des Concerts du Conservatoire, Paris
OSM	Orquesta Sinfonica de Madrid	SF	San Francisco Symphony Orchestra
OT	Orchestre de Chambre de Toulouse	SL	St. Louis Symphony Orchestra
PAS	Orchestre de l'Association des Concerts Pasdeloup	SR	L'Orchestre de la Suisse Romande
PC	Paris Conservatory Orchestra	SUD	Südwestfunk Orchester, Baden-Baden
PH	Philharmonia Orchestra	SUDW	Südwestdeutsches Orchester
PHO	Philharmonia Hungarica Orchestra	T	Tibor Serly and His Orchestra
PI	Pittsburgh Symphony Orchestra	TCE	Orchestre du Théâtre des Champs-Elysées
PM	Pro Musica Chamber Orchestra, Stuttgart	TNO	Orchestre du Théâtre National de l'Opéra de Paris
PO	Philadelphia Orchestra	TNOC	Orchestre du Théâtre National de l'Opéra-Comique
PP	Paris Philharmonic Orchestra		
PPO	Philharmonic Promenade Orchestra	USSR	USSR State Philharmonic Orchestra
PRM	Pro Musica Symphony, Vienna	USSRC	USSR State Philharmonic Choir
PSL	Philharmonic Symphony Orchestra of London	UT	Utah Symphony Orchestra

VCO	Vienna Chamber Choir	WES	Westminster Symphony Orchestra
VOP	Vienna State Opera Orchestra	WI	Winterthur Symphony Orchestra
VOPC	Vienna State Opera Chorus	WIQ	Wind Quintet of the Orchestre National de la Radiodiffusion Française
VPO	Vienna Philharmonic Orchestra		
VSO	Vienna Symphony Orchestra	Z	Zimbler Sinfonietta
WE	Westphalia Symphony Orchestra	ZU	Zurich Chamber Orchestra

RECORD LABELS

A	Angel	COOK	Cook
ABC	ABC-Paramount	CSS	Colosseum
AC	Academy	CT	Counterpoint
AEOLIAN-SKINNER		CY	Contemporary
	Aeolian-Skinner	D	Decca
AL	Allegro	DE	Delta
AM	Amadeo	DG	Deutsche Grammo-
ARGO	Argo		phon
ARION	Arion	DIAL	Dial
ASCO	ASCO (American	DO	Dover
	Stereophonic	DOT	Dot
	Corp.)	DR	Draco
AT	Artia	DT	Ducretet-Thomson
AU	Austin	DV	Da Vinci
AUD	Audiophile	E	Epic
B	Boston	ED	Educo
BAM	Bärenreiter-	EL	Electrola
	Musicaphon	EMS	EMS
BK	Bartók	ES	Esoteric
BN	Bruno	EV	Everest
BOI	Boîte à Musique	F	20th Fox
BV	Belvedere	FCO	French Columbia
C	Capitol	FE	Festival
CA	Camden	FW	Folkways
CAM	Cambridge	FY	Fantasy
CAMEO	Cameo-Parkway	GC	Golden Crest
CAN	Cantate	GIA	Gregorian Institute
CANTERBURY CHORAL			of America
	SOCIETY	IN	Internos
	Canterbury Choral	J	Jupiter
	Society	K	Kapp
CC	Crowell-Collier	KE	Kendall
CD	Concert-Disc	L	London
CH	Concert Hall Society	LANIER	Lanier
CI	Circle	LDF	Les Discophiles
CL	Classic Edition		Français
CN	Carillon	LION	Lion
CO	Columbia	LL	L'Oiseau-Lyre
COM	Command	LV	Louisville
CON	Concordia	LY	Liberty

Record Labels

LYR	Lyrichord	SP	Spanish Music Center
MG	Music Guild		
MGM	MGM	SPA	SPA
MI	Mirrosonic	ST	Stand
MK	MK	STRAD	Stradivari
MLL	Montilla	SU	Supraphon
MLR	Music Library	TE	Telefunken
MON	Monitor	TIME	Time
MY	Mercury	TOPS	Tops
N	New Records	U	Urania
O	Odéon	UA	United Artists
OM	Omega	UI	University of Illinois
OV	Overtone	UN	Unicorn
P	Philips	UNIV	University of Oklahoma
PAT	Pathé-Marconi		
PE	Period	V	RCA Victor
PHIL	Philharmonia	VEGA	Véga
POL	Polymusic	VERVE	Verve
PR	Parliament	VG	Vanguard
PRO	Pro Musica	VI	RCA Italiana
Q	Qualiton	VOX	Vox
R	Richmond	W	Westminster
RIT	Rittenhouse	WA	Washington
RIV	Riverside	WL	Westminster (LAB Series)
RONDO	Rondo		
SI	Siena	WORD	Word
SO	Somerset	ZAFIRO	Zafiro
SON	Son-Nova		

357

MALCOLM ARNOLD

ORCHESTRAL

A Grand Grand Overture
★★★—in "Music from The Hoffnung Music Festival Concert," Morley College Sy. Orch., Arnold, A 35500.

Beckus the Dandipratt Overture
★★★—RP, Arnold, E 3422.

English Dances
The Boult release is more vitally performed, but the companion music on the Irving record (additional Arnold and by Britten) is more engaging than the oversentimentalized Elgar under Boult.
—LPO, Boult, L 1335   —PH, Irving, C 7105.

Four Scottish Dances, Op. 59
Everest's sound gives all the details and is balanced expertly. Irving does well with Arnold; his engineers less so.
—LPO, Arnold, EV 6021(S)   —PH, Irving, C 7105.

Symphony No. 2, Op. 40
★★—RP, Arnold, E 3422.

Symphony No. 3, Op. 63
★★—LPO, Arnold, EV 6021(S).

Tam O'Shanter Overture, Op. 51
The best Arnold presentation is Epic's triple offering, which includes Arnold conducting two of his own works.
—RP, Hollingsworth, E 3422   —in "Witches' Brew," NSO, Gibson, V 2225(S).

BAND

River Kwai March
Expertly played in as expertly an unexciting manner. The collection in which this is contained is not precisely titled. On the album cover the recording reads as listed below. On the other side of the jacket the heading is "March Around the World," and on the record label there is a third identification: "Hi-Fi March Around the World." The original release was numbered 9015 (USD 1033); the reorganized Urania firm has given a new number to the stereo reissue.
—in "Marches Around the World," Musikkorps der Bundeswehr, Hamburg (Official West German Army Band), Scholz, U 9015(S).

ORCHESTRA AND BAND

Excerpts from The United Nations
Contained in a titanic assemblage of musical humor, ranging from a
brilliant exposé of the post-Webern school to a Tchaikovsky medley,
the latter played on recorders and other ancient instruments. There
are seven other lampoons.
—in "The Hoffnung Interplanetary Music Festival," Hoffnung Sy.
Orch., Band of the Royal Military School of Music, Arnold, A
35800(S).

SOLO INSTRUMENT WITH ORCHESTRA

CONCERTO

Guitar Concerto, Op. 67
★★★★—Melos Ensemble, Bream (*g*), Arnold, V 2487(S).

CHAMBER MUSIC

Piano Trio in D minor, Op. 54
★★★—Lyric Trio, CD 1234(S).

Three Shanties for Wind Quintet
★★★★—London Wind Quintet, ARGO 326(S).

BALLET

Homage to the Queen
★★—PH, Irving, V 2037.

FILM MUSIC

The Bridge on the River Kwai (original sound track recording)
★—(no Orch. or conductor indicated), CO 1100.

The Inn of the Sixth Happiness (music from the original sound track)
★—LRP, Arnold, F 3011(S).

BÉLA BARTÓK

ORCHESTRAL

Concerto for Orchestra
For lucidity, dramatic authority, and virtuosity on behalf of the
music, Reiner's performance is an unqualified triumph. Both Ormandy's and Dorati's versions are excellent; the former emphasizes the

359

rhythmic content, the other is a full-blooded, quite elemental presentation.

The superb Boston aggregation plays with a neoclassically cool demeanor. The "Concerto for Orchestra" requires more gutsy impulsiveness. On the other hand, the sound has far more realistic presence than any other release. There's too much personal display in Bernstein's ideas and Bartók lands in second place. The disconnective phrases in the piece must be denoted fluidically, not rhapsodically.

—CHI, Reiner, V 1934(S)   —M, Dorati, MY 50033   —PO, Ormandy, CO 4973   —BSO, Leinsdorf, V 2643(S)   —NY, Bernstein, CO 5471(S)   —BR, Fricsay, D 9951   —SR, Ansermet, L 9184(S)   —H, Stokowski, EV 6069(S)   —RP, Kubelik, C 7186(S)   —CG, Haitink, E 3772(S)   —PH, von Karajan, A 35003   —BM, Hollreiser, VOX 10480(S).

Dance Suite

Proper performance of this score demands robustness and expressivity as equal ingredients. The best offering comes from the London Philharmonic, led by the Budapest-born Janos Ferencsik. Oddly enough the same orchestra, under Solti's direction, plays unevenly. The Hungarian musicians give a good reading, though not a brilliant, virtuoso outfit.

Fricsay fully inhabits the Bartók kingdom, despite ragged tempi control. The Dutch orchestra plays expertly, but there are many more interesting points in the suite than are displayed by Haitink's direction.

—LPO, Ferencsik, EV 6022(S)   —PHO, Dorati, MY 50183(S) —RIAS, Fricsay, D 9747   —CG, Haitink, E 3772(S)   —LPO, Solti, L 709   —NSO, Autori, BK 304   —NSO, Autori, BK 302 —LZ, Pflüger, U 7173.

Deux Images, Op. 10

Serly probes the poetry of the first of these "pictures" and underlines the hedonism of the other. In part one of the Artia disk the music sounds as though coming through muslin and conveys much hiss from the tape original. Worse, careless editing left the introductory beats on the cutting room floor. Epic's disk is fine in the initial section. Conversely, it is dull, hazy, and lifeless in part two, while the Artia rendition is bright and ethnically on course.

—NSO, Serly, BK 307   —HRS, Lehel, AT 124   —VSO, Paul, E 3635(S).

Hungarian Peasant Songs
★—HS, Ferencsik, AT 124.

Hungarian Sketches
Both interpretations are excellent though Reiner emphasizes the contrasts a bit more than Dorati.
—CHI, Reiner, V 2374(S)   —M, Dorati, MY 50151   —M, Dorati, MY 50132(S).

Hungarian Sketches ("Bear Dance")
★★—in "Adventures in Music—Grade 3, Vol. 2," N, Mitchell, V 1003(S).

Hungarian Sketches ("Evening in the Village")
★★—in "Adventures in Music—Grade 5, Vol. 2," N, Mitchell, V 1007(S).

Mikrokosmos Suite (arranged by Tibor Serly)
★★★—NSO, Serly, BK 303.

Mikrokosmos Suite ("Bourrée" and "From the Diary of a Fly") (arranged by Tibor Serly)
★★★—PHO, Dorati, MY 50183(S).

Mikrokosmos Suite ("From the Diary of a Fly") (arranged by Tibor Serly)
Music from Leroy Anderson and Cole Porter to Colin McPhee and Gunther Schuller is also represented here.
—in "Music and Plunk, Tinkle, Ting-A-Ling," PHO, Dorati, MY 50338(S).

Mikrokosmos Suite ("Jack-in-the-Box") (arranged by Tibor Serly)
★★—in "Adventures in Music—Grade 2," N, Mitchell, V 1001(S).

The Miraculous Mandarin, Suite from the Ballet, Op. 19
Dorati probes the dramatic detail in his performance, while Irving infuses more poetry by somewhat underplaying the boldness of the writing. Various debits mark the remaining entries.
—CHI, Dorati, MY 50151   —CHI, Dorati, MY 50038   —PH, Irving, C 8576(S)   —SUD, Reinhardt, VOX 12040(S)   —NSO, Serly, BK 301   —RP, Previtali, A 35550.

Suite No. 2 for Orchestra, Op. 4
★—M, Dorati, MY 50098(S).

Two Portraits, Op. 5
With one exception, Fricsay's, the performances are quite good, a shade better in the Capitol release. Of the Bartók disks, I prefer number 303, since the companion piece ("Dance Suite") on number 304 is better represented elsewhere. Millar has a flair for Bartók's work and his version is also recommended.

361

—RP, Kubelik, C 7186(S)   —NSO, Pougnet (*v*), Autori, BK 303
—NSO, Pougnet (*v*), Autori, BK 304   —LSF, Millar, FY 5003(S)
—PHO, Ramor (*v*), Dorati, MY 50183(S)   —HS, Tatray (*v*),
Lehel, AT 124   —RIAS, Fricsay, D 9748.

Two Rumanian Dances, Op. 8a (arranged by Leo Weiner)
★★★—PHO, Dorati, MY 50179(S).

The Wooden Prince, Suite from the Ballet, Op. 13
—SUD, Reinhardt, VOX 12040(S).

CHAMBER ORCHESTRA

Music for Strings, Percussion and Celesta
Reiner is simply without competition. His is a miraculous performance. Second place is a tossup between van Beinum and Kubelik. The
former eschews balanced contrast in the fugue, while the latter is too
benign in the final section.

A special note must be made of Stokowski's reading. It is first the
conductor's ideas and second the composer's music. Stokowski's disregard for the precise tempi Bartók indicated (even to the point of
giving timings for sections *within* the movements) is almost a paraphrase of the original. Yet its egocentric originality is worth consideration. It holds the attention though the interpretation is Bartók
unraveled.
—CHI, Reiner, V 2374(S)   —CG, van Beinum, E 3274   —CHI,
Kubelik, MY 50001   —CHI, Kubelik, MY 50026   —LPO, Solti,
L 9132   —SR, Ansermet, L (6159)   —BPO, von Karajan, A
35949(S)   —in "Percussion!," L. A. Chamber Sy., Byrns, C 8299
—S, Stokowski, C 8507(S)   —BU, Lehel, W 19004(S)   —RIAS,
Fricsay, D 9747   —PM, Reinhardt, VOX 9600   —PPO, Boult,
W 18237   —PPO, Boult, WL 7021.

Rumanian Folk Dances
Winograd does not overargue these miniatures. His steadiness is a
welcome relief from the fidgets that mark so many interpretations.
Dorati plays it straight, yet is a bit too rhythmically anchored.
—MGM Orch., Winograd, MGM 3684   —M, Dorati, MY 50151
—M, Dorati, MY 50132(S).

STRING ORCHESTRA

Divertimento for Strings
The dazzling technique demanded by Bartók's composition can be
taken for granted in all the recorded performances; the drama, rhythmic pungency, and meaning are not always put across. Outstanding
are the Silvestri and Dorati versions containing all the strength neces-

sary and subtle mutations to match. (In making one's choice, the Leo Weiner companion work offered by the latter should not be over-looked; it's a gem.) Once difficult to obtain (because of Unicorn's deletion), the Foss-led version has been reissued by Siena and is worth possessing. The orchestra is small, thus retaining the compact-ness of enlarged chamber music; the presentation warrants the fullest admiration.

De Stoutz's lusty and gusty, clear and precise reading is available on both Austrian and domestic labels; the couplings differ, however. The Moscow ensemble's playing is richly romantic, a lyrical vote that almost eliminates the ictus law and order of Bartók's score. The discipline is magnificent, as is the sound that London has furnished. Similar natural flow-and-let-go is available by the Farberman en-semble. Some may regard this use of string vocalism an ill-placed virtue. It does not exactly express the spirit of the composer and his work.

—PH, Silvestri, A 35643(S)   —PHO, Dorati, E 3513   —in "Con-cert of Modern Music," Z, Foss, SI 100–2   —Z, Foss, UN 1037 —ZU, de Stoutz, VG 1086(S)   —ZU, Goldenberg (*v*), de Stoutz, AM 6204   —MO, Barshai, L 9332(S)   —BCE, Farberman, CAM 803(S)   —RIAS, Fricsay, D 9748   —T, Serly, BK 905   —PPO, Boult, W 18237   —OT, Auriacombe, PAT 279.

Rumanian Folk Dances (arranged by Arthur Willner)
The Swiss group of fourteen, led by their concertmeister, play without muscle. For proper vitality turn to the I Musici rendition.
—in "Music for Strings," I, Michelucci (*v*), P 500–001(S)   —LF, Baumgartner, DG 12016(S).

SOLO INSTRUMENT WITH ORCHESTRA

CONCERTOS

Concerto for Viola and Orchestra
Primrose's command and the noble refinement of his tone is far superior to the other soloist. However, each side is half empty; you get twice as much for your money from Artia.
—NSO, Primrose (*va*), Serly, BK 309   —CZ, Karlovsky (*va*), Ančerl, AT 199(S).

Concerto for Violin and Orchestra (No. 1), *Op. Posth.*
★★★★—PO, Stern (*v*), Ormandy, CO 5677(S).

Concerto for Violin and Orchestra (No. 2)
The Stern-Bernstein disk does justice to the tremendous art of the composer. These musicians do not blemish the work by overconsider-ing its percussive cast, as do Gitlis and Varga. Completely opposite

363

yet remarkably appropriate is the performance by the Hungarian
Garay, an unknown in this country and a new name in the recording
ledger. There isn't an ounce of undue force in his playing and no one
comes close to his lyrical, almost sensuous conclusions. It places the
concerto in a new light and lends a particularly beautiful glow to the
music. (The orchestral support is of a different calibre, being hazy
and undefined. Nonetheless, this should not deter consideration of a
performance in the "sleeper" classification.)
—NY, Stern (*v*), Bernstein, CO 5283(S)   —RU, Garay (*v*),
Kegel, DG 18786(S)   —BPO, Varga (*v*), Fricsay, D 9545
—PRM, Gitlis (*v*), Horenstein, VOX 9020   —PRM, Gitlis (*v*),
Horenstein, DO 211   —M, Menuhin (*v*), Dorati, MY 50140(S)
—PH, Menuhin (*v*), Furtwängler, O 90–070—MSP, D. Oistrakh
(*v*), Rozhdestvensky, PE 338(S)   —MSP, I. Oistrakh (*v*), Rozh-
destvensky, MK 1576.

Concerto No. 1 for Piano and Orchestra
When Serkin plays he is not merely content to reset the notes into
keyboard sound; a fresh spirit that translates the printed score sweeps
through his performances. One need only listen to the Bartók to realize
the presence of a genuine artist.
    Hambro, a brilliant advocate of contemporary music, plays with
sterling command, aided by a good orchestra and an understanding
conductor. Anda is somewhat polite in comparison to Sándor, whose
spontaneity is truly exciting. However, in both cases, and in the
Westminster, the orchestral support is without spark and force.
—COL, Serkin (*p*), Szell, CO 5805(S)   —Z, Hambro (*p*), Mann,
BK 313   —SUD, Sándor (*p*), Reinhardt, VOX 11350(S)   —BR,
Anda (*p*), Fricsay, DG 18708   —HS, Zemplény (*p*), Ferencsik,
W 19003(S).

Concerto No. 2 for Piano and Orchestra
Anda and Wehner are best, understanding the difference existing be-
tween a forceful performance and mere forceful piano playing.
—BR, Anda (*p*), Fricsay, DG 18611(S)   —HS, Wehner (*p*),
Ferencsik, W 19003(S)   —PRM, Sándor (*p*), Gielen, VOX
11490(S)   —VOP, Farnadi (*p*), Scherchen, W 18277.

Concerto No. 3 for Piano and Orchestra
Haas and Anda recognize the almost El Greco order of the concerto;
both describe (with the aid of the same conductor) the nobility and
crystalline quality of Bartók's music. Despite uneven weighting between keyboard instrument and orchestra, Katchen's performance
rates a plus sign.
—RIAS, Haas (*p*), Fricsay, D 9774   —BR, Anda (*p*), Fricsay,
DG 18611(S)   —SR, Katchen (*p*), Ansermet, L 9083   —VOP,

Farnadi (*p*), Scherchen, W 18277   —SL, Pennario (*p*), Golsch-
mann, C 8253   —PO, Sándor (*p*), Ormandy, CO 4239   —PRM,
Sándor (*p*), Gielen, VOX 11490(S)   —CZ, Bernathova (*p*),
Ančerl, AT 199(S).

SOLO PIANO WITH ORCHESTRA

Rhapsody for Piano and Orchestra, Op. 1
Sándor's playing is well-contoured and defines a sustained utterance
that benefits the music. Though Anda performs with decided spirit and
proper style, the supporting orchestra is much too docile.
—SUD, Sándor (*p*), Reinhardt, VOX 11350(S)   —BR, Anda
(*p*), Fricsay, DG 18708(S).

SOLO VIOLIN WITH ORCHESTRA

Rhapsody No. 1 for Violin and Orchestra
All the soloists do brilliantly by Bartók, though Totenberg's more
leisurely pace is not the most propitious. One prefers the opulent
sound of the New Yorkers and the finesse of the smaller California
organization.
—NY, Stern (*v*), Bernstein, CO 5773(S)   —LSF, Rubin (*v*), Millar, FY 5003(S)   —NSO, Vardi (*v*), Autori, BK 307   —VOP,
Totenberg (*v*), Golschmann, VG 1083(S).

Rhapsody No. 2 for Violin and Orchestra
Richly colored performances in all instances. As is the case with the
first rhapsody (*see above*) the orchestras led by Bernstein and Millar
offer the best assistance.
—NY, Stern (*v*), Bernstein, CO 5773(S)   —LSF, Rubin (*v*),
Millar, FY 5003(S)   —NSO, Vardi (*v*), Serly, BK 307.

Two Portraits, Op. 5
See Orchestral *above*.

INSTRUMENTAL

CELLO

Rhapsody No. 1 for Cello and Piano
Marvelous cello playing with superb tonal address. The first listing
offers two concertos (by Boccherini and Mozart), three Kodály
compositions, and a short Leo Weiner item. Designated a "Thrift
Edition," it's a bargain buy.
—in " 'Round the World with Janos Starker," Starker (*c*), Herz (*p*),
PE 1093   —Starker (*c*), Herz (*p*), PE 602   —Starker (*c*), Herz
(*p*), PE 715.

CELLO QUARTET

Fifteen Hungarian Peasant Songs (Nos. 7–15) (arranged by Laszlo Varga)
★—New York Philharmonic Cello Quartet, D 9946.

HARMONICA

Rumanian Folk Dances
★★★—in "Profile," Sebastian (*ha*), Clugston (*p*), D 10025(S).

HARP

Evening in the Country from "Hungarian Sketches"
For Children (arranged by Aristid Von Wurtzler)
★—Aristid Von Wurtzler, ASCO 112.

HORN

For Children (Nos. 17 and 33) (arranged by Joseph Eger)
★★★★—in "Around the Horn," Eger (*hn*), Y. Menuhin (*p*), V 2146.

ORGAN

En Bateau
★★★—in "Organ Music by Modern Composers, Vol. 1," Ellsasser, MGM 3064.

PIANO

Allegro Barbaro
Bartók's small gem does not glow in any of the recorded editions. Most are fairly "allegro," none are "barbaro." Bartók's own interpretation cannot be second-guessed; the sound of his recording is heavy-going for today's ears, however.
—in "The Piano Music of Béla Bartók, Vol. 4," Foldes, D 9804
—in "Bartók Piano Music (Complete), Vol. 2," Sándor, VOX 426(S)   —in "Béla Bartók at the Piano," Bartók, BK 903   —Farnadi, W 18217   —in "Brailowsky Encores," Brailowsky, V 2276(S).

Fifteen Hungarian Peasant Songs
Miss De Toth, a newcomer to the recording field, gives a performance which is hard to criticize. Her phrasing and sensitive range of dynamics are models of this score. Sándor's poetic reading is exceedingly expressive and Foldes' playing is equally eloquent.
—De Toth, DV 204   —in "Bartók Piano Music (Complete), Vol. 2," Sándor, VOX 426(S)   —in "The Piano Music of Béla Bartók, Vol. 3," Foldes, D 9803   —Kraus, ED 3008   —Marik, DR 1331.

366

Fifteen Hungarian Peasant Songs (Excerpts)
Artistic performances of numbers 7–12, 14 and 15.
—in "Béla Bartók at the Piano," Bartók, BK 903.

For Children, Volume 1 (Based on Hungarian Folk Tunes)
Sándor and Pressler consider refinement first. Kozma's rendition
offers more *rapprochement* to Bartók's meaning by giving dynamism
equal billing. Farnadi is very attentive to detail and her conception is
worthy, but Anda insists on dramaticism when the music's temper is
otherwise.
—Kozma, BK 919 —in "Bartók Piano Music (Complete), Vol. 2,"
Sándor, VOX 426(S) —Pressler, MGM 3009 —Farnadi, W
18743 (*both Volumes 1 and 2:* 2226) —Anda, A 35126.

For Children, Volume 2 (Based on Slovakian Folk Tunes)
—Kozma, BK 920 —in "Bartók Piano Music (Complete), Vol.
2," Sándor, VOX 426(S) —Pressler, MGM 3047 —Farnadi,
W 18744 (*both Volumes 1 and 2:* 2226) —Anda, A 35246.

For Children (Excerpts)
Solchany offers excellent insight with his interpretation of fourteen of
the forty pieces in the first volume. Kabos does as well with eight
items also from the initial part. Foldes presents seventeen excerpts
from volume one and eleven from volume two. His tendency to percussiveness alters Bartók's colorations and is to be deplored.

Lili Kraus plays twenty-one selections, nine of which are heard in
both the original and revised versions, making very interesting data
for the perceptive listener. It is unfortunate that Educo's engineers
have given her tinny sound and very little sonority depth. The same
applies to Miss Rev's recording of two samplings from the collection.
Oddly, this negative situation does not exist elsewhere on the disk.
—Solchany, A 45015 —Kabos, BK 917 —in "The Piano Music
of Béla Bartók, Vol. 1," Foldes, D 9801 —in "The Piano Music of
Béla Bartók, Vol. 2," Foldes, D 9802 —Kraus, ED 3008 —in
"Musique pour les Enfants de Bach à Bartók," Rev, PAT 269.

Four Dirges ("Nénies"), *Op. 9a*
★★—in "Bartók Piano Music (Complete), Vol. 3," Sándor, VOX
427(S).

Fourteen Bagatelles, Op. 6
There are subtleties in Sándor's pianism that are not found in Kozma's
performances. Still, the latter's fluidic conception is extremely worthy.
—in "Bartók Piano Music (Complete), Vol. 3," Sándor, VOX
427(S) —Kozma, BK 918.

Fourteen Bagatelles, Op. 6 (No. 2)
★★★★—in "Béla Bartók at the Piano," Bartók, BK 903.

Improvisations, Op. 20
Hambro and Sándor set their playing to match the fantasy of the "Improvisations"; Foldes adopts a more neutral demeanor.
—Hambro, BK 902   —in "Bartók Piano Music (Complete), Vol. 3," Sándor, VOX 427(S)   —in "The Piano Music of Béla Bartók, Vol. 2," Foldes, D 9802.

Improvisations, Op. 20 (Nos. 3, 4, 5, and 6)
★★—in "The History of Music in Sound, Vol. X," Foldes, V 6092.

Mikrokosmos
Sándor's surveyal of the complete opus (available on two different labels) is most revealing. He gives each piece—even the smallest and simplest—particular meaning. Farnadi also has sensitive response though she is less plastic in her playing.
—in "Bartók Piano Music (Complete), Vol. 1," Sándor, VOX 425(S)   —Sándor, CO 229   —Farnadi (*Books 1 and 2*), W 18182   —Farnadi (*Books 3 and 4*), W 18183   —Farnadi (*Books 5 and 6*), W 18184.

Mikrokosmos (Excerpts)
It is startling, at first, to compare Bartók's playing of the thirty-five excerpts he recorded for Columbia with other performances. In many cases he is decidedly reticent and aloof, but this taciturnity strengthens his inventions. The sound is dated, but the opportunity of hearing the composer interpret his own music is unique and must not be over-looked. This release should be supplemented by the special Bartók on Bartók album which includes "Staccato" from the fifth book and "Ostinato" from the last part.

Solchany offers artistically flexible performances of nine portions from the last two volumes. His recording unfortunately does not indicate the titles—a serious omission in music as delineative as "Mikrokosmos." Foldes covers much more ground, with six pieces from book four, and eighteen drawn from books five and six, but quality does not match quantity. Volume six is given complete by Irén Marik. She displays intelligence but lacks the verve and spirit demanded by Bartók's music. Katchen's sampling (eight selections) is drawn from the same portion. It is far below his usual high inter-pretative standards—chasteness is unbecoming for these expressive conceptions.
—Bartók, CO 4419   —in "Béla Bartók at the Piano," Bartók, BK 903   —Solchany, A 45015   —in "The Piano Music of Béla Bartók, Vol. 1," Foldes, D 9801   —Marik, DR 1331   —Katchen, L 759.

Nine Little Pieces
In the polyphonic portions Foldes plays with a crispness that is especially effective. Otherwise no one will be either enthused or irritated by any of the soloists.
—in "The Piano Music of Béla Bartók, Vol. 4," Foldes, D 9804
—in "Bartók Piano Music (Complete), Vol. 3," Sándor, VOX 427(S)   —Farnadi, W 18217.

Nine Little Pieces (Nos. 6 and 8)
★★★★—in "Béla Bartók at the Piano," Bartók, BK 903.

Out of Doors
Hambro's interpretative camera is the sharpest of all three. However, see below for the best performance of the final pair of movements.
—Hambro, BK 902   —in "Bartók Piano Music (Complete), Vol. 2," Sándor, VOX 426(S)   —in "The Piano Music of Béla Bartók, Vol. 4," Foldes, D 9804.

Out of Doors (Nos. 4 and 5)
A truly amazing control of color and the deepest scrutiny mark Cianni's playing. The album in which it is contained presents the winners of the International Piano Competition, held in Budapest, in 1961.
—in "Liszt-Bartók International Piano Festival," Cianni, DG 19292(S).

Petite Suite
★★—in "Bartók Piano Music (Complete), Vol. 2," Sándor, VOX 426(S).

Petite Suite ("Bagpipe")
★★★★—in "Béla Bartók at the Piano," Bartók, BK 903.

Rhapsody, Op. 1
★★★★—Hambro, BK 313.

Rumanian Christmas Carols ("Colindes")
All excellent; the best sound is furnished by the Bartók firm. (The cover of the Vox release indicates these pieces incorrectly as "chorales.")
—Kozma, BK 918   —in "Bartók Piano Music (Complete), Vol. 2," Sándor, VOX 426(S)   —in "The Piano Music of Béla Bartók, Vol. 3," Foldes, D 9803.

Rumanian Folk Dances
The best performance is Ann Schein's, who combines strength and delicacy in a distinguished presentation. Solchany and Foldes are quite perceptive.

369

—in "A Piano Invitation to the Dance," Schein, K 9042(S)   —Solchany, A 4505   —in "The Piano Music of Béla Bartók, Vol. 2," Foldes, D 9802   —in "Bartók Piano Music (Complete), Vol. 2," Sándor, VOX 426(S)   —Farnadi, W 18217   —Kozma, BK 918 —in "A 25th Anniversary Program," Slenczynska, D 10000(S).

Second Fantasy
Sándor's three-album set of the "complete" piano music of Bartók, issued by Vox, fails to include this piece.
—in "The Piano Music of Béla Bartók, Vol. 2," Foldes, D 9802.

Seven Sketches ("Esquisses"), *Op. 9*
The soloists do the best that can be expected with these substandard Bartók pieces.
—in "Bartók Piano Music (Complete), Vol. 3," Sándor, VOX 427(S)   —in "The Piano Music of Béla Bartók, Vol. 2," Foldes, D 9802.

Sonata
Of all the performances, Nádas gives the most idiomatic. Pennario plays with a great deal of splash and almost overpowers the already powerful score. Foldes achieves a better balance. Neither Sándor nor Boehm gets below the surface of the notes.
—Nádas, PE 736   —in "The Piano Music of Béla Bartók, Vol. 3," Foldes, D 9803   —Pennario, C 8376   —in "Bartók Piano Music (Complete), Vol. 2," Sándor, VOX 426(S)   —Boehm, F 4007(S).

Sonatina
Foldes, Sándor, and Anda do well with this short work. Kabos' tempo in part one is much too slow and there is only a minimum of flexibility in Kraus's performance. Incidentally, the record label for the latter calls this a "Sonata in D major"!
—in "The Piano Music of Béla Bartók, Vol. 1," Foldes, D 9801 —in "Bartók Piano Music (Complete), Vol. 3," Sándor, VOX 427(S)   —Anda, A 35126   —Kabos, BK 917   —Kraus, ED 3008.

Suite, Op. 14
Solchany's performance is beautifully conceived, representing the fullest comprehension of the composer's dramatic ideas. It is worth comparing with Bartók's own rendition—a "must" album for the collector. All the others are worthy, though not as clear or as illuminating.
—Solchany, A 45015   —in "Béla Bartók at the Piano," Bartók, BK 903   —in "Bartók Piano Music (Complete), Vol. 3," Sándor, VOX 427(S)   —Farnadi, W 18217   —in "The Piano Music of Béla Bartók, Vol. 3," Foldes, D 9803   —Marik, DR 1331.

Ten Easy Pieces
Beautiful playing, intelligently artistic, describes Sándor's version.
Foldes is just a bit less colorful.
—in "Bartók Piano Music (Complete), Vol. 3," Sándor, VOX
427(S)   —in "The Piano Music of Béla Bartók, Vol. 4," Foldes,
D 9804.

Ten Easy Pieces (Excerpts)
Bartók plays the two most popular pieces in the group; the "Evening
in Transylvania" (as does Miss Rev in her survey), and the "Bear
Dance." The album is a collector's item, including some verbal program notes by the composer.
—in "Béla Bartók at the Piano," Bartók, BK 903   —in "Musique
pour les Enfants de Bach à Bartók," Rev, PAT 269.

Three Burlesques, Op. 8c
Solid, musicianly performances from all three soloists. Some raspy
sound on the Decca recording almost fits in with the mood of the
music.
—in "Bartók Piano Music (Complete), Vol. 3," Sándor, VOX
427(S)   —in "The Piano Music of Béla Bartók, Vol. 4," Foldes,
D 9804   —Farnadi, W 18217.

Three Burlesques, Op. 8c (No. 2)
★★★★—in "Béla Bartók at the Piano," Bartók, BK 903.

Three Etudes, Op. 18
Three Hungarian Folk Songs
Three Hungarian Folk Tunes
★★★—in "Bartók Piano Music (Complete), Vol. 3," Sándor, VOX
427(S).

Three Rondos on Folk Tunes
The Sándor reading is tasteful, with all details brought to light. Foldes
also makes everything eminently clear. Kabos overemphasizes the
contrasts and thereby tears the continuity.
—in "Bartók Piano Music (Complete), Vol. 2," Sándor, VOX
426(S)   —in "The Piano Music of Béla Bartók, Vol. 3," Foldes, D
9803   —Kabos, BK 917.

Three Rondos on Folk Tunes (No. 1)
★★★★—in "Béla Bartók at the Piano," Bartók, BK 903.

Two Elegies, Op. 8b
This kind of music is a pianist's meat and potatoes. Sándor and Foldes
gobble it up.
—in "Bartók Piano Music (Complete), Vol. 3," Sándor, VOX

427(S)   —in "The Piano Music of Béla Bartók, Vol. 2," Foldes, D 9802.

Two Rumanian Dances, Op. 8a
Sándor plays this dazzling music to the hilt. Farnadi performs with dash but without Sándor's strength.
—in "Bartók Piano Music (Complete), Vol. 3," Sándor, VOX 427(S)   —Farnadi, W 18217.

Two Rumanian Dances, Op. 8a (No. 1)
★★★★—in "Béla Bartók at the Piano," Bartók, BK 903.

Two Pianos

Sonata for Two Pianos and Percussion
Some of the inner voices are blurred in the Cambridge issue, but otherwise this is a clean, very alive, and stylish conception. In no other recording are the percussion instruments played so accurately and sensitively. As the only recording available in stereo, the Cambridge release enjoys a further distinction.

Decca's and Vox's (VBX-426) releases are for the most part clear and worthy representations, though both are somewhat stiff and academic in the initial movement. Westminster's entry is good, only a little too brilliant in places calling for softer dynamics. The Vox PL-9600 album is a mishmash of blurred sonorities.
—Vosgerchian (*p*), Votapek (*p*), Firth (*per*), Press (*per*), Farberman, CAM 803(S)   —Seeman (*p*), Picht-Axenfeld (*p*), Peinkofer (*per*), Porth (*per*), D 9963   —Sándor (*p*), Reinhardt (*p*), Schad (*per*), Sohm (*per*), VOX 426(S)   —Parry (*p*), Loveridge (*p*), Webster (*per*), Lees (*per*), Austin, W 18425   —Zelka (*p*), Brendel (*p*), Schuster (*per*), Berger (*per*), Minarich (*per*), Zimmermann (*per*), VOX 9600.

Violin

For Children (Excerpts) (arranged by Ede Zathureczky)
★—Zathureczky (*v*), Pressler (*p*), VOX 1.

Rhapsody No. 2 for Violin and Piano
★★★★—in "Modern Masterpieces for the Violin," Shapiro (*v*), Berkowitz (*p*), VG 1023.

Rumanian Folk Dances (arranged by Zoltán Székely)
Superb playing by the first three soloists; Mr. Kooper's harmonics are not all in focus. Oistrakh's program contains some unusual pieces (Kodály's "Kallo Dances" and Vladigerov's "Songs" from the "Bulgarian Suite") and this makes acquisition of the Parliament disk as

worthwhile as Boston's Bartók-Debussy-Ravel combination. Miss Shapiro's modern repertoire includes the only recorded representation of Ernest Bloch's complete "Baal Shem" and cannot be disregarded. Kooper's collection of ten pieces, with a few exceptions, consists of encore bonbons.
—Grumiaux (*v*), Ulanowsky (*p*), B 203   —in "David Oistrakh Violin Recital," Oistrakh (*v*), Yampolsky (*p*), PR 118   —in "Modern Masterpieces for the Violin," Shapiro (*v*), Berkowitz (*p*), VG 1023   —in "Intrada," Kooper (*v*), Ulanowsky (*p*), F 4006(S).

Sonata for Solo Violin
Mann's performance is a perfect re-creation of Bartók's solo saga, glowing, polished, and perfectly pliant. Ricci displays an index of punctilious, punctuated, amazing virtuosity. No note is left unturned or untuned—as though an X ray has been turned on the music. Silverstein's interpretation is exciting and much different from Mann's and Ricci's. It is just as true; merely of different tone in its emphasis on lyrical qualities.
—Mann, BK 916   —in "Ruggiero Ricci Solo Recital," Ricci, L 9261(S)   —Silverstein, CO 5745(S)   —in "The Violin, Vol. 4," Bress, FW 3354   —Gertler, A 35091   —Menuhin, O 80544 —Gitlis, VOX 9020   —Gitlis, DO 211.

CHAMBER MUSIC

Forty-Four Duos for Two Violins
A re-release of Period's two-disk album (SPLP-506). The new edition follows Bartók's sequence exactly, whereas the older one mixed up the order of the pieces for no apparent reason. The performers exhibit tonal and stylistic finesse.
—Ajtay, Kuttner, BK 907.

Sonata No. 1 for Violin and Piano
Mann and Hambro give a definitive performance, which means an exciting experience. The Menuhins confuse the stylistic issue and often try to soften the rough edges of the sonata.
—Mann (*v*), Hambro (*p*), BK 922   —Y. Menuhin (*v*), H. Menuhin (*p*), O 80544.

Sonata No. 2 for Violin and Piano
Druian and Simms struggle with the essential meaning of the music—Bartók's fantasy escapes them. It is fully understood and realized in the other release.
—Schneiderhan (*v*), Seemann (*p*), D 9980   —Druian (*v*), Simms (*p*), MY 50089.

Contrasts for Violin, Clarinet and Piano
The Decca issue, with its oddly disposed sound, offers no competition whatsoever to the vital version released by the Bartók firm. Westminster's entry is also good, though not quite as dynamic.
—Mann (*v*), Drucker (*cl*), Hambro (*p*), BK 916   —Grinke (*v*), Brymer (*cl*), Parry (*p*), W 18425   —Ritter (*v*), Kell (*cl*), Rosen (*p*), D 9740.

String Quartets
The six quartets have been issued as a package by three companies, Deutsche Grammophon, Vox, and Concert-Disc. In the latter instance, the three disks comprising the package can also be secured separately. Columbia, Angel, and Westminster released them only as separate pieces.

The Juilliard Quartet's performances are old standbys and their Bartók conceptions are truly aged in the wood. No other group can really challenge their status as *the* spokesmen for the Bartók string quartets. The Hungarian String Quartet comes closest, especially in terms of lyric loveliness (aided by truly rich engineering) and atmospheric intensity in the slow movements. However, rhythmic resoluteness and frictional depiction are much sharper in the Juilliard's conception. While the Vegh foursome is an excellent team, one expects greater passion and excitement than they express, as well as a more intense diagnosis of Bartók's fabulous scores.

Security and verve mark the Fine Arts' performances. Unfortunately, the galvanism they produce is not sufficiently strong, nor do they probe the profound meanings of the music. Theirs is an honest re-creation if not a learned one; which cannot be said about either the Ramor or Parrenin presentations. Both these teams refuse to follow Bartók's minute score directions. Crescendi, decrescendi, and sudden dynamic thrusts are glossed over and the electrical juice is short circuited.
—Juilliard Q (*see:* String Quartets Nos. 1, 2, 3, 4, 5, 6)   —Hungarian Sq, DG 18650/2(S)   —Vegh Q (*see:* String Quartets Nos. 1, 2, 3, 4, 5, 6)   —Fine Arts Q, CD 501(S)   —Ramor Q, VOX 19(S)   —Parrenin Q (*see:* String Quartets Nos. 1, 2, 3, 4, 5, 6).

String Quartet No. 1, Op. 7
It will be noted that precise sequence is followed in all of the separate recordings of the Bartók quartets. Regardless of the label involved, the pairing is always the same. In only one instance was a Bartók string quartet companioned by music of another composer (*see:* String Quartet No. 3).
—Juilliard Q, CO 4278   —Vegh Q, A 35240   —Fine Arts Q, CD 1207(S)   —Parrenin Q, W 18531.

String Quartet No. 2, Op. 17
★★★★—Juilliard Q, CO 4278   —Vegh Q, A 35240   —Fine Arts Q, CD 1207(S)   —Parrenin Q, W 18531.

String Quartet No. 3
Worth tracking down is a long-deleted performance by the defunct New Music Quartet. Issued by the Bartók firm (number 901) it also includes five "Mikrokosmos" transcriptions and Stravinsky's "Three Pieces." The playing of the Bartók is a triumph of understanding.
—Juilliard Q, CO 4279   —Vegh Q, A 35241   —Fine Arts Q, CD 1208(S)   —Parrenin Q, W 18532.

String Quartet No. 4
Though elsewhere the sound of the Westminster recordings of the Bartók quartets is good, the sonic coagulation in this case is difficult to understand. The lack of clarity makes the scamper and mystery of the muted movement a pigmental blur and destroys the differences of pizzicato used in movement four.
—Juilliard Q, CO 4279   —Vegh Q, A 35241   —Fine Arts Q, CD 1208(S)   —Parrenin Q, W 18532.

String Quartet No. 5
★★★★—Juilliard Q, CO 4280   —Vegh Q, A 35242   —Fine Arts Q, CD 1209(S)   —Parrenin Q, W 18533.

String Quartet No. 6
★★★★—Juilliard Q, CO 4280   —Vegh Q, A 35242   —Fine Arts Q, CD 1209(S)   —Parrenin Q, W 18533.

VOCAL

Eight Hungarian Folk Songs
A recording that has superior interpretation, and marvelous acoustics. Definitely better than the portion available on Westminster (*see below*) because these songs are more affecting when conveyed by a male voice.
—in "Folk Songs of Hungary, Vol. 1," Chabay (*t*), Kozma (*p*), BK 904.

Eight Hungarian Folk Songs (Excerpts)
Westminster's lack of specific identification is terribly annoying. The record consists of ten bands; the first nine called "Hungarian Folk Songs," the tenth titled "Twenty Hungarian Folksongs—Nos. 16–20." The latter are performed without interruption, minus titles and texts, though Hungarian and English words are supplied for the other songs.
    Bands 1–5 are actually the first five of the "Eight Hungarian Folk

Songs" (recorded in their entirety on Bartók 904). Bands 6–9 actually belong to the same composition as the group of five songs massed on band 10—the "Twenty Hungarian Folk Songs."
—László (*s*), Holetschek (*p*), W 18665.

Five Songs, Op. 15
★★★—László (*s*), Hambro (*p*), BK 927.

Five Songs, Op. 16
★★★—László (*s*), Holetschek (*p*), W 18665.

Twenty Hungarian Folk Songs (Excerpts)
The Bartók firm includes four and nine songs, respectively, in the two albums listed. Westminster presents nine, some of which duplicate the Chabay-Kozma presentation. (In order to make sense of Westminster's confused labeling, refer to the note covering "Eight Hungarian Folk Songs [Excerpts].")
—in "Folk Songs of Hungary, Vol. 1," Chabay (*t*), Kozma (*p*), BK 904   —in "Folk Songs of Hungary, Vol. 2," Chabay (*t*), Kozma (*p*), BK 914   —László (*s*), Holetschek (*p*), W 18665.

Twenty Hungarian Folk Songs (in collaboration with Zoltán Kodály) (Excerpts) (*see also:* Kodály, page 440)
Each album presents a pair of songs of joint authorship, in addition to individual contributions: a dozen by Bartók and a pair by Kodály in the first volume; nine by the former and ten by the latter in the second collection.
—in "Folk Songs of Hungary, Vol. 1," Chabay (*t*), Kozma (*p*), BK 904   —in "Folk Songs of Hungary, Vol. 2," Chabay (*t*), Kozma (*p*), BK 914.

Village Scenes ("Dorfszenen")
Disconcerting applause greets the listener but the actual performance is good.
—in "Irmgard Seefried in Person," Seefried (*s*), Werba (*p*), D 9809.

CHORAL

Five Slovak Folk Songs
Part of an interesting grab bag that includes songs from Japan, Korea, China, the Philippines, Thailand, India, etc. The college group shows good style and ensemble.
—"Songs of the World," Harvard Glee Club, Forbes, CN 122.

Four Slovak Folk Songs
Neither recording can be recommended. The Concert Choir's singing is not clear and their diction is blurred. Everything is wrong with the other performance—ill-chosen tempi, poor balances, and third-grade ideas of style.
—The Concert Choir, Hillis, BK 312 —Texas Tech Choir, Apple (*p*), Kenney, AU 6224.

Twenty-Seven Choruses (Excerpts)
The Concert Choir's presentation of eight choruses is superb. (The recording's label incorrectly gives the total as nine. In Schwann, the listing "Twelve A Cappella Choruses" is also misleading. This is actually a combination of the eight excerpts plus the "Four Slovak folk Songs" [*see above*].)

On the other hand, the "Six Chants Populaires Hongrois" in the Pathé-Marconi album would seem to be a different work. Though descriptively fitting, this is a fictional title covering a half-dozen extracts from the total of twenty-seven. The subtitles create further complications. One example will suffice: "Les Adieux" on Pathé is "Only Tell Me" on Bartók, and so on. For purposes of comparison (painfully difficult because of the lack of separate bands in the Bartók release), the six sung on the French recording are, respectively, numbers 6, 1, 4, 3, 7, and 2 of the set of eight performed by the American group. Jouineau's youngsters sing with sweet expertise, but the tempo of a number of the pieces is dragged and liberties are taken with the score. Nevertheless, owning both disks is enlightening, affording six different aspects of this delightful work—two types of voices, versions in English and French, and *a cappella* singing compared to orchestrally accompanied voices.

Monitor's fascinating release includes three of these Bartók choruses. The first and second are not represented elsewhere; the third ("Ne Hagyi Itt!") is a duplicate of the seventh on the Bartók label (the fifth on Pathé-Marconi). A word of caution, however! The former indicates the translation of this piece as "Only Tell Me," whereas Monitor identifies it as "Do Not Leave Me!" The problem is that practically the same title ("Don't Leave Me") is used for the first of the excerpts on the Bartók release. This is an entirely different portion and should not be confused with the third of the Monitor excerpts. The Hungarian ensemble displays superlative vocalism and musicianship throughout. The entire recording deserves the highest rating possible.
—The Concert Choir, Hillis, BK 312 —LOF, Maîtrise d'Enfants, Jouineau, PAT 247 —in "Madrigals & Motets," Budapest Madrigal Ensemble, Szekeres, MON 2054(S).

CHORAL WITH ORCHESTRA

Three Village Scenes (On Slovakian Folk Songs)
★★★—BU, BUC, Lehel, W 19004.

Twenty-Seven Choruses (Excerpts)
See Choral *above.*

CANTATA

Cantata Profana
Susskind's release is far and away the best. He directs a beautifully clear performance, one that has proper vigor and intensity as well.
—NSO, NSC, Lewis (*t*), Rothmuller (*bar*), Susskind, BK 312
—USSR, USSRC, Rozhoktvensky, PE 757(S)   —VSO, VCO, Dickie (*t*), Hurshell (*bar*), Hollreiser, VOX 10480.

BALLET

The Wooden Prince, Op. 13
★★—NSO, Susskind, BK 308.

OPERA

Bluebeard's Castle, Op. 11
"Bluebeard" is available in three languages (Hungarian, German, and English). It is also offered with editorial revisions plus cuts (the Deutsche Grammophon release). Only the Bartók recording includes the spoken preamble of some twenty lines.

No one performance is free of criticism. Dorati conveys more tensility than Ormandy. While the polish and technical élan of the Philadelphia Orchestra is far ahead of what the Londoners can muster, Dorati's darker, heavier treatment comes closer to the soul of the work. The vocalists of these productions cancel out each other. Szekely is much more imposing than Hines, who is almost too smooth and urbane. On the other hand, Elias indicates a youthfulness blended with sensuosity that is better than Szönyi, who spoils her interpretation by what can only be described as squawking. These are the best two realizations and purists notwithstanding, there is nothing wrong with the English translation Ormandy uses. (At least Columbia provides a full text, which none of the others do, except the Bartók firm.)
—LSO, Szönyi (*s*), Szekely (*b*), Dorati, MY 50311(S)   —PO, Elias (*ms*), Hines (*b*), Ormandy, CO 5825(S)   —NSO, Lorsy (*n*), Hellwig (*s*), Koreh (*b*), Susskind, BK 310–311   —BR, Töpper (*a*), Fischer-Dieskau (*bar*), Fricsay, DG 18565(S)   —VSO, Steingruber (*s*), Wiener (*bar*), Haefner, VOX 100.

ALBAN BERG

ORCHESTRAL

Interlude before the Final Scene from "Wozzeck," Op. 7
Schippers includes an orchestral section from Berg's stage master-piece with operatic "hit" excerpts from Bizet, Verdi, Puccini, Mascagni, and Humperdinck. Unfortunately, he does not always follow Berg's dynamic markings. As a result, some of the secondary voices are further lessened and merge into a mere color background.
—in "Orchestral Music from the Opera," COL, Schippers, CO 5564(S).

Lulu Suite
Dorati follows the printed score exactly, except for a single insertion from the opera—Lulu's blood-curdling shriek as she is attacked by her murderer. Craft presents an excerpted edition of Berg's concert extracts, and edits the score. The choice is apparent: a complete essay versus a shortened one. Further, while both conductors are truly expert, Dorati's sense of voice balance and inner coloring is clearer and more sensitive.
—LSO, Pilarczyk (*s*), Dorati, MY 50278   —in "Music of Alban Berg," COL, Craft, CO 271(S).

Three Orchestral Pieces, Op. 6
Rosbaud's recording is nothing less than sensational. This conductor, the leader among all in the presentation of the most torturous complicated scores, does not overlook or misjudge the minutest intricacy.
   Craft does quite well, defining the Bergian climate with proper temperature. His viewpoint is more robust, less intense, and a bit more extrovert than Rosbaud's. But there are very few who can match this eminent Austrian musician in the realization of music by Schoenberg, Webern, and Berg.
—SUDW, Rosbaud, W 18807   —COL, Craft, CO 5616(S).

STRING ORCHESTRA

Three Movements from the "Lyric Suite"
★★—in "Music of Alban Berg," COL, Craft, CO 271(S).

BAND

March from "Wozzeck," Op. 7
Contained in a splendid package idea: a group of marches which give examples from the classic, romantic, and contemporary periods, plus the café world of Old Vienna.

379

—in "Austrian Classical Marches," Boston Concert Band, Simon, B 411 (S).

SOLO INSTRUMENT WITH ORCHESTRA

Concertos

Chamber Concerto for Piano and Violin with Thirteen Wind Instruments

Do not be confused by the two top listings enumerating the same soloists and conductor. For some unknown reason, when Lyrichord reissued the concerto, after Vox had withdrawn it, an alias was given the Pro Musica group. If this is an attempt to claim a new performance there's madness without method in such cataloguing subversion. No indication that the Lyrichord version was formerly on Vox is given. Further, the deleted Vox recording can still be secured here and there, so who's kidding who? The playing is expert and tasteful, especially Gitlis's soaring tone. Lyrichord or Vox, a top-drawer item in the contemporary music mart.

In terms of specific instrumental playing the Craft-led entry is better; the musicians are magical virtuosi from the soloists to the double bassoonist. Strangely, the balances are not always what the score shows they should be, and leading voices (Berg's score is meticulous in its marking of primary and subordinate parts) are sometimes submerged. The picture is clearer in the Lyrichord and Vox releases.

—Viennese Wind Ensemble, Gitlis (*v*), Zelka (*p*), Byrns, LYR 94—Pro Musica Wind Instrument Group, Vienna, Gitlis (*v*), Zelka (*p*), Byrns, VOX 8660 —in "Music of Alban Berg," COL, Baker (*v*), Kaufman (*p*), Craft, CO 271 (S).

Violin Concerto

Of all the top-drawer virtuosi only Isaac Stern has seen fit to record this work of musical genius. In doing so he has produced, with Leonard Bernstein, a memorable reading. Both soloist and conductor join in an individual conception without perjuring the music or being presumptive.

Each of the other three executions has something to offer but the first is the finest. However, because Krasner premièred the concerto his rendition has documentary value.

—NY, Stern (*v*), Bernstein, CO 5773 (S) —CLE, Krasner (*v*), Rodzinski, CO 4857 —PH, Gertler (*v*), Kletzki, A 35091 —PRM, Gitlis (*v*), Strickland, VOX 10760 —PRM, Gitlis (*v*), Strickland, VOX 8660.

380

INSTRUMENTAL

PIANO

Piano Sonata, Op. 1
Gould performs with the greatest clarity possible. He presents the perfect illustration of postromantic piano playing syle.
And plaudits are also due Demus. His concept of Berg is as clear and clean as one can demand.
—Gould, CO 5336 —in "Two Centuries of Austrian Piano Music," Demus, MG 23(S).

CHAMBER MUSIC

Lyric Suite for String Quartet
The exactness of tone color differentiation (so important to the "Lyric Suite") makes the Juilliard recording of five-star rating.
While the Ramor group has technical ability it has far from probed the guts of this music.
—Juilliard Sq, V 2531(S) —Ramor Q, VOX 530(S).

String Quartet, Op. 3
To perform this work requires a group who must not only honor the music but believe in every one of its sounds. All the teams represented hold the faith seriously and all toss off Berg's finger-breaking passages with ease.
The Kohon and Juilliard representations are best in exploiting tone color; the luminosity of the former especially telling.
—Kohon Q, VOX 730(S) —Juilliard Sq, CO 4737 —New Music Q, BK 906.

VOCAL

An Leukon
★—in "The History of Music in Sound, Vol. X," Hooke (*s*), Moore (*p*), V 6092.

Four Songs, Op. 2
★—Rowe (*s*), Tupas (*p*), LYR 94.

Four Songs, Op. 2 (Excerpts)
The middle pair of the set. The singing is only fair.
—in "The History of Music, Vol. X," Hooke (*s*), Moore (*p*), V 6092.

Seven Early Songs
Neither performance is exemplary lieder singing. (To obtain this, one must secure the setting with orchestra; *see below*.)
—Steber (*s*), Biltcliffe (*p*), ST 417(S)　　—Rowe (*s*), Tupas (*p*), LYR 94.

VOICE WITH ORCHESTRA

Der Wein, Concert Aria for Soprano and Orchestra
★★★★—in "Music of Alban Berg," COL, Beardslee (*s*), Craft, CO 271(S).

Five Orchestral Songs to Picture Postcard Texts by Peter Altenberg, Op. 4
★★★★—COL, Beardslee (*s*), Craft, CO 5428(S).

Seven Early Songs for High Voice and Orchestra
★★★★—in "Music of Alban Berg," COL, Beardslee (*s*), Craft, CO 271(S).

Three Excerpts from "Wozzeck," Op. 7
★★★★—LSO, Pilarczyk (*s*), Dorati, MY 50278(S).

OPERA

Lulu
Columbia's production (particularly Ilona Steingruber in the title role) is exemplary in the singing and in the singers' understanding of the music. It takes many hearings to uncover the dozens of subtle allusions which move "Lulu" to its conclusion. Nonetheless, the over-all expressivity becomes more and more fascinating as the work moves on. (Berg did not live to complete his opera. It is represented on the recording with the complete first two acts and the finale of the third.)
—VSO, Steingruber, Weiner, Matheis, Riegler, Logau, Kmentt, Libert, Loida, Siegert, Bacher, Wild, Cerny, Häfner, CO 121.

Wozzeck, Op. 7
No operatic record collection is complete without "Wozzeck," a landmark in the medium. This is a release worth acquiring, with excellent voices, and polished orchestral playing.
—NY, Chorus of the Schola Cantorum, Members of the Chorus of the High School of Music and Art, Harrell, Farrell, Jagel, Mordino, Lloyd, Herbert, Eustis, Anderson, Norville, Herdt, Mitropoulos, CO 118.

ARTHUR BLISS

ORCHESTRAL

A Colour Symphony
★★—LSO, Bliss, L 1402.

Dance of Summer from "Adam Zero"
★—in "The Sadler's Wells Ballet: A Silver Jubilee Tribute," OROH,
Irving, A 35521(S).

Discourse for Orchestra
Sometimes the Louisville group has a thin sound (their string body is
not very large and this tells in music of romantic orchestration). This
is to be noted here.
—LOU, Whitney, LV 59–2.

Introduction and Allegro
★★—LSO, Bliss, L 1402.

Suite from the Ballet "Miracle in the Gorbals"
★★★—PH, Bliss, A 35136.

Suite from the Film "Things to Come"
★★—LSO, Bliss, V 2257(S).

Welcome to the Queen
★★—LSO, Bliss, V 2257(S).

STRING ORCHESTRA

Music for Strings
★★★—PH, Bliss, A 35136.

SOLO INSTRUMENT WITH ORCHESTRA

CONCERTOS

Concerto for Piano and Orchestra
Plenty of display opportunities in this work, and Barnard negotiates
everything with the fullest assurance. There is more depth to the
slow movement than he realizes, however.
—PH, Barnard (*p*), Sargent, A 36100(S).

Concerto for Violin and Orchestra
Aside from some nasal sonic blockage in the slow section, the solo
violin is heard with refinement; the orchestral support is good.
—LPO, Campoli (*v*), Bliss, L 1398.

383

SOLO VIOLIN WITH ORCHESTRA

Theme and Cadenza for Violin and Orchestra
—LPO, Campoli (*v*), Bliss, L 1398.

CHAMBER MUSIC

Conversations (Nos. 1 and 5)
★★★—in "The History of Music in Sound, Vol. X," Melos Ensemble, V 6092.

VOCAL

The Buckle
★—Amara (*s*), Benedict (*p*), CAM 704(S).

BALLET

Checkmate
★★★—OROH, Irving, CO 4362.

PIERRE BOULEZ

INSTRUMENTAL

TWO PIANOS

Structures
A performance that meets the superhuman demands of Boulez's music.
—Alfons Kontarsky and Aloys Kontarsky, VEGA 30–278.

CHAMBER MUSIC

Sonatine for Flute and Piano
Both Gazzelloni and Tudor are considered the leading exponents of avant-garde music for their respective instruments. They prove it with their discerning and powerful presentation of Boulez's "Sonatine."
—Gazzelloni (*fl*), Tudor (*p*), VEGA 30–139　　—in "Avant-Garde," Bennett (*fl*), Bradshaw (*p*), DE (18005).

384

VOCAL

VOICE WITH INSTRUMENTAL ENSEMBLE

Le Marteau sans Maître
"The Hammer Without a Master" is available in two recordings (part of one of these is on a foreign disk: *see below*). Despite a performance with the composer directing (and Boulez is a remarkable conductor), Craft's is preferable. It is not so much his conception as it is the clarity expressed by the individual performers.
—MacKay (*a*), Gleghorn (*fl*), Thomas (*va*), Kraft (*vib*), Remsen (*x*), Norman (*g*), Goodwin (*per*), Craft, CO 5275   —Cahn (*cn*), Tiberge (*fl*), Collot (*va*), Stingl (*g*), Delécluse (*vib*), Naudin (*x*), Cavaillé (*per*), Boulez, W 18746.

Le Marteau sans Maître (Excerpts)
The Westminster recording listed immediately above was a transfer from an original Véga release (C-35-A-67). Véga has also issued three extracts from this performance in another album, containing music by Luigi Nono and Karlheinz Stockhausen, plus three works by Anton Webern.

The excerpts consist of movements 3, 6, and 9; thereby representing all the portions using voice, save the fifth part. Because of the fascinating companion compositions the disk containing this sampling is worthwhile, even if one has a recording of Boulez's complete work.
—Cahn (*cn*), Tiberge (*fl*), Naudin (*x*), Delécluse (*vib*), Cavaillé (*per*), Stingl (*g*), Collot (*va*), Boulez, VEGA 30–66.

BENJAMIN BRITTEN

ORCHESTRAL

Four Sea Interludes, Op. 33a and Passacaglia, Op. 33b from "Peter Grimes"
The Boult performance on Westminster is tops. Not only do the conductor and orchestra know the work thoroughly but they play it with devoted consideration. The Lab. package is beautifully recorded (the minute-by-minute, note-by-note progression of the music given in the detailed liner could be dispensed with). Van Beinum's version is well-delivered, but does not probe as deeply.
—PPO, Boult, W 18601(S)   —PPO, Boult, WL 7057   —OROH, Watson (*s*), Pears (*t*), Britten, L (6179)   —CG, van Beinum, L 917.

Matinées Musicales, Op. 24
The performances fall in approximately the same order of preference
as for the "Soirées" (*see below*). Boult is to the point, Irving is al-
most as good, while Braithwaite plays "heavy, heavy, what hangs
over." The sound of the Bostonians' recording is dull and lifeless.
Also, this release does not include the last movement of the "Soirées
Musicales," as indicated on the liner notes.
—PPO, Boult, W 18601   —PPO, Boult, WL 7055(S)   —PH,
Irving, C 7105   —OROH, Braithwaite, MGM 3028   —BP, Fiedler, V 1093.

Sinfonia da Requiem, Op. 20
★—Danish State Radio Sy. Orch., Britten, L 1123.

Soirées Musicales, Op. 9
Boult performs the "Soirées" with proper affection (the Westminster
Lab. version offers little for much). Irving does as well, but the sound
of his disk is less luminous. The Urania entry is surprisingly good
and displays much more snappy sympathy for the music than one
would expect from stolid German musicians.
—PPO, Boult, W 18601   —PPO, Boult, WL 7055(S)   —BR,
Kleimert, U 7136   —PH, Irving, C 7105   —OROH, Braithwaite,
MGM 3333   —OROH, Braithwaite, MGM 3028.

Soirées Musicales, Op. 9 ("March")
★★—in "Adventures in Music—Grade 1," N, Mitchell, V 1000(S).

The Young Person's Guide to the Orchestra, Op. 34
Of the purely orchestral releases (*see* Narrator and Orchestra *below,*
for other version of this work) the van Beinum and Ormandy executions rate a laurel wreath. The Philadelphians excel in the brass and
harp departments. The Europeans play with a deeper golden tone.
The Slatkin-conducted group is a close runner-up. Dorati's performance is one of extreme brilliance; but it lacks breadth in the final
portion. In the Boult releases the soloists are under par. The per-
functory reading of the fugal portion is damning in Frémaux's interpretation, but the vastly superior sound of the disk places it ahead
of the three Westminster representations.
—CG, van Beinum, R 19040   —CG, van Beinum, L 917   —PO,
Ormandy, CO 5183(S)   —CAO, Slatkin, C 8373(S)   —M,
Dorati, MY 50047   —in "Monte Carlo Concert Gala: Album 2,"
MCO, Frémaux, DG 18654(S)   —PPO, Boult, W 18601(S)
—PPO, Boult, W 18737   —PPO, Boult, WL 7056.

CHAMBER ORCHESTRA

Sinfonietta, Op. 1
★—MGM Chamber Ensemble, Solomon, MGM 3245.

STRING ORCHESTRA

Simple Symphony, Op. 4
Top performances: the beautifully conceived edition by the Zagreb group and that led by Sargent. Britten's string symphony (more correctly a suite) appears in a balletic collection because it has been utilized for that purpose; the dance presentation retained the composition's title. Excellent performances: by Goossens, Ristenpart, and the conductorless I Musici. Passable performance: Solomon, for whom the MGM engineers have not done well at all. Questionable performance: the Societa' Corelli (overfast tempo in movement one and some stylistic exaggeration).
—in "English Ballets of the 20th Century," RP, Sargent, A 35889(S) —in "Music for Strings," IZ, Janigro, V 2653(S)   —NSO, Goossens, L 9146   —in "Twentieth-Century Music," Sarre Chamber Orch., Ristenpart, MG 39(S)   —in "Music for Strings," I, P 500001(S)   —MGM String Orch., Solomon, MGM 3074   —Societa' Corelli, VI 20204.

Variations on a Theme of Frank Bridge, Op. 10
It is surprising that this work, which has become one of the few contemporary "standards" in the string-orchestra repertoire, has been bypassed by the recording companies. Angel's release is the only one currently available. It shows good sound, good playing, but not much interpretative depth. Despite certain sonic limitations, the now-extinct London production had much in its favor; principally because Boyd Neel was involved with the work from its birth—it was his request for a composition to be presented at the 1937 Salzburg Festival that resulted in Britten's Opus 10.
—PH, von Karajan, A 35142   —BNSO, Neel, L 801.

NARRATOR AND ORCHESTRA

The Young Person's Guide to the Orchestra, Op. 34
Although Sir Adrian Boult's recordings without narration were not the best he passes them all as a narrator. His voice is clear and charming. The other side of the disk has a somewhat interesting "take" of a rehearsal of Britten's work with orchestra alone.

Both Pears and de Wilde are good; the former has an advantage because the orchestra on Angel is much better than that on Vox. Columbia's entry should have been a smash, it turns out to be quite irritating. The idea of using a youngster for the narration was resourceful, but the infantile lines he was given to speak are a feeble (and unbecoming) substitute for Eric Crozier's beautifully flowing words.

Regardless of "the composer's approval," Maazel's recasting of the text is full of school-marm touches and has a very condescending

387

quality. The worst of the lot is the ineffective diction of Deems Taylor's tailored-for-Americans recital.
—in "Hi-Fi in the Making," PPO, Boult (*n*), Boult, W 18372   —PH, Pears (*n*), Markevitch, A 35135   —PRM, de Wilde (*n*), Swarowsky, VOX 9280   —NY, Chapin (*n*), Bernstein, CO 5768(S) —LOF, Maazel (*n*), Maazel, DG 18746(S)   —M, Taylor (*n*), Dorati, MY 14033(S)   —M, Taylor (*n*), Dorati, MY 50055.

SOLO INSTRUMENT WITH ORCHESTRA

Concerto

Concerto for Violin and Orchestra, Op. 15
★★★—LOU, Kling (*v*), Whitney, LV 626.

Solo Piano with Orchestra

Diversions On a Theme for Piano (left hand) *and Orchestra, Op. 21*
★—LSO, Katchen (*p*), Britten, L 1123.

INSTRUMENTAL

Organ

Prelude and Fugue on a Theme by Vittoria (Victoria)
★★—in "Organ Music by Modern Composers: Vol. 1," Ellsasser, MGM 3064.

Prelude on a Theme by Victoria
★★—in "The King of Instruments: Vol. VI," Wyton, WA 6.

Piano

Holiday Diary, Op. 5
★—Bianca, MGM 3366.

Recorder

Scherzo
★★★—in "Twentieth Century Recorder Music," Manhattan Recorder Consort, CL 1055.

CHAMBER MUSIC

Sonata in C for Cello and Piano, Op. 65
The composer and this great Soviet artist make a perfect team. Remarkable sound. A very strongly recommended release.
—Rostropovich (*c*), Britten (*p*), L 9306(S).

388

Phantasy Quartet for Oboe, Violin, Viola and Cello, Op. 2
★★★—Members of the Galimir Sq, Gomberg (*o*), CT 504.

String Quartet No. 1, Op. 25
The Galimir Quartet disposes of the work in passable fashion. Though more definite underlining of the music's structure can be heard from the Paganini four, the Galimir group sounds richer and more expressive.
—Galimir Sq, CT 504   —Paganini Sq, LY 15000.

VOCAL

Folk Songs
The eight selections represented on the Boston disk are drawn from volumes one and three, representing songs of the British Isles. The tenor sings five of these and shows perfect communication. The soprano is no less an artist, though her diction is not as clear.

Pears and Britten draw their program from the entire set of five volumes. Ten of the seventeen songs they present are British, two are French, and the remainder Irish. The performances are superb. With the composer at the keyboard one must accept the liberties both he and his colleague take with the published editions.
—Pears (*t*), Britten (*p*), L 5693(S)   —Lloyd (*t*), Willauer (*s*), Schanzer (*p*), B 205.

The Holy Sonnets of John Donne, Op. 35
★★—Young (t), Watson (*p*), W 18077.

Let the Florid Music Praise! from "On This Island," Op. 11
★★—in "English Song Recital," Pears (*t*), Britten (*p*), L 1532.

Seven Sonnets of Michelangelo, Op. 22
Pears sings with a nobility which matches Britten's appropriate Italian stylization. The other (Westminster) recording is confused. One of the seven songs is missing and what one expects as the final piece is simply a partial retake of the previous band. Neither release offers a copy of the text, unfortunate for vocal music with words in a foreign language.
—Pears (*t*), Britten (*p*), L 1204   —Young (*t*), Watson (*p*), W 18077.

Six Hölderlin Fragments
A plus sign for a presentation of engaging musicality. A minus sign for the absence of a printed text of any kind.
—Pears (*t*), Britten (*p*), L 5687(S).

Three Canticles

> Canticle I—*My Beloved is Mine, Op. 40*
> Canticle II—*Abraham and Isaac, Op. 51*
> Canticle III—*Still Falls the Rain, Op. 55*

Magnificent performances by the entire cast. Britten had a woman's voice in mind for the alto part (Kathleen Ferrier sang this at the première). However, the use of a boy alto seems more fitting for the role of Isaac, and Hahessey's singing supports this conviction. His voice is both charming and properly poignant.
—Pears (*t*), Hahessey (*a*), Tuckwell (*hn*), Britten (*p*), L 5698(S).

Winter Words, Op. 52
★★★—Pears (*t*), Britten (*p*), L 1204.

VOICE WITH ORCHESTRA

Les Illuminations for Tenor or Soprano Solo and String Orchestra, Op. 18
All three versions are fine examples of recording art. Krebs and Micheau represent the composer best. Though the words are of far less importance than the derived feeling, the German vocalist is most dynamically clear in these intellectually warm images.
—BR, Krebs (*t*), Rother, U 7104   —LAM, Micheau (*s*), Sacher, E 3355   —NSO, Pears (*t*), Goossens, L 5358.

Nocturne, Op. 60
★★★—Strings of the LSO, Murray (*fl*), Lord (*Eh*), de Peyer (*cl*), Waterhouse (*bn*), Tuckwell (*hn*), Blyth (*ti*), Ellis (*hp*), Pears (*t*), Britten, L (6179).

Serenade for Tenor Solo, Horn and String Orchestra, Op. 31
Britten's music is projected beautifully by Lloyd with the assistance of top-flight string players and a horn soloist the equal of any. This Boston recording has a lovely sound. On the other hand Pears is surprisingly uneven and his upper tones are somewhat squeezed, and Brain also is not in top form.
—Members of the BSO, Lloyd (*t*), Stagliano (*hn*), Burgin, B 205
—NSO, Pears (*t*), Brain (*hn*), Goossens, L 5358.

CHORAL

A Ceremony of Carols, Op. 28
The Danish and Texan youngsters perform magnificently. The Canterbury Choristers are just as good, only lacking the distinguishing intimacy of the other two groups. Since Britten wrote his work for

"treble voices" the use of a female chorus is not out of place. However, none have the youthful freshness of the boys' choirs.

(The Concordia disk is titled as though the work were complete, but it is a cut version, omitting four sections.)
—Copenhagen Boys Choir, Simon (*hp*), Britten, L 9146   —Texas Boys' Choir, Boyd, Shockler, Hermann (*hp*), Bragg, D 10060(S) —Choristers of Canterbury Cathedral, Elder and Finch (*trebles*), Korchinska (*hp*), Campbell, L 5634(S)   —Women's Voices of Phila. Oratorio Choir, Dettore (*s*), Brame (*cn*), Costello (*hp*), Ness, RIT 1001   —Robert Shaw Chorale of Women's Voices, Shaw, V 1088   —Concordia Choir, Haukebo (*s*), Hector (*p*), Christiansen, CON 4.

A Ceremony of Carols, Op. 28 ("Procession" and "Wolcum Yole!")
★★★—in "Thirteen Centuries of Christian Choral Art, Vol. 3: 20th Century," Peloquin Chorale, Peloquin, GIA 19 (also obtainable as a set with Vol. 1: 8th to 16th Centuries [GIA 17] and Vol. 2: 17th to 19th Centuries [GIA 18]).

A Ceremony of Carols, Op. 28 ("This Little Babe")
—in "Songs and Choral Music," Women's Lyric Club of L.A., Robinson (*p*), Davis, BV 7095.

A Hymn to the Virgin
★★★—Chorus of the LSO, Malcolm, LL 50206(S).

Choral Dances from "Gloriana," Op. 52
★★—Chorus of the LSO, Malcolm, LL 50206(S).

Hymn to St. Cecilia, Op. 27
There is no doubt that the London group is splendid, vocally clean, properly incisive, and has accomplished a fine rendition. The Columbia University performance is lovely and clear. This group and the Augustana Choir have been molded into impressive organizations; the accuracy of their intonation, plus balance, brings out the freshness of the composer's invention.
—in "Chorus, Organ, Brass and Percussion," Columbia University Chapel Choir, Springer (*s*), Mallon (*a*), Bullard (*t*), Doe (*b*), Wright, K (9057)   —Chorus of the LSO, Malcolm, LL 50206(S) —Augustana Choir, Veld, WORD 4001.

CHORAL WITH ORCHESTRA

Spring Symphony, Op. 44
★★★★—ORCOH, Chorus of Boys from Emanuel School, Wandsworth, Vyvyan (*s*), Proctor (*cn*), Pears (*t*), Britten, L 5612(S).

War Requiem, Op. 66
A distinguished recording. It would be difficult to imagine a presentation that could better this superb and moving performance, supported by brilliant engineering.
The three solo voices have a U.N. type of disposition, with Pears from England, Fischer-Dieskau, from Germany, and Vishnevskaya from the Soviet Union. It had been Britten's hope to have these three for the première, given in England, on May 30, 1962. Vishnevskaya could not arrange her schedule to accomplish this, but she did manage the recording.
—LSO, Melos Ensemble, Bach Choir, LSO Chorus, Highgate School Choir, Vishnevskaya (*s*), Pears (*t*), Fischer-Dieskau (*bar*), Preston (*org*), Britten, L 4255(S).

CANTATA

Cantata Academica (Carmen Basiliense), *Op. 62*
★★★—LSO, LSO Chorus, Vyvyan (*s*), Watts (*cn*), Pears (*t*), Brannigan (*b*), Lester (*p*), Malcolm, LL 50206(S).

Rejoice in the Lamb, Op. 30
★—Canterbury Choral Society, Van Der Schans (*treble*), Boyer (*ms*), Porter (*t*), Shuss (*b-bar*), Lowry (*org*), Walker, CANTERBURY CHORAL SOCIETY 6251.

Saint Nicolas, Op. 42
★★★—Aldeburgh Festival Choir and Orch., Girls' Choir of Sir John Leman School, Beccles, Boys' Choir of the Prep. Dept. of Ipswich School, three boys from the Choir of St. Mary-le-Tower, Ipswich, Pears (*t*), Hemmings (*boy s*), Downes (*org*), Britten, L 1254.

BALLET

The Prince of the Pagodas, Op. 57
★★—OROH, Britten, L 7209.

OPERA

The Little Sweep, Op. 45
★★★★—The English Opera Group Orch., The Choir of Alleyn's School, Hemmings (*boy s*), Vyvyan (*s*), Thomas (*cn*), Cantelo (*s*), Ingram (*boy s*), Baker (*s*), Fairhurst (*boy s*), Soskin (*s*), Vaughan (*boy s*), Anthony (*b*), Pears (*t*), Britten, L 4107.

Noye's Fludde, Op. 59
★★★★—The English Chamber Orch., An East Suffolk Children's Orch., Children's Chorus, Brannigan, Rex, Anthony, D. Pinto,

Angadi, Alexander, Clack, M. T. Pinto, O'Donovan, Garrod, Hawes, Petch, Saunders, Del Mar, L 5697(S).

Peter Grimes, Op. 33
The performance is monumental, especially with Pears who gives marvelous reality to the part of Grimes. Claire Watson is excellent; the work of Owen Brannigan makes him one of the stars of this production. The others are no less impressive.
—ORCOH, Pears (*t*), Watson (*s*), Pease (*b*), Kelly (*b*), Brannigan (*b*), Elms (*ms*), Watson (*cn*), Studholme (*s*), Kells (*s*), Nilsson (*t*), Lanigan (*t*), Evans (*bar*), Norman, Britten, L 4342(S).

The Turn of the Screw, Op. 54
Under the composer's direction the performance is a study in subtle coloring and meaningful vocal inflections. Though at times Vyvyan is somewhat in cold, rather unpleasant voice, she fulfills her role admirably. Pears is magnificent, and the two young singers are exceptionally well cast. The release is fully documented with story, background material, and libretto. A triumph for Britten and for the London firm.
—The English Opera Group Orch., Pears (*t*), Vyvyan (*s*), Hemmings (*treble*), Dyer (*s*), Cross (*s*), Mandikian (*s*), Britten, L 4219.

LUIGI DALLAPICCOLA

ORCHESTRAL

Variazioni per Orchestra
The Louisville Orchestra's ability to cope with Dallapiccola's difficult music speaks highly of its development, and just as nobly for its conductor.
—LOU, Whitney, LV 545–8.

SOLO INSTRUMENT WITH ORCHESTRA

SOLO VIOLIN WITH ORCHESTRA

Tartiniana for Violin and Orchestra
Posselt plays with a big tone and she is well supported by Bernstein of the pre-Philharmonic era.
—COL, Posselt (*v*), Bernstein, CO 4996.

VOCAL

Quattro Liriche di Antonio Machado
★★—in "Splendori della Vocalita' Italiana - Il '900," Martino (*s*), Ghiglia (*p*), VI 20148.

VOICE WITH ORCHESTRA

Cinque Frammenti di Saffo ("Five Fragments of Sappho")
★★★—Instrumental Ensemble, Soederstroem (*s*), Prausnitz, E 3706(S).

Concerto per La Notte di Natale dell'anno 1956 ("Christmas Concerto for the Year 1956")
★★★—Instrumental Ensemble, Soederstroem (*s*), Prausnitz, E 3706(S).

VOICE WITH INSTRUMENTAL ENSEMBLE

Cinque Canti per Baritone e Alcuni Strumenti ("Five Songs for Baritone and Several Instruments")
Fuller delivers the pieces with a white voice which is somewhat unbecoming, and thereby belies the dramatic direction of Dallapiccola's songs.
—Instrumental Ensemble, Fuller (*bar*), Prausnitz, E 3706(S).

Due Liriche di Anacreonte ("Two Anacreontics")
★★★—Instrumental Ensemble, Soederstroem (*s*), Dallapiccola, E 3706(S).

Goethe Lieder
★★★—Instrumental Ensemble, Soederstroem (*s*), Dallapiccola, E 3706(S).

Goethe Lieder (Nos. 2, 3, 5, and 6)
—in "The History of Music in Sound, Vol. X," Hooke (*s*), Dobree (*cl*), Moore (*cl*), Hambleton (*b. cl*), V 6092.

CHORAL

CHORAL WITH ORCHESTRA

Canti di Prigionia
★★★★—ANSC, Markevitch, A 35228.

MANUEL DE FALLA

ORCHESTRAL

El Amor Brujo ("Love, the Magician")
Only one version hits par for the course: that conducted by a little-known name, Jean Meylan. Surinach directs a dull, feeble-tempoed presentation and the same pertains to Collins' truncated setting (containing less than half of the total suite).
—CZ, Meylan, PR 137   —ORS, Surinach, MLL 142 (S)   —LPO, Collins, R 19032.

El Amor Brujo ("Love, the Magician") ("Ritual Fire Dance")
Any orchestra of professional standing can play this exciting bit blindfolded. Naturally, all the readings are contained within miscellaneous collections or as a filler with the recording of a major-sized work. Choice is thus mainly conditioned by what comes with what, and very little by who is interpreting Falla's excerpted dance. However, the best of all performances of the "Ritual Fire Dance" remains that contained in the recording of the complete work by Leopold Stokowski on Columbia ML-5479 (MS-6147), *see* Voice with Orchestra *below*.
—in "Hi-Fi a la Española," ER, Fennell, MY 50144(S)   —in "Music of Spanish Masters," RP, Rodzinski, C 7176(S)   —in "Melodies of the Masters, Vol. 2, 'Rhythms of Spain,' " RP, Rodzinski, C 8564(S)
—in "Jungle Drums," G, Gould, V 1994(S)   —VOP, Scherchen, W 18733   —VOP, Scherchen, WL 7066   —in "Fire and Jealousy," KO, Kostelanetz, CO 1898(S)   —in "Grand Tour," NY, Kostelanetz, CO 981   —in "Favorites," KO, Kostelanetz, CO 791
—in "Lure of Spain," KO, Kostelanetz, CO 943   —in "Light Classics," BP, Fiedler, V 2547(S)   —in "In the Latin Flavor," BP, Fiedler, V 2041   —in "Pops Stoppers," BP, Fiedler, V 2270(S)
—in "Concert Brilliants," CSO, Dragon, C 8559(S)   —in "Echoes of Spain," HB, Dragon, C 8275(S)   —in "The International Pop Orch. . . . 110 Men," *no conductor indicated,* CAMEO 2001(S)
—in "España," Sinfonia de Granada, Savino, K 1220(S).

El Sombrero de Tres Picos ("The Three-Cornered Hat") (Suites Nos. 1 and 2)
Rodzinski delivers a good reading, despite a lack of verve. Giulini displays the greatest mastery of this half-of-the-total ballet score. There is a rightful aggressiveness and a rhythmic friction in his por-

395

trayal that makes it the best of the releases that cover the excerpted double suite.

A large choice is offered below of the most often presented second suite, and a number of versions of the complete ballet are on the market. The many wonderful sections one never hears in the concert hall or in the recorded suites suggest serious consideration of the entire score. Otherwise, the larger sampling (Suites 1 and 2) is preferable.

—PH, Giulini, A 35820(S)   —in "Music of Spanish Masters," RP, Rodzinski, C 7176(S)   —ONE, Argenta, L 9196(S).

El Sombrero de Tres Picos ("The Three-Cornered Hat") (Suite No. 1)
—International Symphonic Orch., Stern, TOPS 1616.

El Sombrero de Tres Picos ("The Three-Cornered Hat") (Suite No. 2)
[*The recording companies persist in identifying this suite with a freedom far from their right. The designations include "Ballet Suite," "Dances," "Three Dances," "Suite," and "Suite No. 2." No matter what the title disguise, they all mean the same thing. Correctly "Suite No. 2," the compilation consists of "The Neighbors," "The Miller's Dance," and a "Final Dance."*]
Rosenthal directs with dynamic brilliance and Reiner matches this by quiet intensity.

Fiedler, Golschmann, and Markevitch are all quite satisfactory, without four-starred distinction. The latter's tempi are in some places exceedingly slow in order to permit a greater accelerando. Such tempo compression bends the music out of shape.

—TNO, Rosenthal, W 18798(S)   —in "Spain," CHI, Reiner, V 2230(S)   —in "Slaughter on Tenth Avenue and Other Ballet Selections," BP, Fiedler, V 1726, *also* 2294(S)   —in "Getting Friendly With Music," BP, Fiedler, V 1995   —SL, Golschmann, C 8257   —PH, Markevitch, A 35008   —PH, Markevitch, A 35152   —BM, Lehmann, D 9775   —PC, Wolff, L 9256(S)   —NY, Mitropoulos CO 5172.

El Sombrero de Tres Picos ("The Three-Cornered Hat") ("The Miller's Dance")
Markevitch's reading is a segment in an anthology devoted to ballet scores; Rodzinski's is part of a crosspatch of music by Spanish composers and Spanish music by French composers. Both are excerpted from recordings of the suites drawn from Falla's ballet (*see above:* for Rodzinski, under "Suites Nos. 1 and 2"; for Markevitch, under "Suite No. 2"). The six sides of Angel's production are packaged with unusual beauty and care. Expensive, but worth it.

—in "Homage to Diaghilev," PH, Markevitch, A 3518C   —in "Melodies of the Masters, Vol. 2, 'Rhythms of Spain,' " RP, Rodzinski, C 8564(S).

Homenajes ("Homage")—*Suite Sinfonica for Orchestra*
The sonic felicity of the RCA Victor recording is superior to Angel's, which lacks textural clarity.
—Rome Sy. Orch., Castro, V 2143   —LOF, Halffter, A 35134.

La Vida Breve ("Life is Short") (Interlude and Dance)
It takes clear insight (as in the case of Reiner), magnificent color shaping and just tempo (Ansermet), or the more personal, but cogently expressed viewpoint of Mitropoulos to reveal the magnetism of Falla's operatic portions. (Reiner's example is identified as "Intermezzo and Dance"—the first part of this title is the equivalent of the "Interlude.")
—in "Spain," CHI, Reiner, V 2230(S)   —SR, Ansermet, L 9292(S)   —NY, Mitropoulos, CO 5172   —M, Dorati, MY 50146(S)   —LSO, Poulet, MGM 3073.

La Vida Breve ("Life is Short") ("Dance")
Fancy-free titling accompanies the plentiful recorded performances. The list includes "Danza Español," "Danza Española," "Spanish Dance," "Spanish Dance No. 1," "Dance No. 1," and so on.
    If it were not for poor engineering (harsh and somewhat strident sound), Surinach's interpretation would take first place. He plays the piece vividly and with special understanding of its style, introducing the dance with a ripping-spitting chord that starts things colorfully. Ansermet also leads into the dance, by way of some introductory measures. He reads the score with artless literacy.
    Surprisingly, since he is a Spaniard, Jorda's presentation is drab. Despite inferior sound and a numerically weak orchestra, Marrow's much older recording (which was reissued on the more economical Lion label) is far better in comparison. All the rest of the listings will be found acceptable.
—in "Orchestral Favorites," SR, Ansermet, L 9153   —ORS, Surinach, MLL 162   —in "La Danza!," HB, Dragon, C 8314(S)   —in "Tempo Español," CSO, Dragon, C 8487(S)   —in "Melodies of the Masters, Vol. 2, 'Rhythms of Spain,'" CSO, Dragon, C 8564(S)   —in "Fire and Jealousy," KO, Kostelanetz, CO 1898(S)   —in "Lure of Spain," KO, Kostelanetz, CO 943   —Orch., Kostelanetz, CO 763   —in "Adventures in Music: Grade 6, Vol. 1," N, Mitchell, V 1009(S)   —in "'Pop' Concert Favorites, Vol. 1," MGM Orch., Marrow, LION 40007   —in "'Pop' Concert Favorites, Vol. 1," MGM Orch., Marrow, MGM 3136   —in "The Music of Spain," PC, Jorda, R 19052.

ORCHESTRAL ARRANGEMENTS

Dance of the Miller's Wife from "El Sombrero de Tres Picos" ("The Three-Cornered Hat")

Novelty of transcription (for an orchestra of plectral instruments) and rare performance (all the players are blind) mark this album.
—in "Serenata Española," Popular Concert Orch. of Madrid, Albert, UA (6065).

Ritual Fire Dance from "El Amor Brujo" ("Love, the Magician")
Caveat emptor. In Hayman's album, Falla's piece is tossed onto a merry-go-round of musical arrangement.

The Verve releases are titled differently for the mono and stereo issues, but have the same contents. If you insist on this kind of molasses in your musical diet, then at least get the stereophonic version.
—in "Richard Hayman Conducts Pop Concert In Sound!," Richard Hayman and His Orch., Hayman, MY 2010(S)   —in "Percussion King–Gene Krupa," Orch., Williams, VERVE 8414 (S in "Classics in Percussion! Gene Krupa").

SOLO INSTRUMENT WITH ORCHESTRA

SOLO PIANO WITH ORCHESTRA

Noches en los Jardines de España ("Nights in the Gardens of Spain"), *Symphonic Impressions for Piano and Orchestra*
A reviewer has a right to his preferences, but he would be silly to designate any of the top listings given below as *the* best.

Novaes achieves the most poetic result. Curzon evokes a sensitive atmosphere, but the orchestra is weak. Loriod is best for color. Soriano displays the most defined Spanish character, but, with Argenta conducting, the piano and orchestra are not always in sonic balance. The collaboration with Frühbeck de Burgos is far better and has subtle intensity. Dominant overstatement of the rhythmic shapes makes Casadesus' playing somewhat stiff, whereas Haskil is too reticent. Ciccolini is over-spirited. Both Rubinstein and del Pueyo are a trifle restrained; the piano tone of the former is brittle and the total sound is quite shallow.

The Telefunken stereo release constitutes a bargain buy, but is a mystery entry with no soloist listed. The unnamed keyboard performer does nicely; the orchestra is metrically bound, constricting Falla's score.
—PRM, Novaes (*p*), Swarowsky, VOX 8520   —NSO, Curzon (*p*), Jorda, L 1397   —SDCC, Soriano (*p*), de Burgos, A 36131(S) —ONE, Soriano (*p*), Argenta, L 9212(S)   —TNO, Loriod (*p*), Rosenthal, W 18803(S)   —NY, Casadesus (*p*), Mitropoulos, CO 5172   —SF, Rubinstein (*p*), Jorda, V 2181   —LAM, Haskil (*p*), Markevitch, P 500034(S)   —LAM, del Pueyo (*p*), Martinon, E

3305 —LOF, Ciccolini (*p*), Halffter, A 35134 —in "Dukas-Falla-Ravel Program," Sy. Orch. of the Belgian National Radio, André, TE (18008).

INSTRUMENTAL

CELLO

Ritual Fire Dance from "El Amor Brujo" ("Love, the Magician")
Either cellist will satisfy. However, Bruno's is the more attractive compendium, presenting three great Soviet musicians in addition to Shafran; namely, David Oistrakh, Igor Oistrakh, and Leonid Kogan.
—in "Music of Spain," Shafran (*c*), Musinian (*p*), BN 14015 —in "Round the World, Volume 1: Music of Spain," Starker (*c*), Pommers (*p*), PE 584 —Shafran (*c*), Musinian (*p*), VG 6028.

Seguidilla Murciana from "Siete Canciones Populares Españolas" ("Seven Popular Spanish Songs")
Full, hearty playing. The album has some good and some dubious originals, and also some doleful transcriptions (as single examples of each category: Bloch's "Prayer" from "Jewish Life"; Kunc's "Notturnino," Op. 45, and Rimsky's "Flight of the Bumble Bee").
—in "Cello Encores," Janigro (*c*), Bagnoli (*p*), W 18004.

Spanish Dance No. 1 from "La Vida Breve" ("Life is Short")
★★—in "Recital," Gendron (*c*), Gallion (*p*), E 3753(S).

Suite Populaire Espagnole
Starker gives Falla's musical outpour its head while the Russian cellist tends to detail. Starker's instrument has a more golden tone. This does not discount Shafran. His performance is merely smaller, more intimate.
—in "Round the World, Volume 1: Music of Spain," Starker (*c*), Pommers (*p*), PE 584 —in "Music of Spain," Shafran (*c*), Musinian (*p*), BN 14015 —Shafran (*c*), Musinian (*p*), VG 6028.

GUITAR

Canción del Fuego Fátuo ("Song of the Will-o'-the-Wisp") *from "El Amor Brujo"* ("Love, the Magician")
—in "Music of Spain," Almeida, C 8295 —in "Virtuoso Guitar," de la Torre, E 3479.

El Círculo Mágico—Romance del Pescador ("The Magic Circle"— "The Fisherman's Song") *from "El Amor Brujo"* ("Love, the Magician")
Capitol uses the main title, Epic the subtitle, but it is the same piece

(part six of the orchestral suite). Almeida plays with taste. De la Torre is a discriminating performer.
—in "Music of Spain," Almeida, C 8295   —in "Virtuoso Guitar," de la Torre, E 3479.

Homenaje: Pour le Tombeau de Debussy ("To the Memory of Debussy")
Segovia's instrument sings with effortless grace, beautiful clarity and comprehensive knowledge of line; Diaz is a junior master. Comparing the engineering on these disks with the next two listed is like examining two sides of a coin. The sound equipment has picked up every move of de la Torre's and Bream's hands, and the ear is treated to assorted "pings," and swishes.
—in "An Andrés Segovia Concert," Segovia, D 9638   —in "Masterpieces of the Spanish Guitar," Diaz, VG 1084   —in "The Romantic Guitar," de la Torre, E 3564   —in "Spanish Guitar Music," Bream, W 18135   —in "Spanish Music for Guitar," Yépès, L 9105   —in "Guitar Extraordinary," Gomez, D 4312(S).

TWO GUITARS

The Miller's Dance from "El Sombrero de Tres Picos" ("The Three-Cornered Hat")
Two-by-one, via the technique of over-dubbing. We are not amazed.
—in "The Spanish Guitars of Laurindo Almeida," Almeida, C 8521(S).

HARMONICA

Ritual Fire Dance from "El Amor Brujo" ("Love, the Magician")
★★★—in "Profile," Sebastian (*ha*), Clugston (*p*), D 10025(S).

HARP

Dance of the Corregidor from "El Sombrero de Tres Picos" ("The Three-Cornered Hat")
★★—in "Spanish Classics," Zabaleta, PE 745(S).

Jota from "Siete Canciones Populares Españolas" ("Seven Popular Spanish Songs")
★★—in "El Amor d'España," Grandjany, C 8473.

Spanish Dance from "La Vida Breve" ("Life is Short")
Vito is recorded very close-in, thereby permitting finger contacts and pedal changes to interfere with clear sound. Grandjany takes first place and serves up a more artistic rendition.
—in "El Amor d'España," Grandjany, C 8473   —in "Harp Recital," Vito, PE 704.

400

ORGAN

Ritual Fire Dance from "El Amor Brujo" ("Love, the Magician")
—in "A Hi-Fi (Stereo) Fantasy in Pipe Organ and Percussion,"
Montalba, SO 8400(S).

PIANO

Canción and El Paño Moruno from "Siete Canciones Populares Españolas" ("Seven Popular Spanish Songs")
★★—in "Piano Music from Spain," de Groot, E 3175.

El Amor Brujo ("Love, the Magician") (Excerpts)
Echániz offers the "Ritual Fire Dance," the "Récit du Pêcheur" ("The
Fisherman's Song") (representing part six from the original suite with
its main title "The Magic Circle"), as well as the "Dance of Terror,"
and the "Pantomime." The playing passes approval.
—in "Ritual Fire Dance and the Complete Piano Music of Manuel
de Falla," Echániz, W 18434.

El Amor Brujo ("Love, the Magician") ("Dance")
This is the "Canción del Fuego Fátuo" ("Song of the Will-o'-the-
Wisp"), magnificently portrayed.
—in "Spanish Piano Music," Copeland, MGM 3025.

El Amor Brujo ("Love, the Magician") ("Dance of Terror")
In effect, a Spanish tarantella. It registers best in the hands of de
Larrocha.
—in "Piano Music of Manuel de Falla," de Larrocha, CO 5640
—in "World-Wide Favorites," Iturbi, V 1967.

El Amor Brujo ("Love, the Magician") ("Ritual Fire Dance")
It seems that pianists are defeated by Falla's war-horse. Actually, none
of the dozen noted below are without a blemish of some kind. For
some reason, the "Ritual Fire Dance" (on the piano) is never *wholly*
a piece. Continuity is constantly destroyed by dynamic poking, teasing
of phrases, and false tempo shifts. Rubinstein, Sanromá, Levant, and
de Groot are closest to the ideal. Iturbi would be included, but the
sound of his recording is poor. In the middle range stand Pressler, with
a dynamic reading, and young Hollander, who puts a number of his
elders to shame.
—Rubinstein, V 2566(S) —Sanromá, POL 1011 —in "Levant's
Favorites," Levant, CO 1134 —in "Piano Music from Spain," de
Groot, E 3175 —Pressler, MGM 3071 —in "Discovering the
Piano," Hollander, CA 460 —in "World-Wide Favorites," Iturbi,
V 1967 —in "Julius Katchen Encores," Katchen, L 9304(S)
—in "El Pianoforte Español (Spanish Piano Classics)," Cortes, SP

1022 —in "Brailowsky Encores," Brailowsky, V 2276(S) —in "Piano Recital," Foldes, DG 1909(S) —in "Spanish Piano Music," Frugoni, VOX 9420.

El Sombrero de Tres Picos ("The Three-Cornered Hat") (Excerpts)
Echániz toils mightily and produces musical dilution in three dances from the original score. The cause is not his lack as a pianist; the fault lies in his choice of literature.
—in "Ritual Fire Dance and the Complete Piano Music of Manuel de Falla," Echániz, W 18434.

El Sombrero de Tres Picos ("The Three-Cornered Hat") ("The Miller's Dance")
All three soloists are very convincing. The most stimulating album is Rubinstein's, which includes "Nights in the Gardens of Spain" and shorter items.
—Rubinstein, V 2181 —in "Levant's Favorites," Levant, CO 1134 —in "Encore: Byron Janis," Janis, MY 50305(S).

El Sombrero de Tres Picos ("The Three-Cornered Hat") ("The Miller's Dance" and "Neighbor's Dance")
In comparison with other performances (*see above*) of the first of this pair of excerpts, Miss de Larrocha comes in fourth, due to neutral coloration. However, some may overlook this in preference to the double portion.
—in "Piano Music of Manuel de Falla," de Larrocha, CO 5640.

Fantasía Bética
A fantasy must never sound like a potpourri. Of all the soloists Miss de Larrocha best understands the basic purity and depth of Falla's piece.
—in "Piano Music of Manuel de Falla," de Larrocha, C0 5640 —in "Ritual Fire Dance and the Complete Piano Music of Manuel de Falla," Echániz, W 18434 —Soriano, B 304 —Pressler, MGM 3071.

Homenaje: Pour le Tombeau de Debussy ("To the Memory of Debussy")
★★—in "Ritual Fire Dance and the Complete Piano Music of Manuel de Falla," Echániz, W 18434.

La Vida Breve ("Life is Short") (Danza No. 2)
Not to be confused with the very familiar "Spanish Dance No. 1" (the excerpt has been given many different titles but this is the most pertinent). It is not (as indicated on the liner copy) "the most frequently heard part of the score." In fact, it is rarely performed and

has not been transcribed for other media. Played with excellent style.
—in "Piano Music of Manuel de Falla," de Larrocha, CO 5640.

La Vida Breve ("Life is Short") ("Spanish Dance")
★★—in "Piano Music from Spain," de Groot, E 3175.

Nocturno
★★—in "Ritual Fire Dance and the Complete Piano Music of Manuel de Falla," Echániz, W 18434.

Pour le Tombeau de Paul Dukas ("To the Memory of Paul Dukas")
★★★—in "Ritual Fire Dance and the Complete Piano Music of Manuel de Falla," Echániz, W 18434.

Quatre Pièces Espagnoles ("Four Spanish Pieces")
Unfortunately, Sanromá's thrilling performance is on an old deleted recording. The best substitute is de Larrocha.
—Sanromá, POL 1011   —in "Piano Music of Manuel de Falla," de Larrocha, CO 5640   —in "Ritual Fire Dance and the Complete Piano Music of Manuel de Falla," Echániz, W 18434   —Pressler, MGM 3071   —in "Piano Music from Spain," de Groot, E 3175.

Quatre Pièces Espagnoles ("Four Spanish Pieces") ("Andaluza")
Andalusian musical zip and zeal needs razor-edge rhythmic performance. Milgrim supplies it wonderfully. Frugoni is far behind.
—in "The Romantic Music of Spain," Milgrim, K 9058(S)   —in "Spanish Piano Music," Frugoni, VOX 9420.

Quatre Pièces Espagnoles ("Four Spanish Pieces") ("Andaluza" and "Cubana")
★—in "Airs of Spain," Bolet, B 300.

Quatre Pièces Espagnoles ("Four Spanish Pieces") ("Montañesa")
★—in "The History of Music in Sound, Vol. X," Crowson, V 6092.

Serenata Andaluza
Take your choice of a pair of good pianists.
—in "Ritual Fire Dance and the Complete Piano Music of Manuel de Falla," Echániz, W 18434   —Pressler, MGM 3071.

Valse Capriccio
★★—in "Ritual Fire Dance and the Complete Piano Music of Manuel de Falla," Echániz, W 18434.

TWO PIANOS

Jota and Nana from "Siete Canciones Populares Españolas" ("Seven Popular Spanish Songs")
★—in "A Night in Spain," Whittemore and Lowe, C 8500(S).

Ritual Fire Dance from "El Amor Brujo" ("Love, the Magician")
Get L. & N. rather than W. & L. The tempo employed by the younger
pair causes a raising of the eyebrows. None of the others has anything
to offer.
—in "Two-Piano Favorites," Luboshutz and Nemenoff, CA 198
—in "A Night in Spain," Whittemore and Lowe, C 8500(S)   —in
"Pop Hits for Two Pianos," Whittemore and Lowe, CA 470   —in
"Popular Classics," Ferrante and Teicher, ABC 437(S)   —in "Concert for Two Pianos," J. Lang and D. Lang, GC 4070.

VIOLIN

Asturiana and Jota from "Suite Populaire Espagnole"
★★★★—in "Vignettes," Milstein (*v*), Pommers (*p*), C 8396.

Canción Populare from "Suite Populaire Espagnole"
★★★—in "The Art of Fritz Kreisler," Kreisler (*v*), Lamson (*p*), CA
518.

Jota from "Suite Populaire Espagnole"
The Russian portrays great art and the listener is transfixed; the
young Bolivian illustrates a very good violinist and we listen—politely, that's all. (A larger portion of the suite is presented by Milstein, whose performance of the "Jota" is as beautifully conceived as
Oistrakh's—*see above:* "Asturiana and Jota" from "Suite Populaire
Espagnole.")
—in "Oistrakh Encores," Oistrakh (*v*),Yampolsky (*p*), A 35354(S)
—in "Presenting Jaime Laredo," Laredo (*v*), Sokoloff (*p*), V
2373(S).

Nana (Berceuse) *from "Suite Populaire Espagnole"*
★★—in "Presenting Jaime Laredo," Laredo (*v*), Sokoloff (*p*), V
2373(S).

Pantomime from "El Amor Brujo" ("Love, the Magician")
★★★—in "Heifetz Encores," Heifetz (*v*), Bay (*p*), V 1166.

Spanish Dance from "La Vida Breve" ("Life is Short")
Oistrakh's playing of Falla's music is ravishing. You can hear this
master on two different labels, but the Monitor disk is a shade better.
    The Kreisler album contains seven other transcriptions in addition
to Falla's beautiful invention. It is a graduate course in listening to
hear the Russian's and the Austrian's treatment. Both are so different
and yet both are wonderfully musical. The last two words describe the
playing of Friedman (a protégé of Heifetz) in his solo recording
debut.
—in "Oistrakh Plays from Albéniz to Zarzycki," Oistrakh (*v*), Yam-

polsky (*p*), MON 2003 —in "Music of Spain," Oistrakh (*v*), Yampolsky (*p*), BN 14015 —in "The Art of Fritz Kreisler," Kreisler (*v*), Lamson (*p*), CA 518 —in "Virtuoso Favorites," Friedman (*v*), Smith (*p*), V 2671(S) —in "Imperial Kreisler," PM, Gimpel (*v*), Cremer, VOX 25150 —in "Intrada," Kooper (*v*), Ulanowsky (*p*), F 4006(S).

CHAMBER MUSIC

Concerto for Harpsichord (or Piano), *Flute, Oboe, Clarinet, Violin and Cello*
Best is the dramatic conception of Soriano and his colleagues. It has a single drawback—the middle movement contains none of the "energico" in Falla's tempo indication.
—Debost (*fl*), Casier (*o*), Boutard (*cl*), Nérini (*v*), Cordier (*c*), Soriano (*hps*), de Burgos, A 36131(S) —Concert Art Players, Marlowe (*hps*), C 8309 —Soloists of the ONE, Veyron-Lacroix (*hps*), Argenta, L 9213(S).

VOCAL

Seguidilla
★—in "The Art of Lucrezia Bori," Bori (*s*), Copeland (*p*), CA 343.

Siete Canciones Populares Españolas ("Seven Popular Spanish Songs")
Each one of the performances is a re-creative gem. Each deserves a place in a collector's library.
—in "20th Century Spanish Songs," de los Angeles (*s*), Soriano (*p*), A 35775(S) —in "Teresa Berganza Sings Music of Spain," Berganza (*ms*), Lavilla (*p*), L 5517(S) —in "Spanish Songs," Merriman (*ms*), Moore (*p*), A 35208.

Siete Canciones Populares Españolas ("Seven Popular Spanish Songs") ("Asturiana" and "Nana")
★—in "Soprano Assoluto: 35 Years of Recordings," Ponselle, ASCO 125.

Siete Canciones Populares Españolas ("Seven Popular Spanish Songs") ("Jota," "Canción," and "Polo")
—in "For My True Love," Terri (*ms*), Almeida (*g*), C 8461(S).

Siete Canciones Populares Españolas ("Seven Popular Spanish Songs") ("Seguidilla Murciana")
—Amara (*s*), Benedict (*p*), CAM 704(S).

VOICE WITH ORCHESTRA

El Amor Brujo ("Love, the Magician")
Stokowski's performance offers a fantastic auditory experience. Not a single measure is permitted to go by casually. It is a glorious illustration of a conductor in pursuit of white-heated orchestral volatility. Peculiarly, his earlier version is the opposite, perhaps due to the orchestra; the Hollywoodians were never Stoky's orchestra. The impact and fire of Martinon's reading puts all but the Philadelphia Orchestra version into the shade.
—PO, Verrett-Carter (*ms*), Stokowski, CO 5479(S)   —LAM, Vozza (*cn*), Martinon, E 3305   —SDCC, Iriarte (*ms*), Argenta, A 35089   —SR, de Gabarain (*ms*), Ansermet, L 9153   —TNO, de Prulière (*ms*), Rosenthal, W 18803(S)   —HB, Merriman (*ms*), Stokowski, V 1054   —in "Popular Spanish Classics for Orchestra," BPO, Eustrati (*ms*), Lehmann, D 9775   —NE, Delorie (*cn*), Goehr, CC 128.

Two Arias from "La Vida Breve" ("Life is Short")
★★★—in "Cantos de España," SDCC, de los Angeles (*s*), de Burgos, A 35937(S).

CHORAL

Five Songs
★★—Agrupación Coral de Pamplona de España (Pamplona Choir of Spain), J. Olaz (*t*), C. Olaz (*s*), Zubillaga (*cn*), Zabalza (*ms*), Morondo, CO 5278.

BALLET

El Sombrero de Tres Picos ("The Three-Cornered Hat")
"Par excellence" describes the first three performances listed.

Ansermet has twice recorded the complete ballet with the same orchestra for London. The older offering (CM-9055) (reissued on the bargain-priced Richmond label) is rather tame. Placid temperament tempers Falla's ballet; rhythmic realism and virtuosic-timed discipline bring out its richnesses. In the later presentation there is much more exuberance and sufficient vitality.

Van Remoortel turns out only a fair reading. It lacks pertinent crispness and proper tempi selection.
—LOF, Rubio (*ms*), Toldra, A 35553   —LSO, Howitt (*s*), Jorda, EV 6057(S)   —OCM, Langa (*s*), Arámbarri, CO 5358   —SR, Berganza (*ms*), Ansermet, L 9292(S)   —SR, Danco (*s*), An-

sermet, L 9055   —*the same,* R 19100   —VSO, Madeira (*cn*), van Remoortel, VOX 11920(S).

OPERA

El Retablo de Maese Pedro ("Master Peter's Puppet Show")
The pointed exactness of Argenta's direction, the precise following of Falla's vocal instructions, and the performance's declarative quality make London's release the superior one.
—ONE, Bermejo (*s*), Munuia (*t*), Torres (*bar*), Argenta, L 9213(S)   —LOF, Aragon (*s*), Renom (*t*), Ausensi (*bar*), Toldra, A 35089   —VPO, Steingruber (*s*), Kmentt (*t*), Wiener (*b*), Adler, SPA 43.

La Vida Breve ("Life is Short")
★★★—Orchestre Symphonique de l'Opéra de Barcelone, Chorus of the "Capilla Clásica Polifónica," Pujol (*t*), Gomez (*ms*), Cartaña (*t*), Gombau (*s*), Tello (*s*), Turullols (*ms*), de los Angeles (*s*), Civil (*t*), Pava (*bar*), Simorra (*bar*), Puigsech (*ms*), Cachadina (*bar*), Halffter, PAT 326/7.

PAUL HINDEMITH

ORCHESTRAL

Concert Music for String Orchestra and Brass Instruments, Op. 50
The vote must go to the composer, despite the excitation brought about by the Philadelphians' reading. And Angel's sonic blend will make any recordphile happy.
—PH, Hindemith, A 35489(S)   —PO, Ormandy, CO 4816.

Concerto for Orchestra, Op. 38
★★★—BPO, Hindemith, D 9969.

Cupid and Psyche, Ballet Overture (1943)
★★★—BPO, Hindemith, D 9969.

Nobilissima Visione ("St. Francis"), *Suite for Orchestra* (1938)
The Hindemith-led recording supersedes in every way the earlier release by the same orchestra on the same label.
—PH, Hindemith, A 35490   —PH, Klemperer, A 35221   —HP, Keilberth, TE 66055.

Sinfonietta in E (1950)
★—LOU, Whitney, LV 605.

Symphonia Serena (1946)
★★★★—PH, Hindemith, A 35491(S).

Symphonic Dances (1937)
★★★—BPO, Hindemith, D 9818.

Symphonic Metamorphosis of Themes by Carl Maria von Weber (1943)
Hindemith skims along in the first movement, which is a deviation from the designated tempo; the music does not get settled at that point and it should. Kubelik's ideas are much more adequate and the music benefits thereby.
—CHI, Kubelik, MY 50024   —CHI, Kubelik, MY 50027   — BPO, Hindemith, D 9829   —HP, Keilberth, TE 66055.

Symphonic Metamorphosis of Themes by Carl Maria von Weber ("March")
★★★—in "Symphonic Marches," CLEP, Lane, E 3763(S).

Symphony "Die Harmonie der Welt" (1951)
★★★—BPO, Hindemith, D 9765.

Symphony in E♭ (1940)
Boult keeps things moving, but the effect is somewhat aloof, almost distressingly ascetic.
—LPO, Boult, EV 6008(S).

Symphony "Mathis der Maler" (1934)
Ormandy's reading is superb. He has rarely surpassed it with any other work. Silvestri's and Steinberg's considerations are creditable, but the former does not have the sheen of the latter, and the latter does not have the golden glow that suffuses Ormandy's recording.
—PO, Ormandy, CO 4816   —PI, Steinberg, C 8364(S)   —PH, Silvestri, A 35643(S)   —BPO, Hindemith, D 9818   —BPO, von Karajan, A 35949(S).

CHAMBER ORCHESTRA

Kammermusik No. 1, Op. 24, No. 1
★★★—LSF, Millar, FY 5001.

STRING ORCHESTRA

Eight Canons in First Position for Violin Choir, Op. 44, No. 2
★★—in "Educational Music for Instrumental Ensembles," MLS, Levine, MGM 3161.

Eight Pieces in First Position for String Choir, Op. 44, No. 3
Levine's ensemble (a group formed for recording the four Hindemith items included in the MGM issue) plays moderately well, though the string quartet version is far better. However, the Circle recording is the product of a long-defunct firm, so it will be exceedingly difficult to find.
—Radio Artists Sq, CI 51-100   —in "Educational Music for Instrumental Ensembles," MLS, Levine, MGM 3161.

Five Pieces in First Position for String Orchestra, Op. 44, No. 4
Levine's reading is not of sufficient depth and cannot compare to the strength of Goldberg's conception. However, MGM's production offers the rare opportunity of hearing the complete Opus 44, headed "Schulwerk für Instrumental-Zusammenspiels" ("Educational Music for Instrumental Ensembles"), devoted to sets of pieces in increasing performance difficulty.
—NCO, Goldberg, E 3356   —in "Educational Music for Instrumental Ensembles," MLS, Levine, MGM 3161   —LF, Baumgartner, DG 12016(S)   —Folkwang-Kammerorchester, Essen, Zoerb (v), Dressel, BAM 30-1517.

Nine Pieces in First Position for Violin Choir, Op. 44, No. 1
★★—in "Educational Music for Instrumental Ensembles," MLS, Levine, MGM 3161.

BRASS INSTRUMENTS

Morning Music from "Plöner Musiktag" ("A Day of Music at Plön") (1932)
Both versions (three are listed, but the performance on Classic is a transfer from the discontinued Circle recording) are worthwhile, though differing in performance conception and instrumentation. The Classic-once-Circle release follows a more stately idea of tempi, for the most part, and utilizes two trumpets plus one each of horn, trombone, and tuba; Kapp employs pairs of trumpets and trombones.
—in "The Modern Age of Brass," Roger Voisin and His Brass Ensemble, K 9020   —Shuman Brass Choir, CL 1041   —Shuman Brass Choir, Shuman, CI 51-100.

BAND

Symphony in B♭ for Concert Band (1951)
There is little choice between the pair of performances noted below. Hindemith moves his music a bit more slowly and his style is less athletic than Fennell. Both men do not overindulge themselves (Hindemith certainly wouldn't!). It is really worth owning both recordings.
—PH, Hindemith, A 35489(S)   —EW, Fennell, MY 50143(S).

SOLO INSTRUMENT WITH ORCHESTRA

CONCERTOS

Concerto for Cello and Orchestra (1940)
★—CZ, Tortelier (*c*), Ančerl, SU 474.

Concerto for Clarinet and Orchestra (1947)
★★★★—PH, Cahuzac (*cl*), Hindemith, A 35490.

Concerto for Horn and Orchestra (1949)
Performed with a rich, calid tone and illustrative of Dennis Brain's manifold artistic credits. Hindemith wrote his concerto for Brain, who introduced it in 1950; the recording was one of the last he made prior to the auto accident in which he met his death.
—PH, Brain (*hn*), Hindemith, A 35491(S).

Concerto for Trumpet, Bassoon and String Orchestra (1949)
★★★—LSF, Haug (*tp*), Ojeda (*bn*), Millar, FY 5001.

Concerto for Violin and Orchestra (1939)
Fuchs' performance is brilliantly styled and Everest's sound is marvelous. This is a sleeper if there ever was one.

Aside from Oistrakh's impeccable fiddle diction, London's entry is especially worthy because of the substance of the orchestral playing. In this respect it is better than Everest's, despite the use of the same ensemble by both companies. Gitlis' reading is very rewarding, though his tone is thinner than the other soloists. It also enjoys the advantage of being paired with another Hindemith work, if the buyer is interested only in that composer.
—LSO, Fuchs (*v*), Goossens, EV 6040(S)　—LSO, Oistrakh (*v*), Hindemith, L 9337(S)　—WE, Gitlis (*v*), Reichert, VOX 11980.

Concerto for Woodwinds, Harp and Orchestra (1949)
★★★—LSF, Subke (*fl*), Duste (*o*), Bibbins (*cl*), Ojeda (*bn*), Adams (*hp*), Millar, FY 5001.

SOLO ORGAN WITH ORCHESTRA

Kammermusik No. 7 (Organ Concerto) *for Organ and Chamber Orchestra, Op. 46, No. 2*
★★★★—COLC, Biggs (*org*), Burgin, CO 5199.

SOLO PIANO WITH ORCHESTRA

Concert Music for Piano, Brass Instruments and Two Harps, Op. 49
★★★—BPO, Haas (*p*), Hindemith, D 9969.

The Four Temperaments (Theme with Four Variations) *for Piano and String Orchestra* (1940)
The Berliners give a convincing performance, though a more engaging and less routined version comes from the Hollanders, with distinguished playing by the pianist, Leon Fleisher. Neither of the last two listings is especially worthwhile.
—NCO, Fleisher (*p*), Goldberg, E 3356   —BPO, Otte (*p*), Gieseler (*v*), Hindemith, D 9829   —OT, François (*p*), Auriacombe, PAT 279   —VSO, Holetschek (*p*), Swoboda, W 18716.

SOLO TROMBONE WITH ORCHESTRA

Trauermusik ("Music of Mourning") *for Trombone and Strings*
—Radio Artists Strings, Shuman (*tb*), CL 1041   —Radio Artists Strings, Shuman (*tb*), CI 51-100.

SOLO VIOLA WITH ORCHESTRA

"Der Schwanendreher" (Concerto for Viola and Small Orchestra) (1935)
Primrose, first and all the way. His tone has none of the somewhat coarse, somewhat nasal, somewhat heavy-handed negative qualities heard from the other soloist.
—COLC, Primrose (*va*), Pritchard, CO 4905   —VSO, Breitenbach (*va*), Haefner, VOX 11980.

Trauermusik ("Music of Mourning") *for Viola and Strings* (1936)
Though Epic's sound is better, the solo violist must take second place to Vardi.
—MGM String Orch., Vardi (*va*), Solomon, MGM 3432   —NCO, Godwin (*va*), Goldberg, E 3356   —Strad Chamber Ensemble, Persinger (*va*), STRAD 608.

SOLO VIOLIN WITH ORCHESTRA

Kammermusik No. 4 (Violin Concerto) *for Violin and Large Chamber Orchestra, Op. 36, No. 3*
★—WI, Rybar (*v*), Swoboda, W 18716.

INSTRUMENTAL

HARP

Sonata (1939)
Both harpists are in full command. Zabaleta's album contains much better music, however. (Be warned: the Counterpoint disk will probably have reverse labeling.)

—in "Contemporary Harp Music," Zabaleta, CT 523　—in "Music for the Harp," Grandjany, C 8420.

ORGAN

Sonata No. 1 (1937)
Exemplary performance and sound mark the Lyrichord disk. Although Biggs' registration is neat, Hindemith can stand a more colorful presentation. And the same goes for Reda's overly sober delivery. The final listing offers an excellent consideration of Hindemith's beautiful score, but the brightness of Noehren's conception is lacking.
—Noehren, LYR 53　—Biggs, CO 5634(S)　—Reda, BAM 30-1516　—in "Organ Music from Sweelinck to Hindemith," Heitmann, TE 66037/8.

Sonata No. 2 (1937)
For the second organ sonata alone and without considering the companion offerings the MGM album ranks above the others.
—in "Organ Music by Modern Composers, Vol. 1," Ellsasser, MGM 3064　—Noehren, LYR 53　—Biggs, CO 5634(S).

Sonata No. 3 (1940)
Noehren's playing can hardly be bettered. His phrasings especially show a musician of deep understanding at work. Of all three sonatas, Biggs plays this one best.
—Noehren, LYR 53　—Biggs, CO 5634(S).

PIANO

Fuga Octava in D from "Ludus Tonalis" (1942)
★★—in "The History of Music in Sound, Vol. X," Foldes, V 6092.

Kleine Klaviermusik (Easy Five-Tone Pieces), *Op. 45, No. 4*
★★—in "Piano Music for Children by Modern Composers," Richter, MGM 3181.

Shimmy and Rag from "Suite '1922'," Op. 26
★★★★—in "The Masters Write Jazz," Smit, DOT 3111.

Sonata No. 1 (1936)
Badura-Skoda fulfills all the music's power and derring-do.
—Badura-Skoda, W 18200; *reissued as* W 9309.

Sonata No. 3 (1936)
In the hands of Tupas and Previn, Hindemith's sonata is beautifully effective. It almost is in the case of Yudina. However, she condemns her fluent technique by not respecting Hindemith's explicit dynamic directions, by the insertion of *subitos* which destroy line, plus a love of ritardandi and rubati that are as annoying as an untuned fiddle. Badura-

Skoda, who does a superb job with the first piano sonata, tends to overheat Hindemith's music, and thereby waters it down. (A very old recording by Muriel Kerr—made in 1951—on the short-lived Hyperion label is worth mentioning. She does very well with the sonata. Another note: MK indicates this piece as being "in B flat major." However, the music bears no key designation, and employs no key signatures. Regardless of the fact that the sonata begins and concludes in B flat, such freedom in titling is to be criticized.)
—Tupas, LYR 15   —Previn, CO 5369(S)   —Yudina, MK 1567
—Badura-Skoda, W 18200; *reissued as* W 9309.

PIANO DUET

Sonata for Piano, Four Hands (1938)
Seldom has piano ensemble music been so advantageously presented as Hindemith's piece by Demus and Badura-Skoda. The restraint of the other team makes the music stiff and dull.
—Demus and Badura-Skoda, MG 22(S)   —G. Dichler and J. Dichler, SU 10185.

VIOLA

Sonata for Viola Alone, Op. 25, No. 1
Magnificently performed and sensitively recorded. Question: What price stereo for a single four-stringed instrument?
—Ulmer, CD 1218(S).

VIOLIN

Sonata for Violin Alone, Op. 31, No. 1
Sonata for Violin Alone, Op. 31, No. 2
★★★★—in "Ruggiero Ricci Solo Recital," Ricci, L 9261(S).

CHAMBER MUSIC

Kleine Sonate for Viola d'Amore and Piano, Op. 25, No. 2
Included in a very unusual compilation (the first such in recorded form) of viola d'amore music. The noncontemporary examples include fascinating rarities by Haydn, Biber, Toeschi, and others.
—in "Die Virtuose Viola d'Amore," Stumpf (*va. d'amore*), Mrazek (*p*), AM 6261.

Sonata for Bassoon and Piano (1938)
★★—Garfield (*bn*), Lettvin (*p*), EMS 4.

Sonata for Cello and Piano, Op. 11, No. 3
Starker gives a magnificent performance, playing with rich tone despite the terrifying passage work. His pianistic companion does not sound as courageous. Period had two couplings for this Hindemith work, but

413

the second one has been deleted from its current catalogue—it is listed here for the sake of completeness. The descriptive title of Period's 741 is incorrect. It contains sonatas by Breval and Debussy, and an arrangement of a violin sonata by Francoeur, but it also offers short pieces by Couperin and Ravel. (The "Serenade" by Poulenc, indicated on the label, but significantly not on the liner copy, may be in Period's vaults—it's not on the record.)
—in "Sonatas for Cello & Piano," Starker (*c*), Pommers (*p*), PE 741 —Starker (*c*), Pommers (*p*), PE 715 —Stern (*c*), O'Neil (*p*), SPA 8.

Sonata for Cello and Piano (1948)
★—Piatigorsky (*c*), Berkowitz (*p*), V 2013.

Sonata for Clarinet and Piano (1939)
The clear designs of Hindemith's sonata require no interpretative paraphrase. Forrest understands his role as a functionary whereas Kell aims for more personal regulation of the music's conduct.
—Forrest (*cl*), Tupas (*p*), LYR 15 ˙ —Kell (*cl*), Rosen (*p*), D 9570.

Sonata for English Horn and Piano (1941)
★★★—Speyer (*Eh*), Barnett (*p*), UN 1028.

Sonata for Flute and Piano (1936)
Try to better Kincaid's polished tone and exquisite styling! Caratelli is not a poor second. He, too, is an excellent musician.
—in "Music for the Flute," Kincaid (*fl*), Sokoloff (*p*), CO 4339 —Caratelli (*fl*), Manley (*p*), NR 406.

Sonata for Oboe and Piano (1938)
Though Speyer's reading is good and Unicorn's sound is well-defined, it must take second place to the expressive, sensitively engineered Columbia issue.
—Gomberg (*o*), Mitropoulos (*p*), CO 5603 —Speyer (*o*), Barnett (*p*), UN 1028.

Sonata for Trombone and Piano (1941)
The difficulties of this sonata are artistically conquered by both Smith and Shuman. However, the former plays with more perception and tonal liquidity. Shuman's performance on Golden Crest (as part of a highly interesting program) is the better of the two he has made.
—Smith (*tb*), Lettvin (*p*), EMS 4 —Shuman (*tb*), Hambro (*p*), GC 7011 —Shuman (*tb*), Raphling (*p*), CI 51-100.

Sonata for Trumpet and Piano (1939)
★★—Wilson (*tp*), Lettvin (*p*), EMS 4.

Sonata (No. 4) *in C for Violin and Piano* (1939)
★★★★—Schneiderhan (v), Seemann (p), D 9980.

Sonata (No. 2) *in D for Violin and Piano, Op. 11, No. 2*
★—Kaufman (v), Balsam (p), C 8063.

Sonata (No. 1) *in E♭ major for Violin and Piano, Op. 11, No. 1*
★★★★—Oistrakh (v), Yampolsky (p), MON 2009.

Sonata (No. 3) *in E for Violin and Piano* (1935)
The Szigeti-Bussotti reading has lusty strength, perhaps not as much relaxation as the music should have. More serious is Szigeti's wobbly vibrato and hairy tone, absent from the rich, intelligent performance of the other team.
—in "Album of 20th Century Music," Posselt (v), Sly (p), AC 304
—Szigeti (v), Bussotti (p), CO 5178.

Trio for Recorders from "Plöner Musiktag" ("A Day of Music at Plön") (1932)
Good recorder players are rare. Classic Editions has issued a number of top-flight albums devoted to recorder music and all are worth attention.
—in "Twentieth Century Recorder Music," Manhattan Recorder Consort, CL 1055.

Trio for Violin, Viola and Cello, Op. 34
★★★—Pougnet (v), Riddle (va), Pini (c), W 18593.

Trio No. 2 for Violin, Viola and Cello (1933)
★★—Pougnet (v), Riddle (va), Pini (c), W 18593.

String Quartet No. 3, Op. 22
It is shocking that only this quartet of the six Hindemith has composed is represented on current recording lists.
    Kroll and his colleagues give a defined reading of the score, boldly stating the positive contrapuntalism and accentuating its color span. The Hollywood group gives an exemplary performance, though the sound is below par.
—Kroll Q, E 3779(S)   —Hollywood Sq, C 8151   —Fine Arts Q, CD 1225(S).

Kleine Kammermusik for Five Wind Instruments, Op. 24, No. 2
The Philadelphians cast the proper smartness on the music, yet a more cohesive portrayal comes from the New York gentlemen, aided in great part by the depth and profiled depiction granted by stereo. Straightforwardness and nonopinionated readings are given by the Fairfield and the Fine Arts groups. The Chicago ensemble disappoints

415

with a rather dry version, *sans* bite, whereas the French five offer pungency, but minus any cadential grins.
—NYW, CD 1205(S)   —PW, CO 5093   —FA, C 8258   —FAI, STRAD 606   —in "Masterworks of Quintet Literature," CSW, AUD 15(S)   —WIQ, A 35079.

Octet (1958)
Stereo or monaural, either way the rating is tops.
—Members of the Fine Arts Q and the NYW, Siegel (*double b.*), CD 1218(S).

VOCAL

Das Marienleben (1948)
Gerda Lammers' performance has good style. Her voice is somewhat dramatic, but is also often breathless, and thin in the upper register. James's assets are good pitch and aesthetic rapport. Her debits are a sense of vocal strain and pushing of the voice, plus a tendency to compress the dynamic range to a *sotto voce* level.

Tourel's recording was made in 1954 and her voice at that time was fresh, with an appetizing sound. Nonetheless, her interpretation suffers by the sheer fact that the range of Hindemith's cycle is too much for a mezzo-soprano's comfort; the upper tessitura is strained in her performance. Otherwise, Tourel's is a musically satisfying portrayal of a virtuosic score. (As far as the pianists are concerned they are all equally excellent.)

Three postscripts are required to the above remarks. Tourel's rendition is in the deleted category. Second, the Bärenreiter album is not banded—an exasperating point for those who wish to choose portions from the set of songs. Last, Lyrichord originally issued "Das Marienleben" on two disks (catalogue number LL-6). This issue is still available. However, it has been supplanted by a single record release (as noted below). This is the same uncut presentation as the first; the compactness having been accomplished by the technical progress in mastering records, which allows finer groove cutting without loss of fidelity.
—Lammers (*s*), Puchelt (*p*), BAM 30-1514/15(S)   —James (*s*), Brough (*p*), LYR 97   —Tourel (*ms*), Kahn (*p*), CO 196.

Das Marienleben (Excerpt)
An extremely haunting projection of the twelfth song of the cycle, "Stillung Mariä mit dem Auferstandenen" ("The Consolation of Mary by the Risen Christ").
—in "The History of Music in Sound, Vol. X," Hooke (*s*), Moore (*p*), V 6092.

416

Geistliche Motetten (Three Motets) *for Soprano and Piano* (1941–1944)
★—in "Irmgard Seefried Concert," Seefried (*s*), Werba (*p*), D 9768.

CHORAL

Liederbuch für Mehrere Singstimmen (Five Songs on Old Texts), *Op. 33* (Excerpts)
A truly elegant performance; the voices beautifully blended. Three of Hindemith's pieces are contained in this exciting compilation.
—in "German Choral Music from the 16th to the 20th Centuries," Chorus of Radio Berlin, Koch, MON 2047.

Six Chansons (1939)
—Berkeley Chamber Singers, Aird, MLR 7075.

CHORAL WITH ORCHESTRA

Requiem "For Those We Love" (1946)
Everest's release is rather misrepresented. Though no credit is given, it is actually a transfer from a very old Vox album (PL-1760) consisting of two ten-inch records. Furthermore, Everest states "first in 35 mm. recording." This is an impossibility, in view of the fact that the Vox disks were made in the pre-stereo days of 1950. No amount of doctoring can produce authentic stereo.

Aside from all this the recording does not do justice to Hindemith's work. There are a number of imbalances, and the diction is blurred. Braun is a fair vocalist; the mezzo-soprano is downright weak and often has a wavery delivery.
—VSO, VOPC, Höngen (*ms*), Braun (*bar*), Hindemith, EV 6100(S).

BALLET

The Demon, Ballet Pantomime, Op. 28
—Scarlatti Orch. di Napoli, Caracciolo, CSS 1036.

Hérodiade (1944)
★—MGM Chamber Orch., Winograd, MGM 3683.

OPERA

Mathis der Maler (1934) (Excerpts)
In view of the reticence of opera companies to produce "Mathis der Maler" a unique opportunity is offered by this single recording of

hearing seven portions of the work, plus two purely orchestral sections. The sampling only emphasizes that the failure to mount Hindemith's opera is artistic injustice.

—BR, Fischer-Dieskau (*bar*), Lorengar (*s*), Grobe (*t*), Ludwig, DG 18769(S).

GUSTAV HOLST

ORCHESTRAL

Egdon Heath, Op. 47
★★★—LPO, Boult, L 9324(S).

The Perfect Fool—Ballet Suite, Op. 39
Sargent's viewpoint raises no questions; the score is realized in all of its virtuosic brilliance and the sonics are marvelous. Boult plays Holst's suite rather blandly, but the music's strength comes through nonetheless.

Of the two Boult representations the preferable one is the first listed, containing the only recorded versions of "Egdon Heath" and "The Hymn of Jesus." It has the additional advantage of being available in stereo.

—in "English Ballets of the 20th Century," RP, Sargent, A 35889(S)
—LPO, Boult, L 9324(S)   —in "A Concert of English Music," LPO, Boult, L 9122.

The Perfect Fool—Ballet Suite, Op. 39 ("Spirits of the Earth")
This represents the initial section of the ballet.
—in "Adventures in Music: Grade 6, Vol. 2," N, Mitchell, V 1008(S).

The Planets, Suite for Large Orchestra, Op. 32
The conductor should understand that the imagery is paramount, that the dramatic thrusts must be pinpointed, that every juicy and subtle nuance must be given its full quota of registration. This exactly describes the Stokowski recording—truly a beautiful musical feat.

Sargent's consideration of the work is not as succulent or as exciting as the picturesque maestro's, though it is closer to the actual score. Oddly enough, the older disk Sargent made with the Londoners is better than that with the BBC group (the last, however, is available in stereo and such sound-spread, engineered with superiority, gives this version the upper hand). Boult has to take third place in this survey. Though he knows each slur and dynamic of the Holst work, Boult is defeated by his performers on both records. Von Karajan's reading is no better or worse than Boult's.

—LA, Women's Voices of the Roger Wagner Chorale, Stokowski, C 8389(S) —BBC, Women's Chorus, Sargent, C 7196(S) — LSO, Chorus of Female Voices, Sargent, L 9101; *the same,* R 19095 —PPO, LPC, Boult, W 18252 —VOP, Vienna Academy Chorus, Boult, W 18919(S) —VPO, VOPC, von Karajan, L 9313(S).

STRING ORCHESTRA

St. Paul's Suite, Op. 29, No. 2
★—Societa' Corelli, *no conductor,* VI 20204.

BAND

First Suite in E flat, Op. 28a
Fennell's playing of Holst's suite could hardly be bettered.
—in "British Band Classics," EW, Fennell, MY 50088 —in "Yale Band," Yale University Band, Wilson, CN 109 —NTS, McAdow, AU 6226 —in "An Album of Military Band Music," Band of the Grenadier Guards, Harris, L 1622.

Hammersmith: A Prelude and Scherzo, Op. 52
★★★★—in "British Band Classics: Vol. 2," EW, Fennell, MY 50197(S).

Mars from "The Planets," Op. 32
Truly an oddball. The subtitle of Riverside's album reads "Stirring Arrangements of Family Favorites." Since when has any part of Holst's suite been a "family favorite"? The music is indicated as "The Planets," but only the "Mars" movement is heard. The band is a pickup group, its name fashioned for the occasion, and no conductor is credited. Holst did not transcribe any of the seven movements of "The Planets" for band, but the identity of the arranger is not made known. The liner notes are laughable, describing "Mars" as "an excursion into the *semiclassical* field" (my italics)!
—in "Concert in the Park," Regis Symphonic Band, (*no conductor given*), RIV 7529(S).

Second Suite in F, Op. 28b
Magnificent is the rating for both performance and engineering of the record.
—in "British Band Classics," EW, Fennell, MY 50088.

VOCAL

Persephone, Op. 48, No. 9
The single Holst song available in the recorded catalogue. It is sung by Pears with good style and artistic restraint. The album covers not

419

only contemporary composers but music of the Elizabethan age (Julian Bream accompanies this group on the lute).
—in "English Song Recital," Pears (*t*), Britten (*p*), L 1532.

CHORAL

Abroad As I Was Walking
—Stanford Chorale, Schmidt, MLR 7022

A Dirge for Two Veterans
★★—in "Hymns and Songs of Brotherhood," Mormon Tabernacle Choir, Schreiner and Asper, organists, Condie, CO 5714(S).

A Dream of Christmas
★★—in "Choral and Organ Music," Stanford University Choir, Nanney (*org*), Schmidt, MLR 6995-6.

Eternal Father
★★★★—in "Chorus, Organ, Brass and Percussion," Columbia University Chapel Choir, Springer (*s*), Kneeream (*org*), Wright, K 9057(S).

Lullay My Liking
★★★—in "Christmas Music," Choir of Trinity Church, New Haven, Conn., Clarke (*t*), Byles, OV 11.

Matthew, Mark, Luke and John, Op. 36, No. 3
★★★★—in "Madrigals, Ballets and Folk Songs of Four Centuries," The English Singers of London, A 35461.

Personent Hodie
★★—in "On Christmas Night," Choir of King's College, Cambridge, Preston (*org*), Willcocks, ARGO 333(S); *the same*, L 5735(S).

CHORAL WITH ORCHESTRA

The Hymn of Jesus, Op. 37
★★★★—BBC, B.B.C. Chorus, Boult, L 9324(S).

148th Psalm
★—in "The Lord's Prayer," PO, Schreiner and Asper, organists, Mormon Tabernacle Choir, Ormandy, CO 5386(S).

ARTHUR HONEGGER

ORCHESTRAL

Chant de Joie ("Song of Joy")
Scherchen's performance is brilliant and to the point. Denzler offers a slightly less detailed viewpoint. (The Westminster "Lab." version is, as in all instances, beautifully executed, but is not economical for the purchaser.)
—PSL, Scherchen, W 18486   —PSL, Scherchen, WL 7032   —PC, Denzler, L 1296.

Mouvement Symphonique No. 3
Though Scherchen's reading is strong in character, the playing is not always clear; the brass section compromises matters several times.
—PSL, Scherchen, W 18486   —PSL, Scherchen, WL 7010.

Pacific 231 (Mouvement Symphonique No. 1)
The cleanest playing is found in the Cook recording (though different names are given the performing groups the Rondo is simply a reissue of the Cook disk), while the cleanest sound is on the London disk. In the latter instance the most definitive picture of the simulated train is obtained—bearing in mind that for music of this sort performance precision is second in importance to musical effect.
—SDCC, Ansermet, L 9119   —in "Modern Orchestral Textures," New Orchestral Society of Boston, Page, COOK 10683(S)   —Boston Orch., Page, RONDO (502)   —SDCC, Tzipine, PAT 187/188   —PSL, Scherchen, W 18486   —PSL, Scherchen, WL 7010   —in "Pops," HP, Walther, MGM 3144.

Prelude, Fugue and Postlude
The two-record album in which this composition is contained is of fascinating interest, including one work each by the six French composers, plus a spoken introduction by Jean Cocteau. Angel's usual high level of recording plus packaging is present. (Each of the two records in the album is obtainable separately, but the composite release is not only a genuine treat but a real bargain.)
—in "Le Group des Six," SDCC, Tzipine, A 3515-B   —SDCC, Tzipine, A 35117.

Prelude to "La Tempête" ("The Tempest")
Scherchen realizes Honegger's purposes in his noisy, quite overtheatrical piece.
—PSL, Scherchen, W 18486   —PSL, Scherchen, WL 7010.

421

Rugby (Mouvement Symphonique No. 2)
Of all the works that Scherchen conducts on his all-Honegger disk, "Rugby" is performed the best. However, the inner electricity shines brighter in Tzipine's exposition.
—SDCC, Tzipine, PAT 187/188   —PSL, Scherchen, W 18486
—PSL, Scherchen, WL 7010.

Suite Archaïque
★★—LOU, Whitney, LV 615.

Symphony No. 3 ("Liturgique")
Baudo's orchestra has an uncanny way with Arthur Honegger's music. They describe its keen vitality, but in so doing do not overlook the *musical* purpose. Unfortunately, the Parisians do not achieve the composer's intent. Theirs is top surface playing, with sonic plangency, but minus depth.
—CZ, Baudo, SU 10143   —PC, Denzler, L 1296.

Symphony No. 5 ("Di Tre Re")
★★★★—LAM, Markevitch, D 9956.

CHAMBER ORCHESTRA

Concerto da Camera for Flute, English Horn, and String Orchestra
Though beautifully performed and recorded, Capitol's older release is not as sharply conveyed as Epic's collection of four works (each featuring the flute with a different combination). Nor is it as easily purchased.
—in "Music for a Golden Flute," Cleveland Sinfonietta, Sharp (*fl*), McGuire (*Eh*), Chalifoux (*hp*), Lane, E 3754(S)   —L.A. Chamber Sy., Gleghorn (*fl*), Kosinski (*Eh*), Byrns, C 8115.

Pastoral d'Eté ("Summer Pastoral")
All the conductors recognize Honegger's mood thoroughly. All versions being practically equal, the compendiums must guide a person's choice.
—in "French Orchestral Music," LAM, Martinon, E 3058   —CAO, Golschmann, C 8244   —PSL, Scherchen, W 18486.

STRING ORCHESTRA

Symphony No. 2
The Czech presentation directed by Serge Baudo cannot be praised sufficiently for its vigor, conviction, and technical finish. Similar strength radiates from Ansermet's execution but there is more tension in Baudo's conception. The Bostonians play with rare (but appropriate) potent power.

—CZ, Baudo, SU 10143   —SR, Ansermet, L 5686(S)   —BSO, Munch, V 1868   —MGM String Orch., Baker (*tp*), Solomon, MGM 3104.

BAND

La Marche sur la Bastille ("The March on the Bastille")
★★★★—in "The Sound of the Goldman Band," Goldman Band, Goldman, D 8931(S).

SOLO INSTRUMENT WITH ORCHESTRA

SOLO PIANO WITH ORCHESTRA

Concertino for Piano and Orchestra
It is good to hear Viennese performers play Honegger's music without schmaltz and slickness. Jacquinot's playing is equally good but the MGM sound is not crystal clear. However, the frankness and "let-go" quality of Jacquinot is preferable to the lugubrious, unfitting Reger-Kaminski ideas that pervade Miss Weber's pianism.
—PRM, Klien (*p*), Hollreiser, VOX 10840(S)   —PH, Jacquinot (*p*), Fistoulari, MGM 3041   —BR, Weber (*p*), Fricsay, D 9900.

INSTRUMENTAL

FLUTE

Danse de la Chèvre ("Dance of the Goat")
DeLaney is little known; his recording may help to focus attention on his flute mastery. Nicolet is as good but has been miked so close in that one hears every breath he takes.
—in "Flute Contest Music," DeLaney, LANIER (*no call number*)
—Nicolet, D 2849.

ORGAN

Choral
★★—in "The First International Congress of Organists: Vol. II," Trevor, MI 1004.

CHAMBER MUSIC

Second Sonata for Violin and Piano
★—Wiener (*v*), Shorr (*p*), MLR 7094.

Sonatine for Cello and Piano
★★★★—Bex (*c*), Lee (*p*), BOI 059.

423

Sonatine for Two Violins
The twin-brother team gives a richly cogent performance, which is better balanced than that presented by the Oistrakhs.
—G. Beal and W. Beal, MON 2008   —D. Oistrakh and I. Oistrakh, MON 2058(S).

Sonatine for Violin and Cello
Outstanding clarity of performance marks this excellent release.
—Gendre (*v*), Bex (*c*), BOI 059.

Petite Suite for Two Instruments and Piano
★★—Nicolet (*fl*), Schneeberger (*v*), Souvairan (*p*), D 2849.

Rapsodie for Flute, Oboe, Clarinet and Piano
★★—in "French Moderns," Berkshire Ensemble, Zighera (*p*), UN 1005.

CHORAL

CHORAL WITH ORCHESTRA

Cantique de Pâques
A special worthwhile release, since the "Cantique de Pâques" is hardly ever heard in the concert hall.
—Maîtrise d'Enfants, LOF, Jouineau, PAT 247.

CANTATA

Cantate de Noël ("Christmas Cantata")
Reacting to the persuasiveness manifested in Honegger's work, both groups of performers are sympathetic and deeply convincing in their interpretations. London's vivid stereo recording serves the composition especially well.
—SR, Le Choeur des Jeunes de Lausanne, Le Choeur de Radio-Lausanne, Le Petit Choeur du Collège de Villamont, Mollet (*bar*), Ansermet, L 5686(S)   —LAM, Elisabeth Brasseur Choir, Petits Chanteurs de Versailles, Roux (*bar*), Duruflé (*org*), Sacher, E 3153.

ORATORIO

Jeanne d'Arc au Bucher ("Joan of Arc at the Stake")
★★★★—PO, Zorina (*n*), Gerome (*n*), Yeend (*s*), Long (*s*), Lipton (*cn*), Lloyd (*t*), Smith (*b*), Brown (*boy s*), Carrere (*n*), Mahieu (*n*), Juilliard (*n*), Temple University Choirs, St. Peter's Boys' Choir, Ormandy, CO 178.

424

Le Roi David ("King David")
Abravanel has turned out a thrilling representation of Honegger's fascinating musical fresco. He has the advantage of a magnificent narrator, in the person of Singher, the best of any I have ever heard in this part. Another exquisitely delineated segment is the chilling "Incantation" for speaking voice and orchestra, narrated by Madeleine Milhaud, the composer's wife. This release is a triumph. Of the two older versions the better re-creation is that by Ansermet.
—UT, University of Utah Chorus, Davrath (*s*), Sorenson (*t*), Preston (*ms*), Singher (*n*), M. Milhaud (*speaker*), Abravanel, VG 1090/1(S)   —SR, Choeur des Jeunes de l'Eglise Nationale Vandoise, Danco (*s*), de Montmollin (*ms*), Martin (*ms*), Hamel (*t*), Audel (*n*), Ansermet, L 1651/2   —LOF, Chorale Elisabeth Brasseur, Micheau (*s*), Collard (*cn*), Mollet (*bar*), Hervé (*n*), Duruflé (*org*), Honegger, W 204; *the same,* DT 8342–3.

Les Cris du Monde
One of the most telling recordings in the Honeggerian discography. Soloists, chorus, and orchestra join in an exciting translation of Honegger's score.
   Nothing exciting about Pathé-Marconi's production ideas. They should be severely criticized for issuing a recording without text of any kind and minus a solitary word about composer or composition.
—LOF, Choeurs de la Radiodiffusion Française, Monmart (*s*), Roux (*bar*), Collard (*cn*), Tzipine, PAT 649.

DRAMATIC WORK

Nicolas de Flue
★★—SDCC, Chorale Elisabeth Brasseur, Les Petits Chanteurs de Versailles, Davy (*n*), Tzipine, PAT 187/188.

JACQUES IBERT

ORCHESTRAL

A Louisville Concerto
—LOU, Whitney, CO 5039   —LOU, Whitney, LV 545-5.

Escales ("Ports of Call")
For subtlety, yet mastery of style, the palm goes to Stokowski (in the older Victor version; available separately or in a three-record anthology; Capitol's suffers by an inferior finale and not enough juice in the

425

middle movement). The *playing* by the Philadelphia group is sheer virtuosity and Columbia's sound corresponds. (John de Lancie's oboe styling in the second piece is truly incomparable.) Munch is graphic, but in a very quiet manner—the music is more a silhouette than one drawn in oils; while Paray plays the score rather than permitting the score to play him (as so often happens).

The other performances lack animation, both are limited representations.

—S, Stokowski, V 9029   —in "The Tone Poem," S, Stokowski, V 6129   —in "Ports of Call," PO, de Lancie (*o*), Ormandy, CO 5878(S)   —PO, Ormandy, CO 4983   —in "The Sea," BSO, Munch, V 2111(S)   —DET, Paray, MY 50313(S)   —DET, Paray, MY 14030(S)   —DET, Paray, MY 50056   —LOF, Stokowski, C 8463(S)   —LAM, Fournet, E 3478   —Paris Opera Orch., Ibert, C 18004.

L'Amours de Jupiter
★★—Paris Opera Orch., Ibert, C 18004.

The Little White Donkey from "Histoires"
★★—in "Adventures in Music: Grade 2," N, Mitchell, V 1001(S).

CHAMBER ORCHESTRA

Capriccio
★—WI, Swoboda, W 18520.

Clowns' Dance from "Invitation to the Dance"
★★★—in "Musical Merry-Go-Round," Sinfonia of London, Irving, C 7244(S).

Divertissement
Surinach's version is deadly incorrect. He slows the tempi to such an extent that one believes the record turntable to be out of order. By far the best are the performances of Désormière and Martinon. Both have a cleanness of delivery and complete recognition of Ibert's extrovert style. Martinon takes second place only because the opening movement is not as chiseled in its contours as it should be. Fiedler's and Ormandy's ideas are almost as excellent; their players better, but both play this graphic conception too straight—a little rakish demeanor is fitting; the French were born with it.

—PC, Désormière, R 19028   —PC, Martinon, L 9269(S)   —BP, Fiedler, V 2084(S)   —PO, Ormandy, CO 5849(S)   —CAO, Slatkin, C 8270   —WI, Swoboda, W 18520   —MGM Chamber Orch., Surinach, MGM 3514.

Divertissement ("Parade")
★★—in "Adventures in Music: Grade 1," N, Mitchell, V 1000(S).

Suite Symphonique "Impressions of Paris"
★★—MGM Chamber Orch., Winograd, MGM 3414.

SOLO INSTRUMENT WITH ORCHESTRA

SOLO SAXOPHONE WITH ORCHESTRA

Concertino da Camera
★★★—LAM, Deffayet (*sax*), Fournet, E 3478.

INSTRUMENTAL

ORGAN

The Little White Donkey from "Histoires"
—in "The Power and the Majesty," Salvador, CO 144.

Trois Pièces
★★★—in "Organ Music by Modern Composers: Vol. 2," Ellsasser, MGM 3585.

PIANO

Histoires (Ten Short Piano Pieces)
★★★—Pressler, MGM 3042.

CHAMBER MUSIC

Entr'acte
★★—in "Duets with the Spanish Guitar," Almeida (*g*), Ruderman (*fl*), C 8406(S).

Jeux—Sonatine for Flute and Piano
★★★—in "Flute Contest Music: Vol. 2," DeLaney (*fl*), Reeves (*p*), LANIER(*no call number*).

"Le Jardinier de Samos"—Prelude to Act Two
Merely a filler on the disk below.
—Urban (*v*), Hubert (*c*), CL 1005.

Trio for Violin, Cello and Harp
Though recorded by a firm no longer in existence, copies can still be purchased in the various outlets that specialize in the unusual, the deleted, and so on. Worth acquiring.
—S. Shulman (*v*), A. Shulman (*c*), Newell (*hp*), PHIL 102.

String Quartet in C
★★★—Parrenin Q, W 18659.

Trois Pièces Brèves
The two French versions cannot compare with those made in America. The latter add strength by way of subtlety, whereas the French play with somewhat astringent tone and almost monotonous straightforwardness. The Philadelphians and New Yorkers reveal the sparkling life of Ibert's wind pieces. Honorable mention belongs to the Chicagoans. The Fairfield group play well, but the engineering is not of the best.
—PW, CO 5093   —in "Woodwind Encores," NYW, EV 6092(S)
—in "French Woodwind Music," NYW, ES 505   —in "Masterworks of Quintet Literature," CSW, AUD 15   —FAI, STRAD 606
—FWQ, LL 50122   —WIQ, A 35079.

VOCAL

VOICE WITH ORCHESTRA

Suite Elizabethaine
★★★—VSO, Loose (*s*), Women's Choir of the Vienna Akademie Kammerchor, Swoboda, W 18520.

LEOŠ JANÁČEK

ORCHESTRAL

The Ballad of Blaník
★—BSP, Bakala, SU 10053.

The Fiddler's Child, Ballad for Orchestra
★★—BSP, Bakala, SU 10053.

Lachian Dances
★★★—BRS, Bakala, AT 122.

Sinfonietta
Bakala's performance is a triumph of understanding. For some reason, Ančerl refuses to accept the pathos of the third section, and this aloofness is unacceptable. But the difficult final (fifth) movement, with its almost outlandishly grotesque scoring, is particularly clear under his baton.
—CZ, Bakala, AT 122   —CZ, Ančerl, PR 166(S)   —PRM, Horenstein, VOX 9710   —RU, Neumann, U 7030.

Taras Bulba, Rhapsody
Both Ančerl (with sharper contrasts) and Horenstein emphasize the sonority scheme. Swoboda underplays this factor, while Kubelik attempts to purify it, and, in so doing, waters it down. The first pair of recordings listed are the most truthful (the Ančerl is available in stereo).
—CZ, Ančerl, PR 166(S) —PRM, Horenstein, VOX 9710 — RP, Kubelik, C 7159 —VSO, Swoboda, W 18069.

STRING ORCHESTRA

Suite for String Orchestra
Both recordings are acceptable; the Supraphon easier to come by.
—Prague Chamber Orch. (*no conductor*), SU 10053 —WI, Swoboda, W 18069.

SOLO INSTRUMENT WITH ORCHESTRA

SOLO PIANO WITH ORCHESTRA

Capriccio
By far the superior release is by the Bostonians, who bring out all the discovery and invention of the composer and play with perfection of ensemble. The MK disk has adumbrated balances, and the microphoning nullifies and distorts some of the scoring. Further, for no apparent reason, the Russians have substituted a trombone for the tenor tuba.

The Boston disk was produced for private distribution in the "Bristol Collectors' Classic Series" (BL-2) sponsored by the Bristol Laboratories, Inc. and available only to the medical profession. It has been announced that Boston Records will shortly release the record for general sale. For that reason it is included here, though without any call number.
—Palenicek (*p*), Korneyev (*fl and pic*), Popov (*tp*), Gevorkyan (*tp*), Bastashov (*tb*), Klyuchinsky (*tb*), Fedorovich (*tb*), Petrov (*tb*), MK 1559 —Boston Brass Ensemble, Hambro (*p*), Pappoutsakis (*fl and pic*), Simon, B.

Concertino for Piano and Chamber Orchestra
The Philadelphians play with much more beauty and sensitivity than the others, but their magnificent resource is too absorbent and professional for Janáček's music; he needs not only strength but clear-cut roughage.

The best conception comes from Klien and his colleagues. The two Westminster releases are by the same group, though designated differently. They play with the tense sound that fits this music. MK's edition is slightly marred by some instrumental slips, as well as scratchy surfaces.

—PRM, Klien (*p*), Hollreiser, VOX 10840(S)   —BE, W 18750
—Holetschek (*p*), Vienna Philharmonic Wind Group, Barylli Q,
W 18173   —Palenicek (*p.*), Abramenkov (*v*), Polees (*v*), Talalyan
(*va*), Tupikin (*cl*), Afanasiev (*hn*), Kurpekov (*bn*), MK 1559
—Firkusny (*p*), Krachmalnick (*v*), Madison (*v*), Lifschey (*va*),
Gigliotti (*cl*), Schoenbach (*bn*), Jones (*hn*), CO 4995.

INSTRUMENTAL

PIANO

In the Threshing House
★★★—in "The Piano Music of Leoš Janáček," Firkusny, CO 4740.

October 1, 1905
★★★—in "The Piano Music of Leoš Janáček," Firkusny, CO 4740.

On the Overgrown Path—Set I
Firkusny brings a special element of contrast and picture painting to
the music. While Hurník plays with sensitivity he tends to stress the
improvisational quality of the suite. Both viewpoints are germane.
—Hurník, SU 307   —in "The Piano Music of Leoš Janáček," Firkusny, CO 4740.

On the Overgrown Path—Set II
★★★—Hurník, SU 307.

VIOLIN

Dumka for Violin and Piano
★★—Barylli (*v*), Holetschek (*p*), W 18750.

CHAMBER MUSIC

Sonata for Violin and Piano
The rhythmic divergences emerge most vividly in the terse dramatic
statements of the Barylli-Holetschek performance. The richness and
polish of the Druian and Simms reading is not so fitting in this instance.
—Barylli (*v*), Holetschek (*p*), W 18750   —Druian (*v*), Simms (*p*),
MY 50090.

String Quartet No. 1
★★★★—Smetana Q, AT 109.

String Quartet No. 2 ("Intimate Letters")
There is no question that the Smetana foursome focuses the heat and
drive of the score into a wonderfully exciting and sensitively dis-

tinguished performance. (The Artia liner notes for this recording
translate the subtitle as "Secret Pages.") The Janáček Quartet plays
exactly, pristinely, and the music's edges become dulled. The Galimir
version does not compare to either of the others.
—Smetana Q, AT 109   —Janáček Q, D 9851   —Galimir Q,
STRAD 619.

Mládí ("Youth")
★★★★—PW, Lester (*b. cl*), CO 4995.

VOCAL

The Diary of One Who Vanished
The Czech language, used in the Artia recording, has a vital rhythm,
while the German, utilized for the Epic disk, is extremely clear.
Despite Häfliger's richer voice, Blachut and the other protagonists in
this unconventional work produce as good a performance.
—Häfliger (*t*), Meyer (*ms*), De Nobel (*p*), three members of the
Netherlands Chamber Choir, E 3121   —Blachut (*t*), Stepanova
(*a*), Palanicek (*p*), Czech Women's Chamber Ensemble, Kuhn
(*choirmaster*), AT 102.

The Diary of One Who Vanished (Excerpts)
★★★—in "The History of Music in Sound: Vol. X," Bielecki (*t*),
Moore (*p*), V 6092.

CHORAL

Elegy on the Death of Daughter Olga
Only the word "Elegy" is denoted as the title of Janáček's piece on this
recording. Thus the personal documentation that caused the music's
composition is lost.
—in "Leoš Janáček: Choral Works," Czechoslovak Radio Chorus,
Zidek (*vocal soloist*), Panenka (*p*), Kasal, SU 10064.

Folk Nocturnes
★★—Czech Singers' Chorus, Hála (*p*), Kühn, SU 475.

Male Voice Choruses
   Oh! The War!
   O Love

Male Voice Folk Choruses
   Our Birch Tree
   The Wreath

Moravian Male Voice Choruses
   Evening Witch
   If You Only Knew
   Parting
★★—in "Leoš Janáček: Choral Works," The "Moravian" Academic Chorale, Veselka, SU 10064.

Songs of Hradčany
★★★—Moravian Women Teachers Chorus, Wysoczanska (*solo voice*), Kašlík (*fl*), Součková (*hp*), Bakala, SU 475.

Three Mixed Choruses
   Autumn Song
   Our Song
   Wild Duck
These beautifully executed pieces together with the "Elegy" (*see above*) form the first side of a disk devoted to twelve choral compositions. However, the record label incorrectly designates this set of three "for male choir," whereas all are scored for mixed voices. It is the second side that is exclusively for male voices.
—in "Leoš Janáček: Choral Works," Czechoslovak Radio Chorus, Kasal, SU 10064.

Truthful Love
★★—in "Leoš Janáček: Choral Works," The "Moravian" Academic Chorale, Veselka, SU 10064.

The Wolf's Footprints
★—Moravian Women Teachers Chorus, Bakalová (*solo voice*), Švábová (*p*), Bakala, SU 475.

CHORAL WITH ORCHESTRA

CANTATA

Amarus, Lyric Cantata for Soli, Mixed Chorus and Orchestra
★★★★—BSP, Žídek, Pokorná, Bauer (*vocalists*), Neumann, SU 10387.

MASS

Slavonic (Glagolitic) *Mass*
Urania's release was on the market a number of years before the same performance was issued by Supraphon. The credits on the for-

432

mer are devoid of the names of the soloists and the orchestra's name is shortened, but the disks are identical.

High praise must be accorded everyone concerned with the presentation. Bakala has his forces keyed to the emotional sincerity that fills the work; the solo voices (with very taxing parts) and chorus, the organist and orchestra are all magnificent.

—BRS, Moravian Mixed Chorus, Michálek (*org*), Domanínská, Juřenová, Válka, Hromádka (*vocalists*), Bakala, SU 251 —BRSO, Moravian Mixed Chorus, Michálek (*org*), Bakala, U 7072.

OPERA

The Cunning Little Vixen
★★★—OCPT, Members of the Jan Kuhn Children's Chorus, Asmus, Belanova, Votava, Halíř, Joran, Vojta, Cadikovicova, Cupalova, Lebedova, Bohmova, Domanínská, Hanzalikova, Prochazkova, Tattermuschova (*vocalists*), Neumann, AT 88B/L.

The Cunning Little Vixen (Finale)
★★—Orch. of the Janáček Theater in Brno, Kroupa (*b*), Domanínská (*s*), Liška, SU 450.

From the House of the Dead
★★—Orch. and Choir of the Netherlands Opera, Jongsma, Scheffer, van Mantgem, van Trirum, Gorin, Holthaus, Taverne, Wozniak, Genemans, van Gent, Borelli, van Woerkom, van de Meent, Reumer, Broecheler, Voogt, Smith (*vocalists*), Krannhals, E 6005.

From the House of the Dead (Excerpts)
Termed "highlights from the opera," this disk presents the introduction, and four sections, two each from the second and third acts. The coverage is approximately half of the opera and offers far more than the usual portions.

—BSP, Chorus of the Janáček Opera in Brno, Ulrych, Soušek, Hrubeš, Jaroš, Jakubík, Placar, Mikulica, Kurfirst, Steinerová, Halíř, Sauer, Bauer, Pelc (*vocalists*), Bakala and Vogel, SU 10095.

Jenůfa
A powerful recording, at times a little too frenzied, but this is a minor dissent to an otherwise outstanding performance.

—OCPT, Cadikovicova (*a*), Blachut (*t*), Zidek (*t*), Krasova (*s*), Jelinkova (*s*), Kalas (*bar*), Jedenactik (*b*), Vesela (*ms*), Musilová (*ms*), Hanzalikova (*ms*), Fidlerova (*s*), Subrtova (*s*), Kourimska (*a*), Vogel, AT 80C/L.

433

Jenůfa (Aria of Kostelnitschka)
★★★—Orch. of the Janáček Theater in Brno, Steinerová (*ms*), Jílek, SU 450.

Jenůfa (Jenůfa's Prayer)
★★★—Prague National Theater Orch., Domanínská (*s*), Sachs, SU 450.

Kata Kabanová
★★★★—OCPT, Kroupa (*b*), Blachut (*t*), Komancova (*cn*), Vich (*t*), Tikalova (*s*), Koci (*t*), Mixova (*ms*), Jedlicka (*bar*), Hlobilova (*ms*), Lemariova (*ms*), Krombholc, AT 85B/L(S).

The Makropulos Affair (Excerpts)
Three portions are presented in this sampler. It is worth listening to, though these snippets give no hint of the opera's story.
  Through the mishaps of translation Supraphon labels this composition "Matter Makropulos." Another title that has been used is "The Makropulos Secret."
—OCPT, Hrnčířová (*s*), Blachut (*t*), Šrubař (*bar*), Asmus (*b*), Musilová (*s*), Vonásek (*t*), Vogel, SU 450.

ANDRÉ JOLIVET

ORCHESTRAL

Suite Française
★—ACC, Jolivet, FCO 724.

Suite Transocéane
★★★—LOU, Whitney, LV 57–2.

CHAMBER ORCHESTRA

Rapsodie à Sept
★—Alès (*v*), Laugerot (*double b*), Boutard (*cl*), Allard (*bn*), Delmotte (*tp*), Suzan (*tb*), Passeronne (*per*), Jolivet, FCO 724.

Suite Delphique
★★★★—Martenot (*om*), Marseau (*fl and pic*), François (*o and Eh*), Boutard (*cl*), Barboteux (*hn*), Coursier (*hn*), Delmotte (*tp*), Galiègue (*tb*), Passerone (*ti*), Dejean and Dillies (*per*), Borot (*hp*), Jolivet, FCO 639.

STRING ORCHESTRA

Andante for Strings
★★—TCE, Bour, W 5239.

SOLO INSTRUMENT WITH ORCHESTRA

CONCERTOS

Concerto for Bassoon, String Orchestra, Harp and Piano
★★★—in "Twentieth-Century Music," Cento Soli Orch., Allard (*bn*), Albert, MG 39(S).

Concerto for Harp and Chamber Orchestra
Laskine's performance is a heady one (the solo demands are of Paganinian order), but her tone is uneven and lacks the percussiveness necessary to explain the music's dimensions.
—TNO, Laskine (*hp*), Jolivet, W 18360.

Concerto for Ondes Martenot and Orchestra
A recording true to every point of measurement and affording a rare opportunity of hearing this special instrument in a solo capacity.
—TNO, Martenot (*om*), Jolivet, W 18360.

Concerto for Piano and Orchestra
The crucifying demands made on the soloist are carried out excellently by Descaves, and the other participants share in the glory. Muddied reproduction at times.
—TCE, Descaves (*p*), Bour, W 5239.

SOLO TRUMPET WITH ORCHESTRA

Concertino for Trumpet, Piano and String Orchestra
(The composition is titled incorrectly as a "Concerto.")
★★★★—TCE, Delmotte (*tp*), Baudo (*p*), Bour, W 5239.

INSTRUMENTAL

PIANO

Chanson Naïves (Excerpts)
Crystal clear playing of these two extracts: "En Regardant les Mouches Voler" and "Chanson pour une Poupée Bretonne."
—in "Musique pour les enfants de Bach à Bartók," Rev, PAT 269.

Mana
★★—in "Musique Française pour Piano," Gobet, VEGA 30–88.

435

CHORAL

Épithalame
★★★★—Ensemble de Madrigal de la Radiodiffusion Française, Mas-michel (*s*), Henry (*s*), Letellier (*s*), Macaux (*ms*), Duché (*cn*), Lanco (*cn*), Gallet (*t*), Husson (*t*), List (*bar*), Abdoum (*bar*), Richez (*b*), Hetzel (*b*), Jolivet, FCO 639.

ZOLTÁN KODÁLY

ORCHESTRAL

Concerto for Orchestra
Kodály's own performance is miles ahead of the older Urania version.
—BUP, Kodály, DG 18687(S)   —DRE, Bongartz, U 7138(S).

Dances of Galanta
Solti gets intense excitement from his players, while Rodzinski has his orchestra shape the phrases in classically restrained fashion, thus adding a great deal of warmth. Decca's number 9870 release is notable for the fact that for once Kodály is not bracketed with Bartók (Liszt is the companion composer). Fricsay considers the dances almost tenderly and they gain much by such underplaying; the sound is excellent but with less depth than in the London and Westminster recordings. Dorati does well, but not his engineers; the sound is not typical of Mercury.
—LPO, Solti, L 709   —PSL, Rodzinski, W 18775   —PSL, Rodzinski, WL 7020   —RIAS, Fricsay, D 9870   —PHO, Dorati, MY 50179(S)   —BM, Perlea, VOX 9500   —BPO, de Sabata, D 9518.

Háry János Suite
Kempe's is undoubtedly the smoothest, most refined, and neatest projection of the suite in a very large catalogue of LP performances.
"Háry János" is not harmed by bright interpretative lighting. Hence, the Dorati and Rodzinski performances are highly recommended. The same goes for Leinsdorf's; a beautifully chiseled affair, with delightful definition of the score's colors.
Solti (on London's label) expands the sonority somewhat in places that should have a lighter touch; the playing is beyond reproach, however, as is Tibor Paul's. Mitropoulos is also good, but beware if you would like to sample a separate movement; the recording is unbanded.

—VPO, Leach (*ci*), Kempe, A 35975(S) —M, Dorati, MY 50132(S) —LPO, Rodzinski, W 18775 —LPO, Rodzinski, WL 7034 —PH, Leinsdorf, C 8508(S) —LPO, Solti, L 9132 — VSO, Paul, E 3752(S) —NY, Mitropoulos, CO 5101 —PH, Schuechter, MGM 3019 —BAV, Solti, D 9518 —CG, van Beinum, E 3290 —NBC Sy. Orch., Toscanini, V 1973 —RIAS, Fricsay, D 9855.

Háry János Suite ("Dance of the Hussars") ("Intermezzo")
★★★—in "A Program of Songs and Dances," Hungarian National Ballet Co., Baross, E 3735.

Háry János Suite ("Entrance of the Emperor and His Court")
★★—in "Adventures in Music: Grade 4, Vol. 2," N, Mitchell, V 1005(S).

Háry János Suite ("Viennese Musical Clock")
Mitchell plays this excerpt acceptably. Though the album in which it is included was prepared for school use, the compendium is extremely worthwhile for the general listener. Dorati's excellent offering is part of a colorful sampling Mercury has made from its inventory of releases.
—in "Music and Plunk, Tinkle, Ting-A-Ling," M, Dorati, MY 50338(S) —in "Adventures in Music: Grade 2," N, Mitchell, V 1001(S).

Marosszék Dances
Rodzinski plays the dances naturally, understands the rhythmic joys to be found in the score; Westminster's sound is lovely. Dorati is neutral, having no special sensitivity for the music. Fricsay seems bored, there isn't any excitement and there should be.
—PSL, Rodzinski, W 18775 —PSL, Rodzinski, WL 7020 — PHO, Dorati, MY 50179(S) —RIAS, Fricsay, D 9773.

Peacock Variations (Variations on a Hungarian Folksong)
Dorati's forces match Kodály's exhilarating, constructivistic expansion of theme with tremendous color and change of pace. Solti's players do not give their all. They perform with *savoir-vivre,* which is far from the pointedness of this work.
—CHI, Dorati, MY 50038 —LPO, Solti, L 1020.

Symphony
★—LOU, Whitney, LV 631.

Theatre Overture
★★—VSO, Swoboda, W 18455.

CHAMBER ORCHESTRA

Summer Evening
Although Winograd's older recording is first-rate and he deserves plaudits for his musicianship, the much better version is led by Kodály. (The release is incorrectly titled "Summer Night," whereas the liner notes properly refer to the work as "Summer Evening.")
—BUP, Kodály, DG 18687(S)   —MGM Orch., Winograd, MGM 3631.

INSTRUMENTAL

CELLO

Sonata for Cello Solo, Op. 8
For unabashed performance glamour plus blazing virtuosity the honors belong to Starker. Nelsova is almost as eloquent and exciting. However, both have edited the music. The former changes many dynamics, refuses to follow the snarling "sul ponticello" indications, and disfigures the metrical definition of the slow movement by clipping many beats. Nelsova does not observe the "sul ponticello" requirement either. Further, she changes double stops, and blithely substitutes *spiccato* for *legato* in wholesale fashion. Both slice 23 measures out of the slow movement. Starker also deletes 54 measures in the finale and Nelsova cuts 57 measures from that section.
—in " 'Round the World with Janos Starker," Starker, PE 1093
—Starker, PE 510   —Starker, A 35627   —Nelsova, L 1252 —
Parisot, CT 569(S).

PIANO

Children's Dances (Nos. 1–5 and 7–12)
★★—Foldes, D 9913.

Marosszék Dances
★★★—Foldes, D 9913.

Seven Piano Pieces, Op. 11
★—Kabos, BK 917.

Seven Piano Pieces, Op. 11 (Nos. 1–3, 5 and 6)
★★★—Foldes, D 9913.

Seven Piano Pieces, Op. 11 (No. 3)
★★★—in "Musique pour les enfants de Bach à Bartók," Rev, PAT 269.

Viennese Musical Clock, Song, and Intermezzo from "Háry János"
★★—Foldes, D 9913.

VIOLIN

Adagio for Violin and Piano
★—in "International-Americana," Kaufman (*v*), Saidenberg (*p*),
CH 58.

Dances from the Village of Kálló
★★★★—in "David Oistrakh Violin Recital," Oistrakh (*v*), Yampolsky (*p*), PR 118.

Three Hungarian Folk Dances for Violin and Piano
Oistrakh's tone is flawless, a gorgeous sound whether heard on Angel
or Monitor.
—in "Oistrakh Encores," Oistrakh (*v*), Yampolsky (*p*), A 35354(S)
—in "Oistrakh Plays from Albéniz to Zarzycki," Oistrakh (*v*), Yampolsky (*p*), MON 2003.

CHAMBER MUSIC

Duo for Violin and Cello, Op. 7
The great instrumentalists that perform for RCA Victor do not fully
confirm the chamber-music spirit of Kodály's duet. There is too much
solo display, especially in Heifetz's playing (string changes on repeated sounds accentuate what should remain subtle), and overemphasis on the native elements. In short, less teeming passion
strengthens this music. Period's release is certainly more to the stylistic point. RCA Victor's sound is, of course, superior.
—in " 'Round the World with Janos Starker," Eidus (*v*), Starker
(*c*), PE 1093   —Eidus (*v*), Starker (*c*), PE 510   —Eidus (*v*),
Starker (*c*), P 720   —Heifetz (*v*), Piatigorsky (*c*), V 2550(S).

Sonata for Cello and Piano, Op. 4
—in " 'Round the World with Janos Starker," Starker (*c*), Herz (*p*),
PE 1093   —Starker (*c*), Herz (*p*), PE 602   —Starker (*c*), Herz
(*p*), PE 720.

Serenade for Two Violins and Viola, Op. 12
★★★—Classic String Trio, CL 1033.

String Quartet No. 1, Op. 2
The Roth foursome do not present high-class quartet playing here.
Their tone is forced, strident in the higher zones, and they are guilty
of intonation lapses.
—Roth Sq, MY 50094.

String Quartet No. 2, Op. 10
A little more polish in the Hollywood reading and better recorded
sound, but this does not mean the Walden's performance is less

439

worthy. Vegh's rendition is satisfactory, but this very old London release has been deleted for many years.
—Hollywood Sq, C 8472(S)   —Walden Q, LYR 22   —Vegh Q, L 865.

VOCAL

Hungarian Folk Music (Excerpts)
Both singers are accomplished vocalists as well as thorough musicians. Chabay offers ten songs, László, six of the collection.
—in "Folk Songs of Hungary: Vol. 2," Chabay (*t*), Kozma (*p*), BK 914   — László (*s*), Hambro (*p*), BK 927.

Recruiting Song
Soldier's Song
★★★—in "Folk Songs of Hungary: Vol. 1," Chabay (*t*), Kozma (*p*), BK 904.

Six Songs, Op. 9 (Excerpts)
The three songs represented here are sung in a pale fashion.
—Batic (*cn*), Leukauf (*p*), N 405.

Twenty Hungarian Folk Songs (in collaboration with Béla Bartók) (Excerpts) (*see also:* Bartók, page 376)
Each recording has a pair of songs from the jointly published collection.
—in "Folk Songs of Hungary: Vol. 1," Chabay (*t*), Kozma (*p*), BK 904   —in "Folk Songs of Hungary: Vol. 2," Chabay (*t*), Kozma (*p*), BK 914.

CHORAL

A Christmas Carol
The contents of the stereophonic album are quite different from the monophonic. Only a piece by Jean Berger ("In a Time of Pestilence") and Kodály's carol are duplicated in the former, which is titled "Concordia Choir in Stereo: Volume 1."
—Concordia Choir, Christiansen, CON 7(S).

Akik Mindig Elkésnek ("Those Who Are Always Late")
Sung with chilling effect. However, the presentation is marred by the fact that although the original text is contained on an inserted page in the record envelope, no translation is offered. Quite odd, since English versions are given of some of the other twenty-one pieces in the album.
—in "Madrigals & Motets," Budapest Madrigal Ensemble, Szekeres, MON 2054(S).

Christmas Dance of the Shepherds
★★—Phila. Oratorio Choir, Boehl (*pic*), Ness, RIT 1001.

Evening
—Texas Tech Choir, Kenney, AU 6224.

Jesus and the Traders
★★★—Thomanerchor Leipzig, Ramin, CAN 640217.

Scenes from the Mátra District (Mátra Pictures) (Excerpts)
Genuinely satisfying conception of genuine music. (Two movements
are performed: "Vidrócki's Hunting," and "The Farewell.")
—San Francisco State College A Cappella Choir, Tegnell, MLR
6997.

Stabat Mater
★★★—in "Madrigals & Motets," Budapest Madrigal Ensemble,
Szekeres, MON 2054(S).

Veni, Veni Emmanuel
★★★—in "Madrigals & Motets," Budapest Madrigal Ensemble,
Szekeres, MON 2054(S).

CHORAL WITH ORCHESTRA

Kálló Double Dance
Very interesting offbeat Hungarian hillbilly music, played and sung
as it should be by those who should know how.
—Orch. and Chorus of the Hungarian State Folk Ensemble, Csenki,
MON 368(S).

Psalmus Hungaricus, Op. 13
In addition to the composer's own direction of his work on Artia,
"Psalmus Hungaricus" is available in three different languages (in
English on the Everest and London labels, in German on Decca, while
Artia employs the original Hungarian). Kodály's own version is quite
disappointing, principally because the tenor soloist is poor.
    Fricsay's viewpoint is splendid. Solti conducts with fervor and
excitement. The Everest performance is uneven, though flawless in
terms of engineering.
—RIAS, Choir of St. Hedwig's Cathedral, RIAS Choir, Häfliger (*t*),
Fricsay, D 9773 —LPO, LPC, McAlpine (*t*), Solti, L 1020 —
LPO, LPC, Nilsson (*t*), Ferencsik, EV 6022(S) —HCO, Budapest
Chorus, Rösler (*t*), Kodály, AT 152.

Te Deum (Budavari Te Deum)
Westminster's recording is far superior in voices, sound, and acoustic
balances than Kodály's presentation.

—VSO, Vienna Chorus, Jurinac (*s*), Wagner (*a*), Christ (*t*), Poell (*b*), Swoboda, W 18544   —HCO, Budapest Chorus, Szecsody (*s*), Tiszay (*a*), Udvardy (*t*), Farago (*b*), Kodály, AT 152.

MASS

Missa Brevis (in Tempore Belli) ("In Time of War")
The Peloquin's is a restrained, yet fairly telling performance, given with organ in place of orchestra. The same instrumental support is used in the other presentation—satisfactory, save for some stridency in the earlier portions.
—Peloquin Chorale, Hokans (*org*), Peloquin, GIA (205)   —Canterbury Choral Society, Dreher (*s*), Terrell (*s*), Boyer (*ms*), Porter (*t*), Shuss (*b. bar*), Lowry (*org*), Walker, CANTERBURY CHORAL SOCIETY 6251.

Missa Brevis (in Tempore Belli) ("In Time of War") ("Gloria")
★★—in "Thirteen Centuries of Christian Choral Art: Vol. 3, 20th Century," Peloquin Chorale, Hokans (*org*), Instrumental Ensemble, Peloquin, GIA 19 (also obtainable as a set with Vol. 1: 8th to 16th Centuries [GIA 17], and Vol. 2: 17th to 19th Centuries [GIA 18]).

OPERA

Háry János
If the auditor wishes to hear Kodály's "Háry János" music he would best choose the "top cream" represented by the orchestral suite. For the complete document, of course, the recording will serve, but without understanding the Hungarian language most of it will be a boring marking of time until some music appears.
—BUP, Chorus of the Hungarian State Opera House, Children's Chorus of the Horváth Mihály tér General School, Palló (*bar*), Tiszay (*ms*), Maleczky (*bar*), Lendvay (*bar*), Báthy (*s*), Sándor (*ms*), Rösler (*t*), Melis (*bar*), Megyaszay, Szönyi, Lux, Molnar, Fekete, Rajner, Ordelt, Berkes, Bako, Bende (*speaking parts*), Ferencsik, Q 1023–5.

The Spinning Room
Since an English translation of the libretto is not furnished, Kodály's nebulous tale is bewildering to the listener. Nevertheless, the music of "The Spinning Room" is a definite contribution; a must for Kodály fans.
—HRS, Chorus of the HRS, Tiszay (*cn*), Palló (*bar*), Uher (*cn*), Udvardy (*t*), Szecsödi (*s*), Rösler (*bar*), Ferencsik, Q 1009–10.

ERNST KRENEK

ORCHESTRAL

Eleven Transparencies
★—LOU, Whitney, LV 56–3.

STRING ORCHESTRA

Music for String Orchestra
—San Francisco Chamber Ensemble, *no conductor indicated,* MLR 7029.

BAND

Drei Lustige Märsche ("Three Merry Marches"), *Op. 44*
A "sleeper" in this collection of wonderful music by Beethoven, Schubert, Johann Strauss, and Berg. The performance is magnificent.
—in "Austrian Classical Marches," Boston Concert Band, Simon, B 411(S).

SOLO INSTRUMENT WITH ORCHESTRA

CONCERTO

Double Concerto for Violin, Piano and Small Orchestra
★★—MGM Orch., A. Ajemian (*v*), M. Ajemian (*p*), Solomon, MGM 3218.

INSTRUMENTAL

ORGAN

Sonata, Op. 92
★★★—Andrews, UNIV 2.

PIANO

Sonata No. 3, Op. 92, No. 4
The way Gould plays this work exemplifies sheer, brilliant artistry. (Long out of print is an old Spa recording [No. 4], with Krenek as the performer, also playing two sets of pieces composed in 1925 and 1946. The sound of the disk is very poor, though the playing is

443

naturally authentic. However, it cannot begin to compare with Gould's graphic conception.)
—Gould, CO 5336.

Sonata No. 4
[*There is some confusion in the releases of this sonata and the fifth sonata* (see below). *MLR-7014 now consists of "Sonata No. 4" and the "Four Bagatelles," Op. 70, though at one time the former work was listed similarly as MLR-7014 but shared a disk with "Sonata No. 5," numbered MLR-7029. This double numbered recording is no longer in the catalogue, although it was sent to the author for review* (*it can still be obtained in some shops*). *MLR-7029 has been revamped to include the fifth sonata plus "Music for String Orchestra," and the "Sonata for Viola and Piano."*

[*The covers and liner notes for MLR-7014 and the old MLR-7014-7029 are very misleading. Both are identical, listing only the fourth sonata. Neither the "Four Bagatelles" in the first instance nor "Sonata No. 5" in the other appears on the covers, or is mentioned in the liner notes. A note about Abramowitsch* (*who plays the fourth sonata*) *is given, but none for Ajemian who partners Krenek in the "Bagatelles," or Zelka who performs the fifth sonata. The only true guide is on the labeling of the recordings. This extremely sloppy presentation continues in the new MLR-7029 release, which has no titles on the cover and is bare of liner notes.*]
The performance of the German-born pianist (now resident in this country) is quite good. Only fair sound, however.
—Abramowitsch, MLR 7014   —Abramowitsch, MLR 7014 (*with MLR 7029*).

Sonata No. 5
See preliminary note to *"Sonata No. 4"* above.
Zelka fulfills all requirements, plus. Her reading deserves strong approbation.
—Zelka, MLR 7029   —Zelka, MLR 7029 (*with MLR 7014*).

PIANO DUET

Four Bagatelles (Sonata) *for Piano, Four Hands, Op. 70*
★—Krenek and Ajemian, MLR 7014.

CHAMBER MUSIC

Sonata for Viola and Piano
The performance (by the team to whom the work was dedicated) is marred by pitiful sound. The sonata was recorded in 1949 on 78 rpm and this is a bald transfer.
—Molnar (*va*), Hohfeld (*p*), MLR 7029.

444

VOCAL

Fiedellieder, Op. 64
★--Batic (*cn*), Leukauf (*p*), N 405.

VOICE WITH INSTRUMENTAL ENSEMBLE
Sestina for Voice and Instrumental Ensemble
★★★—Beardslee (*s*), Instrumental Ensemble, Krenek, E 3509.

CHORAL

Die Jahreszeiten ("The Seasons") (Parts 1 and 2: Spring, Summer), *Op. 35*
—Texas Tech Choir, Kenney, AU 6224.

Five Prayers Over the Pater Noster as Cantus Firmus
★—University Women's Glee Club, Mathis, UI 7.

Lamentatio Jeremiae Prophetae ("Lamentations of Jeremiah"), *Op. 93*
★★★★—N.C.R.V. Vocaal Ensemble Hilversum, Voorberg, BAM 30-1303/04.

Lamentatio Jeremiae Prophetae ("Lamentations of Jeremiah"), *Op. 93* (Excerpts)
Only a portion of the opening part is given, plus the sixth and seventh sections. There are no bands on the disk and with unclear diction and the lack of a text the auditor is at a disadvantage with this truncated representation.
—Choir of the State School for Church Music in Dresden, Flämig, E 3509.

CHORAL WITH ELECTRONIC SOUNDS
Spiritus Intelligentiae Sanctus, Pfingstoratorium für Singstimmen und Elektronische Klänge—1. Abteilung ("Whitsun Oratorio for Voices and Electronic Sounds—1st Section")
[*With exceedingly few exceptions, ten-inch disks of serious music are no longer manufactured in the United States. However, foreign releases in this category offer certain music otherwise unobtainable. One such recording is noted here (another will be found in the chapter dealing with Stockhausen, see page 486, these being the only exemptions to the exclusion of ten-inch recordings from this survey. Both are examples of electronic music, illustrative of the very latest facet in contemporary musical composition.*]
★★★—Möller-Siepermann (*s*), Häusler (*t*), Krenek (*speaker*), Elec-

tronic Realization by WDR (West German Radio), Cologne, DG 16134 (*10 inch disk*).

OPERA

The Bell-Tower
★—MacDonald, Paschke, Capell, Burton, Olson, Levy, Govich, Fricker, Hudson, Joiner, Kent, Webb, Backus, Bing, Lilya, Rowand, Stevenson, Weiss, Orch., Garvey, UI 5.

GIAN FRANCESCO MALIPIERO

ORCHESTRAL

Fantasie di Ogni Giorno ("Fantasies of Every Day")
★★★—LOU, Whitney, LV 545-11.

La Cimarosiana (Cimarosa-Malipiero)
—OROH, Braithwaite, MGM 3333   —OROH, Braithwaite, MGM 3013.

SOLO INSTRUMENT WITH ORCHESTRA

CONCERTOS

Concerto No. 3 for Piano and Orchestra
★★★—LOU, Owen (*p*), Whitney, LV 604.

Violin Concerto
Too many weaknesses to be pardoned. The playing (soloist and orchestra) is only fair, not carefully colored, and the recorded sound is quite selfish about a balanced bass.
—RU, Kirmse (*v*), Kleinert, U 7112.

INSTRUMENTAL

PIANO

Poemi Asolani
★—H. Schnabel, SPA 15.

CHAMBER MUSIC

String Quartet No. 4
★★★—Quartetto Italiano, A 35296.

446

String Quartet No. 7
—Quartetto della Scala, U 7075.

Sonata a Cinque for Flute, Violin, Viola, Cello and Harp
The record is a deleted issue since the Philharmonia firm has gone into oblivion. To find this disk one must scout the byways of the recording world.

Since Malipiero permits an alternate instrumentation (a violin substituting for the flute and a piano for the harp) this has been considered in the compromise setting used for the recording. A violin has replaced the woodwind instrument, but the harp has been retained. There is a little loss of color but not too much to really matter.
—Stuyvesant Sq, Newell (*hp*), PHIL 102.

VOCAL

Tre Poesie di Angelo Poliziano
Sung with charm and delightful warmth. Martino's voice caresses the ear. There is a bit of confusion in reference to the catalogue number of this album. The record label, album spine, and front cover indicate the call number as ML-48. However, the back of the album has the number indicated below, as does *Schwann*.
—in "Splendori della Vocalita' Italiana-Il '900," Martino (*s*), Ghiglia (*p*), VI 20148.

BOHUSLAV MARTINU

ORCHESTRAL

Estampes
★★—LOU, Whitney, LV 596.

Fantaisies Symphoniques (Symphony No. 6)
The sound of the Boston outfit is rich and their playing of the score is magnificent. Though the recorded sound is no cavatina of hi-fi, the Czech version is just as adequate, despite certain shadowy woodwind passages. Ančerl has insight and proper temperament and these suffice for a fine presentation.
—BSO, Munch, V 2083   —CZ, Ančerl, SU 416.

Intermezzo
★★—LOU, Whitney, CO 4859.

Les Fresques de Piero della Francesca (Three Frescoes)
No criticism can be indicated for either recording. However, one must

447

emphasize the warmth of the Czech strings plus Ančerl's cogent regard for detail.
—CZ, Ančerl, AT 135(S)   —RP, Kubelik, C 7159.

Memorial to Lidice
★★★—CZ, Ančerl, SU 416.

The Parables
★★—CZ, Ančerl, SU 18369.

Serenade
★★—WI, Swoboda, W 18079.

CHAMBER ORCHESTRA

Concerto for Two String Orchestras, Piano and Timpani
★★★★—CZ, Sejna, AT 135(S).

Sinfonietta La Jolla for Chamber Orchestra and Piano
★★—Prague Chamber Orch., Sýkora (*p*), (*no conductor*), SU 10135.

Toccata e Due Canzoni
★★—Prague Chamber Orch., (*no conductor*), SU 10135.

STRING ORCHESTRA

Partita (Suite 1)
★★—WI, Swoboda, W 18079.

BAND

Little Suite from "Comedy on a Bridge"
—in "The Golden Wave Band in Concert," Baylor University Golden Wave Band, Moore, WORD 4008.

SOLO INSTRUMENT WITH ORCHESTRA

CONCERTO

Concerto for String Quartet and Orchestra
★★—VOP, Vienna Konzerthaus Q, Swoboda, W 18079.

INSTRUMENTAL

PIANO

Les Ritournelles
★★★—Rosen, EMS 2.

Three Etudes
★★★—Rosen, EMS 2.

Two Polkas
★★★—Rosen, EMS 2.

CHAMBER MUSIC

Duo for Violin and Cello
It will be extremely difficult to obtain this disk, but do try; the performers' artistry is worth any amount of trouble.
—Posselt (*v*), Mayes (*c*), FE 70–203.

Five Madrigal Stanzas for Violin and Piano
★—Michaelian (*v*), Hagopian (*p*), MLR 7068.

Sonata for Flute and Piano
★★★—Le Roy (*fl*), Reeves (*p*), EMS 2.

Sonatina for Clarinet and Piano
★★★—De Peyer (*cl*), Preedy (*p*), LL 50197.

Three Madrigals for Violin and Viola
★★★★—J. Fuchs (*v*), L. Fuchs (*va*), D 8510.

Trio No. 2 in D minor
The Albeneri group presents this music with fetching treatment. All of their viewpoints are stylistically in place; this is, indeed, superb trio playing.
—Albeneri Trio, MG 24(S).

Piano Quartet No. 1
A team of certified chamber music experts join in a performance that shows constant faith with the score, is never concerned with display. In any chamber work that includes the piano, symphonicism is always a danger—no mishap in this case.
—Schneider (*v*), Katims (*va*), Miller (*c*), Horszowski (*p*), CO 5343.

CHORAL

CHORAL WITH ORCHESTRA

CANTATA

Liederstrauss—auf Worte der Volkspoesie ("Bouquet of Songs—on Words of Folk Poetry")
Sung in the Moravian dialect, but this does not limit its appeal. How-

ever, there is more conflict in the title of this record than in the very folksy music. The cover (front and back) is noted as above, whereas its art work bears out the record label: "Ein Blumenstrauss"—translated as "A Bouquet of Flowers." Whatever its name, the composition falls in the cantata medium.

—CZ, Czech Singers' Chorus, Czech Children's Chorus, Domanínská, Červená, Havlák, Mráz (*solists*), Ančerl, SU 445.

MASS

Field Mass, for Male Chorus, Baritone and Orchestra
★★—Soloists of the CZ, Sýkora (*p*), Kampelsheimer (*org*), Chorus of the Vít Nejedlý Army Ensemble, Šrubař (*bar*), Liška, SU 10387.

OLIVIER MESSIAEN

ORCHESTRAL

L'Ascension (Four Symphonic Meditations)
★★—NY, Stokowski, CO 4214.

Turangalîla Symphony
"Turangalîia" is very expensive but the magnificent performance is worth the cost. Véga has outdone itself with this album, the most sumptuous release of its catalogue (and won a coveted Grand Prix du Disque as a result). The luxuriant packaging includes a handsome large-size booklet with plentiful artwork, pictures, essays, and other data.

The symphony occupies four record sides. In addition there is a double-faced ten-inch disk (in French) devoted to Messiaen's work, his objectives, etc., titled "Conversation with Olivier Messiaen," delivered by Claude Samuel.

—Orchestre National de la R. T. F., Y. Loriod (*p*), J. Loriod (*om*), Le Roux, VEGA 35-339/340.

SOLO INSTRUMENT WITH ORCHESTRA

SOLO PIANO WITH ORCHESTRA

Oiseaux Exotiques
★★★—Orch., Loriod (*p*), Albert, W 18746.

450

INSTRUMENTAL

FLUTE

Le Merle Noir for Flute and Piano
The British flutist is competent enough, but cannot compare with the artistry and virtuosity of the Italian. Furthermore, Delta's sound is not very resonant. The Time release titles the work incorrectly in the plural—"Merles Noir."
—Gazzelloni (*fl*), Kontarsky (*p*), TIME 58008(S)   —in "Avant-Garde," Bennett (*fl*), Bradshaw (*p*), DE (18005).

ORGAN

Apparition de l'Eglise Eternelle
★★—in "Organ Music by Modern Composers: Vol. 2," Ellsasser, MGM 3585.

La Nativité du Seigneur (Nine Meditations for Organ)
Since the Allegro firm has long ceased to exist, this recording will not be easy to find. It really cries for re-release, considering the fine sense of continuity that is communicated in Noehren's distinguished performance.
—Noehren, AL 3030.

La Nativité du Seigneur (Nine Meditations for Organ) ("Desseins Eternels")

★★—in "Concert," Marchal, W 18949(S).

La Nativité du Seigneur (Nine Meditations for Organ) ("Dieu Parmi Nous")
From the engineering standpoint, this is one of the most impressive organ recordings ever issued. The blockbusting sound of the disk is made to order for Messiaen's smashing of the dynamic barrier.

Since Noehren's complete essayal of Messiaen's nine-part composition may be extremely difficult to come by, and Marchal's recital is in the deleted category, the listener will probably have to settle for a pair of excerpts—this one and that included in Mercury's album; *see below.*
—Fox, COM 33-11018(S).

La Nativité du Seigneur (Nine Meditations for Organ) ("Les Bergers")
★★★—in "Marcel Dupré at Saint-Suplice: Vol. V," Dupré, MY 50231(S).

451

Le Banquet Céleste
It is not an easy matter to place music of static quality into proper perspective, especially when the texture is thick. All the performers manage to solve this problem, with Watters' rendition a tinge more vivid than the others.
—Watters, CL 1004   —in "Organ Music by Modern Composers: Vol. 1," Ellsasser, MGM 3064   —in "Marcel Dupré at Saint-Suplice: Vol. V," Dupré, MY 50231(S).

Messe de la Pentecôte
★★★—in "French Organ Music: Vol. III," Crozier, KE 2557.

Prière du Christ montant vers son Père from "L'Ascension" (Four Meditations)
Both are impressive performances. However, Watters presents an interesting program of other Messiaen music nicely contrasted by Schoenberg's "Variations on a Recitative," while Owen devotes the balance of his recital to the pre-Haydn school, with the exception of an unimportant item by Vierne.
For some unknown reason both recordings fail to indicate the full title. Classic uses the first three words, while Washington disposes of the matter by "L'Ascension—Méditation Symphonique No. 4."
—Watters, CL 1004   —in "The King of Instruments: Vol. 3," Owen, WA 3.

Transports de joie d'une âme devant la Gloire du Christ que est la sienne from "L'Ascension" (Four Meditations)
(Note: the title is shortened on both record label and liner note.)
★★—Watters, CL 1004.

PIANO

Cantéyodjayâ
★★★★—Loriod, VEGA 30-139.

Vingt Regards sur l'Enfant Jésus
★★★—Loriod, W 18469/70. W 18469 (*Parts 1–12*), W 18470 (*Parts 13–20*).

TWO PIANOS

Visions de l'Amen
★—Loriod and Messiaen, DIAL 8.

DARIUS MILHAUD

ORCHESTRAL

Kentuckiana (Divertissement on Twenty Kentucky Airs)
★★★—LOU, Whitney, CO 4859.

La Muse Ménagère ("The Household Muse")
Played well, produced stupidly. The lack of bands for a fifteen-movement work is irritating, and doesn't help Milhaud's weak handling of programmaticism.
—VPO, Haefner, SPA 12.

Ouverture Méditerranéenne
★★—LOU, Whitney, LV 545-8.

Protée—Symphonic Suite No. 2
—in "Music of France," SF, Monteux, CA 385.
Only in terms of sound does this recording have any deficiencies, because it is a 78-rpm transfer. Monteux's reading will make a listener overlook the second-rate sonics.

Saudades do Brasil
★★★—CAO, Milhaud, C 8358.

Saudades do Brasil ("Copacabana")
★★—in "Adventures in Music: Grade 4, Vol. 2," N, Mitchell, V 1005(S).

Saudades do Brasil ("Laranjeiras")
★★—in "Adventures in Music: Grade 2," N, Mitchell, V 1001(S).

Serenade
★—VSO, Swoboda, W 18717.

Suite from "Maximilien"
★—VSO, Swoboda, W 18717.

Suite Provençale
The Bostonians play with taste and charm. Munch's direction of this suite is the epitome of stylistic correctness. Milhaud's older presentation is lighter in touch but no less enjoyable.
—BSO, Munch, V 2625(S)   —CAO, Milhaud, C 8358.

Symphony No. 1
★★—CBS Orch., Milhaud, CO 4784.

453

Symphony No. 2
Tzipine's recording is magnificent. As noted below Milhaud's symphony can be secured separately but the full package is more than worth the extra cost.
—in "Le Groupe des Six," SDCC, Tzipine, A 3515   —SDCC, Tzipine, A 35118.

Symphony No. 4 ("1848")
★—Vienna Orch., Adler, SPA 57.

CHAMBER ORCHESTRA

The Globetrotter Suite
★★★—Chamber Orch., Milhaud, D 9965.

The Joys of Life (Homage to Watteau)
★★★—Chamber Orch., Milhaud, D 9965.

Three Rag Caprices
★—VSO, Swoboda, W 18717.

STRING ORCHESTRA

Symphony No. 4 for Strings
First-rate playing, though the sound is a little overbearing in the bass zone. (The Siena is a reissue of the Unicorn disk, with a catchall title.)
—in "Concert of Modern Music," Z, Foss, SI 100-2   —Z, Foss, UN 1037.

BAND

Suite Française
★★★★—in "Winds in Hi-Fi," EW, Fennell, MY 50173(S).

Suite Française ("Provence")
★★★★—in "Curtain Up! Fennell and the 'Pops,'" EW, Fennell, MY 50340(S).

SOLO INSTRUMENT WITH ORCHESTRA

CONCERTOS

Concerto for Percussion and Small Orchestra
The sound of the Columbia release is far better than the older Capitol record, but the playing on the last is no less skillful.
—in "Virtuosi di Philadelphia," PO, Ormandy, CO 5129   —in "Percussion!", CAO, Rees (*per*), Slatkin, C 8299.

Concerto No. 1 for Cello and Orchestra
★★★★—PH, Starker (*c*), Susskind, A 35418(S).

Concerto No. 1 for Piano and Orchestra
—PH, Jacquinot (*p*), Fistoulari, MGM 3041.

Concerto No. 2 for Violin and Orchestra
★★★—Members of the LOF, Kaufman (*v*), Milhaud, C 8071.

Concerto No. 4 for Piano and Orchestra
A professionally smooth exposition by the soloist who commissioned
the work.
—LOF, Skolovsky (*p*), Milhaud, CO 4523.

SOLO PIANO WITH ORCHESTRA

Cinq Etudes ("Five Studies") *for Piano and Orchestra*
Regretfully, the polyphonic turbulence of Milhaud's music is frittered
away by a type of stoic frugality.
—VSO, Badura-Skoda (*p*), Swoboda, W 18717.

Le Carnaval d'Aix
Both performances are sparkling ones; better engineering gives preference to the D.G.G. album.
—in "Monte Carlo Concert Gala: Album 2," MCO, Hellfer (*p*),
Frémaux, DG 18654(S)   —PH, Johannesen (*p*), Tzipine, C 7151.

TWO SOLO PIANOS WITH ORCHESTRA

Concertino d'Automne for Two Pianos and Eight Instruments
★★—Ensemble of the LAM, Joy (*p*), Bonneau (*p*), Milhaud,
E 3666(S).

SOLO TROMBONE WITH ORCHESTRA

Concertino d'Hiver for Trombone and String Orchestra
★★★—Ensemble of the LAM, Suzan (*tb*), Milhaud, E 3666(S).

SOLO VIOLA WITH ORCHESTRA

Concertino d'Eté for Viola and Nine Instruments
★★—Ensemble of the LAM, Wallfisch (*va*), Milhaud, E 3666(S).

SOLO VIOLIN WITH ORCHESTRA

Concertino de Printemps for Violin and Chamber Orchestra
Kaufman's and Goldberg's performances are superb from every point
of view.
—Ensemble of the LAM, Goldberg (*v*), Milhaud, E 3666(S)
—Members of the LOF, Kaufman (*v*), Milhaud, C 8071.

455

Cantate de l'Enfant et de la Mère
★★★—M. Milhaud (*diseuse*), Juilliard Sq, Hambro (*p*), Milhaud, CO 4305.

INSTRUMENTAL

HARMONICA

Chanson du Marin
★★★★—in "John Sebastian: A Harmonica Recital," Sebastian (*ha*), Josi (*p*), DG 12015(S).

ORGAN

Pastorale
★★—in "Organ Music by Modern Composers: Vol. 1," Ellsasser, MGM 3064.

PIANO

L'Album de Madame Bovary
★★★—Johannesen, GC 4060(S).

La Muse Ménagère ("The Household Muse")
★★—Milhaud, CO 4305.

Saudades do Brasil
Engdahl plays with warm tone, shapes the rhythms precisely, and recognizes the music's nostalgia. Her performance is aided by excellent reproduction. Skolovsky's conception is bland and colorless. Hearing the entire set is too much of a good thing; a few "saudades" at a time bring greater rewards.
—Engdahl, MGM 3158   —Skolovsky, CO 4523.

Three Rag Caprices
★★★★—in "The Masters Write Jazz," Smit, DOT 3111.

Touches Blanches and Touches Noires ("White Keys" and "Black Keys")
★★—in "Piano Music for Children," Pressler, MGM 3010.

TWO PIANOS

Scaramouche
All the teams play with eloquent spirit and expertise. The ensemble and dynamism of Luboshutz and Nemenoff (on Vanguard) and of the

Romans emphasize the sparkling wit of Milhaud's score. Vanguard, Kapp, and Decca produce good piano sound and that is always doubly welcome.
—in "Two Pianos, Four Hands," Luboshutz and Nemenoff, VG 1096(S)   —J. Roman and Y. Roman, K 9055(S)   —in "Two Piano Recital," Vronsky and Babin, D 9790   —in "Concert for Two Pianos," J. Lang and D. Lang, GC 4070   —in "Piano Bravo!", L. Effenbach and S. Effenbach, OM 1043(S)   —G. Dichler and J. Dichler, SU 10185   —in "Two-Piano Favorites," Luboshutz and Nemenoff, CA 198.

FOUR PIANOS

Brasileira from "Scaramouche"
★★—Original Piano Quartet, D 10047(S).

VIOLIN

Danses de Jacarémirim
★★—Kaufman (*v*), Balsam (*p*), C 8071.

Saudades do Brasil
In the single extract played by Heifetz (*see below*) he is rather nonchalant about Milhaud's wishes, whereas Shapiro maintains artistic faith in every measure of the transcribed set.
—in "Modern Masterpieces for the Violin," Shapiro (*v*), Berkowitz (*p*), VG 1023.

Saudades do Brasil ("Corcovado")
★—in "Encores," Heifetz (*v*), Bay (*p*), V 1166.

Saudades do Brasil ("Corcovado" and "Sumaré")
★★★—in "Virtuoso's Choice," Kogan (*v*), Mitnik (*p*), W 18629.

Saudades do Brasil ("Ipanema")
Highly recommended, especially because the album includes some wonderful short pieces, difficult to hear otherwise (by Achron, Guarnieri, McBride, etc.).
—in "International-America," Kaufman (*v*), Saidenberg (*p*), CH 58.

CHAMBER MUSIC

Sonata No. 2 for Violin and Piano
★★—B. Urban (*v*), V. Urban (*p*), CL 1005.

Sonatine for Flute and Piano
★★★—Caratelli (*fl*), Manley (*p*), N 406.

457

Pastorale for Oboe, Clarinet and Bassoon
★★★—Gomberg (*o*), Shapiro (*cl*), Garfield (*bn*), EMS 6.

Sonata for Two Violins and Piano
★★★★—G. Beal (*v*), W. Beal (*v*), Wingreen (*p*), MON 2008.

Suite (d'après Corrette)
★★★—in "French Moderns," Berkshire Ensemble, UN 1005.

Suite for Violin, Clarinet and Piano
Of the two productions Period's is preferable, being better integrated in ensemble sonics, while Decca's microphoning emphasizes the piano.
—Parrenin (*v*), Delecluze (*cl*), Haas-Hamburger (*p*), PE 563
—Ritter (*v*), Kell (*cl*), Rosen (*p*), D 9740.

Sonata for Flute, Oboe, Clarinet and Piano
This vividly played program has the special virtue of displaying three different aspects of Milhaud's compositions calling for wind instruments (a trio, a quartet, and a quintet; the first and last for winds alone).
—Baron (*fl*), Gomberg (*o*), Shapiro (*cl*), Kaye (*p*), EMS 6.

String Quartet No. 6 in G (Movement Two)
★★★—in "The History of Music in Sound: Vol. X," Juilliard Q, V 6092.

String Quartet No. 12
Consider this presentation exclusively in terms of Milhaud's piece, played expertly and diagnostically. The Debussy quartet that is coupled with it represents a false reading of the score.
★★★—Quartetto Italiano, A 35130.

Divertissement en Trois Parties for Wind Quintet
★—in "Twentieth-Century Music," Ensemble Instrumental à Vent de Paris, MG 39(S).

La Cheminée du Roi René—Suite for Woodwind Quintet
Tops is the golden-toned exposition by the Philadelphians. Vivid portrayals with exhilarating spontaneity are given in the Audiophile, Everest, and EMS releases. However, in the latter case the sound is entirely too close up and extraneous sounds interfere.
—Phila. Woodwind Ensemble, CO 5613(S)   —in "Masterworks of Quintet Literature," CSW, AUD 15   —in "Woodwind Encores," NYW, EV 6092(S)   —NYW, EMS 6   —FAI, STRAD 606 —WIQ, A 35079.

Two Sketches for Woodwind Quintet
The brightest readings come from the New York group and the French team.
—in "French Woodwind Music," NYW, ES 505 —WIQ, A 35079 —NAQ, CL 1003.

VOCAL

Chansons de Ronsard
★—in "A Song Recital," Streich (*s*), Werba (*p*), D 9972.

Poèmes Juifs
★—Kolassi (*ms*), Collard (*p*), L 919.

VOICE WITH ORCHESTRA

Air de Manuela and Berceuse from "Bolivar"
★★★—SDCC, Micheau (*s*), Milhaud, A 35441.

Chansons de Ronsard
★★★★—SDCC, Micheau (*s*), Milhaud, A 35441.

Fontaines et Sources
★★★—SDCC, Micheau (*s*), Milhaud, A 35441.

Les Quatre Eléments
★★★—SDCC, Micheau (*s*), Milhaud, A 35441.

CHORAL

Psalm 121
★★—in "Recital," Pancratius Royal Men's Chorus (Heerlen, Holland) Heijdendael, A 35406.

CHORAL WITH ORCHESTRA

Sabbath Morning Service
★★★—TNO, Choeurs de la Radiodiffusion-Télévision Française, Rehfuss (*bar*), Milhaud, VEGA 30-178.

CANTATA

Cantate Nuptiale
★★—SDCC, Micheau (*s*), Milhaud, A 35441.

Le Retour de l'Enfant Prodigue ("The Return of the Prodigal Child")
★★—Solistes de TNO, Demigny (*bar*), Bacquier (*bar*), Vessières (*b*), Collard (*ms*), Caron (*t*), Milhaud, VEGA 30-284.

459

Les Deux Cités ("The Two Cities")
★★—San Francisco State College A Cappella Choir, Tegnell, MLR 6997.

BALLET

La Création du Monde ("The Creation of the World")
Prêtre and Carewe offer acutely perceptive realizations. Both are purged of fatty symphonicism, whereas Munch lays it on with over-sized virtuosity, bloats the music and blunts its intimacy by employing an augmented string body. Prêtre captures the pungency and swing inherent in the score. Munch is far more sober, shackles the notes with classical demeanor; the jazz quotient is outlined only in the rhythmic patterns, not in the total style. Abravanel's ideas fall between these approaches. They are less square than Munch's interpretation, yet not so punchy as Prêtre's or Carewe's. The Utah conductor's handling of the music is just a bit too antiseptic, one wishes for more grit.

The remaining releases have something special to offer, flawed only by inferior sound. Bernstein shows full understanding with a spirited, stylish reading. Milhaud playing Milhaud cannot be argued. —in "Contemporary Ballets from France," SDCC, Prêtre, A 35932(S) —LSO Chamber Group, Carewe, EV 6017(S) —UT, Abravanel, VG 1090/1(S) —BSO, Munch, V 2625(S) —COL, Bernstein, CO 920 —TCE, Milhaud, LDF (530-300).

Le Boeuf sur le Toit
Both are definitive executions.
—CAO, Golschmann, C 8244 —TCE, Milhaud, LDF (530-300).

Les Rêves de Jacob ("Jacob's Dreams")
★★★—Pierlot (*o*), Gendre (*v*), Lequien (*va*), Lepinte (*c*), Cazauran (*b*), Milhaud, BOI 029.

L'Homme et Son Désir
★★—Ensemble Roger Désormière, Milhaud, BOI 029.

OPERA

Le Pauvre Matelot
The cast does well. However, the orchestral sound is somewhat rough and suffers from rumble.
—Members of TNO, Giraudeau (*t*), Brumaire (*s*), Vessières (*b*), Depraz (*b. bar*), Milhaud, W 11030.

460

Les Choéphores
Bernstein brings clarity to Milhaud's score. His direction is thorough, responsive, and responsible; the result of a composer who is a brilliant conductor and a conductor who understands the purposes of a composer. A spectacular release, marred a bit by having over twenty-two minutes of music on one side and a mere eleven-plus on the other. Decca's older release is, therefore, a better bargain, offering a splendid Honegger companion piece ("Symphony No. 5"). This, too, is a first-rate presentation, only faulted by too prominent microphoning of the narrator. Neither Columbia nor Decca offers a text.
—NY, Schola Cantorum of New York, Zorina (*n*), Boatwright (*bar*), Jordan (*ms*), Babikian (*s*), Bernstein, CO 5796(S) —LAM, Chorale de l'Université, Nollier (*n*), Moizan (*s*), Bouvier (*a*), Rehfuss (*bar*), Markevitch, D 9956.

Les Malheurs d'Orphée
★★★—Members of the TNO, Brumaire (*s*), Collart (*s*), Collard (*ms*), Neuman (*cn*), Demigny (*bar*), Cussac (*bar*), Versoub (*t*), Vessières (*b*), Milhaud, W 11031.

CARL ORFF

ORCHESTRAL

Entrata after William Byrd
★★★—in "Scherchen Conducts Music for Multiple Orchestra," VOP, Scherchen, W 19013(S).

CHORAL

CHORAL WITH INSTRUMENTAL ENSEMBLE

Music for Children ("Das Schulwerk") ("The School Work")
The recordings (selected from the first two of the five volumes comprising the work) are for either listening and/or participating. Naturally, the first should lead almost immediately into the second. Listen in segments; this is not a continuous music drama!

In the case of the German version one can obtain either of the two disks comprising the release; Angel's recording is a boxed totality.
—Chorus of the Children's Opera Group, Chorus of the Bancroft School for Boys, Speech Ensemble from the Italia Conti School, Instrumental Ensemble, Orff, Keetman, Jellinek (*conductors*), A

3582-B   —Chor der Augsburger Singschule, Kinderchor des Trapp'-schen Konservatoriums München, Münchner Chorbuben Kindersprech Chor, Instrumental Ensemble, Keetman and Orff (*conductors*), O (or EL) 80-107/108.

STAGE WORKS

Antigone
★★★★—Members of the BAVR, BRC, Borkh (*s*), Hellmann (*ms*), Alexander (*bar*), Stolze (*t*), Uhl (*t*), Haefliger (*t*), Borg (*b*), Plumächer (*cn*), Engen (*b*), Leitner, DG 18717/19(S).

Antigone (Excerpts)
For some unexplained reason Columbia has designated this album as "Scenes IV and V." Since none of the five acts of "Antigone" contains more than three scenes, the designation is totally misleading. "Scene IV" actually represents the second and third scenes of the third act and the first part of the next act. "Scene V" covers the opening part of the fifth (final) act (the "Chorus of Theban Elders") followed by the three scenes that complete the work.
—Members of the VSO, VOPC, Goltz (*s*), Uhde (*bar*), Greindl (*b*), Roessl-Majdan (*a*), Hollreiser, CO 5038.

Carmina Burana ("Trionfi"—Part 1)
Stokowski's attention to minute dynamic distinctions, his control of pace and timbre and Ormandy's more restrained, but just as forceful consideration make these the preferable recordings. The most precise vocalism is to be found in the Angel release. This is a smooth, well-nigh perfect exposition of the score, beautifully engineered, and with a soprano that is easily the best of the lot, but Angel does not have Stokowski or Ormandy on its side and that tells the tale.
—H, Houston Chorale; Houston Symphony Boy's Choir, Babikian (*s*), Gardner (*bar*), Hager (*t*), Stokowski, C 8470(S)   —PO, Rutgers University Choir, Harsanyi (*s*), Petrak (*t*), Presnell (*bar*), Ormandy, CO 5498(S)   —CR, German Radio Chorus, Geibel (*s*), Cordes (*bar*), Kuén (*t*), Sawallisch, A 35415   —HAR, Hartford Sy. Chorale, Stahlman (*s*), Ferrante (*t*), Meredith (*bar*), Mahler, VG 1007(S)   —BAVR, BRC, Trötschel (*s*), Braun (*bar*), Kuén (*t*), Hoppe (*bar*), Jochum, D 9706   —*the same*, DG 18303   —in "Trionfi," *the same*, DG 18483/85   —CZ, Czech Singers Choir, Subrtova (*s*), Tomanek (*t*), Šrubař (*bar*), Smetáček, PR 161(S).

Catulli Carmina ("Trionfi"—Part 2)
Vox's production of Orff's phonogenic composition has a good tenor, offset by a rather uneven, sometimes squeaky soprano; it has better

diction than the other release. Decca's version (later reissued by Deutsche Grammophon) is much less dynamic than Orff should be; the voices are only fair, and Jochum's control is somewhat lax. Though neither performance exactly follows the letter of Orff's score, the vote is in favor of Vox.

—Kamper, Mrazek, Gielen, Klien (*pianists*), VCO, Roon (*s*), Loeffler (*t*), Hollreiser, VOX 8640 '—Weissenbach, Faith, Karr-Bartoli, Prestl (*pianists*), BRC, Kupper (*s*), Holm (*t*), Jochum, D 9824 —in "Trionfi," ,*the same*, DG 18483/85.

Catulli Carmina ("Odi et Amo" and "Ah Miser Catulle")
This pair of segments consists of the eighth and eleventh sections drawn from "Actus III." (The eighth part is note for note the same as the first, included in the "Songs of Catullus" portion—*see below*.)

In this performance, stylistic identity is good, but dynamic distinctions are lacking. In a word, not enough guts.
—Madrigal Choir of the University of Münster, Kramm, CN (105).

Catulli Carmina ("Praelusio")
A stunning exposition if one merely desires a portion of Orff's hot musical potion. The dynamic strata are so intensely realized that the reading is electrifying.

No mention is made on the record cover of the Orff piece, nor can it be found excerpted in Schwann. These catch-all titles are often perplexing even when they cover a miscellaneous group—when music of major length is included it should be singled out somehow in the heading.
—in "Virtuoso!", Roger Wagner Chorale, C 8431(S).

Catulli Carmina ("Songs of Catullus")
★★★—in "The Branko Krsmanovich Chorus of Yugoslavia at Carnegie Hall," Branko Krsmanovich Chorus, Babich, MON 576(S).

Der Mond ("The Moon")
★★★★—PH, Philharmonia Chorus, Christ (*t*), Schmitt-Walter (*bar*), Graml (*bar*), Kuén (*t*), Lagger (*b*), Peter (*bar*), Hotter (*bar*), Rösner, Holloway, Delcroix, Kurzinger, Harsdorff, Wisheu, Hunkele (*speaking parts*), Sawallisch, A 3567-B/L(S).

Die Bernauerin ("The Bernauer Woman") (Excerpts)
The portions heard here do not contain the arresting choral number that opens the work, descriptive of the charms of Agnes, the leading character of the legend. Otherwise, this recording, *as* a recording, is only interesting in terms of listening to the sound of the Bavarian tongue.
—BAVR, BRC, Gold and Liewehr (*speakers*), Holm (*t*), Leitner,

463

DG 18408   —in "Musica Nova, Zweite Serie: 1958," *the same,*
DG 18404-9.

Die Kluge ("The Story of the King and the Wise Woman")
★★★—PH, Cordes (*bar*), Frick (*b*), Schwarzkopf (*s*), Wieter (*b*),
Christ (*t*), Kusche (*b. bar*), Kuén (*t*), Prey (*bar*), Neidlinger
(*b. bar*), Orff (*speaker*), Sawallische, A 3551-B/L(S).

Trionfo di Afrodite ("Trionfi"—Part 3)
Here, the score is quite often made the point of departure rather
than the point of kinship. Accents and dynamics are baldly passed by
in a performance that can only be given a passing grade—the defini-
tive version is still to be produced.
—BAVR, BRC, Kupper (*s*), Lindermeier (*s*), Wiese-Lange (*s*),
Holm (*t*), Delorko (*t*), Böhme (*b*), Jochum, D 9826   —in
"Trionfi," *the same,* DG 18483/85.

FRANCIS POULENC

ORCHESTRAL

Les Biches—Suite for Orchestra
Prêtre's conception is stylish and quite chic compared to the more
straightforward, older MGM and London recordings.
—in "Contemporary Ballets from France," SDCC, Prêtre, A
35932(S) —LSO, Fistoulari, MGM 3415 —LSO, Fistoulari,
MGM 3098 —SDCC, Désormière, L 624.

CHAMBER ORCHESTRA

Suite Française
★★★—in "Twentieth-Century Music," Ensemble of Soloists, Poulenc,
MG 39(S).

SOLO INSTRUMENT WITH ORCHESTRA

CONCERTOS

*Aubade, a Choreographic Concerto for Piano and Eighteen Instru-
ments*
—Members of the WES, Jacquinot (*p*), Fistoulari, MGM 3415
—Members of the WES, Jacquinot (*p*), Fistoulari, MGM 3069.

Concert Champêtre for Harpsichord (or Piano) *and Orchestra*
Played, in each instance, with technical excellence and musical taste.
The results are stunning.

—SDCC, van de Wiele (*hps*), Prêtre, A 35993(S)   —SDCC, van de Wiele (*hps*), Dervaux, FCO 677.

Concerto for Piano and Orchestra
—PAS, Haas-Hamburger (*p*), Dervaux, PE 563.

Concerto in D minor for Two Pianos and Orchestra
What kind of Poulencian bubbly water do you like? If a brilliant *sec,* then it's Gold and Fizdale; if a mellower vintage, choose Poulenc and Février.
   Whittemore and Lowe are only less compelling because their playing is more athletic than *galant.*
—SDCC, Poulenc (*p*), Février (*p*), Prêtre, A 35993(S)   —SDCC, Poulenc (*p*), Février (*p*), Dervaux, FCO 677   —NY, Gold (*p*), Fizdale (*p*), Bernstein, CO 5792(S)   —PH, Whittemore (*p*), Lowe (*p*), Dervaux, C 8537(S)   —RCA Victor Sy. Orch., Whittemore (*p*), Lowe (*p*), Mitropoulos, V 1048.

Concerto in G minor for Organ, Strings and Timpani
The most dramatic performance is given by Duruflé and Prêtre. The Biggs with Ormandy and Zamkochian with Munch considerations are less dynamic, emphasizing the contrasted timbres of organ and orchestra.
—FRT, Duruflé (*org*), Prêtre, A 35953(S)   —BSO, Zamkochian (*org*), Firth (*ti*), Munch, V 2567(S)   —PO, Biggs (*org*), Ormandy, CO 5798(S)   —COL, Biggs (*org*), Burgin, CO 4329 —HP, Ellsasser (*org*), Winograd, MGM 3361.

NARRATOR AND PIANO

The Story of Babar the Little Elephant
★★—Cumming (*p*), Livesey (*n*), MLR 7053.

INSTRUMENTAL

HORN

Elégie
★★★—in "French Horn Masterpieces: Vol. II," Stagliano (*hn*), Ulanowsky (*p*), B 212(S).

PIANO

Humoresque
Used as a filler in both albums, but unfilling music.
—Johannesen, GC 4042   —Haas-Hamburger, PE 563.

Improvisations, Books I and II
★—Kassman, LYR 61.

Improvisations, Book II
★★★—Johannesen, GC 4042.

Improvisations (No. 5 in A minor)
Of the two pianists concerned, Casadesus has the better insight to this portion.
—in "French Piano Music," J. Casadesus, A 35261 —Haas-Hamburger, PE 563.

Improvisations (No. 7 in C major)
★—Cumming, MLR 7053.

Les Animaux Modelés
★★—Johannesen, GC 4042.

Mélancolie
★★★★—in "French Piano Music," Previn, CO 5746(S).

Mouvements Perpétuels
All of the charming wit of the music is defined in Pennario's playing. In the third piece ("alerte") he does not take off on a tempo caper, whereas Levant does and thereby spoils an otherwise good performance. Maclean realizes the irony of the score, but fails to project the intimacy necessary for the music's warmth. Cumming does a little better, but his tone has little depth and some of the bass lines are mechanical. The surprise is Poulenc's unbalanced reading; it's a jumble and has value only in the historical sense.
—in "Pennario Plays," Pennario, C 8469(S) —in "Levant's Favorites," Levant, CO 1134 —Cumming, MLR 7053 —Maclean, MLR 7082 —Poulenc, CO 4399.

Mouvements Perpétuels (No. 1)
Irresponsible production annoyingly spoils a good project in this instance. It remains to say that Martin's playing is excellent and her performance suggestions have real meaning.
—in "Fifty Years of French Music: Vol. 2," Martin, ED 5008.

Nocturne No. 4 in C minor (Bal Fantôme)
★★★—in "Piano Recital Andor Foldes," Foldes, DG 19099(S).

Nocturne No. 6 in D major
★★—Poulenc, CO 4399.

Novelette in C major
★—Cumming, MLR 7053.

466

Pastourelle from the Ballet "L'Eventail de Jeanne"
A delightful execution by both pianists. In terms of reproduction, Columbia's harsh piano tone makes its disk a poor second. (In the Levant album neither record label nor liner notes indicate the source of the "Pastourelle," leading one to believe it is one of the composer's miscellaneous piano pieces.)
—in "Famous Classics for the Piano," Lympany, A 35995(S)   —in "Levant's Favorites," Levant, CO 1134.

Presto in B flat
★★★★—in "French Piano Music," Previn, CO 5746(S).

Seven Pieces for the Piano
Under this devised title, Cumming has grouped the seventh of the dozen "Improvisations," a "Novelette," the "Pastorale" and "Toccata" from the "Trois Pièces," and the complete "Mouvements Perpétuels." (His performances are considered under the titles of the compositions concerned.)
—Cumming, MLR 7053.

Suite Française
Previn's portrayal is very proper to this bright-eyed music. However, Johannesen's all-Poulenc program (distinctively presented) cannot be dismissed. And, even with many reservations in regard to his interpretation of the "Mouvements Perpétuels," one cannot bypass the significance of Poulenc playing his own compositions and those of Satie. For those of affluence the advice is to own all three disks.
—in "French Piano Music," Previn, CO 5746(S)   —Johannesen, GC 4042   —Poulenc, CO 4399.

Three Pieces
Like the "Seven Pieces for the Piano," this coined identification embraces a combination of isolated pieces—"Humoresque," the fifth of the "Improvisations," and the "Valse in C." (Consideration of the recording will be found under each of these titles.)
—Haas-Hamburger, PE 563.

Trois Pièces
★★★★—in "French Piano Music," Previn, CO 5746(S).

Trois Pièces ("Pastorale" and "Toccata")
★—Cumming, MLR 7053.

Valse in C from "Album des Six"
The woolly sound of Period's release interferes with the brightness of Poulenc's gay piece.
—Johannesen, GC 4042   —Haas-Hamburger, PE 563.

Villageoises
★★★★—Johannesen, GC 4042.

PIANO DUET

Sonata
Hambro and Zayde toss off Poulenc's piece with brilliance and impeccable style. In contrast, the Lang sisters miss all the subtlety of the music and confuse Poulenc's bubbling spirit with an invitation to play loudly.

Poulenc's four-handed "Sonata" (composed in 1918) must not be confused with his "Sonata" for two pianos (composed in 1953) since both teams play the duet on two pianos (it does not change matters whatsoever, merely gives them more performing space). Doubtless this is the reason why the Schwann catalogue errs and lists this early composition as the later two-piano "Sonata."
—Hambro and Zayde, COM 11013(S)   —in "Concert for Two Pianos," J. Lang and D. Lang, GC 4070.

TWO PIANOS

Sonata
★★★—in "The Art of Francis Poulenc," Gold and Fizdale, CO 5918
(S)   —Gold and Fizdale, CO 5068.

CHAMBER MUSIC

Sonata for Flute and Piano
★★★—Pellerite (*fl*), Miller (*p*), GC 7010.

Sonata (To the Memory of García Lorca) *for Violin and Piano*
★—Kaufman (*v*), Balsam (*p*), C 8063.

Sonata for Horn, Trumpet and Trombone
★★★—Glantz (*tp*), Pulis (*tb*), Berv (*hn*), STRAD 605.

Trio for Oboe, Bassoon and Piano
★★★—in "French Moderns," Berkshire Ensemble, Zighera (*p*), UN 1005.

Sextet for Piano, Flute, Oboe, Clarinet, Bassoon and Horn
The Philadelphians ("ensemble" or "quintet," it's the same group), give a vivid performance. The New Yorkers play artistically, but their recording (issued by different firms) does not have the brightness (either instrumental or engineering) of the Columbia product. Incidentally, watch out—the labeling on Concert-Disc's review copy was reversed.

468

—Poulenc (*p*), Phila. Woodwind Ensemble, CO 5613(S)   —in "The Art of Francis Poulenc," Poulenc (*p*), PW, CO 5918(S) —Glazer (*p*), NYW, CD 1221(S)   —*the same,* EV 6081(S) —Lurie (*p*), FA, C 8258   —Français (*p*), WIQ, A 35133.

VOCAL

Air Vif
★★★—in "A French Song Recital," Tourel (*ms*), Reeves (*p*), CO 4158.

Attributs
★★—in "The Artistry of Theodor Uppman," Uppman (*bar*), Rogers (*p*), IN 0001.

Banalités
Both recordings present the leading interpreter of Poulenc's songs, with the composer at the piano. Their many joint recitals were memorable events, representing the peak of artistic collaboration between a vocalist and a contemporary composer.
—in "Francis Poulenc: Mélodies," Bernac (*bar*), Poulenc (*p*), VEGA 30–293   —Bernac (*bar*), Poulenc (*p*), CO 4333.

Banalités ("Hotel")
Farrell scales her voice with skill and sings Poulenc's quiet vocal poem with sensitive artistry. She is matched by Tourel's keen musicianship. Swarthout is smooth, but gives less evidence of understanding Poulenc's aesthetic objective.
—in "An Eileen Farrell Recital," Farrell (*s*), Trovillo (*p*), CO 5484(S)   —in "The Art of Francis Poulenc," Tourel (*ms*), Bernstein (*p*), CO 5918(S)   —in "French Songs," Swarthout (*ms*), Trovillo (*p*), V 1793.

Banalités ("Voyage à Paris")
Because of her insight, Tourel's interpretation is the most distinctive of the three available.
—in "The Art of Francis Poulenc," Tourel (*ms*), Bernstein (*p*), CO 5918(S)   —in "A French Song Recital," Tourel (*ms*), Reeves (*p*), CO 4158   —in "An Eileen Farrell Recital," Farrell (*s*), Trovillo (*p*), CO 5484(S)   —in "French Songs," Swarthout (*ms*), Trovillo (*p*), V 1793.

"C" from "Deux Poèmes"
Bernac's performance is historically important (he gave the première with Poulenc, and is admittedly the perfect Poulenc singer); Farrell's

469

version is an exceptional example of vocalism, and constitutes an ideal interpretation, richer and more effective than Tourel's.
—in "Critic's Choice," Bernac (*bar*), V 1156   —in "An Eileen Farrell Recital," Farrell (*s*), Trovillo (*p*), CO 5484(S)   —in "The Art of Francis Poulenc," Tourel (*ms*), Bernstein (*p*), CO 5918(S).

Calligrammes
★★—in "Francis Poulenc: Mélodies," Bernac (*bar*), Poulenc (*p*), VEGA 30–293.

Ce Doux Petit Visage
★★—in "A Program of Song," Price (*s*), Garvey (*p*), V 2279(S).

Chanson à Boire and La Belle Jeunesse from "Chansons Gaillards"
★★—in "The Artistry of Theodor Uppman," Uppman (*bar*), Rogers (*p*), IN 0001.

Chansons Villageoises
★★★—Bernac (*bar*), Poulenc (*p*), CO 4333.

Fiançailles pour Rire
★★★—in "Gloria Davy Concert Recital," Davy (*s*), Favaretto (*p*), L 5395.

Fiançailles pour Rire ("Fleurs")
According to Poulenc's directions, "Fleurs" is to be performed "luminously." Farrell's singing follows this instruction, avoiding any exaggeration. However, Mr. Trovillo's inflexibility mars his piano accompaniment.
—in "An Eileen Farrell Recital," Farrell (*s*), Trovillo (*p*), CO 5484(S).

Fiançailles pour Rire ("Violon")
★★★—in "A French-Italian Program," Tourel (*ms*), Ulanowsky (*p*), D 10013(S).

Le Travail du Peintre
★★★—in "Francis Poulenc: Mélodies," Bernac (*bar*), Poulenc (*p*), VEGA 30–293.

Les Chemins d'Amour
★★—in "French Songs," Swarthout (*ms*), Trovillo (*p*), V 1793.

Main Dominée par le Coeur
★★—in "A Program of Song," Price (*s*), Garvey (*p*), V 2279(S).

Miroirs Brûlants
★★—in "A Program of Song," Price (*s*), Garvey (*p*), V 2279(S).

470

Reine des Mouettes
★★—in "An Eileen Farrell Recital," Farrell (*s*), Trovillo (*p*), CO 5484(S).

Tel Jour Telle Nuit
★★★—in "Francis Poulenc: Mélodies," Bernac (*bar*), Poulenc (*p*), VEGA 30–293.

CHORAL

Litanies à la Vierge Noire
The choice depends on a listener's preference for either children's or women's voices. Poulenc's score is effective both ways. The performances listed are excellent (the French youngsters are a bit more appealing) and offer realistic sound.
—Maîtrise d'Enfants, Roget (*org*), Jouineau, PAT 247   — Peloquin Chorale, Hokans (*org*), Peloquin, GIA (205).

O Magnum Mysterium from "Quatre Motets pour le Temps de Noël"
("Four Christmas Motets")
—in "Christmas Music at Stanford," Stanford University Choir, Schmidt, MLR 7069.

Tenebrae Factae Sunt from "Quatre Motets pour un Temps de Pénitence" ("Four Penitential Motets")
A lightness in the lower voices harms a performance which is otherwise of quality. (Watch for incorrect labeling: the Poulenc, indicated as band one on side one, actually occupies the second band.)
—in "Sing Unto the Lord," Walter Ehret Chorale, Ehret, GC 4032(S).

Videntes Stellam from "Quatre Motets pour le Temps de Noël" ("Four Christmas Motets")
In the first-listed instance the singing is beautifully styled, in the other it is somewhat erratic (the Music Library recording was made during a concert).
—in "Thirteen Centuries of Christian Choral Art; Vol. 3: 20th Century," Peloquin Chorale, Peloquin, GIA 19 (also obtainable as a set with Vol. 1: 8th to 16th Centuries [GIA 17] and Vol. 2: 17th to 19th Centuries [GIA 18])   —in "Choral and Organ Music," Stanford University Choir, Schmidt, MLR 6995/6.

Vinea Mea Electa from "Quatre Motets pour un Temps de Pénitence" ("Four Penitential Motets")
★★★—Concordia Choir, Christiansen, CON 2.

471

CHORAL WITH ORCHESTRA

Gloria in G major
★★★★—FRT, French National Radio-Television Chorus, Carteri (*s*),
Prêtre, A 35953(S).

CANTATA

Le Bal Masqué
There is no arguing against Bernac's abilities and the better sound of
Westminster compared to the older Esoteric disk. However, Galjour
and Fendler are keen diagnostic artists and correctly consider the
music as a nonet rather than a vocal vehicle with accompaniment. The
results are most effective.
—Chamber Orch., Galjour (*bar*), Fendler, ES 518   —Instrumental
Ensemble of Members of TNO, Bernac (*bar*), Poulenc (*p*), Frémaux,
W 18422.

Sécheresses
Two versions have been issued by Angel. One is in a two-record set
which includes music by Poulenc's colleagues in the days of "Les
Six," plus an introduction spoken by Jean Cocteau. (The release is
beautifully packaged in the Soria specialty fashion.) The other is a
single record from the set, covering four of the six compositions contained therein. Either way, it's a French musical feast.
—in "Le Groupe des Six," SDCC, Chorale Elisabeth Brasseur,
Tzipine, A 3515   —SDCC, Chorale Elisabeth Brasseur, Tzipine,
A 35117.

ORATORIO

Stabat Mater
★★★—ACC, Chorale de l'Alauda, Brumaire (*s*), Frémaux, W 18422.

MASS

Mass in G major
★—Robert Shaw Chorale, Fogelson (*s*), Metz (*cn*), Leadwick (*t*),
Shaw, V 1088.

OPERA

La Voix Humaine
★★★★—TNOC, Duval (*s*), Prêtre, V 2385(S).

Les Dialogues des Carmélites
★★—TNO, Chorus of the Théatre National de l'Opéra de Paris,
Duval (*s*), Scharley (*ms*), Crespin (*s*), Gorr (*s*), Berton, Fourrier

(*ms*), Desmoutiers (*ms*), Finel (*t*), Rialland (*t*), Romagnoni (*t*), Bianco (*bar*), Forel (*bar*), Conti (*bar*), Depraz (*b*), Mars (*b*), Charles-Paul (*b*), Dervaux, A 3585 C/L.

Les Mamelles de Tirésias
(The original release by Pathé-Marconi is still in the catalogues; the Angel duplicate, made for American release, is not. Nevertheless, copies of the latter are still available in a number of stores.)
★★★★—TNOC, Chorus of the Paris Opéra-Comique, Duval (*s*), Legouhy (*ms*), Giraudeau (*t*), Rallier (*t*), Leprin (*t*), Jeantet (*bar*), Hivert (*bar*), Rousseau (*b*), Thirache (*b*), Jullia (*b*), Cluytens, A 35090 —*the same,* PAT 230.

ALBERT ROUSSEL

ORCHESTRAL

Bacchus et Ariane, Suites Nos. 1 and 2, Op. 43
Martinon's recording is the only one extant covering both suites, important because of the rareness of hearing a performance of the first suite (with some cuts). For a more virtuoso reading of the second suite, *see below.*
—LAM, Martinon, E 3165.

Bacchus et Ariane, Suite No. 2, Op. 43
For Munch, the word is superb, plus impressive recorded sonics. For Markevitch, wonderful response and conductorial rapport in an electrifying, mercurial rendition. Up to the final section, Ormandy's version (which has some deletions) is rather bland. He then sets the score on fire, but it's too late to cancel the neutrally cool effect of the first two-thirds of the performance. For Rucht, the rapport is "professional,"—only faint condemnation.
—in "The Ballet," BSO, Munch, V 6113 —LAM, Markevitch, DG 12040(S) —PO, Ormandy, CO 5667(S) —BR, Rucht, U 7037.

Concerto for Small Orchestra, Op. 34
★★★★—LAM, Sacher, E 3129.

Petite Suite for Orchestra, Op. 39
Epic's version is played with proper classical registration; a black and white scheme is contrasted and no lushness permitted. Ansermet's is just as good, but may not be readily available.
—LAM, Sacher, E 3129 —SR, Ansermet, L 1179.

Suite in F, Op. 33
Paray allows the sonorous brilliance to blend the contrapuntalism, rather than permit its voices their individuality. Tzipine's old recording has only superficial identification with what Roussel has written.
—DET, Paray, MY 50145   —LAM, Tzipine, C 8104.

Symphony No. 3 in G minor, Op. 42
Ansermet's performance is not clear enough in the first movement, nor is he too careful a judge of line and climax in the slow movement; thereafter he improves. But his is thrice as good as the Urania entry, which is loud, brassy, and uncompelling.
—SR, Ansermet, L 1495   —Leipzig Radio Orch., Borsamsky, U 7037.

Symphony No. 4 in A major, Op. 53
Ansermet's performance (similar to that of the third symphony, with which the work is paired) is short of his usual ability to shape a composition properly. Tzipine's impressive reading is superior.
—LAM, Tzipine, C 8104   —SR, Ansermet, L 1495.

Chamber Orchestra

Le Marchand de Sable qui Passe ("The Sandman"), *Op. 13*
★★★—PP, Leibowitz, ES 511.

String Orchestra

Sinfonietta, Op. 52
★—LAM, Sacher, E 3129.

SOLO INSTRUMENT WITH ORCHESTRA

Concerto

Concerto for Piano and Orchestra, Op. 36
Bravo to both soloists, but a bigger one to Omega for fine stereophonic engineering, with sensitive directionality and good depth.
—Cento Soli Orch. of Paris, Helffer (*p*), Baudo, OM (15) — LAM, Gousseau (*p*), Sacher, E 3129.

INSTRUMENTAL

Guitar

Segovia, Op. 29
Both Segovia and Bream present ideal readings.
—in "Music for the Guitar," Segovia, D 10046(S)   —in "Segovia

Golden Jubilee," Segovia, D 148 —in "The Art of Julian Bream," Bream, V 2448(S).

HARP

Impromptu, Op. 21
(This writer's copy had Roussel on the "B" side, though listed on the reverse.)
★★★—in "Contemporary Harp Music," Zabaleta, CT 523.

PIANO

Sonatine, Op. 16
Previn performs in a distinguished manner. Petit is efficient, but her interpretation lacks shading.
—in "French Piano Music," Previn, CO 5746(S) —Petit, LL 50221(S).

Suite pour Piano, Op. 14
★★—Petit, LL 50221(S).

Trois Pièces, Op. 49
Played by Previn with a charming, unstudied air that invests the music with proper urbanity. Played by Petit nicely and neatly, though much more seriously.
—in "French Piano Music," Previn, CO 5746(S) —Petit, LL 50221(S).

CHAMBER MUSIC

Trio for Flute, Viola and Cello, Op. 40
The Decca group creates a beautiful coloristic synthesis in Roussel's trio, whereas the Bostonians are more soloistic. There is little difference in the long run.
—Baker (*fl*), L. Fuchs (*va*), H. Fuchs (*c*), D 9777 —Dwyer (*fl*), de Pasquale (*va*), Mayes (*c*), B 208.

Trio for Violin, Viola and Cello, Op. 58 (First Movement)
Unfortunately only one-third of the work has been recorded, and that in a symposium dealing with contemporary trends. It is played well.
—in "The History of Music in Sound: Vol. X," London String Trio, V 6092.

String Quartet in D major, Op. 45
★★★★—Parrenin Q, W 18659.

Serenade for Flute, Violin, Viola, Cello and Harp, Op. 30
★★★—Melos Ensemble, Ellis (*hp*), LL 50217(S).

BALLET

Le Festin de l'Araignée ("The Spider's Feast"), *Op. 17*
Ansermet tends to ponderosity, though he does bring out many fine points lacking in the other renditions. Exquisite balance and a highly polished projection of the composer's evocative ideas mark the Paray version, and almost as good, though more direct and of lesser subtlety is Epic's release. Leibowitz's interpretation is a marvel of detail and color, and ranks as one of the best.
—DET, Paray, MY 14036(S)   —DET, Paray, MY 50035   —in "French Orchestral Music," LAM, Martinon, E 3058   —PP, Leibowitz, ES 511   —SR, Ansermet, L 1179   —Cento Soli Orch. of Paris, Albert, OM (15).

ARNOLD SCHOENBERG

ORCHESTRAL

Begleitungsmusik zu einer Lichtspielszene ("Accompaniment to a Cinema Scene"), *Op. 34*
★★★—COL, Craft, CO 5616(S).

Choral Prelude—"Komm, Gott, Schöpfer, Heiliger Geist" ("Come, God, Creator, Holy Ghost") (Bach-Schoenberg)
Choral Prelude—"Schmücke Dich, O liebe Seele" ("Deck Thyself, Bright Soul") (Bach-Schoenberg)
★★★—in "J. S. Bach: Orchestral Transcriptions," UT, Abravanel, VG 1092(S).

Five Pieces for Orchestra, Op. 16
Kubelik heeds the score, but the sound is not Mercury's best. Craft's version lacks string body and healthy sound. Further, he tends to emphasize points in the score when he should not.
—CHI, Kubelik, MY 50024   —CHI, Kubelik, MY 50026 — COL, Craft, CO 5428(S).

Pelleas und Melisande, Op. 5
★★★—in "The Music of Arnold Schoenberg: Vol. 2," CBC, Craft, CO 294(S).

Prelude and Fugue in E flat major ("St. Anne") *for Organ* (Bach-Schoenberg)
★★★—in "J. S. Bach: Orchestral Transcriptions," UT, Abravanel, VG 1092(S).

Variations for Orchestra, Op. 31
Much more is demanded than we are given in these performances. In both cases the flattening out of dynamic levels neutralizes and discolors the textures. Yet the unidentified orchestra (undernourished in the string section) which Craft directs does exceedingly well. In terms of smoothness it is a shade or two better than the Canadian group.
—Orch., Craft, CO 5244 —in "The Music of Arnold Schoenberg: Vol. 2," CBC, Craft, CO 294(S).

CHAMBER ORCHESTRA

Kammersymphonie for 15 Solo Instruments ("Chamber Symphony"), *Op. 9*
The report on the recording is one of dissent. There are departures from the score, in terms of agogic determination, accentuation, and above all, tempi.
—SUD, Horenstein, VOX 10460.

Second Chamber Symphony, Op. 38
★—VSO, Häfner, CO 4664.

Three Little Orchestra Pieces
★★★—in "The Music of Arnold Schoenberg: Vol. 2," CBC, Craft, CO 294(S).

STRING ORCHESTRA

Verklärte Nacht ("Transfigured Night"), *Op. 4*
The majority of the recordings listed are worthwhile. One especially could have been noteworthy (Kletzki's), except that it is blemished by editorial blue-penciling that gives us less than Schoenberg gave.

Winograd plays the work almost coolly, yet there is a chamber-music hand holding the baton and the results are musical and quite fitting. Ormandy has a tremendous body of string players and it shows in his rather poetic (orchestral *not* chamber) style. The better sound of Columbia's disk gives its release the nod over the MGM issue.

The Stokowski recordings were made almost a dozen years apart. Time has not cooled Stoky's performance; it is still as hot as Hades. The newer performance on Capitol is clear, to be sure, almost of chamber-music definition, but the damning result of moderation is fatal.
—PO, Ormandy, CO 4316 —MGM Orch., Winograd, MGM 3630
—S, Stokowski, V 2117 —S, Stokowski, V 1739 —S, Stokowski, C 8433 —in "The Music of Arnold Schoenberg: Vol. 2," CBC, Craft, CO 294(S) —Strings of the NY, Mitropoulos, CO 5285(S)
—SUD, Horenstein, VOX 10460(S) —IP, Kletzki, A 3526B.

BAND

Theme and Variations, Op. 43a
★★★★—EW, Fennell, MY 50143(S).

SOLO INSTRUMENT WITH ORCHESTRA

CONCERTOS

Concerto for Piano and Orchestra, Op. 42
Of these three performances the vote goes to Gould and Craft, who produce a reading of clarity and marvelous insight. As for the Vox and Period productions, the former is one of fidelity, the other merely of identity.
—CBC, Gould (*p*), Craft, CO 5739(S)   —SUD, Brendel (*p*), Gielen, VOX 10530   —ORS, Helffer (*p*), Leibowitz, PE 568.

Concerto for Violin and Orchestra, Op. 36
Marschner has a rounder tone, a warmer insistence than the others. Baker plays with such ease as to belie the horrendous difficulties found in every measure. A feeling of resistance in the solo voice would better define the repercussiveness of the musical material. Krasner performs with force and informative power, stressing the outgo of Schoenberg's musical prosody. This gives almost ugly (but correct) sounds and throws harshness into relief. Choice of performance? The answer to that dilemma is a well-lined purse.
—SUD, Marschner (*v*), Gielen, VOX 10530   —in "The Music of Arnold Schoenberg: Vol. 1," CBC, Baker (*v*), Craft, CO 279(S) —NY, Krasner (*v*), Mitropoulos, CO 4857.

INSTRUMENTAL

ORGAN

Variations on a Recitative, Op. 40
Watters' rendition is in no way as clear and as pronounced as that by his female counterpart.
—Mason, ES 507   —Watters, CL 1004.

PIANO

Five Piano Pieces, Op. 23
Expert musicians. Steuermann's execution is particularly good, especially in matters of phrasing and tonal quality.
—in "Schoenberg: Complete Piano Music," Steuermann, CO 5216
—in "Das Gesamte Klavierwerk," Kraus, BAM 30-1503.

Piano Piece, Op. 33a
Piano Piece, Op. 33b
Rosen shows superb insight in his performance of these pieces, considering them with passionate concern. Steuermann is no less expressive, delineating the melodic aspects to an amazing degree. On the other hand, both Kraus and Stein play with hard tone and the *cantabile* quality is rather dormant.
—Rosen, E 3792(S) —in "Schoenberg: Complete Piano Music," Steuermann, CO 5216 —in "Das Gesamte Klavierwerk," Kraus, BAM 30-1503 —Stein, CO 5099.

Six Little Piano Pieces, Op. 19
The pale abstraction of Kraus's interpretation cannot compare with Steuermann's depth of understanding.
—in "Schoenberg: Complete Piano Music," Steuermann, CO 5216
—in "Das Gesamte Klavierwerk," Kraus, BAM 30-1503.

Suite for Piano, Op. 25
Rosen's performance is a triumph, rich with transparent detail. A much more aloof view is taken by Field in underlining the formal content. In comparison, Steuermann coldly displays Schoenberg's transmutation of eighteenth-century dance movements. So does Miss Kraus. She is too rigid, which Schoenberg is not.
—Rosen, E 3792(S) —Field, PE 568 —in "Schoenberg: Complete Piano Music," Steuermann, CO 5216 —in "Das Gesamte Klavierwerk," Kraus, BAM 30-1503.

Three Piano Pieces, Op. 11
Gould's playing is extremely clear. He fulfills the function of each piece so that it is an entity. Steuermann and Kraus invoke more lights and shadows, attending to the minute instructions that swamp the music. Either of their performances is an artistic victory. The other pianist's tone makes the music angular, causing a stylistic anachronism.
—in "Schoenberg: Complete Piano Music," Steuermann, CO 5216
—in "Das Gesamte Klavierwerk," Kraus, BAM 30-1503 —Gould, CO 5336 —Field, PE 568.

VIOLIN

Phantasy for Violin with Piano Accompaniment, Op. 47
★★—in "The Violin: Vol. 4," Bress (*v*), Reiner (*p*), FW 3354.

CHAMBER MUSIC

Canon for String Quartet
★★—Wade (*v*), Sushel (*v*), Figelski (*va*), Sargeant (*c*), CO 5099.

479

String Quartet No. 1 in D minor, Op. 7
★★★★—Juilliard Sq, CO 4735 —in "The Complete String Quartets of Arnold Schönberg," Juilliard Sq, CO 188.

String Quartet No. 2 in F sharp minor (with Soprano Voice in Movements 3 and 4), *Op. 10*
The Ramor group's reading can in no way compare with the deeply realized, significant performance given by the Juilliard foursome.
—Juilliard Sq, Graf (*s*), CO 4736 —in "The Complete String Quartets of Arnold Schönberg," Juilliard Sq, Graf (*s*), CO 188
—Ramor Q, Escribano (*s*), VOX 730(S).

String Quartet No. 2 in F sharp minor, Op. 10 (Movement One)
★★—in "The History of Music in Sound: Vol. X," Koeckert Q, V 6092.

String Quartet No. 3, Op. 30
★★★—Juilliard Sq, CO 4736 —in "The Complete String Quartets of Arnold Schönberg," Juilliard Sq, CO 188.

String Quartet No. 4, Op. 37
★★★★—Juilliard Sq, CO 4737 —in "The Complete String Quartets of Arnold Schönberg," Juilliard Sq, CO 188.

Quintet for Flute, Oboe, Clarinet, Horn, and Bassoon, Op. 26
There is a curious, sphinxlike definition of the surging that flows within the quintet. The constant crescendi-decrescendi (minute, but precise) are often overlooked or played down to the point where they do not register. Further, certain ritards are not followed and accelerandi are similarly discounted.

The Philadelphians are without doubt five of the greatest wind players in the country. With such artists one expects much more than is heard in this recording.
—PW, CO 5217.

Verklärte Nacht ("Transfigured Night"), *Sextet for Two Violins, Two Violas and Two Cellos, Op. 4*
This music demands passionate inculcation; the Marlboro six supply it. Though the other renditions identify excellent ensemble playing neither portrays sufficient heat.
—in "Chamber Music from Marlboro," Galimir (*v*), Briemeister (*v*), Zaratzian (*va*), Rhodes (*va*), Grebanier (*c*), Rosen (*c*), CO 5644(S) —Hollywood Sq, Dinkin (*va*), Reher (*c*), C 8304 — Ramor Q, Lorincz, Deaky, VOX 530(S).

Suite, Op. 29
—Johnston (*small cl*), Raimondi (*cl*), Ulyate (*b. cl*), Baker (*v*), Figelski (*va*), Neikrug (*c*), Stein (*p*), Craft, CO 5099 — Kreisel-

480

man (*small cl*), Neidich (*cl*), Keil (*b. cl*), Aitay (*v*), Layefsky (*va*), Sophos (*c*), Sherman (*p*), Schuller, PE 705.

Serenade, Op. 24
Only the healthy number of Schoenberg works contained on the Columbia disk would warrant its choice over the really magnificent performance conducted by Maderna. Mitropoulos recorded this work in 1949 and it does not measure up to standards demanded now. Still, it is closer to the mark than Craft's ideas.
—Melos Ensemble of London, Case (*bar*), Maderna, LL 250(S)
—Brody (*cl*), Simon (*b. cl*), Piccardi (*m*), Smith (*g*), Krasner (*v*), Hersh (*va*), Barab (*c*), Galjour (*bar*), Mitropoulos, ES 501 —Raimondi (*cl*), Ulyate (*b. cl*), Gralnick (*m*), Norman (*g*), Wade (*v*), Figelski (*va*), Sargeant (*c*), van Ducen (*b*), Craft, CO 5244.

Serenade, Op. 24 ("March")
Four musicians of this group are members of the Melos Ensemble that recorded the entire work (*see above*). They help to give a representative performance in this interesting survey of contemporary music.
—in "The History of Music in Sound: Vol. X," de Peyer (*cl*), Hambleton (*b. cl*), d'Alton (*m*), Phillips (*g*), Goren (*v*), Aronowitz (*va*), Weil (*c*), Seiber, V 6092.

VOCAL

Fifteen Songs from "Das Buch der Hängenden Gärten" ("The Book of the Hanging Gardens"), *Op. 15*
Bethany Beardslee's performance cannot be praised sufficiently, and Robert Helps is as absorbing. The other release is also recommended, despite some disparity between the voice and the keyboard instrument.
—Beardslee (*s*), Helps (*p*), SON 2(S) —Kibler (*ms*), Albersheim (*p*), LYR 42.

Songs
  Eight Songs for Voice and Piano, Op. 6
  Four Songs with Piano, Op. 2
  Six Songs with Piano, Op. 3 (Nos. 4 and 6)
  Two Songs for Voice and Piano, Op. 14

    Alles, Op. 6, No. 2
    Am Wegrand, Op. 6, No. 6
    Der Wanderer, Op. 6, No. 8
    Erhebung, Op. 2, No. 3
    Erwartung, Op. 2, No. 1
    Freihold, Op. 3, No. 6
    Ghasel, Op. 6, No. 5

481

Hochzeiteslied, Op. 3, No. 4
Ich Darf Nicht Dankend, Op. 14, No. 1
In Diesen Wintertagen, Op. 14, No. 2
Jesus Bettelt, Op. 2, No. 2
Lockrung, Op. 6, No. 7
Mädchenlied, Op. 6, No. 3
Traumleben, Op. 6, No. 1
Verlassen, Op. 6, No. 4
Waldsonne, Op. 2, No. 4
★★★—Steingruber (*s*), Haefner (*p*), SPA 32.

Three Songs for Low Voice, Op. 48
★★★★—McKay (*ms*), Stein (*p*), CO 5099.

Voice with Instrumental Ensemble

Herzgewächse, Op. 20
★★★—Nixon (*s*), Shik (*hp*), Stein (*ce*), Kuhnle (*har*), Craft, CO 5099.

Pierrot Lunaire, Op. 21
There is one version by which all others can be measured; that conducted by Schoenberg himself. However, this old Columbia disk is a dubbing made from a 78 rpm. affair and has many sonic drawbacks. As a historical document it should be in every collector's hands. So should the performance starring Bethany Beardslee. She is closely rivaled by Alice Howland, whose deeper voice is, at times, even more favorably disposed toward the dynamic character of the score. Howland's earlier (MGM) recording is almost as good, its sound the reverse. Westminster's entry is marred by performance liberties that have no right to be taken, despite the conductor's reputation as a Schoenberg scholar.

Now, Schoenberg's score is sufficiently clear in its demand for a course *between* song and speech—to sing is false. And Steingruber sings most of the time. This prettifies the work, deprives the music of its urgency and nightmarish fantasy.
—in "The Music of Arnold Schoenberg: Vol. 1," Beardslee, Helps (*p*), Panitz (*fl and pic*), Bright (*cl and b. cl*), Cohen (*v and va*), McCracken (*c*), Craft, CO 279(S)   —Howland (*Sprechstimme*), Kalish (*p*), Burge (*fl and pic*), Milosovich (*cl and b. cl*), Loft (*v and va*), Sopkin (*c*), Zipper, CD 1232(S)   —Stiedry-Wagner (*recitation*), Steuermann (*p*), Posella (*fl and pic*), Bloch (*cl and b. cl*), Kolisch (*v and va*), Auber (*c*), Schoenberg, CO 4471   —Howland (*speaker*), Steuermann (*p*), Schaefer (*fl and pic*), Lituchy (*cl*), Kalina (*b. cl*), Koff (*v and va*), Barab (*c*), Winograd, MGM 3202
—Semser (*reciter*), Parry (*p*), Walker (*fl and pic*), Fell (*cl*), Lear

(*b. cl*), Bentley (*v*), Edwards (*va*), de Mont (*c*), Leibowitz, W 18143 —Steingruber (*s*), Graf (*p*), Pfersmann (*fl and pic*), Eichler (*cl and b. cl*), Schneiderhan (*v and va*), Reichert (*c*), Golschmann, VG 1082(S).

CHORAL

Canon: The Parting of the Ways from "Three Satires," Op. 28, No. 1
★★—Nixon (*s*), Gayer (*a*), Robinson (*t*), van Ducen (*b*), Craft, CO 5244.

Friede auf Erden, Op. 13
★★★★—in "German Choral Music from the 16th to the 20th Centuries," Chorus of Radio Berlin, Koch, MON 2047.

CHORAL WITH INSTRUMENTAL ENSEMBLE

Four Pieces for Mixed Chorus, Op. 27
★—Nixon (*s*), Gayer (*a*), Robinson (*t*), van Ducen (*b*), Gralnick (*m*), Raimondi (*cl*), Wade (*v*), Sargeant (*c*), Craft, CO 5244.

CHORAL WITH ORCHESTRA

Friede auf Erden, Op. 13
Nothing wrong with the singing, much wrong with the synthetic use of orchestral support. To really enjoy "Friede auf Erden" in all of its pure power, choose the unaccompanied original (*see above*).
—in "The Robert Shaw Chorale 'On Tour'," Orch., Robert Shaw Chorale, Shaw, V 2676(S).

Gurre-Lieder
Originally issued (in 1954) by the defunct Haydn Society, this recording shows its age and deficiencies. While the solo voices are good, the choral ensembles lack clarity, and much of the orchestral finesse is pulverized. Further, the grand scale of the piece is crushed by engineering that gives no perspective.
—Orch. of the New Sy. Society of Paris, Chorus of the New Sy. Society of Paris, Lewis (*t*), Semser (*s*), Tangeman (*ms*), Riley (*b*), Gruber (*t*), Gesell (*speaker*), Leibowitz, VOX 204.

Kol Nidre, Op. 39
★★★—VSO, Academie Chamber Chorus, Jaray (*n*), Swarowsky, CO 4664.

Prelude to "The Genesis Suite," Op. 44
The entire suite for orchestra, chorus, and narrator, recorded almost two decades ago by Capitol (P-8125), is a collector's rarity. Thus,

Schoenberg's contribution to the project, included in Columbia's anthology, constitutes a real novelty.
—in "The Music of Arnold Schoenberg: Vol. 2," CBC, Festival Singers of Toronto, Craft, CO 294(S).

CANTATA

A Survivor from Warsaw, Op. 46
The performance in the Columbia anthology is superb, impeccably organized. Horton's narration is intense, colored to the ultimate in expressivity.

In general, the Viennese exhibit is excellent also, especially the effect of untrained voices singing the climactic scene in Hebrew. The single drawback is Jaray's narration. His diction is clear, but his English has a strong foreign accent.
—in "The Music of Arnold Schoenberg: Vol. 1," CBC, Festival Singers of Toronto, Horton (*n*), Craft, CO 279(S)   —VSO, Academie Chamber Chorus, Jaray (*n*), Swarowsky, CO 4664.

The New Classicism from "Three Satires," Op. 28, No. 3
★—Robinson (*t*), Scharbach (*b*), Figelski (*va*), Arkatov (*c*), Stein (*p*), Mixed Chorus, Craft, CO 5099.

OPERA

Die Glückliche Hand, Op. 18
★★★—in "The Music of Arnold Schoenberg: Vol. 1," COL, Columbia Chorus, Oliver (*b*), Craft, CO 279(S).

Erwartung, Op. 17
★★★★—in "The Music of Arnold Schoenberg: Vol. 1," Orch. of the Opera Society of Washington, Pilarczyk (*s*), Craft, CO 279(S).

Moses und Aron
★★★—Orch. of the Norddeutscher Rundfunk, Chorus of the Norddeutscher Rundfunk, Fiedler (*speaker*), Krebs (*t*), Steingruber-Wildgans (*s*), Zollenkops (*a*), Kretschmar (*t*), Günter (*bar*), Rieth (*bar*), Förster-Georgi (*s*), Pfeffer-Düring (*s*), Tamm (*a*), Bettke (*a*), Hüger (*ms*), Stuckmann (*t*), Sellenpin (*bar*), Lühr (*b*), Rosbaud, CO 241.

KARLHEINZ STOCKHAUSEN

ORCHESTRAL

CHAMBER ORCHESTRA

Kontra-punkte ("Counterpoint")
★★—Instrumental Ensemble, Baulez, VEGA 30-66.

Zeitmasse ("Tempi")
Though this is controversial music there is no argument regarding
either of the recordings. It takes dedicated performers to grasp the
point of such music as "Zeitmasse" (on the Véga disk the work is
titled "Zeitmasze").
—Gleghorn (*fl*), Muggeridge (*o*), Leake (*Eh*), Christlieb (*bn*),
Ulyate (*cl*), Craft, CO 5275 —Maisonneuve (*o*), Castagner (*fl*),
Taillefer (*Eh*), Deplus (*cl*), Rabot (*bn*), Boulez, VEGA 30-139.

PERCUSSION ORCHESTRA

Refrain
Because of the predominant ambiguity of its text any performance of
"Refrain" has its own built-in security. How can one criticize the
playing of music that has no fixed point of departure?
—A. Kontarsky, B. Kontarsky, Caskel, TIME 58001(S).

INSTRUMENTAL

PERCUSSION

Zyklus ("Cycle")
The entire philosophy of chance music is that it never repeats
itself, that no two hearings will ever be the same, that its indetermi-
nancy means an ever-renewal, a new reckoning each and every instance. A recording "freezes" a performance and Stockhausen's
"Zyklus" is to be heard therefore as permanently fixed music with all
chance removed.
—Caskel, TIME 58001(S).

PIANO

Klavierstück 6 ("Piano Piece 6")
★★★—Tudor, VEGA 30-278.

485

ELECTRONIC COMPOSITIONS

Gesang der Jünglinge I ("Song of the Youths I")
Since sonic separation is a fundamental part of the composition's structure, the earlier monophonic disk is a poor substitute. Only the stereophonic recording imparts the true kaleidoscopic mobility of Stockhausen's commanding creation.
—Electronic Realization by WDR (West German Radio), Cologne, DG (138811) —*the same,* DG 16133 (*10-inch disk*).

Kontakte
★★★★—Electronic Realization by WDR (West German Radio), Cologne, DG (138811).

Studie I
Studie II
★★—Electronic Realization by WDR (West German Radio), Cologne, DG 16133 (*10-inch disk*).

ERNST TOCH

ORCHESTRAL

Circus, an Overture
★★—in "Bravo!", NY, Cordon (*bull whip*), Kostelanetz, CO 758.

Notturno, Op. 77
Excellent projection of Toch's sensitive score.
—LOU, Whitney, LV 545-3.

Peter Pan, A Fairy Tale for Orchestra in Three Parts, Op. 76
Few performances by the Louisville group can match this one.
—LOU, Whitney, LV 612.

Third Symphony, Op. 75
A truly superb performance by those who gave the first concert presentation of the symphony. Because of Toch's unique scoring, the stereo version is much the superior one.
—PI, Steinberg, C 8364(S).

INSTRUMENTAL

PIANO

The Juggler, Op. 31, No. 3
★—Maclean, MLR 7082.

Ten Studies for Beginners, Op. 59
★★—in "Piano Music for Children by Modern Composers," Richter, MGM 3181.

CHAMBER MUSIC

Serenade in G major, Op. 25
★★—Westwood String Trio, CY 6002(S).

Sonatinetta for Flute, Clarinet and Bassoon, Op. 84
Couldn't be played better; the textures are as pliable as creamy butter.
—Members of the PW, CO 5788(S).

String Trio, Op. 63
★★★—Vienna String Trio, CY 6005(S).

String Quartet in D flat major, Op. 18
★★★—Westwood Sq, CY 6002(S).

String Quartet No. 10 (on the Name "Bass"), *Op. 28*
★★★—American Art Q, CY 6008(S).

String Quartet No. 12, Op. 70
★★—Zurich Sq, CY 6005(S).

String Quartet No. 13, Op. 74
The Roth group is sufficiently expert, but their tone is wiry and Feri Roth's phrasing is not always objectively concerned.
—Roth Q, CY 6008(S).

Quintet for Piano, 2 Violins, Viola and Violoncello, Op. 64
★★★★—Previn (*p*), American Art Q, CY 6011(S).

Five Pieces for Wind Instruments and Percussion, Op. 83
A sheer joy for the ear. (Label error: Ward O. Fearn is listed as a percussionist; he plays second horn.)
—PW, Fearn (*hn*), Hinger (*per*), Owen (*per*), CO 5788(S).

VOCAL

VOICE WITH ORCHESTRA

The Chinese Flute, for Soprano and Chamber Orchestra, Op. 29
★★—Renzi (*s*), MGM Chamber Orch., Surinach, MGM 3546.

JOAQUÍN TURINA

ORCHESTRAL

Danzas Fantásticas, Op. 22
Of all the performances listed, Argenta's is in a class by itself. It is the second movement in quintal rhythm that upsets conductors. Argenta's choice of tempo shapes this indigenous metrical plan beautifully and succinctly; in the final movement he maintains chiseled clarity even with a generous rate of motion. Irving's energetic and bright realization is very good. Save for some phlegmatic phrases in the first movement, the Monte Carlo release is acceptable.
—SDCC, Argenta, L 9082   —RP, Irving, C 7130   —in "Monte Carlo Concert Gala: Album 2," MCO, Frémaux, DG 18654(S)   — SR, Ansermet, L 9263(S)   —PH, Schuechter, MGM 3018   — OSM, de Freitas Branco, W 5320.

La Procesión del Rocío, Op. 9
Argenta defines all the pageantry and fervor of the piece in a brilliant manner. All the other versions are sympathetic; the best of these is the one led by Irving which has stylistic feeling and sharpness of color detail.
—in "España: Vol. 1," ONE, Argenta, L 9175(S)   —RP, Irving, C 7130   —in "The Music of Spain," PC, Jorda, R 19052   —OSM, de Freitas Branco, W 5320   —LSO, Poulet, MGM 3073.

Rítmos (Choreographic Fantasy)
—ORS, Surinach, MLL 162(S).

Sinfonía Sevillana, Op. 23
Though Winograd is not a descendant of the Hispanic tradition and his orchestra is not to be compared to Argenta's, his performance deserves attention for its vivid coloristic depiction. Only London's superior sound makes it the superior version.
—ONE, Argenta, L 9196(S)   —HP, Winograd, MGM 3435.

String Orchestra

La Oración del Torero, Op. 34
Top valuation goes to Gould, Fennell, and Freitas Branco. Gould's reading is magnificent; the music is given full-scale, total-sweep playing, and all differences are emphasized in proper proportion. Rich sound frames Fennell's wonderful realization of the dynamic properties and tonal pigments, while Freitas Branco stresses the poetical aspects, thereby properly classifying the colors of the score. The fastest

tempi this writer has ever heard used for this composition are on display on the Argenta disk. Nonetheless, the playing is superlative; the despair of the slow-tempo sections is quite moving.
—in "Living Strings," G, Gould, V 2317(S)   —in "Hi-Fi a la Española," ER, Fennell, MY 50144   —OSM, de Freitas Branco, W 5320   —in "España: Vol. 1," ONE, Argenta, L 9175(S)   —in "The String Orchestra," (*no orchestra listed*), Stokowski, C 8458(S) —in "Castles in Spain," Orquesta Zarzuela de Madrid, Torróba, D 9763   —in "String Enchantment," Alfred Newman and His Orch., Newman, D 8194.

SOLO INSTRUMENT WITH ORCHESTRA

SOLO PIANO WITH ORCHESTRA

Rapsodia Sinfónica for Piano and String Orchestra, Op. 66
Presented with gentle reasonableness in both recordings; the richer sound of London's disk gives it preference.
—ONE, Soriano (*p*), Alonso, L 9271(S)   —HP, Bianca (*p*), Winograd, MGM 3510.

INSTRUMENTAL

GUITAR

Fandanguillo
The greatest dynamic contrast belongs to Segovia. His drum effects and musical proclamation are very exciting; the bass passages are tonally magnificent. Diaz's and Almeida's performances are very clarified as is de la Torre's; the latter's tone has less body. Yoghurtjian plays more convincingly than Yépès, who minimizes color differentials. Bream's guitar is exceedingly bright and somewhat harshly recorded. All the performers suffer from microphoning which serves up many a hand sweep, finger glide, and squeak.
—Segovia, CO 4732   —in "Masterpieces of the Spanish Guitar," Diaz, VG 1084   —in "Vistas d'España," Almeida, C 8367   —in "Virtuoso Guitar," de la Torre, E 3479   —in "Great Guitar Music," Yoghurtjian, ARION 72859   —in "Spanish Music for Guitar," Yépès, L 9105   —in "Spanish Guitar Music," Bream, W 18135.

Homenaje a Tárrega: Garrotín and Soleares
Bream's command is eloquent; Almeida's very good. However, the former's album includes only original music for the plucked instrument, while some of the transcriptions on Almeida's program can well be questioned.
—in "Spanish Guitar Music," Bream, W 18135   —in "Music of Spain," Almeida, C 8295.

489

Ráfaga
Both performers yield properly to the music's native temper which permits individuality without damage to the composition. Thus two different representations, each beautifully styled.
—in "Vistas d'España," Almeida, C 8367		—in "Spanish Guitar Music," Bream, W 18135.

Sacro-monte from "Danzas Gitanas," Op. 55
★—in "Vistas d'España," Almeida, C 8367.

Sevillana
★★—in "Vistas d'España," Almeida, C 8367.

Sonata, Op. 61
★★—in "The New World of the Guitar," Almeida, C 8392.

Sonata, Op. 61 (Andante)
Warning! The listing of this item on liner notes and record label as "Andante from Sonatina in D minor," is a blatant error. It is not a portion of a "Sonatina," but is the second movement of the work (discussed immediately above), which Turina composed in 1932.
—in "Spanish Guitar Music," Bream, W 18135.

HARP

Sacro-monte from "Danzas Gitanas," Op. 55
Both harpists play "Sacro-monte" slower than most pianists. Although Grandjany's compendium is exclusively Spanish material, Zabaleta's assortment of "Spanish Classics," includes other countries (examples: Glinka from Russia and Fauré from France).
—in "El Amor d'España," Grandjany, C 8473		—in "Spanish Classics," Zabaleta, PE 745(S).

PIANO

Ciclo Pianístico
	Partita in C major, Op. 57
	Preludios 1–5, Op. 80
★★—in "Alicia de Larrocha Plays Turina," de Larrocha, D 9750.

Cuentos de España, Series 1, Op. 20
Cuentos de España, Series 2, Op. 47
★★—Sánchez, C 18039.

Danzas Fantásticas, Op. 22
The performances are effective, save that both pianists play the middle movement far too slowly. There is some disturbing surface hiss on the Decca disk.
—Echániz, W 18185		—in "Alicia de Larrocha Plays Turina," de Larrocha, D 9750.

490

Danzas Fantásticas, Op. 22 ("Ensueño" and "Orgía")
(No comparison with the performances of the complete opus [*see above*].)
—Soriano, B 304.

Danzas Fantásticas, Op. 22 ("Exaltación")
★—in "Spanish Piano Music," Frugoni, VOX 9420.

Danzas Gitanas, Series 1, Op. 55
Miss Regules sets her compass points perfectly and is the most persuasive exponent of these pieces. But the sound of the Siena instrument is not convincing after a little while, and its twang and tweak twist the ear.
   Personally, I would accept Echániz's more introspective performance, with just (thank goodness) ordinary grand piano sound.
—Echániz, W 18185   —in "The Siena Pianoforte," Regules, ES 3002.

Danzas Gitanas, Op. 55 ("Sacro-monte")
The three performances vary considerably. Milgrim's is the best balanced, especially his artistic concept of attack; Copeland zigzags his tempi and smothers the piece with a flashy grip, while Cortes plays quite poetically, softly (in comparison to the others) and with the slowest tempo. His version is almost ideal, but needs a bit more zip and better sound for its display.
—in "The Romantic Music of Spain," Milgrim, K 9058   —in "El Pianoforte Español (Spanish Piano Classics)," Cortes, SP 1022   —in "Spanish Piano Music," Copeland, MGM 3025.

Le Jeudi Saint à Minuit from "Sevilla, Suite Pittoresque"
The only criticism is that the recording fails to indicate that "Le Jeudi Saint à Minuit" forms the middle portion of a three-movement opus.
—Echániz, W 18185.

Mujeres Españolas, Op. 17
★★—Echániz, W 18185.

Mujeres Españolas, Op. 17 (Movements Two and Three)
Do not be confused. RCA Victor's recording lists Turina's work with the French equivalent ("Femmes d'Espagnole") and naturally follows suit with the subtitles. (The performance is marred by unpleasant tonal quality.)
—in "Spanish Music," A. Iturbi, V 1788.

Niñerias, Op. 21
★★★—Sanromá, POL 1011.

Poema Fantástico, Op. 98
★★★—in "Piano Music from Spain," Masselos, MGM 3165.

Recuerdos de la Antigua España, Op. 48
★★—in "Alicia de Larrocha Plays Turina," de Larrocha, D 9750.

CHAMBER MUSIC

Second Sonata (Sonata Española) *for Violin and Piano, Op. 82*
★—Figueroa (*v*), Miquel (*p*), N 401.

Trio No. 2 in B minor, Op. 76
★★★—Pro Musica Trio, PRO 202.

String Quartet—"De la Guitarra"
★★—Cuarteto Clasico de Madrid, ZAFIRO 1.

Escena Andaluza for Viola, Piano and String Quartet, Op. 7
This Strad issue is no longer in the current lists. It is worth seeking.
—R. Persinger (*va*), L. Persinger (*p*), Strad Sq, STRAD 608.

VOCAL

Farruca from "Triptico"
The partnership of Victoria de los Angeles and Gerald Moore is exquisitely displayed. The same goes for the glorious program presented by Berganza and her husband. The performance of de los Angeles and Soriano is also a model of artistic collaboration. Though not possessed of an overly dramatic voice, Merriman sings her program with knowledge and conviction.
—in "Recital," de los Angeles (*s*), Moore (*p*), PAT 326/7   —in "A Program of Spanish and Italian Songs," Berganza (*ms*), Lavilla (*p*), L 5726(S)   —in "20th Century Spanish Songs," de los Angeles (*s*), Soriano (*p*), A 35775(S)   —in "Spanish Songs," Merriman (*ms*), Moore (*p*), A 35208.

La Giralda from "Canto a Sevilla," Op. 37
(The complete version with the original orchestral background is available in a top-flight presentation: *see* Voice with Orchestra.)
—in "Spanish Songs," Merriman (*ms*), Moore (*p*), A 35208.

Las Locas por Amor
—Amara (*s*), Benedict (*p*), CAM 704(S).

Poema en Forma de Canciones, Op. 19
★—in "Gloria Davy Concert Recital," Davy (*s*), Favaretto (*p*), L 5395.

Poema en Forma de Canciones, Op. 19 ("Cantares")
Compared to Miss Davy's performance of this movement (*see above*)
there is no question that Tebaldi is supreme.
    The other disk is a professional performance, but one of tepid
emotion.
—in "Renata Tebaldi Recital of Songs and Arias," Tebaldi (*s*), Favaretto (*p*), L 5267   —in "Frances Yeend Sings," Yeend (*s*),
Benner (*p*), DV 203.

Saeta en Forme de Salve a la Virgen de la Esperanza
★★★★—in "A Program of Spanish and Italian Songs," Berganza (*ms*),
Lavilla (*p*), L 5726(S).

Tu Pupila es Azul
★★★★—in "The Fabulous Victoria de los Angeles," de los Angeles
(*s*), Moore (*p*), A 35971(S).

Voice with Orchestra

Canto a Sevilla, Op. 37
★★★★—LSO, de los Angeles (*s*), Fistoulari, A 35440.

Canto a Sevilla, Op. 37 (Excerpts)
The four vocal-orchestra settings from the complete work (*see
above*). Miss de Aragon has a well-balanced voice, but with far less
brilliance than de los Angeles.
—OSM, de Aragon (*s*), de Freitas Branco, W 5320.

RALPH VAUGHAN WILLIAMS

ORCHESTRAL

A London Symphony (No. 2)
★★★★—LPO, Boult, L 9052.

A Sea Symphony (No. 1)
    (*see* Choral with Orchestra)

English Folk Song Suite
Regardless of English or Viennese musicians, with Boult as their
conductor this music of Vaughan Williams is played as it should be.
—PPO, Boult, VG 1093   —PPO, Boult, W 18248   —VOP, Boult,
W 18928(S).

Norfolk Rhapsody No. 1 in E minor
—PPO, Boult, VG 1093   —PPO, Boult, W 18248.

493

Pastoral Symphony (No. 3)
★★★—LPO, Ritchie (*s*), Boult, L 9063.

Sinfonia Antartica (No. 7)
   (*see* Choral with Orchestra)

Symphony No. 4 in F minor
Though both versions are exemplary, the virtuosic affinity of the New
Yorkers gives the Columbia release first place. Mitropoulos under-
lines every iota of the violence, brutality, and anger of the piece.
Boult is much more chaste.
—NY, Mitropoulos, CO 5158   —LPO, Boult, L 9094.

Symphony No. 5 in D major
Barbirolli's long association with this piece (he made the initial recording during the 78-rpm era) shows in a reading that captures
every nuance of Vaughan Williams's lyrical blend. Boult's version is
compelling, not as vocal, tighter, and thereby less emotional. (He
takes a slightly faster pace, especially in the "Romanza.")
—PH, Barbirolli, A 35952(S)   —LPO, Boult, L 9095.

Symphony No. 6 in E minor
Boult's conception is more truthful and thereby more expressive than
Stokowski's. Furthermore, London offers a short speech by Vaughan
Williams, made at the time of the recording. It is historical and to be
cherished.
—LPO, Boult, L 9096   —NY, Stokowski, CO 4214.

Symphony No. 8 in D minor
Both British conductors do beautifully with Vaughan Williams's score
and either performance is worth obtaining.
—Hallé Orch., Barbirolli, MY 50115(S) —LPO, Parfitt (*v*),
Boult, L 9189(S).

Symphony No. 8 in D minor (Scherzo alla Marcia)
★★—in "The Orchestra," S, Stokowski, C 8385(S).

Symphony No. 9 in E minor
Vaughan Williams was scheduled to be present during the recording
of his ninth symphony, but died just seven hours before the session
took place. He would have been fully satisfied with this splendid performance, reproduced with the ultimate in fidelity.
—LPO, Boult, EV 6006(S).

The Wasps, Suite
All performances being equal, the choice of recording depends on
what Vaughan Williams music one wishes (all three disks being devoted to this composer).

—LPO, Boult, L 7205   —PPO, Boult, W 18251   —PPO, Boult, W 18250.

The Wasps ("March Past of the Kitchen Utensils")
★★—in "Adventures in Music: Grade 3, Vol. 1," N, Mitchell, V 1002(S).

The Wasps (Overture)
Sargent's presentation is discriminative. As a sampling of the music for "The Wasps" it cannot be bettered. Copies of the old, but truly excellent Westminster Lab. release are still to be found and are worthy of acquisition.
—LSO, Sargent, A 35564   —PPO, Boult, WL 7048.

CHAMBER ORCHESTRA

Fantasia on "Greensleeves"
Sargent's orchestra plays warmly and the reproduction is excellent. Collins, Barbirolli, and Vardi deserve top credits for performance and programming. The Philadelphia strings are magnificent but the sound is rather souped up and this burdens the music's simplicity. Sensitive flute playing by a master is the cardinal point of the Zagreb presentation; the speed at which this group plays the middle section can be argued.
—LSO, Sargent, A 35564   —in "The Voice of the Strings," Strings of the Kapp Sinfonietta, Vardi, K 9059(S)   —Strings of the Sinfonia of London, Barbirolli, A 36101(S)   —Strings of the NSO, Collins, L 9053   —Strings of the PO, Ormandy, CO 5187, *also* CO 5624(S)   —in "Notturno," IZ, Baker (*fl*), Jelinek (*hp*), Janigro, VG 1095(S)   —in "Liebestraum," BP, Fiedler, V 2546(S)   —in "Boston Tea Party," BP, Fiedler, V 2213(S)   —in "Music for Frustrated Conductors," BP, Fiedler, V 2325(S)   —VOP, Boult, W 18928   —PPO, Boult, VG 1093   —PPO, Boult, W 18248   —PPO, Boult, W 18250   —PPO, Boult, W 18249   —PPO, Boult, WL 7048   —in "Adventures in Music: Grade 6, Vol. 2," N, Mitchell, V 1008(S)   —BNSO, Neel, UN 1044.

STRING ORCHESTRA

Fantasia on a Theme by Thomas Tallis
Steinberg guides Vaughan Williams's score with magnificent cogence. His orchestra displays a warm, fully interfused sonority that fits the music like a glove. While neither Collins' nor Boult's various releases were made in stereo they are no less striking. Only the latter's presentation with the Vienna group is disappointing, especially in the lack of cohesion of the solo players and the over-all neutrality of the performance. A minimal amount of chiseled detail mars Barbirolli's otherwise richly sounding disk.

Stokowski's old recording is worth considering because it illuminates the religious atmosphere. Tonal power and sonority with a sufficient outpour are to be found in the Mitropoulos recording, but so is a contrapositive instability; the music surges and falls back instead of flowing. A much more damning verdict applies to von Karajan's consideration. V.W.'s music is far from V.K.'s fatherland and the coolness of the playing proves it.

—PI, Steinberg, C 8383(S)   —PPO, Boult, VG 1093   —PPO, Boult, W 18248   —PPO, Boult, W 18249   —PPO, Boult, W 18250   —PPO, Boult, WL 7048   —Strings of the NSO, Collins, L 9053   —Strings of the Sinfonia of London, Barbirolli, A 36101(S)   —VOP, Boult, W 18928(S)   —S, Stokowski, V 1739   —Strings of the NY, Mitropoulos, CO 5285(S)   —BNSO, Neel, UN 1044 — PH, von Karajan, A 35142.

Partita for Double String Orchestra
★★★—LPO, Boult, L 9189(S).

BAND

English Folk Song Suite
Fennell's performance is the only one that has conviction, authority, and artistic balance.
—in "British Band Classics," EW, Fennell, MY 50088   —NTS, McAdow, AU 33-6015   —in "Great Band Music," Cities Service Band of America, Lavalle, V 1133.

Toccata Marziale
Only superlatives can be used to describe Fennell's performance.
—in "British Band Classics," EW, Fennell, MY 50088   —South Park High School Band, Hutchinson, AU 33-6211.

SOLO INSTRUMENT WITH ORCHESTRA

CONCERTOS

Concerto for Oboe and Strings
★★—Saidenberg Little Sy., Miller (*o*), Saidenberg, MY 10003.

Concerto in D minor (Concerto Accademico) *for Violin and String Orchestra*
The musicianship, taste, and artistry of these violinists are peerless. Concert Hall is no longer on the market. However, its recording has been reissued by the Record Hunter shop in New York as part of its "Rarities Collection." Both disks are beguiling offerings.
—Z. Fuchs (*v*), D 9625   —Concert Hall Sy. Orch., Kaufman (*v*), Goehr, CH 1253.

INSTRUMENTAL

CLARINET

Six Studies in English Folk Song for Clarinet and Piano
★★—Kell (*cl*), Smith (*p*), D 9941.

ORGAN

The Old Hundredth
★★—in "The Virtuoso Organ," Fox, C 8499(S).

Prelude on the Welsh Hymn "Hyfrydol" (No. 3 of "Three Preludes Founded on Welsh Hymn Tunes")
★★—in "Organ Music by Modern Composers: Vol. 1," Ellsasser, MGM 3064.

Prelude on the Welsh Hymn "Rhosymedre" (No. 2 of "Three Preludes Founded on Welsh Hymn Tunes")
—Mueller, MLR 7049.

TWO PIANOS

Fantasia on "Greensleeves"
★—in "Concert for Two Pianos," J. Lang and D. Lang, GC 4070.

VIOLA

Suite for Viola and Piano
★★★—Gromko (*va*), Wingreen (*p*), CL 1038.

CHAMBER MUSIC

Sonata in A minor for Violin and Piano
★★★—Grinke (*v*), Mulliner (*p*), L 1382.

VOCAL

Folk Songs
   The Cuckoo and the Nightingale
   Down by the Riverside
   The Jolly Plough Boy
   My Boy Billy
   The Painful Plough
★★★★—in "Vaughan Williams Folk Song Album," Deller (*ct*), Dupre (*lute*), VG 1055(S).

497

Linden Lea
★★—in "Songs of Travel and Other Songs; English Sea Ballads,"
Standen (*b*), Stone (*p*), W 18710.

Seven Songs from "The Pilgrim's Progress"
★★★—Cameron (*bar*), Kells (*s*), Bartlett (*s*), Watson (*p*), W 18097.

Silent Noon (No. 2 from "The House of Life")
★★—in "Songs of Travel and Other Songs; English Sea Ballads,"
Standen (*b*), Stone (*p*), W 18710.

Songs of Travel
★★—in "Songs of Travel and Other Songs; English Sea Ballads,"
Standen (*b*), Stone (*p*), W 18710.

The Watermill
★★—in "Songs of Travel and Other Songs; English Sea Ballads,"
Standen (*b*), Stone (*p*), W 18710.

Voice with Instrumental Ensemble

On Wenlock Edge
★★★—Young (*t*), Watson (*p*), Sebastian Sq, W 18097.

CHORAL

All People That on Earth Do Dwell (The "Old Hundredth" Psalm
Tune)
★★—in "The King of Instruments, Vol. X: Music of the Church,"
Choir of the First Presbyterian Church, Kilgore, Texas, Austin College Choir, Perry (*org*), AEOLIAN-SKINNER 80 P (*now:* WA 10).

A Song of Thanksgiving
Very disappointing. The liner notes mention that the performance
is an "abridgment." This is certainly not the proper description for
presenting a three and one-quarter minute snippet of a composition
approximately sixteen minutes in length!
—in "Hymns and Songs of Brotherhood," Mormon Tabernacle Choir,
Schreiner (*org*), Asper (*org*), Condie, CO 5714(S).

At the Name of Jesus
★★—in "Hymns and Anthems," University of Redlands Choir, Jones,
CO 4866.

Down in Yon Forest (from "Eight Traditional English Carols")
—in "Christmas Music at Stanford," Stanford University Choir,
Schmidt, MLR 7069.

Five English Folk Songs
★★★★—in "Vaughan Williams Folk Song Album," Deller Consort, VG 1055(S).

Five English Folk Songs ("Wassail Song")
Choose the Angel album. The record label on the Music Library release defines the catalogue number as 7101, the cover as 7071; no mention is made on the cover that the recording represents the second volume of "Christmas Music at Stanford," causing confusion with the undesignated initial album (MLR 7069). The banding identification on both label and liner note is incorrect. Most important, the singing is poor.
—in "Madrigals, Ballets and Folk Songs of Four Centuries," English Singers, A 35461   —in "Christmas Music at Stanford: Vol. No. 2," Stanford University Choir, Stanford Chorale, Schmidt, MLR (7101).

Folk Songs
    A Farmer's Son So Sweet
    An Acre of Land
    Bushes and Briars
    Ca' the Yowes
    Greensleeves
    John Dory
    Loch Lomond
    Ward the Pirate
★★★★—in "Vaughan Williams Folk Song Album," Deller Consort, VG 1055(S).

Linden Lea
★—in "Recital," Pancratius Royal Men's Chorus (Heerlen, Holland), Heijdendael, A 35406.

Lord Thou Hast Been Our Refuge
A worthy effort by the Augustana group, with one drawback. Vaughan Williams's division of the chorus into large and small groups is not made clear. Avoid the other release; the singing is strictly amateurish and the recording of poor quality.
—Augustana Choir, Veld, WORD 4001   —in "Rhapsody in White and Baylor Bards," Choral Ensemble of Baylor University, Harrell (*p*), Barkema, AU 6241.

Oh How Amiable
★★★—in "Music of the Episcopal Church," Choir of the Cathedral of St. John the Divine, New York City, Wyton (*org*), Wyton, WORD 4014.

Prayer to the Father of Heaven
—San José State College A Cappella Choir, Erlendson, MLR 7065.

The Souls of the Righteous
★★—Augustana Choir, Veld, WORD 4012.

The Turtle Dove
The Deller group is inspired in its rendition. The English group sings with good style, while the Stanford organization leadens the piece with a heavy texture.
—in "Vaughan Williams Folk Song Album," Deller Consort, VG 1055(S) —in "Madrigals, Ballets and Folk Songs of Four Centuries," English Singers, A 35461 —Stanford Chorale, Schmidt, MLR 7022.

CHORAL WITH INSTRUMENTAL ENSEMBLE

O Clap Your Hands
★★★—in "Chorus, Organ, Brass and Percussion," The Columbia University Chapel Choir, Brass and Percussion Ensemble, Kneeream (*org*), Wright, K 9057(S).

CHORAL WITH ORCHESTRA

A Sea Symphony (No. 1)
★★★★—LPO, LPC, Baillie (*s*), Cameron (*bar*), Boult, L 7205.

Fantasia on Christmas Carols
★★★—in "On Christmas Night," LSO, Choir of King's College, Cambridge, Alan (*b. bar*), Preston (*org*), Willcocks, ARGO 333(S)
—*the same,* L 5735(S).

Five Tudor Portraits, A Choral Suite
Deleted from the current catalogue, the suite deserves re-recording.
—PI, Mendelssohn Choir, Rankin (*ms*), Anderson (*b. bar*), Steinberg, C 8218.

Serenade to Music
Angel's version is of unreserved beauty. For this music the words are quite incidental and the lack of a printed text to follow is relatively unimportant.
Bernstein's performance is certainly satisfactory. However, "Serenade to Music" is only one-quarter of a very posh, super-duper album (Columbia's "Legacy Series") that is expensive. The extra cost is only worth it for those that wish an aural facsimile, including audience applause, of the initial concert given at the hall.
—LSO, Chorus, Morrison (*s*), Thomas (*cn*), Robertson (*t*), Anthony (*b*), Sargent, A 35564 —in "First Performance—Lincoln

Center," NY, Addison (*s*), Amara (*s*), Farrell (*s*), Chookasian (*ms*), Tourel (*ms*), Verrett-Carter (*ms*), Bressler (*t*), Tucker (*t*), Vickers (*t*), London (*b. bar*), Flagello (*b. bar*), Bell (*b. bar*), Bernstein, CO 1007(S).

Sinfonia Antartica (No. 7)
Each movement of the composition is preceded by a quotation, indicating the objective of the music. Though serving as a guide, they are not meant to be actually delivered by a narrator. That they are heard in London's superb recording is a novel touch and deserving of a listener's appreciation.
—LPO, LPC, Ritchie (*s*), Gielgud (*speaker*), Boult, L 9097.

Toward the Unknown Region
★★★—LSO, Chorus, Sargent, A 35564.

ORATORIO

Sancta Civitas ("Holy City")
In the only recording ever issued (why?), an organ substitutes for the orchestra, thereby subtracting some of the oratorio's influential color.
—San Francisco Bach Choir, Harmon (*bar*), Mueller (*org*), Jacobsen, MLR 7049.

MASS

Mass in G minor
Capitol's version, especially in stereo, vividly outlines the majestic antiphony within Vaughan Williams's mass. The Campbell-led entry is less dramatically presented. It has a much more liturgical cast than Wagner's conception.
—Roger Wagner Chorale, McNelly (*s*), Yates (*a*), Carolan (*t*), Scharbach (*b*), Salamunovich (*cantor*), Wagner, C 8535(S)
—Choristers of Canterbury Cathedral, Renaissance Singers, Wells (*s*), Whitworth (*a*), English (*t*), Bevan (*b*), Campbell, L 5634(S)
—Augustana Choir, Veld, WORD 4012   —Fleet Street Choir, Lawrence, L 805   —Texas Tech Choir, Suttle (*s*), Maddox (*a*), Pummill (*t*), Benningfield (*bar*), Kenney, AU 6224.

Mass in G minor (Kyrie Eleison)
★—in "Choral and Organ Music," Stanford University Choir, First Methodist Chancel Choir, Schmidt, MLR 6995/6996.

BALLET

Job, A Masque for Dancing
London's older recording has sharper playing and clearer outlines than the newer Everest, despite the same orchestra and conductor for both.

501

—LPO, Shadwick (*v*), Boult, L 1003   —LPO, Datyner (*v*), Boult, EV 6019(S).

Old King Cole
Boult is willin' but there's not much excitement that he can engender in this composition. Neither could anyone else.
—PPO, Boult, W 18251   —PPO, Boult, W 18249.

WILLIAM WALTON

ORCHESTRAL

Crown Imperial: Coronation March, 1937
Walton's performance is very good. However, a march's best friend is a band and for that purpose the collector is strongly advised to get Fennell's exceptional, block-busting rendition (*see* Band).
—PH, Walton, A 35639.

Façade—Suites Nos. 1 and 2
None of the executions of the "Façade" orchestral suites really hit the bull's-eye. The Fistoulari portrayal lacks highly polished playing and Walton subverts his own music by making it innocent of all satire. Irving is entirely too formal in his approach.
—OROH, Fistoulari, V 2285(S)   —PH, Walton, A 35639   —LSO, Irving, L 771.

Façade (Excerpts)
Both recordings consist of the entire first suite with portions drawn from the second; the sequence of movements being very free. Kostelanetz splices one piece from the second suite in between the fourth and fifth parts of the first suite. Sargent's presentation is listed as "Suite No. 1 & Suite No. 2—Nos. 2, 5 & 6." This is statistically true, but only in terms of total coverage. The playing order does not follow suit, employing the continuity selected for the ballet production. On a recording this is rather pointless, especially since Walton's concert arrangement makes better musical sense. (In order to rearrange the movements to conform to Walton's "Suite No. 1" plan and then follow the succession of the indicated extracts from "Suite No. 2" the listener will have to play the eight parts in the following pattern: 3-5-2-7-8-1-6-4.)
　　Columbia's haphazard identification (titled simply "Façade") continues in the naming of the movements—numbers 4, 5, and 6 are all shortened. Properly, the "Tango" should read "Tango-Pasodoblé,"

the "Song" is actually a "Popular Song," and the "Tarantella" is much more, being a "Tarantella, Sevillana."

Though the labeling of Walton's music is sloppy, the performances are the direct opposite. Throughout, both are in the vein, with stylistic savvy, sharp color, and sparkling playing. Kostelanetz's special perception of the snide side of Walton's whim-whams makes one hope he will record the entire score.

—in "Encore!", NY, Kostelanetz, CO 1135(S)   —in "English Ballets of the 20th Century," RP, Sargent, A 35889(S).

Façade ("Valse")
★★—in "Adventures in Music: Grade 6, Vol. 2," N, Mitchell, V 1008(S).

Johannesburg Festival Overture
Either performance will satisfy.
—PH, Walton, A 35639   —in "A Kostelanetz Festival," NY, Kostelanetz, CO 5607(S).

Orb and Sceptre: Coronation March, 1953
Fennell's and the composer's performances are the best; the former adds a little pepper to the score.
—in "Marches for Orchestra," ER, Fennell, MY 50271(S)   —PH, Walton, A 35639   —LSO, Sargent, L 9070.

Partita for Orchestra
The brilliance of the Clevelanders is undeniable.
—CLE, Szell, E 3568(S)   —PH, Walton, A 35681(S)..

Portsmouth Point—An Overture
Both versions are included in all-Walton disks, and both are played with proper gusto. However, Angel offers better sonics than the older London release.
—PH, Walton, A 35639   —LPO, Boult, L 1165.

Scapino—Comedy Overture
★★—LPO, Boult, L 1165.

Symphony (No. 1)
Now deleted. A new recording is urgently needed.
—PPO, Boult, W 18374(S).

Symphony No. 2
★★★—CLE, Szell, E 3812(S).

The Wise Virgins—Ballet Suite (Bach-Walton)
Capitol's recording is available in defined, full range stereo. Otherwise, it is no better than the much older Vanguard disk.

503

—CAO, Irving, C 8583(S)   —VOP, Litschauer, VG 440   —LPO, Boult, L 1165.

CHAMBER ORCHESTRA

Siesta
★★—LPO, Boult, L 1165.

STRING ORCHESTRA

Two Pieces for Strings from the Film "Henry V"
★★★—in "Music from the Films," CLEP, Lane, E 3809(S).

BAND

Crown Imperial: Coronation March, 1937
Fennell communicates Walton's march in a magnificently exciting way and shows a superb knowledge of proper pace.
—in "British Band Classics: Vol. 2," EW, Fennell, MY 50197(S)
—in "More March Favorites," EW, Fennell, MY 50325(S)   —in "All-Star Band Concert: Vol. II," Burke-Phillips All-Star Concert Band, Burke and Phillips (*conductors*), GC (4040).

Orb and Sceptre: Coronation March, 1953
★—NTS, McAdow, AU 33-6104.

SOLO INSTRUMENT WITH ORCHESTRA

CONCERTOS

Concerto for Cello and Orchestra
★★★—BSO, Piatigorsky (*c*), Munch, V 2109.

Concerto for Viola and Orchestra
★★★★—RP, Primrose (*va*), Sargent, CO 4905.

Concerto for Violin and Orchestra
★★★★—PO, Francescatti (*v*), Ormandy, CO 5601(S).

NARRATOR AND CHAMBER ENSEMBLE

Façade (an Entertainment with Poems by Edith Sitwell)
London presents the complete work. The ninth of the set ("Tarantelle") is omitted from Sitwell's Columbia album and the order of the poems is totally different after the sixth of the group (two of these six are given different titles: "Long Steel Grass" on the London disk is called "Trio for Two Cats and a Trombone" on Columbia's, for

504

example). The contrast between female and male voices makes London's release preferable (Horner narrates only one poem).
—English Opera Group Ensemble, Sitwell and Pears (*reciters*), Collins, L 4104 —Chamber Orch., Sitwell and Horner (*reciters*), Prausnitz, CO 5241 —PO, Zorina (*reciter*), Ormandy, CO 5849(S).

CHAMBER MUSIC

Sonata for Violin and Piano
★—Rostal (*v*), Horsley (*p*), W 18024

Quartet for Piano and Strings
★★—Robert Masters Q, W 18024.

String Quartet in A minor
The performance is masterly; however, a warning about the liner notes. They are full of purple patches without any semblance of reality, containing such built-in nonsense as this remark concerning the last movement—". . . the character of a determined drive toward an affirmative answer to the problems of mind and soul which it explores."
—Hollywood Sq, C 8054.

VOCAL

Three Songs
★★★—in "A Recital of Songs by English Composers," Brown (*t*), McNamee (*p*), J 00A5.

CHORAL

Make We Joy Now in This Fest
★—in "Choral and Organ Music," Stanford University Choir, Schmidt, MLR 6995/6.

Set Me As A Seal Upon Thy Heart
★★—in "The First International Congress of Organists: Vol. III," Choir of St. John's College, Cambridge University, Guest, MI 1006.

CHORAL WITH ORCHESTRA
ORATORIO

Belshazzar's Feast
Boult's and Ormandy's versions both possess magnificent drive, a fine sense of line and requisite brilliance. Roger Wagner's entry is also

eloquent. The solo baritone is undoubtedly the best of all represented below. Only the orchestra lacks the thrust and composite balance of Ormandy's.

—PO, Rutgers University Choir, Cassel (*bar*), Ormandy, CO 5667(S)
—PPO, LPC, Noble (*bar*), Boult, W 5248   —RP, Roger Wagner Chorale, Cameron (*bar*), Wagner, C 8577(S)   —PH, Philharmonia Chorus, Bell (*bar*), Walton, A 35681(S)   —Royal Liverpool Philharmonic Orch., Cooper (*org*), Huddersfield Choral Society, Milligan (*b. bar*), Sargent, C 7141.

Belshazzar's Feast (Excerpt)
Excerpt?! Nothing more than the attempt to convey what must have been a clever sight gag at the musical shenanigans of the third Hoffnung Festival. On a recording it is the epitome of ridiculousness. After a minute and thirty-five seconds of applause and introductory remarks by one T. E. Bean, the "music" totals *one* short, clangorous chord, conducted with a flyswatter! No humor, no reason, no excerpt.
—in "The Hoffnung Astronautical Music Festival 1961," Hoffnung Sy. Orch., Walton, A 35828(S).

OPERA

Troilus and Cressida (Excerpts)
The recording presents two sections from the first act, three from act two, and two scenes from the last act. It is an excellent presentation, even though a sampling of the opera.
—PH, Schwarzkopf (*s*), Lewis (*t*), Wells (*t*), Hauxvell (*bar*), Thomas (*t*), Sinclair (*cn*), Walton, A 35278.

FILM MUSIC

Henry V
(A seven-minute synthesis of the score.)
—in "Film Spectacular," London Festival Orch., Black, L (44025).

ANTON WEBERN

ORCHESTRAL

Fuga (Ricercata) *a 6 Voci* ("Six-Voice Fugue")—*No. 2 from "Das Musikalisches Opfer"* ("The Musical Offering") (Bach-Webern)
Abravanel's reading is splendid, and where it can afford to be, even

more dynamic and robust than Craft's. However, the latter's men achieve perfect smoothness and a chamber-music quality in their playing. Each and every note in the score is delineated, not one sound being of secondary importance in this remarkable music.
—in "J. S. Bach: Orchestral Transcriptions," UT, Abravanel, VG 1092(S)   —in "Anton Webern: The Complete Music," Orch., Craft, CO 232.

German Dances (October 1824) (Schubert-Webern)
★★★—COL, Craft, CO 5744(S).

Passacaglia, Op. 1
★★—in "Anton Webern: The Complete Music," Orch., Craft, CO 232.

Six Pieces for Large Orchestra, Op. 6 (Original Scoring)
Craft's direction is beyond criticism, though oddly enough he plays the revised version (*see below*) quite faster (the performance time of this example is 10:54, that of the second orchestration is 9:32).
—COL, Craft, CO 5616(S).

Six Pieces for Large Orchestra, Op. 6 (Revised Scoring)
It is certainly a rare and happy situation that both versions of Webern's Opus 6 are available (*see above* for the initial setting). Though the sound of Columbia's disk is better, Westminster's is preferable because Rosbaud knew this style of music even better than the very knowledgeable Craft. Obtain Rosbaud's performance of this edition and Craft's of the original and all purposes will be served.
—SUDW, Rosbaud, W 18807   —in "Anton Webern: The Complete Music," Orch., Craft, CO 232.

Variations for Orchestra, Op. 30
★—in "Anton Webern: The Complete Music," Orch., Craft, CO 232.

CHAMBER ORCHESTRA

Concerto, Op. 24
★★—in "Anton Webern: The Complete Music," Gleghorn (*fl*), Pope (*o*), Raimondi (*cl*), Decker (*hn*), Remsen (*tp*), Ulyate (*tb*), Schaeffer (*v*), Figelski (*va*), Stein (*p*), Craft, CO 232.

Five Pieces for Orchestra, Op. 10
★★★—in "Anton Webern: The Complete Music," Orch., Craft, CO 232.

Symphony, Op. 21
Craft's performance is transparent and authoritative; that by Boulez unbalanced and improvisational.

—in "Anton Webern: The Complete Music," Orch., Craft, CO 232
—Orch., Boulez, VEGA 30-66.

STRING ORCHESTRA

Five Movements for String Orchestra, Op. 5
★—COL, Craft, CO 5428(S).

INSTRUMENTAL

PIANO

Variations, Op. 27
★★★—in "Anton Webern: The Complete Music," Stein, CO 232.

CHAMBER MUSIC

Four Pieces for Violin and Piano, Op. 7
Though all the teams play with equal muscular solidity or precise evanescence, as required, it is simply a matter of preferable reproduction for this highly concentrated, translucent music. The rather dry sound of the MGM disk frames the music best.
—A. Ajemian (*v*), M. Ajemian (*p*), MGM 3179   —in "The Violin: Vol. 5," Bress (*v*), Reiner (*p*), FW 3355   —in "Anton Webern: The Complete Music," Schaeffer (*v*), Stein (*p*), CO 232.

Three Small Pieces for Cello and Piano, Op. 11
★★★—in "Anton Webern: The Complete Music," Sargeant (*c*), Stein (*p*), CO 232.

String Trio, Op. 20
★★★—in "Anton Webern: The Complete Music," Wade (*v*), Figelski (*va*), Sargeant (*c*), CO 232.

Five Movements for String Quartet, Op. 5
All three versions are first-rate; the latest Juilliard presentation (RCA Victor) the most minutely searching in its unfoldment. This release revises the title to "Five Pieces," but the original German "Fünf Satze" must read "Five Movements."
—Juilliard Sq, V 2531(S)   —Juilliard Sq, CO 4737   —in "Anton Webern: The Complete Music," Wade (*v*), Fenley (*v*), Thomas (*va*), Sargeant (*c*), CO 232.

Quartet for Violin, Clarinet, Tenor Saxophone and Piano, Op. 22
★★★—in "Anton Webern: The Complete Music," Lurie (*cl*), Ulyate (*t. sax*), Schaeffer (*v*), Stein (*p*), CO 232.

Six Bagatelles for String Quartet, Op. 9
The foursome that play this work in the "complete music" album fail to heed Schoenberg's statement (in his preface for the published score), ". . . every trace of sentimentality must be banished," whereas the Juilliard achieve the utmost concentration and project the innermost expression of the pieces. The Juilliard's subtle reticence creates soft thunderbolts of effect.
—Juilliard Sq, CO 2531(S)   —in "Anton Webern: The Complete Music," Wade (*v*), Sushel (*v*), Figelski (*va*), Sargeant (*c*), CO 232.

String Quartet, Op. 28
★★★—in "Anton Webern: The Complete Music," Wade (*v*), Sushel (*v*), Figelski (*va*), Sargeant (*c*), CO 232.

Quintet for String Quartet and Piano
★★—in "Anton Webern: The Complete Music," Wade (*v*), Fenley (*v*), Thomas (*va*), Sargeant (*c*), Stein (*p*), CO 232.

VOCAL

Five Songs, Op. 3
Five Songs, Op. 4
Four Songs, Op. 12
Three Songs, Op. 23
Three Songs, Op. 25
★★★★—in "Anton Webern: The Complete Music," Nixon (*s*), Stein (*p*), CO 232.

VOICE WITH INSTRUMENTAL ENSEMBLE

Five Canons on Latin Texts, Op. 16
★★★★—in "Anton Webern: The Complete Music," Martin (*s*), Lurie (*cl*), Ulyate (*b. cl*), Craft, CO 232.

Five Sacred Songs, Op. 15
★★★★—in "Anton Webern: The Complete Music," Instrumental Ensemble, Martin (*s*), Craft, CO 232.

Four Songs, Op. 13
For a proper presentation with quality choose the Craft-conducted version.
—in "Anton Webern: The Complete Music," Instrumental Ensemble, Martin (*s*), Craft, CO 232   —Instrumental Ensemble, Héricard (*vocalist*), Boulez, VEGA 30-66.

Six Songs, Op. 14
★★★★—in "Anton Webern: The Complete Music," Instrumental Ensemble, Martin (*s*), Craft, CO 232.

Three Songs, Op. 18
★★★—in "Anton Webern: The Complete Music," Martin (*s*), Raimondi (*E flat cl*), Marshall (*g*), Craft, CO 232.

Three Traditional Rhymes, Op. 17
★★★—in "Anton Webern: The Complete Music," Martin (*s*), Lurie (*cl*), Ulyate (*b. cl*), Schaeffer (*v*), Figelski (*va*), Craft, CO 232.

Two Songs, Op. 8
The French recording does not have the fluidity of the American release, nor is the vocalist as sensitive.
—in "Anton Webern: The Complete Music," Instrumental Ensemble, Martin (*s*), Craft, CO 232   —Instrumental Ensemble, Héricard (*vocalist*), Boulez, VEGA 30-66.

CHORAL

Entflieht auf leichten Kähnen, Op. 2
★★★—in "Anton Webern: The Complete Music," Chorus, Craft, CO 232.

CHORAL WITH INSTRUMENTAL ENSEMBLE

Two Songs, Op. 19
★★★—in "Anton Webern: The Complete Music," Instrumental Ensemble, Nixon (*s*), Martin (*a*), Robinson (*t*), Scharbach (*b*), Craft, CO 232.

CHORAL WITH ORCHESTRA

Das Augenlicht, Op. 26
★★★—in "Anton Webern: The Complete Music," Orch., Chorus, Craft, CO 232.

CANTATA

Cantata No. 1, Op. 29
Cantata No. 2, Op. 31
★★★★—in "Anton Webern: The Complete Music," Orch., Chorus, Nixon (*s*), Scharbach (*b*), Craft, CO 232.